# AWAKE & SINGING

## NEW EDITION

# AWAKE &
# SINGING
## NEW EDITION

## SIX GREAT AMERICAN
## JEWISH PLAYS

EDITED AND WITH AN INTRODUCTION BY

## ELLEN SCHIFF

**APPLAUSE**
THEATRE & CINEMA BOOKS

*Awake & Singing, New Edition*
*Six Great American Jewish Plays*
Copyright © 2004 by Ellen Schiff

Cover and interior photos reprinted with permission from Michael Brosilow, Marc Bryan-Brown, Magnum Photos, TimePix, and Williamstown Theatre Festival.

Art direction: Michelle Thompson

Library of Congress Control Number: 2003113273

**APPLAUSE THEATRE & CINEMA BOOKS**
151 West 46th Street, 8th Floor
New York, NY 10036
Phone: (212) 575-9265
Fax: (646) 562-5852
Email: info@applausepub.com
Internet: www.applausepub.com

*Sales & Distribution*
NORTH AMERICA:
Hal Leonard Corp.
7777 West Bluemound Road
P. O. Box 13819
Milwaukee, WI 53213
Phone: (414) 774-3630
Fax: (414) 774-3259
Email: halinfo@halleonard.com
Internet: www.halleonard.com
UNITED KINGDOM:
Roundhouse Publishing Ltd.
Millstone, Limers Lane
Northam, North Devon
Ex 39 2RG
Phone: 01237-474474
Fax: 01237-474774
Email: roundhouse.group@ukgateway.net

# CONTENTS

EDITOR'S NOTE and ACKNOWLEDGMENTS  9
INTRODUCTION
The Coming of Age of the American Jewish Repertoire  13

**COUNSELLOR-AT LAW**
Elmer Rice  53
Headnotes  63
Play  65

**AWAKE AND SING!**
Clifford Odets  175
Headnotes  185
Play  189

**MORNING STAR**
Sylvia Regan  243
Headnotes  251
Play  253

**THE TENTH MAN**
Paddy Chayefsky  323
Headnotes  331
Play  333

**CONVERSATIONS WITH MY FATHER**
Herb Gardner  409
Headnotes  419
Play  421

**BROKEN GLASS**
Arthur Miller  507
Headnotes  517
Play  519

# EDITOR'S NOTE AND ACKNOWLEDGMENTS

This book pays tribute to the development and accomplishment of the American Jewish repertoire. Five of its six plays are reprinted from my collections, *Awake and Singing* and *Fruitful and Multiplying* (Penguin/Mentor, 1995 and 1996). I am delighted to add *Broken Glass*, Arthur Miller's first play to focus entirely on American Jewish life. A revised and expanded introductory essay brings up to date an overview of American Jewish playwriting.

The enormous contribution of Jews to the American repertoire is at last capturing the critical recognition it merits. This is the place to salute the increasing number of theatre scholars, historians and critics drawn to the fertile field that lies between the Yiddish theatre and the international proliferation of plays by and about Jews. In citing by name exemplary scholars like Joyce Antler, Sarah Blacher Cohen, Julius Novick, Robert Skloot and Stephen J. Whitfield, I mean to acknowledge the work of all those whose study of American Jewish drama deepens our understanding and appreciation of its genesis and multi-faceted evolution.

In this excellent company, I recognize myself with a shudder as a serial anthologist. What chutzpah! How can a handful of scripts, however exceptional, represent an entire repertoire, especially one as abundant and flourishing as this one? Even supposing that were possible, how to tell which plays offer the best examples? Well, the operative words cannot be "best," any more than a hillside of flowers can be gathered in a single bouquet. The plenitude of fine plays is a solid reason for more collections; meantime, I am happy to explain my choices for this one.

There were several criteria. The plays have proven artistic value. Beautifully written, they are good entertainment. They are dramatically vital on the page, as on the stage. All had respectable initial runs and have enjoyed recent revivals. For example, *Counsellor-at-Law* was remounted at the Shaw and the Williamstown Theatre Festivals in 1993; *Awake and Sing!* in New York in 1984, Chicago in 1992, and Phoenix in 2002. Lincoln Center Theatre opened its 1989 season with a new production of *The Tenth Man*; Chicago's Steppenwolf Theatre revived *Morning Star* in 1999. Notable among the many post-New York productions of *Conversations With My Father* across the country was that of Atlanta's Jewish Theatre of the South in 1999. *Broken Glass* traveled from New York to London, Paris and Munich; it was performed in Yiddish in Montreal in 1995, and Joseph Chaikin directed it at Atlanta's Seven Stages in 2003.

"Documents" seems a stodgy term to apply to the lively art displayed here. Still, these works are valuable because they bring to life before our eyes many of the seminal events that shaped the American Jewish experience through the last century: immigration, family life and generational conflicts, the Great Depression, "making it" in America, encounters with anti-Semitism, the Triangle Fire, assimilation, two world wars, the Holocaust and Israel nationhood. Interestingly, through a variety of subjects and viewpoints, each of these works incorporates what sociologist Steven M. Cohen calls the "competing impulses: the urge to *integrate* into modern America and the urge to *survive* as Jews."[1] So the plays tell us a good deal about Jewish self-perception. And, because the theatre is both topical and public — these plays are, after all, intended for general audiences — they serve as an index of how Jews see America and how America sees Jews.

In no sphere have Jewish artists influenced the Jewish image in America more than in the performing arts. Playwrights, who inherit an old, deeply entrenched tradition of formulaic stage Jews, have played an important role. They have reversed stereotypes and replaced them with a more varied and credible population of Jewish characters. My choice of scripts in this volume suggests this broader, more multiform census. The doctor, the lawyer and the materfamilias are here, but so are the Jew as confused first generation American, struggling businessman, doubting rabbi, anomic modern professional, successful writer, military hero, would-be entertainer, and the pious elderly hard put to cope with the indifference of the secular world. Alongside the upright and estimable, there are characters here who are not looking for admiration; they are disaffected, insecure, intermarried and at war with their own Jewishness. There are images of changing gender roles and the early appearance of fresh dramatis personae who will have long stage lives.

And sometimes — all right, once — I included a play just because I liked what it said and how it said it and believed it deserved a new life in print. That play is *Morning Star* and, as its headnotes detail, my faith was well placed.

The collection's deficiencies are, of course, solely my doing, but a number of people cooperated in the book's realization and I am indebted to them. I am grateful to Glenn Young, for his belief in the project; to Irene Backalenick and Jay Novick, close and generous readers; to Greg Collins and John J. O'Sullivan, whose editing often saved me from myself; to Carole Kessner, who came out to plays she might have preferred to miss; and to Dan Berley, whose loving support and uncommon patience defy qualification.

—ELLEN SCHIFF
New York, 2003

# INTRODUCTION
## THE COMING OF AGE OF THE
## AMERICAN JEWISH REPERTOIRE

### I. DRAMATIC BEGINNINGS

The American Jewish repertoire is a national treasure some eight decades old. It consists of hundreds of plays, written in English, usually by Jewish dramatists, which explore some aspect of the American Jewish experience. This book pays tribute to the canon by tracing its development and illustrating its accomplishment with six important works.

The role of Jews in the making of American theatre is difficult to over-estimate. According to one estimate, "by 1905, half the people working in the entertainment business were Jewish."[2] From producers and impresarios — Erlanger, Zimmerman, the Frohmans, the Shubert brothers, Belasco and Fields — to the writers and performers who animated this country's vaudeville circuits, burlesque shows, musical halls, and pioneer theatres, Jews have worked shoulder to shoulder with fellow Americans in the making of a national theatre. Jewish participation and presence have been so constant in the indigenous American theatre since its coming of age in the post-World War I years that it took the perspective of an outsider, British director Tyrone Guthrie, to observe that if Jews withdrew from the American theatre, it "would collapse about next Thursday."[3]

Their efforts did not take place in a vacuum, or, for that matter, in a climate of tolerance. Nativism, well entrenched as the 20th century got under way, manifested itself in its first decades as what historian John Higham terms "inflamed racial nationalism."[4] Though the resurgent Ku Klux Klan and various ideological firebrands threatened all foreigners, Jews were the specific target of new quotas and restrictions on immigration that, in 1924, effectively ended their mass influx to these shores.[5] Higham records the nation's most severe eruption of anti-Semitism in the years surrounding World War I, the pestilence breaking out again "in the 1930s, stimulated by the Great Depression and the example of European fascism."[6]

Whatever inroads racism made in the arts, it did not deter Jewish playwriting. In disregard or defiance, distinguished critic and author Gilbert Seldes used the pages of *The Menorah Journal* in 1922 to implore dramatists to translate to the stage "the poetry and the richness and the hard certain solidness of our fantastically mingled existence [as Americans and Jews.]"7 Nonetheless, sensitivity to intolerance probably accounts for the reserve with which some dramatists treated their ethnicity, a practice that continued well into mid-century. So, for example, Samuel Shipman calls his transparently Jewish characters in *Cheaper to Marry* (1924) Jim Knight and Charlie Tyler. Other *dramatis personae* are endowed with Jewish names, but no distinguishing Jewish substance, as in Edna Ferber and George S. Kaufman's *Minick* (1924). Or they have Jewish identifying traits so trite as to be meaningless, a signature practice of the prodigiously successful George S. Kaufman.

Other cultural forces influenced the development of American Jewish drama. The early years of the century ushered in new uses of leisure. Cultural historians note that Americans were increasingly drawn to passive diversions. For instance, Russell Lynes credits the invention of the phonograph and, later, film and radio with "creating a mass audience of listeners and watchers out of a people who … seem to have preferred to do rather than to be done by…."8 The growth of audiences was crucial in fostering the development and popularity of all the arts.

The role of Jews as arts patrons, especially German Jews who had prospered since their arrival earlier in the 19th century, has been well documented. Less spectacular, but equally consequential were the recreational habits of the newcomers from Eastern Europe. Irrespective of the work they did in this country, many immigrant Jews brought with them middle-class tastes. These included a frequently indulged affinity for theatre, to which the enormous popularity of the Yiddish stage well into the thirties bears testimony.9 It is no surprise that this predominantly East European immigrant population has augmented the ranks on both sides of the footlights in America.

Since the twenties — the date by which "the American theater began to function as a world-class vehicle of dramatic literature"10 Jews have been writing often and with distinction for the American stage. A few statistics confirm their warm reception. Elmer Rice, the first Jew awarded the Pulitzer Prize for drama — for *Street Scene* in 1929 — heads a roster that currently includes twenty-six Jewish laureates. Since the establishment of the Tony Awards in 1947, plays and books for musicals written by Jews have been nominated virtually every year. To commemorate the authoritative *Best Plays and Year Book of the Drama in America's* 75th anniversary, the 1993-94 edition listed authors whose works it had selected four or more times since 1919. Five of the first ten dramatists were Jewish. George S. Kaufman was second on the list with eighteen plays, followed by Neil Simon with fifteen.

The sheer volume of plays in English *by* Jews may divert attention from the important number of plays *about* Jews that are only now beginning to attract the recognition they deserve. To arrive at the focus of this book, we need identify those plays that, by virtue of their explicit Jewish content constitute the American Jewish repertoire. We can make the critical distinctions by posing some defining questions.

*What is an American Jewish play?*

Like any attempt to define anything Jewish, beginning with the classic conundrum, "What is a Jew?", this query invites multiple, contradictory opinions. For some, a Jewish play is any written by a Jew, a judgment that does not consider whether Jewishness infuses the work in any meaningful way. Others hold the view that no play written in English can be a Jewish play (an issue to be addressed shortly). The matter is further complicated by the existence of countless works whose subjects or characters are not specifically Jewish, but whose themes and values undeniably are.

*Death of a Salesman* springs immediately to mind, although by the 1949 premiere of Arthur Miller's masterwork, Jews had already written a body of plays inspired by traditional concern for the rights and welfare of the working class. Social consciousness, along with typically left-wing political activism, pervades the drama of American Jews in the twenties and thirties. At the same time, as cultural historian Stephen Whitfield points out, the essentially competitive nature of a mercantile society undermined the community ethos of the Jews. As early as the twenties, American Jewish dramaturgy addressed a theme that continues to dominate it, "the collision of *menshlichkeit* [uprightness] with business."[11]

Numerous scripts dramatize the plight of America's downtrodden, typically portrayed as victims of capitalism. Industry's unconcern for the individual was represented in the depersonalized expressionist style of Elmer Rice's *The Adding Machine* (1923) and Paul Sifton's *The Belt* (1927). The despair and fury that fuel workers' revolts furnished the subject of plays like John Howard Lawson's *Processional* (1925), set against a West Virginia mine strike, Albert Bein's *Let Freedom Ring* (1935), a reckoning of the shattering cost of job action for southern mill workers, and, perhaps most famously, Clifford Odets's agitprop play about a taxi drivers' strike, *Waiting for Lefty* (1935). Claire and Paul Sifton leveled a scathing indictment of the human suffering caused by unemployment in 1931 (1931); Albert Maltz dramatized the bitter life of coal miners in *Black Pit* (1935). The sociopolitical bias of these works reveals traditional Jewish emphasis on community responsibility, human worth, and integrity. Elmer Rice's *Street Scene* offered a sympathetic display of the urban frustrations that engender violence. The cry for social justice was taken up by John Wexley in reaction to the Scottsboro case in which nine blacks were wrongly convicted of rape in *They Shall Not Die* (1934).

Concern with ethical behavior finds eloquent and sustained expression in the works of Arthur Miller, whose early play *No Villain* (1936) dealt with a beset smalltime garment manufacturer whose Jewish values put him at odds with the strike-breaking tactics of big business. "Maybe it's honest for steel companies to work this way, but I can't see it's the way for Jewish men to act," he agonizes.[12] While Miller did not again focus specifically on American Jewish life in subsequent works until *The American Clock* (1982) and *Broken Glass* (1994), his entire canon is informed by his preoccupation with individual integrity and social responsibility, concerns that he makes clear in his autobiography derive from his Jewish heritage.[13]

Since serious (if high-spirited) dramatizations of social and political concerns are also effectively set to music, a very broad definition of a Jewish play might also include musical theatre. For instance, Harold Rome's revue *Pins and Needles* (1937) portrayed the garment industry through the eyes of its workers. With a cast of amateur players drawn from the International Ladies Garment Workers Union, the show had an impressive run of 1109 performances. Marc Blitzstein's *The Cradle Will Rock*, despite its sponsorship by a federal relief program, the Works Projects Administration, made a searing anti-capitalist statement that provoked government watchdogs to attempt unsuccessfully to squelch its premiere in 1938. Better-natured but deliciously barbed was the musical trilogy written by Morrie Ryskind, George S. Kaufman, and George and Ira Gershwin. *Strike Up the Band* (1930) targeted industry's profiteering from weapons sales, while *Of Thee I Sing* (1933), the first musical to win the Pulitzer Prize, jauntily skewered the inanity of presidential electioneering based entirely on vacuous slogans. The lightheartedness of its sequel notwithstanding, *Let 'Em Eat Cake* (1933) imagined the triumph of anarchy ("Down with all majorities/Also all minorities... Down with books by Dostoevksy/Also Boris Tomashevsky") or of totalitarianism (the Blue Shirts establish a "dictatorship of the proletariat"). In a nice bit of early feminism, clever and assertive women save the day.

But the enormous contribution of Jews to American musical theatre — from Irving Berlin and Jerome Kern to Jerry Bock and Sheldon Harnick and Stephen Sondheim — is a rich and important subject that has elsewhere received the critical attention it merits.[14] The musical stage, in common with plays like those previously mentioned that are not explicitly Jewish, lie outside the focus of this essay, which deals with drama that specifically is. There are other distinctions to be made.

*What languages do Jewish plays speak?*

The use of English as the language of Jewish creativity presents an important issue, not just for the drama. Ethnic writing in English is sometimes seen as a dilution of the identity typically conferred by language. Cynthia Ozick, among the most prolific and intellectual of American Jewish writers, flatly declared, "there are no major works of Jewish imaginative genius written in any Gentile language."[15] Scholar and critic Robert Alter agrees, "Though Jews have lived in many different cultures and have been profoundly influenced by them, they have never created a distinctly imaginative literature except in indigenous Jewish languages."[16] (The issue is not uniquely Jewish. Social philosopher Horace Kallen assumed that "cultural pluralism" would involve "each nationality [cultivating] its own dialect in English under the influence of its national culture."[17]) But what *is* the "indigenous Jewish language" for American Jews, who often have none other than English?

The question has international analogues. The native languages of many countries have come to function admirably as vehicles for "distinctly imaginative literature" by and about Jews. There are significant examples in all the literary genres. To cite a few for the theatre: the English-language drama celebrated in this collection has its parallels in Canada in the plays of Aviva Ravel and Jason Sherman, and in England in those of Julia Pascal and Arnold Wesker. The Jewish stage speaks French in the plays of Liliane Atlan and Jean-Claude Grumberg, German in those of Nelly Sachs and Peter Weiss, and Spanish in the Argentinian theatre of Diana Raznovich and Jorge Goldenberg.

Casting doubt on the authenticity of Jewish art in non-exclusively Jewish languages or challenging the contribution of such writing to the Jewish literary tradition scants the art itself and undervalues the very symbiosis that animates Diaspora creativity. Surely both cultural and aesthetic considerations are more appropriately served by accepting these works for what they are: reflections of every dimension of Jewish identity and Jewish life in pluralistic societies. What more appropriate medium can there be to express the dominant theme of modern Jewish creativity — the imperatives and challenges of dual identity — than the idiom of those countries where Jews live?

Prefixing "American Jewish" before such words as "play," "drama," "theatre," or "repertoire" invites dissent of another sort. The "American" notwithstanding, the association of Jewish theatre with the Yiddish stage is inevitable and unyielding. Semantics is partly to blame. For instance, when in 1980 the newly formed Jewish Theatre Association (JTA) of the National Foundation for Jewish Culture convened the First Jewish Theatre Conference/Festival, it felt obliged to explain the title of the event, "Exploring the Dimensions of Jewish Theatre." In its registration form, the JTA welcomed "all theatre expressions which relate to the Jewish experience, life, and culture." The Festival's four morning-to-late-night days of performances, readings, demonstrations, workshops, and panel discussions surpassed its organizers' most optimistic expectations by serving up overwhelming evidence of the breadth and depth of Jewish theatrical activity across the nation — all in English.

Although English has superseded Yiddish as the Jewish lingua franca (Israeli scholar Moshe Davis observes that English "is the mother tongue for the majority of world Jewry"[18]), the conflation of "Yiddish" and "Jewish" persists, perhaps nowhere more enduringly than in reference to the theatre. And this tendency persists despite the disproportion between the number and availability of productions in English and those in Yiddish. Potential ticket-buyers regularly call the box offices of the Association of Jewish Theatres, the network of producing companies across North America that has succeeded the JTA, seeking assurance that their productions are in English. At least some of the tenacity of the confusion can be explained.

The Yiddish theatre has hardly disappeared. New York City is the home of the oldest continuous theatrical producing institution in the United States, the Folksbiene (People's Theatre), a wing of the Workmen's Circle, founded in 1915. Yiddish lives in the active programming of the Saidye Bronfman Yiddish Theatre of Montreal, and on Yiddish-speaking stages in Argentina, Europe, Israel and Mexico. Still, however vigorous contemporary Yiddish theatrical activity worldwide, even its most zealous advocates would not argue that "Jewish theatre" means exclusively the Yiddish stage.

However, classics of the Yiddish stage are readily available in English, notably the collections translated and edited by Joseph C. Landis and Nahma Sandrow.[19] Not meant just for reading, they are smartly refitted for the stage. New York's Jewish Repertory Theatre scored a tremendous hit in 1983 with Nahma Sandrow, Raphael Crystal, and Richard Engquist's *Kuni Leml*, based on Avrom Goldfadn's delightful farce. *The New York Times* hailed Joseph Papp's production of Leivick's *The Golem*, directed by Richard Foreman at the Public Theater in 1984, as "a play of imperishable ideas." The Jewish Repertory Company initiated its new space in 1992 by commissioning a fresh adaptation by Stephen Fife of Sholom Asch's powerful *God of Vengeance*, a work that subsequently has become something of a hot property, inspiring several adaptations, including the play Pulitzer Prize-winner Donald Margulies based on Joachim Neugroschel's translation (2000). Caraid O'Brien has made a specialty of lively translations toothsomely punctuated with Yeshivish, an amalgam of Yiddish, Aramaic and English. O'Brien's *God of Vengeance* was produced by Theater J in Washington D.C. in 2001 as part of a four-play bill titled, "Sex and Guilt in the Jewish Theatre." Another Pulitzer laureate, Tony Kushner, reworked Anski's best-known play as *A Dybbuk* (1995), produced at the Public Theater in 1997.

Irving Howe's observation about the original *Dybbuk* once seemed applicable to the Yiddish repertoire itself. Howe wrote that Anski's work "for all its brilliant darkness... offered no path of development for the Yiddish theatre: it was a work sealed into the past, which could be imitated but not enlarged upon."[20] There are those who would argue (I am among them) that the

Margulies, Kushner, and O'Brien adaptations, which integrate recent, relevant Jewish experience into the givens of the original, offer a serious rebuttal. Moreover, it is very difficult to think what these English-language adaptations of Yiddish plays are if not American Jewish drama.

The persistent identification of Jewish theatre with Yiddish also may be attributable to a precept much honored in the Jewish world — the injunction to remember. The Yiddish stage fulfills what Francine Prose, in a very different context, calls a "moral and spiritual obligation."[21] Nourished by memory, animated by historical consciousness, the Yiddish stage comments on traditional Jewish mores and values. It is a reminder of the Baal Shem Tov's aphorism, "Exile comes from forgetting. Memory is the source of redemption." It resonates with another significance, revivifying not only roots, but also the places where roots once flourished. Often set in East European communities, Yiddish plays evoke painful awareness of a world obliterated. The delight with which the Polish villagers greet the advent of the railroad and its promise of travel to wonderful places in Kushner's *A Dybbuk* is unbearably poignant to a post-Holocaust audience.

Then too, New York's Second Avenue and its equivalent venues for Yiddish theatre across the country remain a treasured part of the recollections of many American Jews, frequently because their earliest, most indelible impressions of theatre were fashioned by the Yiddish stage. This experience is hardly unique to senior citizens. Emily Mann, born in 1952, a versatile playwright and director who heads Princeton's Tony award-winning McCarter Theatre, told me that she knew where she wanted to spend her professional life when as a teenager she saw Anski's *The Dybbuk* and "fell under the spell of the girl in white." Mann's experience echoes that of innumerable Jewish artists who have brought to their careers in the American theatre the humor, vitality, artistic standards, and social consciousness of the Yiddish stage at its finest. It is quite possible that simply because prized memories remain so vivid and cherished, they overshadow any "other" theatre that calls itself Jewish.

Although the Yiddish and the American Jewish stages have had much in common, particularly in the first decades of the 20th century, they are poised on separate axes and serve different constituencies. The Yiddish theatre faces inward, speaking its own language. Like all theatre, the Yiddish stage engages us because it entertains, and to that end, the American Yiddish stage graciously makes provisions for theatregoers who are, as musician Moishe Mlotek puts it, "Yiddish-impaired." Still, its appeal is keenest for those who can appreciate the cadences and nuances of its language and rejoice in hearing it spoken or sung well. The Yiddish stage comes as close as any in the modern world to replicating the original function of drama, to affirm the identity and beliefs of a people. It energizes its legends of romance, mystery, devotion, naiveté and martyrdom. It furnishes a forum for good-natured mockery and self-parody. How can one not relax and rejoice where it is acceptable (and often funny) to see Jews portrayed with all their warts and foibles? Yet how not to admit that this special kind of gratification in the theatre is an ethnic secret, impenetrable for general audiences, as well as for countless non-Yiddish-speaking Jews, in a multicultural society?

*What happens when the Jewish stage speaks English?*

Just there lies a problem. Linguistic barriers secured the Yiddish theatre as a safe place to laugh at Jewish foolishness, weep at Jewish misfortune and assert secular Jewish identity. That haven is compromised — some would say threatened — when such frank portraiture of Jewish life is made accessible beyond the "in" group. The sensitivity of Jews to their public depictions has exacted formidable demands on those who would write about them in the vernacular. "Is it good for the Jews?" endures as an important criterion in some quarters. When Aaron Hoffman's *Welcome Stranger*, a comic but extremely forthright treatment of Yankee anti-Semitism[22], was mounted at a special Jewish New Year's performance in 1920, it raised hackles. Though the audience laughed heartily, it completely missed the play's vigorous assertion of the rights of Jews to avail themselves of America's opportunities. Instead theatregoers complained that Hoffman had turned his back on the opportunity to "do the Jew in America a fine service by explaining his attitude toward the age-old racial antagonisms his people are supposed to have created."[23] The same touchiness created a regrettable chapter in American theatre history in 1922 when Rudolph Schildkraut's world-renowned production of Sholom Asch's *God of Vengeance* played in New York in English. Although the earlier Yiddish production had raised no eyebrows, the English language debut of *God of Vengeance* met a stormy reception. Scandalized by the play's frank depiction of a Jewish brothel keeper and his lesbian daughter, uptown Jews turned the production into an historic moment: the first instance in American jurisprudence of a play's being closed down and its principals brought to trial on obscenity charges.[24]

American Jewish theatre can be seen as a challenge to Jewish exclusiveness. From its inception, the American Jewish stage has faced in exactly the opposite direction from the Yiddish — outward. Where the Yiddish stage is specific, the American Jewish theatre is allusive. In its vanguard stood vaudeville, where the acts of Jewish comics resonated with the analogous experiences of other new Americans, making the Jew what Alfred Kazin aptly termed "the representative national entertainer."25 Notwithstanding the camouflage or disappearing act imposed by nativism and the Hitler years, by mid-century Jews had forged their way into the center of American life. Then history ushered in what Leslie Fiedler called an "apocalyptic period of atomization and uprooting" in which "the image of the Jew tends to become the image of everyone."26 Jews increasingly used the stage to reflect on society as they saw it and as it saw them — both as Americans and as Jews. Given the myriad reasons for tension and incompatibility between identities, American Jews became symbolic of the conflicted, alienated, and vulnerable.

However, the distinctions made here between the Yiddish and the American Jewish theatres and the argument for the legitimacy of the latter as unquestionably Jewish are not meant to imply that the two are mutually exclusive. Contemporary Yiddish-English revues consciously borrow from the American stage. For instance, in their adaptation of Itsik Manger's biblical poetry for the Joseph Papp Yiddish Theater's *Songs of Paradise* (1989), Miriam Hoffman, Rena Berkowicz Borow, and Rosalie Gerut incorporated rock and roll, and "traditional Jewish beats."27 The influence in the other direction is far more consequential, going well beyond the adaptations mentioned above. Nahma Sandrow concludes her essay "Yiddish Theater and American Theater" by observing that it is, "not surprising that many of the passionate reformers of the twentieth-century American theatre, so many critics, so many sponsors and patrons, so many experimenters, came out of Yiddish culture."28 The repertoire itself demonstrates that the Yiddish theatre's bequest to the American Jewish stage extends well beyond the older institution's stock of plots, characters, legends, and music. The legacy includes informed respect of the Old World repertoire, especially the inspiration of the modern European masters of dramaturgy and production.29 And one thing more: a level of artistic achievement, notably on the part of its actors, that earned the respect of this country's reputation-making drama critics, a predominantly non-Jewish coterie, the likes of Brooks Atkinson, Robert Benchley, John Mason Brown, Alexander Woollcott and Stark Young.

While the achievements of the Yiddish theatre may persist in blinding its admirers to any other Jewish theatre, its dazzling reputation is more often perceived by English-language theatre practitioners as a heritage to build on. For what finally most sets American Jewish drama apart from the Yiddish is precisely the dual citizenship explicit in its name. Nathan Glazer and Daniel Patrick Moynihan usefully pointed out that changes wrought on immigrant cultures as they integrated into American society may have "transformed [them] into something other than what they had been in the old country [but they] did not make them any less distinctive or identifiable — or any less significant to those adhering to them."30

The American Jewish stage tells the story of Jews in America and, increasingly, of Jews in the world. It is customarily the work of Jewish playwrights collaborating with non-Jews in the production of scripts typically populated by both Jews and non-Jews, enacted by casts in which Jews do not always play Jewish roles, and performed for audiences and critics comprising the gamut of multicultural theatregoers.

As the works collected here demonstrate, American Jewish drama often grows out of playwrights' experiences of being Jewish in a pluralistic country whose liberties, like its prejudices, inspire them to ponder what being Jewish means. One of the most intriguing phenomena of American Jewish theatre history is the use artists have made of their freedom to decide how to write as a Jew — or even if they should. Their choices range from Montague Glass and Charles Klein's exploiting the good-natured vulgarity of their Yiddish-inflected jargon-spouting buffoons, Abe Potash and Mawruss Perlmutter, to Lillian Hellman's ignoring Jewish subjects almost entirely. A much-trod middle path is one taken by all the authors included here, a practice so common as to serve as a characteristic practice of American Jewish dramatists: their Jewish plays form part of oeuvres that also include works with no Jewish content at all.

## II. A TIME TO SOW, A TIME TO REAP
*The Postwar Years*

Well into the second half of the century, Jewishness on the American stage continued to be regarded as exotic. In 1959, when Paddy Chayefsky reworked Anski's Yiddish classic, *The Dybbuk* as *The Tenth Man,* he set his play in a

present-day Long Island synagogue and took measures to ensure broad intelli-
gibility to Broadway audiences. So, for instance *tallisim* are "praying shawls"
and a *minyan* becomes a "quorum." Kenneth Tynan's *New Yorker* review
suggests the general perceptions of the play. Tynan was quick to focus on
Chayefsky's "Jewish dialogue,"calling it "as meaty as any I have heard since the
heyday of Clifford Odets." "I failed to understand all the Jewish expressions,"
he went on, agreeably, "but like most Gentiles, I laughed anyway."[31]

Tynan's appreciation reflects the prevailing climate in which sea changes were
taking place, on stage and off. It is impossible to determine which altered more
drastically in the last half of the 20th century: the image of Jews in America or
the America in which Jews live. Both transformations — they are, of course,
interconnected — are everywhere apparent in post-World War II arts and letters. The widening opportunity for and increasing eminence of Jewish
intellectual and artistic activities fortified the position of Jews in a society ever
more familiar with Jewish presence. "The American Jew has entered the cultural life in all its aspects, has made important contributions and exerts signal
influence," noted historian Abraham I. Karp in 1969. "A good deal of American
culture today has taken on a kind of Jewish coloration.... Being Jewish is no
handicap today in American cultural life or in American life in general."[32]

Three years earlier, Marshall Sklare and Theodore Solotaroff introduced a collection entitled, *Jews In the Mind of America* by quoting poet Robert Lowell's
observation that by the sixties, "Jewishness became the theme of our literary
culture,"[33] The fifties and sixties have come to be known as the "Jewish literary
renaissance." The term pays homage to accomplishments like the brilliant
fiction of Saul Bellow, Bernard Malamud and Philip Roth and the incisive literary criticism of Irving Howe, Alfred Kazin and Lionel Trilling. Even Robert
Alter, not altogether ready to accept the fact of a Jewish literary renaissance,
grants that the "illusion" of such a golden age would have to be demarcated
from the publication of Bellow's *The Adventures of Augie March* in 1953 to that
of *Herzog* in 1964."[34]

But where were the Jewish playwrights? It is true that the postwar efflorescence
of American Jewish drama did not occur in the same time frame or manner as
the explosion of American Jewish letters. Rather, the period between 1953 and
1964 is more appropriately viewed as prologue to the expansion of sophisticated and ever more ethnic-specific drama that begins the seventies. It is not

until the eighties and nineties that American Jewish dramatists achieve the dominance and authority that the prose writers and critics had earned earlier. Which is not to say that there were no worthwhile Jewish plays on stage between 1953 and 1964. Since this collection aims to demonstrate that American Jewish plays have historically been part of the national repertoire, a look at what *was* on stage during those twelve years is very much in order.

For starters, works that drew on a variety of classic Jewish texts. By pure coincidence, Alter's bracketing dates correspond to Arnold Perl's *The World of Sholem Aleichem* (1953) and Joseph Stein's *Fiddler on the Roof* (1964), whose resounding successes signify renewed appreciation of the celebrated Yiddish storyteller made available in English. The Bible became a wellspring of inspiration for Odets in *The Flowering Peach* (1954) and Paddy Chayefsky in *Gideon* (1961). Both plays dramatized the conflict between self-determination and complete trust in God's will, a tension that may well have reflected choices troubling American Jews for whom following opportunity meant abandoning orthodox practices. A recasting of the story of Noah as a Jewish tale, *Peach* was selected by the *Year Book of the Drama in America* as a Best Play of 1954. The eponym of *Gideon* vies with God for credit for his military victory.

During these twelve years, there were dramatic treatments of a gamut of concerns that were on many American minds: life in the military, making a living, and getting away from it all. Perplexities troubling Jews who wore their country's uniform in the all-American platoons of World War II were probed by Herman Wouk in the courtroom drama he adapted from his novel *The Caine Mutiny Court-Martial* (1954), and by Arthur Laurents in his work about the psychosomatic ravages of combat, *Home of the Brave* (1960). Various aspects of the needle trade, long a locus of Jewish commercial life, provided the setting of Sylvia Regan's *The Fifth Season,* launched on an extended Broadway run in 1953, Paddy Chayefsky's *Middle of the Night* (1956), Erik Moll's *Seidman and Son* (1962), Joseph Stein's *Enter Laughing* (1963), and Harold Rome's *I Can Get It for You Wholesale* (1963).[35] The fortunes and misfortunes of Jews in the entertainment industry furnished the subject of Herb Gardner's *A Thousand Clowns* (1962), Saul Bellow's *The Last Analysis* (1964), and the musical comedy based on Budd Shulberg's *What Makes Sammy Run?* (1964).

Problematic topics destined to develop into major themes emerged on stage. Intermarriage, depicted so lightheartedly in Anne Nichols's *Abie's Irish Rose*

(1922), became for Jewish playwrights a topic to treat thoughtfully, if gingerly. Audiences found it difficult to reproach the lonely widower, played charmingly by Edward G. Robinson, who gambled on a few more years of happiness with a Gentile woman his daughter's age in Chayefsky's *Middle of the Night* (1956). Gertrude Berg, whose radio career since 1929 had already convinced fans of her infallibility, hardly risked disillusioning them as the sympathetic widow who accepts a dashing Japanese suitor in Leonard Spigelgass's *A Majority of One* (1959). For all its improbabilities, Spigelgass's play boldly — it takes place less than two decades after Pearl Harbor — demonstrates parallels between people bereaved by wartime losses and similarities of Jewish, Buddhist and Shinto mores.

"Alter's era" also includes one of the earliest and still best known American Holocaust plays, the work of non-Jewish Hollywood scriptwriters. Albert Hackett and Frances Goodrich's *The Diary of Anne Frank,* which premiered in 1955, ran for 717 performances, and won the Pulitzer Prize and New York Drama Critics Circle Award.[36]

A troublesome issue that will become a major theme inverts the pattern earlier dramatized by Rice and Odets. Here promising young Jews, alienated from the values of their upbringing and rudderless, come to a sad end (a fate spared Arthur Brooks in *The Tenth Man*). S. N. Behrman treats the subject artfully in his autobiographical *The Cold Wind and the Warm* (1959), Meyer Levin, more sensationally in adapting his novel *Compulsion* to the theatre (1957).

Meyer Levin was not the only well-known American Jewish prose writer to whom the stage beckoned between 1953 and 1964. Saul Bellow made his playwriting debut with the one-act *The Wrecker* (1956), in which tenants of a condemned building refuse to move out until they have vented their rage on the walls that have witnessed their disappointments. It is a fascinating footnote to cultural history that when Bellow's only full-length play, *The Last Analysis,* was produced on Broadway in 1964, its author thought that what he labeled a farce would be better received than his contemporaneous novel, *Herzog.*[37] *Herzog* became one of Bellow's most celebrated novels; *Analysis* lasted for twenty-eight performances. In a perceptive *Herald Tribune* review, critic Walter Kerr faulted Bellow's "frightening naïveté," as a playwright, while hinting at what public expectations of Bellow, as a Jewish intellectual, must have been.

Observing that "laughter *has* grown lame in a world resigned both to holocaust and to television" (TV is central to Bellow's play), Kerr wrote that of course Bellow "knows farce can no longer mean what it used to mean in a simpler and saner time."[38]

During this era two of America's most celebrated Jewish playwrights departed from their customary universalism to treat explicitly Jewish subjects. Lillian Hellman wrote her only play about American Jewish life, *My Mother, My Father and Me* (1963), an absurdist adaptation of Burt Blechman's novel about a family as unhappy as it is implausible. In *Incident at Vichy* (1964) Arthur Miller addressed two daunting subjects: a roundup of Jews in wartime France, and the question of moral responsibility for evil. Hellman's play closed after seventeen performances. A frank experiment, it was an atypically frivolous play.

*Incident at Vichy*'s modest run (99 performances) might be attributed to other commitments in the Lincoln Center repertory season. It is likely, however, that despite generally respectful reviews from clearly uncomfortable reviewers, audiences were not yet ready to be disconcerted by the play's relentless questions about guilt and accountability, and by its brilliant redefinition of the Jew as "the man whose death leaves you relieved that you are not him." Again Walter Kerr's response was trenchant: "The matter," wrote Kerr, "is so recent and so serious, and we are all of us so engaged in it, that we scarcely dare acknowledge our dissatisfaction with its theatrical cloaking."[39] In 1964, Americans had neither the head nor the heart to confront the unprecedented issues raised by the Holocaust unless they were packaged in the comfortable Broadway format cannily used by Goodrich and Hackett in *The Diary of Anne Frank*.

"Alter's era" ends spectacularly with the premiere of *Fiddler on the Roof* in 1964. Its 3,242 performances established the long run record it held until 1980. *Fiddler* signals a milestone in the popular acceptance of Jewish images in American theatre.[40] Although musical comedy admittedly has wider box office appeal than straight drama, the acclaim won by this profoundly Jewish work suggests that the perception of Jews in America had undergone revision. Leslie Fiedler was right about the enhanced relevance of the image of the Jew: the historical Jewish experience of vulnerability and uprootedness had come to be viewed as broadly representative. In addition, Joseph Stein, author of *Fiddler's* book, observed that the pertinence of the Sholem Aleichem stories could be attributed to the contemporary "breakdown of the traditional cultural forms and beliefs under the buffeting of social change and hostile forces."[41]

## *The Pyrotechnic, Ever-More Ethnic Sixties*

The upheaval Joseph Stein refers to touched off fireworks in the theatre. While plays like those just mentioned were delighting Broadway audiences, dramatic events of quite another order were taking place beyond the Great White Way. The political and social cataclysms of the sixties — the war in Vietnam, the civil rights movement, the eruption of ethnic pride, the emergence of the women's movement, and the steady inroads of cultural pluralism — would modify much of what had characterized America at mid-century. The theatre swiftly and broadly reflected the disruption of the status quo. The Age of Aquarius fostered innovation and experiment. New venues multiplied, as did playwrights, scripts, audiences, and, most critically, sources of support. The powerful forces loosed in the sixties fueled the explosion of American Jewish plays and playwrights that marks the century's last decades.

Chief among the transforming influences was the proliferation of noncommercial and experimental theatre that took root and flourished Off-Broadway, ultimately spilling over into Off-Off-Broadway.[42] Animated by the Zeitgeist, Off-Broadway grew into a worthy heir of the Little Theatre movement, whose influential successes in the teens and twenties mark the coming of age of the indigenous American stage.[43] The burgeoning of Off-Broadway in the sixties redefined American theatre, diversifying its goals and functions, enlarging its authority, and increasing the demands it made of audiences. In subsequent years, the role of Off-Broadway has intensified enormously. By 1985 *Best Plays* observed, "Off-Broadway was looking more and more like the major creative stimulus in the New York theatre, holding a virtual monopoly on innovation and generating a vigor essential to the survival of the fiercely commercial theatre uptown."[44]

There is no mystery about the appeal of Off- and Off-Off-Broadway to people working in theatre in the turbulent sixties. Having plenty to say, bursting with a passion for performance and new ideas for using the stage, heady with the opportunity to pursue artistic, rather than monetary or even critical success, they turned coffeehouses, firehouses, churches, even old Second Avenue (once

Yiddish) theatres into laboratories and greenhouses. There was a "found space" to express every point of view and an audience for every innovation.

The climate of openness encouraged pride in identity, particularly in ancestral roots. One result was the establishment of producing companies devoted to developing the work of specific ethnic and cultural groups. Among them were the Jewish Repertory Theatre and the American Jewish Theatre, about which more presently. Continuing the tradition of Jewish contribution to the making of American theatre, many pioneers of the Off-Broadway movement were Jewish: Julian Beck, Judith Malina, Joseph Chaikin, Theodore Mann, Charles Marowitz and Richard Schechner. Among the playwrights who were early nurtured in Off-Broadway and alternative theatres and whose work reflects their Jewishness were Rosalyn Drexler, Jules Feiffer, Israel Horovitz, Arthur Kopit, Karen Malpede, Harvey Perr, Leeny Sack and Susan Yankowitz.

In a figurative sense, the Off-Broadway movement covered the entire United States. The multiplication of professional regional theatres across the country, and of professional resident theatres at universities following the lead of Princeton, Michigan, and UCLA, provided greatly increased opportunities for play development and, of course, for audiences. The expansion and professionalism of regional houses signify a revised American attitude toward theatre. They gradually won acceptance as cultural institutions, which, as theatre scholar and critic Julius Novick pointed out in 1968, "exist to provide a public service for their communities like the local library, art gallery and symphony orchestra."[45] Their impact, however, has broadened far beyond their home cities. At the end of the century, theatre historian Gerald M. Berkowitz wrote that, "Without question the establishment of resident theatres all across America and the broad cultural acceptance of theatre as not-for-profit activity deserving of subsidy were the most positive things to happen to the American theatre in the 20th century."[46]

The regionals have contributed significantly to the development and production of American Jewish plays. For example, Shirley Lauro's *The Contest* premiered at Houston's Arena Stage; Dick Goldberg's *Family Business* at the Berkshire Theatre Festival (Stockbridge, Massachusetts); Mark Harelik's *The Immigrant*, at the Denver Center Theatre Company; and James Sherman's *Beau Jest* at Chicago's Victory Gardens Theater. Chicago's Goodman, Organic and St. Nicholas Theaters have nurtured David Mamet's work. Israel Horovitz refines his plays at the Gloucester (Massachusetts) Stage Company, which he founded in 1980. The Seattle Repertory Theatre has launched an impressive number of hits, including Wendy Wasserstein's *The Sisters Rosensweig* and Herb Gardner's *I'm Not Rappaport* and *Conversations With My Father.* The South Coast Repertory (Costa Mesa, California) commissioned Donald Margulies's *Sight Unseen*, and Jon Robin Baitz's *The Substance of Fire* premiered at the Long Wharf Theatre (New Haven, Connecticut).

In addition to fostering playwrights and launching new works into the repertoire, certain regional theatres across the country have cultivated an esprit de corps that has promoted American Jewish theatre in another way. Let Chicago's Second City exemplify a company that has served all three functions impressively. An improvisational theatre founded in 1959, Second City quickly became the forum for first-rate talent, proudly appropriating the *New Yorker* put-down from which it defiantly took its name. The talent of some of its actors included playwriting: Shelley Berman (*First Is Supper*), Joan Rivers (*Fun City*), and Elaine May (*Adaptation* and *Mr. Gogol and Mr. Preen*). David Mamet, who as a teenager worked as a busboy at Second City, acknowledges the influence of the episodic format of the work he saw there.[47]

At least as significant as American Jewish plays and players that emerged from Second City is the unmistakably Jewish tone it legitimized. Playwright Jeffrey Sweet notes the prevalence of scenes that "emphasized irony and skepticism, drew attention to ethical contradictions and lapses in the logic of authority figures. Conventional wisdom … was constantly being questioned and challenged.… This may not seem like such a big deal today, when much of mainstream popular culture has 'an attitude,' but coming out of Eisenhower's fifties, with McCarthyism fresh in mind, the effect on contemporary audiences was bracing."[48]

One easily recognizes in witty social satire and caustic comedy inveterate hallmarks of Jewish creativity: the skepticism of those who view the establishment as outsiders, the defense the defenseless find in mocking the empowered. Like the merciless stand-up comics — Mort Sahl, Lenny Bruce — Second City artists figure among the heirs of Yiddish satirists and the irreverent early Jewish vaudevillians in America. In expressing Jewish defiance of prevailing mores, these entertainers spoke for multitudes. They are a conduit through which brilliant comic impudence and rapier wit continue to enrich the American mainstream in all the performing arts.[49]

*The NFJC, the AJT and New Jewish Theatres*

The awakening of ethnic awareness — one observer aptly termed it the "postwar revival of peoplehood"[50] — prompted the establishment of a number of arts supporting institutions. Among them was the National Foundation for Jewish Culture (NFJC), founded by the Council of Jewish Federations in 1960. Dedicated to "the enhancement of Jewish life in America through the arts and humanities," the NFJC has been since the late seventies an influential advocate and generous supporter of Jewish theatre. The Foundation has provided for translations and productions of Hebrew and Yiddish plays, convened conferences and festivals of Jewish playwrights and productions, and published various resources for the field. Since 1994, the NFJC has sponsored an annual New Play Commission in Jewish Theatre competition. Dozens of new scripts have been nurtured; more than twenty of them developed through to full productions; a number of these plays will appear in an anthology presently in preparation. The Foundation is planning a national Jewish play reading series.

Some of the most energetic activity in Jewish theatre is taking place in the producing companies of the Association for Jewish Theatre (AJT) whose primary mission is fostering plays relevant to Jewish life and values. Founded in 1980 under the aegis of the NFJC as the Jewish Theatre Association, restructured several times since, the AJT is now an autonomous entity. Its membership includes a network of three-dozen nonprofit theatres across North America and some fifty individuals with a variety of professional interests in Jewish theatre. The AJT brings together well-established companies, like Cleveland's Halle Theatre, which has been running since 1951 and Phoenix's Arizona Jewish Theatre, the largest independent Jewish theatre west of the Mississippi, with fledglings like the Jewish Theatre of Pittsburgh, which presented its first season in 2002. Veteran affiliates like the Winnipeg Jewish Theatre and the Saidye Bronfman Yiddish Theatre have been joined recently by members from other Canadian cities and overseas.

Virtually all the AJT affiliates are dedicated to developing and producing new plays. So, for example, Barbara Lebow's *A Shayna Maidel* was launched when it won the Halle Theatre's Dorothy Silver competition; Detroit's Jewish

Ensemble Theatre provided early support to Donald Margulies's *The Model Apartment* and produced the American premiere of Israeli playwright Motte Lerner's *Else, or Exile in Jerusalem.* Washington D.C.'s Theatre J, under the artistic direction of Ari Roth, has distinguished itself in presenting series of works that provide a variety of perspectives on a single subject. A recent season, for instance, was devoted to "American-Moscow Fusion," and included Neil Simon's *The Good Doctor*, Josh Kornbluth's *Red Diaper Baby*, and Roth's own *Life In Refusal.*

Two professional Jewish theatres were established in New York in 1974. In its twenty-eight year run, Stanley Brechner's American Jewish Theatre made an award-winning name for itself, not only with revivals of Yiddish classics, many in fresh translations (David Pinski's *The Treasure;* Peretz Hirschbein's *Green Fields)*, but also in the development and production of new works. They include the Israel Horovitz trilogy *(Today I Am a Fountain Pen, A Rosen by Any Other Name,* and *The Chopin Playoffs)* and Alan Brody's *Invention for Fathers and Sons.* Also in 1974, Israeli Ran Avni inaugurated the Jewish Repertory Theatre. In addition to producing Yiddish classics, like Sholem Asch's *God of Vengeance* in an adaptation by Stephen Fife, the JRT has mounted European plays of Jewish content (Michel de Ghelderode's *Pantagleize,* John Galsworthy's *Loyalties).* Edward M. Cohen, associate director through 1994, headed the JRTs playwrights-in-residence and writers' lab programs that developed the work of a number of new dramatists.[51] Award-winning plays first staged at the JRT have gone on to healthy runs at commercial venues (*Kuni Leml, Crossing Delancey, Cantorial, Shmulnik's Waltz*).

Since 1994, Tuvia Tennenbom's Jewish Theatre of New York has been producing plays in lower Manhattan as well as in Belgium and Germany. The acclaimed artist-led ensemble, A Traveling Jewish Theatre, founded in California in 1982, lives up to its name by performing across the country and around the world its unique programs of poetry, storytelling, mysticism, history, and music—from jazz to sacred chant.

That First Jewish Theatre Conference/Festival in 1980 which so emphatically demonstrated the extent of Jewish theatre activity in the United States was followed two years later by an international festival at Tel Aviv University. That vanguard event confirmed the vigor of Jewish dramatic activity in many languages, a vitality that has grown even more exuberant in the ensuing years. The annual conference in 2003 drew some 150 attendees: artistic directors, play-wrights, performers, critics and scholars from the United States, Canada, Israel, Austria, England, and South Africa. In the first decade of the 21st century, the AJT is working closely with the Global Theatre Initiative of the Jewish Agency of Israel in developing several Israeli-Diaspora projects such as an international playwriting collaborations and the resources of the Internet website, *www.jewish-theatre.com.*

*A Self-Confident and Sophisticated Repertoire*

Yet another stimulus energized and shaped the postwar American Jewish repertoire. It is perhaps the prime mover. While radically revised attitudes toward ethnicity in general account for significant changes in public percep-tions of Jews, the fundamental difference occurred in Jewish self-image and self-assurance. It seems almost unimaginable today that in 1954, an anxious Garson Kanin, monitoring the dramatization of the Anne Frank *Diary*, cautioned scriptwriters Goodrich and Hackett, "The fact that in this play the symbols of persecution and oppression are Jews is incidental, and Anne, in stating the argument so, reduces her magnificent stature."[52]

Although by the sixties, American Jewish playwrights had long since left behind the deliberate de-ethnicization of patently Jewish characters that had seemed prudent earlier in the century, by today's standards of explicitness, even the most recognizably ethnic voices of that decade sound muted. The only timidity in Neil Simon's first comedy, *Come Blow Your Horn* (1961), is the unspecified identity of its transparently Jewish protagonists. No such misgiv-ings stay Simon's hand in his autobiographical "BB" trilogy, *Brighton Beach Memoirs* (1984), *Biloxi Blues* (1985), and *Broadway Bound* (1987). Similarly, Herb Gardner makes little of the obvious Jewishness of Murray Burns, the writer at the center of *A Thousand Clowns* (1961). Thirty years later, Gardner incorporates whole chapters of the American Jewish experience in Eddie (né Itzik) of *Conversations With My Father.*

Beyond the social, cultural, and intellectual activities that brought Jews even closer to the mainstream — or the other way about — the impact of two his-toric events transformed the way American Jews saw and expressed themselves. The first was the dawning understanding of the devastation of the Holocaust; the second, the creation of the state of Israel. For many American Jews too young or too disaffected in 1948 to be stirred by the implications of a Jewish state, the Six Day War in 1967 and the repeated performance of Jews as brilliant military strategists had far-reaching effects. Assessing the war's impact on identity, scholar Charles Silberman declared it "a watershed between two eras — one in which American Jews had tried to persuade themselves, as well as Gentiles, that they were just like everyone else, only more so, and a period in which they acknowledged, even celebrated, their distinctiveness."[53] Leonard Fein, veteran commentator on Jewish life, pointed out that for many Jews the Six Day War took on theological significance. Fein writes that the war propelled Israel to "the center of the Jewish religious consciousness and consensus. In a very precise way, Israel had now become the faith of the American Jew."[54]

Gradually the impact of history became manifest in Jewish creativity. A look back at the arts of the last four decades shows the range of the influence of the Shoah and Israel, which extends well beyond representations of and responses to the events themselves. What emerged from the American Jewish self-image reshaped by the Holocaust and the Jewish state is artistic self-expression unfettered by conventional notions of propriety and caution.

Curiously, these newly confident assertions of Jewish identity are not totally without precedent. Writing of the early 20th-century entertainers like Fanny Brice, Al Jolson and George Burns, Irving Howe noted, "They would declare themselves 'proud to be a Jew'.... But what it meant to be a Jew, or for that matter an American, they seldom bothered about."[55] The wheel has moved ahead as it has come full circle. Playwrights in the last third of the century also assert their Jewish pride — with this significant difference: They frequently use the theatre to examine the implications of being Jewish *and* American. Sometimes this is a matter of Jews accepting a more active role in shaping society's perceptions of them. So, for example, where George Simon in *Counsellor-at-Law* (1931) struggles for acceptance in a WASP society that sees him only as an over-reaching Jew, Norma Teitel, the young actress on the threshold of a major stage career in Jeffrey Sweet's *The Value of Names* (1983) insists on deciding *how* her Jewish name and famous Jewish parentage will influence her image and her professional life. Arthur Laurents's hypersensitive young GI in *Home of the Brave* (1959) is literally paralyzed by what he perceives as an anti-Semitic slur uttered by a trusted friend. By contrast, David Mamet's veteran in *Goldberg Street* (1991), painfully aware of his conflicted reactions to the prejudice he endured in the military, admits his own compliance with the bias.56

A variety of interpretations of being Jewish in today's world remodel the treatment of traditional themes. What, for instance, could be more central to the repertoire than the Jewish family play and its intergenerational conflicts? Recent plays depart from customary patterns in their depiction of the kinds of problems contemporary families have, in the frankness with which they are portrayed, and even in their definition of family. Works like James Lapine's *Table Settings* (1980) remind us that not all members of a Jewish family are Jewish, Harvey Fierstein's *Widows and Children First* (1979), that they are not all heterosexual, and Lapine and William Finn's *Falsettoland* (1989), that divorce does not end Jewish family life.

Jewish family interaction comes in for mocking, occasionally bitter depictions that indicate that critical self-examination can be, well, critical. In Woody Allen's *The Floating Light Bulb* (1982), a painfully shy youngster resists the efforts of both parents to remodel him. His philandering father wants to make him into a slugger; his alcoholic mother would make a performer of him. Loving parents send out mixed signals about self-sufficiency that confound their Harvard-educated daughter struggling to find her own way in Wendy Wasserstein's *Isn't It Romantic* (1983). A Jewish mother cuts up her wedding gown for a Halloween costume in Donald Margulies's *The Loman Family Picnic* (1988), while her meager wage-earning husband agonizes over bills for a pretentious bar mitzvah for which he finally has to appropriate his son's gift money.

It is surely an indication of energized ethos that social responsibility and principled behavior, early established as stimulus and subject of American Jewish playwriting, take on heightened prominence in postwar Jewish plays. Moral behavior, a timeless subject (recall the inability of Arthur Miller's besieged manufacturer in *No Villain* to reconcile his ethics with industry's strikebreaking tactics), is viewed in updated circumstances.

Community responsibility broadens from neighborhood to peoplehood. In a realistic departure from the convention of just rewards and happy endings, concern for the welfare of others can amount to no more than its own best reward. In Leonard Spigelgass's *The Wrong Way Light Bulb* (1969), a young writer tries earnestly, but with limited success, to reconcile the quarrelsome multi-ethnic tenants of an inner city apartment house he has inherited. In Allen Havis's *Haut Goût* (1997) an American Jewish doctor invents an infant formula intended for Third World use. He puts a prestigious practice on hold to serve his humanitarian goals, only to fall victim to a Haitian dictator and betrayal by his own government.

A startling and ironic figuration of ethical Jewish behavior is woven into the immense fabric of Tony Kushner's *Angels in America* (1992). Two fantasy scenes bring together Ethel Rosenberg with her nemesis, government prosecutor Roy M. Cohn. At the height of the "Red Menace" of 1953, Ethel and her husband Julius were convicted of espionage and, due to Cohn's importuning (according to the play), executed. As if in defiance of this ugly history, in Part I: *Millennium Approaches*, Ethel ignores Cohn's spurious denial that he is very ill; she insists on calling an ambulance for him. After Cohn's death in Part II: *Perestroika*, Rosenberg reappears to guide another Jewish character, Louis, through the *kaddish*, the prayer for the dead. This traditional ritual is the last thing one would expect from Ethel Rosenberg, an ardent Communist. The scene ends with an ironic sandwich of Hebrew rite and American street talk:

> ETHEL V'imru omain.
> LOUIS V'imru omain.
> ETHEL You sonofabitch.
> LOUIS You sonofabitch.[57]

The Rosenberg case is the focus of Donald Freed's *Inquest* (1969), a work that postulates that anti-Semitism and possibly Jewish self-hatred (the sentencing judge was a Jew) sealed the couple's doom. Freed's script perpetuates Jewish affinity for the law and fascination with its operation in the courtroom, a tradition that dates at least from Anski's *The Dybbuk*. (Elmer Rice, himself a lawyer, introduced courtroom drama to the American stage in *On Trial* [1914], a play that used flashbacks in the theatre for the first time.) In Herman Wouk's suspenseful *The Caine Mutiny Court-Martial* (1954), a Jewish lawyer's successful defense of the reprehensible conduct of his client, a naval commander, is motivated entirely by the attorney's gratitude to the career military men who protected America's Jews from the fate of their European co-religionists. In her punningly titled docudrama, *Execution of Justice* (1984), Emily Mann takes a wider view of the disaster wrought by bigotry. Using court transcripts, news reports, and TV footage, Mann shows the intolerance that stained the San Francisco trial of Dan White for the assassination of Harvey Milk, a Jewish homosexual, and George Moscone, the Mayor who had appointed Milk as city examiner.

But American Jewish dramatists' enduring interest in morality also takes the form of works that depict lawlessness and unethical behavior. The subject is stated early. In *Success Story* (1932), John Howard Lawson tells the cautionary tale of a fanatic careerist, impatient with Marxism, who rails against capitalism only to be seduced and ultimately undone by its material rewards. Dishonesty in seeking the spoils of Mammon animates a number of newer plays that are unmistakably contemptuous or derisive of their characters. Unscrupulous hotheads with names like Shelly "the Machine" Levene, Sam Aronow, and Dave Moss populate the world of real estate-selling piranhas in David Mamet's *Glengarry Glen Ross* (1983). In Jon Robin Baitz's *Mizlansky/Zilinsky or Schmucks* (1998), two has-been filmmakers plot to regain solvency through a shady tax shelter that will protect sales of shoddy recordings of Bible stories for children. Baitz leavens his characterizations with healthy doses of comic ridicule. So does Jerry Lerner in his portrait of Lawrence Garfinkle (Larry the Liquidator), the ruthless takeover artist in *Other People's Money* (1989), who gets the wire and cable company, the girl and the doughnuts.

Another dramatic inquiry into responsible Jewish behavior focuses on black-Jewish relationships, sometimes drawing on the parallels between two vulnerable peoples. Although the Jewish manager in Howard Sackler's Pulitzer Prize-winning *The Great White Hope* (1968) devotes himself to protecting his brilliant but arrogant heavyweight prizefighter, he is powerless against the prejudice heaped upon the African American. The guardianship notwithstanding, it is always clear that the harried Jew is the employee of the black. A different set of circumstances forges the bond between black and Jew in Alfred Uhry's *Driving Miss Daisy*, the Pulitzer recipient in 1987. The work traces the evolution over an historic quarter-century, 1948–1973, of the evolving friendship between a strong-minded Southern widow and her self-respecting African American chauffeur. In Herb Gardner's Tony Award-winning *I'm Not Rappaport* (1985), black and Jew are both friends and sparring partners as they face the menaces of Central Park, the ravages of age, and the loss of autonomy.

Community concerns acquire even broader horizons as playwrights train their sights beyond the United States. Israel has become a momentous fact of American Jewish life, not only as a source of identity, but as a modern nation whose politics and policies engage the passions. The sweetly innocent appreciation of Don Appell and Jerry Herman's *Milk and Honey* (1961) bears little resemblance to grittier post-1967 plays. For instance, Gordon Rayfield's *Bitter Friends* (1988) depicts the divided loyalties of David Klein, an American employed by the United States Defense Department. Convicted of passing secret military information to Israel, Klein is given a draconian prison sentence. Though Rayfield denies actual references, his work rings strong echoes of the actual Jonathan Pollard spy case. In Josh Ford's *Miklat* (2002), parents visit their son who is studying in Israel and are bewildered to find that he has joined an ultra-Orthodox yeshiva and agreed to an arranged marriage. William Gibson's *Golda's Balcony* was brought to vivid, multi-dimensional life in a one-woman tour de force performed in New York by the award-winning Tovah Feldshuh in 2003. The play recreates the joys and struggles of Meir's lifetime of dedication and service to her adopted country, and underscores her anguish at the Yom Kippur War in 1973 during her administration as prime minister.

Still other scripts represent multiple perspectives on Israelis and Moslems. Marilyn Felt's *Acts of Faith* (1989) depicts the intense struggle for mutual understanding between a pacifistic American woman and the militant Shi'ite Arab who guards her during a hijacking. Felt's *Asher's Command* (2000) gets under the skin of the relationship between an Israeli military officer serving as a commander in the occupied West Bank and a wise, principled Palestinian mechanic. Allan Havis bases *A Vow of Silence* (1992) on the Givati court-martial trial in 1989 where four members of an elite Israeli brigade were exonerated in the death of a detained Palestinian. Havis likens both the trial and the furious reactions to its verdict to the Rodney King affair in America. The playwright scrupulously views the case from several angles to include conflicting Palestinian and American reactions. Theatre J in Washington D.C. has initiated a program of "Voices From a Changing Israel." As these lines are written, J's artistic director Ari Roth is working with Egyptian satirist Ali Salem to dramatize the latter's *A Drive Through Israel*. In his memoir, the Salem recounts his daring post-Oslo Accord journey to get to know his neighbors by actually knocking at their doors.

Elizabeth Swados's 1988 oratorio, *Jerusalem*, celebrates its city's international significance. The action follows a child traveler through the city sacred to Christians, Moslems, and Jews alike, and wracked by contemporary strife. Swados has woven her own material together with folk and liturgical melodies of more than a dozen nations. Deliberately conflated images reinforce this interdenominationalism; for example, the Rachael who weeps for her children is a Moslem mother lamenting her war dead. The script of *Jerusalem* combines the poetry of Yehuda Amichai, the book of Jeremiah and improvisational texts created by its original multi-ethnic LaMama cast. The work offers a quintessential example of Robert Brustein's 1991 observation that, "Transcultural blending may be the most fully acknowledged artistic development of our time."[58]

Having at last penetrated the American psyche, the Holocaust has come to exercise an irresistible imperative on the American creative imagination and a magnet to Jewish playwrights. Even when the Shoah is not the subject of the work, it is a recurring reference. As Neil Simon's *Brighton Beach Memoirs* (1984) ends, the Jerome family is making room for cousins who have managed to escape from Poland. In Elizabeth Swados's *Esther: A Vaudeville Megillah* (1988), the Biblical rescue from planned genocide resonates with contemporary relevance. A Hitler postcard takes on disproportionate significance for the stubborn paterfamilias in Jon Robin Baitz's *The Substance of Fire* (1991).

Despite the formidable challenge of staging its horror, the Shoah has inspired memorable drama.[59] Arthur Miller's *Incident at Vichy* (1964) recreates the fear and suspense of the anteroom of an interrogation chamber where rounded-up Jews await their fate. Miller insists on the universal implications of the erroneously arrested Polish nobleman's sacrifice in giving his pass to freedom to a Jew: "Jew is only the name we give to that stranger, that agony we cannot feel, that death we look at like a cold abstraction. Each man has his Jew; it is the other. And Jews have their Jews."[60] In 1981, Miller adapted a screenplay from *Playing for Time*, the memoirs of Fania Fénelon, a French chanteuse who escaped death at Auschwitz-Birkenau as a musician in the camp orchestra. Harold and Edith Lieberman's *Throne of Straw* (1972) hews closely to the calamitous history of the Lodz ghetto under the eccentric rule of Chief Elder Mordechai Chaim Rumkowski, who, despite delusions of grandeur, did his utmost to save Jewish lives. The play asks audiences not to judge, but rather to consider what they might have done, faced with Rumkowski's "choiceless choices."[61] In *Hannah Senesh* (1985), David Schechter and Lori Wilner use the poetry and diary of the martyred Hungarian heroine to dramatize her renunciation of safety in Palestine in order return to Europe to fight and die in the resistance.

The ordeals of survivorship also come to the stage. Barbara Lebow's *A Shayna Maidel* (1988) reunites two European-born sisters after the war. One, brought to New York as a child, was spared the Nazi terror experienced by her sister, who had been left behind. Reunited, they must find ways of reweaving their lives in America, whose opportunities mean very different things to each of them. In *The Shawl* (1994), Cynthia Ozick brings to America the death camp survivors she created in her famous short story of that name. Rosa and Stella have now to cope not only with the plague of memories, but also with the infamy of Holocaust deniers. Donald Margulies' *The Model Apartment* (1990, 1995) takes a bitterly comic view of an elderly couple, Holocaust survivors. They want only to find peace in their Florida retirement, but the past follows them in the person of their disturbed, importunate daughter, the namesake of the child they lost in the Shoah. The absurdity and comedy in this play scarcely palliate its pain. In *The Gathering* (1997), Arje Shaw portrays a survivor incensed by President Reagan's plan to honor the dead at the cemetery at Bitburg where some S. S. men lie buried. Unable to convince his son, a White House speechwriter, of the outrageouness of the president's trip, the old man kidnaps his grandson, who is preparing for his Bar Mitzvah, and takes him to Bitburg to protest by reciting his *Haftorah* there. Then their encounter with a 24-year-old guard opens the Americans' eyes to the haunting legacy inherited by post-Holocaust Germans. Jeffrey Sweet's *The Action Against Sol Schumann* (2001) tells the story of an Orthodox Jew whose concealed past as a kapo in a labor camp is revealed when a co-religionist, who had suffered at his hands, recognizes his former tormentor's name when he offers a memorial gift to a synagogue where both are members.

Some effective American drama about the Shoah draws on what is genuinely part of the American Jewish experience: understanding what it means *not* to have been personally involved and facing the challenge of trying to understand what it was for those who were. Emily Mann's *Annulla, An Autobiography* (1988) captures the awe of that responsibility as the disembodied voice of the playwright listens to a spunky 74-year-old relate her courageous, sometimes extravagant adventures in enduring the horror. Leeny Sack, whose parents and grandmother sat on her bed at night telling her their stories about the camps, turned what she heard and felt into an extraordinary performance piece, *The Survivor and the Translator: A Solo Work About Not Having Experienced the Holocaust by a Daughter of Concentration Camp Survivors* (1980). Ari Roth's *Born Guilty* (1990) dramatizes Peter Sichrovsky's interviews with the children and grandchildren of Nazis, an endeavor that draws the journalist into the intersection of his own and his subjects' histories.

That oft-used Jewish weapon, irrepressible humor, is unsheathed even in drama about Nazism. In her performance piece, *Punch Me in the Stomach* (1995), Deb Filler turns into black but very funny comedy chapters from her unusual childhood. She describes her father's birthday present to her, a visit to "his" concentration camp. Though it lies outside the scope of this essay, it would be unthinkable not to mention a musical that takes Hitler-era comedy to a new extreme. Updating the tradition of the Jew as intrepid flouter of proprieties, Mel Brooks's *The Producers* (2001) blithely rewrites German history, poking Hitler in the eye with the pointed stick of parody. Without mentioning the Shoah, Brooks' work pertly affirms Jewish survival.

By the late 20th century, the challenge of American Jewish identity becomes impressively complex. "Many things are possible in America," observes Leon Wieseltier, "but the singleness of identity is not one of them."[62] Dual identity is further complicated when still other distinctions compete for inclusion: American Jewish secularist, humanist, feminist, lesbian, homosexual, and person of color. So far, the American Jewish stage has functioned well as a three-way mirror. Consider the 13-year-old in William Finn's *Falsettoland* (1989) who chooses to celebrate his Bar Mitzvah in the hospital room where his father's lover is dying of AIDS. Or Dr. Judith B. Kaufman, black daughter of a Tuscaloosan Baptist mother who ran off with a Jewish Freedom Rider and was Bat Mitzvahed in Brooklyn, who gives thanks she is "half a man" in Wendy Wasserstein's *An American Daughter* (1998).

The very existence of multiple identities and self-images seems only to have encouraged dramatists to pursue the matter of what it means to be Jewish. The question is treated in plays whose characters dilute, deny or abandon their Jewishness. Alfred Uhry's *The Last Night of Ballyhoo* (1997) draws on a long-standing schism in American Jewry. Set in the Atlanta of 1939, the play depicts a coterie of assimilated German Jews who structure their lives in imitation of their admired Episcopalian neighbors. Trimming her Christmas tree, one

"wannabe" explains that, "Christmas is just another American holiday if you leave out all that silly nonsense about Jesus being born." Such accommodation is thrown into relief by the arrival of a New Yorker, happily secure in his East European mores and values. His comfortable Jewish self-assurance makes a young Southern woman realize that for her, "there's just a big hole where the Judaism is supposed to be."[63] The curtain falls on her lighting candles as her family celebrates the Sabbath, having welcomed the New Yorker and more traditional Jewishness into their home.

Patricia, a non-Jew in Donald Margulies' *Sight Unseen* (1995) tells her former lover, Jonathan Waxman, "You can't exist in two worlds; you've got to turn your back on one of them." That seems to be what Waxman has tried to do: he has intermarried, he was too busy to sit *shiva* for his father, and he vigorously insists, "I'm an *American* painter. *American* is the adjective, not *Jewish, American*."[64] Waxman protests too much. His behavior and his art are driven by guilt at having abandoned the allegiances and the ethics of his upbringing to pursue fame, fortune and especially, acceptance. An imposing, perceptive German interviewer who persists in seeing him as a Jew exposes his insecurity and rudderlessness. Having turned his back on the truth he pretends to honor, he has lost his moorings. For Jonathan Waxman, the inspiration of Jewish identity and the direction of artistic integrity have become sights unseen.

What happens to Jews when Jewishness vanishes from their lives? That question lies at the angry, anxious heart of the first play of David Mamet's autobiographical trilogy, *The Old Neighborhood*. The ominously entitled *The Disappearance of the Jews* (1982) portrays the return of the middle-aged Bobby Gould to the city of his boyhood. He and his old friend Joey reminisce about their youthful adventures. They lament the mediocrity of their adult lives, laying the blame on assimilation, on having drifted away from the already watered-down Jewishness they were barely conscious of in their boyhood and now recall with rue. Their yearning for meaningful connection to Jewish life leads them fanciful wistfulness. They regret the certainties they might have enjoyed in the Jewish past, like life in the *shtetl* or the early days of Hollywood. Bobby is leaving his Gentile wife, who feels that Jews must have earned their history of persecution; he worries about his son who would be recognized as a Jew sooner by anti-Semites than by any traditional branch of Judaism. These men are utterly detached from any firm foundation in Jewish life on which they could build, bereft of a community in which they could take part as involved contributors. Small wonder they look beyond their old neighborhood to one that is very much older.

These are barely chartered waters and there are no tide charts. What has come to be called "postethnic theory" regards ethnicity not as inherited, but as choice. Horace Kallen's cultural pluralism posited that while Americans cannot choose their forebears, they are free to decide the extent to which ancestry shapes their identity. "Anti-Semites may have conceived of the Jews as a race," writes David Biale, "but American Jews, with their historical origins in Europe and the Middle East and with an intermarriage rate now at least 30 percent, defy racializing stereotypes even more now than ever. In a free society, all Jews are 'Jews by choice' (a term coined recently for converts)." Biale adds the radical but tantalizing suggestion that we learn to reconceptualize intermarriage as a source of "new forms of identity, including multiple identities, that will reshape what it means to be Jewish in ways we can only begin to imagine."[65]

Whatever those ways may be, we can count on meeting them in American Jewish plays.

## III. THE PLAYS: AN OVERVIEW

(NOTE: These précis introduce the subjects of the plays. Individual headnotes that precede each play provide more detailed critical material.)

*Counsellor-at-Law*

George Simon, Elmer Rice's eponymous attorney, seems to have realized the American Dream. He is spectacularly successful in an impressive range of legal specialties. Senators travel from Washington to consult with him, beautiful women throw themselves at him, he lives in Westchester with his wife, a member of the Four Hundred, and he is good to his mother. Still, the first words he speaks are, 'Do you want me?" Being wanted is something Simon cannot get enough of. He needs to be needed; he craves acceptance. He is knocking at the wrong doors. Simon faces two formidable obstacles. The first is the patrician society where, despite his brilliant accomplishments, his fortune and the thin armor of intermarriage, he will never achieve the status he seeks. The second is his personal value system, where decency battles ambition for primacy. Simon's relentless drive anticipates the opportunistic Jewish arriviste at the center of John Howard Lawson's sensational *Success Story* (1932). Unlike Lawson's Sol Ginsburg, Simon does not turn his back on Jewish morality. When compassion leads him to bend the law, he makes himself dangerously vulnerable to the determination of his elite enemies to humiliate him and bring him down. Rice contrasts their impregnable hostility with the respect Simon has earned from his more down-to-earth associates and the appreciation of those who know him for what he is. Rice's big, beautifully crafted play sets a standard for candid depiction of American success seeking recognition in its American Jewish identity.

*Awake and Sing!*

Applying a title borrowed from Isaiah to urban life in the great Depression, Clifford Odets's *Awake and Sing!* is a quintessential American Jewish play. Its depiction of the Bronx and its immigrant speech patterns stamp it with historical and social authenticity. The play sets in action remarkably well-drawn characters who were to become staples (and ultimately, alas, stereotypes) on the American stage: male immigrants, bewildered by the values and demands of American life, discontented youths, avid for a life richer than their parents', and the prototypical Jewish mother, compelled by circumstances to develop her extraordinary talent for effective, if insensitive, solutions to life's predicaments. The depth of the characters and the genuineness of the plot stunned audiences in 1935. Writer Alfred Kazin acclaimed the work's verisimilitude and its turning "blunt Jewish speech" into dialogue. Kazin marveled at "watching my mother and father and uncles and aunts occupying the stage...by as much right as if they were Hamlet and Lear."[66] It is striking how closely Kazin's appreciation of the play, produced under the aegis of the predominately Jewish Group Theatre, echoes the words of Harold Clurman, a co-founder of The Group, about the Yiddish theatre he loved: "Here the problems of [the immigrant audience's] life, past and present, could be given a voice."[67] Time has not subdued that eloquence.

*Morning Star*

The Broome Street address in Sylvia Regan's *Morning Star* (1940) provides a window on three generations of American Jewish life. Personal events — bar mitzvahs and weddings — take place against the background of history,

including the Russian Revolution, the First World War and the Great
Depression. The play's central event is the Triangle Shirtwaist Factory fire of
March 25, 1911, in which 147 women and 21 men perished in flames or in futile
efforts to escape them by plunging from the building's top stories (eerily pre-
figuring an even greater catastrophe ninety years later). The ambitious scope of
the play is repeated in its large cast. Many of the characters are archetypal: the
patient, amorous boarder, the angry radical, the furiously ambitious young
woman, the wise and stalwart materfamilias, and the would-be artist.
Judicious glimpses of the past — Becky Felderman's references to Old World
deprivations, the boarder's account of his miserable passage to America, the
unexpected fate of the Marxist who returns to Russia — provide perspective
for the characters' adjustment to the inequities and disappointments in the
New World. Despite tragedies and setbacks, these Jews demonstrate their
appreciation of life in America. Patriotism pervades the play whose original
title was "Spangled Banner."

*The Tenth Man*

Both psychiatry and renewed ethnic awareness have their place in *The Tenth
Man* (1959), but the matrix of Paddy Chayefsky's play is Anski's Yiddish
classic, *The Dybbuk* (1914). The exorcism of a troublesome spirit that inhabits
the soul of a living person supplies the spectacular coup de théâtre of both
plays. But the solemn ritual staged by ten Hasidim in the East European
shtetl synagogue in Anski's work contrasts starkly with the ceremony conducted by the disparate affiliates of a storefront synagogue in Mineola, Long
Island. The poles of opposition in Anski's play, where two young lovers set
themselves at odds with a homogeneous, hermetic community are fragmented
in the American work into a variety of conflicts roiling Jewish lives in an open,
secular society. The sexton's daily search to round up ten men for a *minyan*
becomes metaphoric of each character's struggle for meaning enough to
get through the day. The past does not meld easily into the present here,
and the future is threatening. Widowers joke heartbreakingly about the inhos-
pitality of their daughters-in-law and visit their own cemetery plots. A
young lawyer's disenchantment with life is driving him to dependence on
alcohol and psychoanalysis; a rabbi's dedication to spiritual leadership is
being eroded by the worldlier demands of his congregants. To these
dilemmas the play proposes a common approach: the restoration of the faith
that fosters love.

45

*Conversations With My Father*

Herb Gardner's autobiographical play sprawls over four decades, delineating the challenges of "making it" in America through the attempts of Eddie Ross (né Itzik Goldberg) to make a go of his Canal Street bar and grill. Determined to forget the pogroms of his East European past, Eddie aspires to be 100 percent American. In his book, that means being tough. His dominant mood is defiance, of the Yiddish actor who boards with him and never lets him forget where he came from, of gangsters who would shake him down, of his sons whose lives he tries to program, and of God. The problem is, Eddie is not sure how deep to bury the Jewishness. He balks at reminders to observe his father's memorial date, while insisting that his son stay in Hebrew school until his Bar Mitzvah so he will "join up with *my* Pop and *his* Pop ... and all the Pops back forever." There is irony in the play's title, since what communication there is between father and sons is either one-sided, or delivered at a pitch that can hardly be called conversational. Though Eddie dominates the play, it makes room for other delightful characterizations. One of them is Eddie's wife Gusta, a Jewish mother who has an atypically small role in this family play. It is Gusta's tenacious hold on traditional Jewish recipes (restored to their Yiddish names which Eddie had imaginatively anglicized) that finally makes a popular success of their establishment when the neighborhood changes. After forty years of chasing after America, America comes to the Jew, and, in fact, to secure American Jews for whom brisket tzimmes seems more fulfilling than Mulligan stew.

*Broken Glass*

Hannah Di Blindeh, a denizen of Eddie Ross' bar in *Conversations With My Father* is blinded by what she saw in the October Pogrom. Sylvia Gellburg in Arthur Miller's *Broken Glass* is paralyzed by what she did not see. While the anti-Semitic violence of Kristallnacht bursts forth in Germany, in Brooklyn Sylvia and her husband Phillip live in a world of repressed emotions, unmentioned resentments and unexpressed love. Miller vividly recreates the climate of 1938 when American Jews, however aware of their threatened European co-religionists, were still caught up in Depression woes. Set three years later than *Awake and Sing!*, *Broken Glass* provides a very different and equally representative perspective on American Jewish life in the thirties. Phillip Gellburg has a well-paying job in a firm that never lets him forget he is a Jew and assigns him the unsavory task of dispossessing people from their homes. It is too easy to dismiss Phillip as a self-hating Jew. His like was common in the thirties and forties — insecure, vulnerable, ready to buy acceptance at the price of self-effacement and the gamble that the children would be more fully accepted Americans. Sylvia, frustrated by Phillip's insistence that she leave the job she loved, settles uncomfortably into the role of middle class housewife. In that, she too is a highly representative figure. But Sylvia becomes a symbol of something much more unique when headlines from abroad shatter her resignation, immobilizing her and engendering the crisis which forces the Gellburgs to face their unfulfilled and inauthentic lives.

These six plays bring to the stage and the reader representative reflections of the kaleidoscope of 20th-century American Jewish life. They offer a solid foundation and a standard of accomplishment for the development of the American Jewish repertoire that, even as the latest of these works were written, was vigorously taking off in new directions.

# NOTES

1. Stephen M. Cohen, ed., *American Modernity and Jewish Identity* (New York: Tavistock, 1983), 25.
2. Quoted by Harley Erdman, *Staging the Jew: The Performance of an American Ethnicity, 1860–1920* (New Brunswick: Rutgers University Press, 1997), 96.
3. Tyrone Guthrie, preface, in Mendel Kohansky, *The Hebrew Theatre* (New York: Ktav, 1969), v.
4. John Higham, "American Anti-Semitism Historically Reconsidered," in Charles Herbert Stember, ed., *Jews In the Mind of America* (New York: Basic Books, 1966), 240.
5. Almost two million Jews came to the United States between 1881 and 1924. In 1880, the beginning of the mass migration from Eastern Europe, 230,000 Jews constituted 0.5% of the total U.S. population. By 1925, America's 4,228,000 Jews represented 3.6% of her population. Sidney Goldstein, "American Jewry, 1970: A Demographic Profile," in Marshall Sklare, ed., *The Jew in American Society* (New York: Behrman House, 1974), 100–101.
6. John Higham, "American Anti-Semitism Historically Reconsidered," 248.
7. Gilbert Seldes, "Jewish Plays and Jew Plays in New York," *The Menorah Journal* 8 (April 1922), 240.
8. Russell Lynes, *The Lively Audience: A Social History of the Visual and Performing Arts in America, 1890–1950* (New York: Harper and Row, 1985), 31. See also Richard Butsch, *The Making of American Audiences: From Stage to Television* (Cambridge, U.K.: Cambridge University Press, 2000), 128.
9. Butsch, 132–135. See also Irving Howe, "The Yiddish Theatre," in his *World of Our Fathers* (New York: Schocken, 1976), 469–496 and Nahma Sandrow, *Vagabond Stars, A World History of Yiddish Theatre* (New York: Harper and Row, 1977), 251–302.
10. Howard M. Sachar, *A History of Jews in America* (New York: Knopf, 1991), 356.
11. Stephen J. Whitfield, *In Search of American Jewish Culture* (Hanover and London: Brandeis University Press, University Press of New England, 1999), 115, 125.
12. Arthur Miller, "No Villain," typescript, New York Public Library for the Performing Arts, Lincoln Center.
13. Arthur Miller, *Timebends* (New York: Harper and Row, 1987), 62–63, 166–167, 179, 338.
14. See, for example, Gerald Bordman, *American Musical Comedy: From Adonis to Dreamgirls* (1982), *American Musical Revue: From The Passing Show to Sugar Babes* (1985); *American Musical Theatre: A Chronicle*, 2nd ed., (1992), New York: Oxford University Press; Stephen J.Whitfield, "Musical Theatre," *In Search of American Jewish Culture*, 59–87.
15. Cynthia Ozick, "Towards a New Yiddish," in *Art and Ardor* (New York: E.P. Dutton, 1984), 152–153, 167, 174. Although Ozick once argued for the creation of a New Yiddish—that is, an English made as "centrally Jewish in its concerns" as German was made into the "Old Yiddish"—she subsequently rejected the possibility of "fashioning a Diaspora literary culture" by the "Judaization of a single language used by a large population of Jews."
16. Robert Alter, "The Jew Who Didn't Get Away: On the Possibility of an American Jewish Culture," in Jonathan D. Sarna, ed., *The American Jewish Experience* (New York: Holmes and Meier, 1986), 277.
17. Quoted in David Biale, "The Melting Pot and Beyond," in Biale, Michael Galchinsky and Susannah Heschel, eds., *Insider/Outsider: American Jews and Multiculturalism* (Berkeley: University of California Press, 1998), 24.
18. Moshe Davis, "The Jewish People in Metamorphosis," in A. Leland Jamison, ed. *Tradition and Change in Jewish Experience* (Syracuse: Syracuse University Press, 1978), 7.
19. Joseph C. Landis, trans. and ed., *Three Great Jewish Plays* (New York: Applause, 1986);

Nahma Sandrow, trans. and ed., *God, Man and Devil* (Syracuse: Syracuse University Press, 1998).

20. Howe, *World of Our Fathers*, 492.

21. Francine Prose, "Protecting the Dead," in David Rosenberg, ed., *Testimony* (New York: Times Books), 113.

22. See footnote 55 for a synopsis of this delightful bellwether play.

23. Chicago Tribune, Sept. 26, 1920.

24. Jewish anxiety about stage portrayals and their insistence on seeing only what was deemed "good for the Jews" clearly influenced the repertoire. In 1943, an ill-tempered George Jean Nathan wrote of his distaste as a critic to see the spate of what he contemptuously called "valueless Jewish-oriented material . . . staged with deliberate appeal to the large proportion of theatergoers of that faith." However, he was heartened to note that "Jewish audiences themselves began to gag, ushering in plays whose characters bear 'all of mankind's faults.'" He correctly singles out as exemplary Rose Franken's *Outrageous Fortune* (1943), rare for its age in including a gay Jew and a wealthy Jewish matron disgruntled with moving in conformity with "the pack." However, Nathan's tone is again testy in his review of S. N. Behrman's adaptation of Werfel's *Jacobowsky and the Colonel*, where the not altogether sympathetic depiction of the Polish Jew "is mixed with timeless truths and the inevitable and changeless trials that the race must bear." *The Theatre Book of the Year 1943–1944* (New York: Knopf, 1944), 263–267.

25. Alfred Kazin, "The Jew As Modern Writer," in Peter I. Rose, ed., *The Ghetto and Beyond* (New York: Random House, 1969), 423. Although Harley Erdman writes (*Staging the Jew*, 159) that the 1910s were "the last decade (until modern times) in which markedly Jewish characters were commonplace in American popular performance," and though it is a matter of history that in between the two world wars the Jewish image in popular culture was often disguised or invisible, it is hard to ignore such phenomena as the *The Goldbergs*, a hugely popular radio show which ran from 1929 to 1934, 1937–1945, and 1949–1950, when it went to television. Or, for that matter, the stage personae of such as Fanny Brice and Sophie Tucker, Sid Caesar and Buddy Hackett, whose stock in trade was the distinctly Jewish humor and music that they exported from the Borscht Belt and adult summer camps like Tamimint and Green Mansions. Acknowledging the caution of Jewish entertainers in the years before mid-century, Irving Howe adds, "Not that 'de-Semitization' was, or could be, total" (*World of Our Fathers*, 568). And, of course, the 1910s and 1920s produced the vanguard of the American Jewish drama represented in this book.

26. Leslie Fielder, "What Can We Do About Fagin? The Jew-Villain in Western Tradition," *Commentary* (May 1949), 418.

27. Richard F. Shepard, "Genesis, Yiddish Version," *The New York Times*, Jan. 24, 1989.

28. Nahma Sandrow, "Yiddish Theater and American Theater," in Sarah Blacher Cohen, ed., *From Hester Street to Hollywood* (Bloomington: Indiana University Press, 1983), 27.

29. Sandrow points out, "Chekhov's *Uncle Vanya*, Strindberg's *The Father*, Romain Rolland's *Wolves*, Schnitzler's *Professor Bernardi*—all were performed in Yiddish translation before they were performed in English. Ibsen's *A Doll's House* and *An Enemy of the People* were staples in the serious Yiddish repertoires." "Yiddish Theatre and American Theatre," 26.

30. Quoted by Charles E. Silberman, foreword, in Stephen M. Cohen, ed., *American Modernity and Jewish Identity*, x.

31. Kenneth Tynan, "The Theatre," *New Yorker*, Nov. 14, 1959, 120.

32. Abraham J. Karp, "At Home in America," in Karp, ed., *The Jewish Experience in America*, v. 5 (Waltham, MA: American Jewish Historical Society and New York: Ktav, 1969), xxxvi.

33. Quoted by Theodore Solotaroff and Marshall Sklare, eds., Introduction, *Jews in the Mind of America* (New York: Basic Books, 1966), 4.

34. Robert Alter, "The Jew Who Didn't Get Away," 270.
35. Nineteen-year-old Barbra Streisand made her show-stopping debut as Miss Marmelstein in *I Can Get It for You Wholesale*. Her electric talent and unabashedly Jewish persona rocketed her to stardom as Fanny Brice the next year in *Funny Girl* (1964). With these performances, Streisand trumped prevailing notions of feminine beauty and won popular acclaim for unmistakably Jewish looks, demeanor, and speech.
36. Actually it was Meyer Levin who first made a play of the Diary. An established fiction writer and journalist, Levin discovered Anne Frank's Diary while on assignment in Europe and quickly realized its dramatic potential. In a lamentable story of intrigue and Jewish infighting, Levin lost out to Goodrich and Hackett in a prolonged dispute that poisoned the rest of his life. The entire story is told in fascinating detail by Lawrence Graver, *An Obsession with Anne Frank: Meyer Levin and the Diary* (Berkeley: University of California Press, 1995).
37. Keith Opdahl, "The Mental Comedies of Saul Bellow," in Cohen, ed., *From Hester Street to Hollywood*, 183.
38. Walter Kerr, "Bellow's 'Last Analysis' — Walter Kerr's Analysis," *New York Herald Tribune*, Oct. 2, 1964, *New York Theatre Critics Reviews*, xxv: 20, 206.
39. Walter Kerr, "Theatre: 'Incident at Vichy' Opens," *The New York Times*, Dec. 4, 1964. *New York Times Theatre Critics Reviews*, xxv: 28, 116.
40. The accuracy of those images has been vigorously challenged by Yiddish specialists, among them, Joseph C. Landis. Landis argues that the musical thoroughly falsifies the original text, the world it depicts, and, most seriously, "Sholem Aleichem's sense of the moral code of his people." See his "Fiddling with Sholem Aleichem," *New York University Bulletin*, LXV, 20 (Spring 1965). 29–33.
41. Joseph Stein, *Fiddler on the Roof* (New York: Crown, 1964), 119.
42. In the 1965–1966 *Best Plays Yearbook of the American Theatre*, editor Otis I. Guernsey, Jr. supplies these useful distinctions: "What is now being called Off-Off Broadway [is] the beehive of experimental play production put on, usually without such formalities as Equity contracts, daily performance schedules or invitations to be seen by critics. In the listing in this volume 'Broadway' is the collection of shows with Broadway union contracts, plus major repertory and visiting groups" in houses of 600 seats. "'Off-Broadway' is the collection of regularly-scheduled professional productions whose union contracts recognize their non-Broadway status with concessions," 34.
43. See Dorothy Chansky. "Composing Ourselves: The Little Theatre Movement and the Construction of a New Audience Rhetoric, 1912–1927," Ph.D. diss., New York University, 1996.
44. 1984–1985 *Best Plays Yearbook*, 20. Off-Broadway and experimental theatre had their origins well before the 1960s. The *Best Plays Yearbook* initiated its report on Off-Broadway in 1934–1935, when it recorded foreign language productions, including Yiddish. By 1953–1954, reviewer Garrison Sherwood observed, "Off-Broadway theatre has gone this year from the 'little theatre class to big business,' attributing success to low ticket prices, more variety, and enhanced opportunities for theatre personnel (356). And by 1981–1982, *Best Plays* editor Otis L. Guernsey, Jr., noting that in that season, Off-Broadway was the "principal repository of American playwriting, predicted, "Off-Broadway could become the main event " (31). Had Guersney added in regional theatres and used "greenhouse" rather than "repository," his prediction would be completely accurate.
45. Julius Novick, *Beyond Broadway: The Quest for Permanent Theatres* (New York: Hill and Wang, 1968), 3.
46. Gerald M. Berkowitz, *New Broadways: Theatres Across America: Approaching A New Millenium* (New York: Applause, 1997), 108. There were other reasons to cheer. Secretary of Labor Arthur I. Goldberg used the pages of *The New York Times* in 1961 to urge government support for the arts as essential to a free society. The National

Endowments for the Arts and the Humanities were founded in 1965. Underwriting began to come from federal monies channeled to state subsidies, thence to arts councils. Foundations, led by the Rockefeller and the Ford, initiated support to regional theatres. By the end of the sixties, critic Martin Esslin confidently included this country among those in the West that regard live theatre as "a social necessity as distinct from a luxury industry confined to metropolitan areas." Looking back some four decades later in less propitious times, one can only sigh with regret that so much promise has been thwarted.

47. Samuel C. Freedman, "The Gritty Eloquence of David Mamet," *The New York Times Magazine*, April 16, 1985, 51.

48. Jeffrey G. Sweet, *Something Wonderful Right Away* (New York: Avon, 1978). I am grateful to Jeff Sweet for his observations about the Jewishness of Second City and have drawn extensively in these paragraphs on information he shared with me.

49. It would be irresponsible and ungrateful to observe how Jewish satire has infused popular culture without mentioning the work of Woody Allen, both on stage and in film, and that of Sid Caesar and the remarkable team of mostly Jewish writers for his television shows, which set rarely equaled standards for topical parody.

50. The phrase was coined by Allen Guttman, *The Jewish Writer in America* (New York: Oxford University Press, 1971), 120–128.

51. Five of JRT-developed plays appear in Edward J. Cohen's *New Jewish Voices* (Albany: SUNY Press, 1985). See also Irene Backalenick's history of the Jewish Repertory Theatre, *East Side Story* (Lanham, MD: University Press of America, 1988).

52. Quoted by Lawrence Graver, *An Obsession With Anne Frank*, 89.

53. Charles E. Silberman, *A Certain People: American Jews and Their Lives Today* (New York: Summit, 1985), 201.

54. Leonard Fein, *Where Are We? The Inner Life of American Jews* (New York: Harper and Row, 1988), 29.

55. Irving Howe, *World of Our Fathers* (New York: Schocken, 1976), 565. Any consideration of the coming of age of Jewish self-assurance must make room for Aaron Hoffman's astonishingly forthright *Welcome Stranger*, one of numerous plays this collection is not spacious enough to accommodate (it appears in the 1995 edition of *Awake and Singing*). Hoffman's 1920 comedy is a scathing indictment of Yankee anti-Semitism and Jewish self-hatred and a ringing assertion of American Jewish citizenship, extraordinary for its time.
A genial immigrant, Isidore Solomon, has left Boston ("they don't *like* Jews") to open a general store in tiny Valley Falls, New Hampshire. He runs directly into the opposition of the pillars of the community, one of whom, a Jew, has successfully passed himself off as a Gentile and becomes mayor. In a spirited confrontation with the town fathers, Isidore asserts his rights as an American ("I've read the Constitution of the United States where it says you can't deprive a man of his rights on account of his race, color, or creed") and as a Jew ("better men than you have been trying to wipe us out . . . you can go all the way back to Pharaoh . . . but they can't"). Yes, Solomon triumphs in the end, even redeeming his errant co-religionist. And when his endorsement of an apparently loony experimenter who has built a generator pays off, Solomon literally brings light to Valley Falls.

56. *The Value of Names, Home of the Brave,* and *Goldberg Street* appear in *Fruitful and Multiplying*, Ellen Schiff, ed., (New York: Mentor, 1996).

57. Tony Kushner, *Angels in America, Part Two: Perestroika* (New York: Theatre Communications Group, 1994), 123.

58. Robert Brustein, "The Use and Abuse of Multiculturalism," *The New Republic*, Sept. 16 and 23 1991, 31–34.

59. See Robert Skloot, ed., *The Theatre of the Holocaust: Four Plays* (1982) and *The Theatre of the Holocaust: Six Plays*, vol. 2 (1999), (Madison: University of Wisconsin Press) and

Elinor Fuchs, ed., *Plays of the Holocaust: An International Anthology* (New York: Theatre Communications Group, 1987).

60. Arthur Miller, *Incident at Vichy* (New York: Bantam, 1971), 105.

61. The apt term was coined by Lawrence Langer, eminent critic of Holocaust literature.

62. Leon Wieseltier "Against Identity," *New Republic,* Nov. 28, 1994, 24–32.

63. Alfred Urhy, *The Last Night Of Ballyhoo* (New York: Dramatists Play Service, 1997), 8–9, 76.

64. Donald Margulies, *Sight Unseen,* in *Sight Unseen and Other Plays* (New York: Theatre Communications Group, 1995), 272, 316.

65. David Biale, "The Melting Pot and Beyond," *Insider/Outsider: American Jews and Multiculturalism,* 31–32.

66. Quoted by Margaret Brenman-Gibson, *Clifford Odets: American Playwright, The Years From 1906 to 1940* (New York: Atheneum, 1982), 324.

67. Harold Clurman, *The Fervent Years* (New York: Hill and Wang, 1945), 4.

# COUNSELLOR-AT-LAW

*Elmer Rice*

*Counsellor-at-Law*, Williamstown Theatre Festival, MA 1993. Photo courtesy Williamstown Theatre Festival. Photo: Richard Feldman

# INTRODUCTION

With the sole exception of Eugene O'Neill, with whom he was often compared, no playwright experimented more boldly or fostered the maturation of the American theatre more enthusiastically than Elmer Rice (1982–1967). A native New Yorker, he dropped out of high school, then took evening courses at New York Law School, from which he graduated cum laude in 1912. He clerked in a Manhattan law office while writing his first plays, which he signed Elmer L. Reizenstein. Intrigued by the notion of unraveling a plot backwards, he introduced the filmic technique of flashback to the theatre in *On Trial* (1914). The innovation was a sensational success. It ensured *On Trial* an extended run and subsequent life in film and radio drama. (The story goes that the 21-year-old instinctively refused veteran producer George M. Cohan's offer of $30,000 for the rights, thus ultimately earning an unheard of $100,000 in royalties.) It also enabled Rice to leave his $15-a-week job to study drama at Columbia and write plays. Henceforth, he signed them Elmer Rice because, he explained, that name was easier to say, spell, and remember.

Although he confessed that after *On Trial* he never again subordinated plot and characters to exploit a technical device, he continued to experiment. To dramatize the tragedy of Mr. Zero, a victim of the mechanized world in *The Adding Machine* (1923), Rice used expressionistic devices: interchangeable characters, distorted exteriors, and staccato dialogue reveal the inner life of Zero and his co-workers. Next, Rice tried a drastically different stage style, domesticating the naturalism he had admired in Europe's playhouses. In *Street Scene* (1929), he recreated the life of a New York tenement neighborhood, representing its multicultural population with seventy-five characters.

The enormous scope and technical demands of *Street Scene* bore unanticipated consequences. Having barely succeeded in attracting a producer, the play was abandoned in mid-casting by its director. Rice stepped forward, undaunted by his lack of professional experience. Under his direction, *Street Scene* won the 1929 Pulitzer Prize and launched its author on a parallel career. Henceforth, he directed his own plays and eventually, those of many colleagues. He became a producer as well, taking in stride the uneven reception of some of his own plays. When one of them bombed, he announced in the press, "In response to public demand Elmer Rice will close his production of *Black Sheep*."

Nevertheless, the triumph of *Street Scene* had dissolved any doubts Rice entertained about whether there was a place for him in the American theatre. He was to find other influential roles there besides directing, producing and writing some three dozen full-length plays, several one-acts and screen and television scripts. In 1938, he and four other leading dramatists, Maxwell Anderson, S. N. Behrman, Robert E. Sherwood and Sidney Howard founded The Playwrights Producing Company. Later they were joined by Kurt Weill, a refugee from Hitler's Europe, who in 1947 collaborated with Rice and Langston Hughes to turn *Street Scene* into a critically heralded opera.

Rice, who had sound business instincts, often expressed a keen appreciation of the interdependence of creativity and merchandising in the American theatre. The Playwrights Company was dedicated to making high artistic standards as crucial as commercial success. Over its twenty-two year history, the enterprise contributed importantly to the national repertoire and the level of production and performance. It furthered the careers of dozens of outstanding actors (Ingrid Bergman, Katharine Cornell, Todd Duncan) and directors (Garson Kanin, Elia Kazan, Joshua Logan) and fostered those of rising stars like José Ferrer, Uta Hagan and Karl Malden, not to mention premier stage and costume designers. In its very first season, it produced Robert E. Sherwood's *Abe Lincoln in Illinois*. Directed by Rice and starring Raymond Massey, the play won the 1938 Pulitzer for drama. Among the company's further triumphs was the premier of Tennessee Williams' *Cat On a Hot Tin Roof* in 1955.

The Playwrights Company gave Rice the gratifying opportunity to promote the work of others. Well informed about the history of the American theatre and deeply committed to its future, he forcefully expressed his views in his autobiography, *Minority Report* (1963), and in a collection of essays, *The Living Theatre* (1959). The latter is at once an analysis and assessment of the accomplishments of the institution seen in the context of world theatre, and an argument for reforming many of its practices.

Rice was an outspoken champion of liberal causes and human rights, a position he associated with his Jewishness. "The minority man I have always been is just a grown-up minority boy," he remarked. He served for many years on the board of the American Civil Liberties Union. Along with Clifford Odets, S. N. Behrman, and Lillian Hellman, he figured among the few American dramatists who spoke out against the rise of fascism in Europe. His first warnings were voiced in *Judgment Day* (1934), a play based on the trial that followed the Reichstag Fire, an arson the Nazis imputed to the Communists. That the play addressed an incredulous or indifferent public can be seen in Burns Mantle's New York *Daily News* review: "It matters very little that Mr. Rice can bring into court evidence to prove that he has not ... overstated the case of Hitler.... The audience does not believe it humanly possible for so vicious and brazen a travesty of justice to have taken place in any civilized state...."

Then Rice wrote a pair of works about a menace closer to home. *American Landscape* (1938) tells of the attempt of a Bund group to construct a training camp in Connecticut and casts a critical eye on American isolationism and commercialism. *Flight to the West* (1940) depicts the gamut of political attitudes toward Nazi Germany that prevailed in this country just prior to its entering World War II. One of *Flight's* characters is a young Jew who abandons pacifism to oppose Hitlerism; another is a Jewish refugee from Nazi Europe. While *Flight* is not one of Rice's finer works, it stands as one of the few prewar American plays that dared confront Nazi anti-Semitism.

Rice's commitment to society as well as to the arts asserted itself in his brief tenure as New York regional director of the Federal Theatre Project. He had been instrumental in the organization of this program of the Works Progress Administration, which, between 1935 and 1939, kept thousands of theatre professionals employed and provided welcome diversion to dispirited Americans. Rice energetically advocated one of the FTP's projects, the Living Newspaper, which used documentary materials to dramatize current issues. When State Department censors interfered with the first of these docudramas, an outraged Rice resigned in protest. Such vigorous expression of his principles became Rice's signature. Firmly opposed to the judging of arts and artists by political standards, he withdrew *Counsellor-at-Law* from a TV production in 1951 because John Garfield, who was to play the title role, was blacklisted.

Thus, *Counsellor-at-Law* asks to be viewed as the work of a man of cosmopolitan interests and passionate convictions. Rice's own energy and multiple talents seem to animate the play's protagonist, George Simon. *Counsellor* opened in New York in November 1931, on the heels of his *The Left Bank*, which had premiered just a month earlier. Both were well received, but the accomplished performance of Paul Muni as George Simon made *Counsellor* an "overnight success," as one reviewer put it. Brooks Atkinson of *The New York Times* praised Rice's "Accuracy of observation [and] genius for dialogue," judging George Simon's characterization "the most significant as a fragment of New York." The play ran for 396 performances on Broadway, and sold out through its national tour with Otto Kruger as Simon.

Among its warm reviews, two unusual notices merit attention. The first reminds us of a prevailing perception of the Jew on stage. It comes from critic and editor Burns Mantle, who had earlier expressed admiration for Rice. Considering both *Counsellor* and *The Left Bank* in the 1931–32 *Best Plays* annual, Mantle passed over the former but included *The Left Bank* in his Ten Best list. He explained that *Counsellor* had "a stronger dramatic theme," but judged that the play was "written with a racial consciousness that minimizes its appeal." Second, a performance of *Counsellor* at Sing Sing by a company from the Plymouth Theatre was greeted with a thunderous ovation. In a review that appeared in *The New York Times* of March 27, 1932, an anonymous but wonderfully literate inmate wrote, "We enjoyed keenly the varying shades with which Elmer Rice portrayed the grimness of life.... If one were to ask me for a subtitle for this fine play, I would suggest 'A Slice of Life.'"

So identified was Paul Muni with the role of George Simon that when *Counsellor* was revived in 1942, Louis Kronenberger's *PM* review trumpeted, "Mr. Muni Resumes His Law Practice." Muni had come to English-language theatre and film from a brilliant career on the Yiddish stage as Muni Weisenfreund. However, when his signature role was filmed in 1933, he refused the lead, which went to John Barrymore. In *Minority Report*, Rice supposes that Muni did not want to be typecast in Jewish roles. The power of the character Rice created is apparent in the *Times* film reviewer's appreciative comparison, which flies in the face of Burns Mantle's : "The mere fact that

Mr. Muni is a Jew and that Mr. Barrymore is a Gentile makes little if any difference to the portrayal."

Regardless of the actor who plays him, George Simon remains an enduring representation of an unaccommodated American Jew, struggling to reconcile his Jewish background and its values with the social and economic realities of thirties America.

*Counsellor-at-Law* was presented at the Plymouth Theatre, New York, November 6, 1931, staged by Elmer Rice, settings by Raymond Sovey, with the following cast:

| | |
|---|---|
| Bessie Green | Constance McKay |
| Henry Susskind | Lester Salkow |
| Sarah Becker | Malka Kornstein |
| A Tall Man | Victor Wolfson |
| A Stout Man | Jack Collins |
| A Postman | Ned Glass |
| Zedorah Chapman | Gladys Feldman |
| Goldie Rindskopf | Angela Jacobs |
| Charles McFadden | J. Hammond Dailey |
| John P. Tedesco | Sam Bonnell |
| A Bootblack | William Vaughn |
| Regina Gordon | Anna Kostani |
| Herbert Howard Weinberg | Marvin Kline |
| Arthur Sandler | Conway Washburne |
| Lillian Larue | Dorothy Dodge |
| An Errand Boy | Buddy Proctor |
| Roy Darwin | Jack Leslie |
| George Simon | Paul Muni |
| Cora Simon | Louise Prussing |
| A Woman | Jane Hamilton |
| Lena Simon | Jennie Moscowitz |
| Peter J. Malone | T. H. Manning |
| Johann Breitstein | John M. Qualen |
| David Simon | Ned Glass |
| Harry Becker | Martin Wolfson |
| Richard Dwight, Jr. | David Vivian |
| Dorothy Dwight | June Cox |
| Francis Clark Baird | Elmer Brown |

# SYNOPSIS OF SCENES

The action is laid in a suite of law offices in the midtown section in New York.

## ACT ONE

A morning in Spring.
**SCENE 1:** The reception room.
**SCENE 2:** George Simon's private office.
**SCENE 3.** The reception room.
**SCENE 4.** Simon's office.

## ACT TWO

The next morning.
**SCENE 1:** Simon's office.
**SCENE 2:** The reception room.
**SCENE 3:** Simon's office.

## ACT THREE

A week later.
**SCENE 1:** Simon's office.
**SCENE 2:** The reception room.

# ACT ONE

## SCENE 1

*The reception room of a suite of law offices, high up in a skyscraper, in the midtown section of New York. Two large windows, in the rear wall, look westward upon a view which includes several tall buildings in the middle distance, and the Hudson river and New Jersey shore in the background. Between the windows is a comfortable sofa. In the right wall are two doors. The one downstage is the entrance door to the offices from the public corridor. Upon the opaque glass panel of the door is seen in reverse the following: "Law Offices of Simon and Tedesco." Immediately below this are the names "George Simon" and "John P. Tedesco," then a line and below it, in smaller letters, "Herbert Howard Weinberg" and "Arthur Sandler." The upstage door bears the legend "Mr. Simon" and opens upon a private corridor, leading to the offices of Simon and his secretary. Against the wall, between the doors, is the telephone switchboard, so that the operator sits facing the entrance door. In the upstage right corner, is a small revolving bookstand filled with a miscellany of books and periodicals. In the left wall are two doors, both well upstage. The upper is labeled "Mr. Tedesco," the lower "Library," "Mr. Weinberg," "Mr. Sandler." Below the doors against the left wall is another sofa. In the middle of the room is a rectangular table, with several chairs around it. On the table are scattered law reviews and periodicals.*

**AT RISE:** *At the rise of the curtain,* BESSIE GREEN, *the telephone operator, is at the switchboard. She is young and pretty. Several sets of wires are plugged in, and throughout, she reads a popular movie magazine, with half an eye on the switchboard.* HENRY SUSSKIND, *the office boy, an ungainly youth of 15, is seated at the center table, filling out some legal forms and whistling softly. Across the table from him, a* TALL MAN *is inattentively reading an Italian newspaper. On the sofa, at the left, a stout, swarthy* MAN *is seated, busily covering the back of an envelope with figures. On the sofa, between the windows* SARAH BECKER *is seated. She is* *small, poorly clad and prematurely old. She is obviously frightened and in awe of her surroundings. Every time a door opens, the two men and* MRS. BECKER *look towards it. There is a buzz and* BESSIE, *scarcely looking up from her magazine, disconnects one of the completed calls. Then an incoming call buzzes.*

BESSIE: [*Plugging in.*] Simon and Tedesco—Who is calling, please? Mr. McGee?—Mr. McKee? K like in Kitty? One moment, please—[*Plugging in another wire.*] Mr. McKee of Bartlett, Bartlett and McKee calling Mr. Simon—[*Completing the connection.*] All rightee, go ahead. [*She resumes her magazine. A middle-aged* POSTMAN *enters from the public corridor.*]

THE POSTMAN: Mornin', dearie. Here's a bunch o' love letters for you. [*He slaps down a stack of letters on the switchboard.*]

BESSIE: Don't get so funny.

THE POSTMAN: What's the matter? Get out o' bed the wrong side, this mornin'?

BESSIE: What do you care if I did? An' never mind about that dearie stuff, either.

THE POSTMAN: The voice wit' the smile wins. [*He laughs and exits.*]

BESSIE: Fresh egg! [*An incoming call buzzes*] Simon and Tedesco—Who is calling please?—He's not in, yet. Do you want to talk to Miss Gordon? Well, just a minute, she's on another wire—All right, here she is now—Mr. Simon's brother calling—All rightee, go ahead. [*Turning.*] Mail, Henry.

HENRY: Aw, gee, I gotta get out these notices of trial.

BESSIE: All right. But you know what Mr. Tedesco said, yesterday, about lettin' the mail lay around.

HENRY: Aw, for God's sake! [*Going over and getting the mail*] Can't you even sort it? You're not doing anything.

BESSIE: Say, listen, how many people's work do you think I'm goin' to do around here? [*An incoming call.* HENRY *goes to the table and sorts the mail.*] Simon and Tedesco—Oh, it's you, is it?—Why, I thought you was dead and buried—No, I don't look so good in black—Yeah, sure I missed you: like Booth missed Lincoln—Well, what do you think I've been doing: sittin' home embroiderin' doilies? Gee, I'm glad I'm wearin' long sleeves, so's I can laugh in 'em—All right, now I'll tell one—[*A buzz.*] Wait a minute—Simon and Tedesco—Mr. Tedesco hasn't come in yet—Any minute—What is the name, please?—How do you spell that? —Napoli Importing Company?—All rightee, I'll tell him—Hello—

66

Yeah, I had another call—No, I can't tonight—I can't, I'm tellin' you—I got another date—Ask me no questions and you'll hear no lies—How do you know I want to break it?—Say, you must have your hats made in a barrel factory—

**HENRY:** [*Taking some letters into Simon's office.*] Is that Louis or Jack?

**BESSIE:** [*As HENRY exits.*] Mind your own business, you!—Oh, just a fresh kid in the office, here—No, an' I don't want to see it; I'm sick of gangsters—Wait a minute—All rightee—[*She dials a number.*] Hello—I don't know if I do or not—Yeah? Go on, tell me some more—You know all the answers, don't you?—Wait a minute— Simon and Tedesco— Mr. Weinberg?— One moment, please— Hello, National Security Company?— Mr. Welford, please— Mr. George Simon's secretary— Here's Mr. Welford, Miss Gordon— Hello—[*As the entrance door opens and* MRS. ZEDORAH CHAPMAN *enters.*] Say, you better call me back later. I'm busy now. [*Effusively.*] Well, good morning, Mrs. Chapman!

**MRS. CHAPMAN:** Good morning, Bessie. [*She is an elaborately dressed brunette, in her early 30s.*]

**BESSIE:** Well, you sure must be feeling good, this mornin'.

[*The two* MEN *who are waiting listen with great interest.*]

**MRS. CHAPMAN:** [*Conscious of the sensation she is making.*] I feel just like a new woman that's how I feel.

**BESSIE:** Yes, I'll bet you do. After all you've been through. Excuse me— Simon and Tedesco—No, he hasn't come in yet, Mr. Bellini—All rightee, I'll tell him.

[*Meanwhile,* GOLDIE RINDSKOFF, *a middle-aged, unattractive stenographer, has entered from the library and crossed to* MRS. CHAPMAN.]

**GOLDIE:** [*Effusively.*] Well, good morning, Mrs. Chapman. Congratulations!

**MRS. CHAPMAN:** Well thanks, Goldie. I'm sure glad it's over. You can't imagine what I went through while that jury was out.

**GOLDIE:** I never could have lived through it. Well, anyhow, all's well that ends well.

**MRS. CHAPMAN:** Of course, after Mr. Simon talked to the jury, I had a feeling that everything was going to be all right. Were you there?

**GOLDIE:** No.

**BESSIE:** We never can get away durin' office hours. But I read all about it this mornin'. It must have been wonderful.

**MRS. CHAPMAN:** It was simply marvelous. You certainly missed something worthwhile. Why, do you know, I just sat there and cried like a baby. And I noticed that some of the jury were crying, too.

**BESSIE:** Tt! Gee, I wish I could have heard it.

**GOLDIE:** I guess you're pretty glad you had Mr. Simon.

**MRS. CHAPMAN:** Well, of course, I *was* innocent. It was a clear case of self-defense, just like Mr. Simon told them. Still, that's not saying he wasn't marvelous.

**HENRY:** [*Entering from* SIMON's *office.*] Hello, Mrs. Chapman. Well, how does it feel to be walking around again?

**MRS. CHAPMAN:** It feels wonderful, Henry. It's just as though I suddenly woke up from a bad dream.

**HENRY:** There's a bunch of mail here for you.

**MRS. CHAPMAN:** Oh thanks, Henry. You should have seen the stack that came this morning. Proposals of marriage and goodness knows what all. And the flowers! Why, my apartment looks like a regular conservatory.

**BESSIE:** It must be beautiful.

**GOLDIE:** You ought to take a nice little trip somewhere, now that it's all over.

**MRS. CHAPMAN:** Yes, I think that's just what I'll do, Goldie. I feel as if I was entitled to a rest, after what I've been through.

**BESSIE:** Your sure are.

**GOLDIE:** Well, take good care of yourself, Mrs. Chapman.

**MRS. CHAPMAN:** Thanks, Goldie. [GOLDIE *exits to the corridor.* HENRY *enters the library with more letters.*] Is Mr. Simon in?

**BESSIE:** No, he isn't. But I'll tell Miss Gordon that you're here—Mrs. Chapman is here, Miss Gordon—All rightee—What number?—All rightee—She says she's not sure just when Mr. Simon will be in, but if you want to wait—

**MRS. CHAPMAN:** Well, I think I'll just sit down and read my letters.

**BESSIE:** Yes, sure; just sit down and make yourself comfortable.

[*She dials a number.* MRS. CHAPMAN *crosses to the sofa at the left. The* STOUT MAN *rises, with a courtly flourish.*]

**MRS. CHAPMAN:** [*Sweetly.*] Oh, don't get up, please. There's plenty of room.

[*She seats herself and the* STOUT MAN *sits down beside her. She begins to read her letters.*]

BESSIE: Hello, Gilbert and Gilbert? One moment, please—Here's Gilbert and Gilbert, Miss Gordon—All rightee, go ahead. [CHARLES McFADDEN, *the firm's process server, comes in at the entrance door. He is a small middle-aged man.*] Miss Gordon wants you, right away, Charlie. She's got some papers for you to serve.

McFADDEN: Okay. Good mornin', Mrs. Chapman.

MRS. CHAPMAN: [*Looking up.*] Oh, good morning, Mr. McFadden.

McFADDEN: Well, you're up bright an' early, this mornin'. I thought you'd be sleepin' the clock around, today.

MRS. CHAPMAN: Well, so did I. But the telephone started at seven.

McFADDEN: [*Producing a newspaper.*] Have you seen the *Mirror?*

MRS. CHAPMAN: No, I haven't. It wasn't out, when I left home.

McFADDEN: [*Handing her the paper.*] There's a whole page o' pictures.

MRS. CHAPMAN: Oh, thank you.

McFADDEN: An' I got a whole pack o' letters for you, one of the keepers at the Tombs give me.

MRS. CHAPMAN: Goodness, more letters! I don't know how I'm ever going to read them all.

McFADDEN: Well, that's what happens when you're famous. But did you ever hear anythin' more heartbreakin' than that summin'-up speech of Mr. Simon's?

MRS. CHAPMAN: It was simply wonderful.

McFADDEN: You know, I just sat there an' bawled like a kid. An' I been through a dozen murder trials with him, too. I tell you, there's nobody can come within a mile of him.

[*He exits to* SIMON'S *office.* HENRY *comes out of the library and enters* TEDESCO'S *office.*]

BESSIE: Simon and Tedesco—Oh, hello, Gracie; I was jus' goin' to call you —I'm not feelin' so good, today—I don't know. My stomach don' feel so good. Must be somethin' I ate—Oh, I hate takin' that stuff—Well, maybe I will take a little tonight, before I go to bed—Listen, Fred just called me up—Sure, you do; the one we met on the Iron Steamboat— Yeah, that's the one—Well, so did I, but he says he's been out west—

Wait a minute—Simon and Tedesco—One moment, please, I'll connect you with his secretary—Mr. Hawthorn of the Chase National Bank calling Mr. Simon—All rightee, go ahead—

[HENRY *has come out of* TEDESCO'S *office and resumed his work at the table.* McFADDEN *comes out of* SIMON'S *office and goes toward the entrance door.* MRS. CHAPMAN *drops a letter and the* STOUT MAN *picks it up.*]

MRS. CHAPMAN: [*Smiling sweetly.*] Oh, thanks ever so much.
BESSIE: Charlie, wait a minute.
McFADDEN: I can't. I gotta go right down to Wall Street for Miss Gordon.
BESSIE: Well, listen, get me some lunch on the way back, will you?
McFADDEN: All right. What do you want? Make it quick.
BESSIE: [*Taking a quarter out of her purse.*] I want a tongue on rye and a chocolate malted. Here. [*As he hurries out.*] And tell him I want a lot of Russian dressin'.
McFADDEN: Okay. [*He exits.*]
BESSIE: Hello, Gracie?—I was just orderin' my lunch—No, I don't think I'll go out today, on account of my stomach—Well, listen, I started to tell you. Fred wants me to go out with him, tonight—[*As the door opens and* TEDESCO *enters*]. I'm busy, now; I'll call you back.

[TEDESCO *is a small, dark Italian of American birth. He is in his late 30s.*]

HENRY *and* BESSIE: Good morning, Mr. Tedesco.
TEDESCO: Good morning. [*Both* MEN *who are waiting rise. To the* STOUT MAN.] Hello, Moretti. I'm sorry to keep you waiting.
THE STOUT MAN: Oh, that's all right, counsellor.
TEDESCO: Go right in my office.

[*The* STOUT MAN *smiles and bows to Mrs. Chapman, then enters* TEDESCO'S *office.*]

TEDESCO: Any messages for me?
BESSIE: [*Giving him several slips of paper.*] Yes, sir. Mr. Bellini called twice. He says it's important.

**TEDESCO:** All right. Has G. S. come in?

**BESSIE:** No sir, not yet.

**THE TALL MAN:** [*Timidly.*] *Buon giorno, signor.*

**TEDESCO:** I haven't heard from those people yet. Come in next week. *Lunedi.*

**THE TALL MAN:** All right, signor. Sure. [*He goes out slowly.*]

**MRS. CHAPMAN:** [*As* TEDESCO *crosses to his office.*] Good morning, Mr. Tedesco.

**TEDESCO:** Oh, good morning, Mrs. Chapman. Well, G. S. got you out of it, all right, didn't he?

**MRS. CHAPMAN:** Yes, he was wonderful. But, of course, it was a clear case of self-defense.

**TEDESCO:** Oh, yes, sure; we all knew that. But you always have to convince the jury, you know. Well, excuse me, I got a client waiting. Tell Goldie I want her, Bessie.

**BESSIE:** She just stepped outside, Mr. Tedesco.

**TEDESCO:** Well, as soon as she comes in. And let me know when G. S. comes in.

**BESSIE:** Yes sir [TEDESCO *exits to his office.*] Simon and Tedesco—Who's calling, please?—One moment, please—Wilson and Devore calling Mr. Simon—All rightee, go ahead—Simon and Tedesco—Mr. Weinberg?— Go ahead.

**MRS. CHAPMAN:** What time do you think he'll be in?

**BESSIE:** I don't know. He's in the Supreme Court. [HENRY *exits to the library.*] Simon and Tedesco—Oh, good morning, Mrs. Simon—No ma'am, he hasn't come in yet—No ma'am, he's in court—Miss Gordon is talking on another wire. Do you want to wait?— Yes ma'am—Yes ma'am—Yes ma'am, I'll tell him—Yes ma'am, and he can reach you at the Colony Club—All right, Mrs. Simon— Good-bye. [*To* MRS. CHAPMAN.] That was Mrs. Simon.

**MRS. CHAPMAN:** Does she come around here a lot?

**BESSIE:** Well, not so much. They live up in Westchester. She's one of the four hundred, you know. Her father used to be the governor of some state—Connecticut, I guess it was.

**MRS. CHAPMAN:** Yes, I've seen her picture in the Sunday sections.

**BESSIE:** Didn't you ever meet her?

**MRS. CHAPMAN:** No. I guess she must be kind of ritzy, isn't she?

**BESSIE:** Well, you know the way all these society dames are, sort of proud and haughty. They kind of have a way of lookin' at you, as if they didn't see you.

MRS. CHAPMAN: Yes, they think they're so much better than anybody else, just because they get their names in the paper. Well, I guess I've had my name in the paper as much as any of them.

BESSIE: She can be very nice, though, when she wants to. [*An Italian* BOOTBLACK *enters.*] He's not in yet. Come back later.

THE BOOTBLACK: Okay. [*He exits.*]

BESSIE: You ought to see the clothes she wears. Wait a minute. Yes sir — Yes sir — [*She dials a number.*] I've never seen her wear the same dress twice.

MRS. CHAPMAN: The way he talks about her, you'd think she was a queen or goodness knows what.

BESSIE: He worships the ground she walks on. Hello — Is this the Italian consulate? — Mr. Bellini, please — Hello, Mr. Bellini? — Mr. Tedesco calling — Here's Mr. Bellini, Mr. Tedesco — All rightee, go ahead. He got her her divorce from her first husband and then they ran away and got married.

MRS. CHAPMAN: Yes, I know. The matron in the Tombs was telling me.

BESSIE: She's got two children, too. You know, from her first marriage. An' talk about spoiled kids —

[*She stops abruptly as* REGINA GORDON *enters from* SIMON'S *office.* REGINA *is in her late 20s; an attractive girl, but in her official hours rather severe in dress and manner.*]

REGINA: Where is Mr. Sandler?

BESSIE: He hasn't come back from the courthouse yet.

REGINA: Well, I want to see him as soon as he comes in.

BESSIE: All right, Miss Gordon. I'll tell him. Mrs. Simon called up while you were on the other wire. She wants Mr. Simon to call her, at the Colony Club.

REGINA: Very well.

MRS. CHAPMAN: How do, Miss Gordon? When do you expect Mr. Simon?

REGINA: In a little while. Did he know you were coming in, Mrs. Chapman?

MRS. CHAPMAN: Well, not exactly —

REGINA: He has a very busy day. Isn't there anything I can do?

MRS. CHAPMAN: No. I've got some things to talk over with Mr. Simon.

REGINA: All right, if you want to wait —

MRS. CHAPMAN: Yes, of course, I'll wait.

MRS. BECKER: [*Who has risen timidly.*] Excuse me, lady—

REGINA: Mr. Simon hasn't come in yet.

MRS. BECKER: Please, he's coming soon, now?

REGINA: Yes, I expect him soon.

MRS. BECKER: Please, lady: mine boy—they took him in the police station—

REGINA: Yes, I know. But I can't do anything about it until Mr. Simon gets here. You'll have to wait.

MRS. BECKER: Thank you, lady.

[*She resumes her seat.* HERBERT HOWARD WEINBERG *enters. He is a slender, young intellectual.*]

WEINBERG: Oh, Miss Gordon—

REGINA: [*Turning.*] Mr. Weinberg, Wilson and Devore called me up again about that stipulation in Rosenblatt against the Baltimore and Ohio. They were supposed to have it by ten o'clock.

WEINBERG: I told Arthur to be sure to get it over there. [*To* BESSIE.] Where is Mr. Sandler?

BESSIE: He's down at the courthouse. Hello—What number?—Yes sir— [*She dials a number.*]

REGINA: Mr. Simon promised them that they would surely have it this morning.

WEINBERG: Well, I'll get it out, myself. G. S. wanted that memorandum of law in the Pickford case. That's why I asked Arthur to do it.

REGINA: Well, will you please see that they get it right away?

WEINBERG: Yes, I will.

BESSIE: Hello, Napoli Importing Company?—One moment, please. All right Mr. Tedesco, go ahead.

WEINBERG: [*As* REGINA *is about to go*]. Oh, Miss Gordon. [*She stops*]. A friend has just offered me two tickets for the Boston Symphony Orchestra tonight. Would you care to go with me?

REGINA: No, thank you, very much, Mr. Weinberg. I really don't care to go.

WEINBERG: It's a very fine program: the Brahms First and the Beethoven Violin Concerto, with Heifetz as soloist. I thought perhaps you would have dinner with me somewhere first—

REGINA: No, thanks; I really can't tonight.

WEINBERG: I'm sure you'd enjoy it. If you decide later in the day—

REGINA: I've decided already. I really don't care to go. [*As* ARTHUR SANDLER, *a law clerk of 22, enters.*] Arthur, why didn't you get out that stipulation in Rosenblatt against the Baltimore and Ohio?

WEINBERG: I told you that G. S. wanted Wilson and Devore to have it, this morning.

SANDLER: I had to answer the calendar in Part Three, didn't I? And then I had to go to the Surrogate's Court for Mr. Tedesco.

REGINA: When Mr. Simon promises something, he likes it to be there on time.

SANDLER: All right; I'll get it out right away. Arrow against the Radio Corporation was marked ready and passed. It may be reached Monday.

REGINA: It doesn't matter. Mr. Simon is going to settle it today.

BESSIE: Simon and Tedesco—Yes, who's calling?—Senator Wells? One moment, please—[*To* REGINA.] Senator Wells calling from Washington.

REGINA: All right [*To* SANDLER.] Arthur, please get that stipulation right out.

SANDLER: All right.

[REGINA *exits.*]

BESSIE: One moment, please.

SANDLER: Hello, Mrs. Chapman.

MRS. CHAPMAN: Good morning, Mr. Sandler.

SANDLER: Well, I'll bet you're feeling pretty good this morning.

MRS. CHAPMAN: Yes, indeed, I am.

WEINBERG: [*To* BESSIE.] Please get me Wilson and Devore.

BESSIE: I'll give you a wire. [WEINBERG *starts to protest, then changes his mind and exits to the library.*] Simon and Tedesco—Mr. Simon's secretary is busy on another wire—All rightee—

SANDLER: Where's Goldie?

BESSIE: She'll be back in a minute. But Mr. Tedesco wants her.

SANDLER: God, I have to do everything myself, around here. [*He exits to the library*]

BESSIE: Simon and Tedesco—Yes. Who is this: Jack?—Oh, not so good, Jack—I don't know; I just feel kind of punk—Is that so? Well, if you want to know, I haven't had a drink in a week: not enough to hurt me, anyhow—wait a minute—No, Mr. Tedesco, she hasn't come back yet— Yes, sir—Hello—No, she's still busy—Hello, Jack—Yeah, I had another call—No, I can't tonight, Jack—No, honest I can't—I got another date—With Gracie—Yeah, you know Gracie; Gracie Ferguson—No, I couldn't do that—Why she'd be sore at me, that's why—Yes, sure, I'd like to, but I can't tonight—All rightee; give me a ring tomorrow—Bye-bye—Hello—Here's Mr. Simon's secretary now.

[*The* STOUT MAN *comes out of* TEDESCO'S *office. As he passes* MRS. CHAPMAN, *he smiles and tips his hat. She smiles sweetly at him. He crosses to go to the entrance door, and as he opens it* LILLIAN LARUE, *a young, bleached blonde, flashily dressed, enters. He holds the door open, gallantly, for her, then exits.*]

LILLIAN: I'm Miss Lillian Larue. I got an appointment to see Mr. Simon.
BESSIE: He hasn't come in yet. Take a seat, won't you?
LILLIAN: Yeah. Sure.
BESSIE: I'll tell his secretary you're here?
LILLIAN: [*Seating herself beside* MRS. BECKER.] Yeah, will you? Miss Lillian Larue.

[HENRY *enters and seats himself at the table.*]

BESSIE: Miss Lillian Larue is here to see Mr. Simon. [*To* LILLIAN.] He's expected any minute, Miss Larue.
LILLIAN: Okay.

[*She lights a cigarette, meanwhile staring curiously at* MRS. CHAPMAN. *An* ERRAND BOY *enters and slaps some papers down before* BESSIE.]

THE BOY: Admission of service.
BESSIE: Don't you even know how to say please? [THE BOY *stares at her.*] Here, Henry.

[HENRY *takes the papers and goes into the library.*]

BESSIE: [*To* THE BOY.] Wait. And don't stand right in the doorway, either. Simon and Tedesco—One moment, please—*New York Times* calling Mr. Simon—All rightee, go ahead.

MRS. CHAPMAN: [*Eagerly.*] Is that the *New York Times?*

BESSIE: Yes, ma'am.

MRS. CHAPMAN: I wonder if they want to know anything—

BESSIE: I don't think so—Wait a minute, I'll find out. [*She listens in.*]

MRS. CHAPMAN: Is it?

BESSIE: No, it's just about some bankruptcy case.

MRS. CHAPMAN: [*Disappointed.*] Oh.

HENRY: [*Entering from the library; to the waiting* BOY.] He'll be out in a minute.

THE BOY: Okay. [*He starts to whistle.*]

BESSIE: No whistlin' allowed here. [THE BOY *stops.*]

LILLIAN: [*Rising and going towards* MRS. CHAPMAN.] Pardon me. Aren't you Mrs. Zedorah Chapman?

MRS. CHAPMAN: Why yes, I am.

LILLIAN: [*Seating herself at the table.*] Well, I thought it was you, the minute I came in. You look a lot like your picture.

MRS. CHAPMAN: Well, some of them have been pretty good. The one in the *News* this morning was a dandy one.

LILLIAN: Yeah that's just the one I saw. Well, it certainly is a coincidence to walk in and see you sittin' right here. I wanted to come down to the trial but we've been havin' rehearsals nearly every day.

MRS. CHAPMAN: Oh, are you on the stage?

LILLIAN: Yeah, I'm with the Scandals. I been with Mr. White three years now. He's gonna give me a bit in a black-out in his new show.

MRS. CHAPMAN: I've been thinking maybe I'd like to go on the stage.

LILLIAN: Well, say, it'll be a cinch for you to get a break, with your name.

BESSIE: You oughta ask Mr. Simon to give you some introductions. He knows lots of theatrical people.

MRS. CHAPMAN: Yes, I think maybe I will.

LILLIAN: Say, I wonder if you'd do me a favor? I wonder if you'd write out your autograph for me?

MRS. CHAPMAN: Why, certainly, I'd be glad to. [*They both fumble in their handbags.*]

LILLIAN: I don't think I've got a piece of paper with me. Gee, I wish I'd of known you was gonna be here. I'd of brought my little book.

BESSIE: Here's some paper if you want it.

MRS. CHAPMAN: Never mind, I'll put it on the back of one of my cards. Oh, but I haven't got a pen.

**HENRY:** Here's a pen, Mrs. Chapman.

**MRS. CHAPMAN:** Oh, thank you.

[*She takes the pen from* HENRY *and seats herself at the table.* SANDLER *enters from the library and crosses to the waiting* BOY.]

**SANDLER:** I can't give you admission on this. It was due yesterday. You'll have to leave a copy and make an affidavit of service.

**THE BOY:** [*Stolidly.*] He told me to get admission of service.

**SANDLER:** I don't care what he told you. It's a day late. Go ahead; I'll call up your office.

[THE BOY *hesitates, then goes, with a final look at* MRS. CHAPMAN.]

**MRS. CHAPMAN:** [*With a little laugh.*] I never know just what to write.

**LILLIAN:** Oh, just write anything. It's just the idea of the thing.

**SANDLER:** [*To* BESSIE.] Say, that's some run you've got in your stocking, kid.

**BESSIE:** Where? Oh, God, wouldn't that give you a pain! An' I just put them on clean this mornin'.

**SANDLER:** I'll buy you a new pair, if you let me put them on for you.

**BESSIE:** Say, listen, one more crack like that out of you and you'll get a good smack in the face.

**SANDLER:** Get hot. Get hot.

**BESSIE:** Well, you just remember, that's all. Hello—No, she hasn't, Mr. Tedesco—Yes, sir. [*As the door opens and* GOLDIE *enters.*] Goldie, go right in to Mr. Tedesco. He's been askin' for you, two or three times.

[GOLDIE *nods majestically and, without quickening her pace, crosses to* TEDESCO'S *office.*]

**SANDLER:** [*Crossing to the library.*] Did you have a nice weekend?

**GOLDIE:** Shut your mouth, you!

[*She exits to* TEDESCO'S *office.* SANDLER *laughs and exits to the library.*]

**MRS. CHAPMAN:** Is this all right? To my friend, Miss Larue, from yours sincerely, Mrs. Zedorah Chapman.

LILLIAN: Yeah that's lovely. Thanks ever so much. It's just sort of a hobby of mine. I got a whole book full, home — lots of famous people, too. I got Legs Diamond and Babe Ruth and Belle Livingston — and, oh, I forget who all. And, of course, I got a lot of people in the profession, too. Eddie Cantor gave me one of his pictures. Only after what he wrote on it, I can't show it to nobody.

[*The door opens and* ROY DARWIN *enters: a handsome, well-dressed man of 40.*]

BESSIE: Yes sir?

DARWIN: Will you please tell Mr. Simon that Mr. Roy Darwin would like to see him?

BESSIE: Mr. Simon hasn't come in yet. Have you an appointment?

DARWIN: Why no, I haven't. Just when do you expect him?

BESSIE: Wait a minute — Simon and Tedesco — One moment, please — District attorney's office calling Mr. Simon. And Mr. Roy Darwin is here to see Mr. Simon — All rightee — All rightee, district attorney's office, go ahead. [*To* DARWIN.] Mr. Simon ought to be here, any moment, if you care to wait.

DARWIN: Very well; I'll wait.

[*He crosses to the sofa, and sits beside* MRS. BECKER, *glancing curiously at* MRS. CHAPMAN. *A Western Union* MESSENGER *enters.*]

THE MESSENGER: Simon?

BESSIE: Yes [*She signs the receipt.*] Here, Henry. [HENRY *takes the telegram into* SIMON'*s office.* THE MESSENGER *exits.*]

MRS. CHAPMAN: Mr. Simon is certainly a busy man.

LILLIAN: Well, I guess he's just about the biggest lawyer in New York, isn't he?

MRS. CHAPMAN: [*With a laugh.*] Well, naturally, I think so.

[BESSIE *dials a number.*]

LILLIAN: Say, if you wouldn't, who would?

BESSIE: Hello: Gracie? — Yeah — Say, listen, about tonight — I told you about Fred callin' up, didn't I? — Well, listen, if you happen to see Jack

and he asks you about tonight, I was out with you, see? — Yeah, I know,
but in case you do — Well, listen, tell him —

**HENRY:** [*Entering.*] G. S. is in.

**BESSIE:** I'm busy now, Gracie. I'll call you back.

**REGINA:** [*Entering.*] Get Senator Wells at the Hotel Shoreham, in
Washington, and then get these other numbers. [*She hands* BESSIE *several
slips of paper.* BESSIE *dials.*] Mr. Simon will see you in just a minute,
Miss Larue.

**LILLIAN:** All rightee.

**BESSIE:** Hello, long distance? I want Washington, D.C. — That's right —
Hotel Shoreham — No, Shoreham —

**REGINA:** I'll tell Mr. Simon you're here, Mr. Darwin. But it may be a half-
hour before he can see you.

**DARWIN:** That's quite all right. I don't mind waiting.

**BESSIE:** [*As* REGINA *exits.*] Shoreham — S like in Sammy, H like in Howard,
O like in Oscar, R like in Robert, E like in Eddie, H like in Henry, A like
in Albert, M like in Max. That's right.

[*The scene blacks out.*]

CURTAIN

# SCENE 2

*The inner office. A large room, simply furnished in modernistic style. Two windows in the rear wall face south, affording a panoramic view of lower Manhattan. In the right wall are two doors, the one downstage leading to the corridor which communicates with the outer office: the other leading to* REGINA's *office.* SIMON's *large flattop desk faces the entrance door. Above the desk is a comfortable chair. In the middle of the room is a large sofa. Between the windows is a small desk and a chair. Simon's desk is equipped with a telephone, an interoffice phone and a handsome desk set. There is also a cigarette box, containing several kinds of cigarettes, a cigar box of fine wood, and a photograph of* CORA SIMON *in a leather frame. On the smaller desk are a telephone equipped with a Hushaphone, writing materials and so on.*

*As the lights go up on the scene,* GEORGE SIMON *is seated at his desk, making a connection on the interoffice phone. He is 40, clean-shaven, rather good-looking and well-dressed.*

SIMON: Hello, John, do you want me? — Yes — Yes — Yes, sure I'll see him — all right, let me know when he gets here — All right — Oh say, didn't I tell you I'd get an acquittal in the Chapman case? — Well, I never had any doubt about it — Not after that bunch of buttonhole makers on the jury got a good look at her — Well, maybe I can fix it up for you, John — No, those days are over for me — All right, John. [*He disconnects.* REGINA *has entered, during the preceding conversation, and has stood waiting, unable to conceal her embarrassment.*] Did you get Senator Wells?

REGINA: She's getting him, now. Mr. Darwin is outside.

SIMON: Roy Darwin?

REGINA: Yes sir.

SIMON: What does he want?

REGINA: Shall I ask him?

SIMON: No. But tell him he'll have to wait.

REGINA: I did tell him.

SIMON: And as soon as I'm through with Senator Wells, I want to talk to Mrs. Simon.

REGINA: Yes sir.

SIMON: [*Looking through his mail.*] Take a letter to Judge Wiley. Dear

Clarence. I am in receipt of yours of the ninth, inviting me to be a speaker at the testimonial dinner to be given for Luther Ridgeway, in honor of his appointment as Minister to Austria. Nothing would give me greater pleasure than to do honor to Luther, whom I love and esteem. The fact is, however, that I am leaving next week for a little trip abroad with Cora. We will be married five years on the eighteenth and I have decided to break away, for once in my life, and make a real celebration of it. Please convey—[*The telephone rings.*] See if that's Wells.

[REGINA *goes to her desk and speaks into the Hushaphone.*]

REGINA: Yes sir.
SIMON: Take this down. [*He lifts the receiver of the telephone on his desk.* REGINA *listens in on the other telephone and makes stenographic notes.*] Hello, Senator, how are you?—I'm fine, thanks—Oh, thanks very much—Well, that's all there is in these murder cases: a lot of publicity and damn little money—Yes—Yes, I did—I was instructed to do so by my clients—I understand that, Senator, but as I explained to you, a decrease of two cents a pound is going to put my clients out of business—Now, now, wait a minute, Senator. Don't get excited—Well, what of it? There's nothing illegal about lobbying. If there were, they'd have to lock up half the population of Washington—We're living under a democratic form of government, Senator, and even a corporation has a right to be heard—No, I don't want to block the whole bill. I'm simply acting in what I believe to be the best interests of my client, just as you're acting in what you believe to be the best interests of the people of Montana—Sure, I'm always willing to listen to reason—Well, why not hop on the midnight sleeper and have lunch with me tomorrow?—All right, twelve-thirty tomorrow, at the Lawyers' Club—Fine. And give my regards to that charming daughter of yours—Good-bye. [*To* REGINA.] Make a transcript of that, and send it around to Colonel Adolph Wertheimer, Chairman of the Board of the International Metal Refineries. Oh, you'd better leave out the part about the murder cases. And take this letter to go with it. Dear Colonel Wertheimer. I enclose stenographic transcript of a long-distance conversation with Senator Wells. After you have read and digested it, please communicate with me. Personally, I do not think we have anything to worry about. That's all. You'd better let me see that transcript before it goes out.

REGINA: Yes sir.

SIMON: Is she getting Mrs. Simon for me?

REGINA: I'll remind her [*She speaks into the Hushaphone.*] She's calling her, now.

SIMON: All right. I'll see that blond bedroom artist now. What's her name?

REGINA: Lillian Larue.

SIMON: I'll bet she wasn't born Lillian Larue. Well, let her come in. And get me Mr. Vandenbogen of Woodbridge, McCormick, Vandenbogen and Delancey. [REGINA *talks into the Hushaphone.* SIMON *takes a box of chocolates from the top drawer and helps himself to them, while he continues to look through his mail. Reading a letter.*] Here, I don't want this. Take a letter to that Mrs. Moran, you know the one I mean.

REGINA: Yes sir.

SIMON: Dear Mrs. Moran. I am returning herewith your money order for fifty dollars, as I was actuated— No, strike that out: she won't understand it. As I handled your daughter's case only because of our old friendship and because of my interest in you and your family. I am sorry that it was impossible—[*As* LILLIAN *enters.*] Good morning, Miss Larue. Just take a seat, won't you?

LILLIAN: Yeah, thanks.

SIMON: I'll be right with you, as soon as I've finished this letter.

LILLIAN: Oh, that's all right; go ahead.

REGINA: I am sorry that it was impossible—

SIMON: Impossible to obtain a larger settlement, but inasmuch as there was no liability on the part of the defendant—No, strike that out. But owing to the fact that the trucking company was not to blame, I could not do any better. I hope that Helen will soon be able to walk. Give her my love. All right, that's all [REGINA *exits upstage.*] There's a pathetic case. This young girl, Helen Moran, and a beautiful girl, too. She was in a hurry to get home and crossed against the traffic lights and a truck ran her down.

LILLIAN: God, it's awful! Was she hurt bad?

SIMON: She'll be lame all her life. I managed to get her a few hundred dollars from the trucking company, but that doesn't give her back the use of her legs. Her mother runs a grocery store on Second Avenue. I've known them all my life.

LILLIAN: I guess you must hear plenty of people's troubles. I should think it would make you feel kinda goofy.

SIMON: Well, being a lawyer is like being a doctor. You see a lot and you hear a lot, but you can't take it too much to heart. Will you have a chocolate cream? They're very good.

LILLIAN: N-n. I'm on a diet. But if you've got a cigarette—

SIMON: Oh, excuse me. Here, help yourself. Turkish, Virginia, whatever you want. I don't know one from the other, myself.

LILLIAN: I'll try one of these with the gold tip.

SIMON: I'm getting that lawyer on the phone, now.

REGINA: [*Entering.*] Mrs. Simon is on the phone.

SIMON: Oh yes. [*To* LILLIAN.] Excuse me. [REGINA *exits.*] Hello, darling— Yes, I just got in. How are you?—That's good. Sorry I couldn't get home last night, but the jury didn't come in until after midnight, and by the time I got through with the reports and all, it was nearly two—What is it darling?—Well, why don't you have lunch with me?—All right, you can tell me, then—Can you pick me up here?—All right, darling, whenever you want—Good-bye, sweetheart. [*To* LILLIAN.] What a wonderful woman that is! [*Taking up the photograph.*] There she is. My wife.

LILLIAN: Yeah, you showed it to me last time. She sure looks like a winner. [*She produces lipstick and powder puff.*]

SIMON: It's not only her looks. That's the least important part of it. In every respect, she's a wonderful woman.

REGINA: [*Entering.*] Mr. Vandenbogen on the phone.

SIMON: Here's Schuyler's lawyer, now. [*He takes up the receiver as* REGINA *exits.*] Good morning, Mr. Vandenbogen, how are you today?—That's fine. Well, have you got any word for me, about the little lady in the breach of promise case?—Is that so—Well, I don't think that ten thousand would be acceptable to my client—

LILLIAN: Well, I should say not!

SIMON: [*Motioning her to be silent.*] Well, frankly, Mr. Vandenbogen, I don't think I could conscientiously advise her to take it—I don't agree with you—Well, I've had a good deal of experience with juries, Mr. Vandenbogen, and I know that they are inclined to be extremely sympathetic to a young girl who has entered into an intimate relationship with a man, upon his explicit promise of marriage, especially when the young man is a millionaire and the young lady is obliged to earn her own living—[LILLIAN, *who is busily powdering her face, nods emphatically.*] Not at all. As a matter of fact, she's sitting right here in my office and I don't

**83**

mind telling you that she's taking this thing pretty much to heart — Well, now, don't you think that's a little strong? — But Schuyler met her at a nightclub, not in a convent — Well, this is my position, Mr. Vandenbogen. As a courtesy to you and to the Schuyler family, I've held off bringing suit, because I know it would be very embarrassing to them if those letters — Two days? Yes, I'll wait two days — All right — All right — Thank *you* — Good-bye. Mr. Vandenbogen, remember me to Mr. Woodbridge.

LILLIAN: Ten thousand? Is that what he expects me to take?

SIMON: He came up to fifteen. But I think they'll go twenty-five. It may take a few days, though. [*He rises.*] Call me up in about three days.

LILLIAN: [*Rising.*] The dirty little tightwad. Tryin' to jew me down a few thousand dollars after all the pearls and Rolls-Royces he was goin' to buy me.

SIMON: They seem to think that you had been a little indiscreet before you met Schuyler.

LILLIAN: Well, for God's sake, what do they expect for fifteen thousand dollars: a virgin?

SIMON: I think they'll pay twenty-five. Call me up in three or four days.

LILLIAN: I won't take a cent less. Why, there's words in some of those letter that I wouldn't use in front of my colored maid. Is this the way out?

REGINA: [*Who has entered.*] Yes.

LILLIAN: All right, I'll give you a ring.

SIMON: That's right. Good-bye.

LILLIAN: Good-bye. [*She exits.*]

SIMON: Now that's my idea of a nice, sweet, little girl.

REGINA: How can a woman make herself so cheap?

SIMON: Well, Rexie, when you come right down to it, she's not as bad as that young loafer that buys her diamonds and takes her to Florida on the millions his grandfather made by looting the Pennsylvania Traction Company. Let the good-for-nothing pay. Is that Chapman woman still waiting?

REGINA: Yes. And Mrs. Becker, too.

SIMON: Oh yes. Well, let's get rid of Chapman first.

[REGINA'S *phone rings. She answers it.*]

REGINA: Do you want to talk to Mr. Crayfield?

SIMON: Yes. Hello, Mr. Crayfield—Yes, I read them very carefully—Well, I think you have a very good case—Yes, I'm quite sure that we can break the will—Yes. I'd like to talk to you about it—Well, how soon can you get over?—All right—All right—Good-bye. Have Mrs. Chapman come in. No, wait a minute: first get me Mrs. Richter.

[REGINA *calls the number on her phone.*]

REGINA: You didn't finish the letter to Judge Wiley.

SIMON: Wiley? Oh yes, about the dinner to Ridgeway. What did I say?

REGINA: You said—Oh well, it's just the end. I'll finish it up.

SIMON: All right. And on the day of the dinner, send Ridgeway something from me, with a nice card in it. Something that looks pretty good.

REGINA: How much do you want to spend?

SIMON: Oh, a hundred or a hundred and fifty.

[REGINA's *phone rings.*]

REGINA: Mrs. Richter.

SIMON: Hello, Mrs. Richter—I'm fine, thanks. How's yourself?—How's the baby's cough?—Well, that's fine; I'm glad to hear it—Well, I've got some good news for you—Yes, I had a nice long talk with your husband, last night—Well, I told him that since you had agreed to disagree, I felt it was up to him to see that you and the baby were well provided for— How much do you think?—No, I did better than that—A thousand a week—Well, I thought you'd be pleased—Frankly, it's much more than any court would have given you—Oh, that's all right, don't mention it— Can you come in tomorrow at four to sign the papers?—All right—Not at all. I'm glad I was able to get it for you—Good-bye. [*To* REGINA.] Tomorrow at four for the closing of the separation agreement in Richter against Richter. Notify Klein and Davis to have their client here. Now I'll see that Chapman woman. And then tell Weinberg I want to see him [REGINA g*ives these instructions over the Hushaphone.*] How much of a retainer did we get from Mrs. Richter?

REGINA: Twenty-five hundred dollars.

SIMON: As soon as the separation agreement is signed, send her a bill for five thousand. I want her to get it, while she's still grateful. [*As* MRS. CHAPMAN *enters.*] Hello, Zedorah. Sit down.

MRS. CHAPMAN: Hello, George darling. Well, my goodness, I thought you were never going to see me. [REGINA *throws her a quick look and exits.*]

SIMON: I'm pretty busy, today. What's on your mind: anything special?

MRS. CHAPMAN: No, nothing special. I just dropped in to tell you how wonderful it feels to be a free woman again, and to have a little chat. We really haven't had a chance to talk about anything but that horrible case.

SIMON: I've got quite a lot of clients waiting for me—

MRS. CHAPMAN: Oh well, let them wait. I want to have a chance to thank you and to tell you how much it all means to me. [*Putting her hand on his arm.*] George darling, how can I ever thank you enough?

SIMON: [*Withdrawing his arm.*] You thanked me last night. It's my business to help people when they get into trouble. If you'll take my advice, you'll go away somewhere for a while and forget about it. And, hereafter, don't keep any firearms around the house. It might not turn out so well next time.

MRS. CHAPMAN: Oh, George, you were so wonderful when you talked to the jury. All those beautiful things you said about me. It made me feel that you were the first man that ever really understood me.

SIMON: Well, anyhow, I understand juries. [*Rising and extending his hand.*] It was very nice of you to come in. Any time I can—

MRS. CHAPMAN: [*Rising.*] Why are you so cold to me, George? Don't you know how fond of you I am? Oh, George dear, I've learned to grow so fond of you. [*She throws her arms around his neck and kisses him.*]

SIMON: [*Disengaging himself.*] For God's sake! What do you call this, anyhow? Listen, Mrs. Chapman, I was engaged to defend you on the charge of murdering your husband. There's nothing in the retainer that requires me to sleep with you.

MRS. CHAPMAN: Shut up your mouth, you!

SIMON: That's the way out!

MRS. CHAPMAN: Go to hell. [*She exits as* REGINA *enters with a telegram.*]

SIMON: Why do you leave me alone with that woman?

REGINA: I thought it might be something personal.

SIMON: Personal! [*He rubs his lips with his hand.*] Pfui! So help me God, that's the last one of those goddam female murder cases I'll ever handle. Excuse me, Rexie. What have you got there?

REGINA: It's from Washington. All it says is "Yes," and it's just signed. "X. Y. Z."

SIMON: Aha! Let's see it. [*He looks at the telegram.*] Get me Fishman and Company, right away. I want to talk to Joe Fishman, personally.

[REGINA *gives these instructions on the Hushaphone and exits as* WEINBERG *enters. Simon tears up telegram.*]

Listen, Weinberg, I want you to get out that Richter separation agreement right away. He's to pay her a thousand a week for the support and maintenance of herself and child. The other clauses you know about, don't you?

WEINBERG: Yes. Shall I let the memorandum of law in the Pickford case wait?

SIMON: Yes. They're coming in at four tomorrow to sign the Richter agreement. Then I want — [*The interoffice phone buzzes.*] Yes, John — Is he there now? — All right, I'll be in right away — Oh, John — Say, Weinberg, will you wait outside for just a minute?

WEINBERG: certainly. [*He exits.*]

SIMON: Say, John, listen. I just got a hot tip from Washington that the Supreme Court is reversing the lower court and dismissing the complaint in the Gulf Coast Utilities case — No, neither did I — Yes, I'm going to take a little flier in the stock. Do you want to go fifty-fifty with me — Five thousand shares? — All right, I'll be in as soon as I've talked to Joe Fishman — All right.

REGINA: [*Entering.*] Mr. Fishman. [*She exits.*]

SIMON: Hello, Joe — Fine, how are you? — Say, Joe, what's the last Gulf Coast Utilities? — Well, I want you to buy me ten thousand shares at the market — I know it's a lousy stock, but I've got a hunch it's due for a little whirl — No, I haven't any information; just a hunch, that's all — Well, that's all right, if I lose, I'll have only myself to blame — All right, and say, don't buy it all in one block — All right, Joe — Good-bye. Come in, Weinberg. [WEINBERG *enters.*] Listen, I've been retained by the Crayfield family to oppose the probate of Edward Crayfield's will. They have unquestionable proof that the child is illegitimate. Look these over and then run down a line of cases for me.

WEINBERG: Very well. [REGINA *enters.*]

SIMON: I'm going into Mr. Tedesco's office for a minute.

REGINA: That Mrs. Becker has been waiting since nine o'clock.

SIMON: All right, have her come in. I'll see her in a few minutes. [*He exits.*]

WEINBERG: [*As* REGINA *goes towards the telephone.*] Miss Gordon.

REGINA: Well?

WEINBERG: Won't you change your mind about going to the concert tonight?

REGINA: I've told you I don't care to go, Mr. Weinberg. Did that stipulation go over to Wilson and Devore?

WEINBERG: Yes, the boy is on his way now. Why is my society so distasteful to you?

REGINA: It's not a question of that, Mr. Weinberg. I just don't care to go, that's all. [*At* SIMON's *phone.*] Have Mrs. Becker come in, please.

WEINBERG: Will you go to the theatre with me Saturday night?

REGINA: No, thanks. I'm going to my sister's for dinner.

WEINBERG: You always have some excuse, haven't you?

REGINA: Then why do you keep on asking me?

WEINBERG: I suppose if the great G. S. asked you, you wouldn't refuse.

REGINA: Please keep your remarks to yourself. I don't care to listen to them and what's more, I don't have to.

WEINBERG: What have I ever done to you, to make you treat me like this?

REGINA: Then don't make personal remarks.

WEINBERG: I'm not accustomed to being treated like an office boy; to be ordered out of the room, while my employer has a telephone conversation.

REGINA: You're not the first Harvard Law School man we've had in the office, Mr. Weinberg. You ought to be grateful for the opportunity to get your training from a brilliant man like Mr. Simon.

WEINBERG: It's not difficult to be brilliant, when you make capital of other people's brains.

REGINA: Then, if I were you, I'd take my wonderful brains where they're appreciated more.

WEINBERG: Thank you. I'm glad to know what your sentiments towards me are.

REGINA: I think you're a very ungrateful boy, that's what I think. If I were in your place—Yes, Mrs. Becker, come right in.

MRS. BECKER: I wait here, yes?

REGINA: No, it's all right; come right in. Sit down here. Mr. Simon will be right back. [MRS. BECKER *seats herself, timidly.*] I wish you'd let me know,

Mr. Weinberg, when that stipulation comes back from Wilson and Devore. [SIMON *enters before* WEINBERG *can reply.*]

SIMON: Make a note, Rexie, that I'm having lunch on Tuesday at one-thirty at the Sherry-Netherlands with Mr. Tedesco and Mr. Ferraro.

REGINA: Yes sir.

SIMON: Want to see me, Weinberg?

WEINBERG: No. [*He exits.*]

SIMON: [*Calling after him.*] Get busy on that separation agreement, will you? [*Shaking hands with* MRS. BECKER, *who has risen.*] Well, hello, Mrs. Becker, I'm glad to see you.

MRS. BECKER: Good morning, counsellor. [REGINA *exits to her office.*]

SIMON: Sit down. Sit down. How's your husband?

MRS. BECKER: You don't hoid? He's already dead six years.

SIMON: No! Why, he was always a big, healthy fellow.

MRS. BECKER: Yes, big. But not healthy. He's got in de stomach a cancer.

SIMON: You don't say! Tt! That's terrible. Why I remember him, since I was that high. I used to watch his pushcart when he had to go upstairs for a minute.

MRS. BECKER: [*Weeping.*] Yes. Yes.

SIMON: You've had your share of trouble, hm? Who looks after you now?

MRS. BECKER: I got by the sev'ty-seven street station a newspaper stand.

SIMON: And do you get along all right?

MRS. BECKER: W'en my boy Harry is woikin' is everything oll right.

SIMON: Is Harry old enough to work? Why, Last time I saw him, he was in a baby carriage.

MRS. BECKER: He's already twenty.

SIMON: No! My God, I can't realize it. Well, how is he? Is he a good boy?

MRS. BECKER: He's a good boy. Only oll the time he's getting in trouble.

SIMON: What do you mean trouble? What kind of trouble? With girls?

MRS. BECKER: No, no, counsellor! Mine Harry is a good boy. Only oll the time he's making speeches there should be yet in America a revolution.

SIMON: What do you mean? Harry goes around making Communist speeches?

MRS. BECKER: Oll the time. And from this he is losing oll the time his job. And now they put him in the police station.

SIMON: He's been arrested?

MRS. BECKER: Yes, counsellor. The whole night I don't sleep. So I don't know what I'm going to do. So I'm coming here because you know from the old times mine husband. Oi, counsellor, what I'm going to do, if they're putting my boy in preeson?

SIMON: Don't worry, we won't let them put him in prison. When did this happen: yesterday?

MRS. BECKER: Yes. He's making in Union Square a speech and a policeman comes and hits him with such a club on the head. So they're taking him to the station house. On the whole head, he's got bandages. Counsellor, you wouldn't let them send mine boy to preeson?

SIMON: No, I won't. Don't worry about it. Just leave it to me. You go home and get some sleep and leave everything to me. [*He presses the call button on his desk.*]

MRS. BECKER: Oi, counsellor, every night I'm going to say for you a prayer. [*She covers his hand with kisses.*]

SIMON: [*Patting her head.*] That's all right, Mama Becker. We're old friends. [*Thrusting a bill into her hand.*] Here, take this. [REGINA *enters.*]

MRS. BECKER: No, no. I wouldn't take it.

SIMON: Yes, you take it. Buy yourself some groceries.

MRS. BECKER: Tenks, counsellor, tenks.

REGINA: [*Kindly; taking her by the arm.*] This way, Mrs. Becker.

MRS. BECKER: Tenk you, lady. [*She stops, takes a pocket-book out of a pocket in her petticoat and offers* REGINA *a ten-cent piece.*]

REGINA: No, thanks, I really don't—

MRS. BECKER: Please, please, you take—

REGINA: Well, thank you very much. [*She leads* MRS. BECKER *into the corridor.* SIMON *blows his nose.* REGINA *reenters, wiping her eyes.*] Poor old thing.

SIMON: I used to live in the same house with them. That's a fine joke, that is. The police beat up a kid, who's making a speech, and then they arrest him for disorderly conduct.

REGINA: It's terrible the way some of those rough-neck cops treat people.

SIMON: Well, that's the way it is with a lot of those fellows. You take a fellow that's come up from the gutter and you put a club in his hands and, as likely as not, he'll turn around and use it on his own kind. Listen, this is what I want you to do. Find out where this Becker boy is being held and get me a transcript of the police blotter. Then call up the surety company and arrange for bail. I'll go bail for him, personally. Do that right away.

REGINA: Yes sir. Do you want to see Mr. Darwin now?

SIMON: Yes, let him come in. Oh, and find out the name of the assistant district attorney in charge.

[REGINA *phones these instructions on the Hushaphone.*]

REGINA: Mr. Walter Littlefield is on the wire.

SIMON: All right. Hello, Mr. Littlefield—I'm fine, thanks—Yes—Yes— Yes, I'm very familiar with it—Well, I'm afraid I can't do that—[*As* DARWIN *enters.*] Sit down, Mr. Darwin.

DARWIN: [*Seating himself.*] Thanks.

SIMON: [*Resuming his telephone conversation.*] Well, I can't—Because my partner happens to be the receiver—Yes, I understand; but you can't expect me to represent the principal creditor in a proceeding in which my partner is the receiver—Because that isn't the way I practice law, Mr. Littlefield—I don't care who says it's all right. I know what's right and what's wrong, without asking anybody's opinion—No, I don't have to think it over; I'm telling you right now that I won't have anything to do with it—So am I—Good-bye. Sorry to keep you waiting, Mr. Darwin.

DARWIN: Oh, that's perfectly all right. I'm not in a great hurry.

REGINA: [*Entering.*] Excuse me, but Mr. Crayfield is here.

SIMON: I'll see him in a few minutes.

[REGINA *exits.*]

DARWIN: Excuse me, but is that Rigby Crayfield?

SIMON: Yes, it is.

DARWIN: I don't mean to be impertinent. But that's really one of the things I wanted to see you about.

SIMON: Oh, is that so?

DARWIN: Yes. I heard that the Crayfield family was thinking of retaining you for the purpose of breaking Edward's will.

SIMON: I'm very sorry, Mr. Darwin, but I can't discuss—

DARWIN: Oh, of course, I understand perfectly. I shouldn't think of asking you to violate any professional confidences. But you see, Wilma Crayfield, Edward's widow, happens to be a first cousin of mine.

SIMON: Yes, I know.

DARWIN: And I understand that this will contest would involve her in a

rather painful scandal. So, I'd rather hoped that because of your friendship for Wilma —

SIMON: I scarcely know Mrs. Crayfield.

DARWIN: Well, I mean to say, she's dined at your home, and all that.

SIMON: Once, I believe. And three years ago —

DARWIN: Still —

SIMON: An attorney can't let such considerations stand in the way of his
practice, Mr. Darwin.

DARWIN: Well, of course, I can't very well hope to persuade you. Of course,
she's a friend of Cora's, too.

SIMON: My wife would be the last person in the world, Mr. Darwin, to ask
me to give up an important case because she happens to be socially
acquainted with one of the interested parties.

DARWIN: [*Rising.*] Well, I don't want to take up any more of your time.

SIMON: [*Rising.*] I'm sorry I can't oblige you.

DARWIN: Well, if you can't, you can't. Oh, by the way, I wonder if you could
help me out of a temporary embarrassment?

SIMON: Why, I'd be glad to do anything that's —

DARWIN: Well, you see, I'm a rather heavy holder of Amalgamated Zinc, and
now I've just learned that the miserable beggars have gone and passed
their quarterly dividend. So, for the moment, that leaves me rather up
against it. I was wondering if —

SIMON: How much do you need?

DARWIN: Oh, a couple thousand or so. I'll only need it until July. I've quite
a bit of money coming in then.

SIMON: Well, I guess I can manage that.

DARWIN: Well, thanks very much, old man. I'll be glad to give you my note,
of course.

SIMON: All right. Can you drop in tomorrow morning?

DARWIN: I'll be delighted. About eleven?

SIMON: Yes. Any time in the morning. My secretary will have the check and
the note ready for you.

REGINA: [*Entering.*] Excuse me. But Mrs. Simon is outside.

SIMON: Oh, ask her please to wait in your office, while I see Mr. Crayfield.
And have Mr. Crayfield come in.

[REGINA *telephones on the Hushaphone.*]

**DARWIN:** Well, so long, old man. And thanks ever so much.

**SIMON:** Not a bit. You can get out this way.

**DARWIN:** Why, thanks. I think I'll just say hello to Cora on the way out. Good day.

**SIMON:** Good-bye. [DARWIN *exits.*] Draw a check for two thousand dollars on my personal account to the order of Roy Darwin. And a promissory note payable in three months. He'll be in tomorrow morning.

**REGINA:** Yes sir.

**SIMON:** Oh, and how much did I tell you to send a bill to Mrs. Richter for?

**REGINA:** Five thousand.

**SIMON:** Better make it seventy-five hundred.

**REGINA:** Yes sir. Come right in, Mr. Crayfield.

[*The scene blacks out.*]

CURTAIN

# SCENE 3

*The outer office. Bessie is at the switchboard. A small dark Woman is seated on the sofa between the windows. CORA SIMON is seated on the sofa, downstage left. She is an attractive woman in her late 30s, tastefully and expensively dressed. As the lights go up, DARWIN comes out of the door of SIMON's office and crosses to CORA.*

DARWIN: Hello, Cora.

CORA: Why hello, Roy! What are you doing here? [*They shake hands very cordially.*]

DARWIN: Why, there was something I wanted to talk over with George.

CORA: Tell me, wasn't that Rigby Crayfield who just went into George's office?

DARWIN: Yes, it was. That's why I'm here.

REGINA: [*Coming out of SIMON's office.*] Good morning, Mrs. Simon.

CORA: [*Coolly.*] Good morning, Miss Gordon.

REGINA: Mr. Simon will be busy with a client for about fifteen minutes. Do you mind waiting in my office?

CORA: Thank you. I want to have a word with Mr. Darwin first.

BESSIE: Simon and Tedesco—Who's calling?—One moment, please—[*To REGINA.*] Clerk of the Surrogate's Court calling you.

REGINA: I'll take it in my office. [*She exits.*]

BESSIE: One moment please, I'm getting her for you—All rightee, go ahead.

DARWIN: She's a bustling creature, isn't she?

CORA: Oh yes, very. But George finds her indispensable. Well, Wilma Crayfield called me up this morning. The poor thing is in a terrible state. She's heard that the Crayfield family is engaging George to contest the will. Have you spoken to George about it?

DARWIN: Yes, I have. He's absolutely firm about it.

CORA: Oh, but Roy, he mustn't! Think how awful it would be for poor Wilma.

DARWIN: Well, perhaps you can persuade him. He wouldn't listen to me. [*Lowering his voice.*] Tell me, Cora, is it definitely settled that George is going to Europe with you?

CORA: Yes.

DARWIN: Well that's that. When am I going to see you?

CORA: Well—I don't know, exactly.

**DARWIN:** Are you free for lunch?

**CORA:** No, I'm lunching with George.

**DARWIN:** Oh. How about tea?

**CORA:** Why yes, I can make it for tea. I have an appointment for a fitting, but I can change that.

**DARWIN:** Shall we say four at the Plaza?

**CORA:** Yes.

**DARWIN:** Au revoir, then.

**CORA:** Au revoir. [*He exits.* BESSIE *dials a number.* CORA *rises and crosses towards the door to* SIMON*'s office.*] Bessie, I'm going to wait in Miss Gordon's office. Will you get me Miss Williams at Bergdorf-Goodman, please?

[HENRY *enters and, seating himself at the table, begins to solve a crossword puzzle.*]

**BESSIE:** Yes, ma'am.

**CORA:** Thank you. [*She exits.*]

**BESSIE:** Hello. District attorney's office?—One moment please—Here's the district attorney's office—All rightee, go ahead. [*She looks through the telephone directory.* CHARLIE MCFADDEN *enters with a paper bag.*]

**MCFADDEN:** Here's your tongue on rye and chocolate malted.

**BESSIE:** Thanks, Charlie. Did you tell him to put a lot of Russian dressing on it?

**MCFADDEN:** Yeah; he smeared it on thick.

[*He crosses to the library and exits.* BESSIE *dials a number.*]

**BESSIE:** Hello—Hello, Arthur—Will you take the board now? I want to get my lunch.—He can't. He has to go right out for Mr. Tedesco—Hello—Bergdorf-Goodman?—Miss Williams, please—Hello, Miss Williams?—One moment, please. Here's Miss Williams, Mrs. Simon—All rightee, go ahead—

[WEINBERG *enters from the library and crosses to the entrance door.*]

**WEINBERG:** I'm going to lunch. I'll be back in a half-hour.

**BESSIE:** All rightee.

[WEINBERG *exits.* BESSIE *rises and takes a towel from the drawer of the switchboard.* SANDLER *enters from the library.*]

SANDLER: [*To* HENRY.] Hey, kid, do you know what became of volume M to S of Stoddard's Digest?
HENRY: I'll look around for it. [*He exits to the library.*]
SANDLER: [*To* BESSIE.] All right, peaches and vinegar.
BESSIE: This lady is waiting to see Mr. Tedesco. And G. S. has someone with him. And Mr. Weinberg will be back from lunch in a half an hour.
SANDLER: You wouldn't fool me, would you? [BESSIE *exits to The corridor. A* WOMAN *comes out of* TEDESCO'*s office and exits*]. Hello? — Yes sir — [*To the* WOMAN *who is waiting.*] Are you Mrs. Gardi?
THE WOMAN: Yes.
SANDLER: All right. Mr. Tedesco will see you now. [THE WOMAN *goes into* TEDESCO'*s office.*] Hello — The passenger department of the French Line? — Who is this, please — Oh, all right, Mrs. Simon, I'll get it right away — Don't mention it.

[*He looks up a number in the directory.* HENRY *enters carrying a law book.*]

HENRY: Here it is. It was on the wrong shelf.
SANDLER: Oh, it was, was it? What are you doing: reading up on rape cases again?
HENRY: I was not.
SANDLER: You ought to know them all by heart, by now.

[*He dials a number.* GOLDIE *appears at the door of* TEDESCO'*s office with a letter.*]

GOLDIE: Here, Henry, take this right around to the Napoli Importing Company. [HENRY *takes the letter from her.*] Mr. Tedesco wants it delivered right away. [HENRY *goes to the revolving bookstand and takes his cap from behind it.*] Don't delay now. It's very important.
HENRY: All right. All right. Can't you see I'm going?
GOLDIE: Don't be impudent to me, please.

[HENRY *goes out the entrance door.* GOLDIE *exits to the library.*]

SANDLER: Hello, French Line? — Passenger department, please — Hold the wire a minute — Here's the French Line for Mrs. Simon — Go ahead. [*While he is speaking,* MRS. LENA SIMON *has entered. She is a quiet little woman in her 60s.*] Who do you wish to see, madam?

MRS. SIMON: Is Mr. Simon busy, please?

SANDLER: Yes, he is. Will anybody else do?

MRS. SIMON: I'll wait for him.

SANDLER: He may be busy for quite a while.

MRS. SIMON: Oh, that's nothing. I got plenty time.

SANDLER: All right. Take a seat.

MRS. SIMON: Thank you. [*She sits on the sofa between the windows.*]

SANDLER: Hello — What number? — All right — [*He dials a number.* GOLDIE *enters from the library and crosses to the entrance door.*]

GOLDIE: [*Importantly.*] I'm going to lunch.

SANDLER: All right, beautiful. Can you be reached at the Automat?

GOLDIE: You're very funny — I don't think! [*She exits.*]

SANDLER: Hello — 4979? — Go ahead.

[*He becomes absorbed in his law book.* MCFADDEN *comes out of the library and is about to enter* TEDESCO's *office when he stops and looks curiously at* MRS. SIMON.]

MCFADDEN: Excuse me, ma'am, but ain't you Mr. Simon's mother?

MRS. SIMON: Yes.

MCFADDEN: I thought I recognized you. I guess you don't remember me.

MRS. SIMON: Well, I think I saw you somewhere before.

MCFADDEN: I'm Charlie McFadden that used to be the helper to Barney O'Rourke, the plumber, on Third Avenue.

MRS. SIMON: Oh, of course! When we were living on Eighty-second Street.

MCFADDEN: That's right. An' I was livin' right across the street in number 319. That's many a long day ago.

MRS. SIMON: I should say so. Well, well, what do you think of that!

MCFADDEN: Well, say, you're lookin' great. Why you don't look a day older than the last time I saw you.

**MRS. SIMON:** Yes, sure; you expect me to believe that, you jollier? Next month, I'll be sixty-four.

**McFADDEN:** Well, you sure don't look it.

**MRS. SIMON:** Well, I have my health, thank God. And my boy gives me every comfort. Why shouldn't I look well?

**McFADDEN:** You've sure got reason to be proud of your son, Mrs. Simon. He's a prince among men, that's what he is.

**MRS. SIMON:** Yes, that's just what he is, Mr. McFadden.

**McFADDEN:** An' ain't I the one to know it, too. I guess you know what he done for me, don't you?

**MRS. SIMON:** [*Shaking her head.*] No. I know how to mind my own business, Mr. McFadden. He doesn't tell me anything and I don't ask any questions.

**McFADDEN:** Well, he gave me a new start in life, that's what he did. You know I was nothin' but a jailbird.

**MRS. SIMON:** Tt! Tt!

**McFADDEN:** Yes, sure. I did a couple good long stretches for burglary; and I guess that's where I'd of ended my days if I hadn't happened to meet him on the street one day. Well, it seems he'd heard all about me, so he says to me: "Charlie," he says, "if you'll go straight, I'll give you a job in the office." "On the level," says I. "Sure," says he. "For old time's sake," says he. So I took him at his word and here I've been ever since.

**MRS. SIMON:** You're working here for George?

**McFADDEN:** Yep. Nearly four years now. Process server. And now and again I do a little private detective work. You see, I got ways of findin' things out.

**MRS. SIMON:** What do you think of that!

**McFADDEN:** It's made a new man o' me, Mrs. Simon. I got a good steady job here and I meet lots of fine people and I know all the boys around the courthouse. And it's all his doin'.

**MRS. SIMON:** He's a good, good man, my George.

**McFADDEN:** I'd cut off my right hand for him that's what I'd do. Well, it's mighty nice to be seein' you again, Mrs. Simon. [*He shakes hands with her.*]

**MRS. SIMON:** I've been very happy to see you, Mr. McFadden.

**McFADDEN:** God bless you!

[*He enters* TEDESCO's *office.* PETER J. MALONE *enters from the corridor. He is a plump politician of 55, fastidiously dressed.*]

MALONE: County Clerk Peter J. Malone to see Mr. Simon.
SANDLER: Yes sir. Just take a seat, Mr. Malone, and I'll tell him you're here.
MALONE: All right.
SANDLER: County Clerk Malone to see Mr. Simon—Just a few minutes, Mr. Malone.
MALONE: Okay.
MRS. SIMON: What's the matter, Mr. Malone; don't you remember your old friends?
MALONE: What? Well, will you look who's sittin' there! Why, I didn't see you at all. [*He goes over to her and shakes hands with her.*]
MRS. SIMON: What's the matter? Did I shrink so much that you couldn't see me?
MALONE: Why, no. I thought it was a young girl sittin' there. You know, one of them expensive Park Avenue divorce cases of George's.
MRS. SIMON: Yes, you're a fine one, you are. If anybody believed everything that you say!
MALONE: [*Sitting beside her.*] Well, you're a sight for sore eyes, you are. Why, I ain't seen you since the Dewey Parade. How are you, anyhow?
MRS. SIMON: I'm fine. And you! I don't have to ask you. [*She indicates his bulk.*]
MALONE: Yeah, quite a bay window. But when a fellow gets to be my age, you know.
MRS. SIMON: What are you talking about! Why, you're only a spring chicken.
MALONE: [*Behind his hand.*] Fifty-six. But don't tell anybody. Well, a lot o' water has flowed under the bridge since the old days in Yorkville.
MRS. SIMON: Yes, we're all a little better off than in those days.
MALONE: I'll say we are. Me drivin' a truck and you runnin' a little bakery and George sellin' papers. Well, you ought to be mighty proud of your son, Mrs. Simon.
SANDLER: [*Nervously.*] Excuse me, madam. Are you Mr. Simon's mother?
MRS. SIMON: Yes.
SANDLER: Oh, I'll tell him you're here. I didn't know who you were.

MRS. SIMON: Oh, that's all right. I got plenty time.

[SIMON *enters from his office with a middle-aged* MAN.]

SIMON: All right, Mr. Crayfield. I'll phone you in the morning.
THE MAN: Very well. [*He exits.*]
SIMON: Hello, Pete.
MALONE: [*Rising.*] Hello, George.
SIMON: Hello, Mama. I didn't know you were here. [*He goes over and kisses her affectionately.*]
MRS. SIMON: Hello, George.
SIMON: Have you been here long? [*To* SANDLER.] Why didn't you tell me my mother was waiting?
MRS. SIMON: It's only five minutes, George.
SANDLER: I'm very sorry, Mr. Simon. I didn't know the lady was your mother.
SIMON: What do you mean, you didn't know? Don't you ask people who they are when they come in?
MRS. SIMON: Georgie, please!
SANDLER: I'm very sorry, Mr. Simon.
SIMON: You're going up for your bar examination and you can't even announce a caller.
MRS. SIMON: George, be a good boy.
SIMON: The next time my mother calls, I want her announced immediately, do you understand?
SANDLER: Yes, Mr. Simon.
SIMON: Come in, Mama. Come in, Pete.
MALONE: Say, I can wait.
SIMON: No, no. Come in, both of you. [*They exit to* SIMON'*s office.*]
SANDLER: Hello — Yes — Who's calling? — Wait a minute, I'll see if he's in —

[*The scene blacks out.*]

CURTAIN

# SCENE 4

*The inner office.* REGINA *is at* SIMON's *desk, telephoning.*

REGINA: I'll see if I can find him — Wait, I think he's coming now. Hold the wire.

[SIMON, MRS. SIMON *and* MALONE *enter, downstage.*]

SIMON: Did you have your lunch, Mama?

MRS. SIMON: Yes, of course. A long time ago already.

REGINA: Mr. Fishman on the phone.

SIMON: All right, I'll talk to him. Sit down, Mama. Sit down, Pete.

REGINA: Here he is now, Mr. Fishman.

SIMON: Hello, Joe — That's fine — Well, maybe you're right — No, don't do anything — All right — All right, I'll tell you when to sell — All right — Good-bye, Joe.

REGINA: [*Meanwhile.*] How are you, Mrs. Simon. [*She shakes hands cordially with her.*] You're looking very well.

MRS. SIMON: Oh, I can't complain. I don't get any younger, but otherwise I'm fine.

MALONE: Hello, Rexie. How are you?

REGINA: Oh, I'm all right, thanks, Mr. Malone.

MALONE: I guess George is keeping you pretty busy, ain't he?

REGINA: Oh, I don't mind that. If there's one thing I don't like, it's being idle.

SIMON: [*Hanging up the receiver.*] Where's Mrs. Simon?

REGINA: She's in my office. I think she's telephoning.

SIMON: [*Opening the door of* REGINA's *office.*] Hello, darling.

CORA: [*Offstage.*] Hello, George. I still have another call to make.

SIMON: All right, sweetheart. Come in whenever you're through. [*He closes the door and goes to his desk.*]

MRS. SIMON: George, I'm going to wait outside and you talk with Mr. Malone.

MALONE: No, no, you stay right where you are. I've got to call up Albany. Where's a phone I can use?

SIMON: In the library. Rexie, show Mr. Malone —

REGINA: Yes sir.

MALONE: Never mind, Rexie. I know the way.

SIMON: Go ahead with him, Rexie, and if there's anybody in the library, chase 'em out till Mr. Malone is through. And listen, see that he gets his number. That fathead at the switchboard doesn't know his ear from his elbow.

REGINA: Yes sir.

MALONE: Thanks, I'll see you later.

SIMON: Yes, come back, as soon as you're through.

[MALONE *exits.*]

REGINA: That Becker boy is being held on two thousand dollars bail on a felonious assault charge. I'm arranging the bail and the district attorney's office is going to call me back to let me know who's handling the case.

SIMON: All right. Have the boy come in to see me.

REGINA: Yes sir. [*She exits.*]

MRS. SIMON: That's a nice girl, George, that Miss Gordon.

SIMON: She's a wonderful secretary. I couldn't get along without her. Mama, have a piece of candy.

MRS. SIMON: No, thanks, Georgie.

SIMON: [*Taking several pieces.*] They're very good.

MRS. SIMON: You'll spoil your lunch, Georgie, nasching like that.

SIMON: Nonsense! Why should a piece of candy spoil my lunch?

MRS. SIMON: Georgie, how is it a nice girl like Miss Gordon doesn't find herself a husband?

SIMON: I don't know. I don't think she's interested in men. Mama, do you remember Sarah Becker from Second Avenue?

MRS. SIMON: Becker? No, I don't remember any Becker.

SIMON: Certainly you do. Her husband used to sell neckties from a pushcart. A great big fellow.

MRS. SIMON: Oh yes, of course, of course! It must be twenty years ago. She had a little baby with red curls—little Harry.

SIMON: That's the one. Well, little Harry has been making Communist speeches in Union Square and getting into trouble with the police.

MRS. SIMON: What, that little baby! I can't believe it.

SIMON: He hasn't stayed a little baby all these years, mama.

MRS. SIMON: But you're going to do something for him, George?

SIMON: Yes, I guess I can get him out of it, all right. His mother was in this morning. Becker died of cancer a few years ago, and I think she's been having a pretty hard time of it.

**Mrs. Simon:** *Ach*, the poor thing. I think I'll go and pay her a little visit.

**Simon:** Yes, why don't you do that? Rexie will give you her address. And take her a little fruit or something. The poor thing looks as though she didn't have enough to eat. And I guess she's too proud to go to the charities.

**Mrs. Simon:** Yes, the charities! Don't talk to me about those charities! It's better to starve.

**Simon:** Well, Mama, I've decided to go to Europe with Cora next week.

**Mrs. Simon:** That's good, Georgie. You need a good rest. You work too hard.

**Simon:** Oh, I don't need any rest. Hard work is good for me. But I made up my mind that we'd celebrate our fifth anniversary by taking a trip together. You know, I haven't really had a chance to be alone with Cora since we eloped together.

**Mrs. Simon:** Yes, that's just what you should do, Georgie. A man and wife should be just as close together as they can.

**Simon:** Especially when a man has a wife like Cora. She's a wonderful, wonderful woman, Mama.

**Mrs. Simon:** Well, she has a good husband, in you, too, Georgie.

**Simon:** Oh yes, of course. According to you, nobody would be good enough for me. It's a wonder the King of England never asked me to become his son-in-law.

**Mrs. Simon:** Well, I'm sure his daughters couldn't do any better.

**Simon:** What a *naar*[1] you are, Mama.

**Mrs. Simon:** All right, laugh. It doesn't change my opinion.

**Simon:** Well, anyhow, I wish I deserved a wife like Cora.

**Mrs. Simon:** Georgie, listen, I want to talk to you.

**Simon:** Is anything wrong? Are you feeling all right?

**Mrs. Simon:** Of course, I'm feeling all right, Georgie. You mustn't worry about me.

**Simon:** Well, what's the matter, then? What do you look so serous about?

**Mrs. Simon:** Georgie, you mustn't be angry with me—

**Simon:** I'm not going to be angry. What is it?

**Mrs. Simon:** Georgie, Davie called me up this morning—

**Simon:** Well?

---

[1] Silly.

**MRS. SIMON:** You told me you wouldn't be angry.

**SIMON:** I'm not angry. Go ahead.

**MRS. SIMON:** He needs a little money.

**SIMON:** Money? What does he need money for this time?

**MRS. SIMON:** A check came back from the bank.

**SIMON:** You mean he gave somebody a bum check?

**MRS. SIMON:** He made a little mistake in his balance.

**SIMON:** The hell he made a little mistake in his balance. He's a goddam crook, that's what he is.

**MRS. SIMON:** Georgie, is that a way to talk about your brother?

**SIMON:** Yes, brother. A fine brother he is. All he does is one dirty, crooked thing after another. I no sooner get him out of one thing then he gets himself into another. But I'm through with him. He can get himself out of this one.

**MRS. SIMON:** Georgie, please—

**SIMON:** No, to hell with him. Let him go to jail. That's where he belongs, anyhow.

**MRS. SIMON:** Georgie, be a good boy. It's the last time. He won't do anything again.

**SIMON:** Yes! How many times have I heard that one before, too? I'm through with him, I tell you. That *lausbub*[2] has given me more headaches than my whole practice put together. I'm supposed to be an important lawyer around here. I'm mixed up in more front-page cases than any lawyer in New York. People from old families come in and think I'm doing them a favor if I accept their retainers. If I don't happen to like a millionaire's looks, I throw him out of the office. It's fine for me, isn't it, to have a brother going around getting himself pinched in gambling raids and annoying women in the subway and handing out rubber checks? It's great, isn't it?

**MRS. SIMON:** It won't happen again, Georgie.

**SIMON:** No, I've done all I'm going to do. Let him shift for himself.

**MRS. SIMON:** Georgie, please. For me, do it; not for him.

**SIMON:** No.

**MRS. SIMON:** I don't often ask you for something, Georgie—

**CORA:** [*Entering.*] May I come in? Oh, I'm sorry. I didn't know you were busy.

**SIMON:** It's all right, darling. Come right in.

---

2 While the context makes clear Simon's annoyance with his brother, *lausbub* remains elusive. It could be a corruption of the Yiddish *shlub* [*zhlub*], oaf, or even the Polish *Xobus*, scoundrel.

CORA: [*Shaking hands with* MRS. SIMON.] How do you do, Mrs. Simon?

MRS. SIMON: I'm very well, thank you. And you?

CORA: Quite well, thanks.

MRS. SIMON: That's good. You got a little thinner since the last time I saw you.

CORA: Have I? I don't think so.

REGINA: [*Entering.*] Excuse me, Mr. Simon. Mr. Hirshberg is outside. He has an appointment with you.

SIMON: Oh yes, I forgot about him.

CORA: Shall I clear out?

SIMON: No, stay right here. I'll see him in one of the other offices. Mama, are you sure you won't have a little lunch with us?

MRS. SIMON: No, I must go now.

SIMON: [*Kissing her.*] Well, good-bye, Mama. Take a taxi uptown.

MRS. SIMON: The bus is good enough, Georgie, don't forget.

SIMON: I'll think it over and call you up tonight. I won't be five minutes, darling. Oh, Rexie, write down that Mrs. Becker's address for my mother.

REGINA: Yes, sir.

[SIMON *exits to the corridor,* REGINA *to her office.*]

CORA: Lovely spring weather we're having, isn't it?

MRS. SIMON: Yes, today it's beautiful. I'm always glad when the winter is over.

CORA: Yes, I prefer warm weather, too.

[*A moment of silence.*]

MRS. SIMON: And your children: are they well, too?

CORA: Yes, very well, thank you.

MRS. SIMON: They must be getting big now.

CORA: Yes, Richard is fourteen and Dorothy twelve.

MRS. SIMON: Tt! Tt! Before you know it, they're grown up. It seems like yesterday since Georgie was a little boy.

CORA: I know. They do grow up awfully fast.

MRS. SIMON: They don't mind that you go to Europe and leave them?

CORA: Oh, no! They're quite accustomed to being left. They're very fond of their governess.

MRS. SIMON: Well, I'm glad Georgie is going to have a little vacation. He works so hard.

CORA: Yes, he does work hard. Too hard, in fact.

MRS. SIMON: He always worked hard. Since he was a little boy, he's been working hard. Always working and studying and trying to better himself. That's how he made his success.

CORA: Yes, of course. But now that he's achieved success, there's really no longer any necessity for it.

MRS. SIMON: It's his nature. You can't change his nature.

CORA: Yes, I think perhaps you're right. Marvelous view from here, isn't it?

MRS. SIMON: Yes, it's beautiful.

CORA: [*Looking at her watch.*] Heavens, it's half-past one already.

REGINA: [*Entering.*] Here's the address, Mrs. Simon.

MRS. SIMON: Oh, thank you. Thank you, very much. Well, I think I'll go now.

REGINA: Shall I tell Mr. Simon you're going?

MRS. SIMON: No, no, don't disturb him. [*Extending her hand to* CORA.] Well, good-bye.

CORA: [*Shaking hands.*] Good-bye. Awfully nice to have seen you again.

MRS. SIMON: Maybe I'll see you again before you go to Europe.

CORA: Oh, I hope so.

MRS. SIMON: But in case I don't, I hope you have a wonderful trip and that you come back safe and sound.

CORA: Thanks, very much.

MRS. SIMON: And take good care of my Georgie.

CORA: I'll do my best.

MRS. SIMON: Good-bye, Miss Gordon.

REGINA: Good-bye, Mrs. Simon. Shall I show you the way?

MRS. SIMON: No, no. I know the way.

REGINA: I'm going to come and pay you a little visit soon.

MRS. SIMON: Oh, that will be very nice. Come any time: I don't go out very much. Well, good-bye.

REGINA: Good-bye, Mrs. Simon.

CORA: Good-bye. [MRS. SIMON *exits.* REGINA *is about to go to her office.*] Oh, Miss Gordon!

REGINA: Yes, Mrs. Simon.

CORA: I'd like you to do something for me.

REGINA: Certainly.

CORA: I'd like you, between three and four this afternoon, to call up the French Line and ask for Mr. Morell—M–O–R–E–double L. You'd better write it down, hadn't you?

REGINA: I'll remember it. [*Nevertheless, she takes up a piece of paper and makes some notes.*]

CORA: I want to make sure that our suite on the *Paris* has a serving pantry. I forgot to ask him this morning.

REGINA: And if it hasn't?

CORA: Well, if it hasn't you'd better—No, never mind. In that case, I'll take it up with him, myself. I'm almost certain it has, but I want to make sure. Also I wish you'd ask him to arrange to have a steward named Marcel Lebon—Have you got that?—Lebon—L–E–B–O–N.

REGINA: Yes, I have it.

CORA: I want him assigned to our suite. He's served me several times before, and I prefer to have someone who is familiar with my requirements. You'll attend to that, will you?

REGINA: Yes, ma'am, is that all?

CORA: Yes, thank you. I think that's all. Oh, you'd better phone me about the pantry this evening, at dinner time.

REGINA: I can tell Mr. Simon.

CORA: He's likely to forget. I'd rather you phone me.

REGINA: Very well.

CORA: Thank you. [*As* REGINA *is about to go.*] Oh, I wonder if you'd mind giving me a cigarette. I seem to have run out of them.

REGINA: Certainly. [*She takes the cigarette box over to* CORA.]

CORA: Thanks. Heavens, I seem to be out of matches, too. [REGINA, *without a word, strikes a match and offers* CORA *a light.*] Thanks very much.

SIMON: [*Entering.*] I'm sorry to keep you waiting, darling.

CORA: It doesn't matter.

SIMON: [*To* REGINA, *who is about to exit.*] Rexie, you'd better go get your lunch.

REGINA: I'm in no hurry. [*She exits abruptly.*]

SIMON: That girl's a human dynamo. Why, it's half-past one already! You must be starved, darling.

CORA: Well, I am rather hungry. I had an early breakfast and I've been running errands all morning.

SIMON: Well, sweetheart, I've got to see Peter Malone for a few minutes. Why don't you go ahead and start your lunch and I'll join you in ten or fifteen minutes?

CORA: Perhaps I'll do that. I've lots of things to attend to after lunch. But there's something I must talk to you about first.

SIMON: [*Sitting on the sofa beside her.*] All right, honey. Nothing's wrong, is it?

**CORA:** It's about Wilma Crayfield.

**SIMON:** Oh! Your friend Mr. Darwin has been talking to me about that, too.

**CORA:** Yes, so he told me. George, you're really not thinking seriously of trying to break that will, are you?

**SIMON:** Yes, darling, very seriously. In fact, Rigby Crayfield was in here this morning and engaged me to represent the Crayfield family.

**CORA:** But George, you can't do that!

**SIMON:** Why, darling?

**CORA:** Why, it's a scandalous case!

**SIMON:** It certainly is! Do you know the facts?

**CORA:** No, I don't.

**SIMON:** Well, in a couple of words, it turns out that Madam Wilma played a pretty dirty trick on her husband and that the child to whom he left the bulk of the estate isn't his child after all.

**CORA:** Why, I don't believe it! It's preposterous.

**SIMON:** I've got the proofs right here, darling. You don't think I'd take the case, do you, unless I were convinced of the facts?

**CORA:** I can't understand why you would want to have anything to do with such a case.

**SIMON:** There's a hundred thousand dollar fee in it, if I win. The estate will come to over four million.

**CORA:** You don't need the money. Especially money that you get by such means.

**SIMON:** By such means? I don't understand you, darling.

**CORA:** Think of what this is going to do to Wilma!

**SIMON:** But think of what she did to Crayfield!

**CORA:** Well, he's dead and buried and none the worse off for it.

**SIMON:** I really don't follow your logic, sweetheart. I don't see that there's much reason for sympathizing with a woman who's palmed off a bastard on her husband and then gets found out.

**CORA:** We all make mistakes and do foolish things that we regret. Anyhow, there's no reason why *you* should have anything to do with the nasty mess.

**SIMON:** As an attorney, I owe it to myself to take lucrative and important case when it's offered me. And as a member of the bar, I owe it to the community to see substantial justice done. You don't think Edward Crayfield would have made that will, do you, if he'd known the child wasn't his?

CORA: I don't know anything about it. I do know that Wilma Crayfield is a friend of mine and has been for years. Why, you know her, too, George. She's dined at our house.

SIMON: But so have hundreds of other people, darling. Does that mean that I can't appear in any case in which their interests are involved? It's a pretty high price to pay for having people to dinner.

CORA: You know I don't mean that. This is a very special case. It's a friend's reputation that's involved.

SIMON: Her reputation can't be saved, anyhow. If I didn't take the case, a hundred other lawyers would be glad to.

CORA: Well, at least, you would have made a magnanimous gesture.

SIMON: I should say so! A hundred thousand dollars! That's not the way law is practiced, darling.

CORA: I don't see why it isn't possible to practice law, like a gentleman.

SIMON: [*Rising and walking away.*] I never laid any claims to being a gentleman, dear. The last time I crossed the Atlantic, it was in the steerage.

CORA: I didn't mean it in that way, George. Heavens, nobody admires you more than I for the handicaps you've overcome. I couldn't have given any better demonstration of it, could I, than making a runaway marriage with you, after divorcing the man I'd been married to for eleven years?

SIMON: Well, we've been pretty happy together, haven't we?

CORA: Yes, of course we have.

SIMON: The old saying about marrying in haste and repenting at leisure hasn't held good with us. I know I haven't lived up to all your expectations of me. I told you from the start I wasn't good enough for you. But I've tried my best.

CORA: I'm not complaining, George.

SIMON: I know you're not. You're very sweet to me. But I know there are lots of ways in which I don't measure up to your standards.

CORA: Well, it's only that I feel that now that you've made your success, you should try to disassociate yourself from all these unsavory *affaires de scandale*. Like that awful murder case, for example—

SIMON: I know: the Chapman case. Yes, I'm through with cases of that sort. What do you think, sweetheart, she was in here this morning and tried to steal me away from you!

CORA: What an awful person she must be!

SIMON: Fine chance she had, huh? [*He tries to kiss her.*]

CORA: My mouth, George! I just put it on.

SIMON: I used to be quite a lady-killer, in the old days, too. But that was before I knew you, darling.

CORA: You see it's a little embarrassing for me to have your name constantly associated with these sensational cases. After all, it's my name now, too, you know. And the sort of people I've always known can't help thinking it's a little strange.

SIMON: Sweetheart, the last thing in the world I want to do is cause you any embarrassment. My one object in life is to make you happy and give you everything you want.

CORA: Oh. I didn't mean to imply for a minute that it's been intentional. Only—

SIMON: I don't even want it to be unintentional. Listen, darling, would it make you any happier if I dropped this Crayfield case?

CORA: It would make me feel that I was married to a man who recognizes the value of the social amenities.

SIMON: Okay. [*He pushes the call button on his desk. Almost instantly,* REGINA *enters.*] Take a letter to Rigby Crayfield, Rexie. Dear Mr. Crayfield, I regret to inform you that it will be impossible for me to represent you in the matter of the probate of the will of Edward Crayfield. My reasons for withdrawing from the case have nothing to do with the merits of your claims, but are of a personal nature, the details of which I shall not burden you with. I am enclosing herewith all the papers in the matter, of which kindly acknowledge receipt. Regretting any inconvenience I may have caused you, I am, et cetera. Get that right out and send it around by messenger. And get the papers from Weinberg.

REGINA: Yes sir. [*She throws a swift look at* CORA *and exits.*]

CORA: Thank you, George dear.

SIMON: Feel better, now?

CORA: Yes, much better.

SIMON: Don't I rate a kiss? [CORA *holds up her face. He kisses her on the lips.*] You'll make a gentleman of me, yet.

CORA: I'm sure you've ruined my beautiful mouth. Yes, you have. [*She busies herself with her lipstick.*]

MALONE: [*Appearing in the doorway.*] Am I intrudin'?

SIMON: No, I was just kissing my wife.

MALONE: Well, I'm glad there's some that still do.

SIMON: Darling, this is Pete Malone, who makes governors and presidents.

MALONE: [*Shaking hands with* CORA.] And assemblymen, George. Don't forget the assemblymen.

CORA: How do you do, Mr. Malone?

MALONE: I had the pleasure of meetin' you in Washington, before you and George were married.

CORA: [*Rising.*] Oh yes, of course. Well, George, I think I'll go on to lunch now.

SIMON: All right, darling. Where will you be?

CORA: At the Marguery.

SIMON: I'll be there in fifteen minutes.

MALONE: I won't keep him long.

CORA: All right. Au revoir, George. Good-bye, Mr. Malone. Awfully nice to have seen you again.

MALONE: Thank you, ma'am, it was a great pleasure to see you again, too.

[CORA *exits.* MALONE *seats himself upstage of the desk.*]

SIMON: [*Sitting on sofa.*] God, what a woman that is, Pete! I can't realize, half the time, that I'm really married to her.

MALONE: [*Taking a cigar from the box on the desk.*] Well, you sure are hittin' the high places, George. In the old days, when you were peddlin' papers in the rain and your toes comin' through your boots, it was a million to one, and no takers, that I'd live to see you ridin' around in a Hispano — whaddya-call-it with a Daughter of the American Revolution.

SIMON: Well, you haven't done so badly by yourself, either, Pete.

MALONE: Oh, I'm not complainin'. Only you're on the front page defendin' the beautiful Flossie McFloosie, whilst I'm back amongst the editorials, in a long tail an' stripes, makin' a hearty meal of civic Virtue.

SIMON: Pete, there's something I want to talk to you about. Matter of fact, I meant to give you a ring. I think John Tedesco's got a Supreme Court nomination coming to him.

MALONE: Well, I don't know, George.

SIMON: And there's not a lawyer in the whole judicial department that stands in stronger with the Italian voters than John does.

MALONE: I guess that's right, too. The wops have got another judgeship coming to them. And I don't think anybody's got anything on John. His record's all right. Listen, John and I grew up together. I tell you there's not a whiter man on the face of the earth.

MALONE: Oh, I'm not sayin' anythin' against John. It's just a question if he's big enough for the Supreme Court.

SIMON: What do you mean, big enough? What about some of those horse's piazzas that are decorating the bench now? What about Edgar Thayer?

MALONE: Oh, sure. The trouble is John's father don't happen to be a railroad president. Anyhow, that's what I'm drivin' at. We gotta keep up the standard of the judiciary. There's been an awful lot of bellyachin' lately about keepin' the bench out of politics. We gotta get A-1 men. Now if it was you, George—

SIMON: Nothing doing, Pete. What the hell do I want to be a judge for? I'd get locomotor ataxia sitting up there all day on my fanny doing nothing but looking important. Anyhow, I can't afford it. It costs me a hundred thousand a year to live.

MALONE: A hundred grand would of gone a long way on Second Avenue, George.

SIMON: Sure, it's crazy. I know that just as well as you do. But when you've got that kind of set-up what can you do about it?

MALONE: John ain't so hot on the legal end, is he?

SIMON: Oh, he knows his laws, all right. I don't say he's a Blackstone. But hell, neither am I. I've got a young Harvard boy in the office here, named Weinberg that John can have for his secretary. Believe me, he'll hand down opinions that will give the Court of Appeals an inferiority complex.

MALONE: All right, George, I'll think it over. I'd like to do it for you, if I can, and I think maybe we can work it.

SIMON: I wish you would, Pete. It would mean an awful lot to John.

MALONE: Okay. Tell you why I came in, George. You know my brother Ed, the warden up at Elmira?

SIMON: Yes, sure I know him. How's he getting along up there?

MALONE: Oh, he's getting along all right. Well, he tipped me off to something that I think you oughta know.

SIMON: All right.

MALONE: Do you ever remember handling a case for some fellow named— Wait a minute, till I think of his name. It's some Dutch or Hebrew name, something-or-other-stein. Wait, I think I wrote it down somewhere. Yeah, here it is. Breitstein, Jo-hann Breitstein. Remember him?

SIMON: Yes, I remember. Johann Breitstein, a German boy. I defended him on a larceny charge, about eight or nine years ago, and got him an acquittal. What about it?

MALONE: Was there something about an alibi?

SIMON: Yes, he had an airtight alibi. That's why the jury acquitted him.

MALONE: Yeah. Well, it seems there was a guy named Whitey Cushman who was mixed up in the case. Is that right?

SIMON: Yes. He established the alibi for Breitstein.

MALONE: That's it. Well, this bird Cushman is doin' a stretch up at Elmira and it seems he had a session with your friend Francis Clark Baird, who's a member of the Parole Board.

SIMON: Yes? Well? What about it?

MALONE: Well, this Cushman has been givin' Francis Clark Baird some song-and-dance about the alibi in the Breitstein case bein' framed up.

SIMON: What do you mean framed up?

MALONE: I'm just tellin' you what Ed told me over the phone last night. Is this guy Baird on the grievance committee of the Bar Association, too?

SIMON: Yes, I think so.

MALONE: That's what Ed said. He says he's got a hunch that Baird would like to get something on you. And I guess that's right, too, ain't it?

SIMON: Yes, sure he would. I've licked him to a fare-you-well in half a dozen cases.

MALONE: Yeah. I know you have. Well, accordin' to Ed, Baird thinks he can cook up some kind of a disbarment proceedin' against you out of this Breitstein case. Anyhow, he's havin' Cushman brought down to New York next week to take his deposition.

SIMON: Oh he is, is he? Well, let him! What the hell do I care? He's got nothing on me.

MALONE: Well, that's what I told Ed. "There's nothin' to it, Ed," I says. "George is too smart a boy," I says, "to let himself get mixed up with anything like that." Only I thought I'd better tip you off.

SIMON: Francis Clark Baird: To hell with Francis Clark Baird: He's got nothing on me. I've been practicing law for eighteen years and my record is an open book. It's not the first time this Baird and the rest of those silk-stocking babies in the Bar Association have tired to get me. They've been gunning for me for years. But they haven't got anything on me, yet. No, and they never will. So they're going to disbar me on a crook's deposition, are they? Ho, that's a laugh, that is! Just let Mr. Francis Clark Baird try it, and he'll find himself holding the dirty end of the stick. Jesus

Christ! Some lousy little crook makes a play for a parole and they think they're going to pin something on me. That's funny, that is!

MALONE: That's what Ed said. He says this Cushman is a bad egg and a troublemaker: A guy that throws fits and all that. Well, don't worry about it George. I guess nothin' much will come of it. I just wanted to give you the lowdown that's all.

SIMON: Thanks, Pete. It was damn nice of you to let me know. What do you think of those S. O. B. s trying to pull a thing like that on me!

MALONE: Well, you know how it is, George. These guys that came over on the *Mayflower* don't like to see the boys from Second Avenue sittin' in the high places. We're just a lot of riffraff to them. They've had their knives out for me, for a long time, too, but, hell, it's me that has the laugh when the votes are counted. Well, I got to be getting back to the office. And I guess the missis is getting' tired of keepin' the filly de bee's wax warm for you. So long, George. Come around to the club, some night.

SIMON: Yes, I will Pete. And thanks for the steer.

MALONE: Keep the change. Well, *Scholem aleichem.*

[*He exits. The moment he has gone,* SIMON *slumps down in his chair and stares fixedly ahead of him. Then he suddenly raises both fists and brings then down on the desk.*]

SIMON: Goddam it to hell!

[*He springs to his feet and walks swiftly up and down the office, pounding his palm with his fist. Then he goes to the desk and pushes a button.* REGINA *enters, almost instantly.*]

Listen, Rexie. About eight or nine years ago, I defended a fellow named Johann Breitstein in General Sessions. I want to get hold of Breitstein right away. I met him three or four years ago and at that time he was working as an usher in one of the Warner Brothers' Theatres. Call up Warner Brothers and see if you can trace him and have him come in here as soon as possible. Get McFadden or anybody else to help you, if necessary. Let everything else go until you locate him. Understand?

REGINA: Yes, sir.

SIMON: Then get me all the papers out of the files and have them here for me when I get back from lunch. People against Johann Breitstein. Then send up to General Sessions and order a transcript of the stenographer's minutes of the trial. No, wait a minute! You'd better not do that. No, never mind that. Just get me the papers out of the files. And locate Breitstein: that's the important thing.

**REGINA:** Yes sir.

**SIMON:** Get right on the job, will you? I'm going around to the Marguery to join Mrs. Simon at lunch, and I'll be back in three-quarters of an hour.

[*He exits.* REGINA *sits at* SIMON's *desk and takes up the telephone receiver.*]

**REGINA:** Hello—Get me Warner Brothers' Picture Corporation, please—Yes, that's right.

[*She hangs up the receiver and sits staring at* CORA's *picture. Then with a sudden gesture, she sweeps the photograph off the desk.*]

CURTAIN

# ACT TWO

## SCENE 1

*The inner office.* BESSIE *lies stretched out upon the sofa, in the corner, her eyes closed. Her shoes are on the floor beside the sofa.* REGINA *enters quickly, with a glass in her hand, and crosses to* BESSIE.

REGINA: Here, Bessie, drink this.

BESSIE: [*Opening her eyes.*] What is it?

REGINA: It's just some bromides to quiet your nerves. Drink it.

BESSIE: [*Sitting up.*] Does it taste bad?

REGINA: No, no, it's nothing at all. Take it: it will make you feel better.

BESSIE: I hate taking stuff. [*She closes her eyes, shudders and drains the glass.*]

REGINA: In a little while, you'll feel much better. How do you feel now?

BESSIE: I still feel kinda funny inside.

REGINA: You'd better lie down again.

BESSIE: No, I don't want to. I'm sick o' layin' down.

REGINA: I'll tell you what I'm going to do. I'm going to send you home in a taxi.

BESSIE: No, I don't want to go home, honest I don't. I'll only start thinkin' if I go home.

REGINA: Are you sure?

BESSIE: Yes, I'll be all right in a minute. I think I'll go back to the board. [*As* SIMON *enters.*] Look, here's Mr. Simon. I better get out. [*She gets up, quickly, and puts her shoes on.*]

SIMON: What's the matter? Anything wrong?

REGINA: It's nothing. Bessie had a little shock this morning and it upset her. But she's all right again.

SIMON: You'd better jump into a cab, Bessie, and go home.

**Bessie:** No, I'm all right, again, Mr. Simon, honest I am. I'm goin' back to the board now.

**Simon:** Well, listen, if you're not feeling all right, I want you to go home.

**Bessie:** I'm all right, Mr. Simon. Thanks ever so much, Miss Gordon. [*She exits.*]

**Simon:** What's the matter with her?

**Regina:** She saw somebody jump out of the window of an office building and it gave her a bad shock.

**Simon:** God, that's awful! Where was it?

**Regina:** I don't know exactly where. Somewhere on Fifth Avenue.

**Simon:** It's terrible! Imagine a fellow doing a thing like that.

**Regina:** Well, I suppose if you're tired of living, it's as good a way as any to end it.

**Simon:** What, jumping out of a window like that?

**Regina:** Why not? A few seconds and it's all over. I guess people don't do it unless they have a pretty good reason.

**Simon:** What the hell are *you* so morbid about?

**Regina:** I'm not morbid. Only, we don't ask to be brought into the world, and if we feel like leaving it, I don't see that it's anybody's business but our own.

**Simon:** What's the matter? Don't you feel well or something?

**Regina:** Yes, of course! I'm just talking a lot of nonsense, that's all. I haven't been able to get Mrs. Simon yet. She left home early this morning, with the children. I've left messages at half-a-dozen places. She's sure to get one of them.

**Simon:** Is Breitstein here?

**Regina:** Yes sir; he's waiting outside.

**Simon:** I'll see him right away. Wait a minute. See if you can get me Francis Clark Baird.

[Regina *calls on her telephone.*]

**Simon:** Is there anything important in the mail?

**Regina:** There's a letter from Mr. Upjohn, confirming the terms of settlement in Arrow against the Radio Corporation. And there's a transcript of the minutes of the directors' meeting of the International Metal Refineries.

SIMON: Anything else?

REGINA: Nothing of importance. A check came in from the Murray Packing Company.

SIMON: How much?

REGINA: Ten thousand, plus two hundred and some odd dollars for disbursements. I forget the exact amount.

SIMON: Never mind it. [REGINA's *phone rings.*] See if that's Baird.

[REGINA *answers the phone.*]

REGINA: Mr. Baird is not in.

SIMON: Oh! When is he expected? Wait a minute! Is that his secretary?

REGINA: Yes sir.

SIMON: I'll talk to her, myself. Hello—Is this Mr. Baird's secretary?—This is Mr. Simon speaking; Mr. George Simon—do you know when Mr. Baird will be in?—Oh, I see—Well, do you know where he can be reached?—Well, he's in town, isn't he?—Oh, I see; you don't know that, either—Do you think you're likely to hear from him during the day?—Yes, It's all pretty indefinite, isn't it?—Well, if you do hear from him, will you tell him that I called and ask him if he'll be good enough to call me? Thank you very much—good-bye. [*He hangs up the receiver.*] You'd think that Baird could afford to employ a more convincing liar than that. All right, I'll see Breitstein now. [REGINA's *telephone rings.*] See if that's Mrs. Simon.

REGINA: [*After answering the phone.*] It's Mrs. Schwarzfeld.

SIMON: I'm in court and may not be back today. She can get me in the morning. [REGINA *relays this message.*] Is Breitstein coming in?

REGINA: Yes, sir.

SIMON: All right. And I don't want to be disturbed. Have I any engagements?

REGINA: Lunch at twelve-thirty with Senator Wells.

SIMON: Yes, I must keep that. Anybody else?

REGINA: I've put off all the others. Except that Becker boy. I couldn't reach him.

SIMON: What Becker boy?

REGINA: You know, that young Communist—

SIMON: Oh yes. Well, that's not important. All right, Breitstein, come right in.

[JOHANN BREITSTEIN *enters, a fair German in his early 30s.*]

SIMON: Rexie, see that I'm not disturbed, will you?

REGINA: Yes sir. [*She exits.*]

SIMON: Hello, Breitstein. Glad to see you again.

BREITSTEIN: I'm very glad to see you, Mr. Simon.

SIMON: Sit down. How have you been?

BREITSTEIN: I been fine, Mr. Simon. I got a good job, now.

SIMON: You have? What are you doing?

BREITSTEIN: I'm assistant cameraman for the Pathé newsreel.

SIMON: Is that so? Well, that's great!

BREITSTEIN: I don't need to ask you how you are, Mr. Simon. I read about you in the papers almost every day.

SIMON: Yes, I manage to keep busy. Listen, Breitstein, I'll tell you why I asked you to come in. Oh, have a cigarette, will you? Or a cigar.

BREITSTEIN: Thanks, I'll take a cigarette.

SIMON: Breitstein, has anybody been talking to you lately about that case of yours?

BREITSTEIN: Why no, Mr. Simon, they haven't.

SIMON: Nobody's approached you or asked you any questions?

BREITSTEIN: No sir. Why, is there anything—

SIMON: Well, the reason I've sent for you is that I want to put you on your guard. There's a complication that's come up and you've got to be prepared to answer a lot of questions.

BREITSTEIN: What kind of a complication, Mr. Simon?

SIMON: Well, it seems that this fellow Whitey Cushman has been doing some talking.

BREITSTEIN: Why he's up in Elmira, doing twenty years for manslaughter.

SIMON: I know it; but he's been telling some people that we cooked up that alibi.

BREITSTEIN: Holy Moses, Mr. Simon, does that mean that they're going to come after me again?

SIMON: Yes, they're likely to.

BREITSTEIN: Holy smoke, Mr. Simon. What am I going to do?

SIMON: Now don't get excited, Breitstein. I think maybe everything will be all right, if you just do what I tell you to.

BREITSTEIN: Well, sure I will, Mr. Simon. Gee whiz, I got a wife and family now. I don't know what I'd do if—

**SIMON:** What you've got to do is stick by that alibi story, understand?

**BREITSTEIN:** Yes sure, Mr. Simon, whatever you say. And you think—

**SIMON:** I'll do the best I can for you. And I guess between us, we can fix it up all right. But we've got to stick together, Breitstein. You know it just might happen that somebody would try to make trouble for me, too.

**BREITSTEIN:** For you, Mr. Simon?

**SIMON:** Yes. You know I took an awful chance in order to get you out of that jam you were in. And if this thing were to get up before the Bar Association, there might be a nasty stink about it.

**BREITSTEIN:** Well, gosh, Mr. Simon, I wouldn't want you to get into trouble on account of me. Why, everything I got, I owe to you. Jiminy, if it wasn't for you, I'd be in for life. I'd go through fire and water for you.

**SIMON:** [*Rising.*] All right, Breitstein, thanks. I knew I could count on you. Just keep all this under your hat, and if anybody questions you, just stick to your story and act dumb. And let me know, if you're approached.

**BREITSTEIN:** You betcha. And you think everything's going to be all right?

**SIMON:** Well, I hope it is. Why, don't you?

**BREITSTEIN:** Oh yes, sure. Only I was just thinking—

**SIMON:** What?

**BREITSTEIN:** Well, I was thinking in case they should look up the hospital records.

**SIMON:** What hospital records?

**BREITSTEIN:** The hospital records of Whitey Cushman.

**SIMON:** What hospital records of Whitey Cushman. What the hell are you talking about?

**BREITSTEIN:** Well, you know the day it happened, the day he said I was in his house, he was in the hospital.

**SIMON:** You mean to say that the day you robbed the bathhouse, Whitey Cushman was in the hospital?

**BREITSTEIN:** Yes. He used to have fits—what do you call them?—epileptic fits; and they took him to the hospital.

**SIMON:** Holy—! Are you sure of this, Breitstein?

**BREITSTEIN:** Yes, sure. That's why I had to pay him two hundred dollars to testify. He was afraid they'd find out about him being in the hospital that day. I thought you knew all about it, Mr. Simon.

**SIMON:** It's the first I ever heard of it. What hospital was it, do you know?

**BREITSTEIN:** I think it was the Polyclinic. Mr. Simon—

**SIMON:** All right, Breitstein, I've got to think about this. I may ask you to come in again, in a day or two. Goodbye.

**BREITSTEIN:** Good-bye, Mr. Simon. I hope everything's going to be all right.

**SIMON:** Yes, so do I.

[BREITSTEIN *exits.* SIMON *sits biting his lips and pounding the desk with his fists. Then he pushes the call button, and rising, walks about the office.* REGINA *enters.*]

**SIMON:** What is it, Rexie?

**REGINA:** You rang.

**SIMON:** Did I? Well, I forget what I wanted.

**REGINA:** Your brother is outside.

**SIMON:** Oh, he is, is he? Well, I don't want to see him. No, wait a minute. Let him wait.

**REGINA:** Yes sir. [*She exits.*]

**SIMON:** [*On the interoffice phone.*] Hello—Say, John, I want to talk to you about something—Oh. Well, come in when you're through, will you?— All right. [*He pushes the call button.* REGINA *enters.*] Have my brother come in.

**REGINA:** Yes sir.

[*She exits.* SIMON *goes to the window and looks out.* DAVID SIMON *enters; a slovenly, shifty fellow, some years younger than George.*]

**DAVID:** Morning, Georgie.

**SIMON:** [*Turning.*] What? Oh, it's you, is it? Well, what the hell do you want?

**DAVID:** Well, I just came in to—

**SIMON:** Oh, you just came in, did you? Well, you can just get out again. I don't want to see your dirty mug around here.

**DAVID:** Geez, Georgie, don't get sore. I just wanted to tell you—

**SIMON:** I don't care what you wanted to tell me, you lousy bum. You think I've got time to listen to anything you've got to say? What the hell do you mean by passing around bum checks, you heel?

**DAVID:** Well, that's what I was goin' to tell you, Georgie. You see, I happened to get into a little crap game—

SIMON: What do you mean, you happened to get into a little crap game? What the hell are you, anyhow, a Pullman porter?

DAVID: Geez, Georgie, just give me a chance and I'll—

SIMON: Shut up, you louse! I'm the one that does the talking around here. You listen to what I got to say, do you hear me?

DAVID: Sure, I'll listen, Georgie.

SIMON: You'd better listen, if you know what's good for you. Well, this is what I got to say—and this time I mean it. It's the last time you're going to get anything out of me. Have you got that through your thick head?

DAVID: I certainly appreciate you helpin' me out, Georgie. I wouldn't of asked you, only—

SIMON: Do you think I'd do anything for you, you cockroach? I wouldn't lift my little finger to save you from the electric chair. I only did it because Mama asked me to, that's the only reason.

DAVID: It's the last time, Georgie. I swear to God it is.

SIMON: It better be. The next time you can go to jail, that's what you can do. And what's more, I'll have myself appointed special prosecutor, so that you'll be sure of getting a good, long term. If you haven't got any respect for me, you ought to have some for mama.

DAVID: Geez, Georgie, everybody can make a mistake, once in a while.

SIMON: Yes? Is that so? Well, I guess you're one of God's mistakes. All right, that's all I got to say to you.

REGINA: [*Entering.*] Mrs. Simon is on the phone.

SIMON: All right; I'll talk to her right away. [REGINA *exits.*]

DAVID: Mama tells me you got a swell-lookin' wife, Georgie. Well, give her my regards, even though I guess she never heard of me.

SIMON: All right. Get out, now. And here. [*Tossing him a bill.*] Buy yourself a hat. You look like one of Coxey's army[3].

DAVID: Thanks, Georgie. I hope you have a nice trip to Europe. [*He exits.*]

SIMON: Hello, darling—Sorry to keep you waiting—You're not angry, are you, sweetheart, that I couldn't get home last night? Listen, dear, I've got a little bad news for you—Well, I'm afraid we'll have to postpone the trip to Europe—Something of the utmost importance has come up and I can't get away.—Well, I can't over the telephone. Where are you?—Well, why don't you come in?—That's all right. Bring them along—All right; as soon as you can get here—All right—Good-bye, sweetheart.

---

3 A body of jobless men who, led by social reformer Jacob Sechler Coxey, marched on Washington after the Panic of 1893 to petition Congress for relief measures.

[*He hangs up the receiver and sits motionless for a moment. Then he pushes the call button.* REGINA *enters.*]

SIMON: Rexie: I've changed my plans about going to Europe. [*She looks at him in silence.*] Something has come up and I won't be able to get away for a while.

REGINA: That's a shame.

SIMON: Well, it can't be helped. Just keep it under your hat for the present, will you?

REGINA: Yes sir. [*She stands, looking at him.*]

SIMON: All right; that's all for just now. [REGINA *exits.* TEDESCO *enters.*]

TEDESCO: I couldn't get rid of that woman, George.

SIMON: It's all right, John. Sit down. I want to talk to you.

[TEDESCO *seats himself.* SIMON *paces the room.*]

SIMON: [*At length.*] Listen, John, I'm in a hell of a bad spot. [TEDESCO *looks at him, attentively.*] I'll tell you what it is. You know Francis Clark Baird, don't you? The cornerstone of the Union League Club and the right-hand man of the Lord God Jehovah?

TEDESCO: Yes.

SIMON: Well, he's got something on me; and he's going to break me.

TEDESCO: What do you mean, he's got something on you?

SIMON: Well, you'll think I'm crazy when you hear this, and maybe you're right. But I once helped a fellow out of a jam by putting over a fake alibi.

TEDESCO: For God's sake! Subornation of perjury!

SIMON: They can't get me on a criminal charge. The statute of limitation has run. But what the hell's the difference? They can disbar me, and they will!

TEDESCO: But, George, how did you ever get yourself mixed up in anything like that?

SIMON: Don't ask me! I was just a goddam fool, that's all. I'll tell you how it happened. A kid by the name of Breitstein had stolen twelve dollars out of a locker in a bathhouse. Well, I advised him to plead guilty and get off with a few months, and then I discovered that he was a fourth offender and that a conviction meant a life sentence. Well, I didn't know what the hell to do about it. So, finally, Breitstein said that he could get a fellow named Whitey Cushman to swear that Breitstein was in his house in Jamaica the day the robbery was committed. I couldn't refuse, John. I'd known the kid and family since God knows when. I knew he'd go straight if I got him off—and he has, too! I just couldn't see that kid get a life sentence. So, like a sucker, I went into it. And now, the chickens are coming home to roost.

TEDESCO: But has this fellow Breitstein been squealing?

SIMON: No, Cushman. He's doing twenty years in Elmira and now I guess he's decided to make a play for a Parole. And, of course, Francis Clark Baird has to be on the Parole Board. It's funny, in a way. For years, that Yankee has been trying to get something on me, and every time he's drawn a blank. And now, this one thing that was dead and buried and forgotten, falls right into his lap, and it's as good as if I'd misappropriated a million dollars.

TEDESCO: But can't you bluff it through, George?

SIMON: Well, maybe yes and maybe no. Breitstein was just here. They can't do anything to him, of course, but I've thrown a scare into him and I guess I can rely upon him. The trouble is that the case won't bear any investigating. I've been over the record and it's phony as hell right on its face. And now I've just learned from Breitstein that Cushman was in the hospital on the day of the robbery. That sews it up for me, good and proper.

TEDESCO: God! [*He springs to his feet and paces the room.*]

SIMON: What am I going to do, John? They're going to disbar me, as sure as God made little green apples. It's rich, isn't it?

TEDESCO: I guess there's not much use going to Francis Clark Baird with the whole story?

SIMON: That's a laugh, John. You might just as well throw a biscuit to a man-eating tiger. Anyhow, I've been trying to make an appointment with him and he's been dodging me. I could hear him sharpening his knife, over the phone.

TEDESCO: I know some ways that you could get him that would put an end to his funny business forever.

SIMON: John, listen [*Seizing him by the arms.*] We're a long way from Sicily, boy. Put it out of your mind, for God's sake. You'll make me sorry that I told you, in a minute.

TEDESCO: Well, what good is a rat like that? He's out after *our* scalps, isn't he? And why? Because we came from the streets and our parents talk with an accent.

SIMON: What's the good of talking about all that? He's technically right and he's doing his duty, as a member of the grievance committee. The rest is off the records and not worth a hoot in hell.

TEDESCO: Well, we've got to get you out of it, that's all. Give me some time to think about it.

SIMON: Yes, that's what I want you to do, John. I'm not licked yet. But it's going to take some headwork to get me out of this. I'll pull all the wires I can, or do any goddam thing, so long as I get out of it. God, disbarment! After all these years, and all I've sweated through to get where I am. I don't think I could face it, John.

TEDESCO: George, I don't need to tell you—

SIMON: No, you don't, John. I know I can count on you to the last drop of blood. That's the one bright spot in the picture. I've got you and one or two other friends that'll stick to the finish. And a wife that's one hundred percent. That's the tough part, now, John. I've got to break it to Cora.

TEDESCO: Why do you have to tell her?

SIMON: Oh, I've got to. She's entitled to know. Everything's always been open and above-board between us. Anyhow, I've got to call off this European trip and she has to know why. [*Looking at his watch.*] I'm going around to the Polyclinic Hospital now, to look up those records. [*Extending his hand.*] Thanks, John.

TEDESCO: [*Grasping* SIMON'*s hand.*] George—!

SIMON: I know, boy.

TEDESCO: Don't worry about it, George.

SIMON: Well, it's something to worry about. [REGINA *enters.*] I'm going out for a few minutes. I won't be long.

REGINA: Yes sir. That Becker boy is here.

SIMON: He'll have to wait until I get back. And if Mrs. Simon comes, let her wait in here for me.

[SIMON *exits.* TEDESCO *stands looking out of the window.*]

REGINA: [*After considerable hesitation.*] Mr. Tedesco.

TEDESCO: [*Turning.*] What?

REGINA: I don't want to be inquisitive, but I have a feeling that Mr. Simon is in some kind of trouble. Is he?

TEDESCO: Trouble? No, he's not in any trouble.

REGINA: Well, I know it's none of my business and I shouldn't have asked. But I just wanted to tell you that if there's anything that I can do, it doesn't matter what, you can count on me.

**TEDESCO:** All right, Rexie; I guess Mr. Simon knows that. But there's nothing to worry about.

[*He exits.* REGINA *remains, troubled and deep in thought.*]

**WEINBERG:** [*Entering.*] Oh, isn't G. S. in?
**REGINA:** No.
**WEINBERG:** Here's that Richter separation agreement. He wants to look it over.
**REGINA:** All right. I'll give it to him when he comes in.
**WEINBERG:** Thank you. [*Looking at her.*] Aren't you feeling well today?
**REGINA:** Yes, of course.
**WEINBERG:** You don't look very well.
**REGINA:** I wish you wouldn't worry so much about me, Mr. Weinberg. I'd really prefer it if you didn't.
**WEINBERG:** You might at least be civil to me. Everywhere else I go, people treat me with civility. Everywhere but here.
**REGINA:** I try to be civil to everybody, Mr. Weinberg. But you seem to think that because you work in the same office with somebody, that you have to get personal right away.
**WEINBERG:** All I did was to inquire about your health. I can't see that there's anything in that to take offense at.
**REGINA:** I'm not taking offense, only — [*Impatiently.*] Oh, well, what's the difference! I'll have to ask you to excuse me, Mr. Weinberg. I have a lot of work to do. [*She goes towards her office.*]
**WEINBERG:** Miss Gordon.
**REGINA:** [*Turning.*] What?
**WEINBERG:** Will you have lunch with me today?
**REGINA:** No, I can't. I have some shopping to do.
**WEINBERG:** You don't think up very clever excuses.
**REGINA:** We can't all be clever, Mr. Weinberg.
**WEINBERG:** It isn't necessary to be sarcastic, Miss Gordon. I know what your opinion of me is.
**REGINA:** I'm sorry, but I really can't stand here all day, talking about nothing. Excuse me. [*She exits to her office and closes the door.*]
**WEINBERG:** [*Despairingly.*] Regina, I —

[*He turns and exits abruptly. The scene blacks out.*]

CURTAIN

# SCENE 2

*The outer office.* BESSIE *is at the switchboard. Between the windows,* MRS. BECKER *and* HARRY BECKER *are seated.* BECKER *is a boy of 20, shabbily dressed. His head is entirely swathed in bandages.*

**BESSIE:** Simon and Tedesco — Who's calling, please? — One moment, please — Colonel Wertheimer calling Mr. Simon — Yes, thanks, Miss Gordon, I'm feeling much better — No, I'm all right, honest I am — Hello, here's Mr. Simon's secretary. Go ahead.

[*While she is talking,* WEINBERG *comes out of the door to* SIMON*'s office and crosses to the library.*]

**WEINBERG:** [*Stopping.*] Oh, Bessie, get me the County Lawyers' Association, will you please?

**BESSIE:** I'll give you a wire.

[WEINBERG *is about to protest, then goes into the library.*]

**MRS. BECKER:** Harry, you got bad pains?

**BECKER:** I tell you it's nothing. Forget about it, can't you?

**BESSIE:** Hello — Yes sir —

[*She dials a number.* GOLDIE *come out of the library, humming softly, and crossing to the entrance door, exits.*]

**BESSIE:** Simon and Tedesco — Oh, hello, Gracie — I was jus' gonna call you — Wait a minute — Hello, is Mr. Bellini there? Mr. Tedesco calling — Hello, Mr. Bellini? — One moment, please — Here's Mr. Bellini, Mr. Tedesco — All rightee, go ahead — Hello, Gracie — Say, listen, can you imagine what happened to me this morning? — Well, I was on my way to the office, see, and a man jumps out of about a twelfth-story window almost right in front of my eyes — I'll say it is. It makes me sick to my stomach just to think about it — Wait a minute — Simon and Tedesco — Mr. Weinberg? One moment, please — Hello, Gracie — Oh God, don't talk about it! It was awful — Yeah, it's a wonder I didn't faint —

[SANDLER, *meanwhile, has crossed from the library to the entrance door.*]

SANDLER: I'm going to Special Term Part II, the Surrogate's Court and lunch. Did you hear what I said, Greta Garbo?

BESSIE: Yes, I heard you. I heard you. Go ahead.

SANDLER: I can hardly bear to tear myself away from you. Here's a little present for you. [*He puts a paper clip down her back.*]

BESSIE: Say, quit it, will you! [*She strikes at him.*]

SANDLER: [*His hand to his heart, sings.*] Give me something to remember you by. [*He exits.*]

BESSIE: Fresh egg! [*She reaches down her back for the paper clip.*] What? — Oh, a fresh mugg in the office, putting things down my back — Yeah, I know, they never can keep their hands to themselves — Wait a minute — Hello — Why, she just stepped outside for a minute, Mr. Tedesco — All right, sir, I'll tell her as soon as she comes in — Hello, Gracie — No, I don't think I'll go out to lunch today — Yeah, I know, but I think I better give my stomach a rest — Well, I'll just send out for a chocolate malted or something — Wait a minute — Simon and Tedesco — Who's calling please? — One moment, please — Your sister, Miss Gordon — All rightee, go ahead — Say, Gracie, listen. I was out with Fred last night — Well, it all ended up in an awful fight — Well, wait till I tell you about it — [*As the door opens and* CORA *and her* CHILDREN *enter.*] Listen, I'm busy now. I'll call you back this afternoon — How do, Mrs. Simon? Why, hello, Richard. Hello, Dorothy.

THE CHILDREN: [*Distantly.*] Hello.

CORA: Tell Mr. Simon I'm here, please.

BESSIE: He's not in right now, Mrs. Simon.

CORA: Are you sure? Why, he's expecting me.

BESSIE: I think he'll be back soon. I'll ask Miss Gordon as soon as she's through talking on this wire.

CORA: Well, we may as well sit down, children. I don't understand his not being here. [*They all seat themselves.*]

BESSIE: I don't think he'll be long.

[McFADDEN *enters.*]

McFADDEN: Good morning, Mrs. Simon.

CORA: Good morning.

McFADDEN: Good morning, Miss. Good morning, young man.

THE CHILDREN: Good morning.

McFADDEN: Well, you sure are growin' up, the two of you. [*To* CORA.] Why, the last time I saw them, ma'am, they were little bits of shavers.

CORA: Really! [*To* BESSIE.] Are you sure Mr. Simon didn't leave a message for me?

BESSIE: He probably did with Miss Gordon. She'll be through in just a minute, now.

[McFADDEN *hesitates a moment, then goes into the library.*]

DOROTHY: Who's that man?

CORA: He's one of the employees in the office, here.

RICHARD: People always make such original remarks about how big you're getting. What do they expect you to do, get smaller?

DOROTHY: Look at the man with his head all bandaged, Mother.

CORA: Don't make remarks about people, Dorothy.

BESSIE: Simon and Tedesco—Who's calling, please?—One moment, please: the wire's busy—She's through now—Miss Gordon, Mrs. Simon and the children are here. And Mr. Vandenbogen is on the other wire—All rightee, Mr. Vandenbogen, go ahead—[*To* CORA.] Miss Gordon will be out, just as soon as she's taken this call.

CORA: Well, really—

TEDESCO: [*Coming out of his office.*] Bessie, hasn't Goldie come in, yet?

BESSIE: Not yet, Mr. Tedesco.

TEDESCO: Oh, how do you do, Mrs. Simon?

CORA: How do you do, Mr. Tedesco?

TEDESCO: Are these your children? I don't think I've ever met them, before.

CORA: Haven't you really? Richard, Dorothy, this is Mr. Tedesco.

TEDESCO: [*Shaking hands with them.*] Hello, Richard. Hello, Dorothy.

THE CHILDREN: Hello.

TEDESCO: Well, young man, are we going to have you here in the office, some day?

RICHARD: No.

CORA: My father wants Richard to enter the diplomatic service.

TEDESCO: Well, that's too bad. We could use a bright young fellow around here. Does George know you're here?

CORA: He doesn't seem to be in. I can't understand it. He knew I was coming.

TEDESCO: Oh, yes, that's right. He had to go out for a few minutes on a very important matter. He'll be back soon. Well, if you'll excuse me—

CORA: Certainly.

TEDESCO: Good-bye, Richard. Good-bye, Dorothy. I'm glad to have met you.

THE CHILDREN: Good-bye.

TEDESCO: [*To* CORA.] I didn't expect them to be so grown up. [THE CHILDREN *exchange a look.*]

TEDESCO: [*To* BESSIE.] I want Goldie, as soon as she comes in.

BESSIE: Yes sir.

[TEDESCO *exits to the library.* REGINA *enters from* SIMON'*s office.*]

REGINA: Good morning, Mrs. Simon.

CORA: Good morning, Miss Gordon. I've been waiting quite a while.

REGINA: I'm very sorry. I've been on the telephone. Hello, Richard. Hello, Dorothy.

THE CHILDREN: Hello.

CORA: Isn't Mr. Simon in?

REGINA: No ma'am. But he'll be back in a few minutes. He left word for you to wait in his office.

CORA: I have a thousand things to do this morning. Well, I suppose there's nothing to do but wait.

[*She rises and* THE CHILDREN *rise, too.*]

REGINA: He'll only be a few minutes.

CORA: I think you'd better wait out here, Richard and Dorothy.

[THE CHILDREN *sit down again.*]

RICHARD: Are you going to be long?

CORA: No, I can't stay long. I have too many things to do. [*She exits.*]

REGINA: [*To* THE CHILDREN.] There's a wonderful view from the windows.

RICHARD: We're been up the Chrysler Building and the Empire State.

DOROTHY: And the Woolworth.

RICHARD: The Chrysler and the Empire State are bigger.

DOROTHY: I know it.

REGINA: [*Going to bookcase.*] I'll see if I can find you a magazine to read. I don't know if there's anything that will interest you. Yes, here's the *National Geographic.*

RICHARD: I don't care to read it, thank you.

DOROTHY: Neither do I.

[REGINA *puts the magazine back on the bookcase.*]

BESSIE: Simon and Tedesco—One moment, please—Devore and Wilson calling, Miss Gordon.

REGINA: I'll take it in my office. [*She exits.*]

BESSIE: One moment, please—[GOLDIE *enters.*] Goldie, Mr. Tedesco wants you right away. He's in the library. All rightee, go ahead.

GOLDIE: Goodness! Are these the little Simon children?

RICHARD: I'm Richard Dwight, Jr.

DOROTHY: And I'm Dorothy Dwight.

GOLDIE: [*To* BESSIE.] I guess they still keep their father's name. Goodness, haven't they grown, though! Well, you're both very nice-looking children. Good-bye. [*She pats the cheek of each, then exits to the library.*]

DOROTHY: Who's that awful person?

RICHARD: Oh, some old stenographer or something. How many more people do we have to talk to?

DOROTHY: Yes, that's what I say.

BESSIE: Hello, Bank of America?—Mr. Riccordi, please—Well, leave word for him to call Mr. Tedesco, please—That's right. Thank you—[*To* THE CHILDREN.] Well, I suppose you'll be having lunch with your father today.

RICHARD: Our father lives in Washington.

BESSIE: I mean Mr. Simon.

RICHARD: He's not our father.

DOROTHY: Our father's name is Richard Dwight. He's in the Apartment of State.

RICHARD: *De*partment.

DOROTHY: *De*partment of State.

BESSIE: Oh, I know Mr. Simon isn't your real father. But being married to your mother makes him your father in a way.

131

RICHARD: No, it doesn't.
McFADDEN: [*Entering from the library.*] Well, are you learnin' all about the inside of a law office?

[THE CHILDREN *do not answer.*]

McFADDEN: [*To* BESSIE.] I'm going to 535 Fifth Avenue for Mr. Tedesco— [*Sotto voce.*] They're high and mighty little beggars, ain't they?
BESSIE: I'll say they are. Oh, Charlie, will you get me a chocolate malted and a tongue on rye on the way back?
McFADDEN: All right.
BESSIE: [*Giving him money.*] And don't forget: lots of Russian dressing.

[McFADDEN *exits.*]

BESSIE: [*Taking a box of chocolates out of the drawer.*] Want some chocolates?
RICHARD: No, thank you.
BESSIE: Dorothy, how about you?
DOROTHY: [*After a look at* RICHARD.] No, thank you.
BESSIE: They're good. Chocolate caramels. Sure you don't want any? [*She eats one.*]
RICHARD: No, thank you.
DOROTHY: No, thank you.
BESSIE: Simon and Tedesco—Who's calling, please—One moment, please —Mrs. Axelrod calling Mr. Simon—All rightee, go ahead—[*She listens in on the conversation.*]
DOROTHY: Who is Mr. Tedesco?
RICHARD: He's his partner. Don't you see the name on the door there? Simon and Tedesco.
DOROTHY: Where?
RICHARD: Right there on the door.
DOROTHY: Oh, I see where you mean. Why is it written backwards?
RICHARD: It isn't backwards. You're just seeing it through the glass, that's all.
DOROTHY: But the others don't look like that.
RICHARD: Of course, they don't. You're looking at them from the front, aren't you?
DOROTHY: Oh. But I thought a partner was somebody on your side in a game: like tennis or bridge.

RICHARD: Don't be stupid. It means anybody you're in partnership with.

DOROTHY: Oh. Is he a Jew, too?

RICHARD: No, of course not.

DOROTHY: He has a funny way of talking.

RICHARD: Well, he's some kind of a foreigner. An Italian or something like that. Gosh, I wonder how long we have to sit here. I want to go to a matinée this afternoon.

DOROTHY: I have an appointment with the hairdresser at two.

[HENRY *enters from the corridor, wearing his cap.*]

HENRY: Is Mr. Tedesco in?

BESSIE: What? Yes, he's in the library.

[HENRY *puts his cap in his pocket and crosses to the library.*]

DOROTHY: Who's that?

RICHARD: Oh, just some errand boy or office boy.

DOROTHY: Would you like to be an errand boy?

RICHARD: Of course, I wouldn't! Don't ask so many silly questions.

[HARRY BECKER *suddenly stands up.*]

MRS. BECKER: [*Nervously.*] What's the matter, Harry? Don't you feel good?

BECKER: I'm not going to wait around here all day.

MRS. BECKER: Harry, please, be a good boy. He's coming soon.

[BECKER *silently resumes his seat.*]

DOROTHY: [*Sotto voce.*] Who's he, Richard?

RICHARD: Oh, some gangster, probably, that got into a fight.

DOROTHY: Maybe he's a murderer.

RICHARD: Don't be silly. He'd be in prison, wouldn't he, if he were a murderer?

DOROTHY: Maybe he escaped.

RICHARD: As though an escaped murderer would be sitting around in an office.

DOROTHY: Sh! He can hear us.

**BESSIE:** Hello—Yes sir—[*She dials a number.*]
**RICHARD:** Well, we may as well look at that *National Geographic* as just sit here.

[*He is about to go over and get it when* HENRY *comes out of the library.*]

**RICHARD:** Oh, would you mind handing me that magazine, please?

[HENRY *looks at him a moment, then goes over to the bookcase.*]

**HENRY:** This?
**RICHARD:** Yes, please. [HENRY *takes it over to him.*] Thank you.

[HENRY *goes to the table and begins filling out some forms, every now and then glancing at* RICHARD *and* DOROTHY, *who are looking at the magazine.*]

**BESSIE:** Hello—Goldie, tell Mr. Tedesco that that mumber don't answer, will you?
**RICHARD:** Look, this is the kind of movie camera I want. Albert Adams has one and it's three times as good as that old, cheap one I have.
**DOROTHY:** Why don't you ask mother to buy one for you?
**RICHARD:** I will.
**DARWIN:** [*Entering.*] Mr. Roy Darwin to see Mr. Simon, please.
**BESSIE:** Yes sir.
**DARWIN:** Why, hello, Richard. Hello, Dorothy.
**RICHARD:** Hello, Roy.
**DOROTHY:** Hello, Roy.

[*They both get up to greet him. He shakes hands with* RICHARD *and kisses* DOROTHY]

**BESSIE:** Mr. Roy Darwin to see Mr. Simon—All rightee—Mr. Simon's secretary will be right out, Mr. Darwin.
**DARWIN:** Thank you. Well, what are you fellows doing here?
**DOROTHY:** We came with mother.
**DARWIN:** Oh, really, is your mother here?

RICHARD: Yes, she's in his office, waiting for him.

REGINA: [*Entering.*] Those papers are ready for you, Mr. Darwin, if you'll just step in.

DARWIN: Yes. Thank you. Well, I'll see you later, old dears.

[*He precedes* REGINA *into* SIMON's *office.* HARRY BECKER *rises but* REGINA *has gone before he can speak to her.*]

MRS. BECKER: Hev a little patience, Harry.

[BECKER *resumes his seat.* THE CHILDREN *seat themselves again.*]

DOROTHY: Roy is nice.

RICHARD: Yes, he's a good old scout.

[*The scene blacks out.*]

CURTAIN

# SCENE 3

*The inner office.* CORA *is walking up and down the office impatiently, smoking a cigarette. After a moment, there is a knock at the door of* REGINA'S *office.*

CORA: [*Turning.*] Yes?

DARWIN: [*Opening the door and entering.*] Is it all right? May I come in?

CORA: Hello, Roy, I seem always to be running into you here.

DARWIN: Well, I've had a tiresome business matter to dispose of. And little Miss — the little secretary — said you were in here. So I thought I'd say hello. [*He is about to close the door.*]

CORA: No, don't.

DARWIN: What? Oh, I see what you mean. Little pitchers have big eyes, eh? [*He comes over and kisses her hand.*] How are you, today? You look a little *distrait.* [*He puts his hat and stick on the table upstage.*].

CORA: I'm more than a little *distrait.* I'm quite provoked.

Darwin: Anything wrong? Or isn't it any of my business?

CORA: George tells me now that he can't go to Europe.

DARWIN: Oh, really! He's not going to Europe?

CORA: So he told me a little while ago, over the telephone. Some business matter or something has come up.

DARWIN: Well, that's rather disturbing, isn't it, after all your plans are made?

CORA: Yes, it's most disturbing. But that's George for you. He's so impulsive, so impetuous — one never quite knows what to expect next. He has a way of carrying things by storm, of sweeping you off your feet. You know, he carried me off and married me almost before I knew what was happening. It's rather exciting in a way but — [*Breaking off.*] Well, heavens, I seem to be telling you all my troubles.

DARWIN: You know I'm interested.

CORA: Yes, I do, Roy.

DARWIN: Does this change in plans mean that you won't go to Europe, either?

CORA: I don't know. I haven't had time to think about it. I don't know what to do. I've made all my arrangements here, about the house and the children and all. And I've bought my clothes. And I'm meeting people in London and on the Continent. It's really most upsetting.

DARWIN: It does seem a shame to have to give it all up, now.

CORA: Well, I'll see. Goodness, I wish George would get back. I have a thousand things to do.

DARWIN: Can I help?

CORA: No, thanks, Roy. I'll just have to wait now and hear what George has to say.

DARWIN: Well, if I *can* be of any help —

CORA: Thanks, Roy; you're very sweet. That was a lovely tea yesterday.

DARWIN: *You* were lovely; not that that's anything out of the ordinary.

CORA: I don't feel a bit lovely this morning. I feel horrid.

DARWIN: Will you have a cigarette?

CORA: Yes, thanks; I will.

[*He gives her a cigarette and a light.*]

REGINA: [*Knocking and entering.*] Excuse me.

[*She hurries to* SIMON'*s desk, finds a paper and goes out, at the downstage door.* CORA *watches her exit.* DARWIN *walks over to chair upstage of the desk.*]

DARWIN: Talk about the way of Martha[4]! She's a human beehive. But damned little honey, if you ask me.

CORA: What a vulgar little person!

DARWIN: Was that just the common or secretarial knock, or was it — ?

CORA: Yes, it was!

DARWIN: Oh!

[*A moment of silence.*]

DARWIN: Funny, you know, I've been thinking of going to Europe myself.

CORA: Have you, Roy?

DARWIN: Yes. Chiefly in the hope of running into you somewhere, I confess.

CORA: That would have been nice.

DARWIN: And, now, you're probably not going at all! Well, *c'est la guerre.*

CORA: I wish I knew *what* to do.

[*A moment of silence.*]

DARWIN: Have you ever been to La Baule?

---

4 In medieval Christian literature, Jesus' friend Martha represents the active life, as contrasted with the contemplative.

CORA: Yes, I adore it.

DARWIN: Everyone tells me it's charming.

CORA: You'll love it there.

DARWIN: Well, I don't know what to do, either.

CORA: When would you be sailing, if you did go?

DARWIN: Oh, I don't know. In a week or ten days. I've nothing to keep me here. That is—

CORA: If you go to La Baule, be sure to motor over to Dinard and St. Malo.

DARWIN: I probably shan't be going. [*He rises and walks over to get his hat and stick.*] Am I going to see you soon, Cora?

CORA: Yes, if you want to.

DARWIN: You know I want to. Tea today?

CORA: I can't today; I have Dorothy on my hands.

DARWIN: Tomorrow?

CORA: I wasn't coming in tomorrow. Why don't you drive out and have lunch with me? It's lovely in the country now.

DARWIN: I'd be delighted to. Is it all right?

CORA: Yes, I think so.

DARWIN: About one?

CORA: Yes.

DARWIN: Fine.

[*They shake hands.* DARWIN *starts to exit.*]

SIMON: [*Offstage.*] Are you there, sweetheart?

CORA: Yes.

SIMON: I saw the car downstairs. I'm sorry—Oh, hello, Mr. Darwin.

DARWIN: Hello, George. I've just been keeping Cora company, until you got back.

SIMON: Yes, I had to go out. I'm sorry to keep you waiting, darling.

CORA: Well, it's all right now that you're here.

DARWIN: Well, I'm going along. Good-bye, George.

SIMON: Good-bye, Mr. Darwin. Did my secretary fix you up all right?

DARWIN: Yes, thanks very much.

SIMON: Don't mention it.

DARWIN: Good-bye, Cora.

CORA: Good-bye, Roy. Oh, I'll tell you what you can do for me, if you're not terribly busy.

**Darwin:** Anything you like. I haven't a thing to do for the rest of the day.

**Cora:** Well, I wish you'd take the children to lunch.

**Darwin:** Certainly, I'd like nothing better.

**Cora:** I don't like them sitting out there so long. I don't think it's a particularly good atmosphere for Dorothy.

**Simon:** Oh, are they outside?

**Cora:** Yes, I didn't know you'd be so long.

**Darwin:** I'll take them to the Biltmore, shall I?

**Cora:** Yes, and I'll join you as soon as I leave here.

**Simon:** Wait, I'll have them come in.

**Cora:** Don't bother, George. Roy can pick them up on the way out.

**Darwin:** Yes, of course.

**Simon:** Well, I thought I'd like to say hello to them. I haven't seen them for three or four days.

**Cora:** Well, just as you like.

**Simon:** [*At the telephone.*] Have my son and daughter come in. — Oh, and is Charlie McFadden in? — Well, I want to see him, as soon as he gets in. [*To* Darwin.] I don't have as much time to spend with the children as I'd like to.

**Regina:** [*Offstage.*] This way, children. Right in here.

[The Children *enter, followed by* Regina, *who goes into her own office.*]

**Simon:** Well, hello, strangers. I haven't seen you in a month of Sundays.

**The Children:** [*Indifferently.*] Hello.

[Simon *shakes hands with* Richard.]

**Simon:** And how's my young lady, today?

**Dorothy:** I'm all right.

[*He attempts to kiss her, but she averts her head.*]

**Richard:** Mother, look, this is the kind of a movie camera I want.

**Cora:** I haven't time now, Richard. Roy is going to take you to lunch now.

**Dorothy:** Oh, goody! Are we going to the Ritz?

**Cora:** No, to the Biltmore.

**DOROTHY:** Ah, why not to the Ritz? I like the Ritz better.

**RICHARD:** So do I.

**DARWIN:** I can take them to the Ritz just as easily, if they prefer it.

**CORA:** All right, then, make it the Ritz. I'll join you in a few minutes.

**SIMON:** I'm sorry I can't come along, but I have an important business engagement.

**DARWIN:** All right, old dears, come along. [*He links an arm through each of theirs.*]

**SIMON:** Good-bye.

**THE CHILDREN:** Good-bye.

**SIMON:** Wait, you can get out this way; right through my secretary's office.

[DARWIN *and* THE CHILDREN *exit.*]

**SIMON:** They get along very well with Mr. Darwin, don't they?

**CORA:** Yes, they're very fond of Roy.

**REGINA:** [*Entering.*] Excuse me, Mr. Simon.

**SIMON:** Yes? What is it, Rexie?

**REGINA:** Mr. Vandenbogen called and will call you again this afternoon. And Colonel Wertheimer would like to know the result of your conference with Senator Wells.

**SIMON:** All right. I'd like not to be disturbed now.

**REGINA:** Yes sir.

**SIMON:** Close both doors, will you please?

**REGINA:** Yes sir.

[*She closes the downstage door, then exits to her office, closing the door behind her.*]

**SIMON:** [*Sitting beside* CORA *on the sofa.*] Well, darling, I'm afraid the European trip is off.

**CORA:** So you said over the telephone.

**SIMON:** I know it's a big disappointment to you. And I assure you it is to me, too. I never in my life looked forward so much to anything. But something has come up and I can't get away.

**CORA:** You were so certain, no longer ago than yesterday, that nothing could keep you from going.

**SIMON:** Yes, I know it. That's the funny part of it. I would have sworn yesterday that nothing in the world could have made me call off the trip — barring something happening to Mama. And then this thing had to come up.

CORA: What is it: another hundred thousand dollar fee?

SIMON: Why, darling, you don't think a hundred thousand or five hundred thousand would make me call off our little honeymoon trip, do you? I wouldn't have called it off for a retainer from the United States Steel Corporation.

CORA: Then it's not business that's detaining you?

SIMON: Well, it is and it isn't. I don't know just how to tell you.

CORA: Don't tell me, if you don't want to. I didn't mean to be prying.

SIMON: Why, darling, of course I want to. You don't think I'd have any secrets from you, do you? It's just a little hard to explain, that's all. I'm afraid it's going to upset you a little.

CORA: Well, tell me, George, what it is. It doesn't help matters to pile up the suspense.

SIMON: [*Rising.*] No, I guess you're right. [*With a great effort.*] Well, darling, I'm in trouble: the worst trouble I've ever been in in my whole life. [*He pauses.*]

CORA: Well, tell me.

SIMON: Well, I'm threatened with disbarment.

CORA: Oh, how perfectly awful!

SIMON: I knew it would be a shock to you. That's why it took me so long to get it out. And it's been a shock to me, I can tell you. I didn't know anybody could go through such hell as I've been going through these last twenty-four hours.

CORA: But I don't understand it. Disbarment! Why, I thought —

SIMON: Of all the things that could have happened to me! God, you never know from one day till the next.

CORA: But doesn't disbarment imply —?

SIMON: Yes, it does more than imply. It establishes that a man is guilty of conduct which makes him unworthy to practice his profession. That's what I'm faced with this very minute.

CORA: Then — I mean — I'm quite bewildered —

SIMON: Eighteen years I've been a full-fledged lawyer. Eighteen years and nobody's ever had anything on me. And then this one thing, this one, little thing, that was dead and buried, comes up — and bing, out I go like a candle. God, I can't believe it.

CORA: But, what was it that you did, George?

SIMON: Wait until you hear. Then you'll understand the irony of the whole thing. Once, mind you, once in eighteen years—yes, and with a thousand opportunities to get away with murder—once I overstepped the mark and then it was to save a poor devil from going to prison for life. Do you know what it means to frame up an alibi?

CORA: Yes, I think I do. Getting someone to testify falsely—

SIMON: Yes, that's it. I had a hand in framing up an alibi, so that a kid who had committed a number of petty crimes wouldn't have to spend the rest of his life in prison.

CORA: I don't know much about these things. But wasn't that a dishonest thing to do?

SIMON: [*Seating himself at his desk.*] It was conniving at a lie, to prevent a conviction that nobody wanted, not the judge, nor the district attorney, nor the jury; but that the law made inevitable.

CORA: [*Rising.*] Why do you have anything to do with such people; thieves, criminals?

SIMON: I'm a lawyer, darling.

CORA: All lawyers don't have dealings with such people.

SIMON: Somebody's got to defend people who are accused of crime.

CORA: This boy was guilty.

SIMON: Guilty of stealing a few dollars, yes. I'd known the boy since he was a baby. Why, I never would have had a night's sleep if I'd let that boy go up the river for life.

CORA: And now someone has found out and they are going to disbar you, is that it?

SIMON: Yes, someone has found out. And it's just my luck that it happens to be a man who's had it in for me for years: a gentleman by the name of Francis Clark Baird.

CORA: Francis Clark Baird. Why, he's a very eminent lawyer, isn't he? I think I've heard father speak of him. Isn't he one of the Connecticut Bairds?

SIMON: He may be, for all I know. But that doesn't mean much to me. All that I know is that he's got the drop on me and he's going to make me pay through the nose.

CORA: Why do you always put things on a personal basis, George? Isn't it the duty of a man like Mr. Baird?

SIMON: No man has to break another man, unless he wants to. I've locked horns with this Baird a good many times, and he's always come out on the short end. He doesn't like taking that from a nobody, from an East Side boy that started in the police court.

**CORA:** Is a person who began in the police court necessarily superior to one who grew up in an atmosphere of culture and refinement?

**SIMON:** Why, darling, you're not siding with Baird, are you?

**CORA:** It isn't a matter of siding with anyone. But I can't help resenting a little the constant implication that there's some peculiar merit in having a humble origin.

**SIMON:** I'm not implying that, darling. You ought to know me better than that. I realize my shortcomings. Especially when I compare myself with you. I know that you sacrificed a lot to marry me, and that you've had to put up with a lot of things that you didn't like. And it's because you've been so sweet and understanding about it that I'm putting all my cards on the table: telling you just where I stand and what I'm up against. It's because I know I can count on you to help me through this thing.

**CORA:** I don't see how I can help you, George.

**SIMON:** I don't mean that I want you to do anything, sweetheart. I'm going to do whatever can be done. I'm in a tough spot, but I'm going to take an awful lot of licking before I throw up the sponge. It's just having you with me and knowing that you're standing by me that's going to make all the difference to me. Because in you I've got something worth fighting for.

**CORA:** [*Seating herself.*] I really don't know what to say, George. It's most distressing.

**SIMON:** Yes, it's just about as bad as anything that could have happened. But there's nothing to do but face it. Maybe something will break for me, who can tell? I've got lots of loyal friends, and when you've got your back to the wall, you can do an awful lot of fighting.

**CORA:** Yes, that's all very well, George. I understand thoroughly how you must feel about it. And, of course, I'm quite willing to accept your explanation of the whole thing.

**SIMON:** I knew you would, Cora.

**CORA:** I know how you've had to struggle and work and it's all very admirable. But it's made it possible for you to accept things that are rather difficult for me to accept.

**SIMON:** What things, darling?

**CORA:** Oh, I don't know. There's something distasteful—frankly, something rather repellent—about the whole atmosphere of the thing. This association with thieves and perjurers, and all the intrigue and conniving that goes with it. And now this scandal—it will be a scandal, I'm sure—newspaper publicity and all that.

SIMON: Yes, no doubt about it.

CORA: It's a horrible prospect. I suppose I'll have my picture in the papers, too. And reporters knocking at my door.

SIMON: I'll try to spare you all I can, darling.

CORA: And what are my friends going to say? How am I going to face them?

SIMON: Do they mean more to you than I do?

CORA: That isn't the point. It's something deeply vital to you: your career, your reputation, all the rest of it. But what am I to do? Flutter about pathetically in the background, in an atmosphere of scandal and recrimination? [*She rises.*] No, I can't. The best thing for me to do is to go to Europe as I had planned. If this thing blows over—and let's hope it will—you can join me abroad later. If it doesn't, well, then there's time enough to think about that.

SIMON: You mean you're going to walk out on me?

CORA: That's a very crude way of putting it. And very unfair to me, too. It implies that I'm deserting you when you need me. You know that isn't fair. It isn't as though I could do anything to help you. If there were, I'd be glad to stay. But you've said yourself that there isn't, haven't you now?

SIMON: Yes, I guess I did. It was just that at a time like this, I thought I'd like to have you around, that's all.

CORA: But isn't that just a little selfish, George: to ask me to stay and be subjected to all that miserable business, because it would give you a little satisfaction to have me here?

SIMON: Yes, I guess you're right. I guess it is selfish. I hadn't looked at it in that way. I just thought that maybe you'd want to stay.

CORA: [*Going to him and putting her hand on his shoulder.*] Please don't misunderstand me, George. Please don't think I'm unsympathetic. I assure you I'm terribly upset about this thing. If there were anything I could do, I should be only too happy to do it. Would you like me to ask father to intercede with Mr. Baird?

SIMON: No, I wish you wouldn't do that. [*He goes to his desk.*]

CORA: [*Following him.*] Well, just whatever you say. I do hope sincerely that everything will turn out for the best. And I give you my word, George, that if I could see how giving up my trip could possibly help you out of this difficulty, I'd give it up in a minute. But you know it couldn't.

SIMON: Yes, sure. Just forget about it darling. It was just a foolish idea of mine. But you're perfectly right. I've got to fight this thing out, myself, and there really isn't anybody that can help me.

CORA: If you think of any way at all in which I can be helpful —

SIMON: I'll let you know. Thanks, sweetheart.

CORA: I've really got to run now. Both Dorothy and I must be at the hair-dresser's at two. Will you be coming out to the country tonight?

SIMON: I don't know whether I'll be able to make it or not. I'll phone you, if I can't.

CORA: Yes, do. [*She puts her hand on his.*] Au revoir, George, and I do hope that everything is going to be all right.

SIMON: [*Patting her hand.*] Well, we'll see. Good-bye, sweetheart. Here, you can go out through Rexie's office.

CORA: Don't bother. I know the way. [*She exits.*]

[SIMON *seats himself slowly at his desk, his hands stretched out before him. He looks straight ahead of him. Then his eyes wander to* CORA'*s photograph, and taking it up, he holds it before him, in both hands, and stares at it. There is knock at the downstage door.* SIMON, *startled, puts down the photograph hastily.*]

SIMON: Well? What is it? Come in.

[*The door opens and* MCFADDEN *enters.*]

MCFADDEN: Excuse me, chief, but Bessie said you was askin' for me.

SIMON: Yes. Yes. I was asking for you. Sit down. [MCFADDEN *seats himself.*] Listen, Charlie, there's something I'd like you to do for me.

MCFADDEN: Okay, chief.

SIMON: There's a lawyer by the name of Francis Clark Baird —

MCFADDEN: The one that was attorney for Mr. DeWitt in that alienation case?

SIMON: Yes, that's the one.

MCFADDEN: Sure, I know him. He's right across the street in the French Building.

SIMON: Yes. Well, what I'd like you to do, Charlie, is to see what you can find out about him.

MCFADDEN: You want him shadowed, is that it?

SIMON: Yes. I want to know how he spends his time and who his friends are and where he goes nights.

McFADDEN: I get you.

SIMON: But you've got to go about it carefully, Charlie. I don't want anybody to get on to it, do you understand?

McFADDEN: Oh, don't worry about that, chief. I shadowed that singer—what was his name? Gerchy or Goochy, or somethin' like that—for a whole month nearly I shadowed him and he wasn't any the wiser. Don't you remember, we finally caught him in that little hotel way out on Long Island, with that red-headed jane?

SIMON: Yes, I remember. Well, get on the job now, right away. Let everything else go for the present, understand?

McFADDEN: [*Rising.*] You bet, chief.

SIMON: And give me a daily report of everything he does.

McFADDEN: Leave it to me, chief. I got lots of ways of finding things out.

SIMON: Never mind the expense. Spend whatever is necessary. And whatever you do, keep it under your hat.

McFADDEN: Sure, I got you, chief. Mum's the word.

[*A knock at the door.*]

SIMON: Well? See who it is, Charlie.

[McFADDEN *opens the door and the* BOOTBLACK *enters.*]

SIMON: No, not now, Joe.

JOE: All right, boss. After lunch?

SIMON: Yes. Come back after lunch. Well, no, wait a minute. You'd better shine 'em up now, I guess.

JOE: Sure, boss.

[*He kneels at* SIMON*'s feet and begins to shine his shoes.*]

SIMON: All right, Charlie, that's all.

McFADDEN: Yes, sir.

[*He exits.* SIMON *presses the call button.* REGINA *enters.*]

**SIMON:** I've put Charlie McFadden on a job that will probably keep him busy for several days. I don't want him interfered with. So, if necessary, take on somebody else temporarily to do his work.

**REGINA:** Yes sir. Do you want to see Mrs. Becker and her son?

**SIMON:** Oh, are they still waiting? Tell them to come back tomorrow.

**REGINA:** They've been waiting a long time.

**SIMON:** All right, I'll see them. No, wait a minute. Just have the boy come in. I can talk to him better if he hasn't got his mother here to sympathize with him.

**REGINA:** Yes sir. [*She exits.*]

**JOE:** Well, boss, I hear you gonna take a nice little trip.

**SIMON:** What's that? Oh yes, sure.

**JOE:** You gonna take da missis along, too?

**SIMON:** Yes, I guess so. Make it snappy, will you Joe? I'm busy.

**JOE:** Yes, sure, boss.

**REGINA:** [*Ushering in* BECKER.] Go right in.

[BECKER *enters.* REGINA *goes to her office.*]

**SIMON:** Sit down, Becker.

[BECKER *seats himself.*]

**SIMON:** Now, listen, to what I got to say — [*He breaks off.*] God, they did beat you up, didn't they? Are you badly hurt?

**BECKER:** I'm all right.

**SIMON:** You don't look all right. Well, maybe this will be a lesson to you. Maybe in the future, you'll keep your mouth shut. Now, listen, and I'll tell you what I've done for you. But first I want you to get this straight. The reason I've done it is not because I have any sympathy for you. I think you're just a goddam silly kid. But I've known your mother since you were wearing diapers. She's a good, honest, hard-working woman, and she's had troubles enough in her life, without a young smart aleck like you making more trouble. That's why I'm doing this, do you understand? What's the matter, can't you talk? You seem to be doing a hell of a lot of talking in Union Square.

**BECKER:** I can talk when there's any need to talk.

SIMON: Well, I'm glad to hear it. Now, listen, and I'll tell you what I've done for you. I've got quite a lot of influence with the district attorney's office and the assistant in charge of this case happens to be a boy who used to work for me. So, I explained to him that you're just a crazy kid that likes to hear himself talk and he's agreed to accept a plea of guilty and to ask the court to give you a suspended sentence. That means that you're all right, as long as you behave yourself and keep your mouth shut. And if you ask me, you're damned lucky to get off so easily.

BECKER: I won't plead guilty and I won't keep my mouth shut.

SIMON: Oh, you won't, won't you? Well, listen, kid, as long as I'm representing you, you're going to be guided by my advice, do you understand?

BECKER: I never asked you to represent me.

SIMON: Well, that's a nice way to talk to me, isn't it, when I'm trying to help you out of a jam. Do you know that I put up the bail for you out of my own pocket?

BECKER: What do I care? Keep your charity for your parasites.

SIMON: Say, listen to me, boy—All right, Joe, that'll do.

JOE: All right, boss. Good-bye, boss. [*He exits.*]

SIMON: Good-bye. All right, now that you haven't got an audience, let's cut out the soapbox stuff and get down to cases. I'm used to making grandstand plays to juries, and I know just how you feel about it. But you've got to promise me that hereafter you're going to keep quiet with the Communist stuff.

BECKER: Listen, Simon, you can't make me keep quiet and neither can anybody else. If the Cossacks want to beat me up, let them do it. They killed my grandfather and my uncle, and the only way they can keep me quiet is to kill me, too.

SIMON: What do you mean, Cossacks? What the hell are you talking about? This is America, not Russia.

BECKER: It's worse than Russia ever was under the Czar.

SIMON: Don't talk so foolish. What do you know about Russia under the Czar? Were you ever there?

BECKER: I was born in the steerage.

SIMON: Yes? Well, anyhow, you had better meals coming over than I had. You know what's the matter with you? I'll tell you what's the matter with you. You're very young—

BECKER: Is it a crime to be young, too?

SIMON: You're very young and you've got a lot of crazy ideas. But I think you've got some good stuff in you, otherwise I wouldn't be wasting my time talking to you. I'm pretty nearly old enough to be your father and I'm going to give you some good, practical advice—

BECKER: Who wants your advice? I don't want your advice or your help or your friendship. You and I have nothing in common. I'm on one side of the class war and you're on the other.

SIMON: Get some sense into your head, will you, and stop talking like a goddam idiot. Class war, my backside. You're going to tell me about class wars, are you? You're going to explain to me about the working class, is that it? Do you think I was born with a silver spoon in my mouth? I started working before I was through shedding my milk teeth. I began life in the same gutter that you did. If I were to tell you what I had to go through to get where I am, it would take me a week. Why, you wouldn't have the guts to go through one-tenth of it, you and your Cossacks and your class wars. Do you think I don't know what it is to sweat and to freeze and to go hungry? You're barking up the wrong tree this time, son. I can give you cards and spades and beat you at your own game. Don't come around me with any of your goddam half-baked Communistic bull and expect me to fall for it.

BECKER: Do you think it's to your credit that you started in the working class? You ought to be ashamed of it. You ought to be ashamed to admit that you're a traitor to your class.

SIMON: Oh, so I'm a traitor to my class, am I? Why you, little—

BECKER: Yes, a traitor. A dirty traitor and a renegade, that's what you are.

SIMON: All right, I don't want to hear any more out of you.

BECKER: [*Rising.*] Shut up, Simon. I'm going to do the talking here. How did you get where you are? I'll tell you. By betraying your own class, that's how. By climbing on the backs of the working class, that's how. Getting in right with crooked bourgeois politicians and pimping for corporations that feed on the blood and sweat of the workers.

SIMON: That's enough, do you hear?

BECKER: No, it's not enough. I'm going to tell you what you are, Counsellor Simon, sitting here in your Fifth Avenue office, with a bootblack at your feet and a lot of white-collar slaves running your errands for you. You're a cheap prostitute, that's what you are, you and your cars and your country estate and your kept parasite of a wife.

SIMON: [*Rising.*] Shut up, goddam you!

BECKER: No, I won't shut up. I'll say it again. Your kept parasite of a wife, the daughter of capitalists and slave drivers and her two pampered brats.

SIMON: If you don't stop, I'll—

BECKER: Go ahead. Hit me. Beat me up. I'm used to it. I like it. I'd like to be beaten up by Comrade Simon of the working class, who sits rolling in wealth and luxury, while millions of his brothers starve.

SIMON: Get out.

BECKER: Aren't you going to beat me up? Why not? You've got everything and I've got nothing, so why don't you beat me up? Why don't you be true to the traditions of your class, of the capitalistic class?

[SIMON *points silently to the door.*]

BECKER: You dirty traitor, you!

[*He spits venomously on the floor and exits.* SIMON *slinks down into his chair. His hand taps the desk, idly.*]

REGINA: [*Entering.*] It's time to leave for your luncheon appointment with Senator Wells.

SIMON: What? Oh yes. Is it time to leave?

REGINA: Yes sir.

[SIMON *rises and goes towards the door.*]

REGINA: Excuse me, Mr. Simon.

SIMON: Well?

REGINA: Is there anything wrong?

SIMON: Of course not. Why should there be anything wrong?

REGINA: Because if there were anything I could do—

SIMON: You can mind your own business, that's what you can do.

[*He exits quickly.* REGINA *stands looking after him.*]

CURTAIN

# ACT THREE

## SCENE 1

*The inner office.* REGINA *is seated at* SIMON's *desk, telephoning.*

REGINA: Well, I don't know. It's almost five now, you'd better call him in the morning about eleven. You'll be sure to get him, then — All right. Good-bye. [*She hangs up the receiver. The phone rings again almost instantly.*] Hello — all right, I'll speak to her. [McFADDEN *thrusts his head into the door.*] Not yet, Charlie. [McFADDEN *exits.*] Hello — Good afternoon, Mrs. Simon — No ma'am, he hasn't returned from Washington yet — Are you at the pier, now? — Oh, well, he may have gone from Pennsylvania Station to the pier — No, I haven't heard from him all day; but I know he's planning to see you off — How soon will you be at the pier? All right — All right — Yes ma'am — Yes ma'am — All right, I will — Good-bye, I hope you have a pleasant trip. [*She hangs up the receiver.*] I hope you fall overboard.

[WEINBERG *enters, with some papers.* REGINA *ostentatiously picks up a letter from the desk and reads it.* WEINBERG *looks at her, then puts the papers on the desk. She ignores his presence. He looks at her again, is about to speak, then changes his mind and goes out hastily, almost colliding with* TEDESCO, *who is entering.*]

WEINBERG: I'm sorry.
TEDESCO: Oh, did you get that answer out?
WEINBERG: I'm going to dictate it now. [*He exits.*]
TEDESCO: G.S. isn't back yet?
REGINA: No sir, not yet.
TEDESCO: It's almost five. Maybe he won't come in at all, today.

**REGINA:** I think he may have gone right to the French Line pier. Mrs. Simon's boat sails at six.

**TEDESCO:** Yes, I guess he did. Oh, I forgot to send her a telegram.

**REGINA:** There's still plenty of time.

**TEDESCO:** I guess it's too late for a basket of fruit or some flowers, isn't it?

**REGINA:** Not for flowers. Do you want me to take care of it for you?

**TEDESCO:** Yes, if you don't mind.

**REGINA:** I'll be glad to. How much do you want to spend—about five dollars?

**TEDESCO:** Yes, I guess so. No, you'd better make it ten.

**REGINA:** All right. I'll attend to it, right away. Oh, here's Mr. Simon now.

**SIMON:** [*Entering and seating himself on the sofa.*] Hello, Rexie. Hello, John. [*He is weary and dispirited.*]

**REGINA:** Good afternoon, Mr. Simon.

**TEDESCO:** Hello, George.

**REGINA:** Mrs. Simon just called up about five minutes ago.

**SIMON:** Oh, did she? Well, get her for me.

**REGINA:** Why, I don't think I can get her now. She's on her way to the steamer; I don't think she'll be there for about a half-hour yet. I didn't know whether you'd be back or not.

**SIMON:** Well, call up the pier—No, never mind. I'll go down there in a few minutes. What time does the boat sail—six?

**REGINA:** Yes sir.

**SIMON:** Well, have a taxi ready for me, in about fifteen minutes.

**REGINA:** Yes sir. [*She starts to exit.*]

**SIMON:** Oh, did you arrange about the books and flowers?

**REGINA:** Yes sir.

**SIMON:** Fresh flowers every day, do they understand that?

**REGINA:** Yes sir, it's all taken care of.

**SIMON:** All right. And make a note to remind me to send a radiogram every day.

**REGINA:** Yes sir. Is that all?

**SIMON:** Yes, that's all [REGINA *exits.*] Well, John, Pete Malone and I just got back from Washington.

**TEDESCO:** Well?

**SIMON:** Well, we might just as well have saved ourselves the trip.

**TEDESCO:** Didn't you see him?

**SIMON:** Oh, yes, sure. We saw him. We were with him nearly an hour.

**TEDESCO:** What did he say?

**SIMON:** Oh, he handed out the usual line of bull, about what a great guy I am, and how he loves me like a brother, and about what a tough break it is that this thing had to come up.

**TEDESCO:** Yes, well, is he going to do something about it?

**SIMON:** He's not going to do a goddam thing about it, John. Pete tried to get him to make a personal appeal to Baird, but it wasn't a bit of use.

**TEDESCO:** You mean he refused to do it?

**SIMON:** Well, of course, he wouldn't have the face to refuse right off the bat. He hasn't got the guts to do that. He just talked all around it. You know, he's going to think it over and all that. He can't abuse the power of his office and he can't take advantage of the fact that Baird is his brother-in-law: and this and that. It was pitiable to sit there and watch him crawl. It nearly made me puke.

**TEDESCO:** The yellow mutt? Why didn't you tell him that if it hadn't been for you, he never would have got the nomination?

**SIMON:** What's the use? If he doesn't know it already, it's because he doesn't want to know it. I could have told him too about the stumping I did for him and about the twenty-five thousand I contributed to his campaign fund.

**TEDESCO:** Well, why the hell didn't you?

**SIMON:** I tell you it's no use, John. Didn't you know that when you give somebody a helping hand, he always turns around and kicks you in the pants? You see, John, the little fellow's getting ambitious. He's a statesman now. He dreams about the White House and I hear he's having himself measured for a laurel wreath and a toga. You can't expect a big shot who's headed for the Hall of Fame to get himself mixed up with a little shyster who's been up to some funny business. God, it is to laugh!

**TEDESCO:** I don't blame you for being good and sore: the dirty little sneak.

**SIMON:** Well, what the hell, John? What did you expect? This is a cut-throat game we're in, and it's every man for himself. Well, I'm about at the end of my rope! Tomorrow the grievance committee meets and once it gets before them I can kiss my career good-bye.

**TEDESCO:** They haven't got you licked yet, George. You've got some pretty good friends in the Appellate Division.

**SIMON:** That's not going to help me, John. There's not a thing in the world they can do but disbar me. It's an open and shut case. Technically, I'm as guilty as hell, and any judge that didn't say so wouldn't be fit to be on the bench. No, I don't believe in kidding myself, John. As long as there was a chance of keeping this thing from getting before the Grievance Committee, why maybe I had an out. But I've shot my last bolt. Between us, we've tried everything that could be tried, and now I'm licked. I'm finished — through — kaput.

TEDESCO: The hell you are! We're going to fight and we're going to get you out of it.

SIMON: John, there's not a chance, I tell you. I'm about ready to quit now. Whey the hell shouldn't I? [*He rises and paces the room.*] Why shouldn't I thumb my nose at the whole lot of them and walk right out on them?

TEDESCO: You're crazy?

SIMON: Why? Why am I crazy? Let them disbar me. What the hell do I care? I'll go and get on a boat somewhere and spend the rest of my life enjoying myself. Why shouldn't I? I've been working like a horse ever since I'm eight years old. Why shouldn't I quit and see the world and have a good time? Why, this thing may turn out to be a godsend to me: a chance to get out of harness and live a life of leisure, instead of working myself into an early grave.

TEDESCO: You'd get sick of it in a year, just the same as I would.

SIMON: I don't know about that. Why would I? The world's a big place. There's a lot to see and a lot to do. And when I got tired of sightseeing, I could settle down somewhere and get out into the sun a lot. I could take up golf, maybe. Probably be the best thing in the world for me: I'm beginning to put on a little weight. I could — [*He sits down at his desk.*] Jesus, you're right, John. A year? God, I'd go nuts in six months.

TEDESCO: Forget all about that, will you, George? Just make up your mind that you're going to fight this thing and win out.

SIMON: What am I going to do, John? How am I going to spend the rest of my life? How am I going to face the people I know, the people who think I'm the cat's whiskers? How am I going to put in my time? What am I going to do every morning and every afternoon and every evening? I'm no golf player, John. And I don't know an ace from a king. I don't even know how to get drunk. All I know is work. Take work away from me and what the hell am I: a car without a motor, a living corpse.

TEDESCO: Listen, take my advice, and get some sleep tonight. I guess you haven't been sleeping much, have you?

SIMON: No, not much.

TEDESCO: Well, that's what you need, a good sleep. Why don't you lie down and take a nap now?

SIMON: No, I've got to go down to the boat to say good-bye to Cora. I guess it's time to go. [*He rings the bell.*] this is pretty hard on her, John . A woman with her background married to a lawyer who gets himself kicked out of his profession. [REGINA *enters.*] Is it time for me to go?

REGINA: You still have a few minutes. I don't think Mrs. Simon will be there yet. Mr. Uccello is on the phone for you, Mr. Tedesco.

TEDESCO: All right, I'll take it in my office. George, will you have dinner with me tonight at the club?

SIMON: Yes, all right. I'll meet you there at six-thirty.

TEDESCO: Okay. [*He exits.*]

REGINA: Do you want to go over your mail?

SIMON: No, let it wait.

REGINA: Mr. Fishman called up and said that he had sold your Gulf Coast Utilities at an average price of 28-¼.

SIMON: 28-¼? Let's see, what did I pay for it? About 24. That's four points profit. About forty thousand dollars. What the hell good does it do me?

REGINA: Sir?

SIMON: Nothing. Tell Mr. Tedesco he made twenty thousand dollars profit on the Gulf Coast Utilities deal.

REGINA: Yes sir. [*She is about to go, then stops.*] Oh, I called the Bellevue Hospital a little while ago to inquire about Harry Becker.

SIMON: Yes. Well, how is he getting along?

REGINA: He died early this morning of a cerebral hemorrhage.

SIMON: What? He died?

REGINA: Yes sir. It's terrible, isn't it?

SIMON: It's awful.

REGINA: Think of his poor mother.

SIMON: It's terrible. Listen, I'll tell you what I want you to do. Arrange to have me pay for the funeral expenses. If necessary, buy a little plot somewhere so they don't bury him in Potter's Field. And then, send his mother a check for five hundred dollars. Remind me tomorrow to write her a nice letter. What do you think of that—dead?

REGINA: A young boy like that!

SIMON: Well, maybe he's better off. His troubles are over and, in his own eyes, he died a hero and a martyr to a cause. That's better than living to be old and ending our days in disgrace. Yes, after all, it's not such a bad thing to die at twenty, believing in the millennium and the brotherhood of man. [REGINA *wipes her eyes.*] What are you crying about?

REGINA: Nothing.

SIMON: He's better off where he is.

REGINA: I'm not crying about him.

SIMON: No? Then what are you crying about?

REGINA: It's nothing. Nothing at all. Do you—

SIMON: [*Going over to her.*] What's the matter with you, lately?

REGINA: There's nothing the matter with me.

SIMON: Don't you feel well?

REGINA: Yes, of course.

SIMON: Maybe you've been working too hard. Maybe you ought to have a little vacation.

REGINA: No, I don't want any vacation.

SIMON: [*Turning away from her and going back to his desk.*] Maybe I'll be going away myself, soon. Then you can get a good rest.

REGINA: I don't want a rest. I'll get a cab for you, now.

[*She exits.* SIMON *sits staring ahead of him. Then, suddenly, he rises, goes to the window, throws it open, and looks down. He draws back, with a shudder, and covers his eyes. Then, as he closes the window,* REGINA *enters.*]

SIMON: [*Sharply.*] Well?

REGINA: I forgot to tell you. Charlie McFadden wants to see you about something.

SIMON: It can wait until tomorrow. Are you getting me a cab?

REGINA: Yes sir. Right away.

[*She throws him a quick look, then exits. There is a knock at the downstage door.*]

SIMON: Well?

McFADDEN: [*Entering.*] Excuse me, chief. Can I see you for a minute?

SIMON: Not now. I've got to go down to the boat to see Mrs. Simon off.

McFADDEN: I've got some news for you.

SIMON: What kind of news?

McFADDEN: About our friend across the way.

SIMON: Who? Baird?

McFADDEN: That's him.

SIMON: You've found out something about him?

McFADDEN: I'll say I have.

SIMON: Well, what is it?

McFADDEN: [*Looking about.*] He's leadin' a double life.

SIMON: What do you mean he's leading a double life?

McFADDEN: Wait, till I tell you, chief. Remember my tellin' you the other day how I found out that's he always makin' business trips to Philydelphy?

SIMON: Yes, well?

McFADDEN: [*Seating himself on the sofa.*] Well, yesterday off he goes to Pennsylvania Station and boards a train for Philly, with me right behind him.

SIMON: Well?

McFADDEN: Well, he gets out of the station and hops a taxi, but on account of the noise and bein' afraid of getting' too close to him, all I can hear him say is "Germantown." So I grabs another hack and tells the driver to folly him.

SIMON: Yes. Go on.

McFADDEN: Well, we're goin' along great, when all of a sudden we gets into a traffic jam and by the time it gets straightened out, we loses him.

SIMON: Well, is that all?

McFADDEN: Lord, no. That's jus' the beginnin'.

SIMON: All right, go on.

McFADDEN: Well, I tells the boy to go ahead out to Germantown, thinkin' we might find the cab around somewhere. But, geez, this Germantown is a hell of a big place.

SIMON: Go ahead.

McFADDEN: Well, after cruisin' around for a couple of hours with the old meter clickin' away, I had to give it up, so I goes back to the station and hangs around waitin' to see if the other taxi is gonna come back. Well, after waitin' about three hours, sure enough back it comes—

SIMON: Was Baird in it?

McFADDEN: No, sir, he wasn't.

SIMON: Go on.

McFADDEN: Well, I gets talkin' to the driver and asks him if he remembers

**157**

takin' a party out to Germantown. He says he does and he thinks it was Sycamore Drive, but he can't remember the number. So I gets in, and tells him to take me out there—

REGINA: [*Entering.*] Oh, excuse me. The taxi is ready for you.

SIMON: All right. Let it wait a minute. [REGINA *exits.*] Go ahead.

McFADDEN: Well, he takes me out to this Sycamore Drive, but he can't remember just which house it is. So I gets out, and kinda looks in through the windows of the houses, thinkin' maybe I'll see Baird. But I don't see no sign of him.

SIMON: Yes? Well?

McFADDEN: So I begins gettin' acquainted and askin' a few questions around from the feller in the service station and another guy that's got a little tobacco store. It's a kind of a quiet, family neighborhood, with mostly one and two-family houses.

SIMON: Well, what did you find out?

McFADDEN: Well, I asked if there was any gentleman that came aroun' callin' answerin' to the description of our friend Mr. Baird. At first, nobody seemed to know, but after a while the feller in the tobacco store says: "Why, Yes, that sounds like the uncle of little Mrs. Allen, over at 1217." So I gets him talkin' about this Mrs. Allen, and accordin' to this feller she's a poor little widow woman, an' her husband was killed in an automobile accident when the baby was only two months old. So with the insurance money, she bought this little house in Germantown, and she and the baby have been livin' there now for eight years.

SIMON: She lives there all alone?

McFADDEN: Yes sir: just her and the kid.

SIMON: Well? What else?

McFADDEN: Well, says the feller in the tobacco store, it's a shame about this young widow woman, and all the kith or kin she has in the whole world is this old uncle from Pittsburgh, that comes to see her once in a while.

SIMON: Pittsburgh?

McFADDEN: Accordin' to this feller.

SIMON: All right. Go on.

McFADDEN: So I strolls over to 1217 and it's dark by now, so I looks in the window, and there is the little widow havin' supper with the kid—a pretty, little youngster, too.

SIMON: Was Baird there?

McFadden: No sir, he wasn't.

Simon: Well, what the hell is all this? What proof have you got that he ever was there?

McFadden: Wait a minute, chief. I ain't done yet. I says to myself: "That little lady don't look like no niece to me, an' as for the kid, he's the spitten image of old man Baird."

Simon: Jesus Christ, is that what you call evidence?

McFadden: No sir.

Simon: Go on.

McFadden: Well, I hangs aroun' a little while, but there's nothin' to do till everybody's in bed. So I goes away and has a feed an' takes in a movie, an' along about two o'clock, I goes back to 1217 an' takes a look into the house.

Simon: What do you mean: you broke into the house?

McFadden: I wouldn't want to admit that, chief. I'd be li'ble to arrest an' imprisonment if I did.

Simon: Are you crazy? What the hell did you do a thing like that for?

McFadden: Don't worry about it, chief. It was an easy job an' I ain't as much out of practice, as I thought I'd be. I was back in New York before anybody was the wiser.

Simon: Well, what did you find out?

McFadden: Well, I figgered there'd be letters from him—an' there was.

Simon: You found letters from Baird to this woman?

McFadden: Yes sir. A whole stack of 'em.

Simon: Where are they? What do they say?

McFadden: [*Giving* Simon *a packet.*] Right here, chief. They're all about how much he loves her, an' about how she don't have to worry about her future an' the kid's future, if she'll just keep mum. An' —

Simon: [*Who has been reading the letters.*] Good God! This is a clear admission of the paternity of the child!

McFadden: Yes sir. An' here's his picture an' the kid's picture. They were both in a frame, on her dresser. I didn't think you'd want the frame: it was a kind of a big leather one. But you can see the kid's the spitten image of him.

Simon: [*Absorbed in the letters.*] "Your Frankie" huh? So that's the way the Pilgrim Fathers sign their love letters, is it? I suppose we can verify the handwriting easily enough.

**McFadden:** I've done it, chief. I went through the files in that DeWitt alienation case an' there's three or four letters signed by Mr. Francis Clark Baird. Anybody can see it's the same handwritin'.

**Simon:** Well, what do you know about that? So that's what this old boy has been up to, is it?

**McFadden:** I hope it's what you wanted, chief.

**Simon:** Listen, Charlie, these letters are worth a million dollars to me. You don't know what you've done for me. Only you were a goddam fool to go breaking into that house.

**McFadden:** Well, it's the least I could do, chief, after all you've done for me.

**Regina:** [*Entering.*] You really should go now, Mr. Simon.

**Simon:** What? No, not now. I can't leave now. Get me Francis Clark Baird on the phone right away.

**Regina:** Yes sir. [*She goes to her desk and calls the number.*]

**McFadden:** Well, if you're not needin' me now, chief, I think maybe I'll go home. I didn't get much sleep last night.

**Simon:** Come in to see me in the morning, Charlie.

**McFadden:** Yes sir.

**Simon:** Wait a minute. What is that address: Sycamore Drive?

**McFadden:** Yes sir. 1217.

**Simon:** All right. And Charlie—! [*He puts his finger to his lips.* McFadden *nods and exits.*]

**Regina:** Mr. Baird is busy and can't be disturbed.

**Simon:** Oh, he is, is he? Who is that—his secretary?

**Regina:** Yes sir.

**Simon:** I'll talk to her. Hello, this is Mr. Simon speaking: Mr. George Simon—You say Mr. Baird can't be disturbed? Well, it's extremely important.—Oh, I see. Well, will you take a message for Mr. Baird?—Thank you. Tell him, please, that a client of mine is interested in the property at 1217 Sycamore Drive, Germantown—No, Germantown, Germantown, Pennsylvania.—Yes, that's right—And tell him I'll be here for another half-hour, in case he wants to call me back—Thank you. Listen, Rexie, as soon as Baird calls back put him right on.

**Regina:** It's quarter past five, and the boat sails at six.

**Simon:** All right, listen. Call up the French Line pier and have them connect you with the steamer. If Mrs. Simon is there, I want to talk to her right away. If she hasn't arrived yet, I want her to call me as soon as she arrives. Tell them it's of the utmost importance. No, wait a minute. Take this note. Darling. Don't sail. Get right off the boat. I think that everything is going to be all right and that I'll be able to go with you in a few weeks. Phone me the instant you get this and have your baggage taken off the boat. Hastily and happily. Get that right out and send a messenger down by taxi. No, wait. Get McFadden and have him take it down. Tell him to give it to Mrs. Simon personally, and then to help her to get her baggage off the boat. Hurry up you haven't much time.

REGINA: Yes sir.

[*She hurries out.* SIMON *picks up the letters, and reads them over, laughing and chuckling to himself. Then he walks up and down the office, swinging his arms wildly about and clapping his hands together. Then he goes to his desk and makes a connection on the interoffice phone.*]

SIMON: John, come in, will you?—I've got some hot news.—All right, come in, right away. [*He disconnects and begins pacing the office again.*]

REGINA: [*Entering.*] Do you want to sign this?

SIMON: Yes. Did you tell McFadden?

REGINA: Yes sir: he's waiting.

SIMON: All right. Tell him to take a taxi and get there as quick as he can. And he's to give this to Mrs. Simon, personally.

REGINA: Yes sir.

SIMON: And as soon as Mr. Baird phones, I want to talk to him.

REGINA: Yes sir. [*She exits as* TEDESCO *enters.*]

SIMON: Well, John, I've got that son-of-a-bitch where I want him, at last. Read those.

CURTAIN

# SCENE 2

*The outer office.* BESSIE *is at the switchboard.* MCFADDEN *is waiting, with his hat on.*

BESSIE: Simon and Tedesco—Mr. Weinberg? All rightee. Go ahead.

[REGINA *enters from* SIMON'*s office.*]

REGINA: Here, Charlie. Take a taxi and get right down to the French Line pier with this. And give it to Mrs. Simon personally.
MCFADDEN: Okay.
REGINA: [*As he exits.*] There's very little time.
MCFADDEN: I'll make it, all right.

[REGINA *exits.*]

BESSIE: Simon and Tedesco—Oh, hello, Gracie—Gee, I'm glad you called up. I been tryin' to get you all day—Where you been? Oh. Well, listen, Gracie, there's something I want to ask you—[*She looks about to make sure that she is alone.*] Listen, I want to get the name of that doctor—You know the one I mean—Yeah, that's the one—Wait a minute—[HENRY *comes out of the library, whistling, and carrying a stack of letters to be mailed. He crosses the room and exits to the corridor.*] Hello, Gracie. Somebody was just here—Yeah, you bet I'm worried—Yeah, yeah, I didn't sleep a wink all last night—I feel like the wrath o' God—Yeah, I think I'd better. Gee, I'm scared to death—What is it? P like in Paul?— Yeah, I got it—An' what's the address?—Gee, that's way downtown, ain't it?—Six to seven? Well, I better leave right away, then—Wait a minute, Gracie. [*As* HENRY *re-enters.*] Say, listen, Henry, will you do me a favor?
HENRY: What?
BESSIE: Will you take the board, like a nice boy? I got some shoppin' to do before the stores close.
HENRY: Say, don't you think I wanna get home, too?
BESSIE: Ah, come on, Henry, be nice. They'll all be goin' home in a few minutes. I'll do somethin' nice for you some day.
HENRY: Aw, all right.
BESSIE: Thanks, Henry, you're a nice kid.

HENRY: I'll be back in a minute. [*He goes to the library.*]

BESSIE: Hello, Gracie — Yeah, I was gettin' the office boy to take the board, so's I can get away — No, they never go home around here — Yeah, I'm goin' right away — Listen, do you have to be known or anythin'? Suppose he asks me who I am? Well, I hope so. God, I'm shakin' like a leaf — Yeah, I'll call you up tonight — Well, I don't know. I'll have to go out to call you. Gee, if my family was ever to find out — Yeah, well, don't mention it to nobody, will you, Gracie? — What? — There's somebody comin' now. I'll call you tonight — Good-bye.

[*The outer door opens and a middle-aged* MAN *of dignified bearing enters.*]

THE MAN: I'd like to see Mr. Simon, please. Mr. Baird calling. Mr. Francis Clark Baird.

BESSIE: Just a minute, Mr. Baird. I'll see if Mr. Simon is in.

BAIRD: I'm sure he's in. He telephoned my office just a few minutes ago.

BESSIE: He may have gone out again. Just a moment, please. Hello — Mr. Francis Clark Baird is here to see Mr. Simon, Miss Gordon — No, he's right out here, in the office — All rightee — Just a moment, Mr. Baird — Hello — All rightee — Just a moment, Mr. Baird — Hello — All rightee — Mr. Simon is busy, Mr. Baird, but if you care to sit down and wait, he'll see you in a little while.

BAIRD: Well — is he likely to be long?

BESSIE: She didn't say. But I don't think he'll be very long.

BAIRD: Very well; I'll wait.

[BAIRD *walks to the window and looks out.* BESSIE *begins putting her things away for the day.* GOLDIE *comes out of the library, dressed for the street.* BAIRD *turns as he hears the door open.*]

GOLDIE: I'm going for the day. Good night.

BESSIE: Good night, Goldie.

[GOLDIE *exits.* REGINA *comes out of* SIMON'S *office.* BAIRD *turns again.*]

REGINA: Bessie, if Mrs. Simon or Charlie McFadden calls up, connect them with Mr. Simon right away.

**Bessie:** All rightee.

**Regina:** Are you leaving now?

**Bessie:** I gotta get some medicine made up for my mother on the way home. She needs it very bad. Henry's gonna take the board.

**Regina:** Well, it's all right, as long as someone is at the board. Be sure to tell him—

**Bessie:** Oh, yes, sure, Miss Gordon.

**Regina:** And if anyone else calls, he's gone for the day.

**Bessie:** All rightee.

[Regina *crosses to the library.*]

**Baird:** Excuse me. Do you think Mr. Simon is likely to be busy long?

**Regina:** I don't think very long, Mr. Baird. Why don't you just sit down and make yourself comfortable?

**Baird:** Thank you. I don't care to sit down.

**Regina:** I'm sure he won't be very long. I know he tried to get you a little while ago.

**Baird:** Yes. Thank you.

[Regina *exits to the library.* Tedesco *enters from* Simon's *office.*]

**Tedesco:** Tell Goldie I want her, please.

**Bessie:** She's gone for the day, Mr. Tedesco.

**Tedesco:** Has she? [*He looks at his watch.*] Oh, I didn't know it was so late. Well, never mind. [*He starts to cross to his office, then stops.*] How do, Mr. Baird?

**Baird:** Oh, how do you do?

**Tedesco:** I guess you don't remember me. I'm John Tedesco, Mr. Simon's partner.

**Baird:** Oh yes, of course.

**Tedesco:** We met in Trial Term, Part Eight, during the trial of DeWitt against Carter.

**Baird:** Yes, I remember. Do you think Mr. Simon will be free soon?

**Tedesco:** Well, I really couldn't say. Does he know you're here?

**Baird:** Yes, he does. That is, I assume he does.

**Bessie:** Yes, he does, Mr. Tedesco.

**Tedesco:** Oh. [*As* Regina *enters.*] Rexie, will you remind Mr. Simon that Mr. Baird is waiting?

**Regina:** He said he'd see Mr. Baird in just a few minutes.

**TEDESCO:** Well, remind him again, will you?
**REGINA:** Yes sir. [*She exits to* SIMON's *office.*]
**BAIRD:** Thank you.
**TEDESCO:** Well, I was glad to see you again, Mr. Baird. I hope we meet soon again. [*He shakes hands with* BAIRD.]
**BAIRD:** Thank you.
**TEDESCO:** Good night.
**BAIRD:** Good night.

[TEDESCO *enters his office.* HENRY *enters from the library.*]

**BESSIE:** All right, Henry. Come ahead, will you? I gotta go.
**HENRY:** Yeah? An' what about me? When do I get home?
**BESSIE:** They won't be long. Listen, if Mrs. Simon calls up, or Charlie—
**HENRY:** I know. I know. Miss Gordon tol' me all about it.
**BESSIE:** An' this gentleman is waitin' to see Mr. Simon.
**HENRY:** All right. All right. Go ahead. Beat it.
**BESSIE:** [*Going towards the library.*] Oh, there's some chocolates there, if you want some.
**HENRY:** I don' want no choc'lates.

[BESSIE *enters the library.*]

**REGINA:** [*Entering from* SIMON's *office.*] Mr. Simon will see you now, Mr. Baird.
**BAIRD:** Thank you.
**REGINA:** Right in this way. It's the first door to your right.
**BAIRD:** Thank you. [*He exits to* SIMON's *office.*]
**REGINA:** If Mrs. Simon calls while Mr. Baird is in there, put her on my wire.
**HENRY:** Okay.

[WEINBERG *enters from library, wearing his hat, as* REGINA *is about to exit to* SIMON's *office.*]

**WEINBERG:** Miss Gordon. [REGINA *turns without answering.*] Are you going up on the el[5] tonight?
**REGINA:** No, I'm not. [*She exits abruptly.*]
**WEINBERG:** Well—good night.

---

[5] Elevated train, part of New York City's public transportation system.

[*But she has already gone.* WEINBERG *goes toward the entrance door.*]

HENRY: Going for the day, Mr. Weinberg?
WEINBERG: Yes.

[*He exits.* BESSIE *comes out of the library, dressed for the street.*]

SANDLER: [*Coming out of the library.*] Wait a minute, Cleopatra.
BESSIE: I can't; I'm in a hurry.
SANDLER: Well, can't my chauffeur drop you somewhere?

[*He links his arm through hers.* HENRY *is highly amused.*]

BESSIE: [*Freeing her arm.*] Say, quit it, will you? Can't you keep your hands
to yourself? [*She pushes him away and exits.*]
SANDLER: [*Tossing an imaginary petal in the air.*] She loves me not.

[HENRY *laughs.*]

SANDLER: [*To* HENRY.] Good night, Oswald. If Peggy Joyce calls me, I can
be reached in my box at the Opera.
HENRY: [*Laughing.*] All right. [SANDLER *exits.* HENRY *takes the box of
chocolates out of the drawer and begins to eat them. Then he dials a number.*]
Hello. Sporting Department, please—Have you got the final score of the
Yankees' game?—Gee, they did. Oh, boy! An' what about the Robins—
All right. Thanks. [MRS. LENA SIMON *enters from the corridor.*] Good
evening' Mrs. Simon.
MRS. SIMON: Good evening. Is my son still here?
HENRY: I think there's somebody in there with him.
MRS. SIMON: [*Seating herself to the right of the table.*] It's all right. I'll wait. I
got plenty time.
HENRY: I'll tell Miss Gordon you're here.
MRS. SIMON: So you're a telephone operator, too.
HENRY: Oh, I'm jus' takin' Bessie's place. Mr. Simon's mother is here, Miss
Gordon. Okay. Miss Gordon will be right out.
MRS. SIMON: It's no hurry. What time do you close the office?
HENRY: Well, we're supposed to close at five, but it's all accordin' if Mr.
Simon or Mr. Tedesco stays later or not.
MRS. SIMON: You're going to be a lawyer, too?

**HENRY:** I don' know.

**MRS. SIMON:** My son began just like you. When he was thirteen years old, he was office boy for Hirsch and Rosenthal, for four dollars a week.

**HENRY:** Four dollars! Gee, I started with nine, an' I'm gettin' ten now.

**MRS. SIMON:** Yes, four dollars he started with. And today, he's the biggest lawyer in New York.

**REGINA:** [*Entering.*] Hello, Mrs. Simon. How are you today? [*She goes over to her and shakes hands.*]

**MRS. SIMON:** Oh, I can't complain. And you?

**REGINA:** I'm all right, thanks. I can't disturb Mr. Simon now. There's someone with him. But I don't think he'll be very long.

**MRS. SIMON:** I can wait. Miss Gordon, he's feeling all right, is he?

**REGINA:** Yes, as far as I know. Why?

**MRS. SIMON:** I don't know. Every day when he calls me up, he sounds so blue.

**REGINA:** Well, if there's anything wrong, he hasn't told me.

[*The door to* SIMON'*s office opens.*]

**SIMON:** No, after you.

**BAIRD:** Thank you.

[*He enters, followed by* SIMON.]

**SIMON:** Hello, Mama. What are you doing here?

**MRS. SIMON:** Hello, Georgie.

**SIMON:** Mr. Baird, I want you to meet my mother.

**BAIRD:** How do you do, Mrs. Simon?

**MRS. SIMON:** How do you do?

**SIMON:** She's a regular shrew. If I don't behave myself, she comes after me with a rolling pin.

**MRS. SIMON:** Georgie, how can you talk such foolishness?

**BAIRD:** I'm afraid I really must be going.

**SIMON:** All right, Mr. Baird. Thanks for coming in. Why don't you drop in some day and have lunch with me?

**BAIRD:** Thank you very much. Good day, Mrs. Simon.

**MRS. SIMON:** Good-bye.

[BAIRD *exits.*]

SIMON: That's my pal, Francis Clark Baird. He's one of the finest, handsomest, blue-blooded stuffed shirts I ever met.

MRS. SIMON: What's the matter with you, Georgie?

SIMON: With me? There's nothing the matter with me! Why should there be something the matter with me? I'm just feeling good, that's all. Can't I feel good if I want to?

MRS. SIMON: I'm glad you're feeling good, Georgie.

SIMON: I'm feeling fine, Mama. I never felt so fine in my life. How about a little dance? Come on, Lena, give me a dance. [*He seizes her and whirls her around.*]

MRS. SIMON: Georgie, are you *verruckt*?[6] [*Pushing him away.*]

SIMON: You're a fine dancer, you are. I'll have to give you a few lessons. Come on, I'll give you a lesson right now.

MRS. SIMON: Georgie, be a good boy! Now.

SIMON: That's a beautiful hat you have on, Mama. Is that a new hat?

MRS. SIMON: Yes, of course. Two years ago, it was new.

SIMON: I never saw it before. [*He takes a roll of bills out of his pocket and gives her one.*] Here, buy yourself a new hat.

MRS. SIMON: I don't want a new hat, Georgie.

SIMON: I want you to buy yourself a new hat. Take it.

MRS. SIMON: Georgie! [*She indicates* HENRY, *who is grinning with merriment.*]

SIMON: What? [*He turns.*] Go home, kid. I don't need you any more.

REGINA: You're expecting Mrs. Simon to call.

SIMON: That's all right. I'll take the call, myself. Go on, kid. Beat it.

HENRY: [*Getting his cap.*] Yes sir.

SIMON: [*Giving him a bill.*] And here, treat yourself to the ball game Sunday.

HENRY: Gee, thanks, Mr. Simon. Good night.

THE OTHERS: Good night.

[HENRY *exits.*]

SIMON: I used to be a lummox like that, too.

MRS. SIMON: You were no lummox, Georgie.

SIMON: A lot you know about lummoxes. Rexie, go home.

REGINA: I'm in no hurry.

SIMON: Go home, I tell you. Don't you know there's a law against night work for women?

---

6 Crazy.

[*He takes her by the shoulder and pushes her towards the door of his office.*]

**REGINA:** Are you sure you don't need me?

**SIMON:** Listen, if you don't go right away, I'll drop you out of the window. Go on, run along.

**REGINA:** Well, good night, Mrs. Simon.

**MRS. SIMON:** Good night, Miss Gordon.

[REGINA *exits to* SIMON'*s office.*]

**MRS. SIMON:** Georgie, why do you act like crazy?

**SIMON:** I'm just feeling good, that's all. Don't you like to see me feeling good?

**MRS. SIMON:** I didn't think you were feeling good, Georgie. That's why I came in to see you. It's a whole week since I saw you, and over the telephone you sounded so blue. I was worried about you.

**SIMON:** There's nothing to worry about, Mama. I've been busy, that's all. And I had one or two important things on my mind. That's why I haven't been to see you. But everything is all right now. And I feel great.

**MRS. SIMON:** I knew there was something wrong.

**SIMON:** It's all over now, I tell you, Mama—[*The telephone buzzes.*] Wait a minute. That must be Cora. [*He goes to the switchboard and plugs in.*] Hello—Yes, darling, this is me speaking—Listen, sweetheart, I've got some wonderful news for you—Yes, listen, everything is all right—You know, the Baird matter—Yes, it's all fixed up and it's going to be all right and there's nothing to worry about—I knew you would be. Where are you now?—Well, listen, darling, get right off. You've only got ten minutes—Why, didn't you get my note?—Yes, but I told you I thought I'd be able to go with you, in two or three weeks—But you've still got time to get off. We'll have a little celebration tonight. Just the two of us—But, darling, it's only postponing it two or three weeks—But nothing could interfere now. Everything is all right, now—Oh, oh—You mean you don't want to—I see—Yes—Yes—Yes, sure. I wouldn't want you to do anything unreasonable—Yes, I see—No, it's all right—No—No—Thanks—Well, have a wonderful trip—Good-bye.

[*He disconnects and sits motionless at the switchboard.* MRS. SIMON *watches him anxiously. Then, after a moment, she goes over to him.*]

MRS. SIMON: [*Putting her hand on his shoulder.*] Georgie!

SIMON: [*Startled.*] What's the matter, Mama? What do you want?

MRS. SIMON: Georgie, is something wrong? Tell Mama.

SIMON: There's nothing wrong, Mama. Didn't I tell you there's nothing wrong?

MRS. SIMON: Why don't you tell me, Georgie?

SIMON: Let me alone, Mama. Can't you let me alone?

MRS. SIMON: Yes, Georgie. Only if I can help you—

SIMON: I don't want any help. You can help me by going home, that's how you can help me.

MRS. SIMON: All right, Georgie, if you want me to go, I'll go.

SIMON: Yes, I wish you would. I—I have some work to do.

MRS. SIMON: Good-bye, Georgie. Please take care of yourself.

SIMON: Good-bye, Mama. And stop worrying about me. I'm all right. [*She looks at him, silently, then exits.* SIMON *puts his hand across his eyes, then rises and walks slowly up and down the office. Then, suddenly, he hurries to the switchboard, takes down the telephone directory and looks up a number. Then he seats himself and begins dialing, when* REGINA *enters.* SIMON *abruptly stops dialing.*] I thought you went home.

REGINA: I just wanted to make sure there was nothing else you wanted.

SIMON: No, there isn't. I want you to go home, that's all I want.

REGINA: Yes sir. Good night.

SIMON: Good night. [REGINA *exits.* SIMON *waits to make sure that she has gone, then begins dialing.*] Goddam it! [*He has forgotten the number. He takes down the book and looks it up again, then dials it.*] Hello—9246?—I'd like to speak to Mr. Roy Darwin, please—Oh, is that so? When did he sail?—At six this evening, you mean?—I see—Oh, hello—Do you happen to know the boat he's sailing on?—Thank you.

[*He disconnects and clasps both temples with his hands. It is beginning to grow quite dark.* TEDESCO *comes out of his office.*]

TEDESCO: Oh, hello, George! Well, is everything all right? What's the matter?

SIMON: Nothing. I just thought everybody had gone. Yes, everything's all right.

TEDESCO: Well, thank God! Boy, but I'm happy about it. [*Wringing* SIMON'S *hand.*] Well, you must feel like a new man.

SIMON: Yes, I do. I feel fine.

TEDESCO: Well, what happened, tell me? Did he try to throw a bluff?

SIMON: No, he—Listen, John—I'll tell you about it tomorrow. I'm pretty tired now.

TEDESCO: How about dinner?

SIMON: I think I'll have to call it off, John. I'm pretty tired tonight.

TEDESCO: Well, hell, that's only natural. You've been under an awful strain.

SIMON: Yes, I guess that must be it.

TEDESCO: Well, as long as it turned out all right. A good rest tonight will fix you up.

SIMON: Yes, that's what I need: a good rest.

TEDESCO: Oh, what about Cora? Did you get her?

SIMON: No, I couldn't get her.

TEDESCO: Oh, then she sailed! That's too bad.

SIMON: Yes, she sailed. I couldn't get her.

TEDESCO: Well, you can send her a radiogram.

SIMON: Yes, sure. That's just what I'm going to do: send her a radiogram.

TEDESCO: You look all in, George. Come on, let me take you home.

SIMON: No, I'm all right, John. I've got—I've got one or two things to do before I go.

TEDESCO: Well, good night. I'll see you in the morning.

SIMON: Yes, sure. Good night, John.

TEDESCO: I'm sure glad it's all over.

SIMON: Yes, so am I.

TEDESCO: You know all I wish you, George.

SIMON: Thanks, John.

TEDESCO: Good night.

SIMON: Good night. [TEDESCO *exits. It has grown quite dark.* SIMON *gets up slowly and walks to the window. He stands there, looking out. Then suddenly, he throws the sash wide open, and climbing up on the sofa, stands upright on the windowsill. Then, holding the sash with both hands, he leans out. The entrance door opens and* REGINA *enters. She sees* SIMON *and smothers a scream with her hand.* SIMON *turns and sees her. Hoarsely.*] What do you want? What the hell do you want? [REGINA *does not answer. She stands looking at him, paralyzed with terror.* SIMON *jumps to the floor.*] What do you want here? Didn't I tell you to go home? What's the matter, can't you talk?

REGINA: I—I was in the ladies' room.

**SIMON:** In the ladies' room? What the hell were you doing in the ladies' room? You've been hanging around spying on me—that's what you've been doing.

**REGINA:** No, I haven't—honest, I haven't—I—

**SIMON:** Don't lie to me. You've been spying on me. What the hell do you mean by spying on me?

**REGINA:** I met Mr. Tedesco in the hall—he said you were still here—I was so worried—[*Suddenly beginning to sob.*] Oh, my God!

**SIMON:** Shut up! Shut up, do you hear me, or I'll break every goddam bone in your body. [*He makes a stop towards her, then collapses into the sofa. They remain without speaking,* REGINA *standing near the door, trying to control her sobs,* SIMON *trembling from head to foot. The telephone signal begins to buzz and goes on buzzing. At length.*] Answer that goddam thing. Can't you even answer the telephone?

[REGINA *goes to the switchboard.*]

**REGINA:** Hello—Yes—Yes—I'll see if he's still here. Who's calling, please? It's Mr. Theodore Wingdale, the president of the American Steel Company.

**SIMON:** Tell him to go to hell.

**REGINA:** Shall I say you're not in?

**SIMON:** I don't give a damn what you say.

**REGINA:** I'm afraid he's gone. Mr. Wingdale—Is there anything I can do? This is his secretary speaking—No, I don't—well, just one moment— He says it's a matter of life and death.

**SIMON:** What do I care? Tell him—Is that Wingdale himself?

**REGINA:** Yes sir.

**SIMON:** Well, tell him—Wait a minute, I'll talk to him myself. Let me get there. [*He takes* REGINA*'s place at switchboard.*] Hello, Mr. Wingdale— Yes, this is George Simon talking—Yes, she got me just as I was getting into the elevator. It's after office hours, you know—Yes—Well, what's the trouble? Oh, I see—Is that so? Yes—Yes—Have the police been there?—I see—Well, you haven't made any statement, have you?—No, that's right, don't say anything—And don't let the boy say anything either—Yes—I'll be there within an hour—Wait a minute, until I get the address—[*He fumbles around in the drawer of the desk. To* REGINA.] Put up the lights. [REGINA *switches on the lights.*] One moment, Mr.

Wingdale. [*He takes the box of chocolates from the drawer, then a memorandum pad.*] All right, go ahead—Yes—Yes—All right, I've got it—Yes, I'll be there before eight—One moment. You haven't consulted any other lawyer, have you?—All right—All right—Don't mention it—Good-bye. [*He disconnects. To* REGINA.] Wingdale of the American Steel Company. His twenty-seven-year-old son had a quarrel with his wife this afternoon and shot her dead.

REGINA: How awful!

SIMON: [*Nibbling a chocolate.*] They've only been married two years. And you know who she is, don't you? The daughter of one of the richest oil men in Texas. Can you imagine what a case that's going to be? We've got to get right on the job. Come on!

REGINA: Yes sir.

SIMON: I've got to get my hat.

REGINA: I'll get it for you.

SIMON: Never mind. We'll go out the other way. I'll bet he hasn't got a scrap of defense. Those millionaire's sons: they're a lot of good-for-nothings, that's what they are. Well, we'll have to see what we can dope out. Are you ready?

REGINA: Yes sir.

SIMON: All right, come on. We'll grab a sandwich on the way up.

[*They exit.*]

CURTAIN

173

# AWAKE AND SING!

*Clifford Odets*

*Awake and Sing!*, Circle in the Square, NY 1984. (L. to R.) Thomas G. Waites, Paul Sparer and Harry Hamlin. Photo: Martha Swope/TimePix.

# INTRODUCTION

By 1938, when he was featured on the cover of *Time*, Clifford Odets had already been lionized as "the country's most promising playwright," "the proletarian Jesus," and "the poet of the Jewish middle class." Born in Philadelphia in 1906, Odets grew up in the Bronx, which he would dramatize so vividly. Less interested in formal education than in literature, movies, and the stage, he quit high school to become an actor. He was playing bit parts with the Theatre Guild when he was invited to join those who broke away from the Guild to become charter members of the Group Theatre.

The Group, a producing company founded in 1931 by Cheryl Crawford, Harold Clurman and Lee Strasberg, was emphatically left wing. It was firmly rooted in the concept of community, both as an egalitarian ensemble and in terms of its mission: to dramatize from a proletarian point of view concerns central to American life. The Group's interest in Odets, a bit player, is not as easy to understand as his attraction to the Group.

The young Odets was moody and depressed. He had a stormy relationship with his overbearing father and longed to find a more hospitable home. He found it with the Group, which billed its players alphabetically, paid them equally (if it paid them at all), and lived in communal poverty. Odets confided emotionally to their public diary that he had finally found strong roots. The symbiosis reaped mutual benefits. The Group's distinguished productions of half of Odets's dozen plays rank high in its important contributions to the American theatre. Odets became an overnight success, but not as an actor.

As an understudy waiting in vain to go on for Luther Adler as the driven Jewish careerist in John Howard Lawson's *Success Story*, a "sore" Odets wrote a script called "I Got the Blues." Despite the warm reception of the second act by audiences at Green Mansions, an adult camp, the Group was reluctant to mount the entire work. However, some of its actors did stage Odets's one-act play about the genesis of a taxi drivers' strike. *Waiting for Lefty*'s sensational triumph was instant and unanticipated. It has since become the very definition of an agitprop play, its revolutionary statement earning it national and international acclaim and production. The thunderous reception that greeted *Lefty* in 1935 also changed the Group's mind about Odets the playwright. The company prepared to stage "I Got the Blues," newly revised and retitled *Awake and Sing!*

1935 was a momentous year for Odets. *Lefty*'s remarkable premiere in January was followed a month later by *Awake and Sing!*—a one-two punch that rocketed the former bit player to acclaim. Then in March his anti-Nazi play, *Till the Day I Die*, opened in New York and inspired productions across the country. The play was banned in seven cities; its Los Angeles producer was beaten by Nazi sympathizers. In May, Group actor Morris Carnovsky performed "I Can't Sleep," a powerful monologue by a worker who has betrayed his fellows. Meantime, Odets's championing of proletarian causes and human rights kept him busy offstage. A member of the Communist Party for eight months, he headed an ill-fated mission to Cuba where these would-be investigators of injustice were promptly arrested and deported. The year ended on another disappointment—the failure in December of *Paradise Lost*, a play about the dashed aspirations of two Bronx Jewish families.

Small wonder that, by early 1936, Odets was ready to accept an extravagant Hollywood offer. He got off to a slow start. His first script, *The General Died at Dawn*, provoked critic Frank Nugent's famous gibe, "Odets, where is thy sting?"

However, by 1938, when he became the subject of the *Time* cover story, Odets had redeemed himself in Hollywood and returned to the Broadway stage with *Golden Boy* (1937). Here, as in *The Big Knife* (1949), he developed a theme he had introduced in the earlier, Jewish plays: artistic, sensitive individuals whose quest for self-actualization conflicts with their desire for material success. Almost until his death in 1963, Odets himself lived this tension, alternating between the commercial certainty of screenwriting and the chancier artistry of the theatre.

After *Awake and Sing!* and *Paradise Lost*, Odets did not direct his attention to Jews again until his last play, *The Flowering Peach* (1954). Drawing on family figures rather than on Scripture, he made Jews of the Noah clan. The story of the Flood functions as a metaphor for contemporary life threatened by atomic obliteration and as a context for an exploration of the limits of human responsibility. Sadly, many of the fresh Jewish characters Odets had developed two decades earlier emerge in *Peach* as parodies of themselves. Reviewers of the original production generously accepted Odets's recasting of the powerful material from Genesis as a Jewish family comedy. Although several critics faulted the "repetitious family wranglings," and "petty quarrels," and one was "embarrassed" by the "wise-cracking burlesque," all praised comedian Menasha Skulnik's performance as Noah. The play, which became a Richard Rodgers musical, *Two By Two*, is occasionally revived, though its 1994 production by New York's National Actors Theatre, for example, evoked little enthusiasm. *Peach*'s timeless legend and the universal questions it raises are not well served by its cast of largely stereotyped characters. Among them, however, Noah's youngest son, Japheth, stands out for his stubborn self-sufficiency. Japheth's fierce struggle for independence from parental control echoes Ralph Berger's in *Awake and Sing!* His unshakable belief in humankind, much more focused than Ralph's, provides reassurance that at least one of Odets's memorable early Jewish characters could mature without flattening into a stock type.

The Group had been initially reluctant to stage *Awake and Sing!* because they objected to the play's "small horizon" and "messy kitchen realism," that is, its preoccupation with the assorted miseries of the Bergers. As Odets biographer Margaret Brenman-Gibson has shown, these woes and discontents translate many of Odets's own. The work, in John Gassner's words, had to "emerge out of its private chrysalis" — an evolution explicit in the revised title. To bring the play squarely into alignment with the Group's proletarian view of its times, Odets emphasized conflicting ideologies and the climate of the Depression as forces aggravating tensions in the Berger household. Ironically, in making his work more stageworthy for his predominantly Jewish colleagues, Odets stripped away much of its original Jewish explicitness. Since *Awake and Sing!* remains a profoundly Jewish play, it is interesting to see what was accomplished in the rewriting.

The early drafts of *I Got the Blues* are laden with Yiddish expressions, and Odets reconsidered them judiciously. Sometimes he just translated them (Morty originally said Bessie's cooking "*schmekt gitt*" rather than "smells good"). A few changes simplified the plot (Bessie first opposed Ralph's girlfriend not as "a girl with no parents" [named Miss Hirsch in the final script], but "a *shiksa*!"). But Odets listened carefully to his characters as he revised, turning the language of *Awake and Sing!* into one of the play's notable achievements. Brimming with the vigor, cadences and non sequiturs ("You ain't sunburnt—you heard me") appropriate to its dramatis personae, these speech patterns accurately represent the Yiddishized English and urban idiom of countless American Jews. Critic Grenville Vernon remarked that the dialogue seemed not to be "created by the dramatist, but inherited by him from the speech of his people."

At the same time, in rewriting dialogue, Odets eliminated numerous specifically Jewish allusions, making characterizations contribute more pointedly to the plot. For instance, Jacob's earlier stream of references to "the Jew Bible" is replaced by repeated socialist sentiments ("It needs a new world."). Such statements reorient his objections to the values prevailing in his daughter's house ("In my day the propaganda was for God. Now it's for success") and make clearer his legacy to Ralph (DO!").

Odets eliminated some superb material that fleshed out characterizations without contributing to the forward motion of the play. Morty, harassed by agitation at his shop, originally reflected bitterly on its organizers: "I see even the Jews are changing in modern America—a people who hung together for thousands of years like bananas on a bunch. Who sits shivah nowadays for the dead—to sit seven days on a soap box? Now they talk from the boxes and make strikes. Kikes in Union Square who yell no equality in the country. Crazy!" However perceptive this speech, it came from the mouth of a man who expresses little awareness of Jewishness, his own or others'. Similarly out of character is a beautiful line Odets cut: The cynical Moe's extravagant promises to Hennie originally included the kind of ecstasy experienced by "the kid who stood in the synagogue while the Rabbi sang sad songs."

The transformation of what the Group had first seen as "the cruel Jewish mother" of *Blues* warrants fuller examination. According to Brenman-Gibson, she embodies the resentment Odets felt for his father. Seizing the opportunity to disdain the object of his wrath, Odets at first gave the offending parent no name other than "Mrs." One excised incident vividly dramatizes behavior that Odets found reprehensible. Ralph brings a tramp home for a meal, only to have Mrs. turn him out ("He should eat off our dishes and make germs?"), to which Ralph responds by giving the man his own next day's lunch money—both deeds unmistakable acts of *tsedakah* (charity). Mean-spirited Mrs. has an astonishing speech in which she disparages the men in her life ("Mice from the kitchen"), proclaims herself at fifty ready to "handle two more husbands yet," and vows to "step into the street a free woman." It is easier to view Mrs. as a prescient caricature of angry feminists to come decades in the future than as the prototype of Bessie Berger, one of Clifford Odets's most memorable characters.

In reworking his play, Odets added a dimension to the mother that, by contrast with the emendations noted above, makes the play more authentically Jewish. When Mrs. breaks Jacob's Caruso records in *Blues*, she is energized by the malice that inspires her behavior throughout. By contrast, the Bessie of *Awake and Sing!*, however controlling and insensitive, is not nasty. Other motives explain her one act of violence, and they are not hard to find. The record-smashing scene shows the cost to Bessie of being a dream-buster and the reliable dispenser of workable, if unsavory, solutions. She finally vents her frustrations as a daughter exasperated with her father's ineffectuality, as a wife, disillusioned by the "paradiso" promised in Caruso's arias, but unrealizable in her marriage to a man who never stopped believing the Messiah would come in the form of a hair restorative or a winning sweepstakes ticket, and as a mother who saw her children had what they needed, not what they asked for, or even what she might have liked to give. Bessie Berger may be one of the strongest representations of the Odetsian struggle between idealism and pragmatism. By developing this materfamilias from a personification of spite to a fully dimensional human being, Odets made her represent countless first-generation American Jewish women who, by instinct or from Old World experience, understood "when one lives in the jungle one must look out for the wild life."

Nor does this masterful characterization stand alone. *Awake and Sing!* shaped and sharpened a half dozen carefully drawn types from *Blues*: the restless *belle juive*, the mild husband bewildered by "life in America," the sybaritic money-man, the socialist grandfather, the bitter racketeer, and the sensitive, discontented young hero. They have had long stage lives, not always (as *The Flowering Peach* demonstrates) retaining the sap and dimension with which Odets endowed them in the extraordinary descriptions that precede the play.

The work itself, well received in 1935, was quickly translated into Yiddish, understandably becoming a favorite production of Yiddish units of the Federal Theatre Project. The continuing worldwide popularity of the play belies its grounding in America of the thirties. Writing of the 1992 Chicago production, critic John Lahr saw untarnished the play's "quirky blend of deep Jewish pessimism and a very American desire to shine."

*Awake and Sing!* was presented by the Group Theatre at the Belasco Theatre on the evening of February 19, 1935, with the following members of the Group Theatre Acting Company:

| | |
|---|---|
| Myron Berger | Art Smith |
| Bessie Berger | Stella Adler |
| Jacob | Morris Carnovsky |
| Hennie Berger | Phoebe Brand |
| Ralph Berger | Jules Garfield |
| Schlosser | Roman Bohnen |
| Moe Axelrod | Luther Adler |
| Uncle Morty | J. E. Bromberg |
| Sam Feinschreiber | Sanford Meisner |

The production was directed by Harold Clurman. The setting was designed by Boris Aronson.

*The entire action takes place in an apartment in the Bronx, New York City.*

# THE CHARACTERS OF THE PLAY

All of the characters in *Awake and Sing!* share a fundamental activity: a struggle for life amidst petty conditions.

BESSIE BERGER, *as she herself states, is not only the mother in this home but also the father. She is constantly arranging and taking care of her family. She loves life, likes to laugh, has great resourcefulness and enjoys living from day to day. A high degree of energy accounts for her quick exasperation at ineptitude. She is a shrewd judge of realistic qualities in people in the sense of being able to gauge quickly their effectiveness. In her eyes all of the people in the house are equal. She is naïve and quick in emotional response. She is afraid of utter poverty. She is proper according to her own standards, which are fairly close to those of most middle-class families. She knows that when one lives in the jungle one must look out for the wild life.*

**185**

**MYRON,** *her husband, is a born follower. He would like to be a leader. He would like to make a million dollars. He is not sad or ever depressed. Life is an even sweet event to him, but the "old days" were sweeter yet. He has a dignified sense of himself. He likes people. He likes everything. But he is heartbroken without being aware of it.*

**HENNIE** *is a girl who has had few friends, male or female. She is proud of her body. She won't ask favors. She travels alone. She is fatalistic about being trapped, but will escape if possible. She is self-reliant in the best sense. Till the day she dies she will be faithful to a loved man. She inherits her mother's sense of humor and energy.*

**RALPH** *is a boy with a clean spirit. He wants to know, wants to learn. He is ardent, he is romantic, he is sensitive. He is naïve too. He is trying to find why so much dirt must be cleared away before it is possible to "get to first base."*

**JACOB,** *too, is trying to find a right path for himself and the others. He is aware of justice, of dignity. He is an observer of the others, compares their activities with his real and ideal sense of life. This produces a reflective nature. In this home he is a constant boarder. He is a sentimental idealist with no power to turn ideal to action. With physical facts — such as housework— he putters. But as a barber he demonstrates the flair of an artist. He is an old Jew with living eyes in his tired face.*

**UNCLE MORTY** *is a successful American businessman with five good senses. Something sinister comes out of the fact that the lives of others seldom touch him deeply. He holds to his own line of life. When he is generous he wants others to be aware of it. He is pleased by attention— a rich relative to the Berger family. He is a shrewd judge of material values. He will die unmarried. Two and two make four, never five with him. He can blink in the sun for hours, a*

*fat tomcat. Tickle him, he laughs. He lives in a
penthouse with a real Japanese butler to serve him. He
sleeps with dress models, but not from his own show-
rooms. He plays cards for hours on end. He smokes
expensive cigars. He sees every Mickey Mouse cartoon
that appears. He is a 32-degree Mason. He is really
deeply intolerant finally.*

MOE AXELROD *lost a leg in the war. He seldom forgets
that fact. He has killed two men in extra-marital
activity. He is mordant, bitter. Life has taught him a
disbelief in everything, but he will fight his way
through. He seldom shows his feelings: fights against
his own sensitivity. He has been everywhere and seen
everything. All he wants is Hennie. He is very proud.
He scorns the inability of others to make their way in
life, but he likes people for whatever good qualities
they possess. His passionate outbursts come from a
strong but contained emotional mechanism.*

SAM FEINSCHREIBER *wants to find a home. He is a
lonely man, a foreigner in a strange land, hypersensitive about this fact, conditioned by the humilia-
tion of not making his way alone. He has a sense of
others laughing at him. At night he gets up and sits
alone in the dark. He hears acutely all the small
sounds of life. He might have been a poet in another
time and place. He approaches his wife as if he were
always offering her a delicate flower. Life is a high
chill wind weaving itself around his head.*

SCHLOSSER, *the janitor, is an overworked German whose
wife ran away with another man and left him with
a young daughter who in turn ran away and joined a
burlesque show as chorus girl. The man suffers rheu-
matic pains. He has lost his identity twenty years before.*

**THE SCENE:** *Exposed on the stage are the dining room and adjoining front
room of the Berger apartment. These two rooms are typically furnished. There is
a curtain between them. A small door off the front room leads to Jacob's room.*

*When his door is open one sees a picture of Sacco and Vanzetti on the wall and several shelves of books. Stage left of this door presents the entrance to the foyer hall of the apartment. The two other bedrooms of the apartment are off this hall, but not necessarily shown.*

*Stage left of the dining room presents a swinging door which opens on the kitchen.*

Awake and sing, ye that dwell in dust:
Isaiah 26:19

# ACT ONE

**TIME:** *The present; the family finishing supper.*

**PLACE:** *An apartment in the Bronx, New York City.*

RALPH: Where's advancement down the place? Work like crazy! Think they see it? You'd drop dead first.

MYRON: Never mind, son, merit never goes unrewarded. Teddy Roosevelt used to say—

HENNIE: It rewarded you—thirty years a haberdashery clerk!

[JACOB *laughs*]

RALPH: All I want's a chance to get to first base!

HENNIE: That's all?

RALPH: Stuck down in that joint on Fourth Avenue—a stock clerk in a silk house! Just look at Eddie. I'm as good as he is—pulling in two-fifty a week for forty-eight minutes a day. A headliner, his name in all the papers.

JACOB: That's what you want, Ralphie? Your name in the paper?

RALPH: I wanna make up my own mind about things ... be something! Didn't I want to take up tap dancing, too?

BESSIE: So take lessons. Who stopped you?

RALPH: On what?

BESSIE: On what? Save money.

RALPH: Sure, five dollars a week for expenses and the rest in the house. I can't save even for shoelaces.

BESSIE: You mean we shouldn't have food in the house, but you'll make a jig on the street corner?

RALPH: I mean something.

**BESSIE:** You also mean something when you studied on the drum, Mr. Smartie!

**RALPH:** I don't know ... Every other day to sit around with the blues and mud in your mouth.

**MYRON:** That's how it is—life is like that—a cake walk.

**RALPH:** What's it get you?

**HENNIE:** A four-car funeral.

**RALPH:** What's it for?

**JACOB:** What's it for? If this life leads to a revolution it's a good life. Otherwise it's for nothing.

**BESSIE:** Never mind, Pop! Pass me the salt.

**RALPH:** It's crazy—all my life I want a pair of black and white shoes and can't get them. It's crazy!

**BESSIE:** In a minute I'll get up from the table. I can't take a bite in my mouth no more.

**MYRON:** [*Restraining her.*] Now, Momma, just don't excite yourself—

**BESSIE:** I'm so nervous I can't hold a knife in my hand.

**MYRON:** Is that a way to talk, Ralphie? Don't Momma work hard enough all day? [BESSIE *allows herself to be reseated*]

**BESSIE:** On my feet twenty-four hours?

**MYRON:** On her feet—

**RALPH:** [*Jumps up*] What do I do—go to nightclubs with Greta Garbo? Then when I come home can't even have my own room? Sleep on a day bed in the front room! [*Choked, he exits to front room.*]

**BESSIE:** He's starting up that stuff again. [*Shouts to him*] When Hennie here marries you'll have her room—I should only live to see the day.

**HENNIE:** Me, too. [*They settle down to serious eating.*]

**MYRON:** This morning the sink was full of ants. Where they come from I just don't know. I thought it was coffee grounds ... and then they began moving.

**BESSIE:** You gave the dog eat?

**JACOB:** I gave the dog eat. [HENNIE *drops a knife and picks it up again.*]

**BESSIE:** You got dropsy tonight.

**HENNIE:** Company's coming.

**MYRON:** You can buy a ticket for fifty cents and win fortunes. A man came in the store—it's the Irish Sweepstakes.

**BESSIE:** What?

**MYRON:** Like a raffle, only different. A man came in—

**BESSIE:** Who spends fifty-cent pieces for Irish raffles? They threw out a family on Dawson Street today. All the furniture on the sidewalk. A fine old woman with gray hair.

JACOB: Come eat, Ralph.

MYRON: A butcher on Beck Street won eighty thousand dollars.

BESSIE: Eighty thousand dollars! You'll excuse my expression, you're bughouse!

MYRON: I seen it in the paper—on one ticket—765 Beck Street.

BESSIE: Impossible!

MYRON: He did... yes he did. He says he'll take his old mother to Europe... an Austrian—

HENNIE: Europe...

MYRON: Six percent on eighty thousand—forty-eight hundred a year.

BESSIE: I'll give you money. Buy a ticket in Hennie's name. Say, you can't tell—lightning never struck us yet. If they win on Beck Street we could win on Longwood Avenue.

JACOB: [*Ironically*] If it rained pearls—who would work?

BESSIE: Another county heard from. [RALPH *enters and silently seats himself.*]

MYRON: I forgot, Beauty—Sam Feinschreiber sent you a present. Since I brought him for supper he just can't stop talking about you.

HENNIE: What's that "mockie"[1] bothering about? Who needs him?

MYRON: He's a very lonely boy.

HENNIE: So I'll sit down and bust out crying "'cause he's lonely."

BESSIE: [*Opening candy.*] He'd marry you one two three.

HENNIE: Too bad about him.

BESSIE: [*Naively delighted*] Chocolate peanuts.

HENNIE: Loft's weekend special, two for thirty-nine.

BESSIE: You could think about it. It wouldn't hurt.

HENNIE: [*Laughing.*] To quote Moe Axelrod, "Don't make me laugh."

BESSIE: Never mind laughing. It's time you already had in your head a serious thought. A girl twenty-six don't grow younger. When I was your age it was already a big family with responsibilities.

HENNIE: [*Laughing*] Maybe that's what ails you, Mom.

BESSIE: Don't you feel well?

HENNIE: 'Cause I'm laughing? I feel fine. It's just funny—that poor guy sending me presents 'cause he loves me.

BESSIE: I think it's very, very nice.

HENNIE: Sure... swell!

---

[1] Greenhorn

**BESSIE:** Mrs. Marcus' Rose is engaged to a Brooklyn boy, a dentist. He came in his car today. A little dope should get such a boy. [*Finished with the meal,* BESSIE, MYRON *and* JACOB *rise. Both* HENNIE *and* RALPH *sit silently at the table, he eating. Suddenly she rises.*]

**HENNIE:** Tell you what, Mom. I saved for a new dress, but I'll take you and Pop to the Franklin. Don't need a dress. From now on I'm planning to stay in nights. Hold everything!

**BESSIE:** What's the matter—a bedbug bit you suddenly?

**HENNIE:** It's a good bill—Belle Baker. Maybe she'll sing "Eli, Eli."

**BESSIE:** We was going to a movie.

**HENNIE:** Forget it. Let's go.

**MYRON:** I see in the papers [*as he picks his teeth*] Sophie Tucker took off twenty-six pounds. Fearful business with Japan.

**HENNIE:** Write a book, Pop! Come on, we'll go early for good seats.

**MYRON:** Moe said you had a date with him for tonight.

**BESSIE:** Axelrod?

**HENNIE:** I told him no, but he don't believe it. I'll tell him no for the next hundred years, too.

**MYRON:** Don't break appointments, Beauty, and hurt people's feelings. [BESSIE *exits*]

**HENNIE:** His hands got free-wheeling. [*she exits.*]

**MYRON:** I don't know … people ain't the same. N-O—The whole world's changing right under our eyes. Presto! No manners. Like the great Italian lover in the movies. What was his name? The Sheik … No one remembers? [*Exits, shaking his head*]

**RALPH:** [*Unmoving at the table.*] Jake …

**JACOB:** Noo?

**RALPH:** I can't stand it.

**JACOB:** There's an expression—"strong as iron you must be."

**RALPH:** It's a cock-eyed world.

**JACOB:** Boys like you could fix it some day. Look on the world, not on yourself so much. Every country with starving millions, no? In Germany and Poland a Jew couldn't walk in the street. Everybody hates, nobody loves.

**RALPH:** I don't get all that.

**JACOB:** For years, I watched you grow up. Wait! You'll graduate from my university. [*The others enter, dressed.*]

**MYRON:** [*Lighting.*] Good cigars now for a nickel.

BESSIE: [*To* JACOB] After take Tootsie on the roof. [*To* RALPH]: What'll
you do?

RALPH: Don't know.

BESSIE: You'll see the boys around the block?

RALPH: I'll stay home every night!

MYRON: Momma don't mean for you—

RALPH: I'm flying to Hollywood by plane, that's what I'm doing. [*Doorbell
rings.* MYRON *answers it.*]

BESSIE: I don't like my boy to be seen with those tramps on the corner.

MYRON: [*Without*] Schlosser's here, Momma, with the garbage can.

BESSIE: Come in here, Schlosser. [*Sotto voce.*] Wait, I'll give him a piece of
my mind. [MYRON *ushers in* SCHLOSSER, *who carries a garbage can in each
hand.*] What's the matter, the dumbwaiter's broken again?

SCHLOSSER: Mr. Wimmer sends new ropes next week. I got a sore arm.

BESSIE: He should live so long, your Mr. Wimmer. For seven years already
he's sending new ropes. No dumbwaiter, no hot water, no steam—In a
respectable house, they don't allow such conditions.

SCHLOSSER: In a decent house, dogs are not running to make dirty the
hallway.

BESSIE: Tootsie's making dirty? Our Tootsie's making dirty in the hall?

SCHLOSSER: [*To* JACOB] I tell you yesterday again. You must not leave her—

BESSIE: [*Indignantly.*] Excuse me! Please don't yell on an old man. He's got
more brains in his finger than you got—I don't know where. Did you
ever see—he should talk to you an old man?

MYRON: Awful.

BESSIE: From now on we don't walk up the stairs no more. You keep it so
clean we'll fly in the windows.

SCHLOSSER: I speak to Mr. Wimmer.

BESSIE: Speak! Speak. Tootsie walks behind me like a lady any time, any
place. So good-bye... good-bye, Mr. Schlosser.

SCHLOSSER: I tell you dot—I verk verry hard here. My arms is... [*Exits in
confusion.*]

BESSIE: Tootsie should lay all day in the kitchen maybe. Give him back if he
yells on you. What's funny?

JACOB: [*Laughing.*] Nothing.

BESSIE: Come. [*Exits.*]

JACOB: Hennie, take care...

**HENNIE:** Sure.

**JACOB:** Bye-bye. [HENNIE *exits.* MYRON *pops head back in door.*]

**MYRON:** Valentino! That's the one! [*He exits.*]

**RALPH:** I never in my life even had a birthday party. Every time I went and cried in the toilet when my birthday came.

**JACOB:** [*Seeing* RALPH *remove his tie.*] You're going to bed?

**RALPH:** No, I'm putting on a clean shirt.

**JACOB:** Why?

**RALPH:** I got a girl ... Don't laugh!

**JACOB:** Who laughs? Since when?

**RALPH:** Three weeks. She lives in Yorkville with an aunt and uncle. A bunch of relatives, but no parents.

**JACOB:** An orphan girl—tch, tch.

**RALPH:** But she's got me! Boy, I'm telling you I could sing! Jake, she's like stars. She's so beautiful, you look at her and cry! She's like French words! We went to the park the other night. Heard the last band concert.

**JACOB:** Music...

**RALPH:** [*Stuffing shirt in trousers.*] It got cold and I gave her my coat to wear. We just walked along like that, see, without a word, see. I never was so happy in all my life. It got late ... we just sat there. She looked at me— you know what I mean, how a girl looks at you—right in the eyes? "I love you," she says, "Ralph." I took her home ... I wanted to cry. That's how I felt!

**JACOB:** It's a beautiful feeling.

**RALPH:** You said a mouthful!

**JACOB:** Her name is—

**RALPH:** Blanche.

**JACOB:** A fine name. Bring her sometimes here.

**RALPH:** She's scared to meet Mom.

**JACOB:** Why?

**RALPH:** You know Mom's not letting my sixteen bucks out of the house if she can help it. She'd take one look at Blanche and insult her in a minute—a kid who's got nothing.

**JACOB:** Boychick!

**RALPH:** What's the diff?

**JACOB:** It's no difference—a plain bourgeois prejudice—but when they find out a poor girl—it ain't so kosher.

**RALPH:** They don't have to know I've got a girl.

**JACOB:** What's in the end?

RALPH: Out I go! I don't mean maybe!

JACOB: And then what?

RALPH: Life begins.

JACOB: What life?

RALPH: Life with my girl. Boy, I could sing when I think about it! Her and me together—that's a new life!

JACOB: Don't make a mistake! A new death!

RALPH: What's the idea?

JACOB: Me, I'm the idea! Once I had in *my* heart a dream, a vision, but came marriage and then you forget. Children come and you forget because—

RALPH: Don't worry, Jake.

JACOB: Remember, a woman insults a man's soul like no other thing in the whole world!

RALPH: Why get so excited? No one—

JACOB: Boychick, wake up! Be something! Make your life something good. For the love of an old man who sees in your young days his new life, for such love take the world in your two hands and make it new. Go out and fight so life shouldn't be printed on dollar bills. A woman waits.

RALPH: Say I'm no fool!

JACOB: From my heart I hope not. In the meantime—[*Bell rings.*]

RALPH: See who it is, will you? [*Stands off.*] Don't want Mom to catch me with a clean shirt.

JACOB: [*Calls.*] Come in. [*Sotto voce.*] Moe Axelrod. [MOE *enters.*]

MOE: Hello girls, how's your whiskers? [*To* RALPH.] All dolled up. What's it, the weekly visit to the cat house?

RALPH: Please mind your business.

MOE: Okay, sweetheart.

RALPH: [*Taking a hidden dollar from a book.*] If Mom asks where I went—

JACOB: I know. Enjoy yourself.

RALPH: Bye-bye. [*He exits.*]

JACOB: Bye-bye.

MOE: Who's home?

JACOB: Me.

MOE: Good. I'll stick around a few minutes. Where's Hennie?

JACOB: She went with Bessie and Myron to a show.

MOE: She what?!

JACOB: You had a date?

MOE: [*Hiding his feelings.*] Here—I brought you some halavah.

JACOB: Halavah? Thanks. I'll eat a piece after.

**Moe:** So Ralph's got a dame? Hot stuff—a kid can't even play a card game.

**Jacob:** Moe, you're a no-good, a bum of the first water. To your dying day you won't change.

**Moe:** Where'd you get that stuff, a no-good?

**Jacob:** But I like you.

**Moe:** Didn't I go fight in France for democracy? Didn't I get my goddam leg shot off in that war the day before the armistice? Uncle Sam give me the Order of the Purple Heart, didn't he? What'd you mean, a no-good?

**Jacob:** Excuse me.

**Moe:** If you got an orange I'll eat an orange.

**Jacob:** No orange. An apple.

**Moe:** No oranges, huh? What a dump!

**Jacob:** Bessie hears you once talking like this she'll knock your head off.

**Moe:** Hennie went with, huh? She wantsa see me squirm, only I don't squirm for dames.

**Jacob:** You came to see her?

**Moe:** What for? I got a present for our boy friend, Myron. He'll drop dead when I tell him his gentle horse galloped in fifteen to one. He'll die.

**Jacob:** It really won? The first time I remember.

**Moe:** Where'd they go?

**Jacob:** A vaudeville by the Franklin.

**Moe:** What's special tonight?

**Jacob:** Someone tells a few jokes … and they forget the street is filled with starving beggars.

**Moe:** What'll they do—start a war?

**Jacob:** I don't know.

**Moe:** You oughta know. What the hell you got all the books for?

**Jacob:** It needs a new world.

**Moe:** That's why they had the big war—to make a new world, they said— safe for democracy. Sure every big general laying up in a Paris hotel with a half dozen broads pinned on his mustache. Democracy! I learned a lesson.

**Jacob:** An imperial war. You know what this means?

**Moe:** Sure, I know everything!

**Jacob:** By money men the interests must be protected. Who gave you such a rotten haircut? Please [*Fishing in his vest pocket*], give me for a cent a cigarette. I didn't have since yesterday—

**Moe:** [*Giving one.*] Don't make me laugh. [*A cent passes back and forth* *between them,* MOE *finally throwing it over his shoulder.*] Don't look so tired all the time. You're a wow—always sore about something.

JACOB: And you?

MOE: You got one thing—you can play pinochle. I'll take you over in a game. Then you'll have something to be sore on.

JACOB: Who'll wash dishes? [MOE *takes deck from buffet drawer.*]

MOE: Do 'em after. Ten cents a deal.

JACOB: Who's got ten cents?

MOE: I got ten cents. I'll lend it to you.

JACOB: Commence.

MOE: [*Shaking cards.*] The first time I had my hands on a pack in two days. Lemme shake up these cards. I'll make 'em talk. [JACOB *goes to his room, where he puts on a Caruso record.*]

JACOB: You should live so long.

MOE: Ever see oranges grow? I know a certain place—One summer I laid under a tree and let them fall right in my mouth.

JACOB: [*Off, the music is playing, the card game begins.*] From "L'Africana" ... a big explorer comes on a new land—"O Paradiso." From act four this piece. Caruso stands on the ship and looks on a Utopia. You hear? "Oh paradise! Oh paradise on earth! Oh blue sky, oh fragrant air —"

MOE: Ask him does he see any oranges?

[BESSIE, MYRON *and* HENNIE *enter.*]

JACOB: You came back so soon?

BESSIE: Hennie got sick on the way.

MYRON: Hello, Moe... [MOE *puts cards back in pocket.*]

BESSIE: Take off the phonograph, Pop. [*To* HENNIE.] Lay down ... I'll call the doctor. You should see how she got sick on Prospect Avenue. Two weeks already she don't feel right.

MYRON: Moe...?

BESSIE: Go to bed, Hennie.

HENNIE: I'll sit here.

BESSIE: Such a girl I never saw! Now you'll be stubborn?

MYRON: It's for your own good, Beauty. Influenza—

HENNIE: I'll sit here.

BESSIE: You ever seen a girl should say no to everything. She can't stand on her feet, so—

**HENNIE:** Don't yell in my ears. I hear. Nothing's wrong. I ate tuna fish for lunch.

**MYRON:** Canned goods…

**BESSIE:** Last week you also ate tuna fish?

**HENNIE:** Yeah, I'm funny for tuna fish. Go to the show—have a good time.

**BESSIE:** I don't understand what I did to God He blessed me with such children. From the whole world—

**MOE:** [*Coming to aid of* HENNIE.] For Chris' sake, don't kibitz so much!

**BESSIE:** You don't like it?

**MOE:** [*Aping.*] No, I don't like it.

**BESSIE:** That's too bad, Axelrod. Maybe it's better by your cigar-store friends. Here we're different people.

**MOE:** Don't gimme that cigar-store line, Bessie. I walked up five flights—

**BESSIE:** To take out Hennie. But my daughter ain't in your class, Axelrod.

**MOE:** To see Myron.

**MYRON:** Did he, did he, Moe?

**MOE:** Did he what?

**MYRON:** "Sky Rocket"?

**BESSIE:** You bet on a horse!

**MOE:** Paid twelve and a half to one.

**MYRON:** There! You hear that, Momma? Our horse came in. You see, it happens, and twelve and a half to one. Just look at that!

**MOE:** What the hell, a sure thing. I told you.

**BESSIE:** If Moe said a sure thing, you couldn't bet a few dollars instead of fifty cents?

**JACOB:** [*Laughs.*] "Aie, aie, aie."

**MOE:** [*At his wallet.*] I'm carrying six hundred "plunks" in big denominations.

**BESSIE:** A banker!

**MOE:** Uncle Sam sends me ninety a month.

**BESSIE:** So you save it?

**MOE:** Run it up, Run-it-up-Axelrod, that's me.

**BESSIE:** The police should know how.

**MOE:** [*Shutting her up.*] All right, all right—Change twenty, sweetheart.

**MYRON:** Can you make change?

**BESSIE:** Don't be crazy.

**MOE:** I'll meet a guy in Goldman's restaurant. I'll meet 'im and come back with change.

**MYRON:** [*Figuring on paper.*] You can give it to me tommorrow in the store.

**BESSIE:** [*Acquisitive.*] He'll come back, he'll come back!

**MOE:** Lucky I bet some bucks myself. [*In derision, to* HENNIE.] Let's step out tommorow night, Par-a-dise. [*Thumbs his nose at her, laughs mordantly and exits.*]

**MYRON:** Oh, that's big percentage. If I picked a winner every day…

**BESSIE:** Poppa, did you take Tootsie on the roof?

**JACOB:** All right.

**MYRON:** Just look at that—a cake walk. We can make—

**BESSIE:** It's enough talk. I got a splitting headache. Hennie, go in bed. I'll call Dr. Cantor.

**HENNIE:** I'll sit here… and don't call that old Ignatz 'cause I won't see him.

**MYRON:** If you get sick Momma can't nurse you. You don't want to go to a hospital.

**JACOB:** She don't look sick, Bessie, it's a fact.

**BESSIE:** She's got fever. I see in her eyes, so he tells me no. Myron, call Dr. Cantor. [MYRON *picks up phone, but* HENNIE *grabs it from him.*]

**HENNIE:** I don't want any doctor. I ain't sick. Leave me alone.

**MYRON:** Beauty, it's for your own sake.

**HENNIE:** Day in and day out pestering. Why are you always right and no one else can say a word?

**BESSIE:** When you have your own children—

**HENNIE:** I'm not sick! Hear what I say? I'm not sick! Nothing's the matter with me! I don't want a doctor. [BESSIE *is watching her with slow progressive understanding.*]

**BESSIE:** What's the matter?

**HENNIE:** Nothing, I told you!

**BESSIE:** You told me, but— [*A long pause of examination follows.*]

**HENNIE:** See much?

**BESSIE:** Myron, put down the… the… [*He slowly puts the phone down.*] Tell me what happened…

**HENNIE:** Brooklyn Bridge fell down.

**BESSIE:** [*Approaching*] I'm asking a question…

**MYRON:** What's happened, Momma?

**BESSIE:** Listen to me!

**HENNIE:** What the hell are you talking?

**BESSIE:** Poppa—take Tootsie on the roof.

**HENNIE:** [*Holding* JACOB *back.*] If he wants, he can stay here.

**199**

**MYRON:** What's wrong, Momma?

**BESSIE:** [*Her voice quivering slightly.*] Myron, your fine Beauty's in trouble. Our society lady…

**MYRON:** Trouble? I don't under—is it—?

**BESSIE:** Look in her face. [*He looks, understands and slowly sits in a chair, utterly crushed.*] Who's the man?

**HENNIE:** The Prince of Wales.

**BESSIE:** My gall is busting in me. In two seconds—

**HENNIE:** [*In a violent outburst.*] Shut up! Shut up! I'll jump out the window in a minute! Shut up! [*Finally she gains control of herself, says in a low, hard voice*] You don't know him.

**JACOB:** Bessie…

**BESSIE:** He's a Bronx boy?

**HENNIE:** From out of town.

**BESSIE:** What do you mean?

**HENNIE:** From out of town!

**BESSIE:** A long time you know him? You were sleeping by a girl from the office Saturday nights? You slept good, my lovely lady. You'll go to him… he'll marry you.

**HENNIE:** That's what you say.

**BESSIE:** That's what I say! He'll do it, take *my* word he'll do it!

**HENNIE:** Where? [*To* JACOB] Give her the letter. [JACOB *does so.*]

**BESSIE:** What? [*Reads.*] "Dear sir: In reply to your request of the 14th inst., we can state that no Mr. Ben Grossman has ever been connected with our organization…" You don't know where he is?

**HENNIE:** No.

**BESSIE:** [*Walks back and forth.*] Stop crying like a baby, Myron.

**MYRON:** It's like a play on the stage…

**BESSIE:** To a mother you couldn't say something before. I'm old-fashioned—like your friends I'm not smart—I don't eat chop suey and run around Coney Island with tramps. [*She walks reflectively to buffet, picks up a box of candy, puts it down, says to* MYRON] Tommorow night bring Sam Feinschreiber for supper.

**HENNIE:** I won't do it.

**BESSIE:** You'll do it, my fine beauty, you'll do it!

**HENNIE:** I'm not marrying a poor foreigner like him. Can't even speak an English word. Not me! I'll go to my grave without a husband.

**BESSIE:** You don't say! We'll find for you somewhere a millionaire with a pleasure boat. He's going to night school, Sam. For a boy only three years in the country he speaks very nice. In three years he put enough in the bank, a good living.

JACOB: This is serious?

BESSIE: What then? I'm talking for my health? He'll come tommorrow night for supper. By Saturday they're engaged.

JACOB: Such a thing you can't do.

BESSIE: Who asked your advice?

JACOB: Such a thing—

BESSIE: Never mind!

JACOB: The lowest from the low!

BESSIE: Don't talk! I'm warning you! A man who don't believe in God— with crazy ideas—

JACOB: So bad I never imagined you could be.

BESSIE: Maybe if you didn't talk so much it wouldn't happen like this. You with your ideas—I'm a mother. I raise a family they should have respect.

JACOB: Respect? [Spits.] Respect! For the neighbors' opinion! You insult me, Bessie!

BESSIE: Go in your room, Papa. Every job he ever had he lost because he's got a big mouth. He opens his mouth and the whole Bronx could fall in. Everybody said it—

MYRON: Momma, they'll hear you down the dumbwaiter.

BESSIE: A good barber not to hold a job a week. Maybe you never heard charity starts at home. You never heard it, Pop?

JACOB: All you know, I heard, and more yet. But Ralph you don't make like you. Before you do it, I'll die first. He'll find a girl. He'll go in a fresh world with her. This is a house? Marx said it—abolish such families.

BESSIE: Go in your room, Papa.

JACOB: Ralph you don't make like you!

BESSIE: Go lay in your room with Caruso and the books together.

JACOB: All right!

BESSIE: Go in the room!

JACOB: Some day I'll come out I'll—[Unable to continue, he turns, looks at HENNIE, goes to his door and says with an attempt at humor] Bessie, some day you'll talk to me so fresh...I'll leave the house for good! [He exits.]

BESSIE: [Crying.] You ever in your life seen it? He should dare! He should just dare say in the house another word. Your gall could bust from such a man. [Bell rings, MYRON goes.] Go to sleep now. It won't hurt.

HENNIE: Yeah? [MOE enters, a box in his hand. MYRON follows and sits down.]

MOE: [Looks around first—putting box on table.] Cake. [About to give

MYRON *the money, he turns instead to* BESSIE.] Six-fifty, four bits change...
come on, hand over half a buck. [*She does so. Of* MYRON] Who bit him?

BESSIE: We're losing our Hennie, Moe.

MOE: Why? What's the matter?

BESSIE: She made her engagement.

MOE: Zat so?

BESSIE: Today it happened... he asked her.

MOE: Did he? Who? Who's the corpse?

BESSIE: It's a secret.

MOE: In the bag, huh?

HENNIE: Yeah...

BESSIE: When a mother gives away an only daughter it's no joke. Wait,
when you'll get married you'll know...

MOE: [*Bitterly.*] Don't make me laugh—when I get married! What I think a
women? Take 'em all, cut 'em in little pieces like a herring in Greek salad.
A guy in France had the right idea—dropped his wife in a bathtub fulla
acid. [*Whistles.*] Sss, down the pipe! Pfft—not even a corset button left!

MYRON: Corsets don't have buttons.

MOE: [*To* HENNIE.] What's the great idea? Gone big time, Paradise? Christ,
it's suicide! Sure, kids you'll have, gold teeth, get fat, big in the
tangerines—

HENNIE: Shut your face!

MOE: Who's it—some dope pullin' down twenty bucks a week? Cut your
throat, sweetheart. Save time.

BESSIE: Never mind your two cents, Axelrod.

MOE: I say what I think—that's me!

HENNIE: That's you—a lousy fourflusher who'd steal the glasses off a
blind man.

MOE: Get hot!

HENNIE: My God, do I need it—to listen to this mutt shoot his mouth off?

MYRON: Please...

MOE: Now wait a minute, sweetheart, wait a minute. I don't have to take
that from you.

BESSIE: Don't yell at her!

HENNIE: For two cents I'd spit in your eye.

MOE: [*Throwing coin to table.*] Here's two bits. [HENNIE *looks at him and
then starts across the room.*]

BESSIE: Where are you going?

**HENNIE:** [*Crying.*] For my beauty nap, Mussolini. Wake me up when its apple blossom time in Normandy. [*Exits.*]

**MOE:** Pretty, pretty—a sweet gal, your Hennie. See the look in her eyes?

**BESSIE:** She don't feel well…

**MYRON:** Canned goods…

**BESSIE:** So don't start with her.

**MOE:** Like a battleship she's got it. Not like other dames—shove 'em and they lay. Not her. I got a yen for her and I don't mean a Chinee coin.

**BESSIE:** Listen, Axelrod, in my house you don't talk this way. Either have respect or get out.

**MOE:** When I think about it…maybe I'd marry her myself.

**BESSIE:** [*Suddenly aware of* MOE] You could—What do you mean, Moe?

**MOE:** You ain't sunburnt—you heard me.

**BESSIE:** Why don't you, Moe? An old friend of the family like you. It would be a blessing on all of us.

**MOE:** You said she's engaged.

**BESSIE:** But maybe she don't know her own mind. Say, it's—

**MOE:** I need a wife like a hole in the head… What's to know about women, I know. Even if I asked her. She won't do it! A guy with one leg—it gives her the heebie-jeebies. I know what she's looking for. An arrow-collar guy, a hero, but with a wad of jack. Only the two don't go together. But I got what it takes…plenty, and more where it comes from… [*Breaks off, snorts and rubs his knee. A pause. In his room* JACOB *puts on Caruso singing the lament from "The Pearl Fishers."*]

**BESSIE:** It's right—she wants a millionaire with a mansion on Riverside Drive. So go fight City Hall. Cake?

**MOE:** Cake.

**BESSIE:** I'll make tea. But one thing—she's got a fine boy with a business brain. Caruso! [*Exits into the front room and stands in the dark, at the window.*]

**MOE:** No wet smack…a fine girl… She'll burn that guy out in a month. [MOE *retrieves the quarter and spins it on the table.*]

**MYRON:** I remember that song…beautiful. Nora Bayes sang it at the old Proctor's Twenty-third Street—"When It's Apple Blossom Time in Normandy."…

**MOE:** She wantsa see me crawl—my head on a plate she wants! A snowball in hell's got a better chance. [*Out of sheer fury he spins the quarter in his fingers.*]

**MYRON:** [*as his eyes slowly fill with tears*]: Beautiful...

**MOE:** Match you for a quarter. Match you for any goddam thing you got. [*Spins the coin viciously.*] What the hell kind of house is this it ain't got an orange!!

SLOW CURTAIN

# ACT TWO

## SCENE 1

*One year later, a Sunday afternoon. The front room.* JACOB *is giving his son* MORDECAI [UNCLE MORTY] *a haircut, newspapers spread around the base of the chair.* MOE *is reading a newspaper, leg propped on a chair.* RALPH, *in another chair, is spasmodically reading a paper.* UNCLE MORTY *reads colored jokes. Silence, then* BESSIE *enters.*

BESSIE: Dinner's in half an hour, Morty.
MORTY: [*Still reading jokes.*] I got time.
BESSIE: A duck. Don't get hair on the rug, Pop. [*Goes to the window and pulls down shade.*] What's the matter the shade's up to the ceiling?
JACOB: [*Pulling it up again.*] Since when do I give a haircut in the dark? [*He mimics her tone.*]
BESSIE: When you're finished, pull it down. I like my house to look respectable. Ralphie, bring up two bottles seltzer from Weiss.
RALPH: I'm reading the paper.
BESSIE: Uncle Morty likes a little seltzer.
RALPH: I'm expecting a phone call.
BESSIE: Noo, if it comes you'll be back. What's the matter? [*Gives him money from apron pocket.*] Take down the old bottles.
RALPH: [*To* JACOB.] Get that call if it comes. Say I'll be right back. [JACOB *nods assent.*]
MORTY: [*Giving change from vest.*] Get grandpa some cigarettes.
RALPH: Okay. [*Exits.*]
JACOB: What's new in the paper, Moe?
MOE: Still jumping off the high buildings like flies—the big shots who lost all their cocoanuts. Pfft!
JACOB: Suicides?

**MOE:** Plenty can't take it—good in the break, but can't take the whip in the stretch.

**MORTY:** [*Without looking up.*] I saw happen Monday in my building. My hair stood up how they shoveled him together—like a pancake—a bankrupt manufacturer.

**MOE:** No brains.

**MORTY:** Enough … all over the sidewalk.

**JACOB:** If someone said five, ten years ago I couldn't make for myself a living, I wouldn't believe—

**MORTY:** Duck for dinner?

**BESSIE:** The best Long Island duck.

**MORTY:** I like goose.

**BESSIE:** A duck is just like a goose, only better.

**MORTY:** I like a goose.

**BESSIE:** The next time you'll be for Sunday dinner I'll make a goose.

**MORTY:** [*Sniffs deeply.*] Smells good. I'm a great boy for smells.

**BESSIE:** Ain't you ashamed? Once in a blue moon he should come to an only sister's house.

**MORTY:** Bessie, leave me live.

**BESSIE:** You should be ashamed!

**MORTY:** Quack quack!

**BESSIE:** No, better to lay around Mecca Temple playing cards with the Masons.

**MORTY:** [*With good nature.*] Bessie, don't you see Pop's giving me a haircut?

**BESSIE:** You don't need no haircut. Look, two hairs he took off.

**MORTY:** Pop likes to give me a haircut. If I said no he don't forget for a year, do you, Pop? An old man's like that.

**JACOB:** I still do an A-1 job.

**MORTY:** [*Winking.*] Pop cuts hair to fit the face, don't you, Pop?

**JACOB:** For sure, Morty. To each face a different haircut. Custom-built, no ready-made. A round face needs special—

**BESSIE:** [*Cutting him short.*] A Graduate from the B.M.T. [*Going.*] Don't forget the shade. [*The phone rings. She beats* JACOB *to it.*] Hello? Who is it, please? … Who is it please? … Miss Hirsch? No, he ain't here … No, I couldn't say when. [*Hangs up sharply.*]

**JACOB:** For Ralph?

**BESSIE:** A wrong number. [JACOB *looks at her and goes back to his job.*]

JACOB: Excuse me!

BESSIE: [*To* MORTY.] Ralphie took another cut down the place yesterday.

MORTY: Business is bad. I saw his boss Harry Glicksman Thursday. I bought some velvets ... they're coming in again.

BESSIE: Do something for Ralphie down there.

MORTY: What can I do? I mentioned it to Glicksman. He told me they squeezed out half the people ... [MYRON *enters dressed in apron.*]

BESSIE: What's gonna be the end? Myron's working only three days a week now.

MYRON: It's conditions.

BESSIE: Hennie's married with a baby ... money just don't come in. I never saw conditions should be so bad.

MORTY: Times'll change.

MOE: The only thing'll change is my underwear.

MORTY: These last few years I got my share of gray hairs. [*Still reading jokes without having looked up once.*] Ha, ha, ha—Popeye the sailor ate spinach and knocked out four bums.

MYRON: I'll tell you the way I see it. The country needs a great man now—a regular Teddy Roosevelt.

MOE: What this country needs is a good five-cent earthquake.

JACOB: So long labor lives it should increase private gain—

BESSIE: [*To* JACOB.] Listen, Poppa, go talk on the street corner. The government'll give you free board the rest of your life.

MORTY: I'm surprised. Don't I send a five-dollar check for Pop every week?

BESSIE: You could afford a couple more and not miss it.

MORTY: Tell me jokes. Business is so rotten I could just as soon lay all day in the Turkish bath.

MYRON: Why'd I come in here? [*Puzzled, he exits.*]

MORTY: [*To* MOE.] I hear the bootleggers still do business, Moe.

MOE: Wake up! I kissed bootlegging bye-bye two years back.

MORTY: For a fact? What kind of racket is it now?

MOE: If I told you, you'd know something. [HENNIE *comes from the bedroom.*]

HENNIE: Where's Sam?

BESSIE: Sam? In the kitchen.

HENNIE: [*Calls.*] Sam. Come take the diaper.

MORTY: How's the Mickey Louse? Ha, ha, ha ...

**HENNIE:** Sleeping.

**MORTY:** Ah, that's life to a baby. He sleeps—gets it in the mouth—sleeps some more. To raise a family nowadays you must be a damn fool.

**BESSIE:** Never mind, never mind, a woman who don't raise a family—a girl—should jump overboard. What's she good for? [*To* MOE—*to change the subject.*] Your leg bothers you bad?

**MOE:** It's okay, sweetheart.

**BESSIE:** [*To* MORTY.] It hurts him every time it's cold out. He's got four legs in the closet.

**MORTY:** Four wooden legs?

**MOE:** Three.

**MORTY:** What's the big idea?

**MOE:** Why not? Uncle Sam gives them out free.

**MORTY:** Say, maybe if Uncle Sam gave out less legs we could balance the budget.

**JACOB:** Or not have a war so they wouldn't have to give out legs.

**MORTY:** Shame on you, Pop. Everybody knows war is necessary.

**MOE:** Don't make me laugh. Ask me—the first time you pick up a dead one in the trench—then you learn war ain't so damn necessary.

**MORTY:** Say, you should kick. The rest of your life Uncle Sam pays you ninety a month. Look, not a worry in the world.

**MOE:** Don't make me laugh. Uncle Sam can take his seventy bucks and— [*Finishes with a gesture.*] Nothing good hurts. [*He rubs his stump.*]

**HENNIE:** Use a crutch, Axelrod. Give the stump a rest.

**MOE:** Mind your business, Feinschreiber.

**BESSIE:** It's a sensible idea.

**MOE:** Who asked you?

**BESSIE:** Look, he's ashamed.

**MOE:** So's your Aunt Fanny.

**BESSIE:** [*Naively.*] Who's got an Aunt Fanny? [*She cleans a rubber plant's leaves with her apron.*]

**MORTY:** It's a joke!

**MOE:** I don't want my paper creased before I read it. I want it fresh. Fifty times I said that.

**BESSIE:** Don't get so excited for a five-cent paper—our star boarder.

**MOE:** And I don't want no one using my razor either. Get it straight. I'm not buying ten blades a week for the Berger family. [*Furious, he limps out.*]

**BESSIE:** Maybe I'm using his razor too.

**Hennie:** Proud!

**Bessie:** You need luck with plants. I didn't clean off the leaves in a month.

**Morty:** You keep the house like a pin and I like your cooking. Any time Myron fires you, come to me, Bessie. I'll let the butler go and you'll be my housekeeper. I don't like Japs so much — sneaky.

**Bessie:** Say, you can't tell. Maybe any day I'm coming to stay. [Hennie *exits.*]

**Jacob:** Finished.

**Morty:** How much, Ed. Pinaud? [*Disengages self from chair.*]

**Jacob:** Five cents.

**Morty:** Still five cents for a haircut to fit the face?

**Jacob:** Prices don't change by me. [*Takes a dollar.*] I can't change —

**Morty:** Keep it. But yourself a Packard. Ha, ha, ha.

**Jacob:** [*Taking large envelope from pocket.*] Please, you'll keep this for me. Put it away.

**Morty:** What is it?

**Jacob:** My insurance policy. I don't like it should lay around where something could happen.

**Morty:** What could happen?

**Jacob:** Who knows, robbers, fire... they took next door. Fifty dollars from O'Reilly.

**Morty:** Say, lucky a Berger didn't lose it.

**Jacob:** Put it downtown in the safe. Bessie don't have to know.

**Morty:** It's made out to Bessie?

**Jacob:** No, to Ralph.

**Morty:** To Ralph?

**Jacob:** He don't know. Some day he'll get three thousand.

**Morty:** You got good years ahead.

**Jacob:** Behind. [Ralph *enters.*]

**Ralph:** Cigarettes. Did a call come?

**Jacob:** A few minutes. She don't let me answer it.

**Ralph:** Did Mom say I was coming back?

**Jacob:** No. [Morty *is back at new jokes.*]

**Ralph:** She starting that stuff again? [Bessie *enters.*] A call come for me?

**Bessie:** [*Waters pot from milk bottle.*] A wrong number.

**Jacob:** Don't say a lie, Bessie.

**Ralph:** Blanche said she'd call me at two — was it her?

**Bessie:** I said a wrong number.

RALPH: Please, Mom, if it was her tell me.

BESSIE: You call me a liar next. You got no shame—to start a scene in front of Uncle Morty. Once in a blue moon he comes—

RALPH: What's the shame? If my girl calls, I wanna know it.

BESSIE: You made enough mish mosh with her until now.

MORTY: I'm surprised, Bessie. For the love of Mike tell him yes or no.

BESSIE: I didn't tell him? No!

MORTY: [*To* RALPH.] No! [RALPH *goes to a window and looks out.*]

BESSIE: Morty, I didn't say before—he runs around steady with a girl.

MORTY: Terrible. Should he run around with a foxie-woxie?

BESSIE: A girl with no parents.

MORTY: An orphan?

BESSIE: I could die from shame. A year already he runs around with her. He brought her once for supper. Believe me, she didn't come again, no!

RALPH: Don't think I didn't ask her.

BESSIE: You hear? You raise them and what's in the end for all your trouble?

JACOB: When you'll lay in a grave, no more trouble. [*Exits.*]

MORTY: Quack quack!

BESSIE: A girl like that he wants to marry. A skinny consumptive-looking... six months already she's not working—taking charity from an aunt. You should see her. In a year she's dead on his hands.

RALPH: You'd cut her throat if you could.

BESSIE: That's right! Before she'd ruin a nice boy's life I would first go to prison. Miss Nobody should step in the picture and I'll stand by with my mouth shut.

RALPH: Miss Nobody! Who am I? Al Jolson?

BESSIE: Fix your tie!

RALPH: I'll take care of my own life.

BESSIE: You'll take care? Excuse my expression, you can't even wipe your nose yet! He'll take care!

MORTY: [*To* BESSIE.] I'm surprised. Don't worry so much, Bessie. When it's time to settle down he won't marry a poor girl, will you? In the long run common sense is thicker than love. I'm a great boy for live and let live.

BESSIE: Sure, it's easy to say. In the meantime he eats out my heart. You know I'm not strong.

MORTY: I know... a pussy cat... ha, ha, ha.

BESSIE: You got money and money talks. But without the dollar who sleeps at night?

RALPH: I been working for years, bringing in money here—putting it in your hand like a kid. All right, I can't get my teeth fixed. All right, that a new suit's like trying to buy the Chrysler Building. You never in your life bought me a pair of skates even—things I died for when I was a kid. I don't care about that stuff, see. Only just remember I pay some of the bills around here, just a few... and if my girl calls me on the phone I'll talk to her any time I please. [*He exits.* HENNIE *applauds.*]

BESSIE: Don't be so smart, Miss America! [*To* MORTY.] he didn't have skates! But when he got sick, a twelve-year-old boy, who called a big specialist for the last $25 in the house? Skates!

JACOB: [ *Just in. Adjusts window shade.*] It looks like snow today.

MORTY: It's about time—winter.

BESSIE: Poppa here could talk like Samuel Webster, too, but it's just talk. He should try to buy a two-cent pickle in the Burland Market without money.

MORTY: I'm getting an appetite.

BESSIE: Right away we'll eat. I made chopped liver for you.

MORTY: My specialty!

BESSIE: Ralph should only be a success like you, Morty. I should only live to see the day when he rides up to the door in a big car with a chauffeur and a radio. I could die happy, believe me.

MORTY: Success she says. She should see how we spend thousands of dollars making up a winter line and winter don't come—summer in January. Can you beat it?

JACOB: Don't live, just make success.

MORTY: Chopped liver—ha!

JACOB: Ha! [*Exits.*]

MORTY: When they start arguing, I don't hear. Suddenly I'm deaf. I'm a great boy for the practical side. [*He looks over to* HENNIE, *who sits rubbing her hands with lotion.*]

HENNIE: Hands like a raw potato.

MORTY: What's the matter? You don't look so well... no pep.

HENNIE: I'm swell.

MORTY: You used to be such a pretty girl.

HENNIE: Maybe I got the blues. You can't tell.

MORTY: You could stand a new dress.

HENNIE: That's not all I could stand.

MORTY: Come down to the place tomorrow and pick out a couple from the "eleven-eighty" line. Only don't sing me the blues.

HENNIE: Thanks. I need some new clothes.

MORTY: I got two thousand pieces of merchandise waiting in the stock room for winter.

HENNIE: I never had anything from life. Sam don't help.

MORTY: He's crazy about the kid.

HENNIE: Crazy is right. Twenty-one a week he brings in—a nigger don't have it so hard. I wore my fingers off on an Underwood for six years. For what? Now I wash baby diapers. Sure, I'm crazy about the kid too. But half the night the kid's up. Try to sleep. You don't know how it is, Uncle Morty.

MORTY: No, I don't know. I was born yesterday. Ha, ha, ha. Some day I'll leave you a little nest egg. You like eggs? Ha?

HENNIE: When? When I'm dead and buried?

MORTY: No, when *I'm* dead and buried. Ha, ha, ha.

HENNIE: You should know what I'm thinking.

MORTY: Ha, ha, ha, I know. [MYRON *enters.*]

MYRON: I never take a drink. I'm just surprised at myself, I—

MORTY: I got a pain. Maybe I'm hungry.

MYRON: Come inside, Morty. Bessie's got some schnapps.

MORTY: I'll take a drink. Yesterday I missed the Turkish bath.

MYRON: I get so bitter when I take a drink, it just surprises me.

MORTY: Look how fat. Say, you live once…Quack, quack. [*Both exit.* MOE *stands silently in the doorway.*]

SAM: [*Entering.*] I'll make Leon's bottle now!

HENNIE: No, let him sleep, Sam. Take away the diaper. [*He does. Exits.*]

MOE: [*Advancing into the room.*] That your husband?

HENNIE: Don't you know?

MOE: Maybe he's a nurse you hired for the kid—it looks it—how he tends it. A guy comes howling to your old lady every time you look cock-eyed. Does he sleep with you?

HENNIE: Don't be so wise!

MOE: [*Indicating newspaper.*] Here's a dame strangled her hubby with wire. Claimed she didn't like him. Why don't you brain Sam with an axe some night?

HENNIE: Why don't you lay an egg, Axelrod?

MOE: I laid a few in my day, Feinschreiber. Hard-boiled ones too.

HENNIE: Yeah?

MOE: Yeah. You wanna know what I see when I look in your eyes?

HENNIE: No.

MOE: Ted Lewis playing the clarinet—some of those high crazy notes!
Christ, you coulda had a guy with some guts instead of a cluck stands
around boilin' baby nipples.

HENNIE: Meaning you?

MOE: Meaning me, sweetheart.

HENNIE: Think you're pretty good.

MOE: You'd know if I slept with you again.

HENNIE: I'll smack your face in a minute.

MOE: You do and I'll break your arm. [*Holds up paper.*] Take a look. [*Reads.*]
"Ten-day luxury cruise to Havana." That's the stuff you coulda had. Put
up at ritzy hotels, frenchie soap, champagne. Now you're tied down to
"Snake-Eye" here. What for? What's it get you?...A 2x4 flat on 108th
Street...a pain in the bustle it gets you.

HENNIE: What's it to you?

MOE: I know you from the old days. How you like to spend it! What I
mean! Lizard-skin shoes, perfume behind the ears...You're in a mess,
Paradise! Paradise—that's a hot one—yah, crazy to eat a knish at your
own wedding.

HENNIE: I get it—you're jealous. You can't get me.

MOE: Don't make me laugh.

HENNIE: Kid Jailbird's been trying to make me for years. You'd give your
other leg. I'm hooked? Maybe, but you're in the same boat. Only it's
worse for you. I don't give a damn no more, but you gotta yen makes
you—

MOE: Don't make me laugh.

HENNIE: Compared to you I'm sittin' on top of the world.

MOE: You're losing your looks. A dame don't stay young forever.

HENNIE: You're a liar. I'm only twenty-four.

MOE: When you comin' home to stay?

HENNIE: Wouldn't you like to know?

MOE: I'll get you again.

HENNIE: Think so?

MOE: Sure, whatever goes up comes down. You're easy—you remember—
two for a nickel—a pushover! [*Suddenly she slaps him. They both seem
stunned.*] What's the idea?

HENNIE: Go on...break my arm.

MOE: [*As if saying "I love you."*] Listen, lousy.

HENNIE: Go on, do something!

**MOE:** Listen—

**HENNIE:** You're so damn tough!

**MOE:** You like me. [*He takes her.*]

**HENNIE:** Take your hand off! [*Pushes him away.*] Come around when it's a flood again and they put you in the ark with the animals. Not even then—if you was the last man!

**MOE:** Baby, if you had a dog I'd love the dog.

**HENNIE:** Gorilla! [*Exits. RALPH enters.*]

**RALPH:** Were you here before?

**MOE:** [*Sits.*] What?

**RALPH:** When the call came for me?

**MOE:** What?

**RALPH:** The call came. [JACOB *enters.*]

**MOE:** [*Rubbing his leg.*] No.

**JACOB:** Don't worry, Ralphie, she'll call back.

**RALPH:** Maybe not. I think somethin's the matter.

**JACOB:** What?

**RALPH:** I don't know. I took her home from the movie last night. She asked me what I'd think if she went away.

**JACOB:** Don't worry, she'll call again.

**RALPH:** Maybe not, if Mom insulted her. She gets it on both ends, the poor kid. Lived in an orphan asylum most of her life. They shove her around like an empty freight train.

**JACOB:** After dinner go see her.

**RALPH:** Twice they kicked me down the stairs.

**JACOB:** Life should have some dignity.

**RALPH:** Every time I go near the place I get heart failure. The uncle drives a bus. You oughta see him—like Babe Ruth.

**MOE:** Use your brains. Stop acting like a kid who still wets the bed. Hire a room somewhere—a club room for two members.

**RALPH:** Not that kind of proposition, Moe.

**MOE:** Don't be a bush leaguer all your life.

**RALPH:** Cut it out!

**MOE:** [*On a sudden upsurge of emotion.*] Ever sleep with one? Look at 'im blush.

**RALPH:** You don't know her.

**MOE:** I seen her—the kind no one sees undressed till the undertaker works on her.

**RALPH:** Why give me the needles all the time? What'd I ever do to you?

**MOE:** Not a thing. You're a nice kid. But grow up! In life there's two kinds—the men that's sure of themselves and the ones who ain't! It's time you quit being a selling plater[2] and got in the first class.

JACOB: And you, Axelrod?

MOE: [*To* JACOB.] Scratch your whiskers! [*To* RALPH.] Get independent. Get what-it-takes and be yourself. Do what you like.

RALPH: Got a suggestion?

[MORTY *enters, eating.*]

MOE: Sure, pick out a racket. Shake down the cocoanuts. See what that does.

MORTY: We know what it does—puts a pudding on your nose! Sing Sing! Easy money's against the law. Against the law don't win. A racket is illegitimate, no?

MOE: It's all a racket—from horse racing down. Marriage, politics, big business—everybody plays cops and robbers. You, you're a racketeer yourself.

MORTY: Who? Me? Personally I manufacture dresses.

MOE: Horse feathers!

MORTY: [*Seriously.*] Don't make such remarks to me without proof. I'm a great one for proof. That's why I made a success in business. Proof—put up or shut up, like a game of cards. I heard this remark before—a rich man's a crook who steals from the poor. Personally, I don't like it. It's a big lie!

MOE: If you don't like it, buy yourself a fife and drum—and go fight your own war.

MORTY: Sweatshop talk. Every Jew and Wop in the shop eats my bread and behind my back says, "a sonofabitch." I started from a poor boy who worked on an ice wagon for two dollars a week. Pop's right here—he'll tell you. I made it honest. In the whole industry nobody's got a better name.

JACOB: It's an exception, such success.

MORTY: Ralph can't do the same thing?

JACOB: No, Morty, I don't think. In a house like this he don't realize even the possibilities of life. Economics comes down like a ton of coal on the head.

MOE: Red rover, red rover, let Jacob come over!

JACOB: In my day the propaganda was for God. Now it's for success. A boy don't turn around without having shoved in him he should make a success.

---

2 A mediocre horse, unlikely to win a race.

**Morty:** Pop, you're a comedian, a regular Charlie Chaplin.

**Jacob:** He dreams all night of fortunes. Why not? Don't it say in the movies he should have a personal steamship, pyjamas for fifty dollars a pair and a toilet like a monument? But in the morning he wakes up and for ten dollars he can't fix the teeth. And millions more worse off in the mills of the South—starvation wages. The blood from the worker's heart. [*Morty laughs loud and long.*] Laugh, laugh ... tomorrow not.

**Morty:** A real, a real Boob McNutt³ you're getting to be.

**Jacob:** Laugh, my son ...

**Morty:** Here is the North, Pop.

**Jacob:** North, south, it's one country.

**Morty:** The country's all right. A duck quacks in every pot!

**Jacob:** You never heard how they shoot down men and women which ask a better wage? Kentucky 1932?

**Morty:** That's a pile of chopped liver, Pop.

[Bessie *and others enter.*]

**Jacob:** Pittsburgh, Passaic, Illinois—slavery—it begins where success begins in a competitive system.

[Morty *howls with delight.*]

**Morty:** Oh Pop, what are you bothering? Why? Tell me why? Ha ha ha. I bought you a phonograph ... stick to Caruso.

**Bessie:** He's starting up again.

**Morty:** Don't bother with Kentucky. It's full of moonshiners.

**Jacob:** Sure, sure—

**Morty:** You don't know practical affairs. Stay home and cut hair to fit the face.

**Jacob:** It says in the Bible how the Red Sea opened and the Egyptians went in and the sea rolled over them. [*Quotes two lines of Hebrew.*] In this boy's life a Red Sea will happen again. I see it!

**Morty:** I'm getting sore, Pop, with all this sweatshop talk.

**Bessie:** He don't stop a minute. The whole day, like a phonograph.

**Morty:** I'm surprised. Without a rich man you don't have a roof over your head. You don't know it?

**Myron:** Now you can't bite the hand that feeds you.

³A character in the "colored jokes" (comic strips) Morty reads.

RALPH: Let him alone—he's right!

BESSIE: Another county heard from.

RALPH: It's the truth. It's—

MORTY: Keep quiet, snotnose!

JACOB: For sure, charity, a bone for an old dog. But in Russia an old man don't take charity so his eyes turn black in his head. In Russia they got Marx.

MORTY: [*Scoffingly.*] Who's Marx?

MOE: An outfielder for the Yanks. [MORTY *howls with delight.*]

MORTY: Ha ha ha, it's better than the jokes. I'm telling you. This is Uncle Sam's country. Put it in your pipe and smoke it.

BESSIE: Russia, he says! Read the papers.

SAM: Here is opportunity.

MYRON: People can't believe in God in Russia. The papers tell the truth, they do.

JACOB: So you believe in God . . . you got something for it? You! You worked for all the capitalists. You harvested the fruit from your labor? You got God! But the past comforts you? The present smiles on you, yes? It promises you the future something? Did you found a piece of earth where you could live like a human being and die with the sun on your face? Tell me, yes, tell me. I would like to know myself. But on these questions, on this theme—the struggle for existence—you can't make an answer. The answer I see in your face . . . the answer is your mouth can't talk. In this dark corner you sit and you die. But abolish private property!

BESSIE: [*Settling the issue.*] Noo, go fight City Hall!

MORTY: He's drunk!

JACOB: I'm studying from books a whole lifetime.

MORTY: That's what it is—he's drunk. What the hell does all that mean?

JACOB: If you don't know, why should I tell you.

MORTY: [*Triumphant at last.*] You see? Hear him? Like all those nuts, don't know what they're saying.

JACOB: I know, I know.

MORTY: Like Boob McNutt you know! Don't go in the park, Pop—the squirrels'll get you. Ha, ha, ha . . .

BESSIE: Save your appetite, Morty. [*To* MYRON.] Don't drop the duck.

MYRON: We're ready to eat, Momma.

MORTY: [*To* JACOB.] Shame on you. It's your second childhood.

[*Now they file out,* MYRON *first with the duck, the others behind him.*]

BESSIE: Come eat. We had enough for one day. [*Exits.*]

217

**Morty:** Ha, ha, ha. Quack, quack. [*Exits.*]

[JACOB *sits there trembling and deeply humiliated.* MOE *approaches him and thumbs the old man's nose in the direction of the dining room.*]

**Moe:** Give 'em five. [*Takes his hand away.*] They got you pasted on the wall like a picture Jake. [*He limps out to seat himself at the table in the next room.*]

**Jacob:** Go eat, boychick. [RALPH *comes to him.*] He gives me eat, so I'll climb in a needle. One time I saw an old horse in summer... he wore a straw hat... the ears stuck out on top. An old horse for hire. Give me back my young days... give me fresh blood... arms... give me — [*The telephone rings. Quickly* RALPH *goes to it.* JACOB *pulls the curtains and stands there, a sentry on guard.*]

**Ralph:** Hello?... Yeah, I went to the store and came right back, right after you called. [*Looks at* JACOB.]

**Jacob:** Speak, speak. Don't be afraid they'll hear.

**Ralph:** I'm sorry if Mom said something. You knw how excitable Mom is... Sure! What?... Sure, I'm listening... Put on the radio, Jack. [JACOB *does so. Music comes in and up, a tango, grating with an insistent nostalgic pulse. Under the cover of the music* RALPH *speaks more freely.*] Yes... yes... What's the matter? Why're you crying? What happened? [*To* JACOB.] She's putting her uncle on. Yes?... Listen, Mr. Hirsch, what're you trying to do? What's the big idea? Honest to God. I'm in no mood for joking! Lemme talk to her! Gimme Blanche! [*Waits.*] Blanche? What's this? Is this a joke? Is that true? I'm coming right down! I know, but—You wanna do that?... I know, but—I'm coming down... tonight! Nine o'clock... sure... sure... sure... [*Hangs up.*]

**Jacob:** What happened?

**Morty:** [*Enters.*] Listen, Pop. I'm surprised you didn't—[*He howls, shakes his head in mock despair, exits.*]

**Jacob:** Boychick, what?

**Ralph:** I don't get it straight. [*To* JACOB.] She's leaving...

**Jacob:** Where?

**Ralph:** Out West—To Cleveland.

**Jacob:** Cleveland?

**Ralph:** ... In a week or two. Can you picture it? It's a put-up job. But they can't get away with that.

**Jacob:** We'll find something.

**RALPH:** Sure, the angels of heaven'll come down on her uncle's cab and whisper in his ear.

**JACOB:** Come eat … We'll find something.

**RALPH:** I'm meeting her tonight, but I know—[BESSIE *throws open the curtain between the two rooms and enters.*]

**BESSIE:** Maybe we'll serve you for a special blue plate in the garden?

**JACOB:** All right, all right. [BESSIE *goes over to the window, levels the shade and on her way out, clicks off the radio.*]

**MORTY:** [*Within.*] Leave the music, Bessie. [*She clicks it on again, looks at them, exits.*]

**RALPH:** I know …

**JACOB:** Don't cry, boychick. [*Goes over to* RALPH.] Why should you make like this? Tell me why you should cry, just tell me … [JACOB *takes* RALPH *in his arms and both, trying to keep back the tears, trying fearfully not to be heard by the others in the dining room, begin crying.*] You mustn't cry …

[*The tango twists on. Inside, the clatter of dishes and the clash of cutlery sound.* MORTY *begins to howl with laughter.*]

CURTAIN

# SCENE 2

*That night. The dark dining room.*

**AT RISE:** JACOB *is heard in his lighted room, reading from a sheet, declaiming aloud as if to an audience.*

JACOB: They are there to remind us of the horrors — under those crosses lie hundreds of thousands of workers and farmers who murdered each other in uniform for the greater glory of capitalism. [*Comes out of his room.*] The new imperialist war will send millions to their death, will bring prosperity to the pockets of the capitalist — aie, Morty — and will bring only greater hunger and misery to the masses of workers and farmers. The memories of the last world slaughter are still vivid in our minds. [*Hearing a noise he quickly retreats to his room.* RALPH *comes in form the street. He sits with hat and coat on.* JACOB *tentatively opens door and asks*] Ralphie?

RALPH: It's geting pretty cold out.

JACOB: [*Enters room fully, cleaning hair clippers.*] We should have steam till twelve instead of ten. Go complain to the Board of Health.

RALPH: It might snow.

JACOB: It don't hurt ... extra work for men.

RALPH: When I was a kid I laid awake at nights and heard the sounds of trains ... faraway lonesome sounds ... boats going up and down the river. I used to think of all kinds of things I wanted to do. What was it, Jake? Just a bunch of noise in my head?

JACOB: [*Waiting for news of the girl.*] You wanted to make for yourself a certain kind of world.

RALPH: I guess I didn't. I'm feeling pretty, pretty low.

JACOB: You're a young boy and for yoiu life is all in front like a big mountain. You got feet to climb.

RALPH: I don't know how.

JACOB: So you'll find out. Never a young man had such opportunity like today. He could make history.

RALPH: Ten p.m. and all is well. Where's everybody?

JACOB: They went.

RALPH: Uncle Morty too?

JACOB: Hennie and Sam he drove down.

RALPH: I saw her.

JACOB: [*Alert and eager.*] Yes, yes, tell me.

RALPH: I waited in Mount Morris Park till she came out. So cold I did a buck'n wing to keep warm. She's scared to death.

JACOB: They made her?

RALPH: Sure. She want's to go. They keep yelling at her—they want her to marry a millionaire, too.

JACOB: You told her you love her?

RALPH: Sure. "Marry me," I said. "Marry me tommorow." On sixteen bucks a week. On top of that I had to admit Mom'd have Uncle Morty get me fired in a second... Two can starve as cheap as one!

JACOB: So what happened?

RALPH: I made her promise to meet me tommorow.

JACOB: Now she'll go in the West?

RALPH: I'd fight the whole goddam world with her, but not her. No guts. The hell with her. If she wantsa go—all right—I'll get along.

JACOB: For sure, there's more important things than girls...

RALPH: You said a mouthful... and maybe I don't see it. She'll see what I can do. No one stops me when I get going...

[*Near to tears, he has to stop.* JACOB *examines his clippers very closely.*]

JACOB: Electric clippers never do a job like by hand.

RALPH: Why won't Mom let us live here?

JACOB: Why? Why? Because in a society like this, today people don't love. Hate!

RALPH: Gee, I'm not bum who hangs around pool parlors. I got the stuff to go ahead. I don't know what to do.

JACOB: Look on me and learn what to do, boychick. Here sits an old man polishing tools. You think maybe I'll use them again! Look on this failure and see for seventy years he talked with good ideas, but only in the head. It's enough for me now I should see your happiness. This is why I tell you—DO! Do what is in your heart and you carry in yourself a revolution. But you should act. Not like me. A man who had golden opportunities but drank instead a glass tea. No...

[*A pause of silence.*]

RALPH: [*Listening.*] Hear it? The Boston airmail plane. Ten minutes late. I get a kick the way it cuts across the Bronx every night.

[*The bell rings.* SAM, *excited, disheveled, enters.*]

JACOB: You came back so soon?

SAM: Where's Mom?

JACOB: Mom? Look on the chandelier.

SAM: Nobody's home?

JACOB: Sit down. Right away they're coming. You went in the street without a tie?

SAM: Maybe it's a crime.

JACOB: Excuse me.

RALPH: You had a fight with Hennie again?

SAM: She'll fight once ... some day ... [*Lapses into silence.*]

JACOB: In my day the daughter came home. Now comes the son-in-law.

SAM: Once too often she'll fight with me, Hennie. I mean it. I mean it like anything. I'm a person with a bad heart. I sit quiet, but inside I got a—

RALPH: What happened?

SAM: I'll talk to Mom. I'll see Mom.

JACOB: Take an apple.

SAM: Please ... he tells me apples.

RALPH: Why hop around like a billiard ball?

SAM: Even in a joke she should dare say it.

JACOB: My grandchild said something.

SAM: To my father in the old country they did a joke ... I'll tell you: One day in Odessa he talked to another Jew on the street. They didn't like it, they jumped on him like a wild wold.

RALPH: Who?

SAM: Cossacks. They cut off his beard. A Jew without a beard! He came home—I remember like yesterday how he came home and went in bed for two days. He put like this the cover on his face. No one should see. The third morning he died.

RALPH: From what?

SAM: From a broken heart ... Some people are like this. Me too. I could die like this from shame.

JACOB: Hennie told you something?

SAM: Straight out she said it—like a lightning from the sky. The baby ain't mine. She said it.

RALPH: Don't be a dope.

JACOB: For sure, a joke.

RALPH: She's kidding you.

SAM: She should kid a policeman, not Sam Feinschreiber. Please … you don't know her like me. I wake up in the nighttime and she sits watching me like I don't know what. I make a nice living from the store. But it's no use —she looks for a star in the sky. I'm afraid like anything. You could go crazy from less even. What I shall do I'll ask Mom.

JACOB: "Go home and sleep," she'll say. "It's a bad dream."

SAM: It don't satisfy me more, such remarks, when Hennie could kill in the bed. [JACOB *laughs.*] Don't laugh. I'm so nervous—look, two times I weighed myself on the subway station. [*Throws small cards to table.*]

JACOB: [*Examining one.*] One hundred and thirty-eight—also a fortune. [*Turns it and reads*] "You are inclined to deep thinking, and have a high admiration for intellectual excellence and inclined to be very exclusive in the selection of friends." Correct! I think maybe you got mixed up in the wrong family, Sam.

[MYRON *and* BESSIE *now enter.*]

BESSIE: Look, a guest! What's the matter? Something wrong with the baby? [*Waits.*]

SAM: No.

BESSIE: Noo?

SAM: [*In a burst.*] I wash my hands from everything.

BESSIE: Take off your coat and hat. Have a seat. Excitement don't help. Myron, make tea. You'll have a glass tea. We'll talk like civilized people. [MYRON *goes.*] What is it, Ralph, you're all dressed up for a party? [*He looks at her silently and exits. To* SAM.] We saw a very good movie, with Wallace Beery. He acts like life, very good.

MYRON: [*Within.*] Polly Moran too.

BESSIE: Polly Moran too—a woman with a nose from here to Hunts Point, but a fine player. Poppa, take away the tools and the books.

JACOB: All right. [*Exits to his room.*]

BESSIE: Noo, Sam, why do you look like a funeral?

SAM: I can't stand it …

BESSIE: Wait. [*Yells.*] You took up Tootsie on the roof.

JACOB: [*Within.*] In a minute.

BESSIE: What can't you stand?

SAM: She said I'm second fiddle in my own house.

BESSIE: Who?

SAM: Hennie. In the second place, it ain't my baby, she said.

BESSIE: What? What are you talking about? [MYRON *enters with dishes.*]

SAM: From her own mouth. It went like a knife in my heart.

BESSIE: Sam, what're you saying?

SAM: Please, I'm making a story? I fell in the chair like a dead.

BESSIE: Such a story you believe?

SAM: I don't know.

BESSIE: How you don't know?

SAM: She told me even the man.

BESSIE: Impossible!

SAM: I can't believe myself. But she said it. I'm a second fiddle, she said. She made such a yell everybody heard for ten miles.

BESSIE: Such a thing Hennie should say—impossible!

SAM: What should I do? With my bad heart such a remark kills.

MYRON: Hennie don't feel well, Sam. You see, she—

BESSIE: What then?—a sick girl. Believe me, a mother knows. Nerves. Our Hennie's got a bad temper. You'll let her she says anything. She takes after me—nervous. [*To* MYRON.] You ever heard such a remark in all your life? She should make such a statement! Bughouse.

MYRON: The little one's been sick all these months. Hennie needs a rest. No doubt.

BESSIE: Sam don't think she means it—

MYRON: Oh, I know he don't, of course—

BESSIE: I'll say the truth, Sam. We didn't half the time understand her ourselves. A girl with her own mind. When she makes it up, wild horses wouldn't change her.

SAM: She don't love me.

BESSIE: This is sensible, Sam?

SAM: Not for a nickel.

BESSIE: What do you think? She married you for your money? For your looks? You ain't no John Barrymore, Sam. No, she liked you.

SAM: Please, not for a nickel. [JACOB *stands in the doorway.*]

BESSIE: We stood right here the first time she said it. "Sam Feinschreiber's a nice boy," she said it, "a boy he's got good common sense, with a business head." Right here she said it, in this room. You sent her two boxes of candy together, you remember?

MYRON: Loft's candy.

BESSIE: This is when she said it. What do you think?

MYRON: You were just the only boy she cared for.

BESSIE: So she married you. Such a world ... plenty of boy friends she had, believe me!

JACOB: A popular girl ...

MYRON: Y-e-s.

BESSIE: I'll say it plain out—Moe Axelrod offered her plenty—a servant, a house ... she don't have to pick up a hand.

MYRON: Oh, Moe? Just wild about her ...

SAM: Moe Axelrod? He wanted to—

BESSIE: But she didn't care. A girl like Hennie you don't buy. I should never live to see another day if I'm telling a lie.

SAM: She was kidding me.

BESSIE: What then? You shouldn't be foolish.

SAM: The baby looks like my family. He's got Feinschreiber eyes.

BESSIE: A blind man could see it.

JACOB: Sure ... sure ...

SAM: The baby looks like me. Yes ...

BESSIE: You could believe me.

JACOB: Any day ...

SAM: But she tells me the man. She made up his name too?

BESSIE: Sam, Sam, look in the phone book—a million names.

MYRON: Tom, Dick and Harry. [JACOB *laughs quietly, soberly.*]

BESSIE: Don't stand around, Poppa. Take Tootsie on the roof. And you don't let her go under the water tank.

JACOB: Schmah Yisoeal. Behold! [*Quietly laughing, he goes back into his room, closing the door behind him.*]

SAM: I won't stand he should make insults. A man eats out his—

BESSIE: No, no, he's an old man—a second childhood. Myron, bring in the tea. Open a jar of raspberry jelly. [MYRON *exits.*]

SAM: Mom, you think—?

BESSIE: I'll talk to Hennie. It's all right.

SAM: Tomorrow, I'll take her by the doctor. [RALPH *enters.*]

BESSIE: Stay for a little tea.

SAM: No, I'll go home. I'm tired. Already I caught a cold in such weather. [*Blows his nose.*]

MYRON: [*Entering with stuffs.*] Going home?

**SAM:** I'll go in bed. I caught a cold.

**MYRON:** Teddy Roosevelt used to say, "When you have a problem, sleep on it."

**BESSIE:** My Sam is no problem.

**MYRON:** I don't mean ... I mean he said—

**BESSIE:** Call me tomorrow, Sam.

**SAM:** I'll phone suppertime. Sometime I think there's something funny about me. [MYRON *sees him out. In the following pause, Caruso is heard singing within.*]

**BESSIE:** A bargain! Second fiddle. By me he don't even play in the orchestra —a man like a mouse. Maybe she'll lay down and die 'cause he makes a living?

**RALPH:** Can I talk to you about something?

**BESSIE:** What's the matter—I'm biting you?

**RALPH:** It's something about Blanche.

**BESSIE:** Don't tell me.

**RALPH:** Listen now—

**BESSIE:** I don't want to know.

**RALPH:** She's got no place to go.

**BESSIE:** I don't want to know.

**RALPH:** Mom, I love this girl ...

**BESSIE:** So go knock your head against the wall.

**RALPH:** I want her to come here. Listen, Mom, I want you to let her live here for a while.

**BESSIE:** You got funny ideas, my son.

**RALPH:** I'm as good as anyone else. Don't I have some rights in the world? Listen, Mom, if I don't do something, she's going away. Why don't you do it? Why don't you let her stay here for a few weeks? Things'll pick up. Then we can—

**BESSIE:** Sure, sure. I'll keep her fresh on ice for a wedding day. That's what you want?

**RALPH:** No, I mean you should—

**BESSIE:** Or maybe you'll sleep here in the same bed without marriage. [JACOB *stands in his doorway, dressed.*]

**RALPH:** Don't say that, Mom. I only mean ...

**BESSIE:** What you mean, I know ... and what I mean I also know. Make up your mind. For your own good, Ralphie. If she dropped in the ocean I don't lift a finger.

**Ralph:** That's all, I suppose.

**Bessie:** With me it's one thing—a boy should have respect for his own future. Go to sleep, you look tired. In the morning you'll forget.

**Jacob:** "Awake and sing, ye that dwell in dust, and the earth shall cast out the dead." It's cold out?

**Myron:** Oh, yes.

**Jacob:** I'll take up Tootsie now.

**Myron:** [*Eating bread and jam.*] He come on us like the wild man of Borneo, Sam. I don't think Hennie was fool enough to tell him the truth like that.

**Bessie:** Myron! [*A deep pause.*]

**Ralph:** What did he say?

**Bessie:** Never mind.

**Ralph:** I heard him. I heard him. You don't needa tell me.

**Bessie:** Never mind.

**Ralph:** You trapped that guy.

**Bessie:** Don't say another word.

**Ralph:** Just have respect? That's the idea?

**Bessie:** Don't say another word. I'm boiling over ten times inside.

**Ralph:** You won't let Blanche here, huh. I'm not sure I want her. You put one over on that little shrimp. The cat's whiskers, Mom?

**Bessie:** I'm telling you something!

**Ralph:** I got the whole idea. I get it so quick my head's swimming. Boy, what a laugh! I suppose you know about this, Jake?

**Jacob:** Yes.

**Ralph:** Why didn't you do something?

**Jacob:** I'm an old man.

**Ralph:** What's that got to do with the price of bonds? Sits around and lets a thing like that happen! You make me sick too.

**Myron:** [*After a pause.*] Let me say something, son.

**Ralph:** Take your hand away! Sit in a corner and wag your tail. Keep on boasting you went to law school for two years.

**Myron:** I want to tell you—

**Ralph:** You never in your life had a thing to tell me.

**Bessie:** [*Bitterly.*] Don't say a word. Let him, let him run and tell Sam. Publish in the papers, give a broadcast on the radio. To him it don't matter nothing his family sits with tears pouring from the eyes. [*To* Jacob.] What are you waiting for? I didn't tell you twice already about the dog? You'll stand around with Caruso and make a bughouse. It ain't enough all day long. Fifty times I told you I'll break every record in the house. [*She brushes past him, breaks the records, comes out.*] The next time I say something you'll maybe believe it. Now maybe you learned a lesson. [*Pause.*]

JACOB: [*Quietly.*] Bessie, new lessons... not for an old dog.

[MOE *enters.*]

MYRON: You didn't have to do it, Momma.

BESSIE: Talk better to your son, Mr. Berger! Me, I don't lay down and die for him and Poppa no more. I'll work like a nigger? For what? Wait, the day comes when you'll be punished. When it's too late you'll remember how you sucked away a mother's life. Talk to him, tell him how I don't sleep at night. [*Bursts into tears and exits.*]

MOE: [*Sings.*] "Good by to all your sorrows. You never hear them talk about the war, in the land of Yama Yama..."

MYRON: Yes, Momma's a sick woman, Ralphie.

RALPH: Yeah?

MOE: We'll be out of the trenches by Christmas. Putt, putt, putt... here, stinker... [*Picks up Tootsie, a small, white poodle that just then enters from the hall.*] If there's a reincarnation in the next life I wanna be a dog and lay in a fat lady's lap. Barrage over? How 'bout a little pinochle, Pop?

JACOB: Nnno.

RALPH: [*Taking dog.*] I'll take her up. [*Conciliatory.*]

JACOB: No, I'll do it. [*Takes dog.*]

RALPH: [*Ashamed.*] It's cold out.

JACOB: I was cold before in my life. A man sixty-seven... [*Strokes the dog.*] Tootsie is my favorite lady in the house. [*He slowly passes across the room and exits. A settling pause.*]

MYRON: She cried all last night—Tootsie—I heard her in the kitchen like a young girl.

MOE: Tonight I could do something. I got a yen... I don't know.

MYRON: [*Rubbing his head.*] My scalp is impoverished.

RALPH: Mom bust all his records.

MYRON: She didn't have to do it.

MOE: Tough tit! Now I can sleep in the morning. Who the hell wantsa hear a wop air his tonsils all day long!

RALPH: [*Handling the fragment of a record.*] "O Paradiso!"

MOE: [*Gets cards.*] It's snowing out, girls.

MYRON: There's no more big snows like in the old days. I think the whole world's changing. I see it, right under our very eyes. No one hardly remembers any more when we used to have gaslight and all the dishes had little fishes on them.

MOE: It's the system, girls.

MYRON: I was a little boy when it happened—the Great Blizzard. It snowed three days without a stop that time. Yes, and the horse cars stopped. A silence of death was on the city and little babies got no milk...they say a lot of people died that year.

MOE: [*Singing as he deals himself cards.*]

"Lights are blinking while you're drinking,
That's the place where the good fellows go.
Good-bye to all your sorrows,
You never hear them talk about the war,
In the land of Yama Yama
Funicalee, funicala, funicalo..."

MYRON: What can I say to you, Big Boy?

RALPH: Not a damn word.

MOE: [*Goes "ta ra ta ra" throughout.*]

MYRON: I know how you feel about all those things, I know.

RALPH: Forget it.

MYRON: And your girl...

RALPH: Don't soft soap me all of a sudden.

MYRON: I'm not foreign-born. I'm an American, and yet I never got close to you. It's an American father's duty to be his son's friend.

RALPH: Who said that—Teddy R.?

MOE: [*Dealing cards.*] You're breaking his heart, "Litvak."

MYRON: It just happened the other day. The moment I began losing my hair I just knew I was destined to be a failure in life...and when I grew bald I was. Now isn't that funny, Big Boy?

MOE: It's a pisscutter!

MYRON: I believe in Destiny.

MOE: You get what-it-takes. Then they don't catch you with your pants down. [*Sings out.*] Eight of clubs....

**Myron:** I really don't know. I sold jewelry on the road before I married. It's one thing to—Now here's a thing the druggist gave me. [*Reads*] "The Marvel Cosmetic Girl of Hollywood is going on the air. Give this charming little radio singer a name and win five thousand dollars. If you will send—"

**Moe:** Your old man still believes in Santy Claus.

**Myron:** Someone's got to win. The government isn't gonna allow everything to be a fake.

**Moe:** It's a fake. There ain't no prizes. It's a fake.

**Myron:** It says—

**Ralph:** [*Snatching it.*] For Christ's sake, Pop, forget it. Grow up. Jake's right—everybody's crazy. It's like a zoo in this house. I'm going to bed.

**Moe:** In the land of Yama Yama... [*Goes on with ta ra.*]

**Myron:** Don't think life's easy with Momma. No, but she means for your good all the time. I tell you she does, she—

**Ralph:** Maybe, but I'm going to bed.

[*Downstairs, doorbell rings violently.*]

**Moe:** [*Ring.*] Enemy barrage begins on sector eight seventy-five.

**Ralph:** That's downstairs.

**Myron:** We ain't expecting anyone this hour of the night.

**Moe:** "Lights are blinking while you're drinking, that's the place where the good fellows go. Good-bye to ta ra tara ra," etc.

**Ralph:** I better see who it is.

**Myron:** I'll tick the button.

[*As he starts, the apartment doorbell begins ringing, followed by large knocking. Myron goes out.*]

**Ralph:** Who's ever ringing means it.

[*A loud excited voice outside.*]

**Moe:** "In the land of Yama Yama, Funicalee, funicalo, funic—"

[*Myron enters, followed by Schlosser the janitor. Bessie cuts in from the other side.*]

BESSIE: Who's ringing like a lunatic?
RALPH: What's the matter?
MYRON: Momma...
BESSIE: Noo, what's the matter?

[*Downstairs bell continues.*]

RALPH: What's the matter?
BESSIE: Well, well...
MYRON: Poppa...
BESSIE: What happened?
SCHLOSSER: He shlipped maybe in de snow.
RALPH: Who?
SCHLOSSER: [*To* BESSIE] Your fadder fall off de roof... Ja. [*A dead pause.* RALPH *then runs out.*]
BESSIE: [*Dazed.*] Myron... Call Morty on the phone... call him. [MYRON *starts for phone.*] No. I'll do it myself. I'll... do it. [MYRON *exits.*]
SCHLOSSER: [*Standing stupidly.*] Since I was in dis country... I was pudding out de ash can... The snow is vet...
MOE: [*To* SCHLOSSER.] Scram. [SCHLOSSER *exits.*]

[BESSIE *goes blindly to the phone, fumbles and gets it.* MOE *sits quietly, slowly turning cards over, but watching her.*]

BESSIE: He slipped...
MOE: [*Deeply moved.*] Slipped?
BESSIE: I can't see the numbers. Make it, Moe, make it...
MOE: Make it yourself. [*He looks at her and slowly goes back to his game of cards with shaking hands.*]
BESSIE: Riverside 7 — ...

[*Unable to talk, she dials slowly. The dial whizzes on.*]

MOE: Don't... make me laugh... [*He turns over cards.*]

CURTAIN

# ACT THREE

*A week later in the dining room.* MORTY, BESSIE *and* MYRON *eating. Sitting in the front room is* MOE, *marking a "dope sheet," but really listening to the others.*

BESSIE: You're sure he'll come tonight — the insurance man?

MORTY: Why not? I shtupped hom a ten-dollar bill. Everything's hot delicatessen.

BESSIE: Why must he come so soon?

MORTY: Because you had a big expense. You'll settle once and for all. I'm a great boy for making hay while the sun shines.

BESSIE: Stay till he'll come, Morty...

MORTY: No, I got a strike downtown. Business don't stop for personal life. Two times already in the past week those bastards threw stink bombs in the showroom. Wait! We'll give them strikes — in the kishkas we'll give them...

BESSIE: I'm a woman. I don't know about policies. Stay till he comes.

MORTY: Bessie — sweetheart, leave me live.

BESSIE: I'm afraid, Morty.

MORTY: Be practical. They made an investigation. Everybody knows Pop had an accident. Now we'll collect.

MYRON: Ralphie don't know Papa left the insurance in his name.

MORTY: It's not his business. And I'll tell him.

BESSIE: The way he feels. [*Enter* RALPH *into front room.*] He'll do something crazy. He thinks Poppa jumped off the roof.

MORTY: Be practical, Bessie. Ralphie will sign when I tell him. Everything is peaches and cream.

BESSIE: Wait for a few minutes...

MORTY: Look, I'll show you in black on white what the policy says. *For God's sake, leave me live!* [*Angrily exits to kitchen. In parlor,* MOE *speaks to* RALPH, *who is reading a letter.*]

**MOE:** What's the letter say?

**RALPH:** Blanche won't see me no more, she says. I couldn't care very much, she says. If I didn't come like I said … She'll phone before she leaves.

**MOE:** She don't know about Pop?

**RALPH:** She won't ever forget me, she says. Look what she sends me … a little locket on a chain … if she calls I'm out.

**MOE:** You mean it?

**RALPH:** For a week I'm trying to go in his room. I guess he'd like me to have it, but I can't …

**MOE:** Wait a minute! [*Crosses over.*] They're trying to rook you — a freeze-out.

**RALPH:** Who?

**MOE:** That bunch stuffin' their gut with hot pastrami. Morty in particular. Jake left the insurance — three thousand dollars — for you.

**RALPH:** For me?

**MOE:** Now you got wings, kid. Pop figured you could use it. That's why …

**RALPH:** That's why what?

**MOE:** It ain't the only reason he done it.

**RALPH:** He done it?

**MOE:** You think a breeze blew him off?

[HENNIE *enters and sits.*]

**RALPH:** I'm not sure what I think.

**MOE:** The insurance guy's coming tonight. Morty "shtupped" him.

**RALPH:** Yeah?

**MOE:** I'll back you up. You're dead on your feet. Grab a sleep for yourself.

**RALPH:** No!

**MOE:** Go on!

[*Pushes boy into room.*]

**SAM:** [*Whom* MORTY *has sent in for the paper.*] Morty wants the paper.

**HENNIE:** So?

**SAM:** You're sitting on it. [*Gets paper.*] We could go home now, Hennie! Leon is alone by Mrs. Strasberg a whole day.

**HENNIE:** Go on home if you're so anxious. A full tub of diapers is waiting.

**SAM:** Why should you act this way?

**HENNIE:** 'Cause there's no bones in ice cream. Don't touch me.

**SAM:** Please, what's the matter…

**MOE:** She don't like you. Plain as the face on your nose…

**SAM:** To me, my friend, you talk a foreign language.

**MOE:** A quarter you're lousy. [SAM *exits.*] Gimme a buck, I'll run it up to ten.

**HENNIE:** Don't do me no favors.

**MOE:** Take a chance. [*Stopping her as she crosses to doorway.*]

**HENNIE:** I'm a pushover.

**MOE:** I say lotsa things. You don't know me.

**HENNIE:** I know you—when you knock 'em down you're through.

**MOE:** [*Sadly.*] You still don't know me.

**HENNIE:** I know what goes in your wise-guy head.

**MOE:** Don't run away… I ain't got hydrophobia. Wait. I want to tell you… I'm leaving.

**HENNIE:** Leaving?

**MOE:** Tonight. Already packed.

**HENNIE:** Where?

**MORTY:** [*As he enters followed by the others.*] My car goes through snow like a dose of salts.

**BESSIE:** Hennie, go eat…

**MORTY:** Where's Ralphie?

**MOE:** In his new room. [*Moves into dining room.*]

**MORTY:** I didn't have a piece of hot pastrami in my mouth for years.

**BESSIE:** Take a sandwich, Hennie. You didn't eat all day… [*At window.*] A whole week it rained cats and dogs.

**MYRON:** Rain, rain, go away. Come again some other day. [*Puts shawl on her.*]

**MORTY:** Where's my gloves?

**SAM:** [*Sits on stool.*] I'm sorry the old man lays in the rain.

**MORTY:** Personally, Pop was a fine man. But I'm a great boy for an honest opinion. He had enough crazy ideas for a regiment.

**MYRON:** Poppa never had a doctor in his whole life… [*Enter* RALPH]

**MORTY:** He had Caruso. Who's got more from life?

**BESSIE:** Who's got more?…

**MYRON:** And Marx he had.

[MYRON *and* BESSIE *sit on sofa.*]

**Morty:** Marx! Some say Marx is the new God today. Maybe I'm wrong. Ha ha ha … Personally I counted my ten million last night … I'm sixteen cents short. So tommorow I'll go to Union Square and yell no equality in the country! Ah, it's a new generation.

**Ralph:** You said it!

**Morty:** What's the matter, Ralphie? What are you looking funny?

**Ralph:** I hear I'm left insurance and the man's coming tonight.

**Morty:** Poppa didn't leave no insurance for you.

**Ralph:** What?

**Morty:** In your name he left it — but not for you.

**Ralph:** It's my name on the paper.

**Morty:** Who said so?

**Ralph:** [*To his mother.*] The insurance man's coming tonight?

**Morty:** What's the matter?

**Ralph:** I'm not talking to you. [*To his mother.*] Why?

**Bessie:** I don't know why.

**Ralph:** He don't come in this house tonight.

**Morty:** That's what *you* say.

**Ralph:** I'm not talking to you, Uncle Morty, but I'll tell you, too, he don't come here tonight When there's still mud on a grave. Couldn't you give the house a chance to cool off?

**Morty:** Is this a way to talk to your mother?

**Ralph:** Was that a way to talk to your father?

**Morty:** Don't be so smart with me, Mr. Ralph Berger!

**Ralph:** Don't be so smart with *me*.

**Morty:** What'll you do? I say he's coming tonight. Who says no?

**Moe:** [*Suddenly, from the background.*] Me.

**Morty:** Take a back seat, Axelrod. When you're in the family —

**Moe:** I got a little document here. [*Produces paper.*] I found it under his pillow that night. A guy who slips off a roof don't leave a note before he does it.

**Morty:** [*Starting for* Moe *after a horrified silence.*] Let me see this note.

**Bessie:** Morty, don't touch it!

**Moe:** Not if you crawled.

**Morty:** It's a fake. Poppa wouldn't —

**Moe:** Get the insurance guy here and we'll see how — [*The bell rings.*] Speak of the devil … Answer it, see what happens. [Morty *starts for the ticker.*]

**Bessie:** Morty, don't!

**Morty:** [*Stopping.*] Be practical, Bessie.

**Moe:** Sometimes you don't collect on suicides if they know about it.

**Morty:** You should let... You should let him... [*A pause in which* ALL *seem dazed. Bell rings insistently.*]

**Moe:** Well, we're waiting.

**Morty:** Give me the note.

**Moe:** I'll give you the head off your shoulders.

**Morty:** Bessie, you'll stand for this? [*Points to* RALPH.] Pull down his pants and give him with a strap.

**Ralph:** [*As bell rings again.*] How about it?

**Bessie:** Don't be crazy. It's not my fault. Morty said he should come tonight. It's not nice so soon. I didn't—

**Morty:** I said it? Me?

**Bessie:** Who then?

**Morty:** You didn't sing a song in my ear a whole week to settle quick?

**Bessie:** I'm surprised. Morty, you're a big liar.

**Myron:** Momma's telling the truth, she is!

**Morty:** Lissen. In two shakes of a lamb's tail, we'll start a real fight and then nobody won't like nobody. Where's my fur gloves? I'm going downtown. [*To* Sam.] You coming? I'll drive you down.

**Hennie:** [*To* Sam, *who looks questioningly at her.*] Don't look at me. Go home if you want.

**Sam:** If you're coming soon, I'll wait.

**Hennie:** Don't do me any favors. Night and day he pesters me.

**Morty:** You made a cushion—sleep!

**Sam:** I'll go home. I know... to my worst enemy I don't wish such a life—

**Hennie:** Sam, keep quiet.

**Sam:** [*Quietly, sadly.*] No more free speech in America? [*Gets his hat and coat.*] I'm a lonely person. Nobody likes me.

**Myron:** I like you, Sam.

**Hennie:** [*Going to him gently, sensing the end.*] Please go home, Sam. I'll sleep here... I'm tired and nervous. Tommorow I'll come home. I love you... I mean it. [*She kisses him with real feeling.*]

**Sam:** I would die for you... [Sam *looks at her. Tries to say something, but his voice chokes up with a mingled feeling. He turns and leaves the room.*]

**Morty:** A bird in the hand is worth two in the bush. Remember I said it. Good night. [*Exits after* Sam.]

[Hennie *sits depressed.* Bessie *goes up and looks at the picture calender again.* Myron *finally breaks the silence.*]

**Myron:** Yesterday a man wanted to sell me a saxophone with pearl buttons. But I—

**Bessie:** It's a beautiful picture. In this land, nobody works... Nobody worries... Come to bed, Myron. [*Stops at the door, and says to* Ralph] Please don't have foolish ideas about the money.

**Ralph:** Let's call it a day.

**Bessie:** It belongs for the whole family. You'll get your teeth fixed—

**Ralph:** And a pair of black and white shoes?

**Bessie:** Hennie needs a vacation. She'll take two weeks in the mountains and I'll mind the baby.

**Ralph:** I'll take care of my own affairs.

**Bessie:** A family needs for a rainy day. Times is getting worse. Prospect Avenue, Dawson, Beck Street—everyday furniture's on the sidewalk.

**Ralph:** Forget it, Mom.

**Bessie:** Ralphie, I worked too hard all my years to be treated like dirt. It's no law we should be stuck together like Siamese twins. Summer shoes you didn't have, skates you never had, but I bought a new dress every week. A lover I kept—Mr. Gigolo! Did I ever play a game of cards like Mrs. Marcus? Or was Bessie Berger's children always the cleanest on the block?! Here I'm not only the mother, but also the father. The first two years I worked in a stocking factory for six dollars while Myron Berger went to law school. If I didn't worry about the family who would? On the calendar it's a different place, but here without a dollar you don't look the world in the eye. Talk from now to next year—this is life in America.

**Ralph:** Then it's wrong. It don't make sense. If life made you this way, then it's wrong!

**Bessie:** Maybe you wanted me to give up twenty years ago. Where would you be now? You'll excuse my expression—a bum in the park!

**Ralph:** I'm not blaming you, Mom. Sink or swim—I see it. But it can't stay like this.

**Bessie:** My foolish boy...

**Ralph:** No, I see every house lousy with lies and hate. He said it, Grandpa—Brooklyn hates the Bronx. Smacked on the nose twice a day. But boys and girls can get ahead like that, Mom. We don't want life printed on dollar bills, Mom!

**Bessie:** So go out and change the world if you don't like it.

**Ralph:** I will! And why? 'Cause life's different in my head. Gimme the earth in two hands. I'm strong. There... hear him? The airmail off to Boston. Day or night, he flies away, a job to do. That's us and it's no time to die.

[*The airplane sound fades off as* MYRON *gives alarm clock to* BESSIE, *which she begins to wind.*]

BESSIE: "Mom, what does she know? She's old-fashioned!" But I'll tell you a big secret: My whole life I wanted to go away too, but with children a woman stays home. A fire burned in *my* heart too, but now it's too late. I'm no spring chicken. The clock goes and Bessie goes. Only my machinery can't be fixed. [*She lifts a button: the alarm rings on the clock; she stops it, says "Good night" and exits.*]

MYRON: I guess I'm no prize bag...

BESSIE: [*From within.*] Come to bed, Myron.

MYRON: [*Tears page off calender.*] Hmmm... [*Exits to her.*]

RALPH: Look at him, draggin' after her like an old shoe.

MOE: Punch drunk. [*Phone rings.*] That's for me. [*At phone.*] Yeah?...Just a minute. [*To* RALPH.] Your girl...

RALPH: Jeez, I don't know what to say to her.

MOE: Hang up? [RALPH *slowly takes phone.*]

RALPH: Hello... Blanche, I wish... I don't know what to say... Yes... Hello?... [*Puts phone down.*] She hung up on me...

MOE: Sorry?

RALPH: No girl means anything to me until...

MOE: Till when?

RALPH: Till I can take care of her. Till we don't look out on an airshaft. Till we can take the world in two hands and polish off the dirt.

MOE: That's a big order.

RALPH: Once upon a time I thought I'd drown to death in bolts of silk and velour. But I grew up these last few weeks. Jake said a lot.

MOE: Your memory's okay?

RALPH: But take a look at this. [*Brings armful of books from* JACOB'S *room—dumps them on table.*] His books, I got them too—the pages ain't cut in half of them.

MOE: Perfect.

RALPH: Does it prove something? Damn tootin'! A ten-cent nail file cuts them. Uptown, downtown, I'll read them on the way. Get a big lamp over the bed. [*Picks up one.*] My eyes are good. [*Puts book in pocket.*] Sure, inventory tommorrow. Coletti to Driscoll to Berger—that's how we work. It's a team down the warehouse. Driscoll's a show-off, a wiseguy, and Joe talks pigeons day and night. But they're like me, looking for a chance to get to first base too. Joe razzed me about my girl. But he don't why. I'll tell him. Hell, he might tell me something I don't know. Get teams together all over. Spit on your hands and get to work. And with enough teams together maybe we'll get steam in the warehouse so our fingers don't freeze off. Maybe we'll fix it so life won't be printed on dollar bills.

MOE: Graduation Day.

RALPH: [*Starts for door of his room, stops.*] Can I have … Grandpa's note?

MOE: Sure you want it?

RALPH: Please — [MOE *gives it.*] It's blank!

MOE: [*Taking note back and tearing it up.*] That's right.

RALPH: Thanks! [*Exits.*]

MOE: The kid's a fighter! [*To* HENNIE.] Why are you crying?

HENNIE: I never cried in my life. [*She is now.*]

MOE: [*Starts for door. Stops.*] You told Sam you love him …

HENNIE: If I'm sore on life, why take it out on him?

MOE: You won't forget me to your dyin' day — I was the first guy. Part of your insides. You won't forget. I wrote my name on you — indelible ink!

HENNIE: One thing I won't forget — how you left me crying on the bed like I was two for a cent!

MOE: Listen, do you think —

HENNIE: Sure. Waits till the family goes to the open-air movie. He brings me perfume … He grabs my arms —

MOE: You won't forget me!

HENNIE: How you left the next week?

MOE: So I made a mistake. For Chris' sake, don't act like the Queen of Romania!

HENNIE: Don't make me laugh!

MOE: What the hell do you want, my head on a plate?! Was my life so happy? Chris', my old man was a bum. I supported the whole damn family — five kids and Mom. When they grew up they beat it the hell away like rabbits. Mom died. I went to the war; got clapped down like a bedbug; woke up in a room without a leg. What the hell do you think, anyone's got it better than you? I never had a home either. I'm lookin' too!

HENNIE: So what?

MOE: So you're it — you're home for me, a place to live! That's the whole parade, sickness, eating out your heart! Sometimes you meet a girl — she stops it — that's love … So take a chance! Be with me, Paradise. What's to lose?

HENNIE: My pride!

MOE: [*Grabbing her.*] What do you want? Say the word—I'll tango on a dime. Don't gimme ice when your heart's on fire!

HENNIE: Let me go! [*He stops her.*]

MOE: WHERE?!!

HENNIE: What do you want, Moe, what do you want?

MOE: You!

HENNIE: You'll be sorry you ever started—

MOE: You!

HENNIE: Moe, lemme go—[*Trying to leave.*] I'm getting up early—lemme go.

MOE: No!... I got enough fever to blow the whole damn town to hell. [*He suddenly releases her and half stumbles backwards. Forces himself to quiet down.*] you wanna go back to him? Say the word. I'll know what to do...

HENNIE: [*Helplessly.*] Moe, I don't know what to say.

MOE: Listen to me.

HENNIE: What?

MOE: Come away. A certain place where it's moonlight and roses. We'll lay down, count stars. Hear the big ocean making noise. You lay under the trees. Champagne flows like—[*Phone rings.* MOE *finally answers the telephone.*] Hello?... Just a minute. [*Looks at* HENNIE.]

HENNIE: Who is it?

MOE: Sam.

HENNIE: [*Starts for phone, but changes her mind.*] I'm sleeping...

MOE: [*In phone.*] She's sleeping... [*Hangs up. Watches* HENNIE, *who slowly sits.*] He wants you to know he got home okay... What's on your mind?

HENNIE: Nothing.

MOE: Sam?

HENNIE: They say it's a palace on those Havana boats.

MOE: What's on your mind?

HENNIE: [*Trying to escape.*] Moe, I don't care for Sam—I never loved him—

MOE: But your kid—?

HENNIE: All my life I waited for this minute.

MOE: [*Holding her.*] Me too. Made believe I was talkin' just bedroom golf, but you and me forever was what I meant! Christ, baby, there's one life to live! Live it!

HENNIE: Leave the baby?

MOE: Yeah!

240

**HENNIE:** I can't...

**MOE:** You can!

**HENNIE:** No...

**MOE:** But you're not sure!

**HENNIE:** I don't know.

**MOE:** Make a break or spend the rest of your life in a coffin.

**HENNIE:** Oh God, I don't know where I stand.

**MOE:** Don't look up there. Paradise, you're on a big boat headed south. No more pins and needles in your heart, no snake juice squirted in your arm. The whole world's green grass and when you cry it's because you're happy.

**HENNIE:** Moe, I don't know...

**MOE:** Nobody knows, but you do it and find out. When you're scared the answer's zero.

**HENNIE:** You're hurting my arm.

**MOE:** The doctor said it—cut off your leg to save your life! And they done it—one thing to get another. [*Enter* RALPH.]

**RALPH:** I didn't hear a word, but do it, Hennie, do it!

**MOE:** Mom can mind the kid. She'll go on forever, Mom. We'll send money back, and Easter eggs.

**RALPH:** I'll be here.

**MOE:** Get your coat... get it.

**HENNIE:** Moe!

**MOE:** I know... but get your coat and hat and kiss the house good bye.

**HENNIE:** The man I love... [MYRON *entering*.] I left my coat in Mom's room. [*Exits.*]

**MYRON:** Don't wake her up, Beauty. Momma fell asleep as soon as her head hit the pillow. I can't sleep. It was a long day. Hmmm. [*Examines his tongue in buffet mirror.*] I was reading the other day a person with a thick tongue is feeble-minded. I can do anything with my tongue. Make it thick, flat. No fruit in the house lately. Just a lone apple. [*He gets apple and paring knife and starts paring.*] Must be something wrong with me— I say I won't eat but I eat. [HENNIE *enters dressed to go out.*] Where you going, little Red Riding Hood?

**HENNIE:** Nobody knows, Peter Rabbit.

**MYRON:** You're looking very pretty tonight. You were a beautiful baby too. 1910, that was the year you was born. The same year Teddy Roosevelt come back from Africa.

**HENNIE:** Gee, Pop; you're such a funny guy.

241

**MYRON:** He was a boisterous man, Teddy. Good night. [*He exits, paring apple.*]

**RALPH:** When I look at him, I'm sad. Let me die like a dog, if I can't get more from life.

**HENNIE:** Where?

**RALPH:** Right here in the house! My days won't be for nothing. Let Mom have the dough. I'm twenty-two and kickin'! I'll get along. Did Jake die for us to fight about nickels? No! "Awake and sing," he said. Right here he stood and said it. The night he died, I saw it like a thunderbolt! I saw he was dead and I was born! I swear to God, I'm one week old! I want the whole city to hear it—fresh blood, arms. We got 'em. We're glad we're living.

**MOE:** I wouldn't trade you for two pitchers and an outfielder. Hold the fort!

**RALPH:** So long.

**MOE:** So long.

[*They go, and* RALPH *stands full and strong in the doorway, seeing them off as the curtain slowly falls.*]

CURTAIN

# MORNING STAR

*Sylvia Regan*

*Morning Star*, Steppenwolf Theatre Company, Chicago, 1999. Photo: Michael Brosilow

# INTRODUCTION

Sylvia Regan (nee Hoffenberg) came to playwriting after earlier demonstrating a number of other theatrical aptitudes. A native New Yorker, she studied at the American Academy of Dramatic Arts. In 1926, at 18, she made her professional stage debut in Milton Herbert Gropper and Max Siegel's *We Americans*, a comedy about assimilation in which Paul Muni played his first English-language role. Still in her teens, Regan assisted the social director at Camp Tamimint, an adult resort in the Poconos whose entertainment programs became famous as a training ground for many of the mid-20th century's major headliners in theatre, film and TV. She ran the weekly Saturday night shows, casting them and contributing costumes, choreography and her own acting talents. Turning next to theatrical publicity and public relations, she worked for the Theatre Union and for Orson Welles and John Houseman's Mercury Theatre, where her job, she says, was to "upholster seats with backsides."

During a visit to the beach in the summer of 1937, Regan was so severely sunburned, she had to remain immobile. Casting about for a diversion from her enforced leisure, she set to work on the one theatrical activity she had not yet tried, playwriting. She transformed into a dramatic script a story Clifford Odets, a friend since childhood, had recently told her. (Odets shortly used the same story for *Rocket to the Moon*.) Although her *Every Day But Friday* was not produced, Sylvia Regan had found her métier.

Regan's subsequent plays include *A Hundred Million Nickles, Morning Star, Safe Harbor, 44 West, The Twelfth Hour*, and *Zelda*. Her biggest commercial success came in 1953 with *The Fifth Season*, which ran for 654 performances. It is a work about the vicissitudes of the garment industry, where insiders claim there are five seasons: summer, fall, winter, spring and slack. Menasha Skulnik, renowned comedian of the Yiddish theatre, made his English-language debut, earning critical raves for himself ("one of the funniest men who ever lived") and for the play ("irresistible fun"). Luba Kadison's musical version of *The Fifth Season*, in Yiddish and English, ran for 122 performances in 1975.

In 1940, Regan married composer and musicologist Abraham Ellstein who, with lyricist Robert Sour, had provided the songs for *Morning Star*. Regan and Ellstein collaborated on two musicals, *Marianne* and *Great to Be Alive*. Together they wrote an adaptation of *The Golem*, commissioned by the Ford Foundation and produced in 1962 by the New York City Opera under the direction of Julius Rudel. When Regan finally stopped writing for the theatre, she turned to a new career. She worked for years on a novel, which she left unpublished at her death in 2003.

The inspiration for *Morning Star*, Regan's first produced play, grew out of an early memory. As a three-year-old, she stood across the street from what had been the Triangle Shirtwaist Factory, listening to her mother tell a friend about the 1911 disaster. Had the fire not broken out on Saturday, whose sanctity her grandfather insisted that his daughters observe, Regan's mother and aunts would have been at work in the building. Regan made this historic event the literal center of her script and repeated the motif of a fiery triangle in the destructive relationship of three of her characters. She set the play in a milieu she knew intimately. Although the characters are fictionalized composites, there is a life drawing in the importunate Brownstein. He is modeled on a Marxist who used to bedevil Regan's father, proprietor of a shoe store, who subscribed to both retail trade journals and socialist publications. The marvelous petticoat scene which opens the play originated in Regan's grandmother's home where there were four daughters. On the other hand, there is no precedent in Regan's life or in dramatic literature for Sadie, who transforms from an unrequited lover to an ambitious career woman to a hardheaded, hard-hearted businesswoman.

*Morning Star* got off to an auspicious start. Regan's agent sold it almost immediately to producer George Kondolf. Effectively cast with Joseph Buloff as the admiring boarder, 15-year-old Sidney Lumet as the bar mitzvah boy, and Molly Picon as a diminutive contrast to the more typically ample Jewish mother, the play opened on Broadway on April 16, 1940. Three weeks later, Luxemburg and the Netherlands fell before Nazi Germany's war machine. The news from Europe extinguished New York's enthusiasm for theatre. Despite efforts on its behalf by producer John Golden and fellow writer Rose Franken (whose 1943 play *Outrageous Fortune* has important Jewish content), the play closed.

But the wheel of fortune had not finished turning for *Morning Star*. Published by Dramatists Play Service, the play was promptly launched into a career in stock and amateur productions. Wee and Leventhal made it part of New York's Subway Circuit, in which productions toured the city's five boroughs. *Morning Star* earned enthusiastic reviews off-Broadway and across the country. In a 1963 Los Angeles production, retitled *In Mama's House,* 16-year-old Richard Dreyfuss played the bar mitzvah boy. The Folksbiene Theatre presented Miriam Kressyn's Yiddish adaptation, first called *Broome Street, America* in 1985 and then *An American Family* in 2000. The former impressed one New York reviewer as "as fine a piece of theatre as can be found anywhere on Broadway or off." It was mounted again in English in Los Angeles in 2000 and the following year at the Asolo Theatre in Sarasota, Florida, both times to critical acclaim.

Although *Morning Star* showcases major chapters in the American Jewish experience, the play's international successes demonstrate its wide appeal. It made its European debut in Scotland in 1946 and has entered the repertoire of Glasgow's Jewish Institute Players. In Hempstead, England, retitled this time *The Golden Door,* it sold out for nearly a year. It took first prize as an amateur entry in the British Drama Festival in the early Fifties. A few years later, Tel Aviv's Ohel Theatre produced *Morning Star* in Hebrew. In the mid Fifties, it was mounted in Buenos Aires, in both Spanish and Yiddish productions, the latter starring Bertha Gerston and Jacob Ben Ami. In 1972, it played to full houses in South Wales, Australia.

Its warm New York and overseas reception notwithstanding, *Morning Star* seems destined for continual rediscovery. I had not heard of the play when I came across it as I was preparing the 1995 edition of *Awake and Singing.* I found Regan's characterizations nuanced and compelling and I loved how the play told its story, so I included it in my book.

Then exciting things began to happen. Director Frank Galati was browsing in a bookstore and found my anthology. Intrigued by an unfamiliar title and a dramatist whose name he did not recognize, he sat down on the spot and read it. He recalls being struck by *Morning Star*'s psychological scope and stunned by its emotional power. Galati brought it to the attention of Martha Lavey, artistic director of Chicago's Steppenwolf Theatre who promptly invited him to direct it. The handsome 1999 production—a production photo is on the cover of this book— won popular and critical raves ("intensely moving" ... "a precious jewel" ... "beautifully crafted"). Its run had to be extended twice. New York reviewers joined their Chicago colleagues in heaping praise on Galati, Steppenwolf and the 91-year-old Regan. "*Morning Star*'s achievement," wrote John Lahr in *The New Yorker*, " is to submerge the audience in the vigor of the century's early optimism and outrage, and to bear witness to the immigrant struggle to tame both American labor and the American language."

The tale does not end there. *Morning Star* had found its home and its moment. Richard Pearlman, director of Chicago's Lyric Opera Center for American Artists, had already commissioned a work from composer Ricky Ian Gordon. Hearing the buzz about *Morning Star* at Steppenwolf, Pearlman too found *Awake and Singing* and read Regan's play. He then recommended it to Gordon because, he says, he thought it would appeal to the composer, whose family history bears some strong parallels to the fictional Feldermans' (he has three older sisters and his father discouraged his mother's vocal career). Pearlman's intuition was sound. Gordon responded warmly to the work and shared his enthusiasm with dramatist William Hoffman, who agreed to write the libretto. Together they have made of *Morning Star* a crossover piece between opera and a musical written for operatic voices. *Morning Star* will now have yet another life as musical theatre.

Interviewed in the *Chicago Sun Times* during the Steppenwolf run, Regan remarked, "I guess the revival of my play proves... what I've always believed, which is that if you put something between covers—if you publish it—it will never die."

Such a success story surpasses an anthologist's most extravagant dreams.

*Morning Star* was produced for the first time by George Kondolf at the Longacre Theatre, New York, April 16, 1940, with the following cast:

| | |
|---|---|
| Fanny | Jeanne Greene |
| Becky Felderman | Molly Picon |
| Aaron Greenspan | Joseph Buloff |
| Esther | Cecilia Evans |
| Hymie (as a boy) | Kenneth LeRoy |
| Harry Engel | Martin Blaine |
| Sadie | Ruth Yorke |
| Irving Tashman | David Morris |
| Benjamin Brownstein | Harold J. Stone |
| Myron Engel | Henry Sharp |
| Hymie (as a young man) | Ross Elliott |
| Pansy | Georgette Harvey |
| Hymie Tashman | Sidney Lumet |

## SYNOPSIS OF SCENES

The action takes place in Becky Felderman's home, on the Lower East Side of New York.

## ACT ONE

**SCENE 1:** A December afternoon, 1910.
**SCENE 2:** A month later.

## ACT TWO

**SCENE 1:** Early morning, March 25th, 1911.
[*During this scene the curtain will be lowered twice to denote a passage of time.*]
**SCENE 2:** Early April, six years later.
**SCENE 3:** Eighteen months later.

## ACT THREE

Thirteen years later, November, 1931.

## AUTHOR'S NOTE

Since the language of the play is rich in Jewish idiom and speech color, there is a danger of caricaturing the lines should the accent be used. Therefore, with the possible exception of Aaron's speech, it is suggested that no other accent be used throughout.

**NOTE:** The songs "We'll Bring the Rue de la Paix" and "Under a Painted Smile," by Abraham Ellstein and Robert Sour, are reprinted by permission of Sylvia Regan (Mrs. Abraham Ellstein).

# ACT ONE

## SCENE 1

*Late afternoon in December, 1910. The scene is the combination living room–dining room of the Felderman household, on the lower East Side, New York. A door up* L. *leads to hall. Two doors at* R. *lead to bedrooms. Door* L. *leads to kitchen and door up* L. *to bathroom. There is a neatly curtained window up* R., *which faces on the street. An old leather couch stands downstage* R. *A round table* C., *several hideous straight-backed chairs and a heavy buffet at upstage wall. An old upright piano, the one note of luxury, stands down* L. *At the moment, a dressmaker's form stands in front of window. The fancy calendar of the type given away free by tradesmen, bric-a-brac, and other decoration may be left to the discretion of the director.*

**AT RISE:** *A general feeling of disorder. It is ironing day. A number of freshly ironed petticoats of the period, stiff with starch, stand around the room as though on legs, and take up all the available floor space between table and chairs.*

ESTHER FELDERMAN *is at ironing board. She is a frail girl, no more than 16. Enormous eyes set off her thin, fair-complexioned face.* BECKY FELDERMAN, *her mother, is at dressmaker's form, working on a much-flowered dress.* BECKY *is about 37, with a girlish alive quality.*

FANNY FELDERMAN, *her second daughter, is at piano, hammering out a tune with one finger. She is a little over 17, a dark, buxom peasant beauty, with a vivacious and excitable manner* AARON GREENSPAN, *the boarder, a man of about 40, is stretched out on couch, sleeping the sleep of the dead, snoring occasionally.* BECKY *hums as she works.*

FANNY: [*Looking up. Good-naturedly.*] Mama, those aren't the words.

BECKY: [*singing off-key.*] Ta-ta-ta—ta-ta-ta—It's just like you sing it, no?

FANNY: No, Mama. It goes like this—Ta-ta-ta-ta—ta-ta—

[BECKY *joins in. By this time they are making a terrific racket.*]

AARON: [*Sits up.*] in Grand Central Station it's more quiet!

BECKY: In Grand Central they take in boarders?

FANNY: [*Of the song she has been playing.*] Is this new song beautiful! [*Laughing.*] In "Alma, Where Do You Live?" the man in the music store told me Kitty Gordon takes off all her clothes when she sings it!

BECKY: Such a song you are singing?

FANNY: Mama, please—don't get excited—

BECKY: To ruin your life singing in the Apollo Nickelette every night—

FANNY: If that's how you felt, why'd you have to go to the contest with me?

BECKY: Because I didn't think you could win—

FANNY: What!

BECKY: To sing in a place where they throw on the actors eggs—

FANNY: [*Cutting in hotly.*] On me they throw eggs? They *love* me—

BECKY: Every night I am taking you from the theatre, a dozen bums standing by the back door. Even to me, an old woman, they are making "Hello, baby." That's *love?* That's *respect?*

FANNY: [*As she starts to exit.*] *You* make me so nervous, I can't even practice! [*She is gone.*]

AARON: Aye, Becky, Becky, you need a *man* in the house.

ESTHER: [*Accidentally dropping the iron onto the board*] Ouch!

BECKY: You burned yourself?

AARON: You can't wear it without pressing? Who sees it?

BECKY: And if, God forbid, an accident, you get run down from a horse-car—they take you to the hospital, it looks nice the petticoat should be with wrinkles?

AARON: The trouble is, Becky, you are a *pessimist.*

BECKY: What?

AARON: You can only see from everything the *bad* side!

ESTHER: Mama is always making us feel good when *we* are seeing the bad side—

AARON: All right! She is always seeing the *good* side! You are satisfied? So, if you'll excuse me!

[*The picture of* AARON *treading gingerly between the petticoats as he exits into bathroom is too much for* BECKY *and* ESTHER. *They start to laugh.*]

ESTHER: [*Picking up the much-flowered dress.*] For what Mrs. Smith is paying, without seam binding would be good enough. In Sadie's shop they never sew a piece of seam binding.

BECKY: What can you expect in ready-made? [*A clock strikes.*] Hymie is late from school—

ESTHER: [*Hesitating.*] Mama, please, can I go with Sadie tomorrow?

BECKY: Where?

ESTHER: To the Triangle Shop.

BECKY: Again you ask me? Esther—

ESTHER: When Fanny was in the shop you didn't mind. Sadie, you don't mind. Only me—

BECKY: You're too young.

ESTHER: Mrs. O'Shaughnessy's Annie is only fifteen.

BECKY: Mrs. O'Shaughnessy has also cockroaches in the sink!

ESTHER: Six, seven dollars a week—

BECKY: Esther, what did I tell you yesterday?

ESTHER: You told me "no"—

BECKY: And the day before?

ESTHER: "No" also—

BECKY: And this morning?

ESTHER: "No"—

BECKY: So?

ESTHER: [*Eagerly.*] So I can?

BECKY: No! [BECKY *gets up, starts to take away ironing board.*]

ESTHER: But, Mama, Sadie says to work gives a girl independence.

BECKY: What?

ESTHER: You have money in your pocket, you are the boss!

BECKY: The boss is not the boss? *You* are the boss?

ESTHER: Over yourself, Mama! You don't need to go to anybody for something! [*Inspired*] You are free!

BECKY: [*Settling the matter*] In America everybody is free! Something is on your mind, Esther. Mama can tell—

ESTHER: Mama, please—sometimes I would like to have a pair of lisle stockings! Not cotton—

**BECKY:** [*Smiling.*] That's all? So I'll buy you a pair of lisle stockings. [*Touching* ESTHER's *face, as though seeking the source of her apparent upset.*] Will that make you happier?

[BECKY *exits into kitchen with ironing board.* ESTHER *looks after her a moment, then starts to gather petticoats together, placing one over the other on dressmaker's form.* AARON *enters.* ESTHER *looks away, embarrassed, but he calmly goes on pulling up his suspenders.*]

**ESTHER:** Aaron, please, try to remember, *women* live in this house!
**AARON:** It's my fault conditions is crowded? I'm not exactly complaining, but a boarder has some rights, too! I pay my rent, no?
**ESTHER:** No!
**AARON:** [*Abashed.*] Well—it is my *intention* to pay! It's my fault I'm a millinery worker on straw and the season is late this year? A man can suddenly get hard up! [ESTHER *stares at him skeptically.*] If you have to know, little lady, right this minute, I could be in the millinery business for myself, a boss—if I wanted!
**ESTHER:** [*Still skeptical.*] It doesn't cost money to go into business?
**AARON:** Who says no? My friend Van Brett the blocker—he has the money. He begs me! With his thousand dollars and my brains, the sky is the limitation!
**ESTHER:** So what stops you?
**AARON:** Because I have a conscience! On one side of me, Van Brett! He says to me, "Become a boss, make a million. It's America—one, two, three."
**ESTHER:** Then why don't you do it?
**AARON:** Because on the other side of me is my friend Brownstein the radical. He says to me, "Exploiter! On the backs of the workers you don't climb to success." Can I help it if I have a conscience? I'm completely confused.
**ESTHER:** [*Impressed.*] Please don't tell Mama I said anything about—the rent. I apologize.
**AARON:** [*Grandly.*] I accept—[BECKY *enters.*]
**BECKY:** I didn't study the lesson for today—and Mr. Engel will be here any minute. [*She takes a book from buffet, starts to glance through it.*]
**AARON:** The whole house English lessons! Does a woman have to vote for the President? What does she need citizna papers for?
**BECKY:** My children and I should have a place in the world. To belong here.

AARON: Listen, Becky, why should you bother with examinations, lessons? If you would listen to my proposition—after all—I'm a citizen and in America the law is—

BECKY: You're starting up again?

AARON: What's the use, Becky, you need a man in the house!

BECKY: [*Playfully.*] So you live here, no?

AARON: A boarder ain't the same thing! [BECKY *stares at him.*] All right! I'm not starting up again! But a man can put in a good word for himself?

BECKY: You're not ashamed in front of the world—

ESTHER: [*Giggling.*] Should I go into the kitchen, Mama?

AARON: What I have to say to your mother, I'm not *ashamed the world to hear!* [*To* BECKY, *directly.*] Nu? [BECKY *laughs.*] You ever saw such a woman? Can you tell me please, one objection you could have to me? I'm an honest man, I don't drink, I don't gamble. Thank God, I make a good living—[*He breaks off, embarrassed by this obvious overstatement.*] When I'm working—[*Pause.*] Becky, say the word, I go into partnership with Van Brett, in no time I could dress you up in Hudson sealskin from head to toe! [BECKY *pays no attention.*] You are exactly my type.

BECKY: Aaron, please—

AARON: A beautiful woman like you—a woman full of life. To live out your days without a husband, ain't—ain't natural!

BECKY: Aaron, please, once and for all—to me it's natural a woman should know her responsibility to her four children—

AARON: Children! You can't fool me, Becky! It's Jacob. Jacob Felderman. A man is dead so many years, but in your heart he's lucky! He'll live forever! [BECKY *continues to read her book. A pause.* AARON *sits on couch dejectedly. Suddenly he jumps up, goes to door, puts on his overcoat and hat.*] Ask me where I'm going? [*He exits.*]

BECKY: [*To* ESTHER.] So—where was I?

ESTHER: You're on Columbus, Mama.

BECKY: That's right—Columbus—[*Turning over pages.*] In 1492 Columbus discovered America. [*A knock at door.* ESTHER *remains at table, trying to contain her excitement.* HARRY ENGEL *enters. He is about twenty-three, a slender young man with a gentle scholarly manner.*] Hello, Mr. Engel. Come in—

HARRY: How do you do? And Miss Esther?

ESTHER: Very, very fine, thank you—

**BECKY:** I'm ashamed of myself. I didn't hardly study the lesson today. [*They get settled,* HARRY *and* BECKY *at* table, ESTHER *on couch where she follows his every movement. Occasionally he glances in her direction.* BECKY *puts on spectacles.*] This minute I was looking up when did Columbus discover America. Oy! [*Giggles.*] I forgot it already. Wait! Don't tell me — fourteen, fourteen is right, yes?

**HARRY.** That's right. Fourteen what?

**BECKY:** You have to give the exact *minute* when they ask you?

**HARRY:** I think they'll want to know the year. Shall I tell you?

**BECKY:** What can I do?

**HARRY:** Mrs. Felderman, I'll tell you and when I do, you'll never forget it again. Listen —

"In fourteen hundred and ninety-two
Columbus sailed the ocean blue."

**BECKY:**

"In fourteen hundred and ninety-two
Columbus sailed the ocean blue."

That's wonderful I'll never forget it. [*Pause.*] I better write it down. [*Writing laboriously, she looks up.*] Mr. Engel, what do you think? Am I passing for my "citizna papers"?

**HARRY:** It means a lot to you, doesn't it?

**BECKY:** The world. [*She laughs.*] I could die laughing when I think how many times they caught us by the border. My Sadie used to say, "Mama, there is no America. It's only a dream in your head." But the dream came true. Mr. Engel, I could kiss George Washington's feet for chopping down the cherry tree, we should be free.

**ESTHER:** [*Laughing.*] Mama, he chopped it down and didn't tell a lie.

**BECKY:** Mr. Engel knows what I mean —

**HARRY:** Now tell me, when was the Declaration of Independence signed?

**BECKY:** July the fourth, 1776!

**HARRY:** Good!

**BECKY:** I should say it's good! In Russia when my brother Abraham used to say "Revolution," I laughed, but now I have different ideas—if a Revolution could make a country like this, maybe Abraham was right? [*Harry looks doubtful.*] Was he?

HARRY: [*With a smile.*] Not exactly, Mrs. Felderman. It's never war that makes a country great. It's the work of her people during peace times—

BECKY: You explain things so good—please don't be mad on me, Mr. Engel, but I have to thank you for what you're doing.

HARRY: Mrs. Felderman, it's nothing—

BECKY: Free lessons to Sadie and Esther and me is nothing?

HARRY: I couldn't take money from you. It would be like taking it from my own family—

BECKY: Yes?

HARRY: [*Afraid he has said too much.*] It's good experience for me, too. I'm taking an examination myself in a few weeks. To teach school—

BECKY: That's wonderful—

HARRY: I think so. To me, it's the most important job in the whole world— [*With some enthusiasm.*] Matter of fact, I intend to specialize in American History.

BECKY: Columbus and Lincoln?

HARRY: That's right. [*Enthusiastically.*] Some day I expect to write a textbook for children. A new kind of history book that doesn't glorify "war"!

BECKY: You're so smart, Mr. Engel. Your mother must be proud of you.

HARRY: I have only my father. I think he's proud of me, but not to my face—[HYMIE FELDERMAN *enters. He is not quite 13—a think kid with a sensitive face.*]

HYMIE: [*Going directly to Becky at table.*] Hello, Mama—

BECKY: You're late from school!

HYMIE: The teacher kept us—[*Hesitating.*] Mama, could you come now with me to the Rabbi, to get my speech?

BECKY: My Hymie is being Bar Mitzvah next month, Mr. Engel. I would be very happy if you and your papa could come—

HARRY: Thank you very much—

HYMIE: Mama, could you come now?

BECKY: Mr. Engel, would you please excuse me—I've been promising him for a week already—

HARRY: Certainly—of course—[*Glancing toward Esther.*] We'll give Miss Esther a little more time for her lesson.

Sylvia Regan

**BECKY:** [*Putting on a shawl.*] Well, good bye and thank you, Mr. Engel. I'll
be back soon, Esther— [*Calling out.*] Fanny, get dressed!
**HARRY:** And, Mrs. Felderman, WHEN did Columbus discover America?
**BECKY:** [*Delightedly.*]

"In founteen hundred and ninety-two
Columbus sailed the blue ocean."

[BECKY *and* HYMIE, *exit. The moment they are gone,* HARRY *and*
ESTHER *quickly go toward one another. His manner changes from the
pedantic school teacher of the moment before to a young boy in love,
They are about to embrace, think better of it as* ESTHER *reminds him
by gestures of* FANNY's *presence in next room. They stare at one
another for a moment.*]

**HARRY:** Esther, darling—
**ESTHER:** You were five minutes late—
**HARRY.** I ran all the way from Canal Street. Can you meet me tonight?
Delancey Park, near the fence, like yesterday?
**ESTHER:** [*Giggling.*] Mama can't understand why I'm always wanting to go
down for a walk after supper!
**HARRY:** The minute I pass my examination, we'll tell them— [*Tenderly.*] So
sweet—
**ESTHER:** Harry, do you think Mama will be mad when we tell her? I'm the
youngest. A mother always likes it better when the oldest gets married
first.
**HARRY:** [*Upset.*] But you told me yourself your mother was only sixteen and
three months when Sadie was born, so how can she be mad? Please,
Esther, maybe we ought to tell her right away—
**ESTHER:** Oh, no—please—it wouldn't look nice. We don't know each other
so long—
**HARRY:** You mean you're not sure? [*They draw apart quickly as* FANNY *enters,
still in her kimono. She makes a beeline for bathroom.*] As I was saying—
[*Discovering* FANNY.] Oh—how do you do, Miss Fanny?
**FANNY:** [*Wrapping kimono around her modestly.*] Very fine, thank you. [*With
exaggerated politeness.*] Pardon the appearance. [*She is gone, banging door
behind her.*]
**HARRY:** [*When* FANNY *has gone.*] You didn't answer me. Aren't you sure?
About us?

ESTHER: Please, Harry, I'm sure—I—I would die for you, so sure I am—
HARRY: Gosh, for a minute you had me scared. [*Glancing around.*] If—if I kissed you somebody might see. Look at me. [*Pause.*] I have just kissed you.
ESTHER: [*Slowly.*] I felt it. [*Giggling.*] This is a fine English lesson—
HARRY: [*Laughing happily.*] And did you hear your mother invite us to the Bar Mitzvah? Like being in the family already!
ESTHER: I was holding my breath!
HARRY: I can hardly wait for my father to meet you. I have already told him about you.
ESTHER: [*Frightened.*] Oh—what did he say?
HARRY: He said, "If you love her, I love her." According to my father we could get married tomorrow.
ESTHER: [*Frightened again.*] So soon?
HARRY: In one month I'll be able to support a wife—
ESTHER: Mama'll be so mad on me—
HARRY: Then we better tell her right away—
ESTHER: Oh, Harry, please—no—[SADIE FELDERMAN *enters. She is about nineteen, thin and sallow-complexioned, with a forceful drive in her manner that belies her slight frame.*]
SADIE: [*Pleased to see him.*] Oh—how do you do, Mr. Engel—?
HARRY: Very well. And you?
SADIE: Simply exhausted. The last minute they brought in a hundred and fifty new waists to finish up! Please pardon my appearance—I must look a sight. [*As she goes toward bedroom.*] I'll be back in a moment. [*She exits into bedroom.*]
ESTHER: Harry, please, maybe you better go—
HARRY: But we didn't settle anything. About when we are getting married.
ESTHER: Please, Harry, we can't talk about it now—somebody'll hear.
HARRY: You'll have to meet me tonight so we can talk.
ESTHER: Maybe Mama won't let me go out.
HARRY: [*Adamant.*] I'll wait for you. Same time tonight.
ESTHER: I'll try my best. Good-bye—
HARRY: Until tonight—darling—[*He is at door.*] Mrs. Engel—[*He is gone.* ESTHER *runs to window.*]
FANNY: [*Calling out.*] Esther! He's gone?
ESTHER: Yes—
FANNY: [*Entering, comes toward* ESTHER.] Esther, I—I couldn't help myself, honest, but I heard what you and your boy friend were talking about.

ESTHER: Oh—

FANNY: Don't get scared. I won't tell anyone, darling. Can you keep a secret?

ESTHER: Surely—[FANNY *nods her head vigorously.*] You mean *you*, too?

FANNY: That's right.

ESTHER: Oh, Fanny, Fanny—both of us—[*The girls embrace, giggling happily.*] Is he nice?

FANNY: He's *wonderful!* The way he dresses—you should just see him!

ESTHER: I'm thinking what Mama will say.

FANNY: She'll have to get used to it. We ain't babies! [*Excitedly.*] He's an usher in the Apollo, where I work. But he's only doing it *temporary*. He writes songs!

ESTHER: No!

FANNY: Honest! He's writing a song for me to sing.

ESTHER: Oh, Fanny, please, let's have a double wedding.

FANNY: He didn't *ask* me yet!

ESTHER: Oh—[*Cheerily.*] But don't worry! Harry didn't *really* ask me right away! Maybe he's bashful?

FANNY: [*Laughing.*] Him bashful? He wouldn't be bashful to tell President William Howard Taft to go to the dickens.

ESTHER: Fanny—

FANNY: I mean it. He's got some mouth on him!

ESTHER: What's his name?

FANNY: Irving. Irving Tashman. I'll be *Mrs.* Irving Tashman—if he asks me—

ESTHER: Oh—he will—how could he help it? You're so beautiful. And you sing so beautiful—

FANNY: [*Pleased*] Go on. [*She surveys herself in mirror over buffet, wrapping kimono tightly about her.*] Maybe you're right. I don't know. [*Trying to be modest and hardly succeeding.*] Everybody tells me I'm beautiful. And when I sing everybody *whistles!* [*As though telling a great secret.*] I'm going to tell you something I wouldn't tell a soul. [AARON *enters, disconsolately. The girls draw apart quickly.*]

AARON: [*As he goes toward couch.*] A man can go crazy when he's not working. Sit in the house, it's on your nerves. Take a walk—so where are you going? Aye, confusion! [*He lies full-length on couch.*]

FANNY: [*Whispering to* ESTHER.] Tonight, he's taking me to a *restaurant!*

ESTHER: Mama won't let you go. [BECKY *enters with* HYMIE.]

BECKY: [*To* FANNY.] You're not dressed yet?

FANNY: I'm getting dressed now. [*She exits, making gesture for secrecy to* ESTHER.]

BECKY: Mr. Engel is gone already?

ESTHER: He had to leave—[HYMIE *goes into kitchen.* SADIE *enters.*]

SADIE: [*Looking around disappointed.*] Mr. Engel is gone already?

ESTHER: He had to leave.

SADIE: [*Disappointed, she takes it out on* AARON, *now lying on couch.*] You have to use the living room for a bedroom even in the daytime?

AARON: [*Sitting up.*] Oh, *you're* here.

SADIE: Mama, I asked you—

BECKY: But the living room *is* his bedroom—

SADIE: Even when he don't pay rent weeks already?

BECKY: Sadie!

AARON: Never mind, Miss Smarty. These humiliations! Why do I stand for it? These—these insults! If I had money you would speak to me with kid gloves! I ask you, would Brownstein be such a Socialist, if he had my opportunity to go into business and be treated like a gentleman?

SADIE: And hereafter on a Wednesday night, be so kind as to take a walk for yourself! Last night when I'm taking my lesson, he lays there on the couch talking to himself the whole time!

AARON: Engel doesn't care if I sit here. Who do I hurt?

SADIE: I care! Like living in the middle of Castle Garden,[1] this house! [*She exits lower bedroom.*]

AARON: What did I come to America for? To be insulted I could have stayed in Russia.

BECKY: Don't be mad on her, Aaron. She can't help—it she's the nervous type.

AARON: How is it *you* ain't the nervous type? I know those skinny women already!

BECKY: In her heart is something which pushes her—to build herself up—to improve her life—

AARON: She should learn first to improve her temper!

[FANNY *enters, wearing an evening dress, obviously homemade, but very becoming.* SADIE *follows her in.*]

SADIE: Mama, look at Fanny—

BECKY: The stage dress for eating supper in the kitchen?

FANNY: [*Excitedly.*] Mama, please don't get excited—tonight I am not eating supper home. I am eating in a restaurant.

---

[1] Huge, busy reception center for immigrants arriving in the port of New York.

**BECKY:** A restaurant?

**FANNY:** [*Anxious.*] I was invited!

**BECKY:** [*Quietly.*] Who invited you?

**FANNY:** [*Almost hysterical now.*] Mr. Irving Tashman, he invited me!

**BECKY:** Who?

**FANNY:** Mama, please, don't get excited! He's a Jewish boy!

**BECKY:** All day you're home you couldn't tell me—

**FANNY:** I was afraid to tell you, you might say "no."

**BECKY:** It's still not too late to say "no."

**FANNY:** [*Screaming.*] Mama!

**SADIE:** And who is this Mr. Tashman?

**FANNY:** He works in my theatre and he's a very nice fellow!

**SADIE:** An actor?

**FANNY:** An usher. His Uncle Abe owns the place. And the usher is only
temporary—[*Anxiously to* BECKY.] Mama, please, he's taking me to a
French restaurant!

**BECKY:** French? American ain't good enough?

**AARON:** Aye, Becky, if you had a man in the house!

**FANNY:** [*To* AARON.] Your two cents, too? The company I am keeping is
plenty good enough.

**SADIE:** Fine company! With tramps!

**FANNY:** It's *my* life! I should give a care what you think! When I'm a big star,
you'll be kissing my feet! [*To* BECKY.] Gee, Mom—you got to get used to
it. In America a girl don't wait till the *Shotchun*[2] comes. Here we gotta
meet our own fellows, or how are we going to get a husband?

**BECKY:** From husbands you are thinking already? [*Doorbell rings.*]

**FANNY:** It's him! [*The house is suddenly galvanized into action.* FANNY *runs to
window, opens it, calling out.*] Yoo-hoo—I'll be right down!

**BECKY:** He's not coming upstairs?

**FANNY:** Mama, please—

**BECKY:** You don't go with him one step unless he comes upstairs first. Mama
should take a look at him! [HYMIE *has entered a moment before.*]

**FANNY:** [*Tearfully.*] In this dump? What will he think of me?

**BECKY:** [*Pointing to window, sternly.*] Upstairs first!

**FANNY:** [*Reluctantly calling down again.*] Irving! Mr. Tashman! Please come
upstairs, will you! [*She comes away from window unhappily, spots* AARON
*on couch.*] Aaron, please—

---

[2] Or *shadchen*, a professional matchmaker.

**AARON:** [*Sitting up.*] All right, all right! It's not so terrible he should find me on the couch!

**ESTHER:** Maybe I'll go into the bedroom, the house won't be so crowded?

**FANNY:** [*Gently.*] Please stay, Esther. I want *you* to meet him. [*They all stand around in stiff, expectant attitudes, waiting for* IRVING TASHMAN's *arrival. There is a knock at door.* IRVING *enters. A slender fellow, with a breezy manner His clothes are sporty and perhaps a little too colorful, his hat a little too cocked to one side.*] Hello. This—this is my family. And Mr. Greenspan—a *friend.*

**IRVING:** Pleased to meet ya—everybody—[*Looking around.*] Nice little place you got here.

**FANNY:** It's not fancy exactly.

**IRVING:** But it's home. No place like home, I always say—[*Spotting piano.*] Say, you didn't tell me you had a piano in the house.

**BECKY:** You play the piano?

**IRVING:** [*Trying to be modest.*] Do I play? Tell her.

**FANNY:** Like Paderewski—

**IRVING:** [*About to demonstrate.*] Would you like me to show you something I just knocked out—it's a beaut.

**FANNY:** [*Drawing his attention away from piano.*] Irving—I'm all ready—

**IRVING:** Ready for the big time? Taking her out big-time tonight. Didja tell 'em?

**BECKY:** A *French* place. She told us.

**IRVING:** Best place in town. I always say, you gonna take a girl out? Then take her to the best! That's my motto.

**FANNY:** And, Mama, tonight it's not necessary for you to take me home from the Apollo.

**BECKY:** I'll let you go home alone, Jack the Ripper should catch you?

**FANNY:** [*Looking at* IRVING *shyly.*] Mr. Tashman is escorting me home tonight.

**IRVING:** Don't you worry, Mom—I'll take good care of your little girl. Wouldn't let anything happen to her for the world—

**FANNY:** Irving, are we going?

**IRVING:** [*Breezily.*] Well—glad to 'a' metya—everybody—[*To* AARON.] Have a cigar. Havana. Have 'em made up special for me—

**AARON:** Thanks. It's a pleasure.

**IRVING:** Don't even mention it—[*He and* FANNY *exit.*]

**SADIE:** Cigars made special for him! Two for three cents, I betcha. Candy-store sport! [HYMIE *exits into kitchen.* AARON *has, lighted cigar and now inhales the aroma.*]

**AARON:** If you have to know, Miss Smarty, this cigar costs at least ten cents!
**SADIE:** And how would you know?
**BECKY:** I like him. He's a nice boy. A little bit fresh, but nice!
**SADIE:** [*Laughing.*] Mama, you meet a fellow two minutes, and you know already he's nice?
**BECKY:** One look and I can tell. He's a good boy.
**ESTHER:** [*As she exits into kitchen.*] I think he is very nice.
**SADIE:** Another party heard from—
**AARON:** Well, in my opinion—
**SADIE:** [*Nastily.*] Oh! So you have an opinion, too—
**AARON:** Well, that settles it! [*Jumps up and starts to put on his coat.*]
**BECKY:** Where are you going?
**AARON:** I'm taking myself for a walk to the Bronx to see Van Brett! And believe me, I'm going to tell it to Brownstein. To hell with my conscience! [*He exits, banging door* SADIE *remains behind, absorbed.*]
**SADIE:** [*After a pause, quietly.*] Mama, he was here again today—and again I didn't get a chance to talk to him. [*Bursting out passionately.*] If I could only have more time with him alone!
**BECKY:** He's bashful—
**SADIE:** What could *any* man say with Aaron on the couch, people walking in and out. [*Pause—then quietly.*] All week I wait on pins till Wednesday when he comes to give me the lesson. I have figured out what I am going to say, how I am going to say it. [*Ruefully.*] Comes the time—I sit, shivering, afraid to open my mouth.
**BECKY:** He said something today, makes me wonder—
**SADIE:** What?
**BECKY:** I was thanking him for what he was doing, lessons for nothing, so he said, money he couldn't take, like from his own family.
**SADIE:** He really said that?
**BECKY:** It's a good sign—
**SADIE:** [*Throwing her arms around* BECKY.] Oh, Mama—
**BECKY:** [*Smiling.*] So maybe now you'll feel better?
**SADIE:** [*Gaily.*] I should say so. What's for supper, Mama?

[SADIE *exits. Clock strikes six.* BECKY *steps on a chair, about to turn on gas.* ESTHER *enters.*]

**ESTHER:** Mama, I don't feel so hungry. I—I think I'll take a little walk—

**BECKY:** Now?

**ESTHER:** I was in the house all day. I need a little air.

**BECKY:** So take a walk. Don't stay long. [*ESTHER quickly takes her coat from rack and exits.* BECKY *lights gas. A warm glow of light suffuses the room.* BECKY *steps down, glances at book on table. Reciting, half to herself.*]

"In fourteen hundred and ninety-two
Columbus sailed the ocean blue — "

[*She exits into kitchen as*]

CURTAIN

# SCENE 2

*The same. A month later. The house has a festive air. There are candles in the brass candelabra on buffet. Table is covered with a white cloth and there are new curtains at window.*

**AT RISE**: Irving Tashman *is at piano, playing. He is in his shirtsleeves, and is by now completely "at home."* Becky *and* Fanny, *in new silk dresses, are busy setting table.* Hymie, *in a stiff new suit, is on floor studying a paper in his hand.*

**Hymie:** [*Half to himself.*] "My dear mama and sisters and brother-in-law and — friends. — Today I yam a man. I — I — " [*His nose is back in paper*]

**Fanny:** Mama, you're putting the knives on the wrong side.

**Becky:** What's the difference? A person can tell it's a knife.

**Hymie:** [*Laughing.*] Oh boy, was the Rabbi sore when I told him I'm makin' the speech in English!

**Becky:** I told him to tell the Rabbi he shouldn't be mad. After all, God can understand English and in America you have to do like the Romans do. [*To* Fanny.] Oh, I forgot! We have to make another setting. I told Aaron to invite his friend Brownstein.

**Fanny:** Him? Tonight? Gee, Mom — why?

**Becky:** The poor man — God knows when he gets something homemade to eat —

**Fanny:** So we have to listen a whole night to his politics? Hymie, get out of the way!

**Becky:** Hymie, your new suit —

[Hymie *exits into upper bedroom, holding paper behind his back, muttering.*]

**Irving:** [*As he plays.*] What's it sound like to you, Mom?

**Becky:** Beautiful —

**Irving:** [*To* Fanny.] C'mon, Kiddo, let's sing the chorus for Mom. [Fanny *and* Irving *sing as he plays, "Under a Painted Smile." They finish song with great aplomb.*]

**Becky:** Beautiful —

**Irving:** And whose little sweetheart am I writing it for?

FANNY: [*Giggling.*] Yours!

IRVING: And what's her name?

FANNY: Mrs. Fanny Tashman!

BECKY: For that I am not forgiving you so easy!

IRVING: [*Getting up, playfully putting his arms around her*] Whatsa matter, Mom! Still sore? I didn't wanna elope. Fanny made me. She took one look at the way I look at you and she got jealous—

BECKY: [*Fighting him off good-naturedly.*] Go away, you loafer, you! I'll go with the broom to you!

FANNY: Irv, let's fix up the cake like you said—[*They exit into kitchen, laughing.* SADIE *and* ESTHER *enter from street.*]

ESTHER: [*Excitedly, as they remove their wraps.*] We ran all the way home!

SADIE: We tried to get off a few minutes early, so the foreman wouldn't let us—

ESTHER: [*Laughing.*] I went up to him and I said, "We don't feel so good—we're sick"—so he says, "Only one of you is allowed to be sick at one time. Make up your mind—" [ESTHER *exits into lower bedroom.* SADIE *goes to window, looks out pensively.*]

BECKY: [*Noticing* SADIE's *absorption.*] Last night he didn't say anything? [SADIE *shakes her head despondently.*] You'll see. He will—

SADIE: What's the use—? [*She turns suddenly.*] All he knows is, I'm a shop girl and he's a school teacher—Why should he even look at me?

BECKY: He's a bashful type boy—

SADIE: I bet if I was a secretary or a bookkeeper—he would look at me then, all right. [*Directly.*] Is Mrs. Gold's Dora smarter than me, Mama?

BECKY: I should say not—

SADIE: That's all I want to know—[*Pause.*] Mama, help me—I want to quit the shop and go to secretary school. I know it's a lot of money, but if you give me thirty dollars I'll pay you back—

BECKY: Why not? Of course I'll give it to you—

SADIE: Oh, Mama, Mama, thank you! And the minute I get a job in an office, have I got plans! The first thing I'm going to do is—throw out that couch—I'm ashamed every time he walks into the house—it's so homely—

BECKY: I don't think it makes a difference to Mr. Engel. He's a very plain boy. He don't expect to get rich.

SADIE: Don't be foolish, Mama. Everybody cares about getting rich. You should see the way people live uptown. You should see what they eat and the way they dress. [*Giggling.*] Honest, Mama, I think he's afraid of girls. He's so polite he still calls me "Miss" Sadie. I'm afraid a boy like him you have to *push* into saying something.

BECKY: [*Smiling.*] So—you want Mama to give him a push for you? [*A knock at door.* BECKY *goes to answer it.* SADIE *exits.* BENJAMIN BROWNSTEIN *enters. He is a large man with a bald head and enormous mustachios. His clothes are those of a poor working man, and he has made no concessions in dress to the occasion.*] Come in, Mr. Brownstein. [HYMIE *enters.*]

BENJAMIN: [*Looking around.*] Greenspan is not home yet?

BECKY: Any minute. Take off your coat.

BENJAMIN: [*Removing coat, he finds a place on couch.*] He told me six o'clock we're eating.

HYMIE: Hello, Mr. Brownstein.

BENJAMIN: [*To* HYMIE, *whom he favors.*] How are you, my boy? [IRVING *and* FANNY *enter*]

IRVING: [*Holding cake under* BECKY's *nose.*] Rector's[3] comes to Broome Street! [*Placing cake on buffet.*] How'ya, Brownstein—

[IRVING *goes back to piano, starts to play.*]

BENJAMIN: Excuse me if I am insulting you, Mrs. Felderman, but this celebration, to me, it's a barbaric bourgeois custom! Gefilte fish and kugel on a boy's thirteenth birthday does not make a man!

HYMIE: [*Listening with all ears.*] What's a bourgeois, Mr. Brownstein?

BENJAMIN: [*About to hold forth.*] A bourgeois—

FANNY: Mr. Brownstein, if it is not too much trouble, *tonight* could we live without a discussion of politics?

BENJAMIN: [*To* HYMIE.] You see, Hymie? That's a bourgeois!

HYMIE: [*Puzzled.*] I see—

FANNY: Honest, I betcha this song sells a million copies!

IRVING: And when it does, you and me'll be living on Riverside Drive and Mama'll be living with us—with a colored cook!

BECKY: I would starve first!

BENJAMIN: Ambitions! To lay a head on a pillow on Riverside Drive when millions ain't got straw to sleep on.

IRVING: That's my fault? Listen to him! I say a man's got one life to live. Make your mark and live it easy. That's my motto.

---

[3] A high-class restaurant.

**BENJAMIN:** Aye, boychick, boychick, comes the Revolution, ideas like yours will not be popular. [ESTHER *enters, wearing new dress.*]

**ESTHER:** [*Pirouetting.*] So—how do I look?

**BECKY:** Even if I made it myself, it looks good!

**IRVING:** Now *that's* what I call class.

**FANNY:** Like a doll! I could get you a job in my theatre any time—

**IRVING:** Seeing as how you don't work there any more?

**FANNY:** [*Petulantly.*] It's just *temporary*—

**BECKY:** When did this happen?

**IRVING:** Yesterday. And it's as permanent as Christmas!

**FANNY:** Ish kabibble,[4] what you say! Monday I'll go see Mr. Shubert and ask him to try me out for the new Winter Garden—

**IRVING:** You'll see Shubert over my dead body—

**FANNY:** You make me sick! The way you carry on, you'd think I was undressing in front of the audience—

**IRVING:** You don't have to undress in front of them! Those guys out front are doin' it for you!

**FANNY:** You just want to ruin my life! All I want is to give pleasure to people—

**BECKY:** You have it in your heart to sing, so sing for Irving's pleasure—for mine—[BECKY *exits into kitchen.*]

**FANNY:** You and Irving are going to make a star outta me? [*Dramatically.*] Can I help it if I have it in my nature to be loved and admired by the world? Do you know what it means to sing for an *audience?* To hear them *whistling* for you?

**IRVING:** Aw, cut it out, Sarah Bernhardt. I'll whistle for you any time—

**FANNY:** Go away from me—you—you—[*She sniffles unhappily.* SADIE *enters, goes to* window, *looks out anxiously.*]

**IRVING:** [*Taking* FANNY *in his arms.*] If it will make you feel better Uncle Abe fired me, too.

**FANNY:** What?

**IRVING:** That's right. I ain't workin' for him any more—

**FANNY:** Why didn't you tell me?

**BENJAMIN:** Aha! I told you, workers of the world unite!

**IRVING:** So I'm *united* with Fanny. So we both lost our jobs! [BECKY *enters with a challis bread wrapped in napkin.*]

**FANNY:** Did you hear, Mama? Irving lost his job, too!

---

[4] Comic character whose name became synonymous with "I should worry."

**BECKY:** That's terrible. How did it happen?

**IRVING:** Uncle Abe is selling the Apollo to Jack Greenfal — so he had to fire us on account Greenfal will have to hire *his own* relatives.

**BECKY:** He's selling the theatre?

**IRVING:** [*Laughing skeptically.*] To go to Califomia to make those moving pictures!

**FANNY:** Gee — Irv — maybe he'll take us with him?

**IRVING:** You looney? Go all the way out there, we should have to walk back?

**FANNY:** In the meantime we'll starve —

**BECKY:** What are you talking about? Tomorrow you move out of the furnished room into the house —

**SADIE:** [*Who has been listening, all ears, unhappier by the moment.*] The house isn't already overstuffed?

**BECKY:** [*Firmly.*] We'll find room. Tomorrow you move in —

**IRVING:** Gee, thanks. You'll get it back. With interest. See if you don't. [*AARON enters from street, dressed in what he considers the well-dressed businessman should wear.*]

**SADIE:** [*Disappointed.*] Oh — it's you.

**AARON:** Hello. Hello. Mazeltuff! And how is my friend Brownstein?

**BENJAMIN:** You said six o'clock — we're eating. [*ESTHER sticks her head through door.*]

**ESTHER:** [*Disappointed.*] Oh — it's you —

**AARON:** What is this? They are expecting the King of England and it's only me? [*He hands HYMIE a package, ostentatiously.*] For you, Hymie. On the occasion of your thirteenth birthday! That's why I was late!

**BECKY:** Aaron — you shouldn't —

**AARON:** [*Grandly.*] Why not? I can afford it!

**HYMIE:** [*Fingering package shyly.*] Should I open it up now? [*SADIE and ESTHER exit lower bedroom.*]

**BECKY:** Why not? [*All eyes are on him as he opens package. It contains a large white silk handkerchief.*]

**AARON:** I asked the fellow, "For the Bar Mitzvah of a boy who is playing the violin, what would be suitable?" So he said, "For under the chin when you play violin, a white silk handkerchief is very suitable."

**HYMIE:** Gee — thanks —

**BENJAMIN:** [*Reluctantly taking package from his coat pocket.*] You might as well take this, too.

**HYMIE:** [*Opening it quickly.*] Thank you, Mr. Brownstein —

**BECKY:** You shouldn't —

**BENJAMIN:** [Angrily.] Why not? From *him* is all right and not from me? [HYMIE *opens package.*]

**BECKY:** A book!

**BENJAMIN:** [*Looking directly at* AARON.] I asked *myself* for the Bar Mitzvah of a boy who wants to be a *man!* Take a look, Mr. Greenspan! *The Writings of Karl Marx*—by Marx! [AARON *takes a large envelope from his pocket, nonchalantly throws it on table.*]

**AARON:** And *furthermore*—open this up, Mrs. Felderman, mine darling, and get yourself an excitement.

**BECKY:** What is this?

**AARON:** Open it up!

**BECKY:** [*Opening envelope, takes out sheaf of money.*] I'm dying! Look what he throws on the table like a newspaper!

**AARON:** [*Pompously to* BENJAMIN.] Seventy-five dollars, cash money! [*Sorting bills, hands* BECKY *several.*] And this, mine sweet Becky, is yours. In full payment of my just debts!

**BENJAMIN:** [*Bursting out violently.*] Blood money!

**BECKY:** [*Disregarding* BENJAMIN'S *outburst. She fingers bills, worried.*] That means you're moving out?

**AARON:** Who said? Even if the couch is not so comfortable, the landlady is one in a million! For the rest of my life, you can count on me! [BENJAMIN *continues to glare at* AARON.] And out of next month's profits, the first thing I am going to buy is a new couch. A comfortable bed is a good investment. [*To* BECKY *pointedly.*] Unless, Mrs. Becky, you are changing your mind. Mine proposition is still good! [BECKY *glares at him.*] All right! All right! Forget I said it! [ESTHER *and* SADIE *enter.* SADIE *carries small package, which she gives to* HYMIE.]

**SADIE:** Hymie!

**HYMIE:** [*Overwhelmed.*] I'm getting a present from you, too? [*Hastily opens package, takes out a small watch.*]

**SADIE:** From Esther and Mama and me—

**HYMIE:** [*Putting it to his ear*] It ticks! Mama—it ticks!

**BECKY:** [*Proudly.*] Sure it ticks. [HYMIE *swallows hard, trying to contain his emotion and pleasure. He gathers his bundles together and runs into bedroom.*]

**ESTHER:** [*Laughing, exiting after him.*] Hymie! Don't cry! You have to laugh, not cry! [SADIE, FANNY *and* ESTHER *exit after him, laughing.*]

**BECKY:** [*Sniffing.*] The fish! [*She exits into kitchen. A moment's pause.* BENJAMIN *glares at* AARON.]

**BENJAMIN:** [*Unable to contain himself.*] Exploiter!

**AARON:** Please! You are starting up again? Don't confuse me now! A man is entitled to make a living!

**BENJAMIN:** Five hundred percent profit is a *living* for you and a *dying* for the man on the machine who does all the work!

**IRVING:** Don't you guys ever get tired? [*He exits into kitchen.*]

**AARON:** Don't exaggerate! Five hundred percent profit I'm not making—yet! And even if I was, who is stopping anybody from doing the same? You'll excuse me, it's a free country!

**BENJAMIN:** A free country, you'll excuse *me*, to starve!

**AARON:** You're starving? You been working steady in a bakery since the first day you came here!

**BENJAMIN:** Fourteen hours a day in a dirty bakery cellar. Five men side by side in a room half like this. No windows. Every five minutes somebody mops the floor. Water? No! Sweat! Sweat I said? Blood! The blood of the workers is in every piece of bread you eat!

**AARON:** I don't taste it!

**BENJAMIN:** [*Almost apoplectic.*] You will! [*A knock on door* BECKY *enters to answer it.*]

**BECKY:** Aaron—Mr. Brownstein—please, the company! [*She opens door* HARRY ENGEL *and his father,* MYRON *enter.* MYRON ENGEL *is a 50-year-old edition of his son. Quiet, pedantic, scholarly.*]

**HARRY:** Papa, this is Mrs. Felderman. And this is my father, Myron Engel.

**MYRON:** How do you do?

**BECKY:** I'm glad you came—[*Calling out.*] Girls! Sadie! The company is here! [HYMIE *and the girls enter.* IRVING *comes out of kitchen.*] Meet my family. This is Mr. Engel's father—and this is my Fanny's husband, Mr. Tashman—and Mr. Greenspan and Benjamin Brownstein—

**HYMIE:** How about me? It's my birthday—

**BECKY:** The most important one we forgot—this is my Hymie—[*Laughing.*] If you'll excuse me, I have to see to the dinner. Fanny! Esther! [BECKY *exits.* ESTHER *glances at* HARRY *shyly, then she and* FANNY *follow their mother into kitchen.*]

**SADIE:** [*Trying to gain* HARRY'S *attention.*] Won't you be seated, Mr. Engel? [*To* MYRON.] And you, Mr. Engel—won't you make yourself comfortable?

**MYRON:** [*As he sits.*] Thank you.

**AARON:** What line are you in, Mr. Engel?

**MYRON:** You might call it the *hospital* line.

**AARON:** A doctor?

**MYRON:** I am in what you might call the cleaning up line in the hospital.

[*With a smile.*] Not exactly a professional man—but my son, Harry, is—
[*Proudly.*] He has just passed his examination to teach public school.

SADIE: Congratulations!

HARRY: Thank you.

BENJAMIN: A worthy profession, teaching. But, unfortunately, the school system is a tool of the bosses!

AARON: My friend is slightly inclined toward the Socialistic system—[BECKY *enters.* FANNY *and* ESTHER *follow her in, carrying plates of food.*]

BECKY: It's ready, gentlemen. The dinner.

MYRON: A pleasure to sit at the table with such a nice family—

IRVING: C'mon, folks! Let's dig in!

MYRON: Everything looks delicious. [HARRY *whispers into* ESTHER'*s ear.*]

SADIE: Secrets, Mr. Engel?

ESTHER: You're going to tell them now?

HARRY: You said tonight at the Bar Mitzvah—

ESTHER: [*Looking around embarrassed, then suddenly.*] All right—now.

HARRY: [*He clears his throat nervously.*] My dear friends—

AARON: Hear! Hear! He's going to make a speech!

HARRY: I—we—that is to say—Esther and I—well—well—I can't make a speech, but Esther and I—well—

MYRON: [*Beaming.*] Don't be nervous, son. [HARRY *looks around tongue-tied*] They are engaged!

HARRY: Thank you, Papa, for telling it for me. [SADIE *stares straight ahead, trying to contain herself during following.*]

[*Simultaneously:*]

FANNY: [*Screaming happily.*] I knew it all the time, but I didn't tell. Not even to Irving!

BECKY: [*Her voice choked.*] It's a great surprise—

AARON: Those quiet fellows certainly put it over on us.

FANNY: [Embracing Irving.] They'll love married life, won't they, Irving?

ESTHER: [*To* BECKY.] You're not mad we kept it a secret?

BECKY: How could I be mad? He's a fine boy—

**MYRON:** [*Shaking* BECKY'*s hand, solemnly.*] Your daughter is a lovely girl. My son is lucky.

**BECKY:** [*Glancing toward* SADIE, *words do not come easily.*] My daughter is lucky too.

**HARRY:** [*To* SADIE.] I can't thank you enough for bringing me into the house to teach you, Miss Sadie.

**SADIE:** [*Dryly.*] You can call me Sadie now, without the *Miss.*

**MYRON:** You have settled on a day for wedding? [HARRY *and* ESTHER *nod vigorously.*]

**ESTHER:** [*Shyly.*] Harry wants it soon.

**HARRY:** And you are all invited to the wedding!

**AARON:** Right away is the best. Once I was engaged to a girl, I found out so much about her, I didn't marry her! [*General congratulations and laughter.*] So kiss the bride!

[*They all tap on glasses with silverware. The tinkling sound continues as* HARRY *kisses her tenderly. Everyone applauds.*]

**MYRON:** Aren't you forgetting something, my son?

**HARRY.** Oh, for goodness' sakes! In my pocket—[*He tenderly extracts a small box, taking out ring.*] It's for you—[*He puts it on* ESTHER'*s finger.*]

**ESTHER:** Oh, Harry—you shouldn't—

**HARRY:** My father went with me to pick it out.

**ESTHER:** It must have cost so much.

**HARRY:** In Greenhut's they have inaugurated a new system. If you are reliable, they give it to you for a dollar a week for two years!

**FANNY:** Listen to that—

**AARON:** The man who thought it up will make a million. They charge ten percent interest—[HYMIE, *completely neglected, has been watching proceedings with great interest.*]

**HYMIE:** Don't anybody want to hear my speech? [*No one pays any attention to him.*]

**ESTHER:** Sadie, isn't the ring wonderful! You didn't say anything!

**SADIE:** I—I wish you everything.

**ESTHER:** I can't tell you how happy I am—

**SADIE:** [*Dryly.*] You should be!

**MYRON:** [*Getting up.*] Let us drink a toast to the bride-to-be. [*Holding up his glass.*] To Esther, my future daughter. A long life and a happy one! [*They all drink, exclaim happily.*]

**FANNY:** Now you, Mama—you make a toast!
**BECKY:** Me?
**IRVING:** C'mon, Mom—it ain't hard—
**MYRON:** Just say what's in your heart, Mrs. Felderman.
**BECKY:** [*Getting up.*] I—I don't know what—[*She clears her throat.*]
**AARON:** [*Applauding.*] Hear! Hear! [*They are seated now, as follows:* BECKY, *table* R., AARON, FANNY, IRVING, *from* R. *to* L., *backs facing audience,* HYMIE *at table* L., MYRON, SADIE, HARRY, ESTHER *and* BENJAMIN *from* R. *to* L., *facing audience.*]
**BECKY:** A lifetime it would take to say what's in my heart. [*They are quiet now.* BECKY *looks from one to other then last at* SADIE. *In an effort to give* SADIE *courage,* BECKY *decides to make speech. Quietly.*] I look around this table and I see: My Fanny has a good husband who loves her. [FANNY *takes* IRVING'S *hand.*] For my Esther and her Harry … life is just beginning. [*Pause.*] Then I see my Hymie sitting in the place where his father would be sitting—and I think, today he is a man. I remember, where we came from was chances only for a man to die—and here— here they beg you to take the chances for living—[*She pauses, then fixes her gaze on* SADIE, *who sits, head bowed.*] Then I took at my Sadie, and for her, too, my heart is happy. [SADIE *looks up sharply.*] Oh, yes! She also has an important announcement surprise. My Sadie is going to give up working in the shop and will go to a school to become a secretary! [*General exclamation, "A secretary"— "That's wonderful!" etc.*] Oh, yes! My Sadie knows in America are chances for everybody to be somebody! [*She lifts her glass.*] So, if it is allowed we should drink, not to a person, but to a place—then please—to America! [*Pause.*] Because we know only good can come to us here! [*She looks around.*] Now should we drink?

[*They are all visibly affected by* BECKY'S *speech.* BENJAMIN *has taken out his handkerchief and chooses at this point to blow his nose vigorously. The spell is broken. They begin to drink and eat, all except* SADIE, *who continues to stare straight ahead, as though in a trance.*]

**HYMIE:** [*Suddenly.*] Mama! Please! Now can I make my speech? [*He gets up.*] My dear mother and sisters and brother-in-law and friends! Today I yam a man—[*As*]

CURTAIN

# ACT TWO

## SCENE 1

*The same. Early morning of Saturday, March 25, 1911. Aaron's couch is disheveled, sheets thrown in a lump, etc. Sadie is at window, wan and dispirited. Becky enters from kitchen. She goes to upper bedroom door and knocks.*

BECKY: Fanny!

FANNY: [*Off.*] I'm up! [*Yelling.*] Irving! Get up—

BECKY: Let him sleep.

FANNY: [*Entering.*] If I can get up at six, he can get up at six! [BECKY, *folding* Aaron's *sheets, watches* SADIE *in deep concern.* FANNY *making a beeline for bathroom.*] I'm first. [*She is gone.*]

BECKY: [*To* SADIE.] Maybe you won't go to the shop today?

SADIE: [*Wearily.*] I'm all right.

BECKY: Sadie, please, do me a favor, don't go.

SADIE: Why shouldn't I go? It's *my* wedding? Tell her to stay home. She's the bride! [*A pause.*] *I* know. You're afraid I'll say something—

BECKY: Did I say it?

SADIE: That's what you're thinking, isn't it? [*Getting up wearily.*] Don't worry, I won't say anything. [*Passionately.*] But you can't stop a person's *thoughts!* Today I'll be sitting at the machine, biting my tongue to keep from running to the window and throwing myself out of it!

BECKY: You don't go to the shop today! I'll tie you with ropes to the bed—

SADIE: Don't worry. They say when a person talks about it, he doesn't do it.

BECKY: Sadie—please—I'll give you breakfast.

SADIE: I'm not hungry.

BECKY: You're killing yourself! A whole month not to eat—

SADIE: I don't know what you want from me. Leave me alone—[*She exits into bedroom.* BECKY *stares unhappily at her retreating form.*]

FANNY: [*Entering.*] I'm out! Who's next? [*She stops when she sees* BECKY'*s expression.*] What's the matter? [BECKY *nods toward door*] Sadie? She'll get over it.

BECKY: It's easy for somebody else to say it.

FANNY: [*Calling out as she exits into upper bedroom.*] Irving! Get up! [BECKY *continues to fold sheets as* ESTHER *enters. She is half dressed.*]

ESTHER: Sadie is sick?

BECKY: She didn't sleep so good—

ESTHER: [*She laughs.*] I guess I made her nervous. Pinching myself all night—[*With a sigh.*] Today, the last day in the shop. Tomorrow I'm getting married. Me! [*Pause.*] Mama, could I ask you a question?

BECKY: Why not?

ESTHER: Were you scared, Mama—when the time came? [*She runs to* BECKY.] Last night when Harry was here, I got so frightened, I wanted to say, "Please excuse me, but I can't do it." I wanted to run away. Is that how you felt?

BECKY: [*Smiling gently.*] If you want to know, I *did* run away. I got up early in the morning and I ran into the fields. I buried my head in the grass and I said to myself, no—no—I wouldn't go back! [*Laughing.*] An hour later, I got hungry, I went back.

ESTHER: [*Laughing, incredulous.*] No!

BECKY: That evening I married Papa—

ESTHER: Mama, Mama, I'm so nervous, I wish it were tomorrow already!

BECKY: Hurry up, get dressed; you'll be late!

ESTHER: [*Gaily, as she exits into bathroom.*] If I'm late today, the foreman can fire me! [BECKY *looks after her a moment, then at door where* SADIE *is. With a sigh she exits into kitchen.* FANNY *enters dressed for street.*]

FANNY: [*In high agitation.*] You'll see if I'll stand for it!

IRVING: [*Coming to door, in his bathrobe.*] Give me one good reason why I have to get up at six-thirty?

FANNY: It's the principle!

IRVING: What principle? Six-thirty you have to hand me four-syllable words?

FANNY: All right—I don't mind working in the shop again. I know it's only *temporary.* But when my back is breaking over the machine, I feel ten times worse if I know you're laying in bed!

IRVING: Have a heart—darling. I'm dead on my feet.

FANNY: The thing that tears me up—this minute I could be turning over on the other side! If you'd only let me go back on the stage... Milton Glaser, the agent, came looking for me—

IRVING: [*Angrily.*] All over again? Half the night wasn't enough? I'm a mild man, Fanny, but—

FANNY: Go ahead! Hit me, why don't you!

IRVING: [*Falling into chair, half asleep.*] I'm too tired.

FANNY: If I knew I'd have to give up my career when I married you, I wouldn't—[*breaking off hotly.*] Irving! You're not listening!

IRVING: [*Wearily.*] I'm listening.

FANNY: That man will drive me wild! [IRVING *gets up.*] Where are you going?

IRVING: Back to sleep.

FANNY: That's all the appreciation—

IRVING: Look, baby, I know we're having a hard time. But, honey—look at me—c'mon—look at me. [*His arms on her shoulders.*] Do I look like the kinda fellow that likes his wife to work for him? Do I?

FANNY: [*Reluctantly.*] No—

IRVING: You know it's only *temporary.* [*Reasoning with her.*] And if I go to a publishing house early, I gotta buy lunch outside and lunch means a quarter. So you think I'm gonna spend your hard-earned quarters buying myself lunch? See the point? [*Pause.*]

FANNY: I see it—

IRVING: [*Sitting next to her arm about her.*] Now you're talking! You know it's just a question of minutes! Kitty Gordon is *positively* trying out my song at the new Roseland Palace! It's as good as published already—

FANNY: [*Jumping up. Tearfully.*] And you wrote that song for me!

IRVING: [*Whistling impatiently.*] Sure I did. And I'm even gonna make 'em print it on the sheet! "For My Wife"—just like that! Gee, baby, don't cry —[*Holding her close.*] I'm crazy about you—

FANNY: [*Through her tears.*] Are you?

IRVING: You've got the most beautiful nose in the whole world! [*Kisses her nose.*]

FANNY: Have I?

IRVING: I'll kill anybody says "no"—[*Pause, as he and* FANNY *embrace.*] As if I don't appreciate what you're doin'—and never, *never* throwin' it up to me—[*He breaks off.*] Well—hardly ever. And, baby, will I make it up to you! You'll have so many dresses hangin' in your closet, it'll take you an hour to make up your mind which one to wear.

FANNY: Oh, Irving—[*They embrace again.*]

IRVING: Now can I go back to sleep?

FANNY: [*Tenderly.*] Go back to sleep, Poppy—[*Pause as she watches him go toward door*] Today is pay day. Should I bring you home something, darling? [ESTHER *enters, dressed for street.*]

IRVING: [*Yawning.*] Cuppla Havana Bums Specials — Am I sleepy — [*He is gone.*]

BECKY: [*Calling out from kitchen.*] Girls, come eat breakfast —

ESTHER: Come on, Fanny, we'll be late —

FANNY: [*Still filled with spell of* IRVING'S *presence.*] Married life is wonderful! It's so legitimate! [SADIE *enters.*]

ESTHER: Are you feeling any better, Sadie?

SADIE: This is a wonderful day for you —

ESTHER: I feel — like on air — Fanny, did you feel that way?

FANNY: To tell you the truth, I don't remember *how* I felt! I was so scared Mama would be mad.

ESTHER: I — I feel so empty —

SADIE: [*Quietly.*] *You* feel empty — ?

ESTHER: [*Gaily.*] Wouldn't you? [*She is about to exit into kitchen.*] I don't know how I'll live through this day —

SADIE: You don't know how *you'll* live through this day — [*Forcing* ESTHER'S *attention to her.*] And how do you think *I'll* live through this day? And tomorrow? And for days and days and years after that? For the rest of my life! [ESTHER *stares at her, still uncomprehending.*] That's right! Stand there looking at me as if I were crazy! [*Her voice reaching a wild crescendo.*] You took him away from me! I brought him into the house! He would have married *me!* You took him away from me, do you hear me? — I hate you! I wish you were dead! [BECKY *has entered at sounds of* SADIE'S *hysteria.*]

BECKY: Sadie! No! No! [ESTHER *has been staring at* SADIE — *the full implication of her words dawning gradually. Suddenly, with a cry of deep hurt, she runs from the house.* FANNY *looks at* SADIE *as if she could strike her; quickly takes* ESTHER'S *wraps and her own from rack; exits after* ESTHER.]

SADIE: [*Falling into chair.*] Mama, please — do something — help me! I can't stand it — [*She weeps — dry hacking sobs escaping her* BECKY *looks on — bewildered and unhappy — as — the curtain is lowered to show the lapse of several hours.*]

TIME: *Four-thirty same afternoon.* BECKY *is at table, kneading dough.* AARON *watches her* HYMIE *is at piano, playing "Here Comes the Bride" on his violin.*

AARON: Cakes! Wedding! One by one they'll get married and leave you alone. [BECKY *looks at him, sharply.*] All right! All fight! I didn't say it. [*He goes to couch, sits down.*] A double wedding we could make it. They would even put it in the *Forwartz*. Mother and daughter marry on the same day. [BECKY *continues her work, not looking at him. He lies full-length on couch.*]

BECKY: Hymie! Go downstairs and play! What are you doing, hanging around the house on such a nice day?

HYMIE: I was practicing for tomorrow, I shouldn't make a mistake.

BECKY: If you make one little mistake, who will notice? [HYMIE *puts away violin and exits.* IRVING *enters, yawning.*]

IRVING: To the "Wedding March" I was dreaming. You know, Mom, the kid's got a nice touch. [SADIE *enters from street as* IRVING, *nears bathroom.*]

SADIE: Good morning, Mr. Tashman! Sleep till four-thirty in the afternoon with his wife slaving in the shop! [*As she goes toward bedroom.*] If I had a man like you, I would throw him out of the window. [*She exits.*]

IRVING,: [*As he exits into bathroom.*] I believe you! In your house murder would be an everyday occurrence! [*He is, gone.* AARON *starts fussing with baking utensils on table.*]

BECKY: Aaron! What are you doing?

AARON: Why not? Somebody else helps you around this house?

BECKY: It's very nice of you.

AARON: Becky, Becky, if you would only let me... [BECKY *does not answer. He changes his tack.*] Listen, Mrs. Feldennan—lately, since I am doing business with the outside world, I am subject to *embarrassment!* How can I explain to my friends that I'm not married? Am I twenty-one? A schoolboy? They think there's something the matter with me.

BECKY: Maybe your friends are right, Aaron. A man like you should be married....

AARON: So?

BECKY: Take my advice, look around. You'll find a good woman who can give you a heart one hundred percent for yourself! [*She looks around at doors of her house in concern.*]

AARON: Tell me the truth—if I took your advice, you mean to say you wouldn't miss me? [*A knock at door.*]

BECKY: Answer the door, Aaron. [AARON *opens door* BENJAMIN *enters, greatly perturbed.*]

BENJAMIN: [*Banging on a newspaper*] What did I tell you American justice? Hello, Mrs. Felderman—On the side of the bosses!

AARON: Brownstein, do you ever give yourself a minute's peace?

**BENJAMIN:** In war how can there be peace?

**AARON:** What war?

**BENJAMIN:** [*Banging on paper again.*] They're not ashamed to print the decision in the paper! The New York State ten-hour-a-day legislation for bakers is unconstitutional! Mr. Justice Peckham! The *Supreme* Court! [*Snorting.*] That's justice?

**AARON:** I don't know about you, Brownstein, but I'm hungry.

**BENJAMIN:** Don't change the subject.

**AARON:** It's easier to change the subject than to change the world. The only thing a sensible man can do is take care of himself. [BENJAMIN *glares at him.*] That makes me a criminal? Brownstein, I wouldn't hurt a fly.

**BENJAMIN:** [*Angrily.*] Boss of a nonunion sweat shop, and he wouldn't hurt a fly!

**AARON:** Tell them to get a union, and I'll have a union! I'm stopping them? [BENJAMIN *looks at* AARON, *unable to face force of his logic.*] The trouble is, Brownstein, you are not looking for a system. You are looking for a Heaven! [BECKY *has been listening, all ears.*]

**BECKY:** Mr. Brownstein! My three girls work in the Triangle Shop, and they are not complaining and I am not complaining, so why should you? [*Suddenly.*] Tell me, where you and I came from did we have even a *chance* to work? If you ask me, in America it's a "Paradise" for the workingman.

**BENJAMIN:** [*Almost apoplectic.*] Paradise! Excuse me for insulting you, but you're crazy! [*Watching her as she kneads dough.*] Furthermore, you make me nervous. With the fingers you don't do it! With the hands—the *palms* of the hands— [*He goes at dough.* BECKY *pushes him away.*]

**BECKY:** Wash your hands first!

**BENJAMIN:** [*Examining his hands.*] To hell with it! [*He walks away, brooding.* SADIE *enters.*]

**AARON:** I'm still hungry.

**BENJAMIN:** I could eat myself.

**BECKY:** [*Good-naturedly.*] Two grown men, you can't help yourself? The icebox is full.

**AARON:** Come, Brownstein, I'll make you a sandwich like in Delmonico's Restaurant.

**BENJAMIN:** It doesn't have to be so fancy— [AARON *and* BENJAMIN *exit into kitchen. A moment of pause. From street we hear dimly sounds of fire engines and bells.*]

**SADIE:** Well, why don't you say something?

**BECKY:** What should I say?

**SADIE:** Haven't you any curiosity? Don't you want to know where I went in such a rush?

**BECKY:** I'm hoping in my heart you went to the shop to apologize to your sister Esther for what you did this morning.

**SADIE:** If you have to know, I took myself for a walk to the secretary school! I enrolled! [BECKY *does not answer.*] Nobody in this world will ever have the satisfaction of seeing Sadie Felderman crying her eyes out over a man! From now on, it's something else in my life! You said in America are chances for everybody to be somebody! Well, I'm going to be somebody! And I won't stop at secretary school, either! That's just the beginning! I'll show them! I'll show — [*She breaks completely, dropping into a chair weeping.*]

**BECKY:** [*Gently, going to her*] *Kind, kind,* as if I don't know how you're feeling. Don't I know what it means for a woman to lose the man she loves? I lived with Papa for ten years — and when I lost him, I wanted to die. [*Sounds of engines, sirens and bells playing a strange counterpoint to her voice.*] But I remembered I had other things to live for. I said to myself, "I cannot take out on my innocent children what I feel." Sadie, Sadie, a family is something you have to hold on to with all your strength! You don't tear it to pieces because you lost a man you never had!

**SADIE:** Didn't I try? Did I say something all month? But when I see you making preparations, wedding cake, wedding dresses — a stone couldn't stand it!

**BECKY:** *Kind, kind,* what is the trick in being strong when everything is going your way? [*Firmly.*] Be a *mensch,* Sadie!

[*Door bursts open.* HYMIE *is there gesticulating, wildly, breathlessly.*]

**HYMIE:** Mama — Mama — [*His voice trails off in a wail. Finding his voice, he screams the words.*] The shop — the Triangle Shop — Mama — it's on fire —

**SADIE:** [*Screaming the word.*] No!

[IRVING *has entered from bathroom, face covered with shaving lather.*]

HYMIE: [*Hysterically.*] It's burning —

[*They stand shocked, unable to believe their ears.*]

BECKY: The girls!

[*Following action happens simultaneously.* IRVING *grabs his coat from rack wiping his face with it as he rushes out of door followed by* BECKY. HYMIE, *breathless, stands staring at* SADIE, *then quickly exits after them hurriedly.* SADIE *stands alone, looking at open door not daring to move as —— the curtain is lowered to show the lapse of several hours.*]

TIME: *Midnight.*

SADIE *is at table, her head buried in her arms.* HYMIE *is at window. Restlessly, he looks out.*

HYMIE: Sadie, please, can't I go downstairs?
SADIE: Hymie, I asked you not to —— [*From outside we hear sounds of wailing.*] It's Mrs. O'Shaughnessy — her Annie, she worked in the shop —
HYMIE: [*Frightened.*] I don't care. I'm gonna go. I'm going downstairs to look for Mama — [*He exits quickly.*]
SADIE: [*Calling after him.*] Hymie! Come back — [*Exhausted, she sits, head in arms again. A moment's pause.* IRVING *enters, grimy, disheveled.*] No news? [IRVING *shakes his head. He sits, suddenly doubles up as if in physical pain. She goes toward him.*] Maybe no news is good news —
IRVING: If they're all right, why aren't they *home?* [*The horror pouring out of him.*] Maybe they jumped! The way I seen 'em jump. Cracking the side-walks! At the windows screaming at you. All you could do was watch 'em burn up in front of your eyes. [*He weeps dryly, silently.*] This morning I held her in my arms — was laughing —
SADIE: Stop it —
IRVING: *One* fire escape for eight hundred people. It broke in the middle with twenty, thirty people on it —

[*A pause, both* SADIE *and* IRVING *lost in their own grief. Door opens.*]

FANNY *is there. She stands still, half demented, her clothes hanging about her, wildly.* IRVING *throws his arms around her, hardly believing she is there.*]

**FANNY:** [*In a dull flat tone, almost unrecognizable.*] Where's Esther?

**IRVING:** Fanny—Fanny—[*He kisses her hands over and over again.*]

**SADIE:** She'll be home right away. Didn't you come home? Irving—go quick—find Mama—tell her Fanny is home—

**IRVING:** [*Shaking her trying to impress his words on her*] Fanny—listen to me—I'm going to look for Mama—tell her you're here—[*He suddenly begins to laugh hysterically.*] Fanny—you're home—you're home, darling—laugh! Laugh, Fanny! [*He continues to laugh, his hysteria mounting.*]

**FANNY:** Where's Esther?

**SADIE:** [*Breaking.*] We don't know where she is!

**FANNY:** [*Quietly, after pause.*] I am downstairs. Walking, walking—I ask everybody, where is Esther? Nobody knows. [*She notices* SADIE.]

**IRVING:** Sadie, please, I'll stay here with her. Go try to find Mama—please—

**FANNY:** [*Suddenly, pointing to* SADIE.] *She* did it—she put the curse on her! I heard you! This morning you said to her, "I wish you were dead—"

[SADIE, *frightened, runs to door, exits quickly.* IRVING *holds* FANNY *close, quieting her.*]

**IRVING:** Look, Fanny—it's me, Irving. Remember Irving? Just like yesterday and the day before—your piece of candy—

**FANNY:** [*Quietly.*] I forgot—the pay envelope. Here—[*She takes small envelope out of her pocket, miraculously safe. Suddenly rational.*] The bell is ringing. Everybody talking and laughing. We are going home. Then—we are running—like crazy we are running—screaming. I am near a wall and somebody is pushing me up a ladder. [*Her voice trails off.*] Who is pushing me—Oh, yes—Piney—

**IRVING:** [*Weeping unashamedly.*] I'm going to kiss Piney for that, you'll see, I'll kiss him for pushing you—

**FANNY:** [*Suddenly she breaks away from* IRVING *and starts running around, pushing* IRVING *aside as though he were in the way. She starts screaming.*] I gotta get out. Out—out—help—out—Esther—Esther—

[IRVING, *picks her up, carries her into upper bedroom, where her moans resound for a moment.* AARON *and* BECKY *enter* BECKY *is near collapse.* SADIE *follows them in.*]

**BECKY:** Oh — [*She quickly exits into upper bedroom.* AARON *sits, exhausted.* MYRON *enters.*]

**AARON:** [*Looking up.*] Fanny is home —

**MYRON:** Thank God!

**AARON:** We left Harry in our place in the line — thousands waiting to get into the morgue. All of them had relatives or friends? No. Curiosity seekers. At a time like this, curiosity seekers!

**MYRON:** [*Quietly.*] They'll know soon enough. The morgue has no secrets. Tomorrow the whole East Side will be in mourning. [*Pause.* SADIE *enters.*] For eight hours I have been making the rounds of the hospitals. After what I saw the first five minutes I prayed in my heart I would not find them — better off dead. Better off — [*A pause. The men look at one another.*] You have to hope. Fanny came home.

**AARON:** A child — a baby. [BECKY *enters from bedroom.*]

**BECKY:** Asleep. It's good she can sleep —

**AARON:** [*Placating, to* BECKY.] Becky, where was Fanny all day? Maybe Esther is also walking around like Fanny. They'll find her — they'll bring her home —

**BECKY:** [*In a daze.*] She *got* to come home — tomorrow is the wedding — everything is ready — [*Looking around*] I didn't finish the challis — [*She touches dough, still resting on table where she left it.*] Mrs. O'Shaughnessy's Annie. They found her there — [*Looking around suddenly.*] Where's Hymie?

**SADIE:** He went downstairs — I'll go find him. [*She exits quickly.*]

**BECKY:** [*Dazed.*] Mrs. Pomerantz's two boys and her husband — [*Suddenly she runs to rack, grabs her shawl.*]

**AARON:** [*Gently taking her arm.*] Where are you going?

**BECKY:** Esther is there — somewhere — I have to find her —

**AARON:** [*Gently drawing her away from door*] Please, you have to wait —

**BECKY:** [*To* MYRON *as she walks toward table.*] I have to wait — wait — [*Dropping into chair exhausted.*] Wait — [*A pause. A moment later door opens and* HARRY *enters. He is too quiet. They all look at him with pleading eyes.* HARRY *goes toward* BECKY. *Taking her hand, he opens it, placing* ESTHER's *ring in it.* HARRY *turns away, goes to buffet quietly, his back to* *them. He suddenly doubles up in a spasm of dry, hacking sobs.* BECKY *continues to stare at ring in her hand. Quietly, dazed, unbelieving.*] A dollar a week for two years — [*Her voice breaks as*]

CURTAIN

# SCENE 2

*The same. Early April, 1917. Six years later late afternoon. The set is changed only in so far as six years of living in one place will bring about the inevitable changes of a different set of curtains, a new calendar, perhaps a new chair or two. The old couch has been exchanged for a new sofa in the best Grand Rapids manner of the period. Otherwise everything remains the same.*

**AT RISE:** HYMIE *and* HARRY *in heated discussion.* HARRY *is now close to thirty, he wears glasses and has developed a more scholarly manner* HYMIE *is now nineteen, a good-looking young man with a vivacious excitable manner.*

HYMIE: I tell you it's any minute now, Harry. Did you see where we handed the German Ambassador his walking papers?

HARRY: [*Unnerved.*] Severing of diplomatic relations doesn't necessarily mean war! [HYMIE *takes up violin and plays a bar of scales.*] The *Illinois's* not the first ship that went down. They can still send a note of regret.

HYMIE: Not this time. She told us six weeks ago she's starting unrestricted submarine warfare! They're calling National Guardsmen up for Federal Service already!

[*A knock at door* HYMIE *answers it.* BENJAMIN *enters. The years have made little change in his appearance.*]

BENJAMIN: Greenspan is home?

HYMIE: Not yet—

BENJAMIN: [*Ill at ease, not in his usual manner*] If it's all right with you, I'll wait.

HYMIE: How'ya, Brownstein?

BENJAMIN: [*Absorbed in his own thoughts.*] All right.

HYMIE: [*With a laugh.*] You *should* be all right! Kerensky and your boyfriends sure fixed the Czar!

BENJAMIN: Kerensky! When I think of him, with my two hands I could— [*He makes gesture of choking.*]

HYMIE: You're complaining?

BENJAMIN: The workers made a Revolution to reestablish the old order? No!

[*He gets up, agitated.*] Any minute they'll start sweeping again—they'll sweep him out with the rest of the dirt!

HARRY: [*Suddenly, out of his own absorption.*] Benjamin, do you think America will enter the war?

BENJAMIN: Wall Street, you should excuse me, will sit on its fat behind, and let Gerrnany win? And lose their investment in the Allies?

HYMIE: [*Laughing.*] Speech! Speech! [BECKY *enters from kitchen.*]

BENJAMIN: Go ahead! Make fun! The propaganda presses will start rolling, before you know it you'll be sporting a uniform and acting like it was your own idea! You give your life. Wall Street gets back its money! Fifty-fifty! Fine America! [*He spits disgustedly.*]

BECKY: Mr. Brownstein! This is a free country, but about America please don't spit in my house!

BENJAMIN: What did I tell you? Propaganda presses!

HARRY: [*More and more disturbed.*] I'll never go to war. I'll go to jail first!

HYMIE: [*Laughing.*] I think I'll give up the violin and start playing the bugle!

BECKY: Nothing is settled yet, so Hymie is playing the bugle and Harry is sitting in jail already!

BENJAMIN: [*Quietly.*] And I am on my way to Russia.

BECKY: Russia?

BENJAMIN: Saturday I am sailing.

BECKY: [*Concerned.*] Why should you go to Russia? You're an American citizen—

BENJAMIN: [*Solemnly.*] They *need* me.

BECKY: Without you they made it—How about a bite supper with us, Mr. Brownstein?

BENJAMIN: [*Getting up instantly, follows* BECKY *into kitchen.*] Supper? I wouldn't care if I did. [*They are gone.* HARRY, *greatly upset, continues to read paper anxiously.*]

HYMIE: [*Putting violin back into case. Noticing* HARRY'S *absorption.*] Got you worried, hasn't it—

HARRY: [*Picking up newspaper*] Seven thousand dead—like they were describing a baseball game—Everything I've tried to teach, all being destroyed in front of my eyes! [*Pleading suddenly.*] Wilson was re-elected because he kept us out of it. He can't suddenly turn turkey on us—

HYMIE: He'll do what he has to do! [*Pause as he sees* HARRY'S *expression.*] They're fighting our battle, Harry. How can we avoid it? This is a war to end war!

HARRY. War to end war? Man! There's no such thing!

HYMIE: [*After a pause.*] Well—I'm enlisting—

HARRY: Hymie, my God—why?

HYMIE: Sh—Mom doesn't know yet—

HARRY: Do you mean to say you could go out and kill a man?

HYMIE: About such things you have to be strictly impersonal—

HARRY: What's impersonal about killing a man who wants to live as much as you do?

HYMIE: I don't like that part of it any more than you do! But fellows like you take too much for granted! Freedom, Democracy—just words in a dictionary to you! When I think of that guy and what he's doing over there—I see red!

HARRY: Listen to me, Hymie—you're not going to preserve Freedom and Democracy by killing! You're going to *destroy* it! Just look at your history books—even the rotten books they gave you to read. The books I've had to teach all my life—[*Breaks off.*] Maybe it's my fault. Maybe if I and others like me had done our parts better—maybe if I had *fought* for the things I stood for—[*Pause.*] But I lost interest—[*Pause.*] Do I talk this way because I'm afraid to die? God knows I've thought of death often enough, as a way out—

HYMIE: [*Quietly.*] Harry, don't talk like a fool—

HARRY: Don't do it, Hymie.

HYMIE: [*Quietly.*] Please, I've made up my mind—a man's gotta do what he has to do—

HARRY: [*After pause.*] All right. We see things differently. You want to go—I can't stop you. But I won't go, because I don't believe in it! I have no faith in violence as a means of settling anything.

BECKY: [*Calling out from kitchen.*] Boys! Come eat supper—[HARRY *exits into kitchen.* HYMIE *remains behind absorbed in thought.* AARON *enters. The six years have dealt kindly with him. A few gray hairs add distinction to his appearance.*]

HYMIE: Hello, Mr. Greenspan—

BECKY: [*Calling out again.*] That's you, Aaron?

AARON: Who else?

BECKY: [*Through kitchen door*] Mr. Brownstein, Aaron is here—

AARON: [To HYMIE.] Some warm day for this time of year—[HYMIE *grabs his hat, and exits suddenly.*] Where are you going in such a hurry? [BENJAMIN *enters. To* BENJAMIN.] And how is the world treating you, Brownstein?

BENJAMIN: [*Coming to point.*] Greenspan, I won't waste your time and my time with preliminaries! You can answer "yes" or "no" and I won't be insulted. Last week I told you I am going to Russia. Well—there is a small matter of two hundred dollars for expenses. I need a loan. [AARON *is taken by surprise. Suddenly implication of* BENJAMIN'*s words dawns on him.* AARON *starts to laugh.*] What's the joke?

AARON: [*Laughing heartily.*] You are asking *me,* the dirtiest capitalist exploiter in America, by your own words, to lend you the money to go to Russia to fight a revolution?

BENJAMIN: I thought you wouldn't see it my way. Never mind—

AARON: Wait a minute! Did I say "no"? [BENJAMIN *stops in his tracks.*] Give a man at least a good laugh for his two hundred dollar investment?

BENJAMIN: Please—I don't see the joke!

AARON: Aye, Brownstein, one reason I like you is because you can always be depended on *not* to see the joke!

BENJAMIN: Greenspan, yes or no, do I get the money?

AARON: [*With a smile.*] I'll lend you the money, on *one* condition—

BENJAMIN: [*Almost apoplectic.*] Conditions?

AARON: Yes. On condition that—[*Pretending to be serious.*] comes the Revolution in America, when they are putting me against the wall, you'll tell them, if it weren't for *me*—you would never—

BENJAMIN: [*Cutting in.*] Never! You can't buy your immunity with two hundred dollars, Greenspan.

AARON: [*Laughing.*] Brownstein, Brownstein, you are worth the price of an admission! [*Suddenly serious.*] You want to know the *truth?* Comes the Revolution in America—[*Forcefully.*] they can line me against the wall and to hell with your immunity!

BENJAMIN: So? [AARON *takes out checkbook, makes out check.*]

AARON: [*As he writes.*] Believe it or not, I will miss you, Brownstein.

BENJAMIN: A man must go where his principles send him. [*Ostentatiously, blows his nose. It is evident that* AARON'*s generosity has touched him.* AARON *solemnly hands check to* BENJAMIN.]

AARON: [*Holding out his hand.*] Will I see you again in my life?

BENJAMIN: Where I am going, a man can't make plans for the future.

AARON: So it's good-bye—[*They shake hands.*]

BENJAMIN: Well—[*He fingers check, then shoves it into his pocket, and goes toward kitchen door*] On good-byes and thank-yous, I'm not so good—[*Pause.*] You tell her—[BENJAMIN *is gone.*]

**BECKY:** [*Entering.*] Aaron, supper is ready—where's Brownstein? [AARON *looks after him a moment.*]

**AARON:** He went to Russia—Becky, would you call me a fool? I gave him two hundred dollars to go there.

**BECKY:** Oh—[*Slowly, after a moment.*] I think if a man believes in something so strong he's willing to give up his life for it—[*Shaking her head.*] a person shouldn't stand in his way.

**AARON:** [*Gently.*] That's what I thought, too. [*They smile at each other, a look of understanding passing between them.* HARRY *enters from kitchen, goes to window, pensively.*] What's for supper, mine dear lady? [AARON *exits.* BECKY *remains behind, watching* HARRY. *She is about to exit into kitchen when* FANNY *and* IRVING *enter from street.*]

**BECKY:** How was the picture?

**IRVING:** I never saw such trash—

**FANNY:** Maybe it's trash, but in the meantime your Uncle Abe is in California making thousands out of it, and you're starving to death!

**IRVING:** I'm starving?

**FANNY:** That's right! Take me literal—

**IRVING:** [*As they go toward kitchen.*] The public wants live shows! Movies are a novelty. There's no *future* in it!

**FANNY:** I suppose there's a big future for you in a fortycent table de hote restaurant! Singing for *tips!* [*She is gone.*]

**IRVING:** If you don't stop nagging me, I'll go out of the house, I won't come back! What's for supper? [*He exits after her.*]

**BECKY:** [*Smiling gently.*] They talk like they mean it—[*Going to window, she opens it, sniffing the air.*] It's spring on Broome Street already, Harry— [BECKY *comes away from window, humming.*] "I didn't raise my boy to be a soldier. I raised him up to be my pride and —" [*She stops short, alarm in her voice.*] Harry!

**HARRY:** [*Out of his absorption.*] Yes?

**BECKY:** If—if they declare war—will my Hymie have to go? [HARRY *does not answer.* BECKY *is suddenly filled with the realization that War is the personal business of one's son going.*] Of course he'll have to go. Mrs. Strong's boy is only eighteen and he's a sailor. [*Pause.*] I'm so mixed up, Harry. When I took out my papers I swore to hold up the Constitution —to give my life—my life—gladly—but—but Hymie—[*She breaks off, tries to throw off her mood, hardly succeeding.*] You know what I am?

**293**

Aaron calls me a pessimist. A Calamity Jane—that's me. [*Pleading with* HARRY *for confirmation.*] I bet in a few days the whole thing is over and I'm worrying about Hymie—

HARRY: We stayed out of it so far—there's not a chance in the world— [*Pause.*]

BECKY: [*Seeing* HARRY's *absorption.*] After all these years, Harry—I think of you as if you were my own—

HARRY: [*Looking up, caught by her tone.*] Yes?

BECKY: [*Shaking her head.*] It's no good—Harry—what you have made of your life. [*With some force.*] A man mustn't dig a hole in the ground beside the loved one and lie down in it for the rest of his life! No! Six years of death for the living is a sin!

HARRY: When she died the life went out of me—as if I were blinded—

BECKY: Maybe it's because you have eyes in your head but you won't see what's right under your nose—[*She breaks off, looks closely at him.*] Sadie.

HARRY: You mean Sadie—and me? [BECKY *nods gently. Disquieted.*] But—I never thought of Sadie that way—I—

BECKY: Maybe if you did think about? [HARRY *turns away.*] I worry about you, Harry. I think what you were like, six, seven years ago! You were going to *do* so much! The world was yours—I look at you today, I get frightened. A young man and you never smile. Sitting for hours with your nose in a book, looking for companionship with people who aren't real. Who never lived. Tell me, is that a way for a man to live? Is it healthy? What will become of you? [*Pause.*] My Sadie—I can see how she buries her feelings in the *job*. Why? Because she has to have something to fill up her life—it's no way for a woman to live, either! [*Quietly.*] Believe me, Harry, there is still time for you to make a life for yourself. But you can't do it alone. I think to myself—two fine young people—if they were *together* they would be living for each other, and they would both be happy—[*She breaks off.*] Harry—if you can't do what I said—please forget I said it—

[*Door opens and* SADIE *enters. In six years she has gained a successful, satisfied look. She is well-dressed and her manner is brisk.*]

SADIE: Good evening.

HARRY: How are you?

SADIE: [*Taking off wraps.*] Same as I was last evening and the evening before. Exhausted!

BECKY: The shop is still going overtime? Aaron is home a while already— [*She exits to kitchen.*]

SADIE: He can leave. He's the boss—[AARON *comes to door.*]

AARON: Where's the ketchup?

SADIE: [*Laughing.*] Did you see today's papers, Greenspan? The shop'll be going overtime plenty.

AARON: [*Pompously.*] We're equipped!

SADIE: Aaron, please, put me in charge of production, I'll make a fortune for you! Don't leave me rotting behind that cage!

AARON: What will I do with Van Brett?

SADIE: Get rid of him. What do you need him for?

AARON: [*Angrily.*] What are you talking about—? [*To no one in particular.*] Did you ever see such a hard-boiled—I'm in partners with a man—my friend—

SADIE: [*Cutting in.*] He'll still be your friend when he bankrupts you? [*Sarcastically.*] Production manager! Buys ribbons when they wear feathers, and feathers when they wear flowers and flowers when they want ribbons, and when you ask him *why*, he says he *likes* it!

AARON: We're making enough for a few mistakes. He's an old man—By the way, make a note, I gave Benjamin Brownstein two hundred dollars. A loan.

SADIE: What?

AARON: Don't get excited! I shouldn't have told you.

SADIE: I'm the bookkeeper so I wouldn't find out? Of course, the three hundred dollars you owe me—

AARON: [*Angrily.*] You don't trust me? I'm going to skip town with it?

SADIE: Aaron, Aaron—sometimes, if you weren't my boss I would lose my temper.

AARON: That stops you? [*He exits into kitchen, ketchup bottle in his hand.* HARRY *is at window again, his back to* SADIE. *Her manner softens. We sense her old feeling for this man is still an active part of her.*]

SADIE: [*As she takes some silver out of buffet drawer and sets a place for herself at table.*] Do you think I'm hard-boiled? When all I'm doing is protecting his interests. In business you have to follow the rules of *good* business.

HARRY: I don't understand much about such things—

**SADIE:** [*After pause.*] Did you have your supper?

**HARRY:** Yes, thanks. Earlier —

**SADIE:** And how is the teaching business?

**HARRY:** It's all right — [*Awkward pause.* HARRY *suddenly looks at* SADIE *as though seeing her for the first time. Pointing to her dress.*] Is that what they call violet color?

**SADIE:** [*Pleased.*] More on the purple side. Do you like it? I got it wholesale. [*She laughs.*] For as many years as I know you, never once did you remark on something I wore. You surprise me.

**HARRY:** Sadie — I was wondering if you — [*He breaks off.*]

**SADIE:** [*Starting to eat, newspaper by her side, she glances through it.*] Yes?

**HARRY:** I — I wanted to ask you something —

**SADIE:** [*After pause.*] You were saying — ?

**HARRY:** In — in all the years I have been practically living in the house — you know — eating here every night since Papa died — well — what I'd like to know is — [*Suddenly.*] What do you think of me — that is to say — if you think of me at all? [*From street we hear the faint call of newsboys shouting "Extry" — "Extry" The two pay no attention.*]

**SADIE:** That's a funny question. We think of you as *belonging* in the house. Like a fixture —

**HARRY:** I see. [*Simply.*] I guess I feel that way, too. [*Rationalizing, more for his own benefit than hers.*] This is my home. The only home I've known for a long time. I — I guess somehow I've attached myself to the family — [*Clears his throat.*] I feel very close to *all* of you. [*Pause.*] Do I make myself clear?

[*We now make out cries of "Extry, Extry" as being quite close.*]

**SADIE:** Harry Engel, what are you trying to say to me?

[AARON *enters.*]

**AARON:** They're calling "Extra" —

[BECKY, FANNY, *and* IRVING, *have now entered, rush to window excitedly.*]

**IRVING:** Wait a minute —

AARON: [*To* IRVING.] Run down and get a paper.

BECKY: [*Frightened.*] What could the Extra say? [IRVING *is at door about to exit.* HYMIE *bursts into room. He carries a newspaper. They crowd around him.*] What is the Extra?

HYMIE: [*Throwing paper on table.*] Listen, everybody! Wilson just called another session of Congress—

[HARRY *has picked paper up, scans it anxiously.*]

AARON: An emergency?

HYMIE: Just wants to talk a few things over with them.

SADIE: I thought for a minute war was declared. —

IRVING: This means war, sure as there's hair on my head—

AARON: Why should you care? You're a married man—

[FANNY, IRVING, *and* AARON *exit into kitchen, chattering excitedly.*]

HARRY: Sadie—how—how would you like to take a walk—

SADIE: [*Pleased.*] Why—that would be very nice. [*She goes toward rack, taking her jacket.* BECKY *has picked up newspaper which* HARRY *has dropped.*]

HARRY: [*Pointedly, as he helps* SADIE *on with her coat.*] We'll be back in a little while, Mama—

[BECKY *looks up, torn between her realization that war is imminent and her pleasure that* HARRY *has asked* SADIE *to take a walk, perhaps more may come of it.* HARRY *and* SADIE *exit.*]

BECKY: Come, I'll give you supper, Hymie.

HYMIE: Mom—

BECKY: Yes?

HYMIE: First—I—I—gotta tell you something. [*Goes toward her, takes her hand in his, looking at her.*] Now, Mom, please don't be mad on me—

BECKY: [A *frightened tone in her voice.*] Wait! Don't tell me—[*She glances at paper on table, then quietly.*] I know—

CURTAIN

# SCENE 3

*The same. A year and a half later November, 1918. About six-thirty in the evening.*

**AT RISE:** FANNY *and* BECKY *enter from street. They take off their wraps, put their bundles down.*

FANNY: [*Calling out.*] Irving! We're home! I don't feel my feet any more. [*She waits for his response.*] Asleep! Sometimes I get so mad at that man I could — [*She goes to bedroom door.*] Irving! He's not home. [FANNY *sits disconsolately.*]

BECKY: He said he was going to see Mr. Strauss, the publisher —

FANNY: That's what he tells you. How — how do I know he's not with some — some — ?

BECKY: You're not ashamed to think such a thing? What's got into you — ?

FANNY: I could swear — lately, he's *different.* Mama, I'm going crazy —

BECKY: Foolish girl — he loves you like — I don't know what. [*Sternly.*] You know why he's never in the house? It's because you are making his life miserable, nagging and picking on him — [*Shaking head.*] All because he didn't make a million dollars —

FANNY: [*Defensively.*] Who wants a *million* — just a living —

BECKY: [*Gently.*] Fanny, Fanny, in your condition, a woman always imagines things ten times worse —

FANNY: I'm giving him one last chance! If something doesn't happen by the time the baby comes, we're packing up! [*Pacing nervously.*] Right this minute he could be making fifty dollars a week with his Uncle Abe! Has he the right to bring a third person into the world when he can't take care of himself?

BECKY: The boy hasn't luck —

FANNY: If he found a horseshoe in front of the door, it would be his luck to trip on it, and break his neck!

BECKY: [*Knocking on wood.*] God forbid! [FANNY *sits, exhausted by her tirade. Pause.*] Fanny —

FANNY: Yes, Mama?

BECKY: I believe in Irving. [*Simply.*] When he plays me one of his songs, I sing it in my head for a week. And if I could sing it — somebody else will —

FANNY: [*Suddenly bitter again.*] Mama, Mama—I get so discouraged sometimes—I—I could die!

BECKY: Sh! Don't say it. Never. Even if you feel it, *don't* say it. [*Gently patting* FANNY's *head.*]

FANNY: [*After pause.*] Mama, are my feet *supposed* to hurt—?

[FANNY *gets up. She kisses her mother gently, then exits into bedroom.* BECKY *remains behind looking after her* BECKY *goes to window, raises shade. The raised shade discloses a service flag with a single gold star on it. A moment's pause.* BECKY *goes to buffet and takes a small watch from drawer. She winds it, puts it to her ear. After a moment, a knock at door. Hastily she puts it back into drawer—runs to open door.* HARRY *and* SADIE *enter. A year and a half of marriage has given* SADIE *added confidence in herself. Her manner is brisk, poised.* HARRY, *by contrast, is quieter than ever.*]

SADIE: [*Pecking* BECKY's *cheek.*] How are you, Mom?

BECKY: All right. Hello, Harry.

HARRY: Hello, Mama—

SADIE: [*As she takes off her wraps.*] I'm starved. So busy today, I didn't eat lunch. [*As she comes down* C.] How's Fanny?

BECKY: Fine. She's resting now.

SADIE: Some people can *afford* to have babies. [*Pause.*] Well, Mama—we have wonderful news!

BECKY: Yes?

SADIE: We are going into business for ourselves! Today we settled everything! [HARRY *does not look particularly happy about this, but he nods when* BECKY *looks in his direction.*]

BECKY: You're quitting Aaron?

SADIE: That's right.

BECKY: Now is a good time to go into business? Everybody says the war will be over any minute—

SADIE: So the millinery business will be better than ever. The girls will be so happy the boys are coming home, they'll be dressed to kill!

BECKY: What did Aaron say?

SADIE: I didn't ask his opinion! [*Gaily to* HARRY.] And Harry is going to be my sales manager—

BECKY: Harry? [*She turns toward him.*] You're giving up teaching?

**299**

**SADIE:** Foolish to pay a stranger sixty a week when we can keep it in the family. [BECKY *looks at* HARRY, *searchingly, aware how painful this business must be to him.*] And, Mama—speaking of keeping it in the family, how much money do you have?

**BECKY:** You know what I have—[*A catch in her throat.*] Hymie's—the college money—

**SADIE:** Well, I'm borrowing two hundred—

**HARRY:** [*Cutting in.*] Sadie, I asked you not to—

**SADIE:** She's using it? I'll pay her back with interest! We need cash, don't we? Come on—let's eat—

[SADIE *and* HARRY *exit into kitchen.* BECKY *is about to exit.* AARON *enters from street, visibly shaken.* BECKY *follows his every movement, deeply concerned. He walks to couch, sits down, buries face in his hands.*]

**BECKY:** Aaron—what's the matter?

**AARON:** Mrs. Felderman, you see before you a man at the end of his senses. That daughter of yours, Sadie. If—if I am arrested for committing murder on her, please, you should excuse me, but I am entitled to it!

**BECKY:** What are you talking about?

**AARON:** With her own hands to stick the knife in my back—[*Mops his brow.*] Today she quit Van Brett and Greenspan. A woman has a *right* to quit. [*Quietly, a catch in his throat.*] Just now I find out why she quit! To open a millinery factory next door!

**BECKY:** [*Softly.*] Oh—

**AARON:** Would you call that ethical? A woman works for us seven years— gets on friendly terms with all our customers—gets them all in the bag —and quits us to open up next door! [*Pause.*] To take away our business. For myself, to hell with it! But Van Brett—over sixty years old—a man with a wife and four children—[SADIE *comes to door*] Oh! There you are!

**BECKY:** [*To* SADIE *forcibly.*] Sadie! Is he telling me the truth?

**SADIE:** [*Coldly, without emotion.*] Did you also tell her why I haven't a cent in cash? How much money you owe me in five and ten dollar bills, out of my salary every other week—six hundred dollars! [*Directly to* AARON.] Would you like it better if I put you into bankruptcy? I am entitled to it! But I am simply going into legitimate competition with you!

AARON: Competition to ruin our business?

SADIE: A man like you doesn't have the *right* to be in business! You're an old fool! Now I can tell it to you!

AARON: [*Almost apoplectic.*] I'm a fool? What I forgot about the millinery business, you don't have in your little finger! [*To* BECKY.] You know what she can't stand? Because I have a *union* in my shop!

SADIE: To be the *only* manufacturer on Grand Street with a union shop is to be in the charity business, not the millinery business!

AARON: In my shop I don't want to be ashamed my workingmen should look me in the face! [HARRY *is at door watching proceedings with distaste.* AARON, *in a daze.*] You know what this will do to Van Brett? It will kill him. [*Pleading.*] Please, so I owe you a few cents. [*Pause.*] A man has a season's hard luck. Notes I'll give you—with my life's blood, I'll pay you back—

SADIE: Hard luck? To lose a fortune in a boom period? If you have to know, you're the laughing stock in the whole trade!

AARON: [*Screaming.*] What I forgot about the millinery business—

SADIE: [*Cutting in.*] In my little finger—I know! [*Laughing.*] You shouldn't be afraid of a little competition! It's the life and spirit of American business! On that principle, my dear man, there is room for everybody! I am quoting you, Mr. Greenspan!

[SADIE *exits into kitchen.* HARRY *and* BECKY *remain behind, watching* AARON. *He takes a much-battered suitcase from behind couch, opens buffet drawer and starts to throw his clothes into it.*]

BECKY: What are you doing?

AARON: How will I face Van Brett! [*Paying no attention. Pursues his own train of thought. He throws more clothes into suitcase.*] Van Brett never liked her. But I said to him, "Let's hire her. She's not so good-natured, but she's smart. And she's the daughter of my best friend." So we hired her. [*Goes to bedroom door, takes two suits which hang behind it, packs them into suitcase through the next.*] How can I tell him we had behind our cage a snake in the grass! [*Addressing* HARRY *and* BECKY *directly.*] You heard her! "Room for everybody." Me she was quoting! My own words come home to slap me in the face! [*He continues to pack. Quietly, with resignation.*] America I wanted. In a potato barrel I escaped to come here. For five days and five nights it rained. When they pulled me out on the other side of the border, I was half drowned. [*He laughs, a thin laugh, with no mirth in it.*] You know what, Mrs. Felderman, my darling? I *should* have drowned.

BECKY: [*A frightened strain in her voice.*] You're moving out—

AARON: [*Gently.*] I'll visit you, Becky. She's your daughter. You can't refuse her the house. To meet her accidentally, ten years from now, would be too soon. [*Picks up his suitcase. With nod to* HARRY *and gentle look in* BECKY'*s direction, he exits.* BECKY *looks at* HARRY, *then in direction of kitchen door, as though making up her mind. Suddenly calls out, a forceful dominant quality in her voice.*]

BECKY: Sadie!

SADIE: [*Coming to door*] He's gone?

BECKY: You didn't tell me going into business would mean this—

SADIE: Mama, please, take care of your own life. And I'll take care of mine! In business it's the survival of the *fittest!*

BECKY: With not one penny of mine! [*Pleading.*] Sadie, Sadie, with such ideas—to go through life—[FANNY *enters from bedroom.*]

HARRY: [*Has been listening, now speaks suddenly, agitated*] I never wanted to go into business, anyway!

SADIE: [*Sharply.*] I'll stay home and bake a cake waiting for your twenty-seven dollar pay envelope from the City of New York?

HARRY: But business is not in my nature—I like to teach school. It's useful, important work—

SADIE: Where *promotion* is something the *kids* get! You took the examination, they threw you into 5-B—to sit there till you rot! Well, I want something better from life than a three-room flat in the Bronx, even if it has got an elevator! [BECKY *turns away, the picture of* HARRY *at the mercy of* SADIE'*s bitter tongue too much for her.* SADIE *putting coat on, impatiently.*] I did all the arguing in one day I'm going to—[*To* HARRY.] Get your coat. We're going home. [*To* BECKY.] Never mind your money. I'll get what I need from the bank! [SADIE *is gone. A pause.*]

BECKY: [*Quietly, in self-castigation.*] I begged Aaron to give her the job. [*Pause, as she closes buffet drawer, breaks off.*] And worst of all, Harry, what did I do to you?

HARRY. Don't blame yourself, Mama. A man should be able to face his life like—like a *man.* [*Pause, then wryly.*] I guess I'm a pretty poor excuse for one. [*Taking his coat from rack. With a level glance in* BECKY'*s direction, he exits.*]

FANNY: [*When he is gone.*] Why does he stand for it? If I was him, I'd leave and I'd never come back! [*Torn,* BECKY *goes to window.* IRVING *enters, morose, his appearance has changed considerably. He looks tired, seedy.*]

IRVING: [*With no spirit.*] How'ya, Mom? Hello, honey. [*Managing a wry smile.*] Well—I saw Strauss today—[IRVING *looks at* FANNY.] You win, baby! We're packing for California the minute the kid comes!

BECKY: Something happened, Irving—I can tell—

IRVING: He told me the truth! He can't publish my stuff. And you wanna know why? Because they're *too* sad. They want happy songs! Optimistic songs! Songs that'll make 'em forget we're still fightin' a war—[*Breaking out.*] How in hell can I *write* happy, if I don't feel happy?

FANNY: [*Gently.*] You hate to leave New York, don't you?

IRVING: Like taking poison—

FANNY: Then we *don't* go! No! No! [*To* BECKY.] I'm not doing to my Irving what she's doing to Harry! No, sir! [*Going to* IRVING.] You want to stay here, you stay here, darling! Even if you don't make a million dollars, if *you're* happy, I'm happy! [BECKY *looks on, fighting tears. From outside we hear faint cries and a whistle blowing.*]

IRVING: [*Hugging* FANNY:] God! What a woman! What a woman!

FANNY: Irving, sweetheart, only one thing I'm going to ask you—Promise me, when you become a big songwriter, you'll let me sing your songs.

IRVING: [*Laughing affectionately.*] Okay, I swear! When I write my hit, you can sing it all you want.

FANNY: Oh, Irving—

IRVING: Except on the stage!

FANNY: You rotten thing! [BECKY *goes to window, opens it. Sounds from outside grow louder. She looks out.*]

BECKY: What's all the blowing, Irving? I can't see what—

IRVING: [*Going to window.*] Something in the street—

FANNY: [*She too is at window now. Excitedly.*] It's coming from across the way. Look! Mrs. Gold! She's going crazy! She's banging on the window with a pot!

BECKY: Mr. Sullivan is hanging with his head out yelling—[*Calling down.*] Mr. Sullivan! What's the noise? [*A pause as she listens for his answer*] What? Did you hear him? It's over! IT'S OVER!

[BECKY, IRVING *and* FANNY, *now hysterical, hang over window yelling "Hooray"— "Hooray"— "It's over"— "It's over." Street noises, whistles, sirens, voices have grown to tremendous proportions. The three embrace for a moment, dancing around. Suddenly* BECKY *disengages herself, walks away, lost in her own grief.*]

FANNY: Irving! Quick! Let's go downstairs!

IRVING: [*Rushing to piano.*] Wait a minute! Wait a minute!

FANNY: The war is over and he's at the piano!

IRVING: [*Excitedly, plays something with a stirring martial quality.*] He said he wants it happy, didn't he? Didn't he?

FANNY: Irving, please, take me downstairs!

IRVING: [*Playing four bars over again.*] Just listen to this, will ya? The same tune I wrote last week. I change it from a major key to a minor key — and put it in four, four time! [FANNY *suddenly begins to double over with pain, a surprised look on her face.*] And what a title! "We'll Bring the Rue de la Paix Back to Old Broadway, and Make the Boys Forget Paree" — [*He repeats four bars, playing while he sings.*]

FANNY: [*Calling out suddenly.*] Irving! [*He pays no attention to her. Sounds of sirens, whistles are now joined by a brass band, filling room.* FANNY *screams again.*] Mama!

[*In a moment* BECKY'*s grief is forgotten in* FANNY'*s need of her* BECKY *rushes to* FANNY'*s side.*]

BECKY: Irving! Quick! Run for the doctor! It's her time!

IRVING: [*Frightened.*] Oh, my God —

BECKY: Stop swearing and run for the doctor! You'll talk to God later — [*The room is filled with the sounds of Armistice as*]

CURTAIN

# ACT THREE

NOTE ON SET DECORATION: *It is suggested that a simple change can be effected by the substitution of two wallpaper plugs, one at upstage wall and one at lower L. wall.*

SCENE: *Late afternoon, November, 1931. Thirteen years later. While the set remains the same, considerable change has taken place in its furnishings. The old furniture is gone and a heterogeneous assortment of modern and overstuffed pieces takes its place. The old upright piano has been exchanged for a radio. This is still* BECKY's *home, however, so that the whole suggests a comfortable living atmosphere, in spite of* IRVING *and* FANNY's *overgenerosity in the matter of "buying Mama a nice thing occasionally." The table* C. *is elaborately set with a complete service for seven, including shining glassware and silver.*

AT RISE: PANSY, *the Tashman's colored maid, finishing setting table. She is about* 50, *inclined to fat, with a broad good-humored smile. She hums a tune. Goes to a drawer, takes some linen out of it.* SADIE *and* HARRY *enter. Both are now definitely middle-aged. Sadie is thinner, drier, her voice more carping than ever.* HARRY, *now* 45, *looks closer to* 50. *The years have taken their toll of his health and spirit.*

SADIE: [*As they enter.*] I told Mama the minute I laid eyes on that fellow—
[*Breaks off when she sees* PANSY.] What are you doing here?
PANSY: Mis' Fanny sent me. [*Pompously.*] I'm supposed to be helpin' with the dinner for Mr. Hymie's birthday—[*Exits into kitchen.*]
HARRY: [*Coming down to couch.*] In spite of what the papers say—I never met a finer, more generous fellow than Irving—
SADIE: Why shouldn't he be? Mama didn't do enough for him? [*Laughing.*] Some generous. Carrying on with that Hope—Hope whatever-her-name-is—

HARRY: [As *he sits.*] Please, Sadie—
SADIE: All right! There's nobody around—[*Placing package on buffet which she has brought in with her.*] You think he deserves it, the fresh kid! Image of his father—
HARRY: For his Bar Mitzvah, you could have bought him something better than two shirts. There are a hundred things a boy would enjoy more—
SADIE: Let his father watch out for his son's enjoyment. Eighty-five dollar Erector sets, hundred dollar trains—if I spent my hard-earned money on foolishness like his father—[HARRY *looks at her. She goes to table, sits down.*] I hope Aaron shows up! It's our only chance. Four times I got him to the phone. When I tell him who it is, he hangs up—
HARRY: He can't do anything anyway—
SADIE: [*Getting up impatiently.*] He's influential in the union, isn't he? You'll have to talk to him, Harry—
HARRY: What could I say? He'd be on their side, not yours.
SADIE: Tell him, with thirty-two stores all canceling our orders because the union threatens to picket them, it absolutely ain't fair!
HARRY: They catch you where it hurts the most, so you have to sign with them—
SADIE: What I want to know is, what side are *you* on?

[PANSY *enters with seltzer bottle, places it on table.*]

HARRY: [*Cutting in, patiently.*] Sadie, I've had a hard day. I don't feel well— I'm going to lie down. [*Exits up* R.]
SADIE: [*Following him in.*] I was in the office three hours before you came in—I can hardly stand on my feet—and you don't feel well—

[*They are gone. A moment later* BECKY *enters, carrying a number of bundles. Well preserved, nicely dressed, she still retains her youthful vivacity.*]

PANSY: Lordy, Lordy—what you got there? I thought you was jes' goin' 'cross the street to show Mrs. Gold your dress—
BECKY: [*Handing her bundles.*] A few extra things I figured we would need— [*Surveying herself happily.*] She says I look like a girl in it.
PANSY: Sure do! Cake's finished, ma'am. Stuck a straw in it. It come out clean, so I took it outta the stove—

**BECKY:** [*Smiling.*] On Broome Street you can *smell* a cake is done, Pansy.

**PANSY:** [*Near kitchen door.*] Miss Sadie and Mr. Harry, they're here — and Mr. Tashman, he brung the liquor — [*Whispering.*] And, ma'am — he gimme a note for you. [BECKY *takes it.*] He said nobody else was to see it —

[BECKY *reads note.* PANSY *exits into kitchen.* BECKY *goes to phone. She is about to make a call, when voices of* FANNY *and* YOUNG HYMIE *are heard in hall.* BECKY *puts down receiver drops note in her pocket, opens door.* FANNY *and* YOUNG HYMIE *enter. She is now 38, smartly dressed, inclined to plumpness.* HYMIE *is 13 — a cute, spoiled kid.*]

**FANNY:** I don't feel my feet any more.

**BECKY:** How was the parade, Hymie?

**HYMIE:** [*In a bored tone.*] It was all right —

**FANNY:** Every time I go, I vow never again! If it wasn't for the kid — [*She is sitting now and has removed one* shoe.] Everything is ready, Mama? Pansy was a help to you?

**BECKY:** [*Laughing.*] If somebody told me thirteen years ago Pansy would be making gefilte fish for Hymie's Bar Mitzvah —

**FANNY:** [*Rubbing the aching foot.*] With a bunch of duminies pushing you around like you were nothin'. I don't know if it's from walking or because it's going to rain!

**HYMIE:** [*Speaking up.*] Not enough we gotta *watch* the parade, Mom makes us *follow* it from 34th Street to 59th Street —

**FANNY:** [*Defensively.*] What's the matter? Don't I do it for you?

**HYMIE:** [*Trying to be patient.*] Mom, in my whole life did I ever ask you to take me to a parade?

**FANNY:** Will you listen to that kid, Mama? That's all the appreciation —

**HYMIE:** Well, did I? [BECKY *starts to laugh.*] She's always saying we go to the parade on account of *me.* *I* don't even *like* parades. *She* likes them, that's why we go.

**FANNY:** [*Laughing.*] I'll kill that kid! You're not ashamed to embarrass me in front of Grandma? [FANNY *makes playful dash for him. He eludes her, laughing.*] Hurry up, take your bath —

**HYMIE:** Gee, I had a bath this morning, didn't I — ?

**FANNY:** My hair is turning white —

HYMIE: Okay, okay—[*As he walks toward kitchen door.*] Hey, Mom—do I have to make the speech tonight?

FANNY: I should say so!

HYMIE: Gee—it's so dumb—I don't wanna—

FANNY: What did I tell you out of respect for Grandma?

HYMIE: So can't I make it for her *alone?*

FANNY: You have to make it for everybody, or it's not good luck!

HYMIE: [*As he exits into kitchen.*] Today I yam a man! Crap!

FANNY: [*Laughing.*] I'll die with that kid! Where he picks up those words! [SADIE *enters.*] Hello.

BECKY: How is Harry feeling?

SADIE: I made him lay down a while.

BECKY: He saw the doctor last week?

SADIE: [*Sitting.*] If he were really sick, he'd run! [*Sighing.*] Mama—have I trouble—times are terrible. They've been picketing my place for three weeks already—

BECKY: I thought you were going to settle with them?

SADIE: They should live so, if I'll let a union dictate how my business should be run! I'll starve first!

FANNY: You won't starve.

SADIE: [*Sharply.*] What do you mean by that? [*Hotly.*] Every cent I have is frozen in real estate. Maybe you are not aware we are up to our ears in a depression, the worst in the history—

FANNY: People still pay you rent, or they'd get a dispossess. [*Laughing.*] I should know. Any minute I expect to find them sticking one under *my* door—

SADIE: You're certainly very cheerful about it—

FANNY: Why shouldn't I be cheerful? Even if Irving's royalties only came to a couple of hundred last month, a son's Bar Mitzvah doesn't happen every day in the week. [*Cheerfully rubbing the offending member.*] I bet I walked a hundred blocks today. Oh—those high heels. [HARRY *enters, stands at doorway, stretching.*]

SADIE: [*Relentlessly pursuing subject.*] For a man who's making so little money, he certainly allows himself expensive *pastimes*—

FANNY: [*Hotly.*] Well—we're not like *some* people! We like to live!

SADIE: Evidently you don't read the papers, or you wouldn't be so cheerful—

FANNY: [*Suddenly looking from one to other.*] Wait a minute. What was that remark? [*An embarrassed pause.*]

SADIE: It just struck me funny you don't read the newspapers.

FANNY: [*Beseechingly* to BECKY.] Mama, what is she talking about?

SADIE: [*Casually.*] Turn to page 26 in the *Graphic*—

FANNY: Where's the paper, Mama?

BECKY: I don't know—

SADIE: [*Pointing to table.*] I brought one in—[FANNY *grabs paper hastily scans it.*]

HARRY: Did you have to tell her?

SADIE: [*Defensively.*] Better to hear it from her sister than her poker-playing girlfriends!

[BECKY *looks on, fear growing in her expression.* FANNY *reads item, thrusts paper into* BECKY's *hand. She exits quickly, lower* R., *a sob escaping her.* BECKY *reads item quickly.*]

BECKY: [*Exiting after* FANNY, *calling out as she goes.*] Fanny! Don't believe it! It's not true—

HARRY: [*Too quietly.*] Well, I guess we can go home now.

SADIE: We're staying right here for our family obligations! [*We hear* FANNY's *voice in hysterical weeping.*]

HARRY: Was that a family obligation, too?

SADIE: The *Graphic* has a circulation of a million, so she wouldn't find out? [HARRY *stares at her a moment, turns on his heels.*] Where are you going?

HARRY. Home.

SADIE: You're staying right here to speak to Greenspan tonight!

HARRY: [*With quiet determination.*] This is as good a time as any to tell you. Monday morning won't see me in that shop again. I'm re-applying for my license to teach school, and I'm going back!

SADIE: [*Startled.*] The fact that I need you in the shop more than ever—

HARRY: [*Quietly, but with strange force.*] For my part, lock it up, throw the key in the river!

SADIE: This is my reward, my thanks for fighting to build up some security for our old age?

HARRY. I don't need security for my old age. I'm a sick man, Sadie. I want to live the last few years of my life in *peace!*

[BECKY *enters distracted and upset.*]

SADIE: Did you hear him, Mama? After all these years he wants to go back to 5-B again!

HARRY: [*Cutting in.*] Do we have to talk about it here?

SADIE: Anything I have to say to you, my mother can hear! [*With self-assurance.*] Make up your mind to it, Engel. Monday morning finds you in the office as usual!

HARRY: [*Quietly.*] I'll see you in hell first!

SADIE: [*Aghast.*] Who do you think you are, to talk to me—?

HARRY: [*With a new kind of determination.*] I'm a man! I know you don't think I'm much of a man—but *once* I had a heart and a spirit and a head! I didn't ask for much. A decent useful life with a woman—

SADIE: Well, you had it, so what do you want?

HARRY. No! No! Now I can say it! Never with you! Not for one minute— [*Pause.*] When I married you I was lost and I wanted to find myself again. I thought I could find myself with you! I wanted to love you! For fifteen years I tried! For fifteen years I've watched you violate every code of human behavior—putting money before human decency—playing one dirty trick after another on people who trusted you—what you did to Fanny just now—I just can't take it any longer! Ask me why I'm telling you now! I could have told you when you murdered Van Brett—

BECKY: Harry—no—

HARRY: [*Relentlessly pursuing subject.*] A coincidence—wasn't it, his jumping out of a window just thirteen years ago today! The Armistice bells were still ringing when we got the news! I didn't tell you then because I was afraid of your tongue. Afraid of that cyclone in you that goes through life tearing people up by the roots! Ask me why I'm telling you now! Why I'm no longer afraid—[*Pause.*] Because I'm dying, Sadie. As surely as I stand here.

BECKY: [*Taking step toward* HARRY, *horrified.*] It's not true—you'll see a doctor—

HARRY: It's no use, Mama. On Saturday I saw the best heart specialist in the country. At the most I've got one, maybe two years—

BECKY: [*Heartbroken.*] Harry—Harry—

HARRY: And I'm not sorry, Sadie. No. I deserved what I got. I gave in to you because it was easier than fighting with you. It took me all these years to learn that men who don't fight for the things they believe in deserve to die—

SADIE: [*Turning.*] I hope you're being paid back for what you did to me. You think you fooled me all these years? You think a woman doesn't know when she lives with a man who's in love with a memory? The joke is on

**310**

me! Break my heart over a man for the best years of my life! I finally get him! What do I get? A weak—spineless—impotent—

[*She breaks off. With look of complete contempt,* HARRY *turns, takes his hat, exits without a backward glance.*]

BECKY: Harry, come back—

SADIE: He'll come back. [*After pause.*] Well, we put on a fine show for you, didn't we? Trying to scare me that way—

BECKY: [*Stonily.*] He was telling the truth—

SADIE: Oh, go on—

BECKY: I know Harry. Only if he were dying could he tell you the truth about yourself!

SADIE: That's right—go ahead—

BECKY: [*Flaring out.*] The outside world doesn't do enough to tear a family to pieces, you have to tear it apart from the *inside!* I ask you, can a string of tenement properties and a boxful of printed papers in a bank bring you an ounce of happiness, when there's not a human soul in the world cares if they never saw you again—

SADIE: [*Waving hand grandly.*] My sentiments are ditto for them—

BECKY: All these years watching what you did to Harry—every time I saw you together, my heart broke—*because I told him to marry you!* [SADIE *sits, stunned.*] I didn't have to tell you, but I did it so you would know how it feels to be hurt for no reason—the way you hurt Fanny just now! I should have recognized this terrible thing in you when you were a child! I should have *beat* it out of you! *When*—when will you learn there are other things in life besides building up a fortune! Decency—human decency—

SADIE: [*Going toward rack.*] If you think I'm going to stay here to be insulted!

BECKY: Oh, no, you don't! [*With authority.*] You will sit here tonight at this table, eating Hymie's Bar Mitzvah supper if it kills you. You will talk and be friendly like nothing happened—[*Quietly.*] When you go home tonight—you do not have to come back here again. Never. [SADIE *makes move toward door.* BECKY *shouts.*] You will do as I say!

[*Reluctant and frightened,* SADIE *drops into a chair, weeping.* BECKY *exits into kitchen, a tiny, unhappy figure, torn by her participation in the scene.* FANNY *enters, looks at* SADIE. *Unable to face her gaze,* SADIE *exits into upper bedroom.*]

FANNY: [*Calling out.*] Mama! [BECKY *enters.*] Well, Mama, I've made up my mind!
BECKY: [*Her voice choked.*] Yes?
FANNY: I'm leaving for Reno in the morning!
BECKY: [*Frightened.*] Reno? In the magazines where they get divorces?
FANNY: Not only in magazines. In real life too! [*Pause.*] Well, *say* something! You stand there like the Sphinx in Egypt!
BECKY: Don't do it, Fanny—
FANNY: Mama, Mama, I can't tell you how miserable I've been!
BECKY: Fanny, darling, don't believe it! It's not true—
FANNY: Mama, don't be naive! This isn't the first time! Three years ago when I read he was seen out with that dancer, I didn't believe it either! I let him get away with it. How long can I keep on closing my eyes—when Hope Robert's husband is suing her for divorce and naming Irving co-respondent?
BECKY: The man says in the column he only *thinks* so—
FANNY: He wouldn't dare to print it if it weren't true! He could be sued! [*Pause.*] Why should it happen to me? Am I ugly? Am I like some women married twenty years? I'm still beautiful, even if I do say so myself! [*Her voice breaks. Summoning her courage.*] Well, he won't get away with it! I'm leaving for Reno in the morning and he'll pay alimony through the nose!
BECKY: With what? No song in a show for two years—
FANNY: [*Heatedly.*] Right this minute he could be making three, four hundred a week in Hollywood with his Uncle Abe. [*Determined.*] Anyway, I don't need his money. I'm going back on the stage!
BECKY: Thirty-eight years old, you do not start a career.
FANNY: I'm thirty-seven.
BECKY: If a year could make a difference to your voice—Maybe if you *still* had a voice—
FANNY: All my friends think my voice is grand!
BECKY: [*Firmly.*] They don't *pay* to hear you—[*Sadly.*] It makes me sad to say it, but you sound, you should excuse me, like a duck. [FANNY *stares at* BECKY. *Suddenly she understands* BECKY *is telling her the truth. In a daze she sits, then crumples up, dissolved in tears.*] Fanny—Fanny—
FANNY: [*Miserably.*] Leave me alone—

**BECKY:** I'm sorry I had to be the one to tell you. [*Pause.*] Hymie will not be so happy when he hears you are leaving Irving. [*No response from* FANNY.] I suppose he'll live through it. Children live through worse. [BECKY *has been making up her mind to say something. Now she finds courage to do so.*] You asked me before to say something—[*Quietly.*] What could I say? You see—once I came to my mother with a story—[*The words do not come easily.*] The *same* story—

**FANNY:** [*Incredulous.*] Our papa? You're lying—[*Heatedly.*] You always said he was the finest, the most wonderful—

**BECKY:** [*Cutting in.*] He *was*—the finest, the sweetest man a woman ever had. [*Quickly.*] But he was a *man*—

**FANNY:** A man can't be wonderful in one breath and a cheater in the other!

**BECKY:** [*Angrily.*] Don't you say such a thing about Papa!

**FANNY:** I can't understand it. All these years you talked about him like he was God—

**BECKY:** And he was! Even if he was dead he was alive enough in my heart to help me keep the family together—[*Pleading suddenly.*] Fanny, please, don't do it! I know he loves you—[FANNY *exits lower bedroom in tears. Pause. Torn,* BECKY *goes to phone. Consulting note, dials number. After a pause.*] Hello? Irving? It's Mama. I—just talked to Fanny. She—she didn't sound so—so encouraging.... Sure she knows. [*Pause.*] It's not exactly a *secret*. Irving, I know how you feel. Right now I don't feel so hot myself. But never mind that. It's Hymie's birthday. I think if you came down and brought his mother a little present—or even a big one—[*Pause.*] No, not over the telephone. You'll kiss my feet when you get here. [BECKY *hangs up. In a daze, she walks toward kitchen. Halfway she changes her mind. Goes toward buffet, examines bottle of liquor Making up her mind quickly, she pours some rye into glass, adds seltzer from table.* PANSY *enters. When she notices* PANSY's *expression.*] There is always a first time for everything. [*She takes sip, makes a wry face.*] People drink this for pleasure? [*Pause.*] It tastes terrible.

**PANSY:** My James says it feels mighty good after.

**BECKY:** [*Like a hurt child.*] That's what I want. To feel good after. [*Pause.*] I think I'll sit a while. Have a seat, Pansy.

**PANSY:** Lordy, no, ma'am—I got work to do.

**BECKY:** Sit, sit—on Mr. Tashman's time you can take a little rest—maybe you'll have a drink?

**PANSY:** Lordy, no—not while I'm on the job, ma'am.

**BECKY:** [*Smiling gently.*] When I went to Paris, France, five years ago, I was the only Gold Star mother on the boat who didn't drink cocktails.

**PANSY:** You been that far, ma'am? To Paris, France?

**BECKY:** [*Proudly.*] Oh, yes. My son-in-law, Mr. Tashman, sent me — [*Breaking suddenly.*] Pansy, Pansy — I did a terrible thing tonight.

**PANSY:** You couldn't do anything terrible, Mis' Becky.

**BECKY:** [*Pause.*] Yes, I did. I told a lie — I spoiled Jacob's memory. The only thing I had left, and I spoiled it. [*She is weeping now, unashamedly. A strange new* BECKY, *for whom a first drink of hard liquor has meant a loosening of her tongue and her emotions as well.*] I'm afraid all the perfumes in Arabia won't wash away my sin. [*Pause.*] Lady Macbeth said it.

**PANSY:** [*Admiringly.*] I could lissen to you talkin' all day, Mis' Becky. You sure are powerful eddicated —

**BECKY:** Oh, yes, I am a high school graduate from Night School — [*Her mood changes.*] I went to Washington with my Night School Delegation. I shook hands with President Harding. Afterwards, they said he was a crook. But I never believed it. Such a fine looking man — [*Slightly tipsy now, she is in a reminiscent mood.*] In Washington they took us in buses to Arlington Cemetery. Beautiful. Like a park. Only instead of trees, millions of little crosses growing up from the ground. And flags! So many little American flags on the graves, and when the wind blows, they wave in the breeze like this — [*Waves hand in front of her dizzily. Suddenly getting up.*] I looked for my Hymie there. [*Staring straight ahead, her body erect.*] Then they showed us the place where one soldier is buried. And him they call the Unknown Soldier. And him they never leave alone. Always, day and night, two live soldiers are walking up and down — day and night — [*Breaks off, then simply.*] I think of this place, and I am glad they don't leave him alone. Please, Pansy, don't tell anybody, but *that's* the place where my Hymie is! [*Pause.*] I lost my Esther in the Triangle Fire. After that the inspector came and made me take my plants off the fire escape. It was the law. And after that, the committee from the Garment Workers came to tell me that she didn't die for nothing. And after that — my Sadie got her husband —

**PANSY:** [*Incredulously.*] Lordy, Lordy — [*A pause.*]

**BECKY:** Tell me, Pansy, do *you* think everything in this world happens for the best?

**PANSY:** Hard to say for sure, ma'am — but if you believes it, it makes you feel mighty good when the bad is happenin'.

**BECKY:** I wanted my family to have *life*. That's why I brought them here.

They sing about it. "The Land of the Free and the Home of the Brave."
[*Pause.*] My Hymie was brave. The day before he went away he said to
me, "Mama, don't he a Calamity Jane. Here's my watch. When you get
lonely, just wind it. When it ticks, it'll be me, talking to you." Then he
went away! [*Pause.*] What is left, Pansy? Nothing—not even Jacob's
memory—

PANSY: [*After pause.*] You sure feel bad, don't you, Mis' Becky? [BECKY *looks
up, tries to smile. The smile does not come.*] Down home the ole folks use'n
to say, "The Moming Star, she always shines brighter after a real dark
night." Yes, ma'am—guess as long as she's there every morning, the end a
the world ain't come yet—

BECKY: [*Sitting suddenly, exhausted.*] Life is very hard, but life is wonderful,
no?

PANSY: [*Wiping a tear from her eye.*] It sure is, Mis' Becky—

BECKY: [*Slowly as though this were a revelation.*] I guess a person has to have
patience to live through history while they are making it—[IRVING *enters.
Goes toward* BECKY *like a frightened child.*]

IRVING: Mama—what am I going to do?


[PANSY *exits into kitchen.*]


BECKY: Now you're asking? She's inside. Go—go in to her, look her straight
in the eye and tell her he printed a lie. That you are going to *sue* him
for it!

IRVING: But, Mama—

BECKY: I know it's true—but she'll believe you because she *wants* to believe
you, and if she doesn't—[*Forcefully.*] Make her! Slap her face! Do something anything—but if you let her get away, I'll never talk to you again
as long as I live! You heard me?

IRVING: I heard you—[*Takes off coat, goes to rack, hangs it up.*]

BECKY: [*With great authority.*] And furthermore, tomorrow morning you will
go downtown and buy yourself three tickets to Hollywood, California!

IRVING: [*Coming toward her*] Me?

BECKY: [*Continuing firmly.*] Yes, you! You will take a job with your Uncle
Abe once and for all. You will keep yourself so busy day and night writing
songs for the all-singing pictures, you won't have time to get yourself in
the papers. [*Winking.*] And if you live in California, how can you sue him
in New York?

IRVING: Mom—the only brains in the family—thanks, Mom—

**BECKY:** I am not through yet—[*Roughly.*] Come here! [IRVING *goes toward her.* BECKY *slaps him sharply across face.*] That's for being a bad boy! [*She slaps him again.*] And *that's* in *advance*—if you ever hurt my Fanny again—I, myself, personally will—[*Breaks off, contrite.*] Did I hurt you?

**IRVING:** [*Throwing arms around* BECKY, *bursting with laughter*] Mom, do I love you, do I love you. [*Pause.*] Becky Felderman! What in hell have you been drinking?

**BECKY:** A cocktail! What's wrong with it?

**IRVING:** [*Shouting with laughter.*] Where's my wife?

[*Goes toward upper bedroom.*]

**BECKY:** Not in there. Sadie is in there.

[IRVING *exits lower* R. BECKY *looks after him, smiling, then looks at her* R. *hand, which has so gloriously told* IRVING *off. She salutes it, with a nod of her head.* YOUNG HYMIE *comes out of kitchen.*]

**HYMIE:** Did I hear my pop?

**BECKY:** Don't go in there now, Hymela—

[*Her tone seems odd to* HYMIE. *He exits into kitchen, looking back at her with a puzzled expression.* BECKY *goes to buffet, takes out a small package, placing it at head of table. A knock at door. Out of habit,* BECKY *starts to answer it, but* PANSY *rushes through to door from kitchen.* AARON GREENSPAN *enters. He is now sixty, hair turned white, a tall, straight, boyish figure for his years. Takes off coat and hat, hangs them up.*]

**AARON:** [*Coming toward* BECKY, *hands outstretched.*] Becky, Becky, Mazeltuff—

**BECKY:** Thanks, Aaron, thanks. You are looking very well.

**AARON:** You don't look so bad yourself—

**BECKY:** [*Laughing.*] Thank you—

**AARON:** [*Touching couch.*] Aye, Becky—where is my old good friend—[*Pause.*] It's a great day for you, Becky—

**BECKY:** [*Looking up meaningfully.*] They have an old saying, "Never say a man lived a happy life till he's dead." Anything could happen the last minute.

AARON: [*Laughing.*] Aye, Becky, Becky—still the pessimist!

BECKY: I'm a pessimist? If you have to know, I am the world's biggest optimist. If I wasn't, I would have been dead long ago. [*Pause.* BECKY'*s manner softens.*] A fine way for me to treat a guest. Five minutes in the house, and I'm fighting with you—

AARON: [*Feeling sorry for himself.*] It's all right. Fight all you want. Even a fight is a pleasure for a lonely old man—[*After pause.*] Oh—I knew I had to tell you something funny. The other night I went to a newsreel. I could swear, on my life, standing next to Stalin on the platform was— guess who?

BECKY: Who?

AARON: Benjamin Brownstein!

BECKY: No! Time flies—[*Pause.*] And otherwise, how do you spend your time?

AARON: Work all day. Comes the night, *again* to a movie or a pinochle. Some life for a man, yes? [*Stares at her. She turns away.*] Oh, yes—last night for a change, in Gold's house, we played guess what, a game! That's the style today—to play games. Well, in this game they ask you questions. So, they asked me, "Who would I rather be, in the whole world, if I could positively *not* be Aaron Greenspan?" [*Turning toward her.*] Should I tell you what I answered? [*Pause.*] I said, I would rather be Jacob Felderman.

BECKY: [*Breaking completely.*] Oh—Aaron—Aaron—

AARON: Becky, please—I didn't mean to hurt your feelings—[*Pause.*]

BECKY: *You*—you didn't hurt my feelings, Aaron.

AARON: So—what's wrong?

BECKY: Plenty! [*Slowly.*] Sadie—after tonight, she does not step foot in this house. Irving and Fanny and Hymie? To California. As they say, "New worlds to conquer"—and Harry—[*Shaking head.*] Harry is a sick boy— very sick. [*Pause.*] My world! The reason I lived and breathed. Finished— done—

AARON: Aye, Becky, still the Calamity Jane—

BECKY: [*Angrily.*] If a woman doesn't have the fight to have heartache—

AARON: [*Going toward her.*] If it's a family you want—[*Suddenly angry.*] For years I have been waiting to be your family! As long as you had them—

**317**

damned kids—[BECKY *looks at him sharply. Looks around, afraid he has been overheard.*] We—we could have such a fine, sweet life together. We talk a little—we laugh a little—all right—we *fight* a little—[*Pause.*] Well! Why don't you *say* something?

BECKY: I—I don't know what to say—

AARON: [*Incredulous.*] You mean, you didn't say "no"?

BECKY: Please—Aaron—I have to think—

AARON: If you didn't shut me up with "no"—it's—it's practically a declaration of love!

BECKY: Stop hollering—they'll hear—

AARON: Once in a lifetime a man is entitled to holler! [*Pause.*] Nu? [*A moment of pause.*]

BECKY: [*Quietly.*] Well, consider I said it. [AARON *stares at her, hardly believing his success. Completely overcome with emotion, takes out handkerchief.*]

AARON: All my life I pictured this moment and all I can do is blow my nose—Becky, Becky darling—

BECKY: [*Smiles gently.* AARON *goes toward her, kissing her hand.*] But first, I have a favor to ask—

AARON: Already?

BECKY: Tonight—*no* announcements!

AARON: Your slightest wish is my command, madam!

[*Bows low, takes her hand in his, kissing it in cavalier fashion. Suddenly, as one person, they start to laugh. They are still laughing when* PANSY *enters. She wears a fresh apron and cap and is beaming.*]

PANSY: Dinner's ready to serve now, Mis' Becky—

BECKY: Knock on the door and tell the others—

[PANSY *knocks on upper bedroom door calling out,* "*Supper's ready.*" IRVING, FANNY *and* YOUNG HYMIE *enter arm-in-arm, smiling happily.* PANSY *exits into kitchen.*]

FANNY: [*Showing* BECKY *a bracelet.*] Mama! Look at this! Hello, Aaron.—

BECKY: It's beautiful—

FANNY: Irving, darling, you shouldn't have done it!

IRVING: What else have I got to do, except make you happy?

[SADIE *enters, slightly the worse for a crying fit, in which she has obviously been indulging.*]

FANNY: [*Throwing arms around* IRVING.] I wouldn't care if I never saw another bracelet in my life! It's you I love, not the bracelet! [*To* BECKY, *proudly.*] Irving is bringing suit first thing next week!

IRVING: [*With a wink toward* BECKY.] I should say so! For damages to my reputation and happiness! And, Mom—how'd you like to come to California to live?

FANNY: He's doing a musical for his Uncle Abe!

IRVING: He sold me a bill of goods this afternoon—[*Winking to* BECKY *again.*] I didn't want it, but you don't sneeze at five hundred a week!

AARON: [*Whistling.*] I wouldn't sneeze at it—

FANNY: [*To* SADIE.] You see, it doesn't pay to believe everything you read in the papers! [*Goes toward kitchen.*]

BECKY: [*Giving* HYMIE *small package.*] For you, Hymie—[HYMIE *opens package, takes out watch.*]

HYMIE: Gee, thanks, Grandma—[*Reading inscription.*] "To Hymie, from Mama and Esther and Sadie"—was that Tanta Esther?

BECKY: Yes. Tanta Esther. The watch belonged to your Uncle Hymie.

[HARRY *has entered quietly through the last. Looks up at mention of* ESTHER's *name, quietly takes his place near others. They gather around table. Speaking as they seat themselves in following order:* HYMIE, *head of table* L. BECKY, *head of table* R. AARON *and* SADIE *facing audience.* HARRY *next to* SADIE. FANNY *and* IRVING *with backs facing audience.*]

IRVING: Tonight Mama and Hymie sit at the heads. This is their night.

AARON: Believe me, Irving, judging from the talking moving pictures I seen lately, your mediocrity will be rewarded by great success—

IRVING: My what?

SADIE: And how are you, Greenspan?

AARON: I never felt better in my life!

SADIE: The world is having a depression, but on you evidently it doesn't make a dent!

AARON: Not even a pin scratch. The union scale is very good. That is, for *us*—but not for you, when you'll have to pay it!

SADIE: Never! I'll move to Jersey first!

[PANSY *enters with tray of food.*]

FANNY: You may serve now, Pansy—
PANSY: Ain't we gonna hear Mr. Hymie's speech first?
HYMIE: Aw, gee, didja have to remind her?
FANNY: Hymie! Remember what I said!
HYMIE: [*Getting up reluctantly, takes out crumpled paper, consults it.*] Well—
dear Grandma and Mama and Papa and everything—I mean everybody.
[*In a sing-song manner.*] Today I yam a man. I am thirteen years old. I
promise to be a good boy, I mean man—and, well—[*Quickly.*] If it's
true I'm a man, I guess I better be getting more than a dollar and a
quarter a week spending money—
FANNY: [*Horrified.*] Hymie! That's not in the speech!
HYMIE: Well I put it in—[*Continuing.*] And, dear God, we thank you for
all the blessings—and please bless Grandma and my dear mother and my
dear father—[*As the*]

CURTAIN SLOWLY DESCENDS

# Under a Painted Smile

# We'll Bring the Rue de la Paix!

# THE TENTH MAN

*Paddy Chayefsky*

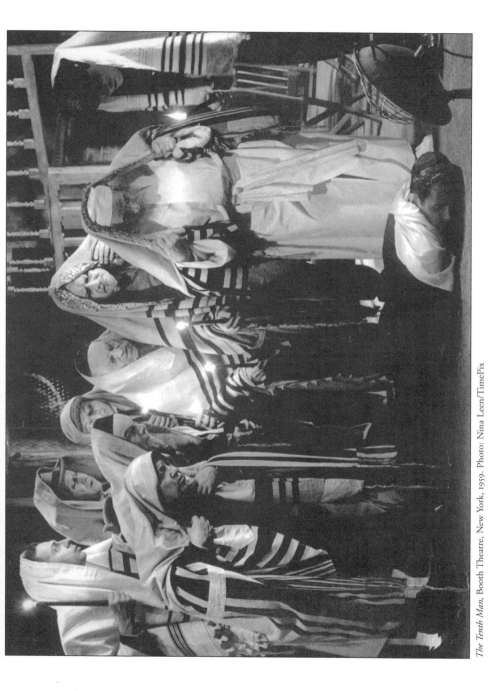

*The Tenth Man*, Booth Theatre, New York, 1959. Photo: Nina Leen/TimePix

# INTRODUCTION

He was Sidney Chayefsky at birth in New York in 1923 and as a student at City College and Fordham University. But on Sunday mornings in the Army, when he chose Mass over K. P., his buddies dubbed him Paddy. The nickname seems apt enough for a Jewish dramatist who set his early works in the Bronx and populated them with lower middle-class ethnic characters. That focus contributed to Chayefsky's reputation as the Clifford Odets of the Fifties.

The comparison with Odets extends to a career that prominently included screenwriting. The film version of Chayefsky's *Marty* (1955), adapted from his TV play, won him the New York Film Critics Award, a Cannes Film Festival Golden Palm, and his first Academy Award. He collected two more Oscars for *The Hospital* (1971) and *Network* (1976). *Network*'s protagonist is a news commentator driven to frustration by the illogic of a dehumanizing society. His broadcast invitation to join him as he raged, "I'm mad as hell, and I'm not going to take it anymore," found a ready audience. The line echoed across the country, a national catch phrase for months. The satirical tone and the cynical treatment of corporate bureaucracy and power struggles in *Network* and *The Hospital* were new vehicles for themes Chayefsky had developed more simply and sentimentally in his early, explicitly Jewish works, like celebrating the power of love and the worth of people who only appear unremarkable in a society misguided by tinsel values.

The later plays also show that Chayefsky's vision had transcended the Bronx and its ordinary people. *The Passion of Joseph D.* (1964) is a "political burlesque" about Stalin's role in the Russian Revolution. The play's episodic and narrative distancing techniques seem influenced by Brecht. *The Latent Heterosexual* (1968) is a bitter comedy in which an Ionescan tyranny of legalese and bureaucratic jargon reduce its hapless central character to protest, "I am being reified, disincarnated and converted into an abstract." Chayefsky was reportedly writing a play about Alger Hiss when he died in 1981.

A strong advocate of Israel, Chayefsky was a social and political activist in the Seventies. He co-founded Writers and Artists for Peace in the Middle East and served as a delegate to the 1971 International Conference on Soviet Jewry. His work, in and out of the arts, was shaped by regard for the individual and concern for a world outgrowing human scale and control. The seriousness of his convictions notwithstanding, he rarely failed to enliven them with the perspective and devices of humor.

Chayefsky first came to public attention during the Fifties golden age of TV drama. Typical of the acclaimed scripts he wrote for the Philco-Goodyear Playhouse is *Holiday Song* (1952). Here the piety of a disaffected cantor is restored when, on the eve of Rosh Hashanah, he is mysteriously led to reunite two Holocaust survivors. Two incidents in *Holiday Song* later found their way into *The Tenth Man* (1959): the rekindling of a disenchanted religious leader's faith, and the pilgrimage made by an elderly Jew through the New York City transit system to consult a chief rabbi. In 1956, Chayefsky adapted another teleplay, *Middle of the Night*, to the Broadway stage. It ran for 477 performances with Edward G. Robinson playing the middle-aged Jewish widower who escapes loneliness and suffocating predictability when he marries a non-Jewish woman half his age, scandalizing his family and hers.

Chayefsky's most thoroughly Jewish plays are *The Tenth Man* and *Gideon* (1961), each cited among its season's Ten Best in the *Best Plays* series. Just as Odets had probed the contemporary relevance of a Bible story in *The Flowering Peach*, Chayefsky reworked the hero of the book of Judges as a man challenged both by divine favor and modern temptations. Like Odets's Judaized characters, Chayefsky's genuine Jew finds himself at odds with a God who lays claim to the unquestioning obedience of a man just learning to value and trust his own judgment. The God of *Gideon* also demands love, but the title character finds it easier to love man than God because, "To love you, God, one must be a god himself."

The source of *The Tenth Man* is the most famous of the classic Yiddish plays, S. Anski's *The Dybbuk* (1914). Maurice Schwartz introduced the play to New York at his Yiddish Art Theater in 1922. Two years later, the Vilna Troupe brought its legendary staging of *The Dybbuk* to the United States, where various members of the company toured with it. Since its English language premier in 1925, the work has had countless productions and inspired notable adaptations. While Chayefsky thus drew on material familiar to many theatre-goers, he had much to do to fashion an American Jewish play of it.

The differences between the two works are as significant as the similarities. The very settings announce the divergences. Anski lays his play in the hermetic, cohesive world of the shtetl, where the generations customarily interrelate within generally accepted mores and practices of Jewish belief. The source of dramatic conflict is, in fact, the violation of those values. By contrast, *The Tenth Man* is set in a storefront synagogue whose hyphenated name proclaims a compromise, and whose affiliates, while hardly a cross-section of American Jewry, suggest the numerous constructions of Jewishness, and even of Judaism, in mid-century America. A side-by-side examination of the two plays reveals the challenges Chayefsky met as he considered equivalences for the mysticism, the opposing forces, and the characters in the masterwork that inspired him. Such a comparison makes the alternate title of Anski's play, *Between Two Worlds*, apply to Chayefsky's with new layers of meaning.

Much of the religious fervor and awed respect for tradition that permeate the Yiddish play get lost in America. *The Tenth Man* shows us how difficult it is to preserve them here. The exigencies of life in a secular, multicultural society keep intruding importunately, even in a modest Orthodox synagogue. *The Tenth Man*'s opening line, "Close the door," is ironic, wishful thinking.

Its single set notwithstanding, the play shows us the much-altered structure of Jewish life beyond the synagogue. Chayefsky makes deft use of humor, the time-honored Jewish response to trouble, to blunt the painful erosion of family and community responsibilies. (For all its earnestness, this play is a comedy, while *The Dybbuk*, of course, is anything but.) So septuagenarian widowers heap Yiddish-style curses on their disrespectful daughters-in-law on whose hospitality they have to depend. Funeral societies having disappeared, they have made their own burial arrangements and joke about the relative merits of their cemeteries. Experience has taught the rabbi to put his duties as social director and club organizer ahead of spiritual leadership. The sexton's daily challenge is to round up ten men for morning prayers.

Only Hirschman, the cabalist, maintains Old World piety. He rarely ventures out of the synagogue, though there may be more pragmatic explanations for his living there. The play deals respectfully with him. His Act II exchange with Arthur Brooks displays his accurate assessment of a world he avoids and another reason for his shunning it. Several of his fellow congregants are more accommodated to life in America, but they can still find it bewildering. While Foreman and Schlissel's foiled pilgrimage in the subway to find the Korpotchniker Rabbi is wildly funny, their search for authoritative answers has obvious symbolic value.

Love plays a central role in both works. In *The Tenth Man*, it ranges from Hirschman's devotion to prayer and study to the more profane expressions of love that account for the presence of a dybbuk in the first place. Several of the congregants confess their accountability for the Whore of Kiev who possesses Evelyn Foreman. They respond out of guilt and the centrality of repentance to Jewish faith, but also according to the ethics of altruism fundamental to the play. Like *The Dybbuk*, *The Tenth Man* celebrates the concern for one's neighbor implicit in the individual's acceptance of responsibility to the community. Small wonder that when Arthur Brooks, paradigm of contemporary cynicism and anomie, finds himself in this rarefied atmosphere, he is totally disoriented. The miracle of Brooks's redemption — and perhaps the only credible explanation for his swift confidence that he can cure Evelyn with his love — stems from his reconnecting with the power of Jewish communal responsibility and of belief.

Although, as several reviewers noted, the redemption of a cynic through religion is a classic theme in Western literature, exorcisms are not routine events, not even in the Yiddish theatre. The enactment of this exotic Jewish rite on the American stage warrants attention. So do the facts that the entire action is set in a synagogue and that there are explanations and directions for ceremonies and rituals. One can question the playwright's substituting of "praying shawl" for *tallith*, or "quorum" for *minyan*, but it is impossible to ignore that this Broadway play makes the morning service an integral part of its plot and the recitation of the confessional Al-Chait prayer a dramatic necessity. Chayefsky brought audiences into an orthodox synagogue as naturally as Odets and Regan had drawn them into Jewish homes several decades earlier. The original production of *The Tenth Man* filled Broadway's Booth Theatre for 623 performances, an index of how far Jews had come in America as it entered the Sixties.

*The Tenth Man* was presented by Saint Subber and Arthur Cantor at the Booth Theatre, New York City, November 5, 1959; directed by Tyrone Guthrie; setting and lighting by David Hays; costumes by Frank Thompson; with the following cast:

| | |
|---|---|
| Hirschman . . . . . . . . . . . . . . . . . . . . | Arnold Marle Sexton |
| David Vardi Schlissel . . . . . . . . . . . . . | Lou Jacobi Zitorsky |
| Jack Guilford Alper . . . . . . . . . . . . . | George Voscovec |
| Foreman . . . . . . . . . . . . . . . . . . . . | Jacob Ben-Ami Evelyn |
| Foreman . . . . . . . . . . . . . . . . . . . . | Risa Schwartz Arthur |
| Brooks . . . . . . . . . . . . . . . . . . . . | Donald Harron Harris |
| Martin Garner Rabbi . . . . . . . . . . . . . | Gene Saks Kessler Boys |
| Alan Manson and Paul Marin Policeman . . . . | Tim Callaghan |

## SYNOPSIS OF SCENES
The action takes place in an Orthodox Synagogue in Mineola, Long Island.

## ACT ONE
Before the Morning Prayers.

## ACT TWO
**SCENE 1:** The Morning Prayers.
**SCENE 2:** Before the Afternoon Prayers.

## ACT THREE
The Exorcism.

# ACT ONE

**SCENE:** *Interior of the synagogue of the Congregation Ateret-Tifereth Yisroel. It is a poor congregation, and the synagogue is actually a converted shop. A raised platform surrounded by a railing contains the lectern and the Holy Ark. This altar is surrounded by rows of plain wooden folding chairs which constitute the seating accommodations for the congregation. On the far side of the altar is an old desk at which the rabbi presides when teaching Hebrew school. A partitioned area downstage right is the rabbi's study, a crowded little cubicle containing a battered mahogany desk and chair, an old leather armchair a worn leather couch, and piles of black prayer books. On the walls are old framed pictures of bearded patriarchs in desolate obsession over their Talmuds and perhaps a few familiar scenes from the Old Testament. Downstage is a metal heating unit. There is a second heating unit upstage, and a door leading apparently to a bathroom. The front door is stage left.*

**TIME:** *It is 6:30 AM on a cold winter day.*

**AT RISE:** *The Cabalist stands in the middle of the synagogue, entirely wrapped in a thick white linen praying shawl with broad black stripes, praying silently from a heavy prayer book that rests on the railing of the altar. Suddenly he pauses in his intense devotions, clutches at the railing as if to hold himself from falling. We have the impression that he is faint, near to swooning. He is a small, bearded man, in his 70s, his face lean and lined, his eyes sunken and hollow. He wears a small black skullcap from beneath which stick out gray forelocks and sidecurls—a testament to his orthodoxy. After a moment, he regains his strength and returns to his prayers. Three men hurry into the synagogue out of the oppressive cold of the street. They are the Sexton, Schlissel and Zitorsky. They all wear heavy overcoats and gray fedoras. Schlissel and Zitorsky are in their early 70s. The Sexton is a small, nervous, bespectacled man of 48. We know he is a sexton because he carries a huge ring of keys and is always doing something. They rub their hands for warmth and huff and puff and dart quick looks at the Cabalist, who is oblivious to their entrance.*

SCHLISSEL: [*Muttering.*] Close the door. [*Light pours down on the synagogue as* THE SEXTON *raises the window curtains.* THE SEXTON *scurries upstage to fuss with the heater in the rear of the synagogue.* SCHLISSEL *and* ZITORSKY *shuffle downstage to a small naked radiator and stand silently—indeed a little wearily—for a moment;* SCHLISSEL *sighs.*] So how goes it with a Jew today?

ZITORSKY: How should it go?

SCHLISSEL: Have a pinch of snuff.

ZITORSKY: No, thank you.

SCHLISSEL: Davis won't be here this morning. I stopped by his house. He has a cold. His daughter-in-law told me he's still in bed.

ZITORSKY: My daughter-in-law, may she grow rich and buy a hotel with a thousand rooms and be found dead in every one of them.

SCHLISSEL: My daughter-in-law, may she invest heavily in General Motors, and the whole thing should go bankrupt.

ZITORSKY: Sure, go have children.

SCHLISSEL: The devil take them all.

THE SEXTON: [*Scurrying downstage; to* THE CABALIST *as he passes.*] Hirschman, are you all right? [*He flutters, a small round ball of a man, to the door of the rabbi's office, which he enters.*]

SCHLISSEL: Foreman won't be here today.

ZITORSKY: What's the matter with Foreman?

SCHLISSEL: His granddaughter today. This is the morning.

ZITORSKY: Oh, that's right. Today is the morning.

SCHLISSEL: Listen, it's better for everybody.

ZITORSKY: Sure.

SCHLLSSEL: I told Foreman, I said: "Foreman, it's better for everybody." The girl is becoming violent. I spoke to her father. He said to me they live in terror what she'll do to the other children. They came home one night, they found her punching one of the little children.

ZITORSKY: Well, what can you do?

SCHLISSEL: What can you do? You do what they're doing. They're putting her back in the institution.

ZITORSKY: Of course. There she will have the benefit of trained psychiatric personnel.

SCHLISSEL: The girl is incurable. She's been in and out of mental institutions since she was 11 years old. I met the psychiatrist there, you know, when I was up there to visit Foreman last week. I discussed the whole business with him. A fine young fellow. The girl is a schizophrenic with violent tendencies.

ZITORSKY: [*Considers this diagnosis for a moment, then sighs.*] Ah, may my daughter-in-law eat acorns and may branches sprout from her ears.

SCHLISSEL: May my daughter-in-law live to be a hundred and twenty, and may she have to live all her years in her daughter-in-law's house.

[*A fourth old Jew now enters from the street, a patrician little man with a Vandyke beard and a black homburg. His name is* ALPER. *He bursts into shrill prayer as he enters.*]

ALPER: [*Chanting.*] As for me in the abundance of Thy loving kindness will I come into Thy house; I will worship toward Thy holy temple in the fear of Thee. How goodly are Thy tents, O Jacob ... [*As precipitously as the prayer had begun, it now drops into nothing more than a rapid movement of lips.* THE SEXTON *acknowledges* ALPER's *arrival from the rabbi's office, where he plunks himself behind the desk and begins hurriedly to dial the phone.* ALPER's *voice zooms abruptly up into a shrill incantation again.*] ... in the truth of Thy salvation. Amen!

SCHLISSEL: Amen.

ZITORSKY: Amen.

[ALPER *joins the other two* OLD MEN *and they stand in silent rueful speculation.*]

THE SEXTON: [*On phone.*] Hello, Harris? This is Bleyer the Sexton. Come on down today, we need you. Foreman won't be here. Davis is sick. We won't have ten men for the morning prayers if you don't come down. Services start in twenty minutes. Hurry up—Wear a sweater under your coat— All right— [*He hangs up, takes a large ledger from the desk and begins to nervously examine its pages.*]

SCHLISSEL: Hirschman slept over in the synagogue again last night. Have you ever seen such pietistic humbug?

ALPER: Well, he is a very devout man. A student of the Cabala. The Rabbi speaks of him with the greatest reverence.

SCHLISSEL: Devout indeed. I assure you this lavish display of orthodoxy is a very profitable business. I was told confidentially just yesterday that his board and food are paid for by two foolish old women who consider him a saint.

**ALPER:** It can't cost them very much. He's been fasting the last three days.

**SCHLISSEL:** And the reason he sleeps in the synagogue so frequently is because his landlady does not give him heat for his own room in the mornings.

**ZITORSKY:** Ah, go be an old man in the winter.

**ALPER:** I must say, I really don't know what to do with myself on these cold days.

**SCHLISSEL:** I'm an atheist. If I had something better to do, would I be here?

**ZITORSKY:** You know what would be a nice way to kill a day? I think it would be nice to take a trip up to Mount Hope Cemetery and have a look at my burial plot. A lovely cemetery. Like a golf course, actually. By the time one gets there and comes back, the whole day has been used up. Would you like to come? I'll pay both your fares.

**ALPER:** Why not? I have never been to Mount Hope. I have my burial lot on Mount Zion Cemetery.

**ZITORSKY:** Oh, that's a beautiful cemetery.

**ALPER:** Yes, it is. My wife wanted to buy plots in Cedar Lawn because her whole family is buried there, but I wouldn't hear of it.

**ZITORSKY:** Oh, Cedar Lawn. I wouldn't be buried in Cedar Lawn.

**ALPER:** It's in such a bad state. The headstones tumble one on top of the other, and everybody walks on the graves.

**ZITORSKY:** They don't take care in Cedar Lawn. My wife once said, she should rest in peace, that Cedar Lawn was the tenement of cemeteries.

**ALPER:** A well-turned phrase.

**ZITORSKY:** She had a way with words, God grant her eternal rest.

**ALPER:** I'd like you to come to Mount Zion sometimes, see my plot.

**ZITORSKY:** Maybe we could make the trip tomorrow.

**SCHLISSEL:** Listen to these two idiots, discussing their graves as if they were country estates.

**ZITORSKY:** Where are you buried, Schlissel?

**SCHLISSEL:** Cedar Lawn.

**ALPER:** Well, listen, there are many lovely areas in Cedar Lawn. All my wife's family are buried there.

**ZITORSKY:** Come with us, Schlissel, and have a look at my grave.

SCHLISSEL: Why not? What else have I got to do?

[ALPER *now slowly goes about the business of donning his praying shawl and phylacteries, which he takes out of a velvet praying bag. Among Jews, prayer is a highly individual matter, and peripatetic to the bargain. The actual ritual of laying on the phylacteries is a colorful one.* ALPER *extracts his left arm from his jacket and rebuttons his jacket so that his shirt sleeved left arm hangs loose. Then, the shirt sleeve is rolled up almost to the shoulders, and the arm phylactery, a long thin black leather thong, is put on by wrapping it around the arm seven times and around the middle finger of the left hand three times. All this is accompanied by rapidly recited prayers, as is the laying on of the head-phylactery. All the while* ALPER *walks bending and twisting at the knees, raising his voice occasionally in the truly lovely words of incantation. In a far upstage corner* THE CABALIST *huddles under his enveloping white praying shawl, his back to everyone else, deeply involved in his personal meditations. The synagogue itself is a shabby little place, the walls yellowed and cracked, and illumined by a fitful overhead bulb. There is indeed at this moment, a sense of agelessness, even of primitive barbarism. During this* THE SEXTON *has dialed a second number.*]

THE SEXTON: Hello? Mr. Arnold Kessler, please — How do you do? This is Mr. Bleyer, the Sexton at the synagogue. Perhaps you recall me — Did I wake you up? I'm terribly sorry. As long as you're up, according to my books, your father died one year ago yesterday, on the eleventh day in the month of Schvat, may his soul fly straight to the Heavenly Gates, and how about coming down with your brother and saying a memorial prayer in your father's name? — Let me put it this way, Mr. Kessler. You know, we can't have morning prayers without a quorum of ten men. If you and your brother don't come down we won't have a quorum — As a favor to me — Kessler, may your children be such devoted sons, and bring your brother. You are doing a good deed. Peace be with you. Hurry up — [*He hangs up, sits frowning, totaling up on his fingers the number of men he has, scowls.*]

ALPER: [*His voice rises for a brief moment.*] and it shall be to Thee for a sign upon Thy hand, and for a memorial between Thy eyes...

THE SEXTON: [*Rises abruptly from his chair and bustles out of the office to the front door of the synagogue. To nobody in particular.*] Listen, I'm going to have to get a tenth Jew off the street somewheres. I'll be right back. Schlissel, will you please fix that bench already, you promised me.

[*He exits.* SCHLISSEL *nods and picks up a hammer. For a moment, only the sing-song murmur of the rapid prayers and the upstage tapping Of* SCHLISSEL'S *hammer fill the stage. The front door to the synagogue now opens, and a fifth old Jew peers in. He is a frightened little wisp of a man named* FOREMAN. *He is obviously in a state. He darts terrified looks all about the synagogue, and then abruptly disappears back into the street leaving the synagogue door open. Nobody is yet aware of his brief appearance. A moment later he is back, this time leading a slim young* GIRL *of 18, wearing a topcoat, who is also distracted. The* OLD MAN *herds her quickly across the synagogue to the rabbi's office, pushes her in, and closes the door behind her. She sits in the rabbi's office, almost rigid with terror. Like his friends,* FOREMAN *wears a heavy winter coat and a warm fedora some sizes too small for him. He stands and watches the others apprehensively. At last* ALPER *reaches the end of his laying on of the phylacteries, his voice climbing to a shrill incantation.*]

ALPER: [*To* FOREMAN, *moving slowly as he prays.*] ... and it shall be for a sign upon Thy hand, and for frontlets between Thy eyes; for by strength of hand the Lord brought us out from Egypt. Amen!
FOREMAN: [*Muttering, his head bobbing nervously.*] Amen!
ALPER: I thought you weren't coming down today, Foreman.
FOREMAN: [*His mouth working without saying anything. Finally says:*] Alper—
ALPER: You seem agitated. Is something wrong?
FOREMAN: [*Staring gauntly at his friend.*] Alper, I have her here.
ALPER: You have who here?
FOREMAN: I have my granddaughter Evelyn here. I have her here in the rabbi's office.
ALPER: What are you talking about?
FOREMAN: I took her out of the house while nobody was looking, and I brought her here. I am faint. Let me sit down. [*He sinks onto a chair.* ALPER *regards him with concern.*]
ALPER: Here, David, let me take your coat.

**FOREMAN:** Alper, I have seen such a thing and heard words as will place me in my grave before the singing of the evening service. Blessed art Thou, O Lord, King of the Universe, Who hath wrought the wonders of the world. [*Suddenly half-starting from his seat.*] I must speak to Hirschman! This is an affair for Hirschman who has delved into the Cabala and the forbidden mysteries of numbers.

**ALPER:** Sit down, Foreman and compose yourself [FOREMAN *sinks slowly back onto his chair.*] Why did you bring her here? Foreman, you are my oldest friend from our days in the seminary together in Rumni in the Province of Poltava, and I speak to you harshly as only a friend may speak. You are making too much out of this whole matter of the girl. I know how dear she is to you, but the girl is insane, for heavens' sakes! What sort of foolishness is this then to smuggle her out of your son's home? To what purpose? Really, Foreman, a gentle and pious man like you! Your son must be running through the streets at this moment shouting his daughter's name. Call him on the phone and tell him you are bringing her back to him.

**FOREMAN:** [*Stares at* ALPER*, his pale eyes filled with tears.*] Alper—

**ALPER:** David, my dear friend, make peace with this situation.

**FOREMAN:** [*Whispering.*] She is possessed, Alper. She has a dybbuk in her. A demon! It spoke to me. [*He stares down at the floor at his feet, a numb terror settling over his face.*] It spoke to me. I went into my granddaughter this morning to comfort her, and I said: "How are you?" And she seemed quite normal. She has these moments of absolute lucidity. [*He looks gauntly at* ALPER *again.*] She seemed to know she was being taken to the institution again. Then suddenly she fell to the floor in a swoon. I said: "Evelyn, what's the matter?" And she looked up at me, and it was no longer her face, but a face so twisted with rage that my blood froze in my body. And a voice came out of her that was not her own. "Do you know my voice?" And I knew it. I knew the voice. God have mercy on my soul. I stood there like a statue, and my granddaughter lay on the floor with her eyes closed, and the voice came out of her, but her lips never moved. "David Foreman, son of Abram, this is the soul of Hannah Luchinsky, whom you dishonored and weakened in your youth, and the gates of Heaven are closed to me." And my granddaughter began to writhe on the floor as if in the most horrible agony, and she began to laugh so loudly that I was sure my son and daughter-in-law in the living room could hear. I flung the door open in panic, and my son and daughter-in-law were sitting there talking, and they heard nothing. And I tell you, shrieks of laughter were coming from this girl on the floor. And I closed the door, and besought God, and finally the dybbuk was silent. May God strike me down on this spot, Alper if every word I tell you is not true.

ALPER: [*Has slowly sat down on an adjacent chair absolutely enthralled by the story. He stares at* FOREMAN.] A dybbuk?

FOREMAN: [*Nodding.*] A dybbuk. Could you believe such a thing?

ALPER: Who did the dybbuk say she was?

FOREMAN: You should remember her. Hannah Luchinsky.

ALPER: The name is vaguely familiar.

FOREMAN: You remember Luchinsky, the sexton of the Rumni seminary with his three daughters? Hannah was the handsome one, who became pregnant, and they threw stones at her, called her harlot, and drove her out of the city.

ALPER: [*Recognition slowly coming over him.*] Oohhh.

FOREMAN: I was the one who debased her.

ALPER: You? You were such a nose-in-the-books, a gentle and modest fellow. Dear me. A dybbuk. Really! What an extraordinary thing. Schlissel, you want to hear a story?

SCHLISSEL: [*Coming over*] What?

ALPER: [*To* ZITORSKY, *who ambles over.*] Listen to this. Foreman is telling a story here that will turn your blood into water.

SCHLISSEL: What happened?

FOREMAN: What happened, Schlissel, was that I went in to see my grand-daughter this morning and discovered that she was possessed by a dybbuk. Now, please, Schlissel, before you go into one of your interminable disputations on the role of superstition in the capitalist economy, let me remind you that I am a follower of Maimonides and—

SCHLISSEL: What are you talking about?

FOREMAN: A dybbuk! A dybbuk! I tell you my granddaughter is possessed by a dybbuk! Oh, my head is just pounding! I do not know which way to turn.

SCHLISSEL: What are you prattling about dybbuks?

ALPER: [*To* SCHLISSEL.] The voice of Hannah Luchinsky spoke to him through the lips of his granddaughter.

ZITORSKY: Oh, a dybbuk.

SCHLISSEL: What nonsense is this?

ALPER: [*To* FOREMAN] Are you sure?

FOREMAN: [*Angrily.*] Am I sure? Am I a peasant who leaps at every black cat? Have I ever shown a susceptibility to mysticism? Have you not seen me engaging Hirschman over there in violent disputation over the fanatic numerology of the Cabala? Have I not mocked to his very face the murky phantasy of the Gilgul with its wispy souls floating in space? Really! Am I sure! Do you take me for a fool, a prattler of old wives' tales? Really! I tell you I heard that woman's voice as I hear the cold wind outside our doors now and saw my granddaughter writhing in the toils of possession as I see the phylactery on your brow this moment. I was a teacher of biology for thirty-nine years at the Yeshiva High School. A dedicated follower of the great Rambam who scoffed at augurs and sorcerers! For heaven's sakes! Really! I report to you only what I see! [*He strides angrily away, and then his brief flurry of temper flows away as abruptly as it flared.*] My dear Alper, please forgive this burst of temper. I am so distressed by this whole business that I cannot control my wits. I assure you that it is as hard for me to believe my own senses as it is for you.

ZITORSKY: When I was a boy in Lithuania, there was a young boy who worked for the butcher who was possessed by the dybbuk.

SCHLISSEL: [*Scornfully.*] A dybbuk. Sure. Sure. When I was a boy in Poland, I also heard stories about a man who lived in the next town who was possessed by a dybbuk. I was eight years old, and one day after school, my friends and I walked barefoot the six miles to the next town, and we asked everybody, "Where is the man with the dybbuk?" And nobody knew what we were talking about. So I came home and told my mother: "Mama, there is no man with a dybbuk in the next town." And she gave me such a slap across the face that I turned around three times. And she said to me: "Aha! Only eight years old and already an atheist." Foreman, my friend, you talk like my mother who was an ignorant fishwife. I am shocked at you.

FOREMAN: Oh, leave me be, Schlissel. I have no patience with your pontificating this morning.

ALPER: Don't let him upset you, Foreman. The man is a Communist.

FOREMAN: He is not a Communist. He is just disagreeable.

SCHLISSEL: My dear fellow, I have never believed in God. Should I now believe in demons? A dybbuk. This I would like to see.

FOREMAN: [*Furiously.*] Then see! [*He strides to the door of the rabbi's office and wrenches the door open. The* OTHERS *gingerly follow him to the opened doorway and peer in. The girl,* EVELYN, *stares at them, terrified. In a thunderous voice,* FOREMAN cries out:] Dybbuk! I direct you to reveal yourself! [THE GIRL *stares at the four patently startled* OLD MEN, *and then suddenly bursts into a bloodcurdling shriek of laughter The four* OLD MEN *involuntarily take one step back and regard this exhibition wide-eyed.*] What is your name?

THE GIRL: I am Hannah Luchinsky.

FOREMAN: Who are you?

THE GIRL: I am the Whore of Kiev, the companion of sailors.

FOREMAN: How came you to be in my granddaughter's body?

THE GIRL: I was on a yacht in the sea of Odessa, the pleasure of five wealthy merchants. And a storm arose, and all were lost. And my soul rose from the water and flew to the city of Belgorod where my soul appealed to the sages of that city. But since I was debauched they turned their backs on me.

FOREMAN: And then?

THE GIRL: Then my soul entered the body of a cow, who became insane and was brought to slaughter, and I flew into the body of this girl as if divinely directed.

FOREMAN: What do you want?

THE GIRL: I want the strength of a pure soul so that I may acquire that experience to ascend to heaven.

FOREMAN: I plead with you to leave the body of this girl.

THE GIRL: I have wandered in Gilgul many years, and I want peace. Why do you plague me? There are those among you who have done the same as I and will suffer a similar fate. There is one among you who has lain with whores many times, and his wife died of the knowledge.

ZITORSKY: [*Aghast.*] Oh, my God.

THE GIRL: [*Laughing.*] Am I to answer questions of old men who have nothing to do but visit each other's cemeteries?

ZITORSKY: [*Terrified.*] A dybbuk—a dybbuk

FOREMAN: Evelyn—Evelyn—She is again in a catatonic state.

[THE GIRL *now sits in the rabbi's chair sprawling wantonly, apparently finished with the interview. The four* OLD MEN *regard her a little numbly. They are all quite pale as a result of the experience. After a moment,* FOREMAN *closes the door of the rabbi's office, and the four* OLD MEN *shuffle in a silent group downstage where they stand each reviewing in his own mind the bizarre implications of what they have seen.* FOREMAN *sinks onto a chair and covers his face with his hands. After a long, long moment,* ZITORSKY *speaks.*]

ZITORSKY: Well, that's some dybbuk, all right.

SCHLISSEL: The girl is as mad as a hatter and fancies herself a Ukrainian trollop. This is a dybbuk?

ALPER: I found it quite an unnerving experience.

ZITORSKY: She caught me dead to rights. I'll tell you that. I was the one she was talking about there, who trumpeted around with women. Listen, when I was in the garment business, if you didn't have women for the out-of-town buyers, you couldn't sell a dozen dresses. Oh, I was quite a gamey fellow when I was in business, a madcap really. One day, my wife caught me in the shop with a model—who knew she would be down-town that day?—and from that moment on, my wife was a sick woman and died three years later, cursing my name with her last breath. That was some dybbuk, all right. How she picked me out! It gave me the shivers.

ALPER: Did you notice her use of archaic language and her Russian accent? The whole business had an authentic ring to me.

SCHLISSEL: What nonsense! The last time I was up to Foreman's the girl confided to me in a whisper that she was Susan Hayward. A dybbuk! Ever since she was a child, Foreman has been pumping her head full of the wretched superstitions of the Russian Pale, so she thinks she is a dybbuk. The girl is a lunatic and should be packed off to an asylum immediately.

ALPER: [*He regards* SCHLISSEL *with a disapproving eye; then takes* SCHLISSEL'S *arm and leads him a few steps away for a private chat.*] Really, Schlissel, must you always be so argumentative? We are all here agreed that we have a dybbuk in our company, but you always seem intent on being at odds with everyone around you. Really, look at poor Foreman, how distraught he is. Out of simple courtesy, really, for an old friend, can you not affect at least a silence on the matter? And, after all, what else have you got to do today? Ride two and a half hours to look at Zitorsky's tombstone? When you stop and think of it, this dybbuk is quite an exciting affair. Really, nothing like this has happened since Kornblum and Milsky had that fistfight over who would have the seat by the East Wall during the High Holidays.

ZITORSKY: [*Ambling over*] That's some dybbuk, all right.

SCHLISSEL: [*Frowning.*] All right, so what'll we do with this dybbuk now that we got it?

**ALPER:** It seems to me, there is some kind of ritual, an exorcism of sorts.

**ZITORSKY:** Maybe we should tell the rabbi.

**SCHLISSEL:** A young fellow like that. What does he know of dybbuks? A dybbuk must be exorcised from the body by a rabbi of some standing. You can't just call in some smooth-shaven young fellow fresh from the Seminary for such a formidable matter as a dybbuk. This rabbi has only been here two months. He hardly knows our names.

**ALPER:** He's right. You have to get a big rabbi for such a business.

**SCHLISSEL:** What has to be done is we must get in touch with the Korpotchniker rabbi of Williamsburg, who has inherited the mantle of the great Korpotchniker of Lwow, whose fame extends to all the corners of the world.

**ZITORSKY:** Oh, a sage among sages.

**ALPER:** I was about to suggest the Bobolovitcher rabbi of Crown Heights.

**SCHLISSEL:** Where do you come to compare the Bobolovitcher rabbi with the Korpotchniker?

**ALPER:** I once attended an afternoon service conducted by the Bobolovitcher, and it was an exalting experience. A man truly in the great tradition of Chassidic rabbis.

**ZITORSKY:** A sage among sages, may his name be blessed for ever and ever.

**SCHLISSEL:** It shows how much you know. The Bobolovitcher rabbi is a disciple of the Korpotchniker and sat at the Korpotchniker's feet until a matter of only a few years ago.

**ALPER:** Listen, I'm not going to argue with you. Either one is fine for me.

**SCHLISSEL:** The Korpotchniker is the number one Chassidic rabbi in the world. If you're going to involve yourself at all, why not go straight to the top?

**ALPER:** All right, so let it be the Korpotchniker.

**ZITORSKY:** For that matter, the Lubanower rabbi of Brownsville is a man of great repute.

**SCHLISSEL:** The Lubanower! Really! He's a young man, for heaven's sakes!

**ALPER:** Zitorsky, let it be decided then that it will be the Korpotchniker.

**ZITORSKY:** I only made a suggestion.

**SCHLISSEL:** The question is how does one get to the Korpotchniker? One does not drop into his home as if it were a public library. One has to solicit his secretary and petition for an audience. It may takes weeks.

**ALPER:** I do think, Schlissel, we shall have to get a more accessible rabbi than that. Ali, here is Hirschman, who I am sure can give us excellent counsel in this matter.

[THE CABALIST *has indeed finished his prayers, and is shuffling downstage, a small, frightened little man.* FOREMAN *leaps from his chair.*]

FOREMAN: Hirschman! [*Everyone crowds around* HIRSCHMAN.]

ZITORSKY: Oh, boy, Hirschman, have we got something to tell you!

ALPER: Zitorsky, please. Hirschman, you are a man versed in the Cabala, a man who prays with all the seventy-two names of the most Ancient of the Ancient Ones.

FOREMAN: [*Blurting out.*] Hirschman, my granddaughter is possessed by a dybbuk!

THE CABALIST: [*Starting back in terror*] A dybbuk!

ALPER: Foreman, please, one does not announce such a thing as baldly as that.

THE CABALIST: Are you sure?

FOREMAN: Hirschman, as a rule, I am not given to whimsy.

THE CABALIST: Was it the soul of a woman wronged in her youth?

FOREMAN: Yes.

THE CABALIST: I heard her cry out last night. I awoke for my midnight devotions, and as I prayed I heard the whimpering of a woman's soul. [*A strange expression of bemused wonder settles over his face.*] I have fasted three days and three nights, and I dismissed the sound of this dybbuk as a phantasy of my weakened state. For only those to whom the Ancient One has raised his veil can hear the traffic of dybbuks. Is this a sign from God that my penitence is over? I have prayed for such a sign. I have felt strange things these past days. Sudden, bursting illuminations have bleached mine eyes, and I have heard the sounds of dead and super-natural things. [*He lifts his worn little face, his eyes wide with wonder. The others are put a little ill-at-ease by this effusive outburst.* FOREMAN, *indeed, is quite overwhelmed.*]

ALPER: Actually, Hirschman, all we want to know is if you knew the tele-phone number of the Korpotchniker rabbi.

THE CABALIST: [*With some effort, he brings himself back to the moment at hand.*] He is my cousin. I will call him for you. [*He moves slowly off, still obsessed with some private wonder of his own, to the wall phone, stage left.*]

ALPER: [*Quite awed.*] Your cousin? You are the Korpotchniker's cousin, Hirschman?

ZITORSKY: [*Hurrying after* THE CABALIST.] You'll need a dime, Hirschman. [*He gives* HIRSCHMAN *the ten cent piece.*]

**ALPER:** Schlissel, the Korpotchniker's cousin, did you hear? Apparently, he's not such a humbug.

**SCHLISSEL:** I tell you, he gives me the creeps, that Hirschman.

[HIRSCHMAN *has dialed a number on the wall phone.* FOREMAN *stands hunched with anxiety at his elbow.*]

**THE CABALIST:** [*To* FOREMAN, *gently.*] Where is she, the dybbuk?

**FOREMAN:** In the rabbi's office.

**THE CABALIST:** You are wise to go to the Korpotchniker. He is a Righteous One among the Righteous Ones. We were quite close as children until I abandoned the Rabbinate. [*On the phone, in soft gentle tones.*] Hello? Is this Chaim son of Yosif—This is Israel son of Isaac. And peace be unto you—There is a man here of my congregation who feels his granddaughter is possessed by a dybbuk and would seek counsel from my cousin. He will bless you for your courtesy. Peace be unto you, Chaim son of Yosif. [*He hangs the receiver back in its cradle, turns to* FOREMAN.] Give me a paper and pencil. [*The* OTHERS, *who have crowded around to hear the phone call, all seek in their pockets for a paper and pencil and manage to produce an old envelope and a stub of a pencil between them.*] That was the Korpotchniker's secretary, and you are to go to his home as quickly as you can. I will write the address down for you. It is in Williamsburg in Brooklyn. And you will be received directly after the morning services. [*He sweeps his praying shawl back over his head and retires upstage again for continued devotions.*]

**FOREMAN:** Thank you, Hirschman. The eye of the Lord will be open to you in the time of your need.

**ZITORSKY:** Oh, Williamsburg. That's quite a ride from here.

**SCHLISSEL:** What are you talking about? Foreman, you take the Long Island Railroad to Atlantic Avenue Station where you go downstairs, and you catch the Brooklyn subway.

**ALPER:** Maybe I should go along with you, David, because a simple fellow like you will certainly get lost in the Atlantic Avenue Station, which is an immense conflux of subways.

**SCHLISSEL:** What you do, Foreman, is you take the Long Island Railroad to the Atlantic Avenue Station where you take the Double G train on the lower level.

**ALPER:** Not the Double G train.

**SCHLISSEL:** What's wrong with the Double G?

**ALPER:** One takes the Brighton Train. The Double G Train will take him to Smith Street, which is a good eight blocks walk.

**SCHLISSEL:** The Brighton Train will take him to Coney Island.

**ALPER:** Foreman, listen to what I tell you. I will write down the instructions for you because an innocent fellow like you, if they didn't point you in the right direction, you couldn't even find the synagogue in the morning. Where's my pencil? [*He has taken the address paper and pencil from* FOREMAN*'s numb fingers and is writing the travelling instructions down.*]

**FOREMAN:** [*Staring off at the wall of the rabbi's office.*] What shall I do with the girl? I can't leave her here.

**ALPER:** Don't worry about the girl. She knows me. I'm like a second grandfather to her.

**FOREMAN:** I don't like to leave her. Did I do right, Alper? Did I do right, kidnapping her this morning and bringing her here? Because the psychiatrist said we must prepare ourselves that she would probably spend the rest of her life in mental institutions. The irrevocability of it! The rest of her life! I was in tears almost the whole night thinking about it. Perhaps, this produced a desperate susceptibility in me so that I clutch even at dybbuks rather than believe she is irretrievably insane. Now, in the sober chill of afterthought, it all seems so unreal and impetuous. And here I am bucketing off to some forbidding rabbi to listen to mystical incantations.

**ALPER:** The Korpotchniker is not a rogue, Foreman. He is not going to sell you patent medicine. He will advise you quite sensibly, I am sure.

**FOREMAN:** [*Buttoning his coat.*] Yes, yes, I shall go to see him. You shall have to hide her till I come back. My son has probably called the police by now, and sooner or later they will come here looking for her.

**ALPER:** Don't worry about it. I won't leave her side for a moment.

**FOREMAN:** I better tell her I'm going. She'll be frightened if she looks for me, and I'm not here. Ah, my coat [*He hurries quickly to the rabbi's office, where he stands a moment, regarding* THE GIRL *with mingled fear and tenderness.* THE GIRL *has sunk into the blank detachment of schizophrenia and stares unseeingly at the floor at her feet.*]

**SCHLISSEL:** So the girl is a fugitive from the police. The situation is beginning to take on charm.

**ALPER:** Look at Schlissel. The retired revolutionary. As. long as it's against the law, he believes in dybbuks.

**SCHLISSEL:** I believe in anything that involves a conspiracy.

[*At this point, the front door bursts open, and* THE SEXTON *returns with the announcement.*]

THE SEXTON: I've got a tenth Jew!

ZITORSKY: Sexton, have we got something to tell you!

SCHLISSEL: [*Shushing him abruptly.*] Sha! Idiot! Must you tell everyone?

THE SEXTON: [*He leans back through the open door to the street and says to someone out there.*] Come in, come in — [*A fine-looking, troubled young fellow in his middle thirties, dressed in expensive clothes, albeit a little shabby at the moment, as if he had been on a bender for the last couple of days, enters. His name is* ARTHUR BROOKS. *He stands ill-at-ease and scowling, disturbed in aspect. His Burberry topcoat hangs limply on him.* THE SEXTON *has scooted to the shelf stage right from which he takes a black skullcap, nervously talking as he does.*] Harris didn't come in yet?

SCHLISSEL: No.

THE SEXTON: The two Kessler boys, I called them on the phone, they didn't show up yet? [*Thrusts the skullcap on* ARTHUR'*s head.*] Here's a skullcap, put it on. [ARTHUR *takes the skullcap absently but makes no move to put it on. He is preoccupied with deep and dark thoughts.* THE SEXTON *heads for the front door.*] The rabbi's not here yet?

SCHLISSEL: He'll be here in a couple of minutes.

THE SEXTON: It's only seven minutes to the services. Listen, I'm going to the Kesslers'. I'll have to pull them out of their beds, I can see that. I'll be right back. [*To* ARTHUR.] You'll find some phylacteries in the carton there. Alper, give the man a prayer book. Sure, go find ten Jews on a winter morning. [*He exits, closing the front door after himself.*]

FOREMAN: [*As he comes out of the office, adjusting his coat about him.*] All right, I'm going. She didn't eat anything this morning, so see she gets some coffee at least. Let's see. I take the Long Island Railroad to Atlantic Avenue Station. Listen, it has been a number of years since I have been on the subways. Well, wish me luck. Have I got money for carfare? Yes, yes. Well — well — my dear dear friends, peace be with you.

ALPER: And with you, Foreman.

ZITORSKY: Amen.

FOREMAN: [*Opening the door.*] Oh, it's cold out there. [*He exits, closing the door.*]

ALPER: He'll get lost. I'm sure of it.

ZITORSKY: Oh, have you ever seen such excitement? My heart is fairly pounding.

ALPER: Oh, it's just starting. Now comes the exorcism. That should be something to see.

ZITORSKY: Oh, boy.

SCHLISSEL: Oh, I don't know. You've seen one exorcism, you've seen them all.

ZITORSKY: You saw one, Schlissel?

SCHLISSEL: Sure. When I was a boy in Poland, we had more dybbuks than we had pennies. We had a fellow there in my village, a mule driver, a burly chap who reeked from dung and was drunk from morning till night. One day, he lost his wits completely, and it was immediately attributed to a dybbuk. I was a boy of ten, perhaps eleven, and I watched the whole proceedings through a hole in the roof of the synagogue. A miracle working rabbi who was passing through our district was invited to exorcise the dybbuk. He drew several circles on the ground and stood in the center surrounded by four elders of the community, all dressed in white linen and trembling with terror. The Miracle Worker bellowed out a series of incantations, and the poor mule driver, who was beside himself with fear, screamed and — Hello, Harris — [*This last is addressed to a very, very old man named* HARRIS, *who is making his halting way into the synagogue at this moment. He barely nods to the others, having all he can do to get into the synagogue and close the door.* SCHLISSEL *continues his blithe story.*] — and fell to the floor. It was a marvelous vaudeville, really. I was so petrified that I fell off the roof and almost broke a leg. The Miracle Worker wandered off to work other miracles and the mule driver sold his mule and went to America where I assume, because he was a habitual drunkard and an insensitive boor, he achieved considerable success. Our little village had a brief month of notoriety, and we were all quite proud of ourselves.

ALPER: Oh, it sounds like a marvelous ceremony.

SCHLISSEL: Of course, they don't exorcise dybbuks like they used to. Nowadays, the rabbi hangs a small amulet around your neck, intones "Blessed art Thou, O Lord," and that's an exorcism.

ALPER: Oh, I hope not.

SCHLISSEL: Really, religion has become so pallid recently, it is hardly worthwhile being an atheist.

**ZITORSKY:** I don't even know if I'll come to see this exorcism. I'm already shivering just hearing about it.

**ALPER:** Well, you know, we are dealing with the occult here, and it is quite frightening. Hello there, Harris, how are you? [*By now, the* OCTOGENARIAN *has removed his overcoat, under which he wears several layers of sweaters, one of which turns out to be one of his grandson's football jerseys, a striped red garment with the number 63 on it. For the rest of the act, he goes about the business of putting on his phylacteries.* ALPER *claps his hands.*] Well, let me find out if we can help this young Jew here. [*He moves towards* ARTHUR BROOKS, *smiling.*] Can I give you a set of phylacteries?

**ARTHUR:** [*Scowling, a man who has had a very bad night the night before.*] I'm afraid I wouldn't have the first idea what to do with them.

**ALPER:** You'll find a praying shawl in one of these velvet bags here.

**ARTHUR:** No, thank you.

**ALPER:** [*Offering a small black prayer book.*] Well, here's a prayer book anyway.

**ARTHUR:** Look, the only reason I'm here is a little man stopped me on the street, asked me if I was Jewish, and gave me the impression he would kill himself if I didn't come in and complete your quorum. I was told all I had to do was stand around for a few minutes wearing a hat. I can't read Hebrew and I have nothing I want to pray about, so there's no sense giving me that book. All I want to know is how long is this going to take because I don't feel very well, and I have a number of things to do.

**ALPER:** My dear young fellow, you'll be out of here in fifteen or twenty minutes.

**ARTHUR:** Thank you. [*He absently puts the black skullcap on his head and sits down, scowling, on one of the wooden chairs.* ALPER *regards him for a moment,; then turns and goes back to his two colleagues.*]

**ALPER:** [*To* SCHLISSEL *and* ZITORSKY.] To such a state has modern Jewry fallen. He doesn't know what phylacteries are. He doesn't want a shawl. He can't read Hebrew.

**ZITORSKY:** I wonder if he's still circumcised.

**ARTHUR:** [*Abruptly stands.*] I'd like to make a telephone call. [*Nobody hears him. He repeats louder.*] I said, I'd like to make a telephone call.

**ALPER:** [*Indicating the wall phone.*] Right on the wall there.

**ARTHUR:** This is rather a personal call.

**ALPER:** There's a phone in the rabbi's office there. [ARTHUR *crosses to the rabbi's office.*]

**SCHLISSEL:** Well, look about you, really. Here you have the decline of orthodox Judaism graphically before your eyes. This is a synagogue? A converted grocery store, flanked on one side by a dry cleaner's and on the other by a shoemaker. Really, if it wasn't for the Holy Ark there, this place would look like the local headquarters of the American Labor Party. In Poland, where we were all one step from starvation, we had a synagogue whose shadow had more dignity than this place.

**ALPER:** It's a shame and a disgrace.

**ZITORSKY:** A shame and a disgrace.

[*In the rabbi's office* ARTHUR *is regarding the girl,* EVELYN, *with a sour eye.*]

**ARTHUR:** Excuse me. I'd like to make a rather personal call.

[THE GIRL *stares down at the floor unhearing, unmoving, off in a phantasmic world of her own distorted creation.* ARTHUR *sits down at the rabbi's desk, turns his shoulder to* THE GIRL *and begins to dial a number.*]

**SCHLISSEL:** Where are all the Orthodox Jews? They have apostated to the Reform Jewish temples, where they sit around like Episcopalians listening to organ music.

**ALPER:** Your use of the word "apostasy" in referring to Reform Jews interests me, Schlissel. Is it not written in Sifre on Deuteronomy, "Even if they are foolish, even if they transgress, even if they are full of blemishes, they are still called sons?" So, after all, is it so terrible to be a Reform Jew? Is this not an interesting issue for disputation? Oh, my God!

[*He wheels and starts back for the rabbi's office. The same thought has been entering the other two old fellows' minds, as has been indicated by a growing frown of consternation on each of their faces. They follow* ALPER *to the rabbi's office, where he opens the door quickly and stares in at* ARTHUR BROOKS. *The latter is still seated at the rabbi's desk, waiting for an answer to his phone call, and* THE GIRL *is still in her immobilized state.* ARTHUR *bestows such a baleful eye upon this interruption that the three* OLD MEN *back out of the office and close the door. They remain nervously outside the door of the office. At last, someone answers the phone call.*]

**ARTHUR:** [*On phone, shading his face, and keeping his voice down.*] Hello, Doctor, did I wake you up? This is Arthur Brooks — Yes, I know. Do you think you can find an hour for me this morning? — Oh, I could be in your office in about an hour or so. I'm out in Mineola. My ex-wife lives out here with her parents, you know. And I've been blind drunk for — I just figured it out — three days now. And I just found myself out here at two o'clock in the morning banging on their front door, screaming — [THE GIRL's *presence bothers him. He leans across the desk to her and says:*] Look, this is a very personal call, and I would really appreciate your letting me have the use of this office for just a few minutes.

**EVELYN:** [*She looks up at him blankly. Hollowly.*] I am the Whore of Kiev, the companion of sailors.

**ARTHUR:** [*This strikes him as a bizarre comment to make. He considers it for a moment, and then goes back to the phone.*] No, I'm still here. I'm all right. At least, I'm still alive. [*Hides his face in the palm of one hand and rubs his brow nervously.*] I've got to see you, Doc, Don't hang up on me, please. If my analyst hangs up on me, that'll be the end. Just let me talk a couple of minutes — I'm in some damned synagogue. I was on my way to the subway. Oh, my God, I've got to call my office. I was supposed to be in court twice yesterday. I hope somebody had the brains to apply for an adjournment. So it's funny, you know. I'm in this damned synagogue. I'll be down in about an hour, Doctor — Okay. Okay — I'm all right — No, I'm all right — I'll see you in about an hour. [*He hangs up, hides his face in the palms of both hands and slowly pulls himself together. After a moment, he looks up at* THE GIRL, *who is back to staring at the floor. He frowns, stands, goes to the door of the office, opens it, gives one last look at* THE GIRL, *and closes the door again. He finds himself staring at the inquiring faces of the three* OLD MEN.] Listen, I hope you know there's a pretty strange girl in there.

[*The* OLD MEN *bob their heads a little nervously.* ARTHUR *crosses the synagogue, his face dark with his emotions. The three* OLD MEN *regard him anxiously. After a moment,* SCHLISSEL *approaches* ARTHUR.]

**SCHLISSEL:** A strange girl, you say?
**ARTHUR:** Yes.
**SCHLISSEL:** Did she say anything?

**ARTHUR:** She said: "I am the Whore of Kiev, the companion of sailors."

**SCHLISSEL:** That was a very piquant statement, wouldn't you say?

**ARTHUR:** Yes, I think I would call it piquant.

**SCHLISSEL:** What do you make of it?

**ARTHUR:** [*Irritably.*] Look, I'm going. I have a hundred things to do. I —

**SCHLISSEL:** No, no, no, sit down. For heaven's sakes, sit down.

**ALPER:** [*Hurrying over.*] Don't go. Oh, my, don't go. We need you for a tenth man. We haven't had ten men in the morning in more than a week, I think.

**ZITORSKY:** [*On* ALPER'*s tail*] Two weeks, at least.

[*At this point,* HARRIS, *who has finally divested himself of his overcoat, muffle, heavy-ribbed button-down sweaters which were over his jacket and is now enwrapt in a praying shawl, bursts into a high, quavering prayer.*]

**HARRIS:** Blessed art Thou, O Lord, our God, King of the Universe, Who hath sanctified us by his commandments and ... [*The words dribble off into inaudibility.* ARTHUR BROOKS *darts a startled look at the* OLD MAN, *not being prepared for this method of prayer, and moves a few nervous steps away from the other* OLD MEN, *where he stands rubbing his brow, quite agitated.*]

**ALPER:** [*Whispering to* SCHLISSEL] So what happened in there? Did she say anything?

**SCHLISSEL:** Yes, she said she was the Whore of Kiev, and the companion of sailors.

**ALPER:** Oh, dear me.

**SCHLISSEL:** I'm afraid we shall have to get her out of the rabbi's office, because if she keeps telling everybody who walks in there that she is the Whore of Kiev, they will pack us all off to the insane asylum. And let us be quite sensible about this situation. If Foreman has kidnapped the girl, he has kidnapped her, however kindly his motives — not that I expect the police to regard a dybbuk as any kind of sensible explanation. Whatever the case, it would be a good idea to keep the girl a little less accessible. [*The wall phone rings.*] Ah! I'll tell you who that is. That's Foreman's son calling to find out if Foreman and the girl are here. [*The phone rings again.*] Well, if you won't answer it, I'll answer it. [*He crosses to the wall phone.*]

**ALPER:** We could take her to my house. Everybody is still sleeping. We'll put her in the cellar. [*The phone rings again.* SCHLISSEL *picks up the phone.*]

**SCHLISSEL:** [*On phone.*] Hello. [*He turns to the others, nods his head and makes an expressive face, indicating he was quite right in guessing the caller. The other two* OLD MEN *move closer to the phone.*] Mr. Foreman, your father isn't here—Listen, I tell you, he isn't here—I wouldn't have the slightest idea—I haven't seen her since I was up to your house last Tuesday. Isn't she home?—If he comes in, I'll tell him—Okay—[*Hangs up, turns to the other two.*] Well, we are in it up to our necks now.

**ALPER:** [*Stripping off his phylacteries.*] So shall we take her to my house?

**SCHLISSEL:** All right. Zitorsky, go in and tell her we are going to take her some place else.

**ZITORSKY:** [*Not exactly inspired by the idea.*] Yeah, sure.

**SCHLISSEL:** [*To* ZITORSKY.] For heaven's sake, Zitorsky, you don't really believe that's a dybbuk in there.

**ZITORSKY:** If that's no dybbuk, then you go in and take her.

**SCHLISSEL:** [*He shuffles slowly to the door of the rabbi's office. Pausing at the closed office door.*] It's getting kind of complicated. Maybe we ought to call Foreman's son and tell him she's here and not get involved.

**ZITORSKY:** Oh, no!

**SCHLISSEL:** Ah, well, come on. What can they do to us? They'll call us foolish old men, but then foolishness is the only privilege of old age. So, Alper, you'll deal with her. You know how to talk to her, and we'll hide her in your cellar. So we'll have a little excitement. Listen, Alper, let's get along, you know. Before the Sexton comes back and starts asking us where we're all going.

**ALPER:** [*He nods apprehensively and takes a few steps into the office. To* THE GIRL, *who doesn't actually hear him or know of his presence.*] How do you do, my dear Evelyn? This is Alper here. [*She makes no answer.* ALPER *turns to the other two.*] She's in one of her apathetic states.

**ZITORSKY:** [*Darting back into the synagogue proper.*] I'll get your coat, Alper.

**SCHLISSEL:** [*Looking around to see if* ARTHUR *is paying any attention to what's going on; he is not.*] Well, take her by the arm.

**ALPER:** Evelyn, your grandfather suggested we take you to my house. You always liked to play with the children's toys in my cellar there, you remember? Come along, and we'll have a good time.

**ZITORSKY:** [*Giving* SCHLISSEL *an overcoat.*] Here. Give this to Alper. [*He hurries off to the front door of the synagogue.*]

**HARRIS:** [*In the process of laying on his phylacteries.*] And from my wisdom, Oh most High God, Thou shalt reserve for me—[*He dribbles off into inaudibility.*]

**ALPER:** [*Placing a tentative hand on* THE GIRL'*s shoulder.*] Evelyn, dear— [*She looks up, startled.*]

**ZITORSKY:** [*Leaning out the front door, searching up and down the street.*] Oh, it's cold out here.

**ALPER:** [*To* SCHLISSEL, *hurriedly, putting on his own overcoat.*] I have a feeling we're going to have trouble here.

**SCHLISSEL:** I've got your coat here.

**ALPER:** Evelyn—[*A strange animal-like grunt escapes* THE GIRL, *and she begins to moan softly.*] Evelyn, dear, please don't be alarmed. This is Mr. Alper here who has known you since you were born. [*He is getting a little panicky at the strange sounds coming out of* THE GIRL, *and he tries to grab her arm to help her to her feet. She bursts into a shrill scream, electrifying everybody in the synagogue with the exception of* THE CABALIST, *who is oblivious to everything.* ZITORSKY, *who has just closed the front door, stands frozen with horror.* ARTHUR, *sunk in despondency, looks up startled. The old man,* HARRIS, *pauses briefly as if the sound has been some distant buzzing, and then goes back to his mumbled prayers. Alarmed.*] Evelyn, my dear girl, for heaven's sakes...

**THE GIRL:** [*Screaming out.*] Leave me alone! Leave me alone!

**ARTHUR:** [*Coming quickly to* SCHLISSEL, *who has shut the office door quickly.*] What's going on in there?

**SCHLISSEL:** It's nothing, it's nothing.

**THE GIRL:** [*Screaming.*] They are my seven sons! My seven sons!

**ALPER:** [*Who is trying earnestly to get out of the office.*] Who closed this door?

**ZITORSKY:** [*Reaching for the front door*] I'm getting out of here.

**SCHLISSEL:** [*To* ZITORSKY] Where are you going? [*But* ZITORSKY *has already fled into the street.*]

**ARTHUR:** [*To* SCHLISSEL.] What's all this screaming?

**ALPER:** [*At last out of the office, he comes scurrying to* SCHLISSEL.] I put my hand on her arm to help her up, and she burst into this fit of screaming.

**ARTHUR:** [*He strides to the open doorway of the office.* THE GIRL *stares at him, hunched now in terror frightened and at bay. To* SCHLISSEL.] What have you been doing to this girl?

**SCHLISSEL:** The girl is possessed by a dybbuk.

**ARTHUR:** What?

**SCHLISSEL:** [*To* ALPER.] Zitorsky ran out in the street like a kangaroo.

**ALPER:** Listen, maybe we should call somebody.

**ARTHUR:** Listen, what is this?

**ALPER:** My dear young man, there is no reason to alarm yourself. There is an insane girl in the rabbi's office, but she appears to have quieted down.

**ARTHUR:** What do you mean, there's an insane girl in the rabbi's office?

**ALPER:** Yes, she is a catatonic schizophrenic, occasionally violent, but really, go back to your seat. There is no cause for alarm.

**ARTHUR:** Am I to understand, Sir, that it is a practice of yours to keep insane girls in your rabbi's office?

**ALPER:** No, no. Oh, dear, I suppose we shall have to tell him. But you must promise, my dear fellow, to keep this whole matter between us. [*To* SCHLISSEL.] Zitorsky, you say, took to his heels?

**SCHLISSEL:** Absolutely flew out of the door.

**ALPER:** Well, I really can't blame him. It was quite an apprehensive moment. I was a little shaken myself. [*Peeks into the office.*] Yes, she seems to be quite apathetic again. I think we just better leave her alone for the time being.

**ARTHUR:** Look, what is going on here?

**ALPER:** My dear fellow, you are, of course, understandably confused. The girl, you see, is possessed by a dybbuk.

**ARTHUR:** Yes, of course. Well that explains everything.

**ALPER:** Well, of course, how would he know what a dybbuk is? A dybbuk is a migratory soul that possesses the body of another human being in order to return to heaven. It is a Lurian doctrine, actually tracing back to the Essenes, I suppose, but popularized during the 13th century by the Spanish Cabalists. I wrote several articles on the matter for Yiddish periodicals. My name is Moyshe Alper, and at one time I was a journalist of some repute. [ZITORSKY *appears in the doorway again, peering nervously in.*] Come in, Zitorsky, come in. The girl is quiet again. [ZITORSKY *approaches them warily.*]

**ARTHUR:** Look, are you trying to tell me you have a girl in there you think is possessed by some demon? Where is her mother or father or somebody who should be responsible for her?

**ALPER:** If there were someone responsible for her, would she be insane in the first place?

**ARTHUR:** Of course, this is none of my business

**ALPER:** You are a good fellow and let me put you at case. The girl is in good hands. Nobody is going to hurt her. Her grandfather, who adores her more than his own life, has gone off for a short while.

**ZITORSKY:** To Williamsburg on the Brighton train.

**SCHLISSEL:** The Brighton train takes you to Coney Island.

**ZITORSKY:** You said the Double G.

**ALPER:** All right, all right.

**ARTHUR:** Of course, this is none of my business.

**ALPER:** [*To* ARTHUR.] I can understand your concern; it shows you are a good fellow, but really the matter is well in hand.

[*The front door opens and there now enter* THE SEXTON *and two young men in their 30s, apparently the* KESSLER *Boys, who are none too happy about being roused on this cold winter morning. They stand disconsolately around in the back of the synagogue.*]

**THE SEXTON:** Here are two more, the Kessler boys.

**ALPER:** Now we'll have ten for a quorum.

**ZITORSKY:** Kessler? Kessler? Oh, yes, the stationery store. I knew your father.

[*There is a general flurry of movement.* THE SEXTON *hurries about the ritual of baring his left arm, donning the praying shawl and phylacteries, walking nervously about, mumbling his prayers rapidly.* ARTHUR, *quite disturbed again, looks into the rabbi's office at* THE GIRL *again, then moves slowly into the office.* THE GIRL *is again in a world of her own. He closes the door after himself and studies* THE GIRL. SCHLISSEL, ALPER *and* ZITORSKY *watch him warily, taking off their overcoats again and preparing to stay for the impending services.* HARRIS'*s shrill quavering voice suddenly leaps up into audibility again.*]

**HARRIS:** Thou shalt set apart all that openeth the womb of the Lord, and the firstling that cometh of a beast which Thou shalt have, it shall belong to the Lord

**SCHLISSEL:** [*To* ALPER.] What are we going to do when the rabbi tries to get into his office? He'll see the girl, and that will be the end of our exorcism. What shall we tell the rabbi?

[*The front door of the synagogue opens, and* THE RABBI *comes striding efficiently in, right on cue. He is a young man in his early 30s, neatly dressed if a little threadbare, and carrying a briefcase.*]

**ZITORSKY:** Peace be with you, Rabbi.

**THE RABBI:** Peace be unto you.

**ALPER:** [*Intercepting* THE RABBI *as he heads for his office.*] How do you do, Rabbi? [THE RABBI *nods as he strides to the door of his office where* SCHLISSEL *blocks the way.*]

**SCHLISSEL:** We have ten men today, Rabbi.

**THE RABBI:** Good. [*Reaches for the door to his office.*] I'll just get my phylacteries.

**ALPER:** [*Seizing* ZITORSKY'*s phylacteries from* ZITORSKY'*s hand*] Oh, here, use these. It's late, Rabbi.

**THE RABBI:** [*Taking the phylacteries.*] Fine. Well, let's start the services. [*He turns back to the synagogue proper.*]

[*From all around, each man's voice rises into prayer as the Curtain falls.*]

# ACT TWO

## SCENE 1

**TIME:** *Fifteen minutes later*

**AT RISE:** ZITORSKY *is reading the prayers. He stands before the lectern on the raised platform singing the primitive chants:*

ZITORSKY: And we beseech Thee according to Thine abundant mercies, Oh, Lord—

THE SEXTON: Young Kessler, come here and open the Ark.

[*The* YOUNGER KESSLER *ascends the platform and opens the Ark by drawing the curtains and sliding the doors apart.*]

ZITORSKY: And it came to pass, when the ark set forward, that Moses said, "Rise up, O Lord, and Thine enemies shall be scattered, and they that hate Thee shall flee before Thee. For out of Zion shall go forth the Law, and the word of the Lord from Jerusalem." [*Immediately, the rest of the* QUORUM *plunge into a mumbled response: "Blessed be Thy name, O Sovereign of the World! Blest by Thy crown and Thy abiding place!" Jewish prayers are conducted in a reader and congregation pattern, although frequently the reader's vocalized statements and the congregation's mumbled responses merge and run along simultaneously. In this specific moment of prayer, where the Ark has been opened and the Torah is about to be taken out, the demarcation between reader and congregation is clearcut. The sliding brown wooden doors of the Ark are now open.* THE SEXTON *is reaching in to take out the exquisitely ornamented Torah, which, when its lovely velvet and brocaded cover is taken off, will show itself to be a large parchment scroll divided on two carved rollers. When* THE SEXTON *gets the Torah out, he hands it carefully to* Zitorsky, *who has been chosen this day for the honor of holding the Torah until it is to be read from.* Zitorsky, *who, as today's reader has been reading along with the congregation although more audibly, now allows his voice to ring out clearly, marking the end of this paragraph of prayers.*] ... May it be Thy gracious will to open my heart in Thy Law, and to grant my heart's desires, and those of all Thy people Israel, for our benefit, throughout a peaceful life. [*Pause.*] Magnify the Lord with me, and let us exalt His name together. [*Again, the* Congregation *leaps into mumbled response. "Thine, O Lord, is the greatness, and the power, and the glory, and the victory, and the majesty," etc.* Zitorsky *marches solemnly to the front of the lectern carrying the Torah before him. Each* Man *kisses the Torah as it passes him. There is now a ritual of removing the velvet cover and the Torah is laid upon the lectern.* Zitorsky, Harris *and* The Sexton *make a hovering group of three old betallithed Jews over it.* The Rabbi *stands rocking slightly back and forth to the left of the lectern. Off the raised platform, but immediately by the railing stands* The Cabalist, *rocking back and forth and praying.* Alper *and* Schlissel *stand at various places, mumbling their responses. The two* Kessler Boys *have removed their coats and wear praying shawls but still stand as close to the front door as they can.* Arthur Brooks *stands, leaning against the wall of the rabbi's office, quite intrigued by the solemn prayers and rituals.* The Girl *is still in the rabbi's office, but she is standing now, listening as well as she can to the prayers. Her face is peaceful now and quite lovely. Again* Zitorsky's *voice rises to indicate the end of a paragraph of prayer.*] Ascribe all of your greatness unto our God, and render honor to the Law.

[*There is now a quick mumbled conference among the three* Old Jews *at the lectern, and* The Sexton *suddenly leans out and calls to the two* Kessler Boys *in the rear*]

The Sexton: Kessler, you want to read from the Torah?
Elder Kessler: No, no, no. Get somebody else.
The Sexton: Alper? [Alper *nods and makes his way to the lectern.* The Sexton's *voice, a high, whining incantation, rises piercingly into the air announcing the fact that* Moyshe, *son of Abram, will read from the Torah.*] Rise up, Reb Moses Hia Kohan, son of Abram, and speak the blessing on the Torah. Blessed be He, who in His Holiness gave the Law unto his people Israel, the Law of the Lord is perfect.

CONGREGATION: [*Scattered response.*] And ye that cleave unto the Lord your
God are alive every one of you this day.

ALPER: [*Now at the lectern, raises his head and recites quickly.*] Blessed is the
Lord who is to be blessed for ever and ever.

CONGREGATION: Blessed is the Lord who is to be blessed for ever and ever.

ALPER: Blessed art Thou, O Lord our God, King of the Universe, who hast
chosen us from all peoples and hast given us Thy Law. Blessed art Thou,
O Lord, who givest the Law.

CONGREGATION: Amen!

THE SEXTON: And Moses said …

[*There are now four mumbling* OLD JEWS *huddled over the lectern.
It all becomes very indistinguishable, although* THE SEXTON'S *piercing
tenor rises audibly now and then to indicate he is reading.* ALPER
*moves into the reader's position and begins to read from the Torah,
bending his knees and twisting his body and hunching over the Torah
peering at the difficult little Hebrew lettering inscribed therein.*
SCHLISSEL *and the* KESSLER BOYS *find seats where they were
standing, as does* THE CABALIST. THE RABBI *and* HARRIS *are seated
on the raised platform. In the rabbi's office,* THE GIRL *has decided to
go out into the synagogue proper. She opens the door and moves a few
steps out.* ARTHUR *hears her and turns to her warily.*]

THE GIRL: [*Quite lucidly and amiably.*] Excuse me, Sir, are they reading from
the Torah now? [*She peers over* ARTHUR'S *shoulder to the* OLD MEN *at the
lectern.*]

ARTHUR: Yes, I think so. [*He watches her carefully. She seems all right now.
Still there is something excessively ingenuous about her, a tentative, wide-eyed,
gently smiling innocence.*]

THE GIRL: Is my grandfather here? [*She peers nervously around the synagogue.*]

ARTHUR: Which one would be your grandfather?

THE GIRL: [*Growing panic.*] No, he's not here. I see Mr. Alper, but I don't
see my grandfather.

ARTHUR: I'm sure he will be back soon. [*His calmness reassures her.*]

THE GIRL: [*She studies this strange young man warily.*] I think all synagogues
should be shabby because I think of God as being very poor as a child.
What do you think of God as?

ARTHUR: I'm afraid I think of God as the Director of Internal Revenue.

**THE GIRL:** [*She laughs brightly and then immediately smothers her laughter, aware she is in a solemn synagogue.*] You're irreverent. [*She goes frowning again into the rabbi's office and plops down on his swivel chair and swivels back and forth, very much like a child.* ARTHUR *follows her tentatively, studying her warily yet taken by her ingenuousness. She darts a quick frightened look at him.*] Were you in here just before?

**ARTHUR:** Well, yes.

**THE GIRL:** Did I—did I say anything?

**ARTHUR:** [*Amiably.*] Well, yes.

**THE GIRL:** [*Sighing.*] I see. Well, I might as well tell you. I've been to several mental institutions. [*She looks quickly at him. He smiles at her.*] You don't seem very disconcerted by that.

**ARTHUR:** Oh, I expect it might be hard to find somebody who couldn't do with occasional confinement in a mental institution.

[*In the synagogue,* THE SEXTON *now calls* HARRIS *to read from the Torah.*]

**THE GIRL:** [*She frowns.*] Did my grandfather say when he would be back or where he was going? [*She starts from her seat, frightened again.*]

**ARTHUR:** I understand he'll be back soon.

**THE GIRL:** Are you the doctor?

**ARTHUR:** No. You don't have to be the least bit afraid of me.

**THE GIRL:** [*She brightens.*] My grandfather and I are very close. I'm much closer to him than I am to my own father. I'd rather not talk about my father, if you don't mind. It's a danger spot for me. You know, when I was nine years old, I shaved all the hair off my head because that is the practice of really orthodox Jewish women. I mean, if you want to be a rabbi's wife, you must shear your hair and wear a wig. That's one of my compulsive dreams. I keep dreaming of myself as the wife of a handsome young rabbi with a fine beard down to his waist and a very stern face and prematurely gray forelocks on his brow. I have discovered through many unsuccessful years of psychiatric treatment that religion has a profound sexual connotation for me. Oh, dear, I'm afraid I'm being tiresome again about my psychiatric history. Really, being insane is like being fat. You can talk about nothing else. Please forgive me. I am sure I am boring you to death.

ARTHUR: No, not at all. It's nice to hear somebody talk with passion about anything, even their insanity.

THE GIRL: [*Staring at him.*] The word doesn't bother you?

ARTHUR: What word?

THE GIRL: Insanity.

ARTHUR: Good heavens, no. I'm a lawyer. Insanity in one form or another is what fills my anteroom. Besides, I'm being psychoanalyzed myself and I'm something of a bore about that too. You are a bright young thing. How old are you?

THE GIRL: Eighteen.

ARTHUR: [*Staring at her*] My God, you're a pretty kid! I can hardly believe you are psychopathic. Are you very advanced?

THE GIRL: Pretty bad. I'm being institutionalized again. Dr. Molineaux's Sanitarium in Long Island. I'm a little paranoid and hallucinate a great deal and have very little sense of reality, except for brief interludes like this, and I might slip off any minute in the middle of a sentence — into some incoherency. If that should happen, you must be very realistic with me. Harsh reality is the most efficacious way to deal with schizophrenics.

ARTHUR: You seem well-read on the matter.

THE GIRL: I'm a voracious reader. I have so little else to do with myself. Will you come and visit me at Dr. Molineaux's Hospital? I am awfully fond of you.

ARTHUR: Yes, of course, I will.

THE GIRL: It won't be as depressing an experience as you might think. If I am not in the violent ward, I will probably be allowed to go to the commissary and have an ice cream soda with you. The worst of an insane asylum is really how poorly dressed the inmates are. They all wear old cable-stitched sweaters. I do like to look pretty. [*A vacuous, atrophied look is beginning to come across her face.*] They ask me to be in a lot of movies, you know, when I have time. Did you see *David and Bathsheba* with Susan Hayward? That was really me. I don't tell anybody that. They don't want me to make movies. My mother, I mean. She doesn't even go to synagogue on Saturday. You're the new rabbi, you know. Sometimes, I'm the rabbi, but they're all afraid of me. The temple is sixty cubits long and made of cypress and overlaid with gold. The burnished Roman legions clank outside the gates, you know. Did you see *The Ten Commandments*? I saw that Tuesday, Wednesday. I was in that. I was the girl who danced. I

was in that. Mr. Hirschman is here, too, you know, and my grandfather.
Everybody's here. Do you see that boy over there? Go away. Leave us
alone. He's insane. He's really Mr. Hirschman the Cabalist. He's making a
golem. You ought to come here, Rabbi.

ARTHUR: [*Who has been listening, fascinated, now says firmly.*] I am not the
rabbi, Evelyn.

THE GIRL: [*She regards him briefly.*] Well, we're making a golem and —

ARTHUR: You are not making a golem, Evelyn.

THE GIRL: [*She pauses, stares down at the floor at her feet. A grimace of pain
winces quickly across her face and then leaves it. After a moment, she
mumbles.*] Thank you. [*Suddenly she begins to cry and she throws herself
upon* ARTHUR's *breast, clinging to him, and he holds her gently, caressing her
as he would a child.*] Oh, I can't bear being insane.

ARTHUR: [*Gently.*] I always thought that since the insane made their own
world it was more pleasurable than this one that is made for us.

THE GIRL: [*Moving away.*] Oh, no, it is unbearably painful. It is the most
indescribable desolation. You are all alone in deserted streets. You cannot
possibly imagine it.

ARTHUR: I'm afraid I can. I have tried to commit suicide so many times now
it has become something of a family joke. Once, before I was divorced,
my wife stopped in to tell a neighbor before she went out to shop: "Oh,
by the way, if you smell gas, don't worry about it. It's only Arthur killing
himself again." Suicides, you know, kill themselves a thousand times, but
one day I'll slash my wrists and I will forget to make a last minute
telephone call and there will be no stomach-pumping samaritans to run
up the stairs and smash my bedroom door down and rush me off to
Bellevue. I'll make it some day—I assure you of that.

THE GIRL: [*Regarding him with sweet interest.*] You don't look as sad as
all that.

ARTHUR: Oh, I have made a profession of ironic detachment. It depresses
me to hear that insanity is as forlorn as anything else. I had always hoped
to go crazy myself some day since I have apparently no talent for suicide.

THE GIRL: I always thought life would be wonderful if I were only sane.

ARTHUR: Life is merely dreary if you're sane, and unbearable if you are
sensitive. I cannot think of a more meaningless sham than my own life.
My parents were very poor so I spent the first twenty years of my life
condemning the rich for my childhood nightmares. Oh, I was quite a
Bernard Barricade when I was in college. I left the Communist Party

when I discovered there were easier ways to seduce girls. I turned from reproaching society for my loneliness to reproaching my mother, and stormed out of her house to take a room for myself on the East Side. Then I fell in love—that is to say, I found living alone so unbearable I was willing to marry. She married me because all her friends were marrying somebody. Needless to say, we told each other how deeply in love we were. We wanted very much to be happy. Americans, you know, are frantic about being happy. The American nirvana is a man and his wife watching television amiably and then turning off the lights and effortlessly making the most ardent love to each other. Television unfortunately is a bore and ardent love is an immense drain on one's energy. I began to work day and night at my law office, and besides becoming very successful, I managed to avoid my wife entirely. For this deceit, I was called ambitious and was respected by everyone including my wife, who was quite as bored with me as I was with her. We decided to have children because we couldn't possibly believe we were that miserable together. All this while I drove myself mercilessly for fear that if I paused for just one moment, the whole slim, trembling sanity of my life would come crashing down about my feet without the slightest sound. I went to a psychoanalyst who wanted to know about my childhood when I could barely remember whether I took a taxi or a bus to his office that day. I began to drink myself into stupors, pursuing other men's wives, and generally behaving badly. One morning, I stared into the mirror and could barely make out my features. Life is utterly meaningless. I have had everything a man can get out of life—prestige, power, money, women, children, and a handsome home only three blocks from the Scarsdale Country Club, and all I can think of is I want to get out of this as fast as I can. [*He has become quite upset by now and has to avert his face to hide a sudden welling of tears. He takes a moment to get a good grip on himself, readopts his sardonic air and says.*] As you see, I have quite a theatrical way when I want to.

THE GIRL: [*Brightly.*] Oh, I think you are wonderfully wise.

ARTHUR: Oh, it was said best by your very own King Solomon, the wisest man who ever lived, when he wrote Ecclesiastes.

THE GIRL: Oh, King Solomon didn't write Ecclesiastes. That was written by an anonymous Jewish scholar in Alexandria. I wouldn't put too much stock in it. Weariness was all the rage among the Hellenized Jews.

ARTHUR: [*Staring at her*] You are an amazing kid.

[*She smiles back at him exuberantly, unabashedly showing her fondness for him. It embarrasses him, and he turns away. He opens the office door and looks out into the synagogue, where the reading of the Torah has come to an end.*]

**THE RABBI:** [*Singing out.*] Blessed art Thou, O Lord Our God, King of the Universe, who has given us the Law of truth, and has planted everywhere life in our midst. Blessed art Thou O Lord, who givest the Law. [*There is a scattered mumbled response from the* OLD MEN *in the synagogue.*]

**ZITORSKY:** [*He, now takes the Torah and holds it up above his head and chants.*] And this is the Law which Moses set before the children of Israel, according to the commandment of the Lord by the hand of Moses. [*The* FOUR MEN *on the platform form a small group as* ZITORSKY *marches slowly back to the Ark carrying the Torah. A mumble of prayer rustles through the synagogue.* ZITORSKY'*s voice rises out.*] Let them praise the name of the Lord; for His name alone is exalted. [*He carefully places the Torah back into the Ark. A rumble of prayer runs through the synagogue. All the* MEN *in the synagogue are standing now.*]

**ARTHUR:** [*Turning to* THE GIRL.] They're putting the Torah back. Is the service over?

**THE GIRL:** No. I have a wonderful book I want to give to you. Mr. Hirschman, our Community Cabalist, gave it to me. It is called *The Book of Splendor* and it is a terribly mystical book. I never met anyone who wanted to know the meaning of life as desperately as you do.

**ARTHUR:** It sounds very interesting.

**THE GIRL:** Oh, I'm glad you think so. I have to get it for you.

[SCHLISSEL *pokes his head into the office and indicates to* ARTHUR *that he is needed outside.*]

**ARTHUR:** I think they need me outside. [*He moves to the door.*]

**THE GIRL:** Yes, we really shouldn't have been talking during the service.

**ARTHUR:** [*He goes out of the office, closing the door behind him. He joins* SCHLISSEL, *who is a few steps away, muttering the prayers. Shaking his head.*] What a pity, really. A lovely girl. What a pity. Now, you look like a sensible sort of man. What is all this nonsense about demons? You really should call her father or mother or whoever it is who is responsible for her.

**SCHLISSEL:** Young man, if we called her father he would come down and take her away.

**ARTHUR:** Yes. That would be the point, wouldn't it?

**SCHLISSEL:** Then what happens to our exorcism?

**ARTHUR:** What exorcism?

**SCHLISSEL:** Listen, we've got to exorcise the dybbuk.

**ARTHUR:** [*Aghast.*] Exorcism!

**THE SEXTON:** [*He leans over the railing of the platform and admonishes them in a heavy whisper.*] Sssshhh!

[SCHLISSEL *promptly turns back to muttering his prayers.* ARTHUR *stares at him in a posture of vague belief.*]

**ARTHUR:** Are you serious?

**ZITORSKY:** [*His voice rises up loud and clear.*] ...And it is said, and the Lord shall be king over all the earth; on that day shall the Lord be One, and His Name One.

[*The* CONGREGATION, *which had sat, now stands again.* THE SEXTON *leans over the railing and calls to the* KESSLER BOYS.]

**THE SEXTON:** Kessler, stand up. Now is the time for your memorial prayers.

[*The two* KESSLER BOYS *nod, stand, and look unhappily down at their prayer books.* THE SEXTON *pokes a palsied finger onto a page to show them where to read, and the two* YOUNG MEN *now begin to read painstakingly and with no idea of what they are reading.*]

**KESSLER BOYS:** Magnified and sanctified by His great Name in the world which He hath created according to His will. May He establish His kingdom in your lifetime and in your days, and in the lifetime of all the house of Israel, speedily and at a near time; and say ye, Amen.

**CONGREGATION:** Amen. Let His great Name be blessed for ever and ever.

**KESSLER BOYS:** Blessed, praised, and glorified, exalted, extolled and honored, adored, and lauded, be the Name of the Holy One, blessed be He, beyond, yea, beyond all blessings and hymns, praises and songs, which are uttered in the world, and say ye, Amen.

**CONGREGATION:** Amen.

[*The front door to the synagogue bursts open and* FOREMAN *thrusts himself in, obviously much distraught, not so distraught, however, that he doesn't automatically join in the "Amen."*]

**KESSLER BOYS:** May there be abundant peace from heaven, and life for us and for all Israel; and say ye, Amen.
**CONGREGATION:** Amen.
**KESSLER BOYS:** May he who maketh peace in his high places, make peace for us and for all Israel, and say ye, Amen.
**CONGREGATION:** Amen.

[*The synagogue bursts into a quick mumble of prayers, except for* SCHLISSEL, *who scurries over to* FOREMAN, *who stares back at him white with panic.*]

**SCHLISSEL:** What happened? You got lost? You took the Long Island Railroad to Atlantic Avenue Station, and you got lost in the Atlantic Avenue Station.
**FOREMAN:** What Atlantic Avenue Station? I couldn't even find the Long Island Railroad.
**SCHLISSEL:** Idiot! You are an innocent child! Really! Services are over in a minute, and I'll take you myself. [ALPER *is leaning over the railing of the platform making obvious gestures as if to ask what had happened. Even* ZITORSKY *looks up from his hunched position at the lectern.* SCHLISSEL *announces in a heavy whisper as he starts to put on his coat again.*] He couldn't even find the Long Island Railway Station. [ALPER *clasps his brow.* THE SEXTON *turns around to* SCHLISSEL *and admonishes him with a heavy "Ssshhh!!!"* FOREMAN *has begun walking about, mumbling the prayers by heart, automatically a part of the service again. As he passes* SCHLISSEL, *he indicates with a jerk of his head that he would like to know the well-being of his granddaughter.*] She's all right. Don't worry about her.

[FOREMAN *nods and continues mumbling his prayers. In the rabbi's office,* THE GIRL, *who has been sitting pensively, now stands, goes out of the office, calmly crosses to the rear of the synagogue, and exits out the front door. Absolutely no one is aware she has gone. The* CONGREGATION *now bursts into a loud prayer obviously the last one of the service, since those* MEN *on the platform begin to meander off,*

*and all those who are still wearing their phylacteries begin to strip*
*them off, even as they say the words of the prayer.*]

CONGREGATION: He is the Lord of the Universe, who reigned ere any
creature yet was formed. At the time when all things were made by His
desire, then was His name proclaimed King. And after all things shall
have had an end, He alone, the dreadest one shall reign; Who was, who
is, and who will be in glory.

[SCHLISSEL, ALPER, ZITORSKY *and* FOREMAN *have all rattled*
*quickly through this final paean, impatient to close off the service,*
*while the others continue the slow, clear and ultimate recital. The four*
OLD MEN *form a huddled group by the front door.*]

THE FOUR OF THEM: [*Rattling it off.*] And with my spirit, my body, also; the
Lord is with me, and I will not fear. Amen.
ALPER: Amen, what happened?
SCHLISSEL: I'm taking him myself right away.
ZITORSKY: What happened, you got lost?
FOREMAN: I asked this fellow in the street, I said: "Could you—"
SCHLISSEL: [*To* ALPER.] Listen, keep an eye on that fellow there. He wants to
tell the rabbi about the girl. All right, listen. I shall have to lead Foreman
by the hand to the Korpotchniker. All right, listen, we're going. Good-
bye. Peace be unto you.
ALPER: Take the Long Island Railroad to the Atlantic Avenue Station. Then
take the Brighton train.
SCHLISSEL: Oh, for heaven's sakes. Are you presuming to tell me how to get
to Williamsburg?
ALPER: All right, go already.
SCHLISSEL: [*Muttering as he leads* FOREMAN *out the door.*] The Brighton
train. If we took the Brighten train, we would spend the day in Coney
Island. [*He exits with* FOREMAN, *closing the door.*]

[*The rest of the* CONGREGATION *has finally come to the end of the*
*service.*]

CONGREGATION: [*Their scattered voices rising to a coda.*] And with my spirit,
my body also; the Lord is with me, and I will not fear. Amen!

SCHLISSEL and ALPER: Amen!

[*There is a flurry of dispersion. The two* KESSLER BOYS *mumble good-byes and disappear quickly out into the street, buttoning their coats against the cold.* HARRIS, *who is slowly and tremblingly removing his phylacteries, continues slowly to redress himself throughout the rest of the scene.* THE SEXTON *now scurries about gathering the various phylacteries and praying shawls and putting them back into the velvet prayer bags and then putting all the velvet bags and prayer books back into the cardboard carton they were all taken from, an activity he pursues with his usual frenetic desperation. Only* THE RABBI *and* THE CABALIST *continue to say a few prayers, "The Thirteen Principles of Faith," etc.* THE CABALIST *reads them sitting down, hunched over his prayer book.* ALPER *and* ZITORSKY *have genuine cause for alarm concerning* ARTHUR BROOKS, *for he has ambled down to the platform where he stands waiting for* THE RABBI *to finish his prayers. They watch* ARTHUR *warily.* HARRIS *suddenly decides to be communicative. He lifts his old face to* ALPER *and* ZITORSKY.]

HARRIS: Ah, am I thirsty!
ALPER: [*Watching* ARTHUR *carefully.*] Good.

[THE RABBI, *having finished his last prayer now turns and starts down from the platform.* ARTHUR *steps forward to meet him.*]

ARTHUR: Rabbi—
THE RABBI: [*Walking by him.*] I'll be with you in just a moment. [*He strides directly to his office.* ALPER *leaps to intercept him.*]
ALPER: Rabbi—
THE RABBI: [*Continuing into his office.*] I'll be with you in a minute, Alper. [*He goes into his office and closes the door.* ALPER *clasps his brow and shrugs.* ZITORSKY *mutters an involuntary "Oy." They both nod their heads and wait with the sufferance that is the badge of all their tribe.* ARTHUR *moves a few steps to the rabbi's door and also waits. In the office,* THE RABBI *has sat down, all business, and has dialed a number on phone.*] I'd like to make a person-to-person call to Rabbi Harry Gersh in Wilmington, Delaware. The number in Wilmington is Kingswood 3-1973—Thank you—[*He hums a snatch of the service.* ALPER *opens the door and comes into the office.*

*He stares just a little open-mouthed at the absence of* THE GIRL. *He tugs at his Vandyke beard in contemplation.*] Yes, Alper?

ALPER: Well, I'll tell you, Rabbi—[*He scowls, a little flustered, then turns and goes out of the office.*] Excuse me.

THE RABBI: [*On phone.*] Locust 6-0931.

ALPER: [*To* ZITORSKY.] She's not there.

ZITORSKY: She's not there?

ALPER: I'll have to go out and look for her. [*Frowning, in contemplation,* ALPER *puts his coat on slowly and exits from the synagogue.*]

THE RABBI: [*His attention is abruptly brought back to the phone. His voice rises into that pitch usually used for long distance calls. On phone.*] Harry, how are you, this is Bernard here, I'm sorry I wasn't in last night, my wife Sylvia said it was wonderful to hear your voice after all these years, how are you, Shirley, and the kids? Oh, that's wonderful. I'm glad to hear it. Harry, my wife tells me you have just gotten your first congregation and you wanted some advice since I have already been fired several times— Good, how much are you getting?—Well, five thousand isn't bad for a first congregation although I always thought out-of-town paid better. And what is it, a one-year contract?—Well, what kind of advice can I give you? Especially you, Harry. You are a saintly, scholarly, and truly pious man, and you have no business being a rabbi. You've got to be a go-getter, Harry, unfortunately. The synagogue I am in now is in an unbelievable state of neglect and I expect to see us in prouder premises within a year. But I've got things moving now. I've started a Youth Group, a Young Married People's Club, a Theatre Club which is putting on its first production next month, *The Man Who Came to Dinner.* I'd like you to come, Harry, bring the wife, I'm sure you'll have an entertaining evening. And let me recommend that you organize a little league baseball team. It's a marvelous gimmick. I have sixteen boys in my Sunday School now— Harry, listen, what do I know about baseball?—Harry, let me interrupt you. How in heaven's name are you going to convey an awe of God to boys who will race out of your Hebrew classes to fly model rocket ships five hundred feet in the air exploding in three stages? To my boys, God is a retired mechanic—Well, I'm organizing a bazaar right now. When I hang up on you, I have to rush to the printers to get some raffles printed, and from there I go to the Town Hall for a permit to conduct Bingo games. In fact, I was so busy this morning, I almost forgot to come to the synagogue—[*He says gently.*] Harry, with my first congregation, I also thought I was bringing the word of God. I stood up in my pulpit every Sabbath and carped at them for violating the rituals of their own religion. My congregations dwindled, and one synagogue given to my charge disappeared into a morass of mortgages. Harry, I'm afraid there are times when I don't care if they believe in God as long as they come to Temple. Of course, it's sad—Harry, it's been my pleasure. Have I depressed you? —Come and see us, Harry—Good luck—Of course. Good-bye. [*He hangs up, stands, starts looking around for his briefcase, strides out into the synagogue still searching for it. He is interrupted by* ARTHUR.]

ARTHUR: Rabbi, I have to hurry off, but before I go I would like to talk to you about that girl in your office. These old men tell me she is possessed by a demon and I think they are intending to perform some kind of an exorcism. I must caution you that that girl should be treated only by competent psychiatrists and the most frightful harm might come to her if she is subjected to anything like—Look, do you know about this exorcism, because I cannot believe you would tolerate any—

THE RABBI: [*Who has been trying very hard to follow all this.*] I'm afraid you have me at a disadvantage.

ARTHUR: I'm talking about the girl in your office.

THE RABBI: I'm somewhat new here and don't know everybody yet by name. Please be patient with me. Now I take it you want to get married.

ARTHUR: [*For a moment he briefly considers the possibility he is not really awake. Pensively.*] This whole morning is beginning to seem absolutely— Rabbi, there is a girl in your office, who is insane.

THE RABBI: In my office? [THE RABBI *is suddenly distracted by* ZITORSKY, *who has been wandering around the synagogue, looking up and down between the rows of chairs, and is now looking into the bathroom at the upstage end of the synagogue.*] Mr. Zitorsky, what are you doing?

ZITORSKY: [*To Arthur, who is moving quickly to the rabbi's office.*] Well, have you ever seen such a thing? The girl has vanished into thin air. [*He shuffles to* THE RABBI, *absolutely awestruck by it all.*]

ARTHUR: [*Now examining the interior of the rabbi's office.*] I suspect something more mundane, like simply walking out the door. [*He moves quickly to the front door which now opens and* ALPER *returns, frowning with thought.*]

ALPER: [*To* ARTHUR.] Well, is that something or isn't it? I looked up and down, I couldn't see her.

[ARTHUR *scowls and goes out into the street, where he stands looking up and down.*]

THE RABBI: Mr. Zitorsky, if you will just tell me what this is all about.

ZITORSKY: [*His eyes wide with awe.*] Rabbi, Mr. Foreman brought his grand-daughter down this morning, and he said: "She is possessed by a dybbuk!" Well, what can you say when someone tells you something like that?

THE RABBI: Oh, Mr. Foreman's granddaughter. Yes, of course, I see.

ZITORSKY. So he took us into your office where she was standing, and it spoke to us! What an experience! You cannot imagine! The voice of the dybbuk spoke to us. It was like a hollow echo of eternity, and the girl's whole body was illuminated by a frame of light! Fire flashed from her mouth—all of us were there, ask Alper here, he'll tell you—I swear this on my soul!—The girl began to rise into the air!

ALPER: Actually, Zitorsky is coloring the story a little bit, but—

ZITORSKY. [*Riveted by the marvelousness of the fantasy.*] What are you talking about? You saw it with your own eyes!

ALPER: Well, it was an experience, I must say.

THE RABBI: And the girl has gone now?

ZITORSKY: Into the air about us.

THE RABBI: And where is Mr. Foreman?

ALPER: He went to Brooklyn.

THE RABBI: What in heaven's name for?

ALPER: To see the Korpotchniker Rabbi.

THE RABBI: [*Quite impressed.*] The Korpotchniker?

ZITORSKY: Certainly! Maybe you don't know this, but Hirschman is his cousin.

THE RABBI: Mr. Hirschman? I have to admit I didn't know that.

ZITORSKY: Oh, sure. Listen, Hirschman is the first-born son of the original Korpotchniker.

ALPER: I am afraid we are drifting from the point.

THE RABBI: [*Frowning.*] The girl probably went home. Why don't you call the girl's home, Mr. Alper, and find out if she's there? I think you are a very close friend of the family.

ARTHUR: [*Who has come back into the synagogue.*] Well, thank God, for the first rational voice I've heard today.

**ALPER:** [*Nodding his head sadly.*] Yes, I suppose I had better call her father.

**ARTHUR:** [*Buttoning his coat.*] Fine. [*Glancing at his watch.*] Gentlemen, if you don't need me for anything any more, I would like to get to my analyst. Good morning. [*He strides to the door.*]

**THE RABBI:** Peace be unto you.

**ARTHUR:** [*He pauses at the front door a little amused at the archaic greeting.*] Peace be unto you, Rabbi. [*He opens the door and goes out.*]

**THE RABBI:** Who was that fellow?

**ZITORSKY:** Who knows? The Sexton found him on the street.

**THE RABBI:** [*Buttoning his own coat.*] Well, I have to be down at the printers. A dybbuk. Really. What an unusual thing. Is Mr. Foreman a mystical man? By the way, Mr. Alper — Mr. Zitorsky — you weren't at the meeting of the Brotherhood last night. I think you should take a more active interest in the synagogue. Did you receive an announcement of the meeting? Please come next time. [*Finds his briefcase.*] Ah, there it is, good. [*Heads for the door.*] I would like to know what the Korpotchniker said about this. Will you be here later today? I'll drop in. Let me know what happens. You better call the girl's family right away, Alper. Good morning. Peace be with you.

**ALPER** and **ZITORSKY:** Peace be with you, Rabbi.

[*THE RABBI exits. The two OLD MEN regard each other a little balefully, and then ALPER shuffles to the wall phone, where he puts his hand on the phone, resting it on the receiver quite depressed by the turn of events. In the synagogue, THE CABALIST is huddled in prayer, and THE SEXTON is sleeping on a bench up right. A long moment of hushed silence fills the stage.*]

**ALPER:** [*Hand still on the phone.*] Zitorsky, let us reason this out.

**ZITORSKY:** Absolutely.

**ALPER:** [*The Talmudic scholar.*] If I call the girl's home, there are two possibilities. Either she is home or she is not home. If she is home, why call? If she is not home, then there are two possibilities. Either her father has already called the police, or he has not called the police. If he has already called the police, then we are wasting a telephone call. If he has not called the police, he will call them. If he calls the police, then there are two possibilities. Either they will take the matter seriously or they will not. If they don't take the matter seriously, why bother calling them? If they take the matter seriously, they will rush down here to find out what we already know, so what gain will have been made? Nothing. Have I reasoned well, Zitorsky?

**ZITORSKY:** You have reasoned well.

**ALPER:** Between you and me, Zitorsky, how many people are there on the streets at this hour that we couldn't spot the girl in a minute? Why should we trouble the immense machinery of the law? We'll go out and find the girl ourselves. [*They are both up in a minute, buttoning their coats and hurrying to the front door where they pause.*]

**ZITORSKY:** [*Regarding* ALPER *with awe.*] Alper, what a rogue you are! [ALPER *accepts the compliments graciously, and they both dart out into the street.*]

[*Then, out of the hollow hush of the stage,* THE CABALIST's *voice rises into a lovely chant as he rocks back and forth, his eyes closed in religious ecstasy.*]

**THE CABALIST:** [*Singing slowly and with profound conviction.*] I believe with perfect faith in the coming of the Messiah, and though he tarry, I will wait daily for his coming. I believe with perfect faith that there will be a resurrection of the dead at the time when it shall please the Creator, blessed be His name, and exalted the remembrance of him for ever and ever.

[*The front door opens, and* THE GIRL *comes rushing in, holding a beautifully bound leather book. She looks quickly around the syna- gogue, now empty except for* THE SEXTON, *and then hurries to the rabbi's office, which is, of course, also empty. A kind of panic sweeps over her and she rushes out into the synagogue again to* THE SEXTON.]

**THE GIRL:** Mr. Bleyer, the young man that was here, do you know—[*She whirls as the front door behind her again opens and* ARTHUR *comes back in. We have the feeling he also has been, if not running, at least walking very quickly. He and* THE GIRL *stare at each other for a moment. Then she says to him:*] I went home to get this book for you. I wanted you to have this book I told you about.

**ARTHUR:** [*Quietly.*] I just simply couldn't go till I knew you were all right. [*For a moment again, they stand poised, staring at each other. Then she sweeps across the stage and flings herself into his arms, crying.*]

THE GIRL: Oh, I love you. I love you. I love you—

[*They stand, locked in embrace.* THE CABALIST'*s voice rises again in a deeply primitive chant, exquisite in its atavistic ardor.*]

THE CABALIST: For Thy salvation I hope, O Lord! I hope, O Lord, for Thy salvation. O Lord, for Thy salvation I hope! For Thy salvation I hope, O Lord! I hope, O Lord, for Thy salvation! O Lord, for Thy salvation I hope!

[*The* CURTAIN *quickly falls.*]

# SCENE 2

**TIME:** *It is around noon, four hours later.*

**AT RISE:** *A silent, dozing quiet has settled over the synagogue. Indeed,* THE CABALIST *has dozed off over a thick tome at the upstage desk on the far side of the altar, his shawl-enshrouded head lying on his book.* THE GIRL, *too, is napping, curled up in the worn leather armchair in the rabbi's office.* THE SEXTON *is sitting like a cobbler on a chair at right.* ALPER *and* ZITORSKY *sit drowsily on two wooden chairs about center stage. Only* ARTHUR *moves restlessly around the synagogue. He looks into the rabbi's office, checking on* THE GIRL, *studies her sleeping sweetness, somehow deeply troubled. All is still, all is quiet. In the synagogue,* THE CABALIST *awakens suddenly and sits bolt upright as if he has just had the most bizarre dream. He stares wide-eyed at the wall ahead of him. He rises, and moves slowly downstage, his face a study in quiet awe. Apparently, he has had a profoundly moving dream, and he puts his hand to his brow as if to contain his thoughts from tumbling out. An expression of exaltation expands slowly on his wan, lined, bearded old face. His eyes are wide with terror.*

THE CABALIST: [*Whispering in awe.*] Blessed be the Lord. Blessed be the Lord. Blessed be the Lord. [*He stands staring out over the audience, his face illuminated with ecstasy. Then he cries out.*] Praise ye the Lord! Hallelujah! Praise ye the Lord! Hallelujah! It is good to sing praises unto our God; for it is pleasant and praise is seemly. Praise ye the Lord! Hallelujah! [ALPER *has been watching* THE CABALIST *with drowsy interest.* THE CABALIST *turns and just stares at him.*] My dear friends, my dear, dear friends … [*Tears fill his old eyes, and his mouth works without saying anything for a moment.*]

ALPER: Are you all right, Hirschman?

THE CABALIST: [*Awed by an inner wonder.*] I was studying the codification of the Law, especially those paragraphs beginning with the letters of my father's name — because today is my father's day of memorial. I have brought some honey cake here, in my father's memory. I have it somewhere in a paper bag. Where did I put it? I brought it here last night. It is somewhere around — and as I studied, I dozed off and my head fell upon the Book of Mishna. — Oh, my dear friends, I have prayed to the Lord to send me a dream, and He has sent me a dream. I dreamt that I was bathing in a pool of the clearest mountain water. And a man of great

377

posture appeared on the bank, and he said to me: "Rabbi, give me your blessing for I go to make a journey." And I looked closely on the man, and it was the face of my father. And I said unto him: "My father, why do you call me Rabbi? For did I not lustfully throw away the white fringed shawl of the Rabbinate and did I not mock the Lord to thy face? And have I not spent my life in prayer and penitence so that I might cleanse my soul?" And my father smiled upon me, and his bearded face glowed with gentleness, and he said unto me: "Rise from your bath, my son, and put upon you these robes of white linen which I have arrayed for you. For thy soul is cleansed and thou hast found a seat among the righteous. And the countenance of the Lord doth smile upon thee this day. So rise and rejoice and dance in the Holy Place. For thine is eternal peace and thou art among the righteous." Thus was the dream that I dreamt as my head lay on the Book of Mishna. [*He lifts his head and stares upward.*] The Lord shall reign for ever. Thy God, O Zion, unto all generations. Praise ye the Lord. Hallelujah! [*He stares distractedly around him.*] Where is the wine, Sexton? The wine! There was a fine new bottle on Friday! I have been given a seat among the righteous! For this day have I lived and fasted! I have been absolved! Hallelujah! Hallelujah!—Ah, the cakes! Here! Good!—[*He is beginning to laugh.*] I shall dance before the Holy Ark! Sexton! Sexton! Distribute the macaroons that all may share this exalted day! The Lord hath sent me a sign, and the face of my father smiled upon me! [*As abruptly as he had begun to laugh he begins to sob in the effusion of his joy. He sinks onto a chair and cries unashamedly.*]

**ALPER:** My dear Hirschman, how delighted we are for you.

**THE SEXTON:** [*Offering some honey cake to* ZITORSKY.] You want some cake there, Zitorsky?

**ZITORSKY:** I'll have a little wine too as long as we're having a party.

[THE SEXTON *scurries to offstage left to get wine.*]

**ARTHUR:** [*Who has been watching all this, rather taken by it.*] What happened?

**ALPER:** Mr. Hirschman has received a sign from God. His father has forgiven him, and his soul has been cleansed.

**ARTHUR:** That's wonderful.

**ZITORSKY:** [*To* THE SEXTON, *now pouring wine from a decanter.*] I'll tell you, Bleyer, if you have a little whiskey, I prefer that. Wine makes me dizzy.

**THE SEXTON:** Where would I get whiskey? This is a synagogue, not a saloon.

**ZITORSKY:** [*Taking his glass of wine.*] Happiness, Hirschman.

**ALPER:** Some wine for our young friend here. [*To* ARTHUR.] Will you join Mr. Hirschman in his moment of exaltation?

**ARTHUR:** [*Who is beginning to be quite taken with these old men.*] Yes, of course. [THE SEXTON, *who is pouring the wine and sipping a glass of his own as he pours, has begun to hum a gay Chassidic tune. He hands* ARTHUR *his glass.*]

**ZITORSKY:** [*Handing his glass back for a refill.*] Oh, will Schlissel eat his heart out when he finds out he is missing a party.

**ALPER:** [*Making a toast.*] Rabbi Israel, son of Isaac, I think it is fitting we use your rabbinical title—we bow in reverence to you.

**THE CABALIST:** [*Deeply touched.*] My dear, dear friends, I cannot describe to you my happiness.

**ZITORSKY:** There hasn't been a party here since that boy's confirmation last month. Wasn't that a skimpy feast for a confirmation—Another glass, please, Sexton. Oh, I'm beginning to sweat. Some confirmation party that was! The boy's father does a nice business in real estate and all he brings down is a few pieces of sponge cake and one bottle of whiskey. One bottle of whisky for fifty people! As much whisky as I had couldn't even cure a toothache. Oh boy, am I getting dizzy. When I was a boy, I could drink a whole jar of potato cider. You remember that potato cider we used to have in Europe? It could kill a horse. Oh, boy, what kind of wine is that? My legs are like rubber already. [*Suddenly stamps his foot and executes a few brief Chassidic dance steps.*]

**ALPER:** This is not bad wine, you know. A pleasant bouquet.

**ZITORSKY:** [*Wavering over to* ARTHUR.] Have a piece of cake, young man. What does it say in the Bible? "Go eat your food with gladness and drink your wine with a happy mind?" Give the boy another glass.

**ARTHUR:** [*Smiling.*] Thank you. I'm still working on this one.

**THE CABALIST:** [*He suddenly raises his head, bursts into a gay Chassidic chant.*]

Light is sown,
sown for the righteous,
and joy for the upright,
the upright in heart.
Oh,
light is sown,
sown for the righteous —

**ZITORSKY:** [*Gaily joining in.*]

and joy for the upright,
the upright in heart.
Oh!

[THE CABALIST *and* ZITORSKY *take each other's shoulders and begin to dance in the formless Chassidic pattern. They are in wonderful spirits.*] and joy for the upright

[THE SEXTON *and* ALPER *join in, clapping their hands and eventually joining the dance so that the four* OLD JEWS *form a small ring, their arms around each other's shoulders, their old feet kicking exuberantly as they stamp about in a sort of circular pattern.*]

**ALL:**

The upright in heart.
Oh!
Light is sown, sown
for the righteous,
and joy for the upright,
the upright in heart.
Oh!
Light is sown,
sown for the righteous,
and joy for the upright,
the upright in heart.

[*Round and round they stomp and shuffle, singing out lustily, sweat forming in beads on their brows. The words are repeated over and over again until they degenerate from shortness of breath into a "Bi-bu-bu-bi-bi — bi-bi-bi-bi-bibibi."* ARTHUR *watches, delighted. Finally,* ALPER, *gasping for breath, breaks out of the ring and staggers to a chair.*]

**THE CABALIST:** A good sixty years I haven't danced! Oh, enough! Enough!

My heart feels as if it will explode! [*He staggers, laughing, from the small ring of dancers and sits down, gasping for air.*]

**ALPER:** Some more wine, Hirschman?

**THE CABALIST:** [*Gasping happily.*] Oh!

[ZITORSKY *looks up, noticing* THE GIRL, *who, awakened by the romping, has sidled out into the synagogue and has been watching the gaiety with delight.* ZITORSKY *eyes her wickedly for a moment; then advances on her his arm outstretched, quite the old cock-of-the walk.*]

**ZITORSKY:** Bi-bi-bi-bi-bi-bi-bi — [*He seizes her in his arms and begins to twirl around, much to her delight. She dances with him, her skirt whirling and her feet twinkling, laughing at the sheer physical excitement of it all.* ZITORSKY *supplies the music, a gay chant, the lyrics of which consist of* ] Bi-bi-bi-bi-bi-bi-bi-bi — [*etc.*] —

**THE CABALIST:** The last time I danced was on the occasion of the last Day of the Holiday of Tabernacles in 1896. I was 17 years old. [*A sudden frightened frown sweeps across his face. He mutters.*] Take heed for the girl, for the dybbuk will be upon her soon.

**ALPER:** [*Leaning to him.*] What did you say, Israel son of Isaac?

**THE CABALIST:** [*He turns to* THE GIRL, *dancing with* ZITORSKY, *and stares at her.*] Let the girl rest, Zitorsky, for she struggles with the dybbuk. Behold. [THE GIRL *has indeed broken away from* ZITORSKY *and has begun an improvised dance of her own. The gaiety is gone from her face and is replaced by a sullen lasciviousness. The dance she does is a patently provocative one, dancing slowly at first, and then with increasing abandon and wantonness.* ZITORSKY *recoils in horror.* THE GIRL *begins to stamp her feet and whirl more and more wildly. Her eyes grow bold and flashing and she begins to shout old gypsy words, a mongrel Russian, Oriental in intonation.* THE CABALIST *slowly moves to* THE GIRL *now, who, when she becomes aware of his coming close, abruptly stops her dance and stands stock still, her face now a mask of extravagant pain.* THE CABALIST *regards her gently and speaks softly to her.*] Lie down, my child, and rest.

**THE GIRL:** [*At this quiet suggestion, she begins to sway as if she were about to faint. Barely audible.*] I feel so faint, so faint. [*She sinks slowly to the floor, not quite in a swoon, but on the verge.* ARTHUR *races to her side.*]

**ARTHUR:** Do we have any water here?

**ALPER:** Wine would be better. Sexton, give her some wine. [THE SEXTON *hurries to her with someone's glass.*]

**ARTHUR:** [*Holding* THE GIRL'S *head.*] Is she a sickly girl?

**ALPER:** [*Bending over them.*] She was never sick a day in her life.

**THE SEXTON:** Here's the wine.

**ZITORSKY:** [*To* THE SEXTON.] Did I tell you? Did I tell you?

**THE GIRL:** I feel so faint. I feel so faint.

**ARTHUR:** [*Bringing the glass of wine to her lips.*] Sip some of this.

**THE GIRL:** [*Murmuring.*] Save me — save me —

**THE CABALIST:** The dybbuk weakens her. I have seen this once before.

**THE SEXTON:** [*To* ZITORSKY.] When you told me about this dybbuk, I didn't believe you.

**ZITORSKY:** So did I tell you right?

**THE SEXTON:** Oh, boy.

**ARTHUR:** Help me get her onto the chair in there.

**ALPER:** Yes, of course.

**THE SEXTON:** Here, let me help a little.

[*Between the three of them, they manage to get* THE GIRL *up and walk her slowly to the rabbi's office, where they gently help her lie down on the leather chair.*]

**THE CABALIST:** [*To* ZITORSKY.] They haven't heard from Mr. Foreman yet?

**ZITORSKY:** No, we're waiting.

**THE CABALIST:** [*Frowning.*] It is not that far to Williamsburg. Well, the girl will sleep now.

[*He walks slowly to the door of the rabbi's office, followed by a wary* ZITORSKY. *In the rabbi's office* ARTHUR *is gently laying* THE GIRL'S *limp sleeping form down on the chair.*]

**ARTHUR:** [*To the others.*] I think she's fallen asleep.

**ALPER:** Thank heavens for that.

**ARTHUR:** [*Straightening.*] Look, I'm going to call her family. She may be quite ill. I think we'd all feel a lot better if she were in the hands of a doctor. If one of you will just give me her home telephone number. [ *Just a little annoyed, for nobody answers him.*] Please, gentlemen, I really don't think it's wise to pursue this nonsense any longer.

**THE CABALIST:** It is not nonsense. I do not speak of dybbuks casually. As a young man, I saw hundreds of people come to my father claiming to be possessed, but, of all these, only two were true dybbuks. Of these two, one was a girl very much like this poor girl, and, even before the black candles and the ram's horn could be brought for the exorcism, she sank down onto the earth and died. I tell you this girl is possessed, and she will die, clutching at her throat and screaming for redemption unless the dybbuk is exorcised. [*He stares at the others, nods his head.*] She will die. Wake the girl. I will take her to the Korpotchniker myself.

**ALPER:** Zitorsky, wake the girl. I will get her coat. Sexton, call a taxicab for Rabbi Israel. [ALPER, *who had been reaching for the girl's coat, is stayed by* ARTHUR. *He looks up at the young man.*] Young man, what are you doing?

**ARTHUR:** Mr. Alper, the girl is sick. There may be something seriously wrong with her.

**ALPER:** Young man, Rabbi Israel says she is dying.

**ARTHUR:** Well, in that case, certainly let me have her home telephone number.

**ALPER:** [*Striding into the rabbi's office.*] You are presuming in matters that are no concern of yours.

**ARTHUR:** [*Following.*] They are as much my concern as they are yours. I have grown quite fond of this girl. I want her returned to the proper authorities, right now. If necessary, I shall call a policeman. Now, let's have no more nonsense.

[ALPER *sinks down behind the desk glowering. A moment of silence fills the room.*]

**THE CABALIST:** The young man doesn't believe in dybbuks?

**ARTHUR:** I'm afraid not. I think you are all behaving like madmen.

**THE CABALIST:** [*He considers this answer for a moment.*] I will tell you an old Chassidic parable. A deaf man passed by a house in which a wedding party was going on. He looked in the window and saw all the people there dancing and cavorting, leaping about and laughing. However, since the man was deaf and could not hear the music of the fiddlers, he said to himself. "Ah, this must be a madhouse." Young man, because you are deaf, must it follow that we are lunatics?

**ARTHUR:** You are quite right. I did not mean to mock your beliefs, and I apologize for it. However, I am going to call the girl's father, and, if he wants to have the girl exorcised, that's his business. [*He has sat down behind the desk, put his hand on the receiver, and now looks up at* ALPER.] Well?

THE CABALIST: Give him the number, Mr. Alper. [ALPER *fishes an old address book out of his vest pocket, thumbs through the pages, and hands the book opened to* ARTHUR, *who begins to dial.*] There is no one home in the girl's house. Her father, who wishes only to forget about the girl, has gone to his shop in the city, and, at this moment, is overeating at his lunch in a dairy restaurant. The step-mother has taken the younger children to her sister's. The girl's doctor has called the police and has gone about his rounds, and the police are diffidently riding up and down the streets of the community looking for an old Jew and his granddaughter. [ARTHUR *says nothing but simply waits for an answer to his ring.* THE CABALIST *sits down on the arm of the couch and contemplates mildly to himself. At last he says:*] I cannot understand why this young man does not believe in dybbuks.

ALPER: It is symptomatic of the current generation, Rabbi Israel, to be utterly disillusioned. Historically speaking, an era of prosperity following an era of hard times usually produces a number of despairing and quietistic philosophies, for the now prosperous people have found out they are just as unhappy as when they were poor. Thus when an intelligent man of such a generation discovers that two television sets have no more meaning than one or that he gets along no better with his wife in a suburban house than he did in their small city flat, he arrives at the natural assumption that life is utterly meaningless.

THE CABALIST: What an unhappy state of affairs.

ARTHUR: [*Returns the receiver to its cradle, muttering.*] Nobody home.

THE CABALIST: [*To* ARTHUR.] Is that true, young man, that you believe in absolutely nothing?

ARTHUR: Not a damn thing.

THE CABALIST: There is no truth, no beauty, no infinity, no known, no unknown?

ARTHUR: Precisely.

THE CABALIST: Young man, you are a fool.

ARTHUR: Really. I have been reading your book — the Book of Zohar. I am sure it has lost much in the translation, but, Sir, any disciple of this abracadabra is presuming when he calls anyone else a fool. [*He produces the book the girl gave him.*]

THE CABALIST: You have been reading The Book of Zobar. Dear young man, one does not read The Book of Zohar, leaf through its pages, and make marginal notes. I have entombed myself in this slim volume for sixty years, raw with vulnerability to its hidden mysteries, and have sensed only a glimpse of its passion. Behind every letter of every word lies a locked image, and behind every image a sparkle of light of the ineffable brilliance of Infinity. But the concept of the Inexpressible Unknown is inconceivable to you. For you are a man possessed by the Tangible. If you cannot touch it with your fingers, it simply does not exist. Indeed, that will be the epithet of your generation—that you took everything for granted and believed in nothing. It is a very little piece of life that we know. How shall I say it? I suggest it is wiser to believe in dybbuks than in nothing at all.

ARTHUR: Mr. Hirschman, a good psychiatrist—even a poor one—could strip your beliefs in ten minutes. You may think of yourself as a man with a God, but I see you as a man obsessed with guilt who has invented a God so he can be forgiven. You have invented it all—the guilt, God, forgiveness, the whole world, dybbuks, love, passion, fulfillment—the whole fantastic mess of pottage—because it is unbearable for you to bear the pain of insignificance. None of these things exist. You've made them all up. The fact is, I have half a mind to let you go through with this exorcism, for, after all the trumpetings of rams' homs and the bellowing of incantations and after the girl falls in a swoon on the floor—I assure you, she will rise up again as demented as she ever was, and I wonder what bizarre rationale and mystique you will expound to explain all that. Now, if the disputation is at an end, I am going to call the police. [*He picks up the receiver again and dials the operator.*]

ALPER: Well, what can one say to such bitterness?

THE CABALIST: [*Shrugs.*] One can only say that the young man has very little regard for psychiatrists.

[*The front door to the synagogue bursts open, and* FOREMAN *and* SCHLISSEL *come hurtling in, breathing heavily and in a state of absolute confusion.* ALPER *darts out into the synagogue proper and stares at them.*]

SCHLISSEL: Oh, thank God, the synagogue is still here!

ALPER: Well?

**SCHLISSEL:** [*Can hardly talk he is so out of breath.*] Well, what?

**ALPER:** What did the Korpotchniker say?

**SCHLISSEL:** Who knows?! Who saw the Korpotchniker?! We've been riding in subways for four hours! Back and forth, in this train, in that train! I am convinced there is no such place as Williamsburg and there is no such person as the Korpotchniker Rabbi! I tell you, twice we got off at two different stations, just to see daylight, and, as God is my witness, both times we were in New Jersey!

**FOREMAN:** Oh, I tell you, I am sick from driving so much.

**ALPER:** Idiot! You didn't take the Brighton train!

**SCHLISSEL:** We took the Brighton train! [*He waves both arms in a gesture of final frustration.*] We took all the trains! I haven't had a bite to eat all morning. Don't tell me about Brighton trains! Don't tell me about anything! Leave me alone, and the devil take your whole capitalist economy! [ZITORSKY, THE SEXTON *and* THE CABALIST *have all come out to see what the noise is all about. Even* ARTHUR *is standing in the office doorway listening to all this.*] We asked this person, we asked that person. This person said that train. That person said this train. We went to a policeman. He puts us on a train. The conductor comes in, says: "Last stop." We get out. As God is my witness, New Jersey. We get back on that train. The conductor says: "Get off next station and take the other train." We get off the next station and take the other train. A man says: "Last stop." We get out. New Jersey!

[*In the rabbi's office,* THE GIRL *suddenly sits bolt up right, her eyes clenched tight in pain, screaming terribly out into the air about her, her voice shrill with anguish.*]

**FOREMAN:** [*Racing to her side.*] Oh, my God! Evelyn! Evelyn! What is it?!

**THE GIRL:** [*She clutches at her throat and screams.*] Save me! Save me! Save me!

[ZITORSKY *and* THE SEXTON *begin to mutter rapid prayers under their breath.*]

**ALPER:** [*Putting his arm around* FOREMAN.] David, she's very ill. We think she may be dying.

**ARTHUR:** [*He has raced to* THE GIRL, *sits on the couch beside her takes her into his arms.*] Call a doctor.

**FOREMAN:** [*In panic to* ALPER, *who is standing stock still in the synagogue.*] He says I should call a doctor.

[ARTHUR *puts his hand to his brow and shakes his head as if to clear it of the shock and confusion within it.*]

**ALPER:** [*Crossing to* THE CABALIST.] Save her, Rabbi Israel. You have had your sign from God. You are among the righteous.

**ARTHUR:** [*He turns slowly and regards the silent betallithed form of the little* CABALIST. *To* THE CABALIST, *his voice cracking under emotions he was unaware he still had.*] For God's sake, perform your exorcism or whatever has to be done. I think she's dying.

**THE CABALIST:** [*He regards* ARTHUR *for a moment with the profoundest gentleness. Then he turns, and with an authoritative voice, instructs* THE SEXTON.] Sexton, we shall need black candles, the ram's horn, praying shawls of white wool, and there shall be ten Jews for a quorum to witness before God this awesome ceremony.

**THE SEXTON:** Just plain black candles?

**THE CABALIST:** Just plain black candles.

[ALPER *moves quietly up to* FOREMAN *standing in the office doorway and touches his old friend's shoulder in a gesture of awe and compassion.* FOREMAN, *at the touch, begins to cry and buries his shaking old head on his friend's shoulder.* ALPER *embraces him.*]

**ZITORSKY:** [*In the synagogue, to* SCHLISSEL.] I am absolutely shaking— shaking.

[ARTHUR, *having somewhat recovered his self-control, sinks down near pulpit, frowning, confused by all that is going on, and moved by a complex of feeling he cannot understand at all.*]

CURTAIN

# ACT THREE

**TIME:** *Half an hour later.*

**AT RISE:** The Girl *is sitting in the rabbi's office, perched on the couch, nervous, frightened, staring down at her restlessly twisting fingers.* Foreman *sits behind the rabbi's desk, wrapped in his own troubled thoughts. He wears over his suit a long, white woolen praying shawl with thick, black stripes, like that worn by* The Cabalist *from the beginning of the play. Indeed, all the* Men *now wear these ankle-length white praying shawls, except* Arthur, *who at rise is also in the rabbi's office, deep in thought.* The Cabalist *sits on pulpit, his praying shawl cowled over his head, leafing through a volume, preparing the prayers for the exorcism.* The Sexton *is standing by the wall phone, the receiver cradled to his ear, waiting for an answer to a call he has just put in. He is more or less surrounded by* Alper, Schlissel, *and* Zitorsky.

Zitorsky: How about Milsky the butcher?

Alper: Milsky wouldn't come. Ever since they gave the seat by the East Wall to Kornblum, Milsky said he wouldn't set foot in this synagogue again. Every synagogue I have belonged to, there have always been two kosher butchers who get into a fight over who gets the favored seat by the East Wall during the High Holy Days, and the one who doesn't abandons the congregation in a fury, and the one who does always seems to die before the next High Holy Days.

Schlissel: Kornblum the butcher died? I didn't know Kornblum died.

Alper: Sure. Kornblum died four years ago.

Schlissel: Well, he had lousy meat, believe me, may his soul rest in peace.

[The Sexton *has hung up, recouped his dime, reinserted it, and is dialing again.*]

Zitorsky: [*To* The Sexton.] No answer?

**THE SEXTON:** [*Shakes his head.*] I'm calling Harris.

**SCHLISSEL:** Harris? You tell an 81-year-old man to come down and make a tenth for an exorcism, and he'll have a heart attack talking on the phone with you.

**THE SEXTON:** [*Dialing.*] Well, what else am I to do? It is hard enough to assemble ten Jews under the best of circumstances, but in the middle of the afternoon on a Thursday it is an absolute nightmare. Aronowitz is in Miami. Klein the Furrier is at his job in Manhattan. It is a workday today. Who shall I call? [*Waiting for someone to answer.*] There are many things that I have to do. The tapestries on the Ark, as you see, are faded and need needlework, and the candelabras and silver goblet for the saying of the Sabbath benediction are tarnished and dull. But every second of my day seems to be taken up with an incessant search for ten Jews — [*On phone.*] Hello, Harris. Harris, this is Bleyer the Sexton. We need you badly down here in the synagogue for a quorum — If I told you why, you wouldn't come — All right, I'll tell you, but, in God's name, don't tell another soul, not even your daughter-in-law —

**SCHLISSEL:** My daughter-in-law, may she grow like an onion with her head in the ground.

**THE SEXTON:** [*On phone.*] Hirschman is going to exorcise a dybbuk from Foreman's granddaughter — I said, Hirschman is — A dybbuk. That's right, a dybbuk — Right here in Mineola — That's right. Why should Mineola be exempt from dybbuks?

**ALPER:** [*Thinking of names.*] There used to be a boy came down here every morning, about eight, nine years ago — a devout boy with forelocks and sidecurls — a pale boy, who was studying to be a Rabbi at the seminary.

**THE SEXTON:** [*On phone.*] Harris, this is not a joke.

**SCHLISSEL:** Chwatkin.

**ALPER:** That's right, Chwatkin. That was the boy's name. Chwatkin. Maybe we could call him. Does he still live in the community?

**SCHLISSEL:** He's a big television actor. He's on television all the time. Pinky Sims. He's an actor.

**ZITORSKY:** Pinky Sims? That's a name for a rabbinical student?

**THE SEXTON:** Put on your sweater and come down.

**ALPER:** [*To* THE SEXTON, *who has just hung up.*] So Harris is coming?

**ZITORSKY:** Yes, he's coming. So with Harris, that makes eight, and I am frankly at the end of my resources. I don't know who else to call.

**ALPER:** This is terrible. Really. God manifests Himself in our little synagogue, and we can't even find ten Jews to say hello.

**THE SEXTON:** I shall have to go out in the street and get two strangers. [*Putting on his coat.*] Well, I don't look forward to this at all. I will have to stop people on the street, ask them if they are Jewish—which is bad enough—and then explain to them I wish them to attend the exorcism of the dybbuk—I mean, surely you can see the futility of it.

**ALPER:** We can only get eight. A disgrace. Really. We shall not have the exorcism for lack of two Jews.

**THE SEXTON:** [*On his way out.*] All right, I'm going. [*He exits.*]

**ZITORSKY.** [*To* SCHLISSEL.] In those days when I was deceiving my wife, I used to tell her I was entertaining out-of-town buyers. I once told her I was entertaining out-of-town buyers every night for almost three weeks. It was a foolhardy thing to do because even my wife could tell business was not that good. So one night, she came down to my loft on Thirty-sixth Street and walked in and caught me with—well, I'm sure I've told you this story before.

**SCHLISSEL:** Many times.

[THE CABALIST *enters the office. Upon his entrance,* THE GIRL *stands abruptly, obviously deeply disturbed and barely in control of herself. She turns from* THE CABALIST *and shades her eyes with her hand to hide her terror.* FOREMAN *looks up briefly. He seems to be in a state of shock.* THE CABALIST *sits down on the couch, lets the cowl of his prayer shawl fall back on his shoulders and contemplates his hands folded patiently between his knees. After a moment, he says:*]

**THE CABALIST:** [*Quietly.*] Dybbuk, I am Israel son of Isaac. My father was Isaac son of Asher, and I wear his fringed shawl on my shoulders as I talk to you. [*Upon these words,* THE GIRL *suddenly contorts her form as if seized by a violent cramp. She clutches her stomach and bends low and soft sobs begin to come out of her.*] Reveal yourself to me.

**THE GIRL:** [*In the voice of the dybbuk.*] I am Hannah Luchinsky.

[*In the synagogue,* ALPER, SCHLISSEL *and* ZITORSKY *begin to edge, quite frightened, to the opened office door.* ARTHUR *watches from his seat in the office.*]

**THE CABALIST:** Why do you possess this girl's body?

THE GIRL: [*Twisting and contorting; in the voice of the dybbuk.*] My soul was lost at sea, and there is no one to say the prayers for the dead over me.

THE CABALIST: I will strike a bargain with you. Leave this girl's body through her smallest finger, doing her no damage, not even a scratch, and I shall sit on wood for you for the First Seven Days of Mourning and shall plead for your soul for the First Thirty Days and shall say the prayers for the dead over you three times a day for the Eleven Months and light the Memorial Lamp each year upon the occasion of your death. I ask you to leave this girl's body.

THE GIRL: [*She laughs quietly. In the voice of the dybbuk.*] You give me short-weight, for you will yourself be dead before the prayers for the new moon.

[*In the office doorway, the three* OLD MEN *shudder.* FOREMAN *looks up slowly.* THE CABALIST *closes his eyes.*]

THE CABALIST: [*Quietly.*] How do you know this?

THE GIRL: [*In the voice of the dybbuk.*] Your soul will fly straight to the Heavenly Gates and you will be embraced by the Archangel Mihoel.

THE CABALIST: Then I enjoin the Angel of Death to speed his way. Dybbuk, I order you to leave the body of this girl.

THE GIRL: [*Her face suddenly flashes with malevolence. In the voice of the dybbuk, shouting.*] No! I seek vengeance for these forty years of limbo! I was betrayed in my youth and driven to the Evil Impulse against my will! I have suffered beyond belief, and my spirit has lived in dunghills and in piles of ashes, and I demand the soul of David son of Abram be cast into Gilgul for the space of forty years times ten to gasp for air in the sea in which I drowned —

FOREMAN: [*Standing in terror.*] No! No!

THE GIRL: [*In the voice of the dybbuk.*] — so that my soul may have peace! A soul for a soul! That is my bargain.

FOREMAN: [*Shouting.*] Let it be then! Leave my granddaughter in peace and I will give my soul in exchange.

THE CABALIST: [*With ringing authority.*] The disposition of David son of Abram's soul will not be decided here. Its fall and ascent has been ordained by the second universe of angels. The bargain cannot be struck! Dybbuk, hear me. I order you to leave the body of this girl through her smallest finger, causing her no pain nor damage, and I give you my word prayers will be said over you in full measure. But if you adjure these words, then I must proceed against you with malediction and anathema.

THE GIRL: [*Laughs.*] Raise not thy mighty arm against me, for it has no fear for me. A soul for a soul. That is my bargain. [*She suddenly begins to sob.*]

THE CABALIST: [*To* ALPER.] We shall have to prepare for the exorcism.

ALPER: I thought that would be the case.

THE GIRL: [*Sitting down on the couch, frightened, in her own voice.*] I am so afraid.

FOREMAN: There is nothing to fear. It will all be over in a minute, like having a tooth pulled, and you will walk out of here a cheerful child.

SCHLISSEL: [*Ambling back into the synagogue proper with* ZITORSKY *and* ALPER.] I tell you, I'd feel a lot better if the Korpotchniker was doing this. If you are going to have a tooth pulled, at least let it be by a qualified dentist.

ZITORSKY: I thought Hirschman handled himself very well with that dybbuk.

SCHLISSEL: [*To* ALPER *and* ZITORSKY.] If I tell you all something, promise you will never throw it back in my face.

ZITORSKY: What?

SCHLISSEL: I am beginning to believe she is really possessed by a dybbuk.

ZITORSKY: I'm beginning to get used to the whole thing.

[THE CABALIST *has stood and moved upstage to the rear wall of the synagogue, where he stands in meditation.* FOREMAN *is sitting again somewhat numbly beside his granddaughter.*]

THE GIRL: [*After a moment.*] I am very frightened, Arthur.

ARTHUR: [*Rises.*] Well, I spoke to my analyst, as you know, and he said he didn't think this exorcism was a bad idea at all. The point is, if you really do believe you are possessed by a dybbuk—

THE GIRL: Oh, I do.

ARTHUR: Well, then, he feels this exorcism might be a good form of shock treatment that will make you more responsive to psychiatric therapy and open the door to an eventual cure. Mr. Hirschman assures me it is a painless ceremony. So you really have nothing to be frightened of.

THE GIRL: Will you be here?

ARTHUR: Of course. Did you think I wouldn't?

[FOREMAN *moves slowly out into the synagogue as if to ask something of* HIRSCHMAN.]

THE GIRL: I always sense flight in you.

ARTHUR: Really.

THE GIRL: You are always taking to your heels, Arthur. Especially in moments like now when you want to be tender. I know that you love me or I couldn't be so happy with you, but the whole idea of love seems to terrify you, and you keep racing off to distant detachments. I feel that if I reached out for your cheek now, you would turn your head or, in some silent way, clang the iron gates shut on me. You have some strange dybbuk all of your own, some sad little turnkey, who drifts about inside of you, locking up all the little doors, and saying, "You are dead. You are dead." You do love me, Arthur. I know that.

ARTHUR: [*Gently.*] I wish you well, Evelyn. We can at least say that.

THE GIRL: I love you. I want so very much to be your wife. [*She stares at him, her face glowing with love. She says quietly.*] I will make you a good home, Arthur. You will be happy with me. [*He regards her for a moment, caught by her wonder. He reaches forward and lightly touches her cheek. She cannot take her eyes from him.*] I adore you, Arthur.

ARTHUR: [*With deep gentleness.*] You are quite mad.

[*They regard each other,* ARTHUR *stands.*]

THE GIRL: You think our getting married is impractical?

ARTHUR: Yes, I would say it was at the least impractical.

THE GIRL: Because I am insane and you are suicidal.

ARTHUR: I do think those are two reasons to give one pause.

THE GIRL: Well, at least we begin with futility. Most marriages take years to arrive there.

ARTHUR: Don't be saucy, Evelyn.

THE GIRL: [*Earnestly.*] Oh, Arthur, I wouldn't suggest marriage if I thought it was utterly unfeasible. I think we can make a go of it. I really do. I know you have no faith in my exorcism —

ARTHUR: As I say, it may be an effective shock therapy.

THE GIRL: But we could get married this minute, and I still think we could make a go of it. I'm not a dangerous schizophrenic; I just hallucinate. I could keep your house for you. I did for my father very competently before he remarried. I'm a good cook, and you do find me attractive, don't you? I love you, Arthur. You are really very good for me. I retain reality remarkably well with you. I know I could be a good wife. Many schizophrenics function quite well if one has faith in them.

ARTHUR: [*Touched by her earnestness.*] My dear Evelyn—

THE GIRL: I don't ask you to have faith in dybbuks or gods or exorcisms— just in me.

ARTHUR: [*He gently touches her cheek.*] How in heaven's name did we reach this point of talking marriage?

THE GIRL: It is a common point of discussion between people in love.

ARTHUR: [*He kneels before her, takes her hand between his. He loves her.*] I do not love you. Nor do you love me. We met five hours ago and exchanged the elementary courtesy of conversation—the rest is your own ingenuousness.

THE GIRL: I do not remember ever being as happy as I am this moment. I feel enchanted. [*They are terribly close now. He leans to her his arms moving to embrace her. And then he stops, and the moment is broken. He turns away, scowls, stands.*] You are in full flight again, aren't you?

ARTHUR: I reserve a certain low level of morality which includes not taking advantage of incompetent minors.

THE GIRL: Why can't you believe that I love you?

ARTHUR: [*Angrily.*] I simply do not believe anybody loves anyone. Let's have an end to this. [*He is abruptly aware that their entire love scene together has been observed by all of the* OLD MEN, *clustered together in the open doorway of the rabbi's office, beaming at them. With a furious sigh, he strides to the door and shuts it in the* OLD MEN's *faces. He turns back to* THE GIRL, *scowling.*] Really, this is all much too fanciful. Really, it is. In an hour, you will be back to your institution, where I may or may not visit you.

THE GIRL: [*She sits slowly down.*] If I were not already insane, the thought that I might not see you again would make me so.

ARTHUR: [*More disturbed than he himself knows.*] I don't know what you want of me.

THE GIRL: [*One step from tears.*] I want you to find the meaning of your life in me.

ARTHUR: But that's insane. How can you ask such an impossible thing?

THE GIRL: Because you love me.

ARTHUR: [*Cries out.*] I don't know what you mean by love! All it means to me is I shall buy you a dinner, take you to the theatre, and then straight to our tryst where I shall reach under your blouse for the sake of tradition while you breathe hotly in my ear in a pretense of passion. We will mutter automatic endearments, nibbling at the sweat on each other's earlobes, all the while gracelessly fumbling with buttons and zippers, cursing under our breath the knots in our shoelaces, and telling ourselves that this whole comical business of stripping off our trousers is an act of nature like the pollination of weeds. Even in that one brief moment when our senses finally obliterate our individual alonenesses, we will hear ringing in our ears the reluctant creaking of mattress springs.

THE GIRL: [*She stares at him, awed by this bitter expostulation.*] You are possessed.

ARTHUR: At your age, I suppose, one still finds theatrical charm in this ultimate of fantasies, but when you have been backstage as often as I have, you will discover love to be an altogether shabby business of cold creams and costumes.

THE GIRL: [*Staring at him.*] You are possessed by a dybbuk that does not allow you to love.

ARTHUR: [*Crying out again in sudden anguish.*] Oh, leave me alone! Let's get on with this wretched exorcism! [*He strides to the door, suddenly turns, confused, disturbed, would say something, but he doesn't know what. He opens the door to find the five* OLD MEN *patiently waiting for him with beaming smiles. This disconcerts him and he turns to* THE GIRL *again, and is again at a loss for words. She stares at the floor.*]

THE GIRL: We could be very happy if you would have faith in me.

ARTHUR: [*He turns and shuffles out of the office. To the* OLD MEN.] It was tasteless of you to gawk at us. [*He continues into the synagogue trailed by the* OLD MEN. *He sits and is immediately surrounded by the* OLD MEN.]

FOREMAN: Are you interested in this girl, young man, because my son is not a rich man, by any means, but he will give you a fine wedding, catered by good people, with a cantor—

ZITORSKY: And a choir.

FOREMAN: —Possibly, and a dowry perhaps in the amount of five hundred dollars—which, believe me, is more than he can afford. However, I am told you are a professional man, a lawyer, and the father of the bride must lay out good money for such a catch.

ALPER and ZITORSKY: Surely—Absolutely.

FOREMAN: Of course, the girl is an incompetent and you will have to apply to the courts to be appointed the committee of her person—

ALPER:—a formality, I assure you, once you have married her.
FOREMAN: As for the girl, I can tell you first hand, she is a fine Jewish girl—
ZITORSKY: Modest—
ALPER: Devout—
FOREMAN:—and she bakes first-rate pastries.
ARTHUR: [*Staring at the gay* OLD MEN *with disbelief.*] You are all mad, madder than the girl, and if I don't get out of here soon, I shall be as mad as the rest.
ZITORSKY: A beauty, young man. Listen, it is said—better a full-bosomed wife than to marry a Rothschild.
SCHLISSEL: Leave the man alone. We have all been miserably married for half a century ourselves. How can you in good faith recommend the institution?
ALPER: The girl is so obviously taken with him. It would be a good match.
FOREMAN: [*Anxiously.*] Perhaps he is married already.
ALPER: [*To* ARTHUR.] My dear fellow, how wonderful to be in love.
ARTHUR: I love nothing!
THE CABALIST: Yes. The girl is quite right. He is possessed. He loves nothing. Love is an act of faith, and yours is a faithless generation. That is your dybbuk.

[*The front door of the synagogue opens, and* THE SEXTON *slips quickly in, quietly closing the door after himself.*]

ARTHUR: [*To* THE CABALIST.] Don't you think it's time to get on with this exorcism?
THE CABALIST: Yes. [*He stands, moves to the pulpit, sits.*]
ALPER: [*To* THE SEXTON.] Did you get anybody?
THE SEXTON: [*He moves in his nervous way down into the synagogue. He has obviously been on the go since he left; sweat beads his brow, and he is breathing heavily. Unbuttoning his coat and wiping his brow.*] Gentlemen, we are in the soup.
SCHLISSEL: You couldn't find anybody?
THE SEXTON: Actually, we have nine now, but the issue of a quorum has become an academic one. Oh, let me catch my breath. The rabbi will be here in a few minutes.
ALPER: The rabbi?
THE SEXTON: I saw him on Woodhaven Boulevard, and he said he would join us. Harris is on his way already. I saw him coming down the hill from his house. But the whole matter is academic.

ALPER: You told the rabbi we need him to exorcise the girl's dybbuk?

THE SEXTON: Well, what else was I to say? He asked me what I needed a quorum for at one o'clock in the afternoon, and I told him, and he thought for a moment, and he said: "All right, I'll be there in a few minutes." He is quite a nice fellow, something of a press agent perhaps, but with good intentions. Oh, I am perspiring like an animal. I shall surely have the ague tomorrow. I have been running all over looking for Jews. I even went to Friedman the Tailor. He wasn't even in town. So let me tell you. I was running back here. I turned the corner on Thirty-third Road there, and I see parked right in front of the synagogue a police patrol car. [*The* OTHERS *start.*]

ALPER: [*Looking up.*] Oh?

THE SEXTON: That's what I mean when I say we are in the soup.

SCHLISSEL: Did they say something to you?

THE SEXTON: Sure they said something. I tell you, my heart gave such a turn when I saw that police car there. They were sitting there, those two policemen, big strapping cossacks with dark faces like avenging angels, smoking cigarettes, and with their revolvers bulging through their blue overcoats. As I walked across the street to the synagogue, my knees were knocking.

ALPER: When was this? It was just now?

THE SEXTON: Just this second. Just before I came in the door—Hello, Harris, how are you?

[*This last to the octogenarian of the first act,* HARRIS, *who, bundled in his heavy overcoat, muffler and with his hat pulled down on his head, has just entered the synagogue.*]

ZITORSKY: [*To* THE SEXTON.] So what happened?

HARRIS: [*In his high shrill voice, as he unbuttons his overcoat.*] Gentlemen! Have you heard about this dybbuk?

SCHLISSEL: Harris, we were all here at the time he called you.

THE SEXTON: Harris, did you see the police car outside?

SCHLISSEL: So what did the policeman say?

THE SEXTON: [*Unbuttoning his collar and wiping his neck with a handkerchief.*] This big strapping fellow with his uniform full of buttons

---

[1] Because Cohmim [Kohanim] and Levites are descendents of priests, they perform certain duties and are accorded first and second honors, respectively, in synagogue worship.

looks up, he says: "You know a man named David Foreman? We're looking for him and his granddaughter, a girl, 18 years old." Well? Eh! Well, are we in the soup or not?

[SCHLISSEL *goes to the front door, opens it a conspiratorial crack, looks out.*]

ARTHUR: I don't think the police will bother you if you get your exorcism started right away. They won't interrupt a religious ceremony, especially if they don't know what it is.

THE CABALIST: [*Who has made his own mind up.*] Sexton, fetch the black candles, one for each man.

[THE SEXTON *scurries to the rabbi's office, where the black candles are lying on the desk, wrapped in brown grocery paper.*]

ARTHUR: [*Moving to the front door.*] I'll stand by the door and talk to the police if they come in.

SCHLISSEL: [*Closing the front door.*] They're out there, all right.

THE CABALIST: [*He looks about the little synagogue, immensely dignified now, almost beautiful in his authority. The* OTHERS *wait on his words.*] I shall want to perform the ablutions of the Cohanim. Is there a Levite among you?

SCHLISSEL: I am a Levite.

THE CABALIST: You shall pour the water on my hands.[1]

[THE SEXTON *scoots across the synagogue carrying black candles to everyone.*]

HARRIS: [*Looking distractedly about.*] What are we doing now? Where is the dybbuk?

ALPER: Harris, put on a praying shawl.

HARRIS: [*Moving nervously to the office door*] Is this actually a serious business then? Where is the dybbuk? Tell me, because Bleyer the Sexton told me nothing—

THE CABALIST: There is nothing in the Book of Codes which gives the procedure for exorcism, so I have selected those passages to read that I thought most apt. For the purpose of cleansing our souls, we shall recite the Al-Chait, and we shall recite that prayer of atonement which begins: "Sons of man such as sit in darkness." As you pray these prayers, let the image of God in any of His seventy-two faces rise before you.

**ALPER:** [*Crossing into rabbi's office.*] I'll get the books.

**THE SEXTON:** [*Giving* SCHLISSEL *a metal bowl.*] Fill it with water.

**SCHLISSEL:** I'm an atheist. Why am I mixed up in all this?

**ALPER:** We do not have a quorum. Will this be valid?

**THE CABALIST.** We will let God decide.

**THE SEXTON:** When shall I blow the ram's horn?

**THE CABALIST:** I shall instruct you when.

**HARRIS:** [*Putting on his shawl.*] What shall I do? Where shall I stand?

**ZITORSKY:** [*To* HARRIS.] Stand here, and do not be afraid.

**FOREMAN:** [*He comes out of the rabbi's office carrying a long white woolen praying shawl which he gives to* ARTHUR.] I will show you how to put it on. [*He helps* ARTHUR *enshroud himself in the prayer shawl.*]

[SCHLISSEL *comes out of the washroom carefully carrying his brass bowl now filled with water. He goes to* THE CABALIST, *who holds his white hands over the basin.* SCHLISSEL *carefully pours the water over them.* THE CABALIST *says with great distinctness:*]

**THE CABALIST:** Blessed are Thou, O Lord our God, King of the Universe, Who hath sanctified us by His commandments, and has commanded us to cleanse our hands.

**ALL:** Amen.

[*The* OTHERS *watch until the last of the water has been poured over his hands. A sudden silence settles over the synagogue. They are all standing about now,* SEVEN MEN, *cloaked in white, holding their prayer books.* THE CABALIST *dries his hands on a towel handed to him by* SCHLISSEL. *He puts the towel down, rolls his sleeves down, takes his long shawl and with a sweep of his arms cowls it over his head, lifts his face, and cries out.*]

**THE CABALIST:** Thou knowest the secrets of eternity and the most hidden mysteries of all living. Thou searchest the innermost recesses, and tryest the reins and the heart. Nought is concealed from Thee, or hidden from Thine eyes. May it then be Thy will, O Lord our God and God of our fathers, to forgive us for all our sins, to pardon us for all our iniquities, and to grant us remission for all our transgressions.

[*As one, the other* OLD MEN *sweep their shawls over their heads and begin the ancient, primitive recital of their sins. They* ALL *face towards the Ark, standing in their place, bending and twisting at the knees and beating upon their breasts with the clenched fist of their right hand. They each pray individually, lifting up their voices in a wailing of the spirit.*]

ALL OF THEM: For the sin which we have committed before Thee under compulsion, or of our own will; And for the sin which we have committed before Thee in hardening of the heart!

For the sin which we have committed before Thee unknowingly:

ZITORSKY: And for the sin which we have committed before Thee with utterance of the lips.
FOREMAN: For the sin which we have committed before Thee by unchastity.
SCHLISSEL: For the sin which we have committed before Thee by scoffing;
HARRIS: For the sin which we have committed before Thee by slander; And for the sin which we have committed before Thee by the stretched-forth neck of pride: [*It is a deadly serious business, this gaunt confessional. The spectacle of the* SEVEN MEN, *cloaked in white, crying out into the air the long series of their sins and their pleas for remission, has a suggestion of the fearsome barbarism of the early Hebrews. They stand, eyes closed, and in the fervor of communication with God, their faces pained with penitence. The last of the old men,* HARRIS, *finally cries out the last lines of supplication, his thin voice all alone in the hush of the synagogue.*] And also for the sins for which we are liable to any of the four death penalties inflicted by the Court — stoning, burning, beheading, and strangling; for Thou are the Forgiver of Israel and the Pardoner of the tribes of Jeshurun in every generation and besides Thee we have no King, who pardoneth and forgiveth.

[*Again, the silence falls over the stage.*]

THE CABALIST. Children of men, such as sit in darkness and in the shadow of death, being bound in affliction and iron, He brought them out of darkness, and the shadow of death.

THE OTHERS: Children of men, such as sit in darkness and in the shadow of death, being bound in affliction and iron, He brought them out of darkness, and the shadow of death.

[*The repetition of these lines has its accumulative effect on* ARTHUR. *His lips begin to move involuntarily, and soon he has joined the* OTHERS, *quietly muttering the words.*]

THE CABALIST: Fools because of their transgressions, and because of their iniquities are afflicted.

ARTHUR and THE OTHERS: Fools because of their transgressions and because of their iniquities are afflicted.

THE CABALIST: They cry unto The Lord in their trouble, and He saveth them out of their distress.

ARTHUR and THE OTHERS: They cry unto The Lord in their trouble, and He saveth them out of their distress.

THE CABALIST: Then He is gracious unto him and saith:

ARTHUR and THE OTHERS: Then He is gracious unto him and saith:

THE CABALIST: Deliver him from going down to the pit; I have found a ransom.

ARTHUR and THE OTHERS: Deliver him from going down to the pit; I have found a ransom.

THE CABALIST: Amen.

THE OTHERS: Amen.

THE CABALIST: Bring the girl in, Mr. Foreman. [FOREMAN *nods and goes into the rabbi's office.*]

ALPER: [*To* SCHLISSEL.] I don't like it. Even if the Rabbi comes, there will only be nine of us. I am a traditionalist. Without a quorum of ten, it won't work.

SCHLISSEL: [*Muttering.*] So what do you want me to do?

[*In the rabbi's office,* FOREMAN *touches* THE GIRL's *shoulder and she starts from the coma-like state she was in, and looks at him.*]

FOREMAN: Come. It is time.

THE GIRL: [*She nods nervously and sits up. There is a vacuous look about her, the vague distracted look of the insane. Quite numbly.*] Where are you taking me? My mother is in Rome. They put the torch to her seven sons, and they hold her hostage. [*She rises in obedience to her* GRANDFATHER'S *arm as he gently escorts her out of the office into the synagogue proper. All the while she maintains a steady drone of rattling gibberish.*] Where were you yesterday? I asked everybody about you. You should have been here. We had a lot of fun. We had a party, and there were thousands of people, Jerobites and Bedouins, dancing like gypsies. [*She suddenly lapses into a sullen silence, staring at the ground, her shoulders jerking involuntarily. The* OTHERS *regard her uneasily.*]

THE SEXTON: Shall I take the ram's horn out?

THE CABALIST: Yes.

[THE SEXTON *produces the horn-shaped trumpet from the base of the pulpit. The front door of the synagogue now opens, and a tall, strapping young* POLICEMAN, *heavy with the authority of his thick blue overcoat, steps one step into the synagogue. He stands in the opened doorway, one hand on the latch of the door his attitude quite brusque as if he could not possibly get his work done if he had to be polite.*]

THE POLICEMAN: Is Rabbi Marks here?

[ALPER *throws up his arms in despair The* OTHERS *alternately stare woodenly at the* POLICEMAN *or down at the floor.* ARTHUR, *still deeply disturbed, rubs his brow.* THE CABALIST *begins to pray silently, only his lips moving in rapid supplication.*]

THE SEXTON: No, he's not.

THE POLICEMAN: I'm looking for a girl named Evelyn Foreman. Is that the girl? [*He indicates* THE GIRL.]

ALPER: [*Moving away, muttering.*] Is there any need, officer, to be so brusque or to stand in an open doorway so that we all chill to our bones?

THE POLICEMAN: [*Closing the door behind him.*] Sorry.

SCHLISSEL: [*To* ZITORSKY.] A real cossack, eh? What a brute. He will take us all to the station house and beat us with nightsticks.

THE POLICEMAN: [*A little more courteously.*] A girl named Evelyn Foreman. Her father has put out a call for her. She's missing from her home. He

said she might be here with her grandfather. Is there a Mr. David
Foreman here? [NOBODY *says anything.*]

**ALPER:** You are interrupting a service, Officer.

**THE POLICEMAN:** I'm sorry. Just tell me, is that the girl? I'll call in and tell
them we found her.

**SCHLISSEL:** [*He suddenly advances on* THE POLICEMAN.] First of all, where
do you come to walk in here like you were raiding a poolroom? This is a
synagogue, you animal. Have a little respect.

**THE POLICEMAN:** All right, all right, I'm sorry. I happen to be Jewish myself.

**ALPER:** [*He looks up quickly.*] You're Jewish? [*Turns slowly to* THE SEXTON.]
Sexton, our tenth man.

**THE SEXTON:** Alper, are you crazy?

**ALPER:** A fine, strapping Jewish boy. [*To* THE POLICEMAN.] Listen, we need a
tenth. You'll help us out, won't you?

**SCHLISSEL:** [*Strolling nervously past* ALPER.] Alper, what are you doing, for
God's sakes?

**ALPER:** We have to have ten men.

**SCHLISSEL:** What kind of prank is this? You are an impossible rogue, do you
know that?

**ALPER:** [*Taking* SCHLISSEL *aside.*] What are you getting so excited about? He
doesn't have to know what it is. We'll tell him it's a wedding. I think it's
funny.

**SCHLISSEL:** Well, we will see how funny it is when they take us to the basement of the police station and beat us with their nightsticks.

**ALPER:** Nightsticks. Really, Schlissel, you are a romantic. [*Advancing on* THE
POLICEMAN.] I tell you, officer, it would really help us out if you would
stay ten or fifteen minutes. This girl—if you really want to know—is
about to be married, and what is going on here is the Ritual of Shriving.

**ZITORSKY.** Shriving?

**ALPER:** A sort of ceremony of purification. It is a ritual not too commonly
practiced any more, and I suggest you will find it quite interesting.

**HARRIS:** [*To* SCHLISSEL.] What is he talking about?

**SCHLISSEL:** Who knows?

**THE POLICEMAN:** [*He opens the door* ZITORSKY *had shut and calls out to his col-
league outside.*] I'll be out in about ten minutes, Tommy, all right? [*He opens
the door further to allow the entrance of* THE *Rabbi, who now comes hurrying
into the synagogue, still carrying his briefcase.*] Hello, Rabbi, how are you?

**THE RABBI:** [*He frowns, a little confused at* THE POLICEMAN'*s presence.*] Hello, officer, what are you doing here? [*He moves quickly to his office, taking stock of everything as he goes, the* SEVEN OLD MEN *and* ARTHUR *in their white shawls*—THE GIRL *standing woodenly in the center of the synagogue.* ALPER *and* ZITORSKY *greet him with hellos, which he nods back.*]

THE POLICEMAN: They've asked me to make a tenth for the shriving.

THE RABBI: [*Frowning as he darts into his office.*] Shriving? [*He opens his desk to get out his own large white shawl, unbuttoning his coat as he does. He notes* ALPER *who has followed him to the doorway.*] What is the policeman doing here?

ALPER: We needed a tenth.

THE POLICEMAN: [*Amiably to* ZITORSKY.] This is the girl, isn't it? [ZITORSKY *nods his head a little bleakly.*] What's really going on here?

[*In his office,* THE RABBI *sweeps his large shawl over his shoulders.*]

ALPER: We have said Al-Chait and a prayer of atonement, and we are waiting now just for you.

[THE RABBI *frowns in troubled thought, slips his skullcap on as he clips his fedora off. In the synagogue,* ZITORSKY *shuffles to* SCHLISSEL.]

ZITORSKY: [*Indicating* THE POLICEMAN *with his head, he mutters.*] He knows, he knows.

SCHLISSEL: Of course. Did Alper expect to get away with such a collegiate prank?

THE RABBI: [*In his office, he has finished a rapid, silent prayer he has been saying, standing with his eyes closed. He looks up at* ALPER *now.*] I would rather not take any active role in this exorcism. I am not quite sure of my rabbinical position. But it would please me a great deal to believe once again in a God of dybbuks. [*He walks quickly past* ALPER *out into the synagogue.* ALPER *follows.*] Well, we are ten.

[*A silence falls upon the gathered* MEN.]

FOREMAN: May God look upon us with the eye of mercy and understanding and may He forgive us if we sin in our earnestness.

THE OTHERS: Amen.

THE CABALIST: Sexton, light the candles. [THE SEXTON *lights each man's candle.* THE CABALIST *advances slowly to* THE GIRL, *who stands slackly, her body making small occasional jerking movements, apparently in a schizophrenic state.* THE CABALIST *slowly draws a line before* THE GIRL *with the flat of his toe. Quietly.*] Dybbuk, I draw this line beyond which you may not come. You may not do harm to anyone in this room. [*The* OLD MEN *shift nervously in their various positions around the synagogue. To* THE SEXTON.] Open the Ark. [THE SEXTON *moves quickly up to the altar and opens the brown sliding doors of the Ark, exposing the several scrolls within, standing in their handsomely covered velvet coverings.* THE CABALIST *moves slowly back to his original position; he says quietly.*] Dybbuk, you are in the presence of God and His Holy Scrolls. [THE GIRL *gasps.*] I plead with you one last time to leave the body of this girl. [*There is no answer.*] Then I will invoke the curse of excommunication upon your pitiable soul. Sexton, blow Tekiah. [THE SEXTON *raises the ram's horn to his lips, and the eerie, frightening tones shrill out into the hushed air.*] Sexton, blow Shevurim. [*Again,* THE SEXTON *raises the ram's horn and blows a variation of the first hollow tones.*] Sexton, blow Teruah. [*A third time,* THE SEXTON *blows a variation of the original tones.*] Sexton, blow the Great Tekiah and, upon the sound of these tones, dybbuk, you will be wrenched from the girl's body and there will be cast upon you the final anathema of excommunication from all the world of the living and from all the world of the dead. Sexton, blow the great Tekiah.

[*For the fourth time,* THE SEXTON *raises the ram's horn to his lips and blows a quick succession of loud blasts. A silence falls heavily on the gathered* MEN, *the notes fading into the air Nothing happens.* THE GIRL *remains as she was, standing slackly, her hands making involuntary little movements.* FOREMAN'*s head sinks slowly on his chest, and a deep expression of pain covers his face.* THE CABALIST *stares steadily at* THE GIRL. *Then, suddenly,* ARTHUR *begins to moan softly, and then with swift violence, a horrible atavistic scream tears out of his throat. He staggers one brief step forward. At the peak of his scream, he falls heavily down on the floor of the synagogue in a complete faint. The echoes of his scream tingle momentarily in the high corners of the air in the synagogue. The* OTHERS *stand petrified for a moment, staring at his slack body on the floor.*]

ALPER: My God. I think what has happened is that we have exorcised the wrong dybbuk.

THE POLICEMAN: [*He starts toward* ARTHUR'*s limp body.*] All right, don't crowd around. Let him breathe.

THE CABALIST: He will be all right in a moment.

ZITORSKY: If I didn't see this with my own eyes, I wouldn't believe it.

THE RABBI: Mr. Hirschman, will he be all right?

THE CABALIST: Yes.

SCHLISSEL: [*With simple devoutness.*] Praise be to the Lord, for His compassion is everywhere.

[THE RABBI *moves slowly down and stares at* ARTHUR *as* SCHLISSEL, ZITORSKY *and* ALPER *help him to a chair.*]

ALPER: How are you, my dear fellow?

ARTHUR: [*Still in a state of bemused shock.*] I don't know.

THE SEXTON: [*Coming forward with some wine.*] Would you like a sip of wine?

ARTHUR: [*Taking the goblet.*] Yes, thank you very much. [*Turning to look at* THE GIRL.] How is she? [*Her schizophrenic state is quite obvious.* ARTHUR *turns back, his face furrowed and his eyes closed now in a mask of pain.*]

SCHLISSEL: Was it a painful experience, my friend?

ARTHUR: I don't know. I feel beyond pain. [*Indeed, his hands are visibly trembling as if from cold, and the very rigidity of his masklike face is a frozen thing. Words become more difficult to say.*] I feel as if I have been reduced to the moment of birth, as if the universe has become one hunger. [*He seems to be almost on the verge of collapse.*]

ALPER: A hunger for what?

ARTHUR: [*Gauntly.*] I don't know.

THE CABALIST: For life.

ARTHUR: [*At these words he sinks back onto his chair exhausted.*] Yes, for life. I want to live. [*He opens his eyes and begins to pray quietly.*] God of my fathers, You have exorcised all truth as I knew it out of me. You have taken away my reason and definition. Give me then a desire to wake in the morning, a passion for the things of life, a pleasure in work, a purpose to sorrow — [*He slowly stands, for a reason unknown even to himself and turns to regard the slouched figure of* THE GIRL.] Give me all these things in one — give me the ability to love. [*In a hush of the scene, he moves slowly to* THE GIRL *and stands before her crouched slack figure.*] Dybbuk, hear me. I will cherish this girl, and give her a home. I will tend to her needs and hold her in my arms when she screams out with your voice. Her soul is mine now—her soul, her charm, her beauty—even you, her insanity, are mine. If God will not exorcise you, dybbuk, I will. [*To* THE GIRL.] Evelyn, I will get your coat. We have a lot of things to do this afternoon. [*He turns to the* OTHERS.] It is not a simple matter to get somebody released from an institution in New York. [*He starts briskly across to the rabbi's office, pauses at the door.*] Officer, why don't you just call in and say you have located the girl and she is being brought to her father? [*To* FOREMAN.] You'd better come along with us. Would somebody get my coat? We will need her father's approval. We shall have to stop off at my office and have my secretary draw some papers.

[MR. FOREMAN *has hurriedly gotten* THE GIRL'S *coat,* ARTHUR'S *coat, and his own. In this rather enchanted state, these* THREE *drift to the exit door.*]

THE POLICEMAN: Rabbi, is this all right?
THE RABBI: Yes, quite all right.
ARTHUR: [*Pausing at the door, bemused, enchanted.*] Oh—thank you all. Good-bye.
ALL: Good-bye.
ZITORSKY: Go in good health.
ALPER: Come back and make a tenth for us sometime.

[ARTHUR *smiles and herds* THE GIRL *and* FOREMAN *Out of the synagogue. The door closes behind them.*]

SCHLISSEL: [*Sitting with a deep sigh.*] Well, what is one to say? An hour ago, he didn't believe in God; now he's exorcising dybbuks.
ALPER: [*Pulling up a chair.*] He still doesn't believe in God. He simply wants to love. [ZITORSKY *joins the other two.*] And when you stop and think about it, gentlemen, is there any difference? Let us make a supposition…

[*As the curtain falls, life as it was slowly returns to the synagogue. The three* OLD MEN *engage in disputation,* THE CABALIST *returns to his isolated studies,* THE RABBI *moves off into his office,* THE SEXTON *finds a chore for himself and* THE POLICEMAN *begins to button his coat.*]

# CONVERSATIONS WITH MY FATHER

*Herb Gardner*

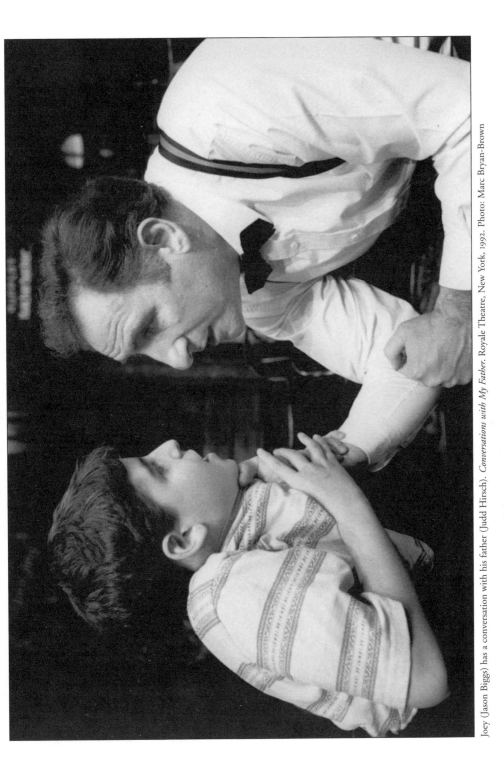

Joey (Jason Biggs) has a conversation with his father (Judd Hirsch). *Conversations with My Father.* Royale Theatre, New York, 1992. Photo: Marc Bryan-Brown

# INTRODUCTION

His national and international successes notwithstanding, Herb Gardner never really left his native New York. His plays take us from the beach at Coney Island, to Manhattan apartments, to a bar and grill very much like the one his father ran on Canal Street. His characters too are New Yorkers, high-spirited and often quirky.

Gardner was born in Brooklyn in 1934. While still at the High School of Performing Arts, he learned his way around Broadway theatres, selling orange drinks and checking coats. At 16, he wrote his first one act, *The Elevator*, which Samuel French published. He studied sculpture and playwriting at Carnegie Tech, then enrolled as an English major at Antioch, but left college without finishing.

As a designer for toy companies, Gardner claims his specialty was faces, especially noses, for stuffed bunnies and walruses. Doubting that kids really wanted cute and clever dolls, he considered creating a homely klutz that just shrugged when squeezed. Instead he drew a shaggy, large-nosed "loser," the Nebbish. It caught on, growing into a cartoon syndicated in newspapers nationwide. A cultural icon, Nebbishes turned up on greeting cards, cocktail napkins and ashtrays. When drawings like the one captioned, "Next week we have to get organized," became bulletin board fixtures, Gardner could stop drawing Nebbishes and get on with playwriting.

It was a good career move. The plays have won every major award; they have become prize-winning films and attracted actors of the stature of Ossie Davis, Sandy Dennis, Judd Hirsch, Yves Montand, Jason Robards and Paul Scofield.

Echoes of his own early history ring in Gardner's writing, beginning with his first hit, *A Thousand Clowns* (1962). Its sharp-witted and defiantly eccentric

Murray Burns quits writing for a children's TV show when, having been asked if he wants an olive in his martini, he automatically answers, "Gosh n' gollies, you betcha." Burns has somehow become the guardian of his precocious 12-year-old nephew. His unorthodox tutelage earns him the boy's devotion and the intervention of the Child Welfare Bureau. Murray also spars with his devoted brother Arnold, who wants him to deal with "the available world" on its terms. The debates between the reasonable, accommodating Arnold and Murray, the wounded but scrappy idealist, announce Gardner's dominant subject.

*The Goodbye People* came next in 1963. Seventy-year-old individualist Max Silverman, having survived a massive heart attack, is bent on making a final protest against non-commitment and compromise. He will reopen, in garish extravagance, his long boarded-up restaurant on the Coney Island boardwalk—in February. Silverman's enthusiasm for the unlikely scheme infects his discontented daughter Nancy, the only one of his children to have his imaginative impulsiveness, and Arthur, a young man (clearly a relative of Murray Burns) trying to muster the resolve to leave his job at the Jingle Bell Display Company. The project is of course doomed, and so is Silverman. But before the final debacle, he has restored Nancy and Arthur's self-confidence and their belief in even the most fanciful possibility.

Following the episodic *Thieves* (1974), which reminded some critics of Elmer Rice's *Street Scene*, the three one-acts under the umbrella title *Love and/or Death* (1979), and a collaboration with Jule Styne in the 1980 Broadway musical, *One Night Stand*, there was a hiatus. In an essay entitled, "Why I Write Plays," Gardner confessed, "It takes me so many years to write anything that I am forced to refer to myself during those periods as a playwrote." The piece appeared in the *Playbill* for *I'm Not Rappaport* in 1985. The wait was worthwhile. *Rappaport* ran for 33 months and won the 1986 Tony for Best Play; produced all over the world, it had a New York revival in 2002.

*Rappaport* portrays the mercurial relationship of two octogenarians, Midge, a black, and Nat, a Jew. From opposite ends of a Central Park bench, they swap stories and reminiscences. They also share the indignities and infirmities of old age, as well as the urban menaces that stalk the vulnerable. The action of the play reaches well beyond a remote corner of the park. It encompasses Midge's problems with the tenants of the building where he and the furnace he tends are about to be replaced by a fully automatic boiler. And it includes wildly

**414**

assorted tales of Nat's fantastic curriculum vita. "Man," protests an irate Midge whom Nat has once again hoodwinked, "You ain't even friendly with the truth." Nat's explanation of his invented personae is illuminating: "I make certain alterations. Sometimes the truth don't fit."

The truth is that Nat is an accomplished and convincing liar. Another Gardner dreamer, Nat has countered life's mediocrities and disappointments by pretending to make himself up as he went along. But clever impersonations fail to protect him against a young hoodlum who beats him up. While Nat will doubtless go on enchanting anyone who will listen to his spectacular fabrications, his audiences will mostly be at the senior center where his daughter, Clara, worried for his safety and as steely-willed as he, insists he start spending his days.

*Clowns*, *Goodbye People* and *Rappaport* set out Herb Gardner's principal themes. From the start, he has drawn dramatic power from the contest between *routiniers*, who stand firmly for compliance with convention, and uncompromising nonconformists, determined to shape life to their own measure. While the latter—Murray in *Clowns*, Max in *Goodbye People*, Nat in *Rappaport*—clearly have the playwright's sympathies, they do not triumph. Exuberant individualism is its own reward.

Nonetheless it is the oddballs who do the teaching. A parent-child relationship figures in all of Gardner's plays. *Clown's* Nick—by whatever name he finally decides to use, his uncle having encouraged him to keep trying different ones until he is 13—is never going to find his life on television. Although Max in *Goodbye People* dies before his daughter has been completely persuaded to challenge her dissatisfactions, he has passed the spirit of rebellion on to Arthur, who will embolden her. *Rappaport's* Clara claims to have abandoned the social activism her father fostered, but she betrays lingering esteem for the fiery factory worker who inspired a strike and for whom she was named.

These themes reappear in *Conversations With My Father*, but with new depth and resonance and a significant addition. Where the characters in the earlier plays are unmistakably, if almost circumstantially Jewish, here Gardner squarely addresses the challenge of being Jewish and American. He focuses on Eddie Ross, formerly Itzik Goldberg, a role memorably brought to life by Judd Hirsch, who won the Tony Award for Best Actor in the play's 402 performances in 1992.

Yiddish is an enduring, even stubborn, presence in the play, which opens with a paean to the world of klezmer, and a demonstration of the savoriness of Yiddish words compared with their juiceless English equivalents. The *lokshen kugel* and brisket *tzimmes* that Gloria (nee Gusta) prepares for the patrons of her husband's tavern appear on the menu as hot apple pie and Mulligan stew. In fervid pursuit of the American dream, Goldberg changes his own and his family's Jewish names. In the same pursuit, he repeatedly alters the name and décor of his establishment.

Unlike young Nick in *A Thousand Clowns,* and Nat Moyer in *I'm Not Rappaport* who are shopping for identities that fit, Eddie knows exactly who he wants to be — an American. He also knows who he does not want to be — an East European Jew. His foil is Zaretsky, the aged, outspoken Yiddish actor who will not let Eddie forget the pogroms of the past or ignore news accounts of deportations and death camps.

The problem is, Eddie does not know what being both American and Jewish means. Quarreling fiercely with Zaretsky, who mocks Eddie's evasions of ethnicity, he cites the fate of his own father, a tavern keeper who met a terrible end during Prohibition when his allegiance to God and the law provided no defense against gangsters. Still, Eddie does not renounce his Jewishness. Instead he makes his own "deal with God," doing what he thinks will keep Him "calm and on his good side." Thus he sends mixed messages to his son, insisting on Joey's going to Hebrew school but scolding him for wearing his *kippah* in the street. "Of course we're still Jewish," Eddie tells him, "we're just not gonna push it." But when two toughs try to muscle in to "protect" the bar, Eddie is galvanized by their anti-Semitic taunts. Turning up the volume of the Yiddish songs on his jukebox, he shows them that a Jew can be a fearless fighter.

Indeed, if any part of the American psyche is absolutely clear to Eddie Ross, it is the fighting spirit. Eddie's defiance is more literal than Gardner's earlier protagonists': Nat, who defends himself against harsh realities with confabulated identities; Murray Burns, with oddball behavior; Max Silverman, with a quixotic project. Eddie wants to do it the American way. His hero, whose name he took as his own, is the formidable boxer, Barney Ross. Eddie's natural mode is combat. Most of the conversations in *Conversations* are really sparring matches, dominated by Eddie. He encouraged his older son to be a professional fighter, only to live with guilt when the boy died a martyr's death as a sailor who would not stop fighting. Perhaps the most poignant upshot of Eddie Ross's lifetime struggle for success in America is not that he does not achieve it, but that he derives only jealousy instead of joy from Charlie, the son who does.

Sadly, Charlie too seems incapable of conversing with his son. In *Awake and Sing!*, the sweetly incompetent paterfamilias, Myron Berger, concedes, "It's an American father's duty to be his son's friend." Six decades later, *Conversations With My Father* shows us that that responsibility is still formidable. There is yet another difficulty. In his determination for recognition as an American, Eddie Ross reinterprets not only fatherhood, but also the faith of his fathers, with sad results. Charlie has no idea how to be a Jew. "No history, no memory," he laments.

Still, Gardner has remarked that there are two things you cannot stop being: a father and a Jew. The very existence of this autobiographical play affirms the sincerity of that conviction.

As these lines are readied for publication, word arrives of Herb Gardner's death. On the heels of sorrow, an irreverent image flashes in my head: I imagine that he is having an endless conversation with his father and "all the Pops back forever"—and that they are all smiling.

*Conversations With My Father* was originally presented by the Seattle Repertory Theatre in April 1991.

The play was subsequently presented by James Walsh at the Royale Theatre in New York City on March 28, 1992. The cast was:

Charlie . . . . . . . . . . . . . . . . . . . . Tony Shalhoub
Josh . . . . . . . . . . . . . . . . . . . . . Tony Gillan
Eddie . . . . . . . . . . . . . . . . . . . . . Judd Hirsch
Gusta . . . . . . . . . . . . . . . . . . . . . Gordana Rashovich
Zaretsky . . . . . . . . . . . . . . . . . . . David Margulies
Young Joey . . . . . . . . . . . . . . . . . . Jason Biggs
Hannah Di Blindeh . . . . . . . . . . . . . . Marilyn Sokol
Nick . . . . . . . . . . . . . . . . . . . . . William Biff McGuire
Finney the Book . . . . . . . . . . . . . . . Peter Gerety
Jimmy Scalso . . . . . . . . . . . . . . . . . John Procacino
Blue . . . . . . . . . . . . . . . . . . . . . Richard E. Council
Young Charlie . . . . . . . . . . . . . . . . David Krumholtz
Joey . . . . . . . . . . . . . . . . . . . . . Tony Gillan

Directed by Daniel Sullivan
Setting by Tony Walton
Costumes by Robert Wojewodscki
Lighting by Pat Collins

# CHARACTERS

CHARLIE
JOSH
EDDIE
GUSTA
ZARETSKY
JOEY, AGE 10
HANNAH DI BLINDEH
NICK
FINNEY THE BOOK
JIMMY SCALSO
BLUE
CHARLIE, AGE 11-13
JOEY, AGE 17

_Herb Gardner_

## SYNOPSIS OF SCENES

The action takes place in The Homeland Tavern—also known as Eddie Goldberg's Golden Door Tavern, The Flamingo Lounge, and The Twin Forties Cafe—on Canal Street, near Broadway, in Lower Manhattan.

## ACT ONE

**SCENE 1:** June 25, 1976, early evening.
**SCENE 2:** July 4, 1936, early morning.

## ACT TWO

**SCENE 1:** July 3, 1944, early morning.
**SCENE 2:** About seven that evening.
**SCENE 3:** August 8, 1945, early morning.
**SCENE 4:** October 15, 1965, early morning.
**SCENE 5:** About eight weeks later, early morning.
**SCENE 6:** June 25, 1976, early evening.

# ACT ONE

**SCENE:** *The interior of The Homeland Tavern on Canal Street near Broadway in Lower Manhattan, June 25, 1976. Although the place is obviously very old, some attempt had been made at one time to give it an Old Tavern style in addition. The original patterned-tin ceiling is there, the pillared walls, the scarred oak bar; the leaded-glass cabinets, the smoked mirror behind the bar; the high-backed wooden booths with their cracked leather seats, the battered and lumbering ceiling fans; but someone has tried to go Old one better here, a kind of Ye Olde Tavern look—a large, dusty Moose head has been placed above the mirror; its huge eyes staring into the room; an imitation antique Revolutionary War musket and powder horn hang on the wall over one of the booths, and over three others are a long-handled fake-copper frying pan, a commander's sword in a rusty scabbard, and a cheaply framed reproduction of "Washington Crossing the Delaware"; a large copy of the Declaration of Independence, with an imitation-parchment-scroll effect and a legend at the bottom saying "A Gift for You from Daitch's Beer," hangs on the back wall next to the pay phone, its text covered with phone numbers; a battle-scarred Old Glory print is tacked up over the yellow "Golden Door" of the entrance and a dozen copies of old oil lamps have been placed about the room with naked light bulbs stuck in them. But the genuinely old stuff is in disrepair—absent panes in the glass panels, missing slats in the booths, gaps in the ceiling design, blades gone from the fans, moth-holes in the Moose-hide, dents in the pillars, the thick heating and water pipes acned by age and too many paint jobs—and the fake old stuff is just too clearly fake and second hand, so the final effect of the place is inescapably shabby. Somehow though, there is still something warm, colorful, and neighbor-hood-friendly about the place; you'd want to hang around in it.*

*The bar runs along the left wall and the four booths run along the right, a few tables and chairs at center: The entrance is down left at the end of the bar; and on the wall behind the bar is a very large but not very good oil painting of four men playing poker and smoking cigars, one of them wearing a green eyeshade. Dozens*

*Herb Gardner* 

*of photographs of Boxers and Performers— the ones of* BENNY LEONARD, BARNEY ROSS *and* EDDIE CANTOR *are autographed— have been taped up around the mirror; as has the December 6, 1933, front page of* The New York Times *heralding the end of Prohibition; a large photo of Franklin D. Roosevelt, a cigarette holder clenched in his broad smile, hangs in a fancy frame over the cash register: Against the wall up center is a glowing red, yellow and orange Wurlitzer Jukebox, Model 800, a beauty; to its left a door with a small circular window opens into the tiny bar-kitchen, and to its right a stairway leads up to the door of the Apartment over the bar where a family once lived.*

**AT RISE:** *Before the curtain goes up we hear the zesty, full spirited voice of* AARON LEBEDEFF, *backed by a wailing Klezmer Band, singing the beginning of an old Yiddish Music Hall song called "Rumania, Rumania"; an invitation to the joys of food, wine, romance, friendship, dancing, and more food. The song speaks of Rumania but it could be telling us about Odessa, Budapest, Warsaw, Lodz, Rody, the places of an older and better world that may never have existed but certainly should have.*

LEBEDEFF'S VOICE:

"Rumania, Rumania, Rumania…
Geven amol a land a zise, a sheyne,
Ah, Rumania, Rumania, Rumania,
Geven amol a land a zise, a fayne,
Dort tsu voyen iz a fargenign,
Vos dos harts glust kentsu krign,
A Mamaligele, a Pastramile, a Karnatsele,
Un a glezele vayn, aaaaaaaah…!"

[LEBEDEFF'S VOICE *and the bouncing Klezmer Band continue as the curtain goes up and we see that the Music is coming from the Jukebox; its pulsing colors and the glow from the open Apartment door at the top of the stairs are the only real light in the bar at first. It is early evening, June 25, 1976; no one onstage, the upended chairs on the tables and the dim, dust filled light tell us that the place has been closed for a while. The Music continues in the empty bar for a few moments*]

422

Lebedeff's Voice:

"Ay, in Rumania iz doch git,
Fun kayn dayges veyst men nit,
Vayn trinkt men iberal—
M'farbayst mit Kashtoval.
Hey, digi digi dam, digi digi digi dam … "

[*A sudden rattle of keys in the entrance door and* Charlie, *early 40s,
casually dressed, enters briskly, crosses immediately to the stairs leading
to the Apartment door, shouts up*]

Charlie: [*trying to be heard above the Music*] Josh! [*Opens Jukebox, turns off
the Music, tries again*] Josh!
Josh's Voice: Yeah?
Charlie: It's five-thirty. [*He shifts his keys from hand to hand, glancing about
the bar; waiting for* Josh; *he clearly doesn't want to stay in the place any
longer than he has to. He looks up at the Moose for a moment, then raises his
hand in farewell*] Well, Morris … goodbye and good luck.

[Josh, *about 20, appears in the Apartment doorway carrying an old
folded Baby-Stroller, an antique samovar, some faded documents, a
few dusty framed photographs*]

Josh: Who're you talking to, Dad?
Charlie: Morris. Morris the Moose. We haven't had a really good talk since
I was twelve. Find some things you want?
Josh: [*coming down the stairs*] Great stuff, Dad, great stuff up there. History,
history. Grandma's closet, just the *closet*, it was like her own Smith*sonian*
in there. [*Putting objects on table*] You sure you don't want *any* of this?
[*Opens Stroller; places it near bar*] Look at this; perfect.
Charlie: Seems a little small for me, Josh. [*Reaches briskly behind bar for
bottle of cold Russian vodka, knowing exactly where to find it, fills shot-glass*]
Josh: Dad, believe me—some of the stuff upstairs, you really ought to take
a look before I pack it up. Some extraordinary *things*, Dad—wonderful
brown photographs full of people looking like *us*—some great old books,
Russian, Yiddish—

CHARLIE: [*briskly*] It's all yours, kid. Whatever you can fit in your place. And anything down here; including Morris. Only the basic fixtures are included in the sale.

JOSH: [*not listening, absorbed in documents*] Perfect, this is perfect, one of Grandpa's bar signs — [*reads from faded posterboard*] "V.J. Day Special, the Atomic Cocktail, One Dollar, If the First Blast Don't Get You, the Fallout Will."

CHARLIE: [*impatiently, checking watch, pointing upstairs*] Josh, it's getting late; pick what you want and let's go.

JOSH: [*reads from old document*] "Declaration of Intention to Become a Citizen"... *Your* Grandpa, listen... "I, Solomon Leib Goldberg, hereby renounce my allegiance to the Czar of All the Russias, and declare my intention to —"

CHARLIE: [*cutting him off*] Got the station wagon right out front; pack it up, let's move.

JOSH: I don't get it; only a month since Grandma died, why does the place have to be sold so fast?

CHARLIE: Leave a bar closed too long it loses its value. Customers drift away. That's how it works. Deal's almost set. [*Points upstairs*] Come on, Josh, let's —

JOSH: I don't get it, I just don't get it... [*Going up stairs*] What difference would another *week* make? What's the hurry, what's the *hurry* here, man...? [*He exits into Apartment.* CHARLIE *sits at bar; then looks up at Moose*]

CHARLIE: He wants to know what's the hurry here, Morris.

[*Silence for a moment,* CHARLIE *lost in thought; the Jukebox glowing brighter as we hear the sudden sound of a full Chorus and Marching Band doing a thunderous rendition of "Columbia, the Gem of the Ocean"*]

CHORUS AND BAND: [*from Jukebox*]

"Three cheers for the red, white and blue,
Three cheers for the red, white and blue,
The Army and Navy forever,
Three cheers for the red, white and blue..."

[*All stage lights, one section after the other, coming up full now in strict cadence to the trumpets, drums and Chorus: the many fake oil lamps, the overheads, the bar-lights, the dawn-light from the street, all coming up in tempo to reveal an image of rampant patriotism only dimly perceived in earlier shadow—red, white and blue crepe bunting hung across the full length of the bar-mirror and on the back of each booth, and several dozen small American flags on gold-painted sticks placed everywhere about the room; the trumpets building, the ceiling fans spinning, as* EDDIE GOLDBERG, *a man in his early 40s who moves like an ex-boxer; bursts out of the Kitchen, a swath of bunting across his shoulders, a batch of foot-high flags in one hand and an individual flag in the other; waving them all to the Music. July Fourth, 1936, and* EDDIE GOLDBERG *have arrived suddenly and uninvited—*CHARLIE *turning slowly from the bar to watch him.* EDDIE *wears a fine white shirt, black bow tie, sharp black pants and noticeably polished shoes—an outfit better suited to an Uptown cocktail lounge than to this Canal Street gin mill. He parks the batch of flags on a nearby table, drapes the bunting with a grand flourish across the Stroller; sticks the individual flag onto the hood—all these movements in strict time to the powerful March Music that continues to blare out of the Jukebox, his spirits rising with the soaring finale of the record, circling the Stroller once and finishing with a fancy salute to the Kid within, kneeling next to the Stroller as the record comes to a trumpet-blasting, cymbal-crashing end*]

CHORUS AND BAND: [*continued*]

"When borne by the red, white and blue,
When borne by the red, white and blue,
Thy banners make tyranny tremble,
When borne by the red, white and blue!"

EDDIE: [*he points to the Moose*] Moose. See? See the nice Moose? Moose, that's an easy one. An "M" at the beginning, "MMMM," and then "OOOO"; Moose. Mmmmooooose. See the pretty Moose? Just look at the Moose. Moose. [*He waits. Silence from the Stroller*] Forget the Moose. We'll wait on the Moose. "Duckie." Hey, how about "duckie"? You had "duckie" last

**425**

Saturday, you had it down cold. "Duckie." [*Reaches under Stroller; takes out wooden duck, presents duck*] Here ya go, here ya go; duckie. *Here's* the duckie. Look at that duckie; helluva duckie, hah? Hah? [*Hides the duck behind his back*] Where's the duckie? You want the duckie? Ask me for the duckie. Say "duckie." [*Silence for a moment; he leans against the bar*] You lost it. You lost "duckie." You had it and you lost it. Now we're losin' what we *had*, we're goin' *back*wards, Charlie. [*Starts to pace in front of bar*] Kid, you're gonna be two; we gotta get movin' here. Goddamn *two*, kid. I mean, your brother Joey—your age—we had a goddamn conver*sationalist* in there! [*Silence for a moment*] Charlie, Charlie, you got any idea how much heartache you're givin' us with this issue, with this goddamn vow of *silence* here? Six words in two years and now *gornisht*, not even a "Mama" or a "Papa." [*Grabs the batch of flags, starts placing one on each table about the room; quietly, controlling himself*] Frankly, I'm concerned about your mother. Granted, the woman is not exactly a hundred percent in the Brains Department her*self*, also a little on the wacky side, also she don't hear a goddamn word anybody says so why should you want to talk to her in the first place—nevertheless, on this issue, my heart goes out to the woman. She got a kid who don't do shit. She goes to Rutgers Square every morning with the other mothers, they sit on the long bench there—in every stroller, right down the line, we got talkin', we got singin', we got tricks; in *your* stroller we got *gornisht*. We got a kid who don't make an *effort*, a boy who don't *extend* himself. [*Leaning down close to Stroller*] That's the *trouble* with you, you don't *extend* yourself. You never did. You don't *now*, you never *did*, and you never *will*. [*Suddenly, urgently, whispering*] Come on, kid, gimme something, what's it *to* ya? I open for business in an hour, every morning the regulars come in, you *stare* at them; I tell 'em you're sick, I cover for you. It's July Fourth, a special occasion, be an American, make an effort. [*Grabs the duck off the bar, leans down to the Stroller with it*] Come on: "duckie," just a "duckie," one "duckie" would be a Mitzvah ... [*Silence from the Stroller; then the beginnings of a sound, barely audible at first;* EDDIE *leans forward, smiling hopefully*] What's that? What ...? [*The sound grows louder, but there is no discernible word, and finally what we hear quite cleary is pure baby-babble, something like "ba-bap, ba-bap, ba-bap ..."*] Oh, shut up. Just *shut* up, will ya! If that's how you're gonna talk, then shut ya goddamn *trap!*

[EDDIE *turns sharply and throws the wooden duck violently across the room—it smashes against the farthest down right booth, barely missing* CHARLIE, *who has been seated in the booth, watching.* CHARLIE *turns, startled, as the pieces of the duck clatter to the floor.* EDDIE *strides angrily over to the bar and then behind it, turning his back to the Stroller, starts to clean glasses from the sink and slap them onto a shelf as the baby-babble continues*]

EDDIE: [*shouting*] The conversation is *over,* kid!

[*The baby-babble stops abruptly. Silence for a moment*]

CHARLIE: [*to Audience; calmly, cordially*] Duck Number Sixteen; other casualties this year include four torn Teddy bears and a twisted metal frog. [*Rising from booth, moving down towards us*] "Gornisht"—in case it wasn't clear to you—means "nothing." "Gornisht *with* gornisht" being less than nothing. The only thing less than that is "bubkes," which is beans, and less than that is "bupkes mit beblach," which is beans with more beans. In Yiddish, the only thing less than nothing is the existence of something so worthless that the presence of nothing becomes more obvious. Which brings me to the story of my life … [*Shrugs, smiling*] Sorry; I can't resist a straight-line, even one of my own. I just—I hear them coming. I am often criticized for this. Oh, but they are everywhere and always irresistible: there are people who are straight-lines—both my ex-wives, for example, and all of my accountants—days, sometimes entire years, whole cities like Newark and Cleveland—"What did you do in Newark last weekend? I dreamt of Cleveland"—and some lifetimes, whole lifetimes like my father's, are set-ups for punch-lines. [*Moving towards Stroller*] That's me in the stroller there and, as you can hear, I *did* finally learn to talk—last year I even started using the word "duck" without bursting into tears—[*We hear the sudden sound of the Kid crying; he leans down to Stroller; whispers gently*] Don't worry, kid … in just a few years they'll be telling you you talk too much.
EDDIE: [*shouting*] Gloria! [*Remains with his back to Stroller; continues briskly cleaning glasses*] Gloria, the kid! Change the kid! [ *The Kid is instantly quieter, comforted by the sound of his father's voice even though he's shouting*] Gloria, the kid! Time to change him! [*Then, louder*] For another kid! [*Turns towards stairway*] Gloria, why don't you *answer* me?!
GUSTA'S VOICE: [*from upstairs, a strong Russian accent*] Because I only been

Gloria two and a half weeks... and I was Gusta for thirty-eight years; I'm waiting to recognize.

EDDIE: I thought you liked the name.

GUSTA'S VOICE: I liked it till I heard it hollered. Meanwhile, your wife, Gloria, she's got a rusty sink to clean.

EDDIE: Hey, what about the *kid* here? I gotta get the bar open!

GUSTA'S VOICE: [*graciously*] A shaynim dank, mit eyn toches ken men nit zayn oyf tsvey simches.

CHARLIE: [*to Audience*] Roughly, that's "Thank you, but with one rear-end I can't go to two parties."

EDDIE: English! English! Say it in *English*, for Chrissakes!

GUSTA'S VOICE: You can't say it in English, Eddie, it don't do the job.

CHARLIE: She's right, of course, English don't do the job. Sure, you can say "Rise and shine!," but is that as good as "Shlof gicher, me darf der kishen," which means "Sleep faster, we need your pillow"? Does "You can't take it with you" serve the moment better than "Tacktrich macht me on keshenes," which means "They don't put pockets in shrouds"? Can there be a greater scoundrel than a paskudnyak, a more screwed-up life than one that is ongepatshket? Why go into battle with a punch, a jab, a sock and a swing when you could be armed with a klop, a frosk, a zetz and a chamalia? Can poor, undernourished English turn an answer into a question, a proposition into a conclusion, a sigh into an opera? No. No, it just don't do the job, Pop. [EDDIE *flips a switch, lighting up the freshly painted entrance to the bar*] Behold... the Golden Door—[*taking in the bar with a sweep of his hand*]—and here, "Eddie Goldberg's Golden Door Tavern"... formerly "Cap'n Ed's Place," "The Café Edward," "Eduardo's Cantina," and "Frisco Eddie's Famous Bar and Grill"; living above it are Gloria and Eddie, formerly Gusta and Itzik, their sons Charlie and Joey, formerly Chaim and Jussel—[*a sweep of his hand up towards the Apartment doorway as* ZARETSKY *enters*] and our boarder, Professor Anton Zaretsky—[*No matter how quietly or subtly, it is impossible for this old actor to come into a room without making an entrance— this same theatrical glow is true of his departures—proceeding purposefully down the stairway to the bar now, carrying his 70 years like an award, his unseasonably long, felt-collared coat draped capelike over his shoulders, his thin cigarette held elegantly, Russian-style, between his thumb and forefinger*]— formerly of Odessa's Marinsky Theatre and the Second Avenue Yiddish Classic Art Players; now, in leaner times, appearing solo and at club meeting as *all* of the Second Avenue Yiddish Classic Art Players, some ascribing this to the Depression and others to the inconvenience of having to work on a stage cluttered by other actors.

[*As* ZARETSKY *arrives at the bar,* EDDIE, *without turning to him, and clearly enacting the ritual of many mornings, briskly pours half a tumbler of straight vodka, places it behind himself on the bar, still without turning, and quickly resumes his busy preparations.* ZARETSKY, *with a sweep of his arm and a sharp flick of his wrist, downs the vodka in one efficient swallow; he places the empty tumbler with a snap on the bar; pauses a moment — then lets go with a truly hair-raising, shattering, siren-like scream of pain. The scream, obviously part of the ritual, is in no way acknowledged by* CHARLIE, *the Kid in the Stroller,* EDDIE — *who continues with his back to* ZARETSKY — *or* ZARETSKY *himself. Silence again for a moment or two*]

ZARETSKY: [*elegant Russian accent, to* KID IN STROLLER *and* EDDIE] Chaim, Itzik, God had two great ideas: beautiful women, and how to drink a potato.

[*He crosses briskly to his usual table at center; opens his newspaper — one of several Yiddish journals he carries with him along with an old carpetbag-style valise — and sits deep into his chair and a world of his own, encircled by his morning vodka and* The Jewish Daily Forward; *all this as* CHARLIE *moves towards the stairway, looks up at Apartment, continues talking*]

CHARLIE: Very important distinction between living behind your store and living *above* it — two years ago we'd made the big move from "living in back" on Rivington to "living over" on Canal; surely goodness and mercy and the Big Bucks would soon be following us.

ZARETSKY: [*not looking up from paper*] For those interested, from today's *Jewish Daily Forward,* an item: "Yesterday morning in Geneva, Stefan Lug, a forty-eight-year-old Jewish journalist from Prague, stood up in the midst of a League of Nations meeting, pulled an automatic pistol from his briefcase, shouted 'Avenol, Avenol,' and shot himself in the chest. In his briefcase a letter to Secretary General Joseph Avenol stating that he has killed himself publicly to awaken the League's conscience to the plight of the Jews in the Reich." [*Silence; waits for response, then turns page*] I thank you all for your attention.

EDDIE: [*slaps the bar with his towel*] O.K., Charlie, I know what's *up*, I know what you're *doin'* ... [*Turns to Stroller; smiling*] And I *like* it! [*Approaching Stroller with diaper and towel*] You're *my kid* and you're not gonna say what you gotta say till you're damn good and *ready*. So I say *this* to you — don't let nobody push you around, and I include *myself* in that remark; got it? Because I would be tickled pink if the first goddamn sentence you ever said was: "Charlie Goldberg don't take shit from *nobody!*" [*Taking dirty diaper out of Stroller*] O.K., now I see you got a hold of your dick there. This don't bother me, be my guest. There's many schools of thought on grabbing your dick, pro and con. Me, I'm pro. I say, go to it, it's *your dick*. What you hope for is that someday some kind person out there will be as interested in it as you are. What you got a hold of there is optimism itself, what you got there in your hand is blind hope, which is the best kind. [*Grips edge of Stroller*] Everybody says to me, "Hey, four bars into the toilet, *enough, forget* it, Eddie — a steady job tendin' *bar*; Eddie, maybe managin' a class place" — I say, "I don't work for *nobody*, baby, this ain't no employee's personality; I sweat, but I sweat for my *own*." [*Deposits slug in Jukebox, making selection*] And I ain't talking about no gin-mill, kid, I ain't talkin' about saloons and stand-up bars — I'm talkin' about what we got *here*, Charlie ... I'm talkin' about America ... [*From the Jukebox we begin to hear a full Chorus and Orchestra doing a gorgeous rendition of "America, the Beautiful," all strings and harps and lovely echoing voices*] We give 'em *America* Charlie — [*Takes in the place with a sweep of his hand as the Music fills the room*] We give 'em a Moose, we give 'em George Washington, we give 'em the red-white-and-blue, and mostly we give 'em, bar none, the greatest American invention of the last ten years — *Cocktails!* [*He flips a switch, illuminating the entire bar area, the mirror glows, a long strip of bulbs running the length of the shelf at the base of the mirror lights up the row of several dozen exotically colored cocktail-mix bottles; he points at the Stroller*] O.K., *Canal* Street, y'say — that's not a cocktail *clientele* out there, these are people who would suck after-shave lotion out of a wet wash cloth — [*Advancing on Stroller as Music builds*] *Nossir!* The trick here, all ya gotta remember, is nobody's equal but everybody *wants* to be — downtown slobs lookin' for uptown class, goddamn Greenhorns lookin' to turn Yankee — New York

**430**

style American Cocktails, Charlie! We liquor up these low-life nickel-
dimers just long enough to bankroll an Uptown lounge—
CHORUS AND ORCHESTRA: [*a Soprano solo rising delicately as* EDDIE *kneels
next to Stroller*]

" ... Thine alabaster cities gleam,
Undimmed by human tears ... "

EDDIE: *Yessir*, that's where we're *goin'*, you and me; I'm lookin' *Up*town, kid,
Madison, Lex—I got a *plan*, see, I'm *thinkin'*—[*Rising with the lush
Soprano*] because there's only two ways a Jew *gets* Uptown; wanna get outa
here, kid, you gotta *punch* your way out or *think* your way out. You're
Jewish you gotta be smarter than everybody else; or cuter or faster or
funnier. Or tougher. Because, basically, they want to kill you; this is true
maybe thirty, thirty-five hundred years now and is not likely to change
next Tuesday. It's not they don't want you in Moscow, or Kiev, or Lodz,
or Jersey City: it's the earth, they don't want you on the *earth* is the
problem; so the trick is to become necessary. If they need you they don't
kill you. Naturally, they're gonna hate you for needing you, but that beats
they don't need you and they kill you. Got it? [*His arms spread wide in
conclusion*] This, kid ... is the whole story.
CHORUS AND ORCHESTRA: [*Full Chorus and Strings as the Music comes to a
lush finale*]

" ... From sea to shining sea!"

ZARETSKY: [*not looking up from newspaper*] Itzik, the only Jew in this room
being persecuted is two years old.
EDDIE: You, Actor; quiet.
ZARETSKY: Fortunately, he understands very few of your dangerously
misguided words, Itzik.
EDDIE: *Eddie*, goddamnit, *Eddie!*
ZARETSKY: Please, enough; I am not feeling very vigorous this morning. You
have kept an entire household awake all night with your terrible noises.
EDDIE: Terrible *noises?* I'm up all night doin' a complete refurbish on the
place, single-handed, top to bottom; I don't hear no comment.
[*Continuing work behind bar*] Guy *lives* here should show an interest.

ZARETSKY: [*he puts down his paper; looks about, nodding thoughtfully*] Ah, yes. Ah, yes … Tell me, Eddie; what period are you attempting to capture here?

EDDIE: Early American.

ZARETSKY: I see. How early?

EDDIE: Revolutionary *War*, shmuck. From now on this place, it's always gonna be the Fourth of July here. How about that Moose?

ZARETSKY: Shocked. Completely shocked to be here. One minute he's trotting freely through the sweet green forest — next thing he knows he's staring out at a third-rate saloon on Canal Street; forever. Yes, shocked and dismayed to be here, in Early America. As am I, *Eddie*. [*He lifts up his newspaper*]

EDDIE: [*turns sharply from bar*] Greenhorn! Greenhorn bullshit! You came here a Grinneh, you *stayed* a Grinneh. *Grinneh* — you were *then*, you are *now*, and you always *will* be! [*Leans towards him*] I *hear* ya, what kinda *noise* is that? "I don't feel wery wigorous" — what *is* that? Ya don't have to *do* that, ya *know* ya don't, you could get *rid* of that. I come here after *you* did, listen to me. Check the patter. I read Winchell, I go to the movies, I know the score —

[*During these last few moments,* GUSTA *has entered from the Apartment above and stopped about halfway down the stairs, her attention caught by the Moose head; small, perpetually busy, near 40, she carries two large pots of just-cooked food, each about a third of her size*]

GUSTA: Eddie, there's an animal on the wall.

EDDIE: It's a Moose.

GUSTA: All right, I'll believe you; it's a Moose. Why is it on the wall?

EDDIE: For one thing, it's a Moose *head* —

GUSTA: Believe me, I didn't think the rest of it was sticking out into Canal Street.

CHARLIE: Hey … she's actually *funny* … [*To* EDDIE] *Laugh*, will ya?

GUSTA: [*crossing quickly to Kitchen*] My favorite, personally, was "Cap'n Ed's Place"; I liked those waves you painted on the mirror, and your sailor hat, *that* was a beauty.

EDDIE: *Captain's* hat, it was a *Captain's* hat — [*Quietly, to Stroller*] Why do I talk to her? Why? *Tell* me. Do *you* know?

GUSTA: [*chuckling, setting pots down on stove*] Meanwhile, I see so far nobody showed up for the Revolution.

EDDIE: Because we ain't *open* yet! *Eight* o'clock, that's the law, I stick to the rules. [*Points to framed Roosevelt photo*] Like F. D. R. says, in that way he's got—"It is by strict adherence to the rules that we shall avoid descent to the former evils of the saloon."

GUSTA: [*indicates F. D. R. photo*] Look at that smile, the man him*self* is half-drunk mosta the time. Your Roosevelt, he says, "There is nothing to fear but fear itself." What, that's not *enough?*

EDDIE: Not another *word*—not another word against the man in my place!

GUSTA: [*approaching Stroller with bit of food on stirring spoon, singing softly, an old Yiddish lullaby*]

"Oif'n pripitchok, brent a faieril,
Un in shtub iz heys,
Un der rebe lerent kleyne kinderlach
Dem alef beys … "

CHARLIE: [*at Kitchen, inhaling the memory*] That food … Brisket Tzimmes, Lokshen Kugel …

GUSTA: [*sitting next to Stroller; gently*]

"Zetje kinderlach, gedenktje taiere,
Voseer lerent daw … "

[ZARETSKY *starts to hum along with her*]

"Zogtje noch amol, un take noch amol,
Kometz alef aw … "

EDDIE: Hey, you people want lullabies, what the hell's wrong with "Rock-a-bye Baby"? A good, solid, American hit—

GUSTA: [*softly, reaching spoon into Stroller*]

"Zogtje noch amol, un take noch amol,
Kometz alef aw … "

CHARLIE: [*softly, kneeling near her*] She's young … she's so young …

**433**

GUSTA: [*smiling sweetly*] Now sing along with me, darling; just "Alef aw" ... [*Singing,* CHARLIE *behind her urging the Kid to respond*] "Kometz alef aw ... alef aw ... " [*No response; she shrugs*] A shtik fleysh mit oygen. [*Goes back to Kitchen*]

CHARLIE: My mother has just referred to me as "a piece of meat with two eyes."

EDDIE: That's why the kid don't talk, he don't know what *language* to speak!

GUSTA: [*laughing to herself, stacking dishes on bar*] Eddie, Ethel called me with two good ones this morning — I mean, *good* ones —

EDDIE: Not now, Gloria, Gimme the Specials. [*Turns to blackboard over bar marked "Today's Specials," picks up chalk*]

GUSTA: So this old Jewish mama, lonely, a widow — her fancy son can't be bothered, sends her a parrot to keep her company —

EDDIE: The *Specials*, Gloria —

GUSTA: This is a five-hundred-dollar parrot, speaks six languages, including Russian and Yiddish —

EDDIE: The pots, the pots, what's in the *pots?!*

GUSTA: A week goes by, he don't hear from her, calls up, "Mama, did you get the parrot?" "Yes," she says, "thank you, Sonny; *delicious.*" [*Breaks up, laughing happily, turns heat down under pots*] Eddie, you want the Specials?

EDDIE: [*to Stroller*] Come on, Charlie, *tell* me, why do I ... ? Yeah.

GUSTA: O.K., in the big pot, Brisket Tzimmes with honey, carrot, sweet potato, a dash raisins.

EDDIE: [*writing in bold letters on blackboard*] "Mulligan Stew."

GUSTA: [*removing apron*] Next to it, still simmering, we got Lokshen Kugel with apple, cinnamon, raisin, a sprinkle nuts.

EDDIE: [*thinks a minute, then writes*] "Hot Apple Pie."

CHARLIE: [*whispering*] No, Pop ... no ...

GUSTA: [*taking school notebook from shelf near phone*] Now I go to Mr. Katz. Don't forget, in a half-hour, you'll turn me off the Lokshen please.

EDDIE: Twelve *years* — twelve years of English with Mr. Katz you're still sayin' "turn me off the Lokshen"!

GUSTA: [*going to entrance door*] It's not just English at the Alliance, we *discuss* things; politics, *Jewish* things.

EDDIE: Goddamn *Commie*, that Katz; he's open Washington's Birthday, *Lincoln's, now* he's teaching on July Fourth!

**GUSTA:** He's not a Communist; he's only an Anarchist.

**EDDIE:** What's the difference?

**GUSTA:** Louder, and fewer holidays. [*Breaks up again, laughing, opens door, waves to Stroller*] Bye-bye, Charlie, when Mama comes back we chapn a bisl luft in droysen, yes?

**CHARLIE:** [*to Audience*] "Catch a bit of air outside."

**EDDIE:** *English,* for Chrissakes, *English*—

**GUSTA:** [*as she exits, laughing*] "Delicious," she says, "delicious" ...

**EDDIE:** [*shouting at door*] English—[*Turning sharply to* ZARETSKY] English! The *two* of ya, the *mouth* on ya, kid's all screwed up, thinks he's livin' in Odessa; meanwhile ya give my *joint* a bad feel. Goddamn Jewish *news*papers all over the place—what're we, advertisin' for *rabbis* here? [*Points to Jukebox*] Goodness of my heart I put some Jew Music on the Box for ya—all I ask ya don't play it business hours or in fronta my kids. Nest thing I know Jack says you're playin' "Rumania" straight through his *shift* last night. The two of ya, I swear, you're discouragin' the proper clientele here, and that's the fact of the matter. Jews don't drink; this is a law of nature, a law of nature and of commerce. [*He slaps the bar with finality; then resumes his work. Silence for a moment*]

**ZARETSKY:** [*singing, from behind his newspaper, a thick brogue*]

"Oh, Danny Boy,
The pipes, the pipes are callin' ..."

**EDDIE:** [*leans forward on bar*] Damn *right,* Mister—damn *right* that's who drinks! You can't sell shoes to people who ain't got no *feet,* pal!

**ZARETSKY:** [*singing*]

"From glen to glen ..."

**EDDIE:** Hey, far *be* it! Far be it from me to discuss makin' a living! [*Coming out from behind bar*] What's that foreign mouth been *gettin'* you, Zaretsky? A once-a-month shot in the Mountains puttin' retired Yiddlach to sleep with old Sholem Aleichem stories? *Pushkin* for the Literatniks? What? When's the last time you saw somebody in a Yiddish theater under a hundred who wasn't dragged there by his Zayde? Read the handwritin' on the goddamn *marquee,* amigo; it's *over.* Gotta give 'em what they *want,* see. That's the Promised Land, pal—find out what they want and *promise* it to them. [*Takes frozen vodka from under bar*] Yessir—[*Pouring half-glass; to Stroller*] A toast to that, Charlie!

CHARLIE: Pop never drank—except to propose a toast, and that toast was always to the same thing...

EDDIE: [*holding glass aloft, towards front door*] The new place, Charlie... to today, the Openin' Day... I lift my lamp beside the Golden Door; bring me your tired, your poor, your drinkers, your winos, your alkies, your—

ZARETSKY: [*lowers his newspaper*] I knew a man once, Itzik Goldberg, with the colors of Odessa and the spirit of a Jew, and I saw this man turn white before my eyes, white as milk—Grade A, pasteurized, homogenized, American *milk!*

EDDIE: [*softly, to Stroller*] Very sad, Charlie; a dyin' man with a dead language and no place to go. [*Downs vodka, turns sharply, shouting*] Check me out, Actor—current cash problems I gotta *tolerate* your crap—soon as this place hits you're out on the *street,* inside a year you're sleepin' in *sinks,* baby; this is a *warning!* [*Slaps glass down*]

ZARETSKY: [*shouting, fiercely*] And a warning to *you,* sir; I shall no longer countenance these threats!

CHARLIE: This exchange, a holler more or less, took place every day, except Sunday, at approximately seven-fifteen A.M. After which, they would usually—[*Sees his father pouring another vodka;* CHARLIE *is suddenly anxious*] Oh, shit, another one...

EDDIE: [*downs second vodka; then, quietly, to Stroller*] Hey, y'know, anything you got to say to me, nobody's gonna know, it's all strictly confidential. [*Takes small red ball from Stroller; tosses it back in pleasantly*] There ya go, pick up the ball and give it back to Papa. [*Silence*] Pick it up... [*A sudden, frightened whisper escapes him*] Oh, kid, don't be dumb... you're not gonna turn out to be dumb, are ya? [*Pause*] Those eyes; don't look at me like that, Charlie... [*Sits on chair next to Stroller, gazing into it*] You got your grandpa's sweet face, see... exactly, to the letter; the soft eyes and the gentle, gentle smile, and it scares the shit outa me. His head in the Talmud and his foot in the grave, the guy come here and got creamed, kid. Not you, Charlie; I'm gonna do good here, but you're gonna do better. There's two kinda guys come off the boat: the Go-Getters and the Ground-Kissers. Your grandpa, though a better soul never walked the earth, was to all intents and purposes, a putz; a darling man and a born Ground-Kisser. In *Hamburg,* in the harbor, we ain't even *sailed* yet and the kissing begins: he kisses the gangplank, he kisses the doorway, he kisses the scummy goddamn *steerage floor* of the S. S. *Pennland.* Nine hundred miles we walk to get to the boat, just him and me, I gotta handle all the bribes. Ten years *old,* I gotta grease my way across the Russian Empire, he don't know how. *Fine* points, this is all he ever knew: *fine* points. *My* grandpa, one o' them solid-steel rabbis, gives Pop a sweet send-off back in Odessa: "Have a good trip, Solomon," he says; "eat kosher or die." So twenty-six days on the boat Pop eats little pieces of bread they give ya with kosher stamps on 'em and a coupla prayed-on potatoes; *I'm* scroungin' everything in sight to stay alive. *Fine* points! Pop loses thirty pounds, *he's* a wreck but the *lips,* the lips are in great shape, the lips are working! New York harbor, he's kissin' the deck, he's blowin' kisses to Lady Liberty, he's kissin' the barge that takes us to Ellis Island. On the mainland, forget it, the situation is turnin' pornographic. Twenty-eight blocks to his brother on Rivington—some people took a trolley, *we* went by lip. On Grand Street I come over to him, this little rail of a man, I say, "Get off your knees, Pop; stand up, everybody's *lookin',* what the hell're ya doin'?" Looks at me, his eyes are sweet and wet, he says, "It's God's will that we come here, Itzik. I show my love for his intentions…" *Fine* points! [*Suddenly rises, bangs his fist on the table next to him, showing the effects of his vodka*] Goddamn *fine* points… [*Gradually turning towards* ZARETSKY, *who remains behind his newspaper*] Opens a joint here on Rivington: Solomon's Tavern. The man is closed Friday night and Saturday by God's law and Sunday by New York's—the income is brought by Elijah every Passover. Comes Prohibition, he sticks to the letter; coffee, soda, three-two beer and no booze—every joint in the neighborhood's got teapots fulla gin and bourbon in coffee cups, we're scratchin' for nickels and lovin' God's intentions. A summer night, late, they come to sell him bootleg: two little Ginzos and this big Mick hench with eyes that died. "Oh, *no,*" says Papa the Putz, "not *me.* Against the *law,*" he says—he's *educatin'* these yo-yo meat grinders, right?—he says he's callin' the cops and the Feds and he's goin' to all the local congregations to talk his fellow Jews outa buyin' or sellin' bootleg. "Do it and you're a dead Yid," says the hench. Pop don't get the message—no, he's got his *own* message now—in a week he hits every landsman's bar he can find, he's tellin' 'em they gotta respect where God has sent them; gets to five, six shuls that week, three on Saturday, he's givin' goddamn public *speeches* in Rutgers Square! A five-foot-six, hundred-and-twenty-pound

Jew has selected Nineteen Twenty-One in America as the perfect time to
be anti-gangster! What the *hell* did he think was gonna protect him? The
*cops?* His *God?* By Sunday morning he is, of course, dead in Cortlandt
Alley over here with his skull smashed in. They hustle me over there at
Seven A.M. to say if it's him; I know before I get there. When they turn
him over I don't look—it's not the bashed-in head I'm afraid of; I'm
afraid I'll see from his lips that with the last breath he was kissing the
dust in Cortlandt Alley. [*Moving briskly up to bar*] The *perfection* of it—
his Jewish God had his soul and America had his heart, he died a devout
and patriotic *putz!* [*Reflexively spashes vodka into glass, downs it in a gulp,
slaps glass onto bar. A moment; he chuckles*] So he don't get thrown outa
heaven, he gives two bucks to this place, the Sons of Moses, to guarantee
his soul gets prayed for; for two dollars they send me a card every year for
the rest of my *life* to remind me to light Pop's Yahrzeit candle and do the
Kaddish for him'; I can't get halfway through the prayer without sayin'
"Go to hell, Pop." I look at the card, I see the alley. And wherever I live,
the card comes. Wherever you go, they find you, those Sons of Moses.
The putz won't leave me be. He wouldn't shut up *then* and he won't shut
up now...he won't shut up...he won't shut up...he won't shut *up*—

[*In one sudden, very swift movement, he kicks over the bar-table next
to him, its contents clattering to the floor;* CHARLIE, *taken completely
by surprise, leaps to his feet in his booth as the round table rolls part-
way across the bar-room floor.* EDDIE, *quite still, watches the table
roll to a stop. Silence for a moment.* ZARETSKY *lowers his newspaper*]

ZARETSKY: [*raising his glass, proudly*] To Solomon Goldberg...who I saw
speak in Rutgers Square against drinking and crime to an audience of
drunks and criminals. Completely foolish and absolutely thrilling. We
need a million Jews like him. [*Downs shot, turns sharply*] You came to the
Melting Pot, sir, and *melted...* melted *away.* [*Slaps glass down*]
EDDIE: [*turns to* ZARETSKY; *quietly*] Whatsa matter, you *forget*, pal? [*Moving
slowly towards* ZARTESKY's *table*] Wasn't that *you* I seen runnin' bare-ass
down Dalnitzkaya Street—a dozen Rooski Goys and a coupla Greek
Orthodox with goddamn *sabers* right behind, lookin' to slice somethin'
Jewish off ya? Only thirty years ago, you were no kid *then*, moving pretty
good considerin'. Did they catch ya, pal? What'd they slice off ya,

Zaretsky? Your memory? They held my grandpa down under his favorite acacia tree and pulled his beard out—his beard, a rabbi's honor—they're tearin' it outa his face a chunk at a time, him screamin' in this garden behind his shul, they grabbed us all there that Saturday comin' outa morning prayers. This chubby one is whirlin' a saber over his head, faster and faster till it whistles—I know this guy, I seen him waitin' tables at the Café Fankoni—"I'm takin' your skull-cap off," he says to my brother Heshy; one whistlin' swing, he slices it off along with the top of Heshy's skull, scalpin' him. Heshy's very proud of this yarmulkeh, he's Bar Mitzvah a month before and wears it the entire Shabes—he's got his hands on his head, the blood is runnin' through his fingers, he's already dead, he still runs around the garden like a chicken for maybe thirty seconds before he drops, hollerin' "Voo iz mine yarmulkeh?... Voo iz mine yarmulkeh?" The kid is more afraid of not being Jewish than not being alive. [*At* ZARETSKY's *table, leaning towards him*] My mother, they cut her ears off; her ears, go figure it, what was Jewish about *them?* Regardless, she bled to death in the garden before it got dark, ranting like a child by then, really nuts. The guy's caftan flies open, the one doin' the job on Ma, I see an Odessa police uniform underneath, this is just a regular beat cop from Primorsky Boulevard, and the waiter too, just another person; but they were all screaming, these guys—louder than my family even—and their women too, watching, screaming, "Molodyets!" "Natchinai!" "good man," "go to it," like ladies I seen at ringside, only happier, all screaming with their men in that garden, all happy to find the bad guys. [*Sits opposite* ZARETSKY] This Cossack's holdin' me down, he's makin' me watch while they do the ear-job on Ma. "Watch, Zhid, watch! Worse to watch than to die!" He holds me, he's got my arms, it feels like I'm drowning. Since then, nobody holds me down, Zaretsky, nobody. I don't even like hugs. [*Grips* ZARETSKY's *wrist, urgently*] The October Pogrom, how could you forget? Livin' with us two *years* now, you don't even *mention* it. You wanna run around bein' Mister Jewish—that's *your* lookout—but leave me and my kids *out* of it. [*Rises, moving briskly to bar*] I got my own deal with God, see; Joey does a few hours a week o' Hebrew School, just enough to make the Bar Mitzvah shot—same with Charlie—I hit the shul Rosh Hashana, maybe Yom Kippur, and sometimes Fridays. Gloria does the candle routine; and that's *it.* You treat God like you treat *any* dangerous looney—keep him calm and stay on his *good* side. Meanwhile ... [*Takes folded legal document from cash register; smiling proudly*] Today, today the Jew lid comes off my boys. [*Striding back to* ZARETSKY'S *table, opening document with a flourish*] Check it out, Anton, you're the first to know—[*Reads from document*] "Southern District Court, State of New York, the Honorable Alfred Gladstone, presiding. Application approved, this Third day of July, of the year Nineteen Hundred and Thirty-Six; Change of Family Name—" [*Holding document aloft*] Yessir; so long, Goldberg; as of One P. M. yesterday you been livin' here with the *Ross* family—outside, take note, the sign says "Eddie Ross' Golden Door"; shit, I just say it out *loud*, I get a shiver. [*Sits next to* ZARETSKY, *pointing to photos over bar*] "Ross," yessir—honor o' Barney "One-Punch" Ross and Mr. Franklin Delano Roosevelt, friend of the Jews, God bless 'im. [*Leans towards* ZARETSKY] Goldberg sat down with ya, pal ... [*Slaps table, stands up*] but Ross rises. [*Striding briskly up towards bar*] And he's got business to do!

ZARETSKY: [*after a moment, quietly*] You didn't mention the feathers ... [EDDIE *stops, turns to him;* ZARETSKY *remains at his table, looking away*] All the goose-feathers, Itzik. Three days exactly, the perfect pogrom; and on the fourth day, in the morning, a terrible silence and feathers everywhere, a carpet of goose-feathers on every street. The Jews of the Moldavanka, even the poorest of them, had goose-feather mattresses and pillows; and this made the Christians somehow very angry. So from every home they dragged out mattresses, pillows, ripped them open and threw the feathers in the streets; thousands of mattresses, millions of feathers, feathers everywhere and so white and the blood so red on them, and the sky so very blue as only could be in Odessa by the sea. All beautiful and horrible like a deadly snow had fallen in the night. This is what I remember. In the big synagogue on Catherine Street they had broken even the highest windows, and these windows stared like blinded eyes over the Moldavanka. And below there are feathers in all the acacia trees on Catherine Street, white feathers in the branches, as though they had bloomed again in October, as though the trees too had gone mad. And crazier still that morning, waddling down the street towards me, an enormous fat man, like from the circus, laughing. I watch him, silent like a balloon on the soft feathers, into one empty Jewish house and then another he goes, growing fatter as he comes, and now closer I see the face of the Greek, Poldaris, from the tobacco shop, and he is wearing one atop the other the suits and cloaks of dead Jews. No, Mr. Ross, they didn't catch me, and no, I didn't forget; this morning even, the fat Poldaris follows me still, laughing, waiting for my clothes. [*Turns to* EDDIE] A picture remains—a picture more disturbing even than the one of Eddie Cantor in black-face you have hung in my room. That first night I am hiding in the loft above the horses in the Fire Station and I see on the street below me young Grillspoon kneeling in the feathers before his house, his hands clasped heavenward, like so. He pleads for his life to be spared by five members of the Holy Brotherhood who stand about him— this group has sworn vengeance on those who tortured their Savior upon the cross, Grillspoon obviously amongst them, and each carries a shovel for this purpose. Now, a Jew does not kneel when he prays, nor does he clasp his hands, and it becomes clear that poor Grillspoon is imitating the manner of Christian prayer, hoping to remind them of themselves. The actor in me sees that this man is fiercely auditioning for the role of Christian for them—and these men for the moment stand aside from him, leaning on their shovels as they watch his performance. Presently, however, they proceed to rather efficiently beat him to death with their shovels. Talk about bad reviews, eh? [*Rises, takes a step towards* EDDIE] Unfortunately, you have decided that the only way to become somebody in this country is first to become no one at all. You are kneeling in your goose-feathers, Mr. Ross. *You,* you who profess to be such a violent Anti-Kneeler.

EDDIE: Go to hell, Actor. [*Turns away sharply, starts briskly stacking glasses behind the bar*]

ZARETSKY: [*moving steadily towards* EDDIE] For God's *sake,* Itzik, they had to *take* your grandfather's beard and your brother's yarmulkeh—but what is yours you will *give* away; and like poor Grillspoon you will reap the disaster of a second-rate Christian imitation. And as a pro*fessional,* I *swear* to you, Itzik—[*bangs his fist on the bar*] you are *definitely wrong for the part!*

[EDDIE *wheels about sharply, about to speak— but* JOEY GOLDBERG *bursts in from the Apartment above, speaking as he enters, cutting* EDDIE *off; a tough-looking ten-year-old, he bounds down the stairs, his Hebrew School books tied with a belt and slung over his shoulder, heading directly for his morning task— a tray of "set-ups" on the bar*]

JOEY: Hey, sorry I'm late, Pop—

Zaretsky: Jussel! A guten tog, Jussel!

Joey: A guten tog, Professor! Vos harst du fun der Rialto!

Eddie: [*anguished, slapping bar*] My God, they got *him* doin' it now too...

Charlie: [*fondly*] Hey, Joey...

Joey: [*passing Stroller*] How ya doin', kid?

Charlie: [*to Audience*] Besides me, Joey loved only two things in this world: the New York Giants and the Yiddish Theatre; for my brother had witnessed two miracles in his life—Carl Hubbell's screwball, and Mr. Zaretsky's King Lear.

Joey: [*carrying set-ups to center table, spotting valise*] Hey, Mr. Zartesky...we got the *satchel*...

Zaretsky: Yes, Jussel—[*grandly lifting valise*] today a journey to Detroit, in Michigan, there presenting my solo concert—"Pieces of Gold from the Golden Years."

Eddie: Hey, Joey, I got the *Moose* up, see—

Joey: [*a quick glance at it*] Yeah, great—[*To* Zaretsky, *fascinated*] "Pieces of Gold"...what's the lineup on that one?

Zaretsky: [*opening valise*] The Program, as follows—

Eddie: Joey, the *set*-ups—

Zaretsky: [*his arms outstretched, setting the scene*] A simple light—possibly blue—reveals a humble satchel, and within—[Joey *and* Charlie, *their arms outstretched, saying the words with him*]—a world of Yiddish Theatre!

Eddie: The *set*-ups, Joey—

[Joey *continuing absently, sporadically, to place set-ups on tables, his gaze fixed on* Zaretsky's *performance*]

Zaretsky: [*takes tarnished gold crown from valise, placing it on his head*] To begin—

Joey: The old guy with the daughters!

Zaretsky: Der Kenig Lear, of course! [*Drops crown into valise*] Three minutes: an appetizer. And then—[*removes a battered plaster skull; studies it, fondly*] "Zuch in vey, umglicklickeh Yorick...ich hub im gut gekennt, Horatio..." [*Briskly exchanging skull for an ornate dagger; a thoughtful gaze, whispering*] "Tzu zein, oder nicht tzu zein...dus is die fragge..." [*Replacing dagger with a small, knotted rope*] The bonds of Sidney Carton, the shadow of the guillotine... [*Looks up; softly*] "Es is a fiel, fiel besera zach vus ich tu yetst, vus ich hub amol getune..." [*Swiftly replacing rope with the fur hat of a Cossack general*] The "Kiddush HaShem" of Sholem Asch, sweeping drama of seventeenth-century Cossack pogroms; condensed. [*Drops Cossack hat into valise*] When they have recovered— [*Places yarmulkeh delicately on his head; directs this at* EDDIE, *busy behind bar*] Sholem Aleichem's "Hard to Be a Jew"... humor and sudden shadows. [*Removes yarmulkeh; his arms outstretched, grandly*] In conclusion, of course, my twelve-minute version of "The Dybbuk," all in crimson light if equipment available; I play all parts... including title role. [*A moment; then he bows his head as though before a huge Jewish Audience in a grand hall; he speaks quietly*] I hear the applause... [*He looks out*] I see their faces, so familiar... and once again I have eluded the fat Poldaris. He shall not have my clothes. [*Silence for a moment; then he picks up his valise, striding briskly to the front door*] Give up my Yiddish Theatre? No, Itzik, I don't think so. Yes, overblown, out of date, soon to disappear. But then, so am I. [*Turns at door*] I go now to the tailor, Zellick, who repairs my robes for Lear. Good morning to you, Jussel; and good morning to you, Mr. Ross, and, of course, my regards to your wife, Betsy.

[ZARETSKY *exits;* EDDIE *instantly intensifies his work behind the bar;* JOEY *not moving, looking off at front door; still in awe*]

EDDIE: *Fake*-o, Joey, I'm tellin' ya—fake-o four-flushin' phony. Man don't make no sense, any manner, shape or form.
JOEY: You should see the way he does that *Dybbuk* goy, Pop, he really—
EDDIE: Joey, the set-ups—what happened to the goddamn *set*-ups here! And the *mail*, kid, ya *forgot* it yesterday.
JOEY: [*picks up books*] Gonna be late for Hebrew, Pop, it's almost Eight—
EDDIE: Then ya shouldn'ta hung around watchin' Cary Grant so long.
JOEY: Ten to Eight, Pop, gotta get goin'—
EDDIE: Bring in the *mail* first, you got obligations here, Mister.
JOEY: [*puts books down*] O.K., O.K.... [*Passing Stroller*] He say anything today?
EDDIE: All quiet on the western front.
JOEY: [*looking into Stroller*] Don't worry about him, Pop; look at the eyes, he's gettin' *everything*. [*As he exits*] He's smart, this kid; very smart, like me.

EDDIE: And modest *too*, I bet. [*Alone now; he pauses for a moment, then goes to the Stroller, peers in thoughtfully*] Everything?

CHARLIE: Every word, Pop.

EDDIE: [*leans forward*] Hey, what the hell're ya *doin'*? This ain't no time to go to *sleep*. You just got *up*, for God's sake—[*Shaking the Stroller*] Let's show a little *courtesy* here, a little common goddamn *courtesy*. [*Stops*] Out. He's *out*. I either got Calvin Coolidge with his dick in his fist or he's *out!*

JOEY: [*entering, thoughtfully, with stack of mail*] Pop, the sign outside, it says "Ross" on it…

EDDIE: That's our new name, you're gonna love it; honor o' Barney himself. [*Takes mail, starts going through it*]

JOEY: You mean not just for the place, but actually our new name?

EDDIE: All done; legit and legal, kid, Al Gladstone presidin'—[*Takes envelope from mail*] Son of a bitch, the Sons of Moses, Pop's Yahrzeit again…

JOEY: So my name is Joe Ross? That's my name now? Joe Ross? Very…brief, that name.

EDDIE: [*studying blue card from envelope*] Fifteen *years*, they find me every time, it's the Royal Mounted Rabbis…

JOEY: Joe Ross; it starts—it's *over*.

EDDIE: Hey, *Hebrew* school—

JOEY: [*suddenly alarmed*] Jeez, went right outa my *mind*—[*Grabs Hebrew texts, races for door; slapping yarmulkeh on his head*]

EDDIE: *Wait* a minute—[*Points to yarmulkeh*] Where ya goin' with *that* on your head? What're ya, crazy? Ya gonna go eight blocks through Little Italy and Irishtown, passin' right through god-damn *Polack* Street, with *that* on your head? How many times I gotta tell ya, kid—that is *not* an outdoor garment. That is an indoor garment *only*. Why don't ya wear a sign on your head says, "Please come kick the shit outa me"? You put it on in Hebrew School, where it belongs.

JOEY: Pop, I don't—

EDDIE: I'm tellin' ya *once* more—stow the yammy, kid. *Stow* it.

JOEY: [*whips yarmulkeh off, shoves it in pocket*] O.K., O.K. [*Starts towards door*] I just don't see why I gotta be ashamed.

EDDIE: I'm not askin' ya to be ashamed. I'm askin' ya to be smart. [*Sees something in mail as* JOEY *opens door; sharply*] Hold it—

JOEY: Gotta go, Pop—

EDDIE: *Hold* it right there—

JOEY: Pop, this Tannenbaum, he's a killer—

EDDIE: [*looking down at mail; solemnly*] I got information here says you ain't *seein'* Tannenbaum this morning. I got information here says you ain't even headed for Hebrew School right now. [*Silence for a moment.* JOEY *remains in doorway*] C'mere, we gotta talk.

JOEY: [*approaching cautiously, keeping at a safe distance*] Hey … no whackin', Pop …

EDDIE: I got this note here; says — [*Takes small piece of cardboard from mail, reads*] "Dear Sheenie Bastard. Back of Carmine's, Remind you, Jewshit Joe, Eight O'clock A. M., Be there. Going to make Hamburger out of Goldberger — S. D." Bastard is spelled here B-A-S-T-I-D; this and the humorous remarks I figure the fine mind of the wop, DeSapio. [*After a moment, looks up, slaps bar*] And I wanna tell ya *good* luck, *glad* you're goin', you're gonna *nail* 'im you're gonna *finish* 'im, you're gonna murder 'im —

JOEY: Wait a minute — it's O. K.? Really?

EDDIE: — and here'a couple pointers how to do so.

JOEY: Pointers? *Pointers?* … I need a *shot*gun, Pop; DeSapio's near twice my size, fourteen years *old* —

EDDIE: Hey, far *be* it! Far be it from me to give pointers — a guy got twenty-six bouts under his belt, *twelve* professional —

JOEY: Yeah, but this DeSapio, he really *hates* me, this kid; he hated me the minute he *saw* me. He says we killed Christ, us Jews.

EDDIE: They was *all* Jews there, kid, everybody; Christ, His mother, His whole crowd — you tell him there was a buncha Romans there too, makes him *directly related* to the guys done the actual hit!

JOEY: I *told* him that, Pop — that's when he *whacked* me.

EDDIE: And I bet you whacked him back, which is appropriate; *no* shit from *no*body, ya stuck to your *guns*, kid —

JOEY: So why're we hidin' then? How come we're "Ross" all of a sudden? [*With an edge*] Or maybe Ross is just our *out*door name, and Goldberg's still our indoor name.

EDDIE: *Hey* —

JOEY: I don't *get* it, this mean we're not Jewish anymore?

EDDIE: Of *course* we're still Jewish; we're just not gonna push it.

JOEY: [*checking watch*] Jeez — three minutes to Eight, Pop, takes five to get there, he's gonna think I'm chicken — [*Starts towards door*]

EDDIE: *One* minute for two pointers; let 'im wait, he'll get anxious —

JOEY: He's *not anxious*, Pop, I promise ya —

**445**

EDDIE: Now, these pointers is based on my observations o' your natural talents: the bounce, the eye, the smarts—
JOEY: [*protesting*] *Pop*—
EDDIE: C'mon, I seen ya take out Itchy Halloran with one shot in fronta the Texaco station; who're we *kiddin'* here? Hey, I was O. K., but *you* got potential I *never* had.
JOEY: But Itchy Halloran's *my height*, DeSapio's twice my *size*—
EDDIE: [*ignoring him*] O. K., first blow; your instinct is go for the belly, right?
JOEY: *Instinct?* His belly is as high as I can *reach*, Pop—
EDDIE: Wrong: first blow, forget the belly. Pointer Number One—ya listenin'?
JOEY: Yeah.
EDDIE: [*demonstrating, precisely*] Considerin, the size, you gotta rock this boy *early*...gotta take the first one up from the *ground, vertical,* so your full body-weight's in the shot. Now, start of the fight, right away, *imm*ediate, you hunk *down*, move outa range; then *he's* gotta come to *you*—and you meet him with a right fist up *off the ground;* picture a spot in the middle of his chin and aim for it—[*demonstrates blow;* JOEY *copies*] then comes the important part—
JOEY: What's that?
EDDIE: Jump back.
JOEY: Jump back?
EDDIE: Yeah, ya jump back so when he falls he don't hurt ya.
JOEY: When he *falls? Murder;* he's gonna murder me. Pop, Pop, this is an *execution* I'm goin' to here! I'm only goin' so I won't be ashamed!
EDDIE: There's only one thing you gotta watch out for—
JOEY: *Death,* I gotta watch out for *death*—
EDDIE: Not death...but there could be some damage. Could turn out to be more than one guy there, you're gettin' ganged up on, somethin' *special*—this *happens*, kid—O. K., we got a weapon here—[*takes framed photo of Boxer from wall*] we got a weapon here, guaranteed. [*Hands photo to* JOEY] What's it say there?
JOEY: [*reading*] "Anybody gives *you* trouble, give *me* trouble. I love you. Love, Vince."
EDDIE: O. K.; June Four, Nineteen Twenty-One, I come into the ring against Vince DiGangi, they bill him "The Ghetto Gorilla"—a shrimp with a mustache, nothin', I figure an easy win. Five *seconds* into Round One

come a *chamalia* from this little Eye-tie—I'm out, I'm on the canvas, your Pop is *furniture*, Joey. I open one eye, *there's* DiGangi on his knees next to me, he's got me in his arms, he's huggin' me, he's kissin' my face, he loves me. I give him his first big win, his first knockout. I *made* him, he says, he's gonna love me forever. And he *does*. That's the nice thing about these Telanas, they love ya or they hate ya, but it's forever; *so, remember*—[*leans towards him*] things get outa hand, you got a group situation, somethin'—you holler "DiGangi è mio fratello, *chiamalo!*" [*Grips his shoulder*] "DiGangi è mio fratello, *chiamalo!*" Say it

JOEY: "DiGangi è mio fratello, chi…amalo!"

EDDIE: That's "DiGangi's my brother, *call* him!" [*Softly, awestruck, imitating their response*] Whoa… "DiGangi"'s the magic word down there, biggest hit since Columbus, lotta power with the mob. Perhaps you noticed, Big Vito don't come around here pushin' protection, whatever. This is the result of *one* word from Mr. Vincent DiGangi. [*Pats* JOEY's *hand*] Very heavy ticket there, kid, you don't want to use it unless the straits is completely dire. [*Slaps bar*] O.K., ya got all that?

JOEY: [*starting towards front door without much spirit*] Yeah; take the first on up from the ground, jump back, and tell 'em about DiGangi if I still got a mouth left. [*As he passes Stroller; softly, sighing*] Well… here I go, Charlie.

CHARLIE: [*speaking on behalf of the silent child*] So long, Joey. Murder 'im.

[JOEY *stops at door; brushes off his shirt, stands up straighter, taller—then puts on his yarmulkeh*]

EDDIE: What're ya doin' *that* for?

JOEY: This'll drive 'im crazy. [*Flings open door; darts off into street, racing past* HANNAH DI BLINDEH *and* NICK, *a matching pair of ragged, aging alcoholics who have been standing in the threshold; they are early morning drinkers who have clearly been waiting at the door for the bar to open, anxious for their first shot of the day. We hear* JOEY's *voice as he races down the street*] They're here, Pop.

EDDIE: [*looks up*] Ah… Fred and Ginger. [*Checks pocket watch*] Eight o'clock; on the button. Dance right in, kids.

CHARLIE: [*gradually remembering, as they enter*] Jesus, it's *them*… Of course, of course… no day could begin without them…

[HANNAH, *near sixty, Russian, and obviously sightless, wears faded, oddly elegant, overly mended clothing that may have been fashionable thirty years earlier:* NICK'S *bushy white beard and matted hair make it hard to read his age, anywhere between early 50s and late 60s depending on the time of day; he has a soiled, ill-fitting suit and shirt, what had once been a tie, a noticeably red nose, and a clear case of the pre-first-drink shakes. During the minute or so of* CHARLIE'S *next speech,* HANNAH, NICK *and* EDDIE *will go through the very specific steps of their morning ritual. Before they reach their assigned bar-stools,* EDDIE *will have dropped a piece of lemon peel into a stemmed glass, filled it halfway with cold vodka and placed it in front of one stool, then snapped a neat row of three shotglasses down in front of the other; briskly filling each with straight bourbon. With due courtliness,* NICK *will escort* HANNAH *to the bar; pull out her stool for her; not sit till she is seated; then she will finish her vodka in three separate delicate sips, saying "Lomir lebn un lachn" before each, while in exactly the same tempo,* NICK *says "You bet" in response to each of her toasts and downs his row of bourbon shots, his shakes vanishing with the contents of the third glass,* HANNAH *finally sighing "Nit do gedacht" as she sets her empty glass down to end the first round; all this beginning and ending with the following speech,* CHARLIE *thoughtful, remembering, as he talks to us*]

CHARLIE: Hannah ... Hannah Di Blindeh—meaning Hannah The Blind One; I used to think Di Blindeh was her last name—and Nick; I didn't know his last name, a problem he often shared with me till his third shot of bourbon—

HANNAH: Lomir lebn un lachn—

NICK: You bet—

CHARLIE: Called "Nick" because, by his sixth shot, he believed—or would like *you* to believe, I was never sure which—that he was, in fact, Santa Claus; you can see the resemblance. In any case, this was an identity preferable to that of forcibly retired police sergeant; it seems that, in celebration of Repeal Day, Nick had managed to shoot out all the street-lamps in front of the Twenty-Second Precinct. He carried this famous Smith and Wesson with him every day to Pop's bar, which allowed them *both* to think of him as a kind of guard-bouncer for the place—God knows if he could still *aim* the damn thing, but Pop loved the street-lamp story and never charged him for a drink. Pop never charged Hannah for a drink either—

HANNAH: Lomir lebn un lachn—

CHARLIE: That's "May we live and laugh."

NICK: You bet—

CHARLIE: She'd been blinded somehow on the second day of the October Pogrom; Hannah didn't remember what she saw that second day, but what she heard still woke her up every morning like an alarm clock—

HANNAH: Lomir lebn un lachn—

CHARLIE: The noise didn't go away till she finished her first vodka.

HANNAH: [*sets her glass down*] Nit do gedacht.

CHARLIE: "May it never happen here."

NICK: [*sets down his third shot-glass*] You bet.

HANNAH: [*same Russian accent as* GUSTA, *as she "looks" about*] Something different here, Itzik. I got a feeling... no more "Frisco Eddie's."

EDDIE: Right; I love you, Hannah—it took *you* to notice.

HANNAH: "Frisco Eddie's"—gone. This includes the Chuck-a-luck wheel, Eddie?

NICK: Yeah; he's got a kinda... museum here now.

HANNAH: A shame; I *liked* that Chuck-a-luck wheel. But a museum, that's unusual. This could be something. The child, Eddie; he speaks yet?

EDDIE: Well, fact is—

HANNAH: [*fondly*] Vet meshiach geboyrn vern mit a tog shpeter.

CHARLIE: "So the Messiah will be born a day later."

NICK: You bet.

HANNAH: Gentlemen—today's Number: I am considering seriously, at this time, betting Number Seven-Seven-Six; this in honor of Our Founding Fathers. Comments, please.

NICK: Seven-Seven-Six it *is;* a fine thought, Hannah.

HANNAH: Next, we make the horse selections. You have brought the sheet, Nick?

NICK: [*takes Racing Form from pocket*] At the ready, darlin'.

HANNAH: Excellent. [*As* NICK *escorts her to their table*] Until such day, which is likely never, they make a Braille Racing Form, you and me is buddies, Nick.

NICK: Longer than that, sweetheart, longer than that...

[FINNEY THE BOOK *suddenly bursts into the room—a tight, tiny bundle of 45-year-old Irish nerves under a battered Fedora, he heads straight for his special upstage booth near the wall—phone. Usually*

**449**

*anxious, depressed and fidgety, he seems in particularly bad shape today; the sound of Nineteen -Thirties Irish New York and the look of Greek tragedy*]

**EDDIE:** Hey, Finney!

**NICK:** Mornin', Finn'.

**CHARLIE:** [*fondly, as* FINNEY *enters booth*] Ah, Finney ... our Bookmaker In Residence; Finney The Book arrives at his office, ready to take bets on the Daily Number, and an occasional horse — early today but tragic as ever, having given up on the Irish Rebellion twenty years ago for a cause with even worse odds ...

**FINNEY:** [*slumps in booth*] Oh, me friends ... me friends ... Nick, Eddie, Hannah ... truly the Tsouris is on me this day!

**HANNAH:** Finney, darling ... what *is* it ?

**FINNEY:** What is it? What is it, y' say? It's the bloody July *Fourth,* is what it is! Every bloody Greenhorn from here to the river bettin' Seven-Seven-Six, every bloody Guinea, Mick, Jew and China-boy bettin' the Independence! [*Rising solemnly in his booth*] "Finney, Finney," I say to m'self the dawn of every Fourth. "Finney, m'boy, stay in your *bed* this cursed and twisted day!" — and *fool* that I am, obliged as I am t'me regulars, I hit the bloody *street!* It's me damned code of *honor* does me in! [*Shoves his hands deep into the pockets of his baggy suit-jacket — we hear now the jingle and rustle of hundreds of quarters in one and hundreds of singles in the other*] Four hundred — four hundred *easy* on Seven-Seven-Six and the mornin' still new yet! Seven-Seven-Six comes in, me entire Mishpocheh's eatin' *toast* for a year! [*Suddenly aware of the dozens of American flags about him*] And what have ya got *here*, Eddie, me bloody *funeral* arrangements?! My God, man, the only thing missin's a bloody fife and drum to march me to me grave!

**NICK:** [*pointing to phone*] Well, you'd best start layin' off some bets then, Thomas —

**FINNEY:** Every damn Book in the *city's* tryin' to lay off the same bloody number, boy! Tom Finney, what's to *become* of ya? Finney, Finney ... [*Suddenly turns to* EDDIE] And while we're on it, Edward — even I do survive this day — I can't be givin' ya no more twenty for' the use o' me booth; it's ten at best, here on.

**EDDIE:** What *is* this, *lep*rechaun humor? [*To* HANNAH *and* NICK] Man's kiddin' me, right? — his own booth, his own personal *booth* Nine till Post Time, *choice* location —

FINNEY: Edward, Edward, all me fondness, ya know damn well I'm bringin' in more pony-people who drink than you're bringin' in drinkers who'll wager — [*Indicates Stroller*] Eight-to-one the boy don't say a word till Christmas. [*Heads briskly to phone*]

EDDIE: The new *place*, I'm *tellin'* ya, it's all gonna turn around —

FINNEY: [*grabs phone*] Better start layin' off now or I'm surely gornisht in the mornin'. [*Dialing anxiously*] Home of the bloody *brave*...

HANNAH: [*handing quarter out towards him*] Finney, darling... twenty-five cents on number Seven-Seven-Seven. May you live and be well.

FINNEY: [*takes coin*] Blessin's on ya — [*Into phone*] Ah, now, is that me sweet Bernie there, the Saint Bernard himself? Finney here, and wonderin' would you care to take two hundred on — [*to the dead phone in his hand*] Star-Spangled bloody Banner... [*Dialing again*] Finney, Finney, you're sendin' an S.O.S. to a fleet o' sinkin' ships...

[*He will continue, quietly, to call several more "Banks" through this next scene; the following dialogue between* NICK *and* HANNAH *will happen at the same time as his call to* BERNIE]

NICK: [*opens Racing Form*] Where ya want to start: Belmont, Thistledown, Arlington Park...?

HANNAH: I say Thistledown; why not?

NICK: Thistledown it *is* then. O.K., first race we got Dancin' Lady, four-year-old filly, Harvest Moon by Wild Time, carryin' one fifteen...

[*They will continue, quietly and with great concentration, to pick horses for the next several minutes — both* FINNEY'S *call to* BERNIE *and their above dialogue happening at the same time as the entrance of two new customers:* BLUE, *followed a few moments later by* JIMMY SCALSO. BLUE *is large, Irish, about 50, slow-moving, powerful, seeming at all times vaguely amused either by something that happened some time ago or something that might happen soon*]

BLUE: [*taps bar*] You got Johnny Red?

EDDIE: [*pouring drink*] Like the choice; *I* got it. [*Snaps it on bar*] Now *you* got it.

[JIMMY SCALSO *enters a few moments later; sleekly Italian, just thirty, wiry, a smiler; wearing the kind of carefully tailored silk suit that demands a silver crucifix on a chain about his neck; he speaks and moves rapidly and surely but is still somehow auditioning for a role he hasn't gotten yet.* Scalso *steps jauntily up to the bar; sits on a stool near* Nick *and* Hannah; Blue *takes his drink to a distant table, opens his newspaper*]

Scalso: You got Daitch on tap, fellah?
Eddie: I got it; like the choice. [*Working tap-spigot*] *I* got it—[*Places full mug on bar*] Now *you* got it.
Scalso: New place, huh? I see the sign outside, "Opening Day." [Eddie *nods pleasantly*] I like the feel. Lotta wood; none of that chrome shit, shiny shit. And the lights: not dark, just… soft; like it's always, what? Evening here. [*Pause; sips his beer*] So here we are, the *both* of us, huh?—workin' on a holiday. Ain't been on a vacation, when?—three, no four, *four* years ago. Four years ago, February. I take the wife and the kid to Miami. O. K., sand, sun, surf; *one* day, it's *over* for me, enough. I'm the kinda guy—
Nick: [*to* Scalso, *quietly*] Do you know who I am?
Scalso: [*ignoring him like the barfly he is*]—kinda guy I am, I don't get the *point* of a vacation. You go, you come back, there you *are* again. I'm the kinda guy, I gotta be movin', workin'.
Hannah: Give him a hint, Nick.
Nick: I give you a hint; "Ho, ho, ho."
Scalso: They say, what?—"don't mix business with pleasure," right? Well, business *is* my pleasure, what can I tell ya? Second day in Miami, second *day*, I'm goin' crazy, I wanna get *outa* there.
Nick: [*speaking confidentially, to* Scalso] You better watch out… you better not cry; better not pout, I'm tellin' you why…
Scalso: Here in town, I'm up, a cup of coffee, a little juice, I'm outa the house—I can't *wait* to go to work. Saturday, *Sun*day, I don't *give* a shit. The wife says to me, "Jimmy, Sunday, we'll go to the park; you, me, the kid, we row a boat." I says to her, "Baby, I hate that shit, I'm *not* that kinda *guy*." She says—
Eddie: [*leans towards him, quietly*] Would you do something for me?
Scalso: What?
Eddie: Shut the hell up.
Scalso: Huh?

EDDIE: Shut your goddamn face. Zip it up. Can it. Button the ruby-reds. Silencio. Got it?

SCALSO: Hey, Mister, what the hell kinda—?

EDDIE: You're boring. I can't stand it. It's killin' me. That Moose up there, he's dead, it don't bother him. Me, while you're talkin' I got individual brain cells up here dyin' one at a time. Two minutes with you, I'm sayin' Kaddish for my brain. Shut up and drink your beer.

NICK: [*confidentially, to* SCALSO] I'm makin' a list ... and checkin' it twice, gonna find out who's naughty and nice ...

SCALSO: How come ya got a guy here half off his *nut*, and *I'm* the one ya—?

EDDIE: Because who he *thinks* he is a hundred times more interestin' than who you *are*. You ain't just borin', buddy, you're a goddamn *pioneer* in the field.

SCALSO: Hey, I come in here for a beer, a little conversation, I don't expect a guy to—

EDDIE: You think the price of a beer you own *one minute* of my time? [*Leans close to him; calmly*] O.K., I got two things I want ya to do for me. The first thing I want ya to do is go away, and the next thing I want ya to do is never come back. That's two things; can ya remember that?

SCALSO: [*slaps bar*] Place is open to the public, I go a right to sit here and drink my beer. Who you *oughta* be throwin' out is these two *drunks* here—

EDDIE: I got a private club here, pal. I got my own rules. You just had a free beer; goodbye.

SCALSO: This ain't no private club.

EDDIE: [*indicating bar-room*] Right, this ain't no private club; but this—[*takes billy-club out from under bar; grips it firmly*] this is a private club. It's called the Billy Club. Billy is the president. He wants you to leave.

[HANNAH *raises her head, listening;* BLUE *looks up from his newspaper;* FINNEY *turns from the phone, watching, tensely twisting his hat*]

SCALSO: [*after a moment*] Ya mean you're willin' to beat the shit outa some guy just because ya think he's *borin'*?

EDDIE: [*taps the club*] Right; self-*defense*, pal. [SCALSO *suddenly starts to laugh, slapping the bar; enjoying himself*]

**BLUE:** [*puts his drink down*] Come on, Jimmy; tell him, we got a long day comin'.

**SCALSO:** Hey, Blue, Blue, I like this guy, I like this guy... *I like this guy!* [*Still laughing;* EDDIE *regarding him stonily, tightening grip on club*] *You* are *great,* Goldberg... you are *some*thin', baby... "A private *club,* the *Billy* Club"... great, great...

**BLUE:** [*rising from table, impatient with him*] Enough now; we got alotta *work* here, boy.

**SCALSO:** [*still chuckling*] Absolutely right, babe. Goldberg... Goldberg, Goldberg, *Goldberg;* you are cute, you are some cute Jew, you are the cutest Jew I ever saw. And tough; I never seen such a tough Jew, I include the Williamsburg Boys. [EDDIE, *his club at the ready, waiting him out*] I'm Jimmy Scalso; maybe you don't hear, various internal problems, Vito had an appointment with the Hudson River, which he kept, Seranno gimme alla his Stops; bye-bye, Big Vito—bon jour, Jimmy. [EDDIE, *absorbing this, lowers club to his side*] Y'know, I seen ya box, barkeep, Stauch's Arena, I'm sixteen—hey, Blue, this was *some*thin', The East Side Savage against Ah Soong, The Fightin' Chinaman—

**BLUE:** Move it along, boy; move it *along,* will ya?

**SCALSO:** Absolutely right, babe. O. K., business, Goldberg; Vito's got fifty-four Stops, fifty-three is solid—some reason he lets one of 'em slide; yours. I'm checkin' the books, ya got no cigarette machine here, ya don't got our *Defense* System, you got a Box should be doin' two and a half a month, you're doin' seventy. *Our* records, selected *hits, thirty* top tunes a month—you take only two. [*Points to Jukebox*] Blue, what's he *got* on there? [*Slaps himself on the head*] Shit, where's my goddamn *manners*— Mr. Goldberg, this is Blue, for Blue-Jaw McCann; called such because the man could shave five times a day, he's still got a jaw turns gun-metal blue by evenin', same color as the fine weapon he carries. A man, in his prime, done hench for Amato, Scalisi, Carafano...

[SCALSO *pauses a moment, letting this sink in.* EDDIE *puts his club down on the bar.* SCALSO *nods, acknowledging* EDDIE's *good sense*]

**BLUE:** [*checking the Jukebox*] All right, he's got eight here by a fella, Leba-Leba—

**HANNAH:** *Lebedeff.* Aaron Lebedeff, the Maurice Che*valier* of the Jewish Stage—

BLUE: Then there's a couple, a fella, Zatz, half-a-dozen Eddie Cantor, some-body Ukelele Ike, Jolson, Kate Smith, The U.S. Army Band, Irish Eyes—

SCALSO: [*his head in his hands*] Stop, stop, stop, *night*mare, it's a *night*mare! Somebody *wake* me, I'm *dreamin'!* Goldberg, Goldberg, you're takin' the joie outa my goddamn *vie* here! [*Looks up mournfully, shouting*] Whatta ya think ya *got* here, Goldberg, a *Victrola?* This is a *Box,* this is *our* goddamn *Box* here, *income, income.* Weird foreign shit, hundred-year-old *losers,* and mosta the plays is your own *slugs!* Where's the *hits,* where's— [*Stops himself; quietly*] O. K., everybody calm down. A new day, a new dollar, right? [*Pacing, to* BLUE] No Butts, no Defense, shit on the Box; Vito musta been crazy…

FINNEY: [*whispering*] Tell him, Eddie; DiGangi…

EDDIE: [*whispering, sharply*] Shut up.

SCALSO: [*pleasantly, a man bestowing gifts*] O. K., new deal, we start fresh— my true belief: everybody's happy. Goldberg, item one, comes tomorrow, A.M., cigarette machine—fifty-fifty split; Butts come certain sources, the price is hilarious. Item two: Angelo Defense System—I hear ya screamin' "Protection racket, ugly Italian behavior, get me outa here!" [*Softly, almost misty-eyed*] My reply: au *contraire,* my darlin' Hebrew, a Wop and a Yid is one heart beatin' here. "Angelo Defense System" meanin' defense against every greasy hand wants *in* your satchel! The cops *alone,* whatta ya pay Christmas? Also Inspectors: Fire, Garbage, whatever— the Angel flies in. Figure what you save, one monthly shot to the Angel; words fail. [*Crossing up to Jukebox*] The Box; tomorrow, A.M., my people come, *out* goes the goddamn funeral music, the Memory Lane Losers, the Hollerin' Hebe— *in* comes forty selected hits; once-a-week collection. Finney here, business as usual; already under the wing, a Defense System who I'm affiliated. *Finale:* same split like Vito on the Box, *plus* you got a one G advance from me on your end, good will, get acquainted, my pocket to yours, this very day. [*Strides back down to bar; takes neatly folded wad of hundreds from jacket, places it on bar in front of the silent* EDDIE, *sits on stool opposite him; then flatly, evenly*] Now, some bannana-nut reason, this deal don't appeal; need I mention, things happen. The Angel come down, fly away with the Liquor License, twenty, thirty days, outa business. Things break, toilets don't work, beer deliveries slow down— [*Suddenly smacks himself on the forehead*] What the hell am I talkin'!? I gotta tell The East Side Savage birds-and-bees basics? You know the story. Gimme the Brocheh, baby; we go in peace. Whatta ya say?

[*Silence; he waits for* EDDIE's *answer as does everyone else in the bar-room. A thoughtful moment, then* EDDIE *picks up the wad of bills*]

EDDIE: [*turns to* HANNAH, *quietly*] Hannah, how about you take Charlie into the kitchen, give him a little something to eat. Brisket's on your right, some Lokshen on the left. [HANNAH, *with some help from* NICK, *wheels the Stroller into the Kitchen and exits as* EDDIE *turns to* SCALSO, *continuing pleasantly*] Fact of the matter, you first come in here, I figure you are definitely not with the Salvation Army; and this guy here, the bulge in the right jacket-pocket is probably not his Holy Bible, I say to myself. [BLUE *chuckles softly,* SCALSO *smiles*] I do *not* know you are a Seranno boy, got alla Vito's Stops now. [*He shrugs apologetically*] Not knowin' this, I do the club thing for ya, kinda demonstrate my attitude and feelings how I run my place. [*A beat; then he tosses the wad of bills into* SCALSO's *lap*] Which remains the exact same. You're boring me to death, Ginzo. [*Continues calmly*] I want your nose and your ass, and everything you got in between, *outa* my business. I don't want your cigarette machine, your records, your advice, and I want your goddamn Angel off my shoulder. I give you the same deal I give Vito on the Box, and that's *it*. And now I want you and your over-the-hill hench outa my joint instantaneous. Goodbye and good luck. [*He picks up the club, raps it sharply on the bar like a gavel*] Conversation over; end of conversation.

[SCALSO *remains quite still,* BLUE *take a small step forward from the Jukebox,* CHARLIE *rises tensely in his booth,* FINNEY *is wringing his Fedora like a wet bathing suit*]

HANNAH'S VOICE: [*softly, from Kitchen*] Pogrom … pogrom … pogrom … pogrom …

SCALSO: [*points to his silver crucifix; quietly*] This here J. C., my Pop give it to me; remind me of Our Savior, but mostly, he says, to do things peaceful before I do 'em hard; this has been my approach with you here. But you know what come to me, I listen to you? Sooner or later, tough or chicken, lucky, unlucky, Jews is Jews. Ain't this the way, Blue? Ain't this the way? Goddamn *guests* in this country, they are—they're here ten minutes, they're tellin' ya how to *run* the place … [*He puts his hand on* EDDIE's *arm*] I pride myself, makin' friends with you Jews—but sooner or later, every *one* of ya—

[EDDIE *reaches forward, gets a firm grip on* SCALSO'S *crucifix and chain and pulls him across the bar with it, holding him firmly down on the bar*]

EDDIE: You was holdin' my arm…
SCALSO: [*struggling*] Hey, my J. C., my J. C. —
EDDIE: You know us Jews, we can't keep our hands off the guy.
SCALSO: *Blue, Blue…*

[BLUE *thrusts his hand into his gun-pocket,* NICK *turns to him;* FINNEY *races up stairs, hovering in Apartment doorway*]

EDDIE: [*retaining firm grip on* SCALSO] Here's the situation: Mr. Blue, whatever you got in mind right now, a fact for ya: Nick here, an ex-cop, got two friends with him, Mr. Smith and Mr. Wesson; there's some say his aim ain't what it used to be, but a target your size he's bound to put a hole in it somewhere; 'sides which, he don't care if he kills ya, he thinks Donder an' Blitzen gonna take the rap for him anyway. [*Lets go of* SCALSO, *holds his billy-club high in the air; all in the room frozen*] Scalso, any part of you makes a move on me, I bust it with Billy. This is the situation, both of ya. Stay and make a move; or go. [*Moving up to Jukebox, watching them carefully*] Meantime, while you're makin' up your mind, I got a need to hear one o' those Hollerin' Hebes; gonna play one of my records on my Box here… [*Quickly deposits slug, makes selection; turns to face them, his club at the ready*] My personal suggestion, we go for a safe and sane Fourth.

[EDDIE'S *eyes dart from* SCALSO *to* BLUE, FINNEY *grips the edge of the Apartment doorway;* BLUE, *his hand firmly in his gun-pocket, looks over at* NICK, *sizing him up.* NICK, *still standing at the far end of the bar; slips his hand into the holster under his jacket, holds it there*]

NICK: [*quietly, to* BLUE] I see you when you're sleepin', I know when you're awake; I know if you've been bad or good, so be good for goodness sake…
FINNEY: [*whispering urgently to* EDDIE] Just tell 'em about DiGangi; we stop all this, Eddie—
EDDIE: [*quietly*] Don't need him, I got it under control. This is mine.

[*Suddenly, from the Jukebox, we begin to hear* AARON LEBEDEFF's *rousing rendition of "In Odessa" and its irresistibly danceable Klezmer Band backup;* LEBEDEFF *sings a dream of the old Moldavanka, inviting us to return to a world of swirling skirts, endless dancing, grand times till dawn in the shoreline cafes of the Black Sea and of course, the food that was served there.* NICK, SCALSO, FINNEY, BLUE *and* CHARLIE *remaining quite still, the pulsing beat of the Klezmer Band filling the silence of this tense moment,* EDDIE *starting to snap the fingers of his left hand to the beat, the billy-club still held high in his right, Music continuing to build through the scene*]

LEBEDEFF'S VOICE:
"In Ades, in Ades, af der Moldavake,
Tantst men dort a Palanez, mit a sheyn tsiganke…"

[SCALSO *rises suddenly from his barstool, going to center of room, forceful, commanding, on top of it again*]

SCALSO: [*shouting, pointing fiercely at* EDDIE] The man *marked* me, Blue; he put a *mark* on me! [BLUE *takes a step forward;* SCALSO *clenches his fists, ready to spring*] O. K., school's in *session* now, barkeep; *lesson* time; Professor Blue and me, we gonna *teach* you something…
JOEY'S VOICE: [*shouting, from street*] Pop! hey, *Pop!*

[ZARETSKY *suddenly bursts through the front door; his arm around a somewhat battered, bloody-nosed, but very proud* JOEY. *A man who knows how to make an entrance,* ZARETSKY *speaks immediately as he comes through the door; using the threshold as his stage; the Group remains frozen*]

ZARETSKY: No, not since David and Goliath have I seen such! Yes, the child bleeds, but wait till you see what this *DeSapio* looks like—
JOEY: He went *down*, Pop, he went *down*—[*Indicatin his bloody nose*] I mean, later he got *up*, but there was—
ZARETSKY: Please, Jussel, allow me—I come upon this child, familiar to me at a distance; opposing him, I tell you, a veritable *Visigoth* of a boy, he— [*His voice trails off; he becomes aware of the stillness in the room*] I feel that I do not have the full attention of this group.

EDDIE: [*quickly, quietly*] Congratulations, kid. Go to Sussman's, pick up the bread order. Now.

JOEY: Pop, I gotta tell ya —

EDDIE: *Suss*man's. *Now.*

JOEY: Christ's sake, Pop —

EDDIE: *Now!*

JOEY: [*as he reluctantly exits*] Christ's sake …

[ZARETSKY *sees the billy-club in* EDDIE'*s hand, glances at the unfamiliar figures of* SCALSO *and* BLUE; EDDIE *remaining quite still, snapping his fingers as the Music continues, swaying slightly to the beat*]

EDDIE: Anton, we got a situation here.

SCALSO: [*grips* BLUE'S *arm, urgently*] Now, Blue, *now;* place is fillin' up Look, Blue, man wants to dance; help him dance, Blue — the feet, go for the feet. I want to see the man *dance,* make him dance, make him *nervous* …

BLUE: [*after a moment; his eyes fixed on* EDDIE] Nervous? You ain't gonna make *this* boy nervous. This boy don't *get* nervous; which is what's gonna kill him one fine day. [*Pulls his empty hand sharply out of his gun-pocket, his gaze never leaving* NICK *and* EDDIE] Now *today*, Jimmy, here's how the cards lay down: what you got here is an ol' shithouse and a crazy Jew. Two and a half on this Box, boy? You give this Jew Bing Crosby in person, you give him Guy Lombardo appearin' nightly, he don't pull in more'n a hundred. Now, tell me, Jimmy-Boy, you want me to go shoot Santa Claus for a hundred-dollar Box?

SCALSO: [*urgently, commanding*] We gatta leave a *mark,* Blue, on *some*body, on *some*thing. Fifty-four Stops, this news travels; there gotta be consequences here, Blue, things *happened* here —

BLUE: *Consequences?* This Jew don't know consequences and don't care. Look at his eyes, Jimmy. He just wants to kill you, boy; don't care if he dies the next minute, and don't care who dies with him. Make it a rule, Jimmy-Boy, you don't want to get into a fight, weapon or no, with a man ain't lookin' to live. [*He turns, walks briskly towards front door*]

SCALSO: [*not moving, rubbing neck-burn*] Things *happened* here, Blue —

BLUE: Seranno ain't gonna give a cobbler's crap about this place — fifty-three Stops to *cover,* Jimmy-Boy, let's go.

SCALSO: [*silence for a moment; then, striding angrily towards* BLUE] Hey,

*hey*—how about you leave off callin' me "Jimmy-Boy," huh? How about we quit that shit, right?

**BLUE:** [*patting* SCALSO'S *shoulder*] In the old Saint Pat's, y'know, over on Prince, we used t'make you Guineas have mass in the basement. Biggest mistake we ever made was lettin' you boys up on the first floor. [*He exits. Scalso remains in doorway, turns towards* EDDIE]

**SCALSO:** [*pointing, fiercely*] O. K., now here's somethin' for *you* and *Billy* and the entire fuckin' *club*—

[*But the* LEBEDEFF *Music has built to an irresistible Freylekeh rhythm— irristible, that is, to any triumphant Jew in the room— and* EDDIE, *holding the billy-club over his head with both hands, begins to spin around the center table to the beat*]

**EDDIE:** Hey, Jimmy-Boy, you wanted to see the man dance … he's dancin' … [*Takes his handkerchief out of his pocket, extends it towards* ZARETSKY, *a gesture of invitation as old as the Music he dances to*] Hey, Actor, Actor … come, come, this Ginzo loves dancin' …

[ZARETSKY *joins* EDDIE *in perhaps the only thing they can ever agree upon, the pleasure of dancing to an old* LEBEDEFF *tune;* ZARETSKY *takes the other end of the handkerchief and, the handkerchief held taut between them over their heads, they dance aggressively towards* SCALSO, *their feet stomping to the beat,* SCALSO *backing away towards the door.*

JOEY *suddenly bursts through the door just behind* SCALSO, *shouting at his back*]

**JOEY:** DiGangi! DiGangi è mio fratello! Chiamalo! Chiamalo!

**SCALSO:** [*surrounded by two dancing Jews and a screaming child; he shouts*] Buncha crazy Hebes here …!

[SCALSO *exits into the street.* ZARETSKY *and* EDDIE *triumphant,* ZARETSKY *swirling to the Music,* EDDIE *beating out the rhythm fiercely with his club,* FINNEY *and* NICK *clapping to the beat,* JOEY'S *arms in the air, shouting*]

JOEY: It *works*, Pop! The *DiGangi* number; it works! It works!

EDDIE: Of *course* it works!

JOEY: [*proudly*] *Comes* to me, Pop, comes to me these guys don't *look* right, see—

EDDIE: Nobody messes with the Ross boys!

JOEY: Who?

EDDIE: Ross! Ross! Joey *Ross*—the kid who beat DeSapio!

JOEY: But I didn't *win*, Pop—

EDDIE: [*prowling the room with his club, his tension unreleased by* SCALSO'S *defeat*] *Sure* you won, kid, we only got winners here, *winners…*

ZARETSKY: [*points a challenging finger*] So then, Itzik, I have seen you rise from your knees—something of your spirit has been touched today!

EDDIE: [*fiercely*] Only thing got touched was my goddamn *arm*, Actor.

HANNAH: [*leaning out of kitchen*] So, the coast, I am assuming, is clear?

EDDIE: Everything under control here, babe.

HANNAH: [*standing in kitchen doorway*] Gentlemen… I got big news…

ZARETSKY: What, Hannah?

HANNAH: Gentlemen… *the child has spoken!* [*The Group cheers, but* EDDIE *cuts sharply through them*]

EDDIE: *What?* What did he say…? [*All fix on* HANNAH *expectantly as* NICK *guides her down into the room*]

HANNAH: Two statements, clear like a bell; The first, very nice, he touches my hand, he says, "Papa." [*All but* EDDIE *responding happily; he remains silent, quite still*] The second statement, a little embarrassing to repeat…..

EDDIE: *What*, Hannah…?

HANNAH: A couple seconds later, he's got my hand again, this time a firm grip, he says—clear like a bell, I tell you—"No shit from nobody!"

[ZARETSKY *applauds lustily, shouting "Bravo,"* NICK *and* FINNEY *cheer loudly, waving their hats, Joey leaps joyously in the air yelling "Hey, Champ";* EDDIE *remains silent, striding sharply away from the cheering Group, his club held tight in his fist*]

EDDIE: [*shouting, fiercely, above the Group*] And no *exceptions*…! [*Raising club violently over his head*] No *exceptions*… nobody…! [*smashing club down on center table*] nobody…!

[*The Group turns to him, startled, quite still, as* EDDIE *continues, out of control now, wildly, striking a chair, another table, killing them like Cossacks, shouting with each blow*]

EDDIE: ... nobody ... nobody ... [*Striking* CHARLIE's *booth,* CHARLIE *rising to his feet, riveted*] Nobody! ... [EDDIE *freezes with this last shout, his club held high in the air, ready to strike another blow as* ... ]

THE CURTAIN FALLS

# ACT TWO

*Before the curtain rises we hear a full Chorus and Marching Band moving up into a thunderous, rousing, next-to-last stanza of "Columbia, the Gem of the Ocean."*

CHORUS:

"Three cheers for the red, white and blue,
Three cheers for the red, white and blue,
The Army and Navy forever,
Three cheers for the red, white and blue..."

**AT RISE:** *The blaring trumpets rise in pitch to herald the final stanza as the curtain goes up.* CHARLIE *alone in the darkened bar—the dim, early evening light of the Present—seated exactly where he was at the beginning of the play, at the far end of the bar near the glowing Jukebox, listening thoughtfully to the triumphant conclusion of the Music to which* EDDIE *first burst into the room.*

CHORUS:

"Three cheers for the red, white and blue,
Three cheers for the red, white and blue,
Thy banners make tyranny tremble,
Three cheers for the red, white and blue..."

*A cymbal-crashing, drum-rolling final;* CHARLIE *continues to look into the colors of the now silent Jukebox for a moment or two, then turns to us.*

CHARLIE: [*indicating Moose*] Well—as Morris will tell you—the Golden Door Tavern did *not* get us Uptown; nor did Eddie Ross' Silver

Horseshoe, the Empire State Sports Club, or even Ed Ross' Riverview, mostly because we didn't have one. [*Inserting slug in Jukebox, making selection*] But then came the summer of Forty-Four, the heyday of Café Society and, of course, its pulsating heart — Sherman Billingsley's Stork Club. [*With a sweeping gesture towards bar*] Eddie's response was swift and glorious: Ladies and Gentleman, July Third, Nineteen Forty-Four... the Opening Day of the Flamingo Lounge.

[*A huge pink and crimson plaster-and-glass chandelier in the shape of a flamingo in flight — its spread wings, thrust-back legs and proudly arched head framed by several dozen glowing pink light bulbs — descends through the ceiling over the bar as we begin to hear the catchy bongo and trumpet Calypso intro to the Andrews Sisters' recording of "Rum and Coca-Coca" coming from the Jukebox*]

ANDREWS SISTERS:

"Out on Mandenella Beach,
G.I. romance with native peach,
All day long make tropic love,
Next day sit in hot sun and cool off, drinkin'
Rum and Coca-Cola..."

[*Music continuing, building, as lights come up full; it's exactly eight years later, about 7 AM on Monday, July 3, 1944, and we see that the bar-room has gone through a transition from general Early American to general Tropical Caribbean, the dominant theme, as always, being Gin-Mill Shabby. The Early American stuff remains but joining it now are coconut-shell candle holders and plastic pineapples on each table, crepe-paper leis hung about on hooks, an incandescent tropical sunset painting over the Jukebox, brightly illustrated placards announcing various rum-punch drinks and their "Reasonable Introductory Prices" tacked up on the walls, running across the bottom of the mirror a red and white banner reading "Welcome to the Flamingo! Opening Day!" and over the door a painting of a flamingo with just the word "Lounge" under it. EDDIE's usual Fourth of July bunting across the top of the mirror and small flags along the bar are in evidence, though the flags have not yet been put on the tables and*]

*booths. In addition, it is the summer of the Fifth Annual "Miss
Daitch" Contest and a string of six small posters, featuring a smiling
head-shot and brief bio of each contestant, hangs across the right wall
just above the booths; beneath these a bright banner states the Daitch
Beer slogan: "There Is a Difference and the Difference Is Daitch";
below that: "Vote here for Miss Daitch, 1944," and next to the far
right booth a ballot-box and a stack of ballots. All this revealed as the
Music and* CHARLIE *continue]*

CHARLIE: And tonight ... the Victory Party, in honor of what we're all sure
will be Joey's twenty-eighth straight win since he got his Amateur Card ...
[*as* JOEY, *almost 18 now, enters from the Kitchen with a tray of plastic
pineapples, places them on tables, his boxer's authority and the tiptow bounce
of his walk distinctly similar to his father's*] ... twenty-three knockouts, six
in the first three rounds, and four decisions. Got his A. A. U. card at
fourteen — two years before the legal age — by using Vice DiGangi's son
Peter's Baptism Certificate, so he's earned a very big reputation over the
last four years for somebody called Pistol Pete DiGangi. [ JOEY *turns,
heading up to bar; the back of his jacket emblazoned with a "Pistol Pete"
logo*] I, of course, was known as the only kid ever to be knocked down by
Cock-Eye Celestini — he being several years my junior, an infant really,
and visually disabled —

EDDIE: [*bursts in from the Kitchen, delighted, waving a folded newspaper*] Hey,
ya see the ad in the "Mirror" this morning? — ya see that? — top of the
*Card* tonight, Joey, top of the *Card.* "Bazooka-Boy" Kilbane, *nobody* —
goddamn *Main Event* even *with* this Mick bozo! This is because ya made
a goddamn *name* for yourself, kid! [*He moves over to* JOEY, *the two of them
sparring, jabbing, ducking, weaving about amidst the tables now, clearly a
morning ritual, as* EDDIE *continues*] Let me tell ya about Kilbane's weak
spot — his *body,* his entire body. Tonight's *pointer?* Bring some stamps
with ya and *mail* the putz home! [*Indicates radio as their sparring
continues*] *Broad*cast — broadcast over the goddamn *air*waves tonight,
Speed Spector him*self* doin' the Blow-by-Blow; *Spector.* Closin' the place
up soon as the fights start, nobody in here unless by special invite; victory
party, champagne, the works. I'd be at ringside, per usual, but I gotta hear
this comin' outa the *Philco,* kid, I *gotta.* After, Spector always does an On-
the-Spot with the Main Event Winner; gotta *hear* it, right? [*As their
sparring ends,* EDDIE — *clearly outboxed and happily exhausted by* JOEY —

*returning to set up bar*] By the way, durin' the On-the-Spot, ya wanna drop a mention there's a new class place openin' on Canal, the Flamingo Lounge, this is optional — [*Suddenly slaps his head*] Will you shut ya *trap*, Eddie?! This is *your* night, kid — don't *mention* me — what the hell am I *talkin'* about?! Would somebody *please* tell me to shut *up?!*

ZARETSKY: [*entering from Apartment*] All right; shut up. [*Moving down to his usual table, folding back page of newspaper*] For all assembled, I have here a certain item...

EDDIE: Shit, the Jew News...

ZARETSKY: Gentlemen, we have here on page twelve of *The New York Times*, amidst ads for Stern's Department Store and a jewelry consultant, an item, five sentences in length, which reports to us that four hundred thousand Hungarian Jews have thus far perished in the German death camps of Poland as of June seventeenth; and further, that three hundred and fifty thousand more are presently being deported to Poland where they are expected to be put to death by July twenty-fourth. *This* on page twelve; however — [*turns to first page*] we find here on the front page of this same jornal, a bold headline concerning today's holiday traffic; I quote: "Rail and Bus Travel Will Set New July Fourth Peak." [*Neatly folding paper*] I offer these items, fellow residents, for the news itself, also an insight into the ironic editorial policies of America's most prominent daily journal; owned, incidentally, by Jews.

[JOEY *has moved down to* ZARETSKY'S *table, clearly absorbed, as always, by* ZARETSKY'S *"Jew News"*]

JOEY: [*quietly, studying newspaper*] Jesus, the next three weeks... that's three hundred and fifty thousand in the next three *weeks*...

EDDIE: [*turns sharply from his work behind the bar*] Come on, Actor, the *truth* — what's it *say* there? That's another one o' those "Informed Sources *say*," "Foreign Authorities *tell* us" goddamn stories, ain't it? If it's true, where's the *pictures?!* How come I never seen it in *Life* magazine? How come I never seen it in the "March of *Time*," they got *every*thing! *Winchell* even! How come *Roosevelt* don't mention — if F. D. R. *believed* all that he'd be doin' somethin' about it this *minute, guaranteed!*

ZARETSKY: [*rising at his table*] Itzik, you are a foolish tender of *bars! Election* year, he's *got* your vote already, he will not stir the *pot!* He will be silent, your Golden Goy. He listens, he hears the old and horrible songs — he knows that nobody believes the Jews are dying, only that somehow Jews are making millions from the war and want it. He will be quiet, Itzik, as quiet now as the Jews of page twelve!

EDDIE: [*shouting*] Do ya *mind*, Zaretsky? Do ya *mind* if we just let the guy go and win the goddamn *war*? Is that *O. K.* with you? The man knows what he's *doin'*, pal—he does *now*, he always *did*, and he always *will*. Meanwhile, you breathe one *word* of that crazy shit durin' Joey's party and you're gonna see *my* twelve-minute version of "The Dybbuk"!

ZARETSKY: [*slams his fist on the table*] I *refuse*—I refuse, sir, to have a conversation of this nature with a man who has just spent the morning putting light bulbs in a huge pink bird! [*Turns to* JOEY, *suddenly pleasant, cordial; one of those instant transitions of which this old actor is very fond*] I am off then to the home of the Widow Rosewald, who, among other favors, now repairs my robes for Lear, and kindly tolerates the aging process, both hers and mine. And, of course, my best with the Bazooka tonight. Bonne chance, Jussel, Joey, Goldberg, Ross, DiGangi—[*patting his cheek*] whoever you are. [*Striding to the front door*] Don't worry, Itzik; tonight I shall sit quietly and cheer appropriately. In future, also, you will have less concern of my Jew News...as there are fewer and fewer Jews, there will be less and less news. [*He exits abruptly*]

[*Silence for a moment;* EDDIE *continues busily setting up behind the bar,* JOEY *studies the newspaper article,* CHARLIE *absorbed, watching all this from near the Jukebox and not his usual booth*]

JOEY: [*quietly*] I think it's all true, Pop.
EDDIE: [*distracted*] What?
JOEY: What Mr. Zaretsky's tellin' us, Pop, I think it's all true. It's *gotta* be—I mean, look at all the shit that's goin' on *here*.
EDDIE: Here is business as usual; maybe a little worse this summer.
JOEY: A little *worse* this summer?—[*Moving down towards him*] Pop, *Brooklyn*, they hit two cemeteries in one *week*. You been on Rivington lately?—Jewish stars with Swastikas painted over 'em, they're poppin' up on the walls like Lucky *Strike* ads. The Gladiators, the Avengers—*Boys'* clubs, they call 'em—they're on the prowl every night beatin' the crap outa Hebrew School kids. Grabbed a kid comin' outa Beth-El Saturday, ripped off his shirt and painted "Jew" on his chest, like maybe he *forgot*—you *hearin'* any of this, Pop?

EDDIE: [*busily stacking glasses, his back to Joey*] It's not I ain't hearin' ya, kid; it's I *heard* it all already; been goin' on since before you was born. But this stuff *Zaretsky's* talkin' about—not even in the old Moldavanka was there ever such.

JOEY: But if it's true—

EDDIE: If it's true then Uncle Nick's got his *sleigh* parked outside! It's all too crazy, kid, I'm tellin' ya. [*Turns to him*] Now lemme *alone*, will ya—I gotta *open* here in twenty minutes! [JOEY *moving thoughtfully up towards phone,* EDDIE *glancing about*] Shit, he ain't done the *set*-ups yet— [*Shouting*] Charlie! Charlie, where are ya?! Charlie! [CHARLIE *hears his name, tenses, looks up*]

YOUNG CHARLIE'S VOICE: [*from Apartment above*] I'm in the studio, writing.

EDDIE: The studio. Is that the same as the toilet?

YOUNG CHARLIE'S VOICE: Sometimes.

EDDIE: [*shouting*] Charlie, *move* it, *now, pronto, down* here!

YOUNG CHARLIE: [*entering from apartment*] I'm coming, I'm in transit...

[YOUNG CHARLIE, *about 11, concerned, thoughtful, and many worlds away, slouches down the stairs carrying a stack of loose-leaf pages and several pens;* EDDIE *leans towards him confidentially*]

EDDIE: Charlie, I got this problem; see, until our book comes out and you become a millionaire, I figured I'd still run my little business here... [*shouting*] so how about ya do the goddamn *set*-ups and help me *open* the place! The set-ups and the *mail,* Mister, you got obligations!

YOUNG CHARLIE: [*quietly getting tray of set-ups from bar*] I got the mail already, it's by the register.

[EDDIE *exits, briskly, to work in Kitchen as* YOUNG CHARLIE *begins to go rather distractedly about the task of placing set-ups on two or three tables;* CHARLIE *watches him silently, intently, for a few moments, then...*]

CHARLIE: Jesus, they were right, I *didn't* pick up my feet. [*Leans towards him*] The shuffling, what's with the *shuffl*ing here? Straighten up, will ya? C'mon, Charlie, what happened to "No shit from nobody"?

YOUNG CHARLIE: [*a forlorn sigh, whispering*] Oh-boy-oh-boy-oh-boy...

CHARLIE: I don't get it, in all the albums I'm always *smiling*... [*Nods*

*thoughtfully*] Yeah, but that's because they kept saying "smile" ...
[*Following, close to him, gently*] Don't worry, kid, you're gettin' out. *Outa*
here. Sooner than you think. What is it, money? You need money? Bucks,
Charlie, *bucks*, the bucks are on their *way* ... Oh, if I could just give you a
coupla dollars, hand you a twenty, right now; a kinda loan, a ... [*During
the above,* YOUNG CHARLIE *will have deposited several slugs in the Jukebox,
punched the same key several times and crossed over to the "Vote Here for
Miss Daitch, 1944" display where he is now clearly entranced, as always, by
the face of Miss Daitch Contestant Number Two, Peggy Parsons, and the
biography beneath it; we begin to hear the Helen Forrest-Dick Haymes
recording of "Long Ago and Far Away" from the Jukebox, their voices drifting
dreamily in the empty bar*] Oh, my God ... Peggy Parsons ... *that's* it ...
[*Turns to us, as it all comes back*] The Miss Daitch Contest of Forty-Four,
our bar has been selected as one of the officially designated polling places
in the neighborhood ... [*Softly, from memory, as* YOUNG CHARLIE *studies
bio*] "Pretty, perky, pert Peggy Parsons, or 'Peggo' as she prefers to be
called, plans to pursue an acting career in motion pictures ... " Peggo,
Peggo ... To say that I had a crush on Peggy Parsons would be to say that
Mao Tse-Tung had a crush on Communism; only the beginning of July
and I had already cast over six hundred ballots in the Greater New York
area. [YOUNG CHARLIE *sits in* CHARLIE'S *usual booth, starts fervently
re-writing whatever is on his loose-leaf pages, all of it clearly inspired by
occasional glances at* PEGGY; *the Music swells, filling the bar*] Yeah, go with
it, Charlie, this is it, it doesn't get better than this ... [*Sits next to him in
booth, leans close*] Very important: love, Charlie, love does *not* make the
world go round, *looking* for it does; this is important ... Also very
important, Charlie, in about ten years you're gonna meet a girl at the
Museum of Modern Art, in front of the *Guernica*—let this painting be a
*warning* to you—don't go out with this girl, don't even *talk* to this girl,
by all means do *not marry this girl*—

JOEY: Hey, Charlie—[*Hangs up phone, comes down towards booth*] Been
settin' up tickets for the guys, everybody tells me—

YOUNG CHARLIE: [*points to pages in* JOEY'S *pocket*] Did you read it?

JOEY: Charlie, *listen*, word's out, the Avengers, the Gladiators, they're gonna
be roamin' tonight, like Memorial Day, or maybe like the Jew Hunt on
Pell Street—whatever, I don't want you walkin' over to Rutgers Arena by
yourself tonight. Gonna work out with Bimmy, then I come *back* for
ya—are you listening?

**YOUNG CHARLIE:** Yeah, after Bimmy's I go with you. Did you *read* it?

**JOEY:** Sometimes, I tell ya, it's like you're not *present* here—

**YOUNG CHARLIE:** [*rising in booth*] Did you read the *letter*, fa Chrissake!

**JOEY:** I *read* the letter, I *read* the goddamn letter! It's completely nuts and wacko. Also hopeless and dumb.

**YOUNG CHARLIE:** If you got a criticism, tell me.

**JOEY:** Charlie, number one: I don't *get* it—[*Indicating the Miss Daitch photos*] These girls, they all got the same *smile,* the same *eyes,* the same *nose*—[*Pointing*] C'mon, tell me, what's the difference between Peggy Parsons… and "Lovely, lively Laurie Lipton" here?

**YOUNG CHARLIE:** The difference? The *diff*erence? Why am I discussing this with a boxer?

**JOEY:** I got to go to Bimmy's—

**YOUNG CHARLIE:** [*holds up loose-leaf pages*] Thirty seconds, Joey—the revised version; I changed key words.

**JOEY:** [*leans against booth*] Twenty.

**YOUNG CHARLIE:** [*reads from pages*] "Mr. Samuel Goldwyn, Metro-Goldwyn-Mayer Studios. Dear Sam: Enclosed please find photo of Peggy Parsons. I think you will agree that this is the outstanding exquisiteness of a Motion Picture Star. You may reach her by the Daitch's Beer distribution place in your area is my belief. If Motion Picture employment is a result you may wish to say to her who recommended her eventually. She or yourself can reach me by post at the Flamingo Apartments, Six Eighty-One Canal Street, New York City. In closing I think of you first-hand instead of Darryl or David because of your nation of origin Poland which is right near my father's original nation Russia. Yours truly, C. E. Ross." [YOUNG CHARLIE *does not look up from the letter, so concerned is he about his brother's response.* JOEY, *sensing this, sits opposite him in the booth*]

**JOEY:** To begin with, that's an exceptionally well-put, well-written letter, Charlie…

**YOUNG CHARLIE:** I know what you're thinkin', but *wild things* happed out there, Joey; they're findin' stars in *drug*stores, *ele*vators—

**JOEY:** Right, and I'm sure the feeling you have for this Peggy is—

**YOUNG CHARLIE:** Peggo, she prefers to be called Peggo—

**JOEY:** Peggo, right—is genuine. So let's follow this through for a moment. Say, thousand-to-one shot, but Goldwyn, somebody in his office, sees the picture, say he gets a hold of her; say she's grateful, comes down to Canal Street to see you, right?

YOUNG CHARLIE: Right, right.

JOEY: And you're eleven.

YOUNG CHARLIE: Joey, I'm *aware* that there's an age problem; I will *deal* with it.

JOEY: [*after a moment, quietly*] Tell ya, sometimes, the similarities, you and Pop, it scares the shit outa me, kid.

YOUNG CHARLIE: [*studying letter*] Maybe "Dear Sam"'s too familiar; maybe "Dear Samuel" or "Mr. Goldwyn," huh?

JOEY: [*pats his shoulder*] Right; that'll do it. [*Rises, starts briskly towards front door*] Gotta get to Bimmy, I ain't worked out since the Chocolate Chopper. [*As* EDDIE *enters, returning from work in Kitchen to go to stack of mail behind bar*] See ya before the fight, Pop; comin' back to pick up Charlie.

EDDIE: [*looks up from mail*] Hey, this kid tonight—an easy win, but the Bazooka's got a little weight on ya and I don't like his left—so go for the kill *early*, the *kill*, Joey. Remember, the boy is *nothin'*; he is *now*, he always *was*—

JOEY: [*as he exits into street*]—and he always *will* be!

CHARLIE: [*to us, from booth*] Brother, brotherly, brotherhood: dynamite, powerhouse words, you could take them up off the ground like a punch; they meant—and still, now, at this moment, mean—Joey. However, take note, the only time Pop talks to me is when his prince is unavailable…

EDDIE: [*behind bar, studying a letter*] Charlie, the *set*-ups, what happened? [YOUNG CHARLIE *leaves booth to continue his task*] You can stick the flags in the pineapples, O. K.? [YOUNG CHARLIE *carries flags and tray of set-ups to center table;* EDDIE, *still looking down at the letter; speaks quietly, solemnly*] Charles…

[YOUNG CHARLIE *freezes at table*]

CHARLIE: "Charles," in this household, is my criminal name.

EDDIE: Charles…I'm lookin' at a letter here from the Star of David School, Rabbi Rubin.

YOUNG CHARLIE: These flags, Pop, they don't fit into the pineapples…

EDDIE: [*still looking down at letter, calmly*] This is *some* letter, this letter. It's got my undivided attention.

YOUNG CHARLIE: Hebrew's been over a week now, Pop; it don't start again
till—

EDDIE: [*continuing calmly*] Turns out it's been over for *you* a very long time
now. About eight months, according to this letter. Also according to this
letter there's been a lot of *other* letters. Says here, Rubin, "I had assumed
from your past responses to my inquiries regarding Charles' religious
training…" Turns out Rubin's been writin' to me, and I been *answerin'*
him on this matter seven months now. Hey, I even got compliments on
"the grace and wisdom of my remarks," says here. He *especially* likes the
graciousness how I keep payin' him anyway even though you ain't goin'
there no more.

YOUNG CHARLIE: Pop, how about we—

EDDIE: [*still calmly, folding letter*] Convenient for ya, you bein' the one gets
the mail. Musta got distracted today, huh? Yeah. Bugsy Siegel don't get
distracted, Frank Costello don't get distracted; Dillinger got distracted
*once*… and now he's dead.

YOUNG CHARLIE: [*moving towards bar*] Pop, I gotta tell ya—

EDDIE: Charlie, look at my hands. Are ya lookin' at my hands?

YOUNG CHARLIE: Yeah.

EDDIE: What I'm doin' here is I'm holdin' onto the edge of the bar because
if I let go I'm gonna beat the crap outa ya.

YOUNG CHARLIE: Here's what—

EDDIE: I'm here loadin' up shickers so you can hang out with God, twenty a
month to the Star of David, hard cash, and you ain't even *there*. [*Quietly,
in awe*] While I'm *sayin'* it, I don't believe it. I don't believe that you're
standin' there in front of me alive, I didn't kill you yet.

YOUNG CHARLIE: It was *wrong*, the whole *thing*, I *know*, but lemme—

EDDIE: My hands, they're lettin' go of the bar— [*Suddenly moving out from
behind bar towards* YOUNG CHARLIE, YOUNG CHARLIE *backing up fearfully
across the room, his hands raised, urgently*]

YOUNG CHARLIE: I gotta tell ya *one* thing, Pop, *one thing!*

EDDIE: [*after a moment*] One thing.

YOUNG CHARLIE: [*keeping his distance; fervently*] That place; you don't know
what it *is* there, the Star of David. It's a terrible place. It's not a Temple or
anything. It's just this ratty place on Houston Street. This ratty room on
the second floor of a building, two Rabbis in a room makin' a buck. Pop,
I swear, God isn't there like you think.

EDDIE: He's *there*, kid. Take my word for it—

**YOUNG CHARLIE:** Over Pedro and Olga's *Dance* Studio? Two ratty guys with bad breath who throw chalk at your head and slam books on your hand every time you miss a trick? I mean real angry guys with bugs in their beards; sometimes they just kick you in the ass on general principles.

**EDDIE:** Yeah, that's God all right; I'd know Him anywhere.

**YOUNG CHARLIE:** That ain't God, those guys—

**EDDIE:** Sure they ain't, I know that; but they're *connected.* That's the whole thing in life: *connections,* kid. [*Relaxes slightly, leans towards him*] First thing, right off, I guarantee you, there's a God. You got that?

**YOUNG CHARLIE:** I'm with you on that. We only disagree on where He's located.

**EDDIE:** Hebrew School, He's located *there;* so you go back there. Sit. [YOUNG CHARLIE *sits obediently at center table;* EDDIE *sits opposite him*] because there's times—you're in trouble, you're really sick, and especially when you die, just before you die—you'll be glad you stayed in touch. That's the payoff. There's gonna be a time, guaranteed, you'll be grateful I made ya go; but the main thing is if ya don't go back I'm gonna kill ya.

**YOUNG CHARLIE:** I don't get it, Pop. Ma lights the candles Friday, starts the prayer, ya say, "Cut the shit and let's eat"; ya *never* go to Temple anymore, the *bar* was open last Rosh Hashana, ya—

[EDDIE *suddenly grabs* YOUNG CHARLIE *by the collar of his shirt with one hand and pulls him halfway across the table*]

**EDDIE:** I stay in *touch*, Criminal! Look, you're makin' me grit my teeth! My goddamn *bridge* is crackin'! I stay in *touch*, Putzolla. Twenty a month to Rubin and the bandits so you should learn the worda the Torah and the worda God—

**YOUNG CHARLIE:** I can't breathe, Pop—

**EDDIE:** That's two shifts a month I'm puttin' out for God here exclusive, same like I done with Joey! Are you breathing?

**YOUNG CHARLIE:** *No*—

**EDDIE:** Then *breathe*—[*Lets him go*] And I got married by a Rabbi, under God, twenty-five years and I stick! How *come* I stick? A woman, we all realize, is at this time a wacky person, nearly deaf; also a rough mouth don't encourage my endeavors whatever. [*Silence for a moment*] This is currently. But there was occasions otherwise. [*Glances up at Apartment door, then leans towards* YOUNG CHARLIE; *quietly*] You hearda the

**473**

expression "raven-haired"? O.K., there's some girls got hair they call "midnight black," very beautiful, but it got no light in it, see. "Raven-hair" is like the bird, glossy, light come *out* of it, got its own light comin' out—this is what she had. First time I seen her she's runnin' down these steps to the beach, this hair is down to her ass, flyin' behind her like wings, her arms is out like she's gonna hug the entire Black Sea, laughin' ... [*Slaps the table*] And then, Sonny-Boy, minutes, *minutes*—I swear to you, minutes after the Rabbi pronounced us the lights went out in her hair like somebody turned off a switch; and the mouth began. Continuing in this manner until she became the totally wacky deaf person we know in our home at this time; she is at this *moment*, stirring a pot, getting wackier and deafer. But I *stick!* [*Slaps the table again*] That's my point, kid: I *stick*. Because there'll be a night one day when the heart attack comes and somebody'll have to call Dr. Schwartzman and the ambulance. And who will do it? The Wacky Ravenhead! In five minutes she covers a fifty-year bet! Why? Because I put my money on a good woman. Wacky and deaf; but good. There's a lot of people got this kind of arrangement. It's called a Coronary Marriage. And when you find a better reason for people staying together, let me know. Love? Forget it. Who are they kidding? It won't be there when you get home and it won't call Dr. Schwartzman for you. [*Leans closer*] Same with God. I *stick*. *I* stick and so will you. Because all God's gotta do is come through *once* to make Him worth your time. Maybe twice. Just one big deal and once when you die so you ain't scared shitless. [*Picks up letter*] O.K., you hang in with Rubin till the Bar Mitzvah shot. Whatta we talkin' about?—a coupla years, tops, it's *over*, you're joined up with *my* Pop and *his* Pop and *his* and all the Pops back forever—you're covered, it's set, I done my job; then ya do whatever the hell ya want. [*Holds out his hand*] Deal ? [*A moment, then* YOUNG CHARLIE *shakes his hand;* EDDIE *rises, starts briskly back towards bar*] C'mon, let's seal it. [YOUNG CHARLIE *follows him,* EDDIE *goes behind bar*] Mine's vodka. What'll ya have?

**YOUNG CHARLIE:** [*sits opposite him, elbows on bar*] Let's see ... you got lemon juice and seltzer?

**EDDIE:** Like the choice; *I* got it—[*A spritz, a splash, places it on bar*] Now *you* got it. [*Pouring his vodka*] Yeah, good; I think this was a good conversation.

**YOUNG CHARLIE:** Me too ... I mean it ain't exactly Andy Hardy and the

Judge, but it's somethin'. [*He laughs at his own joke; soon* EDDIE *laughs too, joining him, they "click" glasses*] Boy, Pop, you're right—

EDDIE: [*still laughing*] *Sure* I'm right—

YOUNG CHARLIE: [*still laughing*] I mean about Mom, she sure is *some* wacky *deaf* person; I mean, she—

[*A sudden, resounding smack in the face from* EDDIE *sends* YOUNG CHARLIE *reeling off his bar-stool, knocking him to the floor.* CHARLIE, *in his booth, holds his cheek, feeling the impact*]

EDDIE: [*shouting*] You will not mock your mother! Even in jest!

YOUNG CHARLIE: [*half-mumbling, still on his knees, his head still ringing, shocked and hurt at once*] Hell with you, *hell* with you, don't make no sense...

EDDIE: [*comes out from behind bar, thundering, pointing down at him*] What's *that?* What do I hear?! Gypsies! Gypsies! The Gypsies brought ya! This can't be mine!

YOUNG CHARLIE: [*scrambling to his feet, screaming*] Oh, I wish to God they *had!* I wish to God the Gypsies brought me! I don't wanna be from *you!* [*Darting from table to table as* EDDIE *stalks him, the boy gradually rising to full, wailing, arm-flailing rage*] Nothin' fits together, nothin' ya *say!* Goddamn switch*eroo* alla time! Her? Her? You! You're the crazy one, *you're* the deaf one, *you're* the one nobody can talk to! [*Whacking pineapples off of tables, wildly, screaming, pointing fiercely at* EDDIE] Loser! Loser! Goddamn *loser!* You're a goddamn crazy *loser* in a goddamn loser *shit*house here!

[EDDIE *suddenly snaps, a moment of pure madness, races towards him, grabbing a chair; raising it over his head, clearly about to smash it down on* YOUNG CHARLIE; YOUNG CHARLIE *drops to the ground, his arms over his head,* EDDIE *lost in rage, all his enemies below him*]

EDDIE: [*roaring*] *You people...!*

[EDDIE *freezes, about to strike, looks down, sees that it's* YOUNG CHARLIE; *he slowly lowers the chair; trembling with rage, looking at it, realizing for a moment what he was about to do, shaken, quite still; he tosses the chair to the ground*]

**YOUNG CHARLIE:** [*rises, unaware of what's happening to his father*] Come on, great, let's see ya do the one thing ya *can* do… [*Shouting, his fists raised, holding his ground*] No. No more hitting this year. This is *it*… Come on, come on, Pop… just one more move, I'm the perfect height; just one more move and I kick you in the balls so hard ya don't straighten up for a *month*… [*Full power now*] One more move and it's right in the balls— right in the *balls*, Pop, I swear to God!

**EDDIE:** Swear to who?!

**YOUNG CHARLIE:** God! I swear to God!

**EDDIE:** [*after a moment, quietly*] See how He comes in handy? [*A pause; then, still a bit shaken, covering*] Well, I… believe I've made my point. Sometimes ya gotta illustrate, y'know… for the full clarity of the thing. [*Sound of* GUSTA *approaching from the Apartment above, humming a few phrases of "In Odessa,"* EDDIE *heading briskly back to bar; pulling himself together*] Now you'll excuse me, I gotta open in five minutes. First day of the Flamingo Lounge.

[EDDIE *takes a quick shot of the vodka he left on the bar; erasing the episode, returning to work as* GUSTA *enters from the Apartment carrying her usual two large pots of just-cooked food, humming brightly,* YOUNG CHARLIE *eventually retreating slowly, thoughtfully to his booth and his loose-leaf pages*]

**GUSTA:** [*placing pots on Kitchen stove*] Today we got the usuals, Eddie— Mulligan Stew, Cottage Fries, General Patton's Pancakes, D-Day Dumplings—

**EDDIE:** General Patton's Pancakes, I forget—

**GUSTA:** Potato Latkes—

**EDDIE:** Potato Latkes, right—

**GUSTA:** [*bringing plate of food to* YOUNG CHARLIE's *booth*] Upstairs, simmering, I got for Joey's party tonight—it's just us, Eddie, I'll use maiden names—Kasha-Varnishkes, also Holishkes with honey and raisin.

**EDDIE:** Great, Gloria, great—

**GUSTA:** [*starts back towards Kitchen*] Joey's boxing-fight, I'll be upstairs; you'll inform me at knockout time, I bring down the food.

**EDDIE:** Don't worry, this guy won't *touch* him, Gloria—

GUSTA: This is how it is with me: I can't watch, so I can't listen either; it hurts.

EDDIE: [*approaching her at Kitchen doorway; quietly*] Hey, for the party tonight, how about ya take the pins outa y'hair ... let it, y'know, free.

GUSTA: I let it free it goes in the soup.

EDDIE: I mean, just loose, y'know, like flowin'.

GUSTA: Who's gonna *see*, Finney, Nick —?

EDDIE: *Me. I'll* see it —

GUSTA: [*suddenly*] Eddie, there's a bird on the ceiling.

EDDIE: It's a *flamingo*.

GUSTA: All right, I'll believe you; it's a flamingo. Why is it on the ceiling?

EDDIE: Gonna be like a *symbol* for us, Gloria, for the place; like I was tellin' Joey: Borden's got a cow, Billingsley's got a stork, Firestone —

GUSTA: How much did the dopey bird cost?

EDDIE: It just so happens this hand-made, hand-crafted, sixty-eight-light Flamingo Chandelier is the only one of its kind in the world.

GUSTA: Two is hard to imagine. [*She goes to Kitchen stove;* EDDIE *continues, high with "Opening Day" fever*]

EDDIE: Gloria, I'm talkin' to Joey this mornin', somethin' *come* to me — somethin' for the *place*, somethin' we never *tried* before — a *word, one word*, a magic word's gonna make all the difference!

GUSTA: Fire.

EDDIE: Advertising!

GUSTA: We'll burn it down and get the insurance. The Moose *alone* puts us in the clover. [*Exits deep into Kitchen, out of sight*]

EDDIE: *Advertising!* Advertising, kiddo! [*Exits into Kitchen, pursuing her, inspired; we hear his voice from inside, his enthusiasm building*] I'm talkin' about a small ad, classy, in there with the Clubs, Gloria — just a picture of a flamingo, one word: *"Lounge,"* under it; under that "Six Eighty-One Canal" — like everybody *knows* already, like it's *in*, Gloria —

CHARLIE: [*during above, rising from booth, moving towards Kitchen*] Leave her alone, Pop, leave her *alone*, it's never gonna *happen* —

EDDIE'S VOICE: Guy comes in here regular, works for the *Journal-American*, runs a heavy tab, I trade him on the *space*, kid —

CHARLIE: [*during above, louder and louder*] — stop, we're never going Uptown; stop, *stop* driving us *crazy* with it, Eddie — this *bar*, this goddamn *bar*!

YOUNG CHARLIE: [*at booth, writing, as* EDDIE's *voice continues*] "Dear Mr. Zanuck... it would not be perfectly candid of me if I did not frankly admit and advise you that I have just previously contacted Sam on this exact matter..."

CHARLIE: [*turns, anguished, caught between the two of them*] My God, you're just as crazy as *he* is...

YOUNG CHARLIE: [*writing, his confidence building*] "...I refer to the enclosed Peggy Parsons. We live in a competitive industry, Darryl, and I do not wish to keep this woman in a basket..."

[*We begin to hear the sound of about Twenty Teen-aged Boys' Voices, quite distantly at first, far down the street outside, singing happily, with great gusto; the sound of the voices and their song growing louder and louder, reaching a peak as we hear them pass the front door, then fading out as they continue along Canal Street;* YOUNG CHARLIE *completely oblivious to this sound of the Boys' Voices, the song drawing him slowly down to the front door as the passing Voices reach their peak; all lights dimming far down now except for the remaining full light on* CHARLIE *at the front door, his face mirroring his almost forgotten but now vividly remembered helplessness and fear at the sound of the Boys' Voices and their song*]

TWENTY BOY'S VOICES: [*to the tune of the Marine Corps Hymn*]

"On the shores of Coney Island
While the guns of freedom roar,
The Sheenies eat their Matzo Balls
And make money off the war,
While we Christian saps go fight the Japs,
In the uniforms thry've made.
And they'll sell us Kosher hot dogs
For our victory parade.
So it's onward into battle
They will send us Christian slobs,
When the war is done and victory won,
All the Jews will have our jobs."

[*Sound of laughter; a crash of glass, then cheering as the Boys' Voices fade into the night*]

CHARLIE: [*shouts towards the fading Voices*] If Joey was here ... if Joey was here you'd never get away with it!

[*The Boys' Voices are quickly obliterated by the sudden sound of a Cheering Crowd, raucous and enthusiastic, and the machine-gun voice of Ringside sportscaster Speed Spector blasting out the blow-by-blow of a fight in progress, the tiny yellow light of the Philco radio dial popping on in the darkness and then glowing brighter as the Cheering Crowd, Spector's Voice and all the bar lights come up full to reveal that night's Party and the Party Guests: HANNAH, NICK and FINNEY, gathered about the radio, EDDIE entering from the Kitchen holding two champagne bottles aloft on a tray full of fancy glasses, a silk vest added to his usual Uptown Bartender's white shirt and black bow-tie, ZARETSKY entering somewhat later from the Apartment above wearing an old but splendid smoking-jacket and cravat for the occasion; CHARLIE remaining at front door looking off towards street, YOUNG CHARLIE no longer onstage*]

SPECTOR'S VOICE: [*from Philco, breathless, one long sentence*] ... toe to toe and here they *go* fourth round another *fight* friends *first* three bouts waltz-time dancin' *darlings* number *four* we got a slammin' *slug*fest here Killer Kalish and and Homicide Hennesy tradin' solid *body* shots instead a *party* favors here tonight forty-five seconds into frame *four*... [CHARLIE *being gradually pulled away from the front door by the much pleasanter memory of* Spector's *Voice*] ... carryin' it to Kalish lightnin' *left* rockin' *right* a stick a jab a hook hook hook roundhouse *right* Killer's outa *business*...

CHARLIE: [*to us, as* SPECTOR *and* CHEERING CROWD *continue*] Well, they didn't call him Speed Spector for nothin, did they? And tonight we waited for *that voice* to talk about *my* brother. First, however, would be the usual pre-Main Event interview with Big Mike Baskin of Big Mike Baskin's Broadway Boys' and Men's Clothes, sponsor of the Tuesday Night Amateurs. We, of course, all knew him as the former Manny Buffalino of Buffalino's Grand Street Garments who gave a silver-plated watch to each of the winners ... and a terrible headache to Pop.

SPECTOR'S VOICE: ... whatta ya think about that whoppin' big *win*, Big Mike?

BIG MIKE'S VOICE: Spid, dis boy, alla tonight win' gonna get a sil' plate wash froma Big Mike. Now, he don' like dis wash, he can hocka dis wash for fifteen doll' —

EDDIE: [*entering with champagne*] Can't stand the *mouth* on that greaseball— [*Turns radio volume way down; they all protest*] Don't worry, Joey's bout ain't on for five minutes anyways—goddamn Steerage *Green*horn; twenty-six locations, man's sittin' on a coupla mil—*nobody* knows what the hell he's *talkin'* about! What's his *angle*, how's he *do* it —?

FINNEY: [*as* ZARETSKY *enters, slapping* ZARETSKY *on back*] Evenin', Mr. Z.; how's Show Business?

ZARETSKY: Mr. Finney; Abbott and *Costello* are in Show Business, Amos and even *Andy* are in Show Business, Franklin Delano *Roosevelt* is in Show Business—

FINNEY: [*pinching* ZARETSKY'S *cheek*] Lost me bearin's, darlin', it's the joy of the night—

EDDIE: [*placing bottles on center table*] I say sixty seconds into Round One this champagne is pourin' and Gloria's down with the goodies!

HANNAH: And Nick wears the *shirt* tonight.

EDDIE: Great...

FINNEY: The shirt, of course...

HANNAH: The occasion demanded.

ZARETSKY: This then is a shirt of some significance, I assume.

NICK: Oh, ya might say. Ya might well say, Mr. Zaretsky. [*Opening old jacket to reveal a faded yellow shirt instead of his usual faded white shirt; there are dark brown stains on the shoulder and collar*] For this then is the blood of Barney Ross, spilled the night he lost the World Welterweight to Armstrong, the greatest Losin' Win I ever saw.

EDDIE: Greatest Losin' Win in the history of the fight game.

FINNEY: Easy.

NICK: Second *row* we are, the four of us; May Thirty-One, Nineteen Thirty-Eight, Round Five, his legs said goodbye to the man, never to return in what was t'be the last bout o' Barney's life. Ref Donovan's beggin' Ross to let 'im stop the thing—"No," Barney says, through the blood in his mouth, "I'm the Champ, he'll have to beat me in the *ring* and *not* on a stool in m'corner!" There then come ten rounds of a horror ya never want to see again, but proud ya saw the once for the grandness that was in it, the crowd is quiet and many look away, but at the end the cheers is for Barney who lost his title and won his pride. [*Looking about at his friends*] Which is why we call it, the four of us...

NICK, EDDIE, FINNEY: ...the Greatest Losin' Win we ever saw!

HANNAH: In my case, heard.

FINNEY: It was in the Twelfth Barney's blood hit the shirt—

HANNAH: A thundering right from Armstrong, yes—
EDDIE: Ya *get* it, Actor—ya see why me and my boys are called *Ross* now?
FINNEY: [*suddenly turns to radio*] My God, the *fight*—
EDDIE: Oh, *shit*—[*He dashes to the radio, quickly turns up volume*]

[*We hear the sound of the Cheering Crowd as* EDDIE *turns the volume up full, the sound building louder and louder as the Crowd chants rhythmically;* CHARLIE *sits solemnly in his booth, nodding, remembering it all too well*]

THE CROWD: Chicken *Pete*... Chicken *Pete*... Chicken *Pete*...
HANNAH: [*confused, frightened*] Chicken Pete, Nick?...
SPECTOR'S VOICE: [*shouting above the chanting Crowd*] ... Listen to *that* Fans! *New* one on Old *Speed* here; got a Referee, one fighter, whole crowd, packed Arena— *one* thing missing: the *other fighter!* Pistol Pete is *not* in that ring, *not* in the locker room, *no*where to be found, friends...

[*All in bar-room stunned at first;* EDDIE, *the others, not moving, riveted by the information as it comes out of the radio; the sound of the chanting Crowd building, filling the room*]

SPECTOR'S VOICE: ... Ref Gordon tells me Pistol Pete's not in the *building*, no *message*, no *word; sounds* like the best explanation of this one's comin' from the crowd itself...
THE CROWD: [*louder and louder*] ... Chicken *Pete*... Chicken *Pete*... Chicken *Pete*....
FINNEY: [*bewildered, staring into radio*] He didn't *show*, Joey didn't *show*...

[*The sound of stomping and clapping joins the rhythmic chant of the Crowd now as* EDDIE *moves slowly out from behind the bar; carefully controlling his fear and confusion*]

EDDIE: [*quietly, evenly*] He's hurt, he's hurt... out *cold;* he'd have to be out *cold* to stay away from that bout... he's hurt... [*Moving towards phone*] *Bimmy's,* maybe somebody at Bimmy's, somebody knows...
ZARETSKY: He leaves with Chaim for the Arena, this is an hour ago...
FINNEY: I heard them Avenger boys was gatherin' on Pell...

**481**

HANNAH: Nit do gedacht…
NICK: [*rising from stool*] I go to the Precinct, get some of the fellahs…
EDDIE: [*picking up phone*] Yeah, yeah…
THE CROWD: [*building to peak now*] …Chicken *Pete*…Chicken *Pete*… Chicken *Pete*…

[*The front door bursts open and Joey rushes in, followed by* YOUNG CHARLIE; *though somewhat shaken, there is something decisive, resolved in* JOEY *as he stands tensely at the center of the room, his "Pistol Pete" jacket gripped in his hand;* YOUNG CHARLIE, *clearly bewildered by the evening's events, stays close to his brother*]

HANNAH: [*trembling*] Jussel, Jussel…?
JOEY: [*gently*] Everything's fine, Hannah.
EDDIE: [*starts towards him; quietly*] Thank God, you're O.K…you're O.K…
JOEY: I'm not O.K. [*Races behind the bar towards the sound of the chanting Crowd, snaps off the radio; the room is silent*] I will be.
EDDIE: The *fight*, kid, the *fight*…what the hell *happened*…?
JOEY: [*slaps his jacket onto the bar; grabs up vodka bottle and shot-glass*] No more fights. No more fights, Pop. Not here. [*Fills his shot glass, downs it*]
EDDIE: Not *here*? Not *here*? What the hell does *that* mean? I need some *explainin'* here, kid, I gotta—
ZARETSKY: Let him *speak*, Itzik.
JOEY: [*quietly*] Pop, this mornin', workin' out with Bimmy—
EDDIE: *Tonight*, kid, I wanna know about *tonight*—
JOEY: [*continuing, firmly*] This mornin', workin' out with Bimmy, we're skippin', we're sparrin', my mind ain't there, Pop. I'm doin' math. Three hundred and fifty thousand Jews in twenty-one days, comes out seventeen thousand five hundred a day, *this* day, today—
EDDIE: A buncha crazy *stories*, Joey, I told ya—[*Wheeling on* ZARETSKY] *You*, it's you and your goddamn *bull*shit—
JOEY: [*moving towards him*] Please, ya gotta be quiet, Pop. That's maybe two thousand just while I'm workin' out. Seventeen thousand five hundred a day. No, it's impossible, I figure; Pop's *right*, it's nuts. I keep punchin' the bag. I come back to pick up Charlie, we're headin' over, not Seven yet; then I hear people hollerin', I look up, I see it. Top of the "Forward" Buildin',

tallest damn buildin' around here, there's the "Jewish Daily Forward" sign, y'know, big, maybe thirty feet high and wide as the buildin', electric bulbs, ya can see it even deep into Brooklyn, *forever,* Pop. What they did is they took out the right bulbs, exactly the bulbs, gotta be hundreds of 'em, so instead of "Jewish Daily Forward" the sign says: "Jew Is For War"; it's goddamn blazin' over the city, Pop, and Charlie and me start runnin' towards it, we're still maybe eight blocks away, we're passin' a lotta people and kids on Canal, pointin' up, laughin', some cheerin', "Son of a *bitch,* son of a *bitch,* we fight the *war* and the Jews get *rich,*" a guy grabs my arm, smilin', musta seen me box, guy my age, he says, "Pete, Pete, let's go get us some Yids, Pete!" and I know that second for sure they are doin' seventeen thousand five hundred a day, somewhere, seventeen thousand five hundred a day and I'm a guy spends his time boppin' kids for a silver-plated watch from Big Mike, hockable for fifteen dollars; right now I wouldn't hock me for a dime. Point is, I'm goin' in, Pop. I'm gettin' into this war and I need your help, now. [*Eddie is silent*] Army don't register me till next month, then it could be a year, more, before they call me. *Navy,* Pop, Navy's the game; they take ya at seventeen with a parent's consent. Eight A.M. tomorrow I'm at Ninety Church, I pick up the consent form, you fill it out, sign it, ten days later Boot Camp at Lake Geneva, September I'm in it, Pop. Korvette, Destroyer, Sub-chaser, whatever, *in* the goddamn thing.

EDDIE: [*after a moment*] Your mother will never—

JOEY: I just need you, Pop. One parent. One signature. [*Silence for a moment*] Do me a favor; take a look outside. Just turn left and look at the sky.

[*During* JOEY'S *story,* HANNAH *has moved instinctively closer to* NICK, *holding his arm;* ZARETSKY *rises*]

ZARETSKY: Come then, Itzik.

[EDDIE *turns towards the door;* ZARETSKY *crosses to the door; exits into street, followed after a moment by* EDDIE *and then* FINNEY; NICK *starts to go but* HANNAH *whispers fearfully to him*]

HANNAH: Stay with me, Nick. They'll look, they'll describe.
NICK: [*embracing her*] Sure, darlin', sure...

[*Silence for a few moments;* CHARLIE, *in his booth, watching the two boys*]

YOUNG CHARLIE: You didn't tell me that part... about goin' in. You didn't mention that.

JOEY: It come to me, Charlie.

YOUNG CHARLIE: [*urgently*] Lotta guys to fight *here*, y'know, the Avengers, the Gladiators; ya don't have to go all the way to *Europe*, ya—

[EDDIE *enters, crosses slowly to bar; sits on stool; he is followed by* FINNEY, *and then* ZARETSKY *who remains at doorway looking out into street*]

FINNEY: [*to* HANNAH *and* NICK] Hangin' over town like a second bloody moon, it is.

EDDIE: [*after a moment, slapping bar*] Get me the goddamn paper, I sign it *now*. Go down to Ninety Church Street, wake the Putzes *up*, bring me the form and I sign it now. All I ask, kid, you're over there, you kill a couple for your Pop, *personally*. [*Starts towards* JOEY; *fiercely*] Kill 'em, Joey *kill* 'em. Show 'em, kid, show 'em how a Jew fights.

JOEY: [*grabs* EDDIE's *fist, holds it proudly in the air*] And in this corner, wearin' the green trunks—The East Side Savage!

[*All cheering, patting* JOEY *on the back, except for* ZARETSKY *and the two* CHARLIES]

YOUNG CHARLIE: [*looking anxiously from one to the other*] Everybody goin' so *fast* here, so *fast*—

NICK: Try to get home for Christmas, kid—

YOUNG CHARLIE: They got *reasons*, y'know, why they don't take guys till they're eighteen, they got—

JOEY: [*turns to* ZARETSKY, *who has remained silent at front door*] You're *with* me, aren't ya?

ZARETSKY: [*after a moment*] Yes... yes, were I your age—[JOEY *rushes forward, embraces him*]

EDDIE: [*holding champagne bottle aloft, rallying the Group*] Hey, hey, *hey*— we still got a *party* goin' here—a *better* one—goddamn Warrior's *send-off* we got here! [*Pops cork at center table as all gather round, except for*

YOUNG CHARLIE *who moves slowly over to his usual booth, sits near*
CHARLIE] First-class Frog juice we got here — *I* got it — [*Pouring for*
JOEY *first*] Now *you* got it, kid — [*As he pours for the others*] Hey, this
ain't just Bazooka Kil*bane* goin' down — I'm talkin' about the whole god-
damn Nazi-Nip *War* Machine here! [*Raising his glass*] To the Winnah
and still Cham*peen!*
HANNAH: [*raising her glass*] So what's wrong with the Bounding Main?
NICK: [*raising his glass*] Right! To the Navy!
FINNEY: [*raising his glass*] To the Navy and Victory!
ALL: [*loudly, raising glasses*] The Navy and Victory!

[*They click glasses just as* GUSTA *enters from the Apartment above
carrying a large tray of Party-food; starts down stairs, confused, seeing*
JOEY *amongst the Group*]

GUSTA: The boxing-fight, Joey, you won already? Nobody informed me.
[*They all turn to her; their six glasses held aloft, poised; she stops near* JOEY]
Ah, no marks; good. O. K., Party-treats — [*Goes briskly to down left table,
a distance from the Group, starts taking dishes from tray, placing them on
table, her back to them; they all remain quite still, watching her*] First, of
course, basics: we got Kasha-Varnishkes, we got Holishkes, special for Mr.
Zaretsky we got Kartoffel Chremsel with a touch apple…
HANNAH: [*quietly*] Eddie signs a paper, Gusta, Joey goes to war.
GUSTA: [*a pause; then she continues briskly*] We got Lokshen Kugel, we got a
little Brisket Tzimmes with honey, special for Charlie we got Cheese
Blintzes, a side sour cream…
JOEY: [*softly, moving towards her*] Ma, did you hear that, Ma…?
GUSTA: And special for Finney and Nick — why not, I was in the mood —
we got Mamaligele Rumanye with a smash strawberry.
JOEY: Ma…
GUSTA: [*a moment; she turns to him*] I hear everything, Sonny. You got some
good news for me? [*Looks over at the Group*] I hear it all. It's just that
twenty years ago I started making selections. [*Walking slowly towards the
Group*] You see, if I listened, I would want to speak. And who would hear
me? Who would hear me? Who would *hear* me?

[*She slaps* EDDIE *hard across the face. A beat; we hear the sudden
sound of a full Marching Band and a Male Chorus doing a blasting,*

*drum-rolling, lusty-voiced rendition of "Anchors Aweigh" as all lights
fade quickly down on the frozen Party Group and the still figures of
GUSTA and EDDIE, Music continuing at full Volume*]

**MALE CHORUS:**

"Anchors aweigh, my boy,
Anchors aweigh,
Farewell to college joys,
We sail at break of day, day, day, day . . . ."

[*During* CHARLIE'S *next speech the pulsing Jukebox lights will come
up again and with them the half-light in which we will see only*
EDDIE *and* YOUNG CHARLIE *remaining onstage and making those
changes in the bar-room that would have occurred during the thirteen
months till the next scene begins;* EDDIE *solemnly draping a length of
black ribbon about the frame of the grinning F.D.R. photo, then
proudly hanging a map of the Pacific Theatre of War over the Jukebox,
happily placing several blue and white Service Stars about the room,
including one over* JOEY'S *boxing photo, finally exiting into Kitchen;*
YOUNG CHARLIE *will take down the Miss Daitch Display— being
careful to keep the Peggy Parsons photo which he stores, among other
treasures, in the hollow seat of the booth he and* CHARLIE *usually use.*
CHARLIE *will have moved down towards us only a moment after the
blackout on the Party Scene, humming a few phrases of "Anchors
Aweigh" along with the Jukebox, then speaking immediately to us
during the action described above*]

**CHARLIE:** Joey called the shot exactly: September, he was in it—desperately
trying to promote his way onto a Convoy-Korvette in the European
Theatre, he ended up on a Destroyer in the Pacific and, as Joey pointed
out, the only dangerous German he ever got to face was our dentist, Dr.
Plaut—but he was *in* it; and, finishing ten weeks of Gunnery School in
four, he became quickly known aboard the Destroyer Campbell as "The
King of the Twin Forties"—double-mounted antiaircraft machine-guns
in a swiveling steel bucket operated by a Gunner and an Ammo Man—
[*Here replicated by* YOUNG CHARLIE *holding two broom handles atop a*

*spinning bar-stool*] Yes, Joey was proud and brave and good and strong—but mostly, he was *gone* [YOUNG CHARLIE *puts on the "Pistol Pete" jacket* JOEY *left on the bar; his posture noticeably straightening*] He was gone and I was here, the house was mine. I was it: star of the show, Top of the Card, the Main Event. Civilians look for job openings in wartime... and there was an opening here for Prince.

[CHARLIE *turns to center as lights come up on* YOUNG CHARLIE *alone onstage, seated comfortably on bar-stool, his feet up, legs crossed at the ankle, on bar; gazing critically at the huge painting of the Four Poker Players over the bar-mirror. Sound of Harry Truman's Voice fading up with the lights as "Anchors Aweigh" record ends on Jukebox*]

TRUMAN'S VOICE: ...on Hiroshima, a military base. We won the race of discovery against the Germans. We have used it in order to shorten the agony of war, in order to save the lives of thousands and thousands of young Americans. We shall *continue* to use it until we completely destroy Japan's power to make war...

EDDIE: [*bursts in from Kitchen*] The Atomic Cocktail, Charlie! [*Holds aloft two large containers of freshly mixed cocktails*] *Two* kindsa rum, light *and* dark, shot o' grenadine-pineapple juice and coconut cream, give a kinda Tropical-Pacific feel. [*Sets containers and handmade placard on bar*] Whatta ya think, kid?

YOUNG CHARLIE: [*still looking at Poker Picture, thoughtfully*] That's a terrible painting, Pop.

EDDIE: [*reads from placard—he's illustrated it with a classic mushroom-cloud Hiroshima photo from a newspaper*] "Atomic Cocktail—One Dollar—If the First Blast Don't Get You, the Fallout Will." How about that, Charlie?

YOUNG CHARLIE: [*squints at Poker Picture*] Not only poorly painted, but look at all the *room* it takes up.

EDDIE: What?

YOUNG CHARLIE: This painting here, Pop; it's no good.

EDDIE: What're ya talkin' about? This here's a handpainted oil picture, seven feet by *six*, fits *exact* over the mirror. This is an original by goddamn Lazlo *Shim*kin; run up a big tab, gimme the picture on a trade-off. Got any idea what this thing's *worth* today?

**YOUNG CHARLIE:** Nothin', Pop.

**EDDIE:** Listen, Putz this picture been sittin' up there since a year before you was *born*. You seen it every day o' ya *life*—all of a sudden it's no *good?*

**YOUNG CHARLIE:** Yes; strange, isn't it?

**EDDIE:** [*quietly*] I gotta open the bar in twenty minutes; otherwise I would immediately take the picture out in the alley and burn it. Only thing I can suggest to you in the meantime, Charlie, is that you *spend the rest of your goddamn life lookin' the other way!* [*Leaning towards him*] Gypsies! Gypsies! The *Gypsies* left ya at my doorstep! *This* can't be *mine!* Before this personally autographed Lazlo *Shim*kin picture goes, *you* go. [*Points*] *Feet* off the bar, and finish the set-ups.

**ZARETSKY:** [*entering from Apartment above*] Ah, I sense artistic differences in the air.

**YOUNG CHARLIE:** [*starts working on set-ups*] 'Morning, Mr. Zaretsky.

**ZARETSKY:** Chaim, you have not yet, I trust, fetched the mail? [*Young Charlie shakes his head*] Good then, it shall be my task. I expect today a cable from Buenos Aires, in Argentina, where still exist two hundred thousand speakers of Yiddish, there confirming my appearance, a full three weeks of concerts; my first since the War. [*Starts towards front door*]

**YOUNG CHARLIE:** [*impressed as always*] Hey, Argen*tina*... Great.

**EDDIE:** [*stacking glasses*] Three weeks without ya, Anton; breaks my goddamn heart. Don't worry, babe, we'll keep y'room *just* the way ya left it.

**ZARETSKY:** Unfortunately. [*Opens front door*] A room in which, for twelve years, sunlight has appeared almost entirely by metaphor. [*Exits into street. Silence for a moment*]

**EDDIE:** [*his back to* YOUNG CHARLIE, *busily stacking glasses*] O.K., just for laughs, Putz, what's so ugly about that picture?

**YOUNG CHARLIE:** For one thing, the light, Pop... [*Eddie squints at the painting*] It's all like... flat, see. It's like the light is coming from *every*where, y'know, so it's not really—

**EDDIE:** Yeah, right, O.K., good this come up. This stuff about where the light's comin' from, also these here poems and stories you been writin'. Take a for-instance—[*takes folded piece of loose-leaf paper from cash register*] this poem ya give me Father's Day.

**YOUNG CHARLIE:** Did ya like it? Ya never mentioned—

**EDDIE:** Sure, sure. [*Hands it to him, sits at their usual center table*] Do y'Pop a favor, O.K.? You read this to me, then I'm gonna ask ya a question. [YOUNG CHARLIE *hesitates for a moment*] Go ahead.

[YOUNG CHARLIE *starts to read as* ZARETSKY *returns with the mail, places all but a few pieces on bar, listens attentively to poem*]

YOUNG CHARLIE: [*reading*] O. K . . . . "Father of the Flamingo; by C. E. Ross: . . . He leadeth them beside distilled waters, he restoreth their credit; and if they be Mick Shickers, he maketh them to lie down in dark gutters. And yea, though I may walk through the valley of the shadow of Little Italy, I shall fear no Goy or evil sound, 'cause my Pop has taught me how to bring one up from the ground."

ZARETSKY: [*applauding*] Bravo, Chaim; bravo! [*He exits upstairs, continuing to nod his approval for the work of a fellow artist*]

EDDIE: O. K., very nice. [*Leaning forward, pleasantly*] O. K., now all I'm askin' is a truthful answer: who helped ya out with that?

YOUNG CHARLIE: Nobody, Pop. I mean, it's a Twenty-Third Psalm take-off, so I got help from the *Bible*—

EDDIE: I *know* that, *besides* that—the thing , the *ideas* in there, how it come together there—you tellin' me nobody helped ya out on that, the *Actor*, nobody?

YOUNG CHARLIE: Nobody, Pop.

EDDIE: [*he pauses, then indicates the chair opposite him;* YOUNG CHARLIE *sits*] O. K., there's times certain Jewish words is unavoidable, I give ya two: Narrishkeit and Luftmensh. Narrishkeit is stuff *beyond* foolish—like what?—your mother givin' English lessons, this would be Narrish-work. Now this Narrishkeit is generally put out by Luftmensh—meanin', literal, *guys* who live on the *air*—from which we get the term "no visible god-damn means of support." Poem-writers, story-writers, picture-painters, we got *alotta* 'em come in here; what ya got is mainly y'Fairies, y'Bust-Outs and y'Souseniks—a blue *moon*, ya get a sober straight-shooter, breaks even. [*Slaps the table*] Now, I'm lookin' at this poem two months now, besides takin note, numerous situations, how you *present* y'self, kid— first-class, flat-out *amazin'*, this poem. [YOUNG CHARLIE *smiles happily,* EDDIE *his son's head* ] It's goddamn Niagara *Falls* in there—now all we gotta do is points it the right way so ya can turn on a coupla *light* bulbs with it. The *answer?* Head like yours, ya know it already, don't ya?

YOUNG CHARLIE: [*confused but flattered* ] No; I don't, Pop.

EDDIE: I speak, of course, of the Legal Profession! Brain like that, how you get them words together, I'm talkin' *Up*town, Charlie, I'm talkin' about the firm o'Ross, Ross, *Some*body and *Some*body; you're gonna be walkin' through places the dollars stick to your *shoes,* y'can't *kick* the bucks off. Hey, looka the experience you got already, huh? — [*rises, arms wide, delightedly struck by the perfect illustration*] — twelve years now you been pleadin' cases before the bar!

[EDDIE *laughs happily at his joke, slapping the bar,* YOUNG CHARLIE *laughing with him, their laughter building with the sharing of the joke,* CHARLIE *joining them*]

CHARLIE: [*chuckling*] Not bad, not bad; one for *you,* Pop... [*Suddenly frightened, remembering; he shouts*] Now — it was *now*—

[*We hear* GUSTA *scream from upstairs* — *a long, wrenching, mournful wail, like the siren of a passing ambulance* — *even at this distance, a stairway and a closed door between them, the sound permeates the barroom. Then silence;* EDDIE *and* YOUNG CHARLIE *frozen for a moment, then both racing towards the bottom of the stairs. Before they can reach the first step, though,* ZARETSKY *enters at the top of the stairs from the Apartment above, closing the door quietly behind himself.* EDDIE *and* YOUNG CHARLIE *remain quite still, several feet from the stairs;* ZARETSKY *takes a step or two down towards them*]

ZARETSKY: The telegram I opened was not for me, Itzik. It is for you and Gusta. Jussel is dead. He was killed two days ago. The first telegram says only [*he reads*] "The Secretary of War desires me to express his deep regret that your son, Petty Officer Second-Class Joseph Ross, was killed in action in defense of his country on August Sixth, Nineteen Forty-Five." [*A moment*] Gusta stays upstairs; she requests to be alone for a while. [EDDIE *and* YOUNG CHARLIE *remain standing quite still at the bottom of the stairs, their backs to us, not a tremor; their emotions unreadable*] There is more; shall I go on? [EDDIE *nods*] Enclosed also, a cable, this from Captain Nordheim of the Destroyer *Campbell.* He begins: "The fanatical suicide attack which caused the death of your son..."

[CHARLIE, *downstage, continuing the cable from memory now as* ZARETSKY *continues reading, inaudibly, on the stairs behind him*]

CHARLIE: "… is tragically consistent with the desperate actions of our enemy at this time of their imminent surrender. On the morning of August Sixth a force of eight Zeros descended upon the *St. Louis* and the *Campbell* at one-minute intervals; the Sixth and Seventh of these craft being destroyed by Petty Officer Ross from his Forward Forty-Millimeter position, the Eighth now aimed directly for his battle-station. With ample time to leave his position for safety, your son, to his undying honor, remained at his weapon, as determined to destroy the target as was the target to destroy his battle-station. As recommended and reviewed by myself and the Secretary of the Navy, it has been deemed appropriate to recognize his selfless valor by awarding the Navy Cross to Petty Officer Second-Class Joseph Ross. In addition, I have respected your son's prior request to be buried at sea, the Kaddish being read by an Ensign Sidney Berman for the name of Jussel Solomon Goldberg, also by the same request."

[*Starting with the first line of the above speech, the action will begin to move forward in time behind* CHARLIE *to the evening of the next day, the first of the seven days of Shiva, the family's mourning period— daylight giving way to night outside and near-darkness in the bar as* CHARLIE *speaks,* ZARETSKY *slowly folding the cable, putting on a yarmulkeh, and then joining* YOUNG CHARLIE *behind the bar where they drape a large piece of black cloth over the long bar-mirror; their movements— and those of the others during this transition— are deliberate, trancelike, ritualized, as though to the beat of inaudible music. During the draping of the mirror,* GUSTA *will have entered from the Apartment, her head covered with a dark shawl, carrying a tray of pastries and* EDDIE'S *black suit-jacket; she places the tray on the center table, drapes the jacket over a chair next to it, then places a piece of black cloth over* JOEY'S *Navy photograph above the Jukebox as* EDDIE, *who has remained quite still at center, slowly puts on his jacket, then sits at center table, blankly, looking off, as though in a dream.* YOUNG CHARLIE *comes up behind* EDDIE, *delicately places a yarmulkeh on his father's head and then one on his own as* NICK, HANNAH, *and then* FINNEY *come quietly through the front door; wearing dark clothes, each bearing a box of pastry, moving slowly, silently, through the half-light of the bar-room;* GUSTA *embracing*

HANNAH, *the two women holding onto each other for a few moments before* NICK *leads* HANNAH *gently away to their table and* GUSTA *sits at the Center table near* EDDIE. *After saying the last few words of the memorized Nordheim cable,* CHARLIE *pauses a moment, then turns to look at* EDDIE *who remains quite frozen, listless, on his chair:* HANNAH *and* NICK *at their usual table now, holding hands,* FINNEY *in the shadows of his booth, his head bowed. Charlie moves close to young* CHARLIE *and* ZARETSKY *now. The old man and the boy, having lit the seven-day memorial candle and placed it on the far left table, sit near its glow, leaning towards each other in quiet conversation*]

**CHARLIE:** I'd never said the Mourner's Kaddish before; I knew what the Hebrew words meant — but suddenly that morning in the synagogue it made no sense to me; here in this ancient, ancient prayer for the dead was not a reference, not a phrase ... not a word about death.

**ZARETSKY:** [*leans towards* YOUNG CHARLIE, *answering his question*] It's not *about* death, Chaim; we have here a prayer about faith only, absolute faith in God and his wisdom. [*Closes his eyes*] Listen, the music of it, "Yisgaddal v'yiskaddash shmey rabboh ... " You praise God, "B'rich Hu": "blessed be He; blessed, praised, glorified, exalted ... "

**EDDIE:** [*quietly, almost to himself, still looking off* ] It's like the Mafia, Charlie ... It's like talkin' to a Mafia Chief after he does a hit, ya kiss the Capo's ass so he don't knock *you* off too: "Hey, God, what a great idea, killin' Joey Ross. Throwin' my cousin Sunny under a garbage truck — I thought *that* was great — but havin' some nutso Nip drop Joey, this is you at the top of your *form*, baby ... " [GUSTA *rises slowly, staring down at him*] Oh, yeah, magnified and sanctified be *you*, Don Giuseppe ... [GUSTA *turns sharply, walks quickly to the stairs and exits into the Apartment;* EDDIE *barely glancing at her; continuing louder now, all in bar turning to him*] Hey, Charlie, that's *it* for Hebrew School. Over and *out* , kid. I hear ya go *near* the goddamn place I bust ya in the chops ... [*Rises, pulls off his yarmulkeh, then yanks off* YOUNG CHARLIE'S] *Hell* with the Bar Mitzvah; I'm takin' ya to Norfolk Street and gettin' ya *laid* that day ... [*As* EDDIE *continues, louder, his rage growing, we begin to hear* GUSTA *singing the old Yiddish lullaby we heard in Act One, distantly, gently, from upstairs*]

**GUSTA'S VOICE:** [*singing*]

"Oif'n pripitchok,

Brent a faierel,
Un in shtub iz heys..."

[*Continuing softly through the scene...*]

EDDIE: ... Three years Joey put in, the prayers, the bullshit, the Bar Mitzvah shot, the goddamn criminal *con* of the whole thing. I *knew* it—[*Shouting, striding fiercely to bar, tearing black cloth off of mirror*] I *told* ya, I knew it all *along* it was a sucker's game! You *watch* me, alla you, *tonight* I go to Beth-*El,* I go to the *East Window* because this is where God's supposed t'hear ya better—and I tell 'im , I tell the Killer Bastard—get *this,* God, I ain't a *Jew* no more! *Over,* pal! Fifty years of bein' a Jew Loser; over, baby! *Take* 'em, take the *resta* them, they're *yours—you* chose 'em, *you* got 'em—
YOUNG CHARLIE: [*quietly*] Shut up...
EDDIE: —every God-fearin' , *death-*fearin', scared-*shit*less *Jew*-creep is *yours—* but not *Eddie,* not—
YOUNG CHARLIE: Shut up, will ya? [*He rises*] You really gonna blame this on *God,* Pop? Really? This is what you *wanted,* Pop: Mr. America, the toughest Jew in the Navy, and you got it; only he's dead. Every *letter, twice* on the phone with him I heard ya—"Kill, kill, *kill* 'em, kid!" Same as you screamed at ringside. And you want God to take the blame for this? [*Pointing fiercely, tears in his eyes*] All for *you,* Pop, the Ring, the Twin-Forties, he was fightin' for *you.* "Kill 'em, kid! *Get* 'em!" No, Pop, no, not *God,* not God—you, it was *you,* it was *you,* Pop. [*He races quickly up the stairs, crying, exits into Apartment, slamming the door behind him*]

[*Silence for a moment, even* GUSTA'S *distant singing has stopped.* EDDIE *goes quickly up the stairs to the door*]

EDDIE: Listen to me, kid; ya got it all wrong, I straighten it out for ya.... [*He tries to open the door, but it has clearly been locked from the inside; he leans closer, raises his voice a bit, trying to talk to* YOUNG CHARLIE *through the door*] Listen to me, Charlie; it's just my wacky Pop, see. Just my wacky Pop all over again. *Fine* points; it's the goddamn *fine* points, kid— [*Louder, almost cracking, his rage holds him together*] He *knows* this Nip Fruitcake is comin' right *for* 'im, but he stays there behind his gun, because he thinks he's *supposed* to! It's my Pop all over again, pal—fine points; goddamn fine points! Wacky, the *both* o' them... *wacky...* [*Silence. He tries the knob again*] Come on, kid; open up. [*Silence*] Let's move it,

**493**

Charlie; let me in. [*Starts banging more forcefully on door*] Let me in, Charlie, Charlie, let me *in*, let me *in!* [*Both fists together now, pounding rhythmically, shouting with each blow*] Let me *in*, let me *in*, let me *in*…

[*He continues banging on the door; his shouting almost like a chant now;* NICK *and* FINNEY *rise as though to come to his aid;* ZARETSKY *remains on his wooden box, his head bowed, intoning loudly above the din*]

ZARETSKY: "Yisgaddal v'yiskaddash shmey rabboh…"

[*A sudden silence, a sharp drop in light, they are all quite still, frozen silhouettes in the dim remaining glow;* CHARLIE *alone in a small spotlight at right, caught by the moment*]

CHARLIE: [*turns to us; softly, a plea*] I didn't mean it, I just… I mean, I was *twelve* at the time, very upset, a *kid*… I was just… ya know what I mean?

[*The sudden sound of Lyndon Johnson's Voice fills the stage, his echoing drawl offering the promise of the Great Society as* EDDIE, ZARETSKY, HANNAH, NICK *and* FINNEY *exit into the shadows of the bar, the Flamingo Chandelier rising into the darkness above it,* CHARLIE *moving slowly down center as this part of his past disappears behind him*]

JOHNSON'S VOICE: Is our world gone? We say farewell. Is a new world coming? We welcome it. And we bend it to the hopes of Man…

CHARLIE: [*turns to us, brightening*] Amazingly… amazingly, life went back to normal after Joey died — Pop quickly resumed living at the top of his voice and the edge of his nerves, battling with Zaretsky in the mornings and me in the afternoons and re-naming the bar "Big Ed's Club Canal." My next bout with Pop oh, there were a few minor exhibition matches about leaving home at seventeen, not going to Law School, not visiting often enough — but our next real bout was more than twenty years later. October Fifteenth, Sixty-Five; I remember exactly because it was the morning the Vatican Council announced that the Jews were no longer responsible for the death of Christ…

[*As he continues, an older* GUSTA, *her raven hair streaked with gray, enters from the Kitchen in the dim half-light behind him, carrying a tray; she will move briskly from table to table as he speaks, clearing away the many plastic pineapples and coconut shells, eventually disappearing back into the Kitchen*]

By then I had become one of the blue-moon Luftmenshen who had *made* it in the Narrishkeit business. This, starting at the age of twenty-*three*, by knockin' out almost one novel a year. The most familiar to you, from the early Sixties, would be *Over at Izzy's Place*, the first of the "Izzy" books, eight and still counting, three best-sellers by then, vast areas of virgin forest consumed by paperback sales, undisputed Middleweight Champ at thirty-four, I had become... unavoidable. And so had Izzy. Izzy, tough but warm, blunt yet wise, the impossible and eccentric Bleecker Street tavern-keeper who won not only your heart in the final chapter, but the Mayor's Special Cultural Award that year for "embodying the essential charm and excitement of New York's ethnic street life." [*Shakes his head, smiling*] Unavoidable, that is, to everyone but Pop. Hard to take it personally, he never read anything longer than Winchell's column or the Blow-by-Blows in the Trib. We were down to maybe four or five visits a year by then—the first half of each being consumed with how long it'd been since the last one and the second half with contractual arrangements for the next—and we didn't meet at the usual family weddings and Bar Mitzvahs because Pop would never again enter a synagogue or any place that resembled one... [*Lights coming up slowly on the bar as he continues;* GUSTA, *who has returned from the Kitchen, sits alone now at the center table, business-like, in charge, wearing glasses, checking a stack of bills, as* CHARLIE *moves about her in the empty bar-room indicating the places where The Regulars once sat*] Hannah was gone by then, and Nick too; I never did learn their last names. Finney—old, but sharp as ever—smelled O.T.B. and Legal Lottery in the wind and was now taking Temperature-Humidity Index bets at a Kosher Delicatessen in Boca Raton. Mr. Zaretsky died in January of Sixty-One, just a week before his ninety-third birthday, during the closing moments of a concert for the Y.M.H.A. of St. Louis, in Missouri, performing his twelve-minute version of "The Dybbuk"; passing away in crimson light, playing all parts... including title role. [*Moving down behind* GUSTA's *chair as she continues busily checking bills*] I called Mom every Sunday to hear her two jokes of the week, but this last call was different—Pop'd had a mild heart attack in Sixty-Four from which he'd quickly recovered, but now she said something had "gone wrong with the health"; I asked for more details but she was already into her second joke by then—[*Sound of* EDDIE *laughing loudly from the kitchen as though at what* CHARLIE *has just said; morning light starts to stream in from outside as* GUSTA *rises with her stack of bills, exits briskly up the stairs into Apartment*]—so I came down early the next morning to check it out myself, and found him as always, in better shape than I was . . . [EDDIE *enters from the Kitchen chuckling happily at something on the front page of* The New York World-Telegram; EDDIE, *though twenty years older, seems spry enough as he walks down towards the far right booth, sharply opening the paper to read the rest of the front-page story that amuses him so much; the front page faces us now and we see a huge banner headline which states: "Vatican Absolves Jews of Crucifixion Blame."* CHARLIE *turns to him*] Pop . . .

EDDIE: [*glances up from paper, pleasantly*] Hey . . . it's *him*. [*Returns to paper*] How ya doin', kid?

CHARLIE: Fine, fine; I'm—

EDDIE: How'd ya get in?

CHARLIE: I got my key. Listen, Pop, I was . . . uh . . . in the neighborhood, stopped by . . .

EDDIE: [*sits in booth, still reading paper*] In the neighborhood?

CHARLIE: Yeah, right . . . [*Approaches booth, indicating headline*] Well, I see you've gotten the big news, Pop.

EDDIE: Winchell had it two days ago. Just sent the Pope off a telegram on the matter; here's a copy. [*Hands him piece of note paper*]

CHARLIE: [*reading*] I don't think they just hand telegrams to the Pope directly, Pop; especially ones that say, "Thanks a lot, you Greaseball Putz."

EDDIE: Well, let's see, must be what?—four, five months now since you last—

CHARLIE: Let's skip that one this time, O.K.? Mom tells me we got a health problem here.

EDDIE: [*slaps table, laughing*] I don't believe it. I don't *believe* it. Six *months* ago I say I'm not feelin' so good, she decides to hear it *now*. That listening thing she does—I'm tellin' ya, kid, it's wackier than ever—the woman hears less and less every week and what she *does* get comes to her entirely by *carrier*-pigeon. [CHARLIE *smiles;* EDDIE *rises from booth*] Old news, kid, I'm fine now; looka me. [*Demonstrates a boxing combination*] Looka me, huh? Also the place is a hit, Charlie; just happened the last few months. Hey not *giant*, but a hit. [*Chuckles, pointing upstairs*] She did it; the Wacky One. Turns out, right near here, starts out a whole new neighborhood, "HoHo"—

CHARLIE: That's "SoHo"—

EDDIE: [*with a sly wink*] I'm tellin' ya, kid, *Ho* Ho—wall-to-wall Luftmensh, blocks and *blocks* of 'em, doin' nothin' but Narrishkeit, and they got these *galleries* here, hustlin' the Narr for 'em; *bucks*, Charlie, bucks like ya wouldn't believe—and all from this Narrishkeit done by these Luftmensh livin' in these Lufts around here.

CHARLIE: Lofts, Pop.

EDDIE: And the *rent* for these Lufts—I'm talkin' *Vegas* money, Charlie. Anyways, maybe five months ago, a coupla these Narrishkeit Hustlers come in here, they're havin' some o' the Mulligan Stew—they go *crazy* for it—

CHARLIE: I don't blame them—

EDDIE: Next thing I know we got a goddamn *army* o' these Narrishkeit people with the fancy Lufts comin' here, they're gobblin' up everything in sight, they love the stuff and they love Mama—under the original *names*, the Varnichkes, the Holishkes—they come in strangers, they go out grandchildren. I put up a new sign outside, musta seen it, "The Homeland"—I up the prices a little, we're a *hit*, not a cha*malia*, but we're doin' O. K. Your Mom done it. [*Sits at center table*]

CHARLIE: She mentioned something about hiring a waitress, but I had no idea—[*sits opposite him*] this is *great*, Pop.

EDDIE: Yeah; so how *you* doin'?

CHARLIE: Well, I'm workin' on a new—

EDDIE: Hey, I seen ya on the TV last week.

CHARLIE: Oh?

EDDIE: Yeah, you was gettin' some prize for somethin', the Mayor was there.

CHARLIE: Right.

EDDIE: Yeah, I seen ya on the TV. You come in old.

CHARLIE: Old?

EDDIE: Yeah; I mean, you're a young fellah, but on TV you come in old.

CHARLIE: Pop, do you happen to recall *which* prize it was and *what* I got it for?

EDDIE: It was one o' them "Dizzy" books.

CHARLIE: "Izzy," Pop, *"Izzy"*—

EDDIE: Maybe it was the tuxedo.

CHARLIE: The tuxedo?

EDDIE: That made you come in old. Yeah, that's what it was.

CHARLIE: O. K., Pop, I'm glad you're feeling well, and I'm delighted about the place. [*Rising to leave*] Now I gotta—

EDDIE: O. K.; give my regards to ... to ... uh ...

CHARLIE: Allison.

EDDIE: What happened to Sally?

CHARLIE: We were divorced three years ago. As you well know.

EDDIE: [*hits his head*] Of course. Of course. Hard to keep track, alla them—

CHARLIE: Pop, I've only been married twice, Sally and *Karen*—

EDDIE: Better catch up; that puts you two behind Rita Hayworth. So what's with this ... uh ... ?

CHARLIE: Allison. You've had dinner with her twice. Last time for three hours. She told you she was editing a book that proved Roosevelt did nothing for the Jews during the War. You broke two plates and walked out. She thought you were cute.

EDDIE: [*after a moment*] Shit, *marry* that one.

CHARLIE: [*starts towards door*] O. K., I really gotta—

EDDIE: Right; hugs to Sarah and Josh—hey, Josh; where's my Josh? Been a coupla *months* now—

CHARLIE: He was hanging around here entirely too much, Pop, it was—

EDDIE: We talk things *over*, we *discuss* things—

CHARLIE: Pop, he's the only ten-year-old at Dalton who drinks his milk out of a shot-glass.

EDDIE: [*laughs happily*] A *pisser*, that kid; goddamn *pisser*—

CHARLIE: [*opens door*] Right; see ya around—

EDDIE: [*quietly*] O. K., them books, I read one. [CHARLIE *turns at door, his hand on knob*] Well, not *read*; I give it a skim. The first one. [*Chuckling*] That's some *sweet*heart, that guy. Who *is* that guy? The bartender with the two sons, comes from Russia; who *is* that sweetie? Got *all* sweeties in there, y'sweet blind lady, y'sweet ex-cop, y'sweet bookie—*three* pages, I got an attack o' diabetes.

CHARLIE: Pop, if I told the truth they'd send a *lynch*-mob down here for ya.
EDDIE: Always glad to see new customers, kid. This guy in the book,
supposed to be a Jewish guy, right? What kinda Jew is that? Don't sound
like no Jew *I* ever heard. Could be anything—Italian, Irish, some kinda
Chink even. [*Turns to newspaper*] Well, what the hell, regardless, I wanna
wish ya good luck with them "Dizzy" books.
CHARLIE: Izzy! [*Closes door, turns to him*] Izzy, Izzy, Izzy. As you know damn
*well.* O.K., that's it. No more, Pop, that was *it.* I am never playing this
fucking game again; it's *over.* [*Moving towards him*] Izzy? You don't like
him? Not Jewish enough for ya? He's *your Jew,* Pop, you made him up.
He's *your* Jew, and so am I; no history, no memory, the only thing I'm
linked to is a chain of bookstores. Vos *vilst* du?—that's Yiddish, Pop, it
means "What do you *want?*" God bothered you, we got rid of him.
Hugging bothers you, we do not touch. Here I am, Pop, just what the
Rabbi ordered; only now you don't like it; now you don't want it. Vos
vilst du, Goldberg? [*Leans towards him at table*] That prize you don't
know the *name* of for the books you never read—I won it, Pop, *me* the
*air*-person, I *did* it—[*bangs fist on table, shouting*]—right here at this bar,
everything you *asked* for. I am an honest-to-God, red-white-and-blue,
*American fucking millionaire.* A *mil,* Pop, a *mil,* a *bundle!* And I never
sleep, only in moving vehicles, I hail a cab to take a nap; I work, I work,
there's like a fire in me and I don't know where it is so I cannot put it
out. And the fire is you. I *did* it, Pop. I won. K. O. in the first *round.* Vos
*vilst* du, Papa? Vos *vilst* du fun mir? What do you fucking *want?*

[*Silence for a moment.* EDDIE *remains quite still*]

EDDIE: [*quietly*] You shouldn't use "fuck" in a sentence, Charlie, you never
put it in the right place. You don't blow good, kid, never did; ya don't
have the knack. Another item: I listen to ya, I don't like the scorin' on
this bout. How about *I* get credit for all the hits and *you* get the credit for
bein' a nervous nut. [*Rises from chair, his old energy*] What're you,
Goddamn Zorro the Avenger? What? You lookin' to come back here with
your empties and get a refund? I didn't *order* this item, you ain't a *cake* I
baked. I wasn't just your Pop, or Joey's neither, I'm Eddie; for this I take
all blame or commendations. Nothin' else. I lived in *my* time, now you
gotta live in *yours,* pal, and you can't send me the goddamn bill. Give it
*up,* kid, give it the hell *up.* Give yourself a rest, you'll waste your life tryin'

to catch me, you'll find y'self twenty years from now runnin' around a cemetery tryin' to put a stake through my heart. Sure I screwed up; now it's *your* turn. Yeah, let's see what *you* do when you look at Sarah or Josh and see your *Pop's* eyes peekin' out at ya; or worse, your *own.* Let's see what ya *do* kid. [*Turns, starts towards bar*] Meanwhile, currently, I admit I give ya a hard time—but, frankly, I never liked Rich Kids. [*He stops, stands quite still; speaks briskly*] O. K., conversation over. End of conversation. See ya around; goodbye—[*Grips back of chair staggers, as though about to faint, whispering*] Shit, here we go again... [*He suddenly falls to the ground, the chair clattering down with him*]

CHARLIE: [*rushing to him, breathless*] Pop, Jesus... Pop...

EDDIE: [*almost immediately, sitting up*] It's O. K., it's O. K., get me a vodka...

CHARLIE: [*helping him up*] Pop, I thought you—

EDDIE: *Vodka,* get me a vodka—[CHARLIE *races behind the bar;* EDDIE, *standing now but still a bit unsteady, leans on the table for a moment*] O. K., O. K. now. Comes, then it goes. [*Walking slowly to bar*] Comes, then it goes. Fine now. Perfect. [CHARLIE, *behind bar, quickly pouring a glass of vodka, handing it out to him— but* EDDIE *grabs the bottle and takes a long swig directly from it*] Excellent. Excellent. [*Sets bottle down on bar; renewed. Silence for a moment*] O. K., I conned ya, Charlie... I got this heart thing; special disease named for some Goy, Smithfield. Your Mother says right off, "How come you got Smithfield's Disease and he don't got yours?" Don't care how old the joke is, what the occasion, she tells it. Turns out that wasn't no heart attack last year, it was this *Smithfield* number. The valve closes up, you keep fallin' asleep, fallin' over—[*Pulls wheelchair out from behind far end of bar*] I'm supposed to sit in this thing alot because I keep droppin' alla time. What kills you is these Embies—

CHARLIE: [*quietly*] I think that's... that's Embolus, Pop...

EDDIE: [*moving wheelchair down left*] Right. Anyways you can shoot off these Embies anytime. They go all over the joint. Musta shot one off four weeks ago, I'm all screwed up, I go in for these tests—turns out I'm the proud owner of a new, fully automatic *Smithfield.* Knocks you off in like six months or maybe next Tuesday. So—[*sits down in wheelchair*] good ya stopped by, we do a wrap-up shot, I got a *job* for ya—

CHARLIE: [*sits next to wheelchair*] The doctors, they're *sure?*—I mean, I can get you—

EDDIE: Minute I get the news I got only one item concerns me, see; I go down to Barney's Tattoo Parlor on Mott, take care of it right off, goddamn relief. Looka here—[*Rolls up both sleeves,* CHARLIE *comes closer to look at the two tattoos*] One says "Pistol Pete," see, nice gun picture there, and this one here—

CHARLIE: [*reading elaborate red and blue tattoo on* EDDIE's *left arm; confused*] "King of the Twin-Forties." I don't—

EDDIE: [*triumphantly*] Hebrew *law*, Charlie—one of the oldest—you can't get buried in *any* Jewish Cemetery if you got tattoos! Twenty *years*, kid, I ain't had to be no kinda *Jew* at *all*—coulda ended up gettin' Kaddished—over, full-out ceremony, then gettin' stuck in some sacred Jew-ground with a buncha Yiddlach for *eternity!* [*Quietly, glancing upstairs*] She ain't to be trusted on this issue; since Joey, the woman is a goddamn religious *fanatic*—candles, prayers, every weird little holiday— [*leans towards Charlie, grips his arm*] So, here's the job, Charlie—*any*-thing goes wrong, I want your personal guarantee—

CHARLIE: Of course, Pop—

EDDIE: [*hands him card from wallet*] Here's where ya put me, kid; place in Queens, no religions whatever, no Gods of any type.

CHARLIE: It's done.

EDDIE: Because the woman, I'm tellin' ya, she's got her eye on this spot in Brooklyn where they planted the Actor. woman thinks dyin' is movin' to the *suburbs*, wants us all *together* there—me, her, Ethel, and *Zaretsky!* Can ya *picture* it, Charlie?—me and Zaretsky, goddamn *room*mates *forever!* Wouldn't get a minute's rest. 'Specially *now*, what I know *now*... [*He looks away. Silence for a moment*]

CHARLIE: *What?* What do you know now?

EDDIE: [*pause; a deep breath, plunges in*] O. K.—*day* before he goes to St. Louis, the man gets a flash he's gonna kick it, makes out a will. Man is ninety-goddamn-*three*, he's first makin' out a will. Brings a lawyer over here, also about a hundred and eight, Ruskin, used to do all his business when he had the New Marinsky on Houston, wants me and Finney to witness, sign the will. I look it over, I see two things—first, I'm not in it; second , whatever he's got is goin' to the State of Israel... whatever he's *got* bein' one million, five hundred thousand dollars and change. A mil and a half, Charlie; the man was sittin on a *mil* and a *half.* And this Ruskin almost as rich; *Ruskin*, with an accent on 'im made Zaretsky sound like George M. *Cohan!* They sell this Marinsky dump for bupkes back in Twenty-Eight; they parlay the bupkes into a fortune, they was good at *business, American business,* and the rest he got from them goddamn *concerts,* Charlie! [*A pause; he rubs the arm of the wheelchair*] I made Finney promise to zip it; I never told you, Gusta, nobody...

CHARLIE: Hey, far as me and Joey were concerned, you were always the *boss* here; wouldn't've made any difference—

EDDIE: A mil and a *half,* Charlie—he's livin' in that little room, takin' shit from me—

CHARLIE: He *loved* it here, Pop—he even liked fightin' with *you,* he—

[CHARLIE *stops in mid-sentence, aware that* EDDIE *has started to nod off to sleep...* EDDIE *suddenly hits the arm of his wheelchair, forcing himself awake*]

EDDIE: [*outraged*] A *millionaire,* Charlie! Workin' in a loser language! He did everything *wrong*—and he was a hit! Can you make sense of this, Charlie? *Zaretsky,* why *him*—why *him* and not *me?* And, you'll forgive me—I wish ya all the best—[*gripping* CHARLIE's *arm*] but why *you,* ya little Putz, you with your goddamn *Narrishkeit*—why *you,* and not me? Why? [*Starting to become drowsy again*] Surrounded by goddamn millionaires here... Can you make *sense* of this... the Bucks, what happened? The Big Bucks, why did they avoid me? Wherever I was, the Bucks never came, and when I went to where the Bucks were they flew away like pigeons... like pigeons in the park... [*his head nodding forward, drifting off*] Got this dream all time I'm at Ellis Island, only I'm the age I'm now. Old days, you had a disease, they wouldn't let ya in. They mark on your coat with chalk, "E" for eye, "L" for lung and they send ya back. In the dream, I got an "H" for heart and they won't let me in... they won't let me in, Joey... [*He falls deeply asleep in the wheelchair. Silence.* CHARLIE *leans anxiously towards him*]

CHARLIE: Pop...? [*Touches his arm gently*] Pop...? [*Silence again.* CHARLIE *rises, carefully turning the wheelchair around so that* EDDIE's *sleep is not disturbed by the morning light that comes in from the front door.* EDDIE *remains with his back to us; during this next scene we will not see his face except perhaps for brief glimpses of his profile.* CHARLIE *speaking to us as he turns the chair*] Six weeks later one o' them Embies shot off into the left side of Pop's brain paralyzing his right arm and leg and taking away his ability to speak. [*Opening small side table on arm of wheelchair, placing ad and pencil on it*] Two weeks back from the hospital he had somehow taught himself to write almost legibly with his left hand — according to this terrific Speech Therapy lady I went to, this meant he could eventually be trained to speak again. But all he was able to produce were these unintelligible, childlike noises, and he refused to see anyone, no less try to *speak* to anyone, including Gusta. He closed "The Homeland" down and sat here. Ten days, like this. On the eleventh day, armed with some hints from the Speech Therapist I came down to take a shot. [*To* EDDIE] Delighted to see me, huh? [EDDIE *shakes his head angrily*] And you're thinkin' what's the sense of trying to learn how to speak again because you figure you *can't,* also why torture yourself if you ain't gonna live that much longer *anyway,* right? [EDDIE *points with his left hand as though to say "You got it," then does a powerful "Go away" gesture*] Right. And there's these clear pictures in your head of all the words you want to say and your mouth just won't do the job, right? [EDDIE *does not respond. Then, after a moment, he nods "Yes"*] O. K., now I don't know *how* this works or *why* this works, but there's a thing you're capable of right now called "Automatic Speech." As impossible as it must feel to you, you are capable, right now, of saying, distinctly as *ever;* certain automatic phrases — ends of songs, if I do the first part, a piece of a prayer, something. And, thing is, you hear yourself *do* that and that'll get you to want to work at the whole talkin'-shot again, see. [EDDIE *scribbles something on the pad on the arm of his wheelchair, hands pad to* CHARLIE] "Go *away. Stay* away." Pop, I gotta try the number here. C'mon, gimme a chance... [CHARLIE *leans forward, singing softly*] "Oh beautiful for spacious skies... " [*Pause, no response.* CHARLIE *tries again*] "Oh beautiful for spacious skies, for amber... " [*Silence for a few moments; then very suddenly, sharply*] You got some ice-cold Daitch on tap, fellah?

EDDIE: [*suddenly*] *I* got it, now *you...* got it. [EDDIE *realizes what he has just done.* CHARLIE *smiles. Silence for a moment;* EDDIE *appears to be chuckling softly*]

CHARLIE: Well, now. Shall we proceed, sir? [*Silence for a moment.* EDDIE *turns away; then looks at* CHARLIE; *he nods*] O. K., now we got some pictures here... [*Takes a stack of eight-by-eleven-inch cards out of an envelope*] Objects, people, animals, O. K.? Double item here, see; there's a picture of the thing and then the word for it printed underneath. You go for either one—word or picture, and *say* what it is. Be patient with yourself on this, O. K.? [EDDIE *nods*] O. K.; animals and birds. [*Looks through cards, stops at one; smiles*] Yeah, here's a good beginning... [*He turns the card around; it is a full-color illustration of a duck*] "Duck." We'll start with "Duck."

[EDDIE *does not move, there is a long silence. Then* EDDIE, *rather forcefully, raises his left arm, the middle finger of his hand jabbing upward, giving* CHARLIE *"The Finger."* EDDIE *continues to hold his hand up firmly; the lights come down, one single light remaining on "The Finger"*]

CHARLIE: [*turns to us*] Well, there it is, my last image of my father: his memorial, his obelisk, his Washington Monument. [*He moves across towards his booth at far right, the light gradually dimming down of "The Finger" during his next speech; only a small spotlight on* CHARLIE, *the rest of the stage in near-darkness*] He died about seven months later; by then he was talking, even hollering, and terrorizing his third Speech Therapist. [*We hear the distant sound of a Cantor singing a phrase of the Kaddish, rising then fading, as the barely visible shape of the older* GUSTA *comes out of the Kitchen; she rolls the wheelchair off into the shadows as* CHARLIE *continues*] Bicentennial's next week, two hundred years since America was born and, two days later, ten years since Pop died. I wish I could tell you that he won my heart in the final chapter, but he did not. I light his Yahrzeit candle every year, though, and say the prayer; I figured Mom would appreciate it. [*After a moment*] It's a month now since *she* died, joking as she closed her act. "I'm thinking of becoming a Catholic," she says, that last night. "And why's that, Ma?" I say, feeding her the straight-line like a good son—[*With* GUSTA's *accent*] "Well, Sonny, I figure better one of *them* goes than one of *us*." [*Takes keys from jacket*] I miss her, of course; but I will not miss this place. [*A beat*] Pop got his wish, of course; I buried him in this aggressively non-sectarian joint called Hamilton Oaks out in Queens. However, one of the reasons I never forget his Yahrzeit is that every year, a week before the Sixth... [*he takes the familiar blue and white card out of his jacket*] this card comes from the Sons of Moses to remind me. For fifty bucks he got them to find me for the *rest of my life*. Los Angeles, *London*, the Virgin fucking *Islands*, they *find* me, those Sons of Moses...

[*The sudden lights of the Present—the early evening light of the beginning of the play—come up in the barroom as* CHARLIE *holds the card up and crushes it fiercely in his hand; he tosses the mangled card on the floor and strides angrily towards the bar, the old Stroller once again down left, his rage building as he slams noisily about behind the bar looking for his glass and vodka bottle*]

CHARLIE: The old switcheroo—the old switcheroo every time! Never made any *sense, never*—his *head,* his *head,* it was *Steeple*chase up there, the goddamn *Roller*-coaster—[*Bangs his fist on the bar*] *None* of it, nothing he said, *none* of it fit together—*none* of it—*still* doesn't—son of a bitch—

JOSH: [*entering briskly from the Apartment above, carrying two cartons; brightly*] Dad...Dad, I've been thinking, how about—why don't we *keep* this place and just get somebody to *run* it for us; y'know, a manager, we'll find a good manager. We *keep* it, Dad we keep it just the way it *is;* I'll help out, weekends, every summer, maybe even—

CHARLIE: [*fiercely, wildly, shouting*] I *told* you, we're *selling* it, we're selling it, you don't *listen*—

JOSH: [*startled*] I just—I just thought maybe we could—

CHARLIE: [*he smashes his fist on the bar, coming quickly out from behind bar towards* JOSH] It's *gone, over,* outa *my* life, outa *yours, over, over*—[CHARLIE, *blindly, violently, his fist raised, advancing on* JOSH, JOSH *backing fearfully away across the room*]—you don't *listen,* you *never did*—you don't *now,* you never *did,* and you never *will*—

[JOSH *is trapped against one of the booths, startled, frozen.* CHARLIE *stops, stands quite still, trembling with his own rage; then gradually begins to focus on his son's frightened eyes; he lowers his fist*]

CHARLIE: [*lost, whispering*] Josh...sorry, I was...

[JOSH *backs away towards the front door; warily, as though from a stranger*]

JOSH: [*softly*] You get yourself together, O.K. ...? I'll wait in the car, O.K ...?

CHARLIE: Josh, I'm sorry...I was...see, I was...

**JOSH:** You get yourself together, I'll be in the car...
**CHARLIE:** [*moving towards him, his hand up*] Josh, what happened, let me explain...

[*But* JOSH *has gone out into the street with his cartons, the door closing behind him.* CHARLIE *stands exhausted at the center of the room, looking at the door; silence for several moments. He turns, looks about at the bar for a moment, sees the crumpled Sons of Moses card on the floor; he picks it up, studies it thoughtfully, then starts straightening it out as he walks slowly towards the bar. We begin to hear the violin introduction to* AARON LEBEDEFF *recording of "Rumania" from the Jukebox, and then* LEBEDEFF'S *rousing voice*]

**LEBEDEFF'S VOICE:**

"Rumania, Rumania, Rumania...
Geven amol a land a zise, a sheyne..."

[*As* CHARLIE *reaches the bar and sits on one of the stools; the old bar lights fade quickly up, the colorful lights of the Thirties and Forties, and* EDDIE *enters briskly from the Kitchen, the younger* EDDIE *with his fine white shirt, black bow-tie and sharp black pants;* EDDIE *goes directly behind the bar, takes a glass and a bottle from the shelf, pours with his usual flourish and sets a drink down next to* CHARLIE; CHARLIE *looking down at the card as the Lebedeff Music fills the room,* EDDIE *leaning forward with his hands on the bar, looking at the front door, waiting for customers, as...*]

THE CURTAIN FALLS

# BROKEN GLASS

*Arthur Miller*

*Broken Glass.* Booth Theatre, New York, 1994. Amy Irving and Ron Rifkin. Photo © Inge Morath/Magnum Photos.

# INTRODUCTION

Arthur Miller's seven-decade-long career is a landmark in American theatre history. From his first commercial success, *All My Sons* in 1947, to *Resurrection Blues*, mounted by the Guthrie Theater in 2002, Miller has brought to the stage the vision, ethics and artistic vitality that have earned him international homage. Writing late in 2002, eminent theatre personage Robert Brustein, not always a Miller fan, saluted him as, "a true public intellectual [who] leaves behind not just a legacy of powerful plays, but also a shining moral example unmatched in American theatre." At a 1997 tribute, director Nicholas Hytner reported, "In England we revere him as one step above God and one step below Shakespeare." He has won all the major awards and prizes, from the Pulitzer (for *Death of a Salesman*) in 1949, to the National Medal of Arts in 1993, to the Jerusalem Prize in 2003.

While Miller is best known for theatrical achievements, he has written screenplays (*The Misfits, The Crucible*), radio scripts, travel books with his late wife, renowned photographer Inge Morath, as well as prose fiction and essays. In *Playing for Time* (1981), he adapted for TV the memoirs of French chanteuse Fania Fénelon, who survived Auschwitz by playing in the camp orchestra.

Between 1965–1968, he served as president of PEN, providing leadership that invigorated the international writers organization and guided its protests against repression. Miller's choice of words in welcoming writers from the Soviet bloc into PEN membership is strikingly Jewish. "The writing community," he exulted, "would at last be a light unto the nations" (*Timebends*, 581).

Arthur Miller was born in New York in 1915. His father's coat manufacturing business fell victim to the Wall Street crash. Thus Miller was alert early to the insecurities of the Depression and the winds of social revolution. They nurtured the concerns that became his signature subjects: the demand for universal justice, the importance of individual responsibility and the effects of social tensions on family relationships. He was also shaped by growing up in a Jewish family in a Jewish neighborhood. He writes in his autobiography *Timebends* of his awareness that his "skin had been absorbing two thousand years of European history" (24). His first play, *No Villain* (1936), depicts the impact of economic crisis on a Jewish coat manufacturer and his family. *No Villain*'s protest against an oppressive economic system and its portrayal of an inharmonious family, if not its level of achievement, were likened to *Awake and Sing!* The comparison must have pleased the young Miller who recognized Odets's poetic verve as trailblazing.

As an artist aspiring to address a universal audience, Miller saw himself in "the psychological role of mediator between the Jews and America, and among Americans themselves as well" (*Timebends*, 82). The second audience is the more dominant. Scholar Enoch Brater has aptly observed that Miller's forte is ethics, not ethnicity.[1] Nonetheless, Jewish characters and content are generously represented in his canon, sometimes more explicitly than others. Miller's lifelong sympathy for the common man, the importance he attaches to meaningful continuity, his alertness to far-off but imminent menace, and the primacy attached to individual and social responsibility in his work are all rooted in profoundly Jewish self-awareness.

There has been prolonged and, for me, largely unrewarding critical attention to unmasking Arthur Miller's supposed crypto-Jews, most famously the *dramatis personae* of *Death of a Salesman*. Miller has never disguised having drawn these characters as composites of relatives and acquaintances, some of whom were Jewish. There seems to be little to gain by forcing an ethnic specificity the playwright did not intend and, in the case of *Salesman,* deliberately avoided in the goal of indicting the fickleness of the American dream. However, when his themes or situations do draw their substance from Jewishness, Miller writes Jews. The distinction is clear in a comparison between his two 1964 works, *After the Fall* and *Incident at Vichy.*

*After the Fall* was inspired by Albert Camus' *The Fall.* The French novel centers on the moral dilemma of a self-styled judge-penitent. He has not intervened to stop a suicide and so is consumed by remorse. Miller wanted to go beyond

---

[1] Enoch Brater, "Ethics and Ethnicity in the Plays of Arthur Miller," in Cohen, ed. *From Hester Street to Hollywood,* 123–126.

the guilt of the observer/survivor, to address the evasion of responsibility that permits people to disavow complicity in their own failures. For Arthur Miller, Jew and citizen of the 20th century, the defining failure, the fall, of modern times is the Holocaust.

*After the Fall* is set in the mind of its protagonist Quentin, a landscape dominated by the tower of a German concentration camp. Having rehearsed his personal betrayals in the shadow of this icon of the most evil and horrendous betrayal of humanity, Quentin cries, "Who can be innocent again on this mountain of skulls!... — my brothers died here... but my brothers built this place; our hearts have cut this stone." The first person indictments are unmistakably universal. There are no specifications of ethnicity in *After the Fall*.

By contrast, the contemporaneous *Incident at Vichy* focuses intensely on the question of guilt and responsibility in an explicitly Jewish context. The play is set in 1942 in the anteroom of a detention center where men rounded up by the police await interrogation and almost certain deportation. At the play's center are three rational and rationalizing men: von Berg, an Austrian prince, who was doubtless arrested erroneously, a French Jewish psychiatrist Leduc, and the German major assigned to oversee this nasty process. In an earlier time, the German and the Frenchman had worn their countries' uniforms and faced off at Amiens in a combat they understood. But in the present situation, the major sees himself as a cog in an inexorable machine, and the psychiatrist cannot give his captor a convincing reason that he is the worthier to exist. Admitting that he would save himself at the expense of another, Leduc recognizes that he has been deceiving himself about the reasonableness of human behavior, particularly his own. The psychiatrist is unmoved by the von Berg's genuine despair that the Nazis have created a world unfit for what used to be human beings. But Leduc does not want the prince's guilt. Rather, he contends that no one can call himself human until he puts himself in the next man's place and feels accountable rather than relieved that he is afflicted. Moreover, his psychiatric practice has taught him that all Gentiles harbor some enmity against Jews. To von Berg's protest, Leduc responds with a startling definition: "Jew is only that name we give to that stranger, that agony we cannot feel, that death we look on like a cold abstraction." This is potent moral suasion. Given his pass to freedom, von Berg presses it on the doctor. Now along with survivor guilt, Leduc must accept responsibility that the prince, descendant of a thousand years of decency and culture, dies as his Jew. Leduc is unlikely to find respite from the imperative to answer the major's question, why he is worthier to live than the next man.

Miller's redefinition of "Jew" as an ethical category is a powerful statement of the definitive expulsion from pre-Holocaust Eden. After Auschwitz, say both these plays, innocence is impossible.

*Incident at Vichy* deepens Miller's examination of individual accountability for barbarity behavior first expressed in his 1945 novel *Focus*. Here, when a Gentile, ambiguously named Lawrence Newman starts to wear glasses, he is taken for a Jew by a bigoted society looking for targets. Ultimately, Newman adopts the ethnicity he once disdained and makes common cause with other victims of anti-Semitism.

In vivid contrast to the non-Jews who adopt Jewish identity in *Focus* and *Vichy* stands the fabulous 89-year-old figure at the center of *The Price* (1968). Gregory Solomon is the used furniture dealer called in to bid on the household effects inherited by two estranged brothers. Solomon could be an elaboration of two theatrical stock types, the old-clothes man and the wanderer, but there are more substantial reasons for his Jewishness. Miller endows him with a *vita* that includes struggling "in six different countries," service in the British navy, recovery from four financial ruins and a career as the bottom man of an acrobatic act that played the vaudeville circuit. The circus act is a wonderfully apt metaphor, for Solomon incarnates whole chapters of Jewish history. He has survived by maintaining his balance and his sense of humor is intact. Solomon is suitably named. In arbitrating between the brothers, he argues the necessity of belief in life, whatever its disappointments and defeats. The curtain scene of *The Price* is among the most unforgettable moments in the Miller canon. Solomon, alone on stage, dwarfed and frightened by his massive purchase, puts an ancient party laugh record on the phonograph and gradually succumbs to hilarity and the life-giving embrace of the comic.

In *The American Clock* (1982), inspired in part by Studs Terkel's portraits of victims of the Great Depression, in part by his own experience of it, Miller paints on a broad canvas. The play's large cast of characters prominently features the Baum family, whose misfortunes parallel Miller's own family's. In *Broken Glass* (1994), he returns to the Depression years, but here Miller narrows and intensifies his focus.

Phillip Gellburg, obsessed with his Jewishness, regards it as a handicap to be overcome. He esteems himself as the only Jew ever to work for the ironically named Brooklyn Guarantee and Trust Company, whose president never lets Phillip forget he is a Jew. He takes pride too in his son as a West Point cadet. Gellburg wants to prove that a Jew can be not only a doctor or a lawyer, but also an Army general. Suspicious and disdainful of other Jews, Gellburg is anxious and fearful. Now his wife Sylvia is too, but for vastly different reasons. Sylvia is terrified by news of the mounting violence against Jews in Germany, culminating in Kristallnacht. Their vulnerability feeds her own; the horrifying threat immobilizes her. For her self-assured doctor, Harry Hyman, intrigued by his paralyzed patient's obsession with atrocities, "It's like she's connected to some ... some wire that goes halfway around the world."

Dr. Hyman believes that people get sick together, not as individuals. The notion of collective malady applies to the morbidity in the Gellburgs' marriage, the anti-Semitism rife in America in the late thirties, and the madness about to engulf Europe. Through the mindset of his characters, Miller illustrates a theme central to his work, the bonds of responsibilities that unite human beings and the antagonisms that make them torment themselves and one another.

Miller has explained that he carried around with him since the thirties the image of a woman who had unaccountably lost the use of her legs. Ultimately he realized she had been paralyzed by hysteria. When he began to read of ethnic cleansing in the nineties, the story came back to him to serve as the driving force in this play—yet another demonstration of Miller's ability to find the junction of the epic and the personal. *Broken Glass* refers both to Kristallnacht, which occurred in November 1938, a few weeks before the action of the play, and to the well-known ritual that concludes a Jewish wedding ceremony.

Following its production at the Long Wharf Theatre in Connecticut, *Broken Glass* opened in New York on April 24, 1994, where it ran for ten weeks and was nominated for a Tony Award for Best Play. It was subsequently mounted in London, where it won the Olivier Award for Best Play, and in Paris and Munich. A splendid production is available on videotape.

The original production of *Broken Glass* was staged at the Long Wharf Theater in New Haven, Connecticut. The play was subsequently presented on Broadway at the Booth Theatre with the following cast:

Phillip Gellburg . . . . . . . . . . . . . . . . . Ron Rifkin
Sylvia Gellburg . . . . . . . . . . . . . . . . . Amy Irving
Dr. Harry Hyman . . . . . . . . . . . . . . . David Dukes
Margaret Hyman . . . . . . . . . . . . . . . . Frances Conroy
Harriet . . . . . . . . . . . . . . . . . . . . . . Lauren Klien
Stanton Case . . . . . . . . . . . . . . . . . . George N. Martin

Directed by John Tillinger

*The play takes place in Brooklyn in the last days of November 1938, in the office of Dr. Harry Hyman, the bedroom of the Gellburg house, and the office of Stanton Case.*

# ACT ONE

## SCENE 1

*A lone cellist in discovered, playing a simple tune. The tune finishes. Light goes out on the cellist and rises on...*

*Office of* DR. HARRY HYMAN *in his home. Alone on stage* PHILLIP GELLBURG, *and intense man in his late 40s, waits in perfect stillness, legs crossed. He is in a black suit, black tie and shoes, and white shirt.*

*MARGARET HYMAN, the doctor's wife, enters. She is lusty, energetic, carrying pruning shears.*

MARGARET: He'll be right with you, he's just changing. Can I get you something? Tea?

GELLBURG: [*faint reprimand:*] He said seven o'clock sharp.

MARGARET: He was held up at the hospital, that new union's pulled a strike, imagine? A strike in a hospital? It's incredible. And his horse went lame.

GELLBURG: His horse?

MARGARET: He rides on Ocean Parkway every afternoon.

GELLBURG: [*attempting easy familiarity:*] Oh yes. I heard about that... it's very nice. You're Mrs. Hyman?

MARGARET: I've nodded to you on the street for years now, but you're too preoccupied to notice.

GELLBURG: [*a barely hidden boast:*] Lot on my mind, usually. [*A certain amused loftiness.*] —So you're his nurse, too.

MARGARET: We met in Mount Sinai when he was interning. He's lived to regret it. [*She laughs in a burst.*]

GELLBURG: That's some laugh you've got there. I sometimes hear you all the way down the block to my house.

**519**

**MARGARET:** Can't help it, my whole family does it. I'm originally from
  Minnesota. Nice to meet you finally, Mr. Goldberg.

**GELLBURG:** — It's Gellburg, not Goldberg.

**MARGARET:** Oh, I'm sorry.

**GELLBURG:** G-e-l-l-b-u-r-g. It's the only one in the phone book.

**MARGARET:** It does sound like Goldberg.

**GELLBURG:** But it's not, it's Gellburg. [*A distinction.*] We're from Finland
  originally.

**MARGARET:** Oh! We came from Lithuania ... Kazauskis?

**GELLBURG:** [*put down momentarily:*] Don't say.

**MARGARET:** [*trying to charm him to his ease:*] Ever been to Minnesota?

**GELLBURG:** New York State's the size of France, what would I go to
  Minnesota for?

**MARGARET:** Nothing. Just there's a lot of Finns there.

**GELLBURG:** Well there's Finns all over.

**MARGARET:** [*defeated, shows the clipper:*] ... I'll get back to my roses.
  Whatever it is, I hope you'll be feeling better.

**GELLBURG:** It's not me.

**MARGARET:** Oh. 'Cause you seem a little pale.

**GELLBURG:** Me? — I'm always this color. It's my wife.

**MARGARET:** I'm sorry to hear that, she's a lovely woman. It's nothing serious,
  is it?

**GELLBURG:** He's just had a specialist put her through some tests, I'm waiting
  to hear. I think it's got him mystified.

**MARGARET:** Well, I mustn't butt in. [*Makes to leave but can't resist.*] Can you
  say what it is?

**GELLBURG:** She can't walk.

**MARGARET:** What do you mean?

**GELLBURG:** [*an overtone of protest of some personal victimization:*] Can't stand
  up. No feeling in her legs. — I'm sure it'll pass, but it's terrible.

**MARGARET:** But I only saw her in the grocery ... can't be more than ten
  days ago ...

**GELLBURG:** It's nine days today.

**MARGARET:** But she's such a wonderful-looking woman. Does she have fever?

**GELLBURG:** No.

**MARGARET:** Thank God, then it's not polio.

**GELLBURG:** No she's in perfect health otherwise.

**MARGARET:** Well Harry'll get to the bottom of it if anybody can. They call him from everywhere for opinions, you know... Boston, Chicago... By rights he ought to be on Park Avenue if he only had the ambition, but he always wanted a neighborhood practice. Why, I don't know—we never invite anybody, we never go out, all our friends are in Manhattan. But it's his nature, you can't fight a person's nature. Like me for instance, I like to talk and I like to laugh. You're not much of a talker, are you.

GELLBURG: [*a purse-mouthed smile:*] When I can get a word in edgewise.

MARGARET: [*a burst of laughter:*] Ha!—so you've got a sense of humor after all. Well give my best to Mrs. Goldberg.

GELLBURG: Gellbu...

MARGARET: [*hits her own head:*] Gellburg, excuse me!—It practically sounds like Goldberg...

GELLBURG: No-no, look in the phone book, it's the only one, G-e-l-l...

[*Enter* DR. HYMAN]

MARGARET: [*with a little wave to* GELLBURG:] Be seeing you!

GELLBURG: Be in good health.

[MARGARET *exits.*]

HYMAN: [*in his early 50s, a healthy, rather handsome man, a determined scientific idealist. Settling behind his desk—chuckling:*] She chew your ear off?

GELLBURG: [*his worldly mode:*] Not too bad, I've had worse.

HYMAN: Well there's no way around it, women are talkers... [*Grinning familiarly:*] But try living without them, right?

GELLBURG: Without women?

HYMAN: [*he sees* GELLBURG *has flushed; there is a short hiatus, then:*] ...Well, never mind.—I'm glad you could make it tonight, I wanted to talk to you before I see your wife again tomorrow. [*Opens cigar humidor.*] Smoke?

GELLBURG: No thanks, never have. Isn't it bad for you?

HYMAN: Certainly is. [*Lights a cigar.*] But more people die of rat bite, you know.

GELLBURG: Rat bite!

HYMAN: Oh yes, but they're mostly the poor so it's not an interesting statistic. Have you seen her tonight or did you come here from the office?

GELLBURG: I thought I'd see you before I went home. But I phoned her this afternoon—same thing, no change.

HYMAN: How's she doing with the wheelchair?

GELLBURG: Better, she can get herself in and out of the bed now.

HYMAN: Good. And she manages the bathroom?

GELLBURG: Oh yes. I got the maid to come in the mornings to help her take a bath, clean up ...

HYMAN: Good. Your wife has a lot of courage, I admire that kind of woman. My wife is similar; I like the type.

GELLBURG: What do you mean?

HYMAN: You know—vigorous. I mean mentally and ... you know, just generally. Moxie.

GELLBURG: Oh.

HYMAN: Forget it, it was only a remark.

GELLBURG: No, you're right, I never thought of it, but she is unusually that way.

HYMAN: [*pause, some prickliness here which he can't understand:*] Doctor Sherman's report ...

GELLBURG: What's he say?

HYMAN: I'm getting to it.

GELLBURG: Oh. Beg your pardon.

HYMAN: You'll have to bear with me ... may I call you Phillip?

GELLBURG: Certainly.

HYMAN: I don't express my thoughts very quickly, Phillip.

GELLBURG: Likewise. Go ahead, take your time.

HYMAN: People tend to overestimate the wisdom of physicians so I try to think things through before I speak to a patient.

GELLBURG: I'm glad to hear that.

HYMAN: Aesculapius stuttered, you know—ancient Greek god of medicine. But probably based on a real physician who hesitated about giving advice. Somerset Maugham stammered, studied medicine. Anton Chekhov, great writer, also a doctor, had tuberculosis. Doctors are often physically defective in some way, that's why they're interested in healing.

GELLBURG: [*impressed:*] I see.

HYMAN: [*pause, thinks:*] I find this Adolf Hitler very disturbing. You been following him in the papers?

GELLBURG: Well, yes, but not much. My average day in the office is ten, eleven hours.

HYMAN: They've been smashing the Jewish stores in Berlin all week, you know.

GELLBURG: Oh yes, I saw that again yesterday.

HYMAN: Very disturbing. Forcing old men to scrub the sidewalks with toothbrushes. On the Kurfürstendamm, that's equivalent to Fifth Avenue. Nothing but hoodlums in uniform.

GELLBURG: My wife is very upset about that.

HYMAN: I know, that's why I mention it. [*Hesitates.*] And how about you?

GELLBURG: Of course. It's a terrible thing. Why do you ask?

HYMAN: [*a smile:*] — I don't know, I got the feeling she may be afraid she's annoying you when she talks about such things.

GELLBURG: Why? I don't mind. — She said she's annoying me?

HYMAN: Not in so many words, but...

GELLBURG: I can't believe she'd say a thing like...

HYMAN: Wait a minute, I didn't say she said it...

GELLBURG: She doesn't annoy me, but what can be done about such things? The thing is, she doesn't like to hear about the other side of it.

HYMAN: What other side?

GELLBURG: It's no excuse for what's happening over there, but German Jews can be pretty... you know... [*Pushes up his nose with this forefinger.*] Not that they're pushy like the ones from Poland or Russia but a friend of mine's in the garment industry; these German Jews won't take an ordinary good job, you know; it's got to be pretty high up in the firm or they're insulted. And they can't even speak English.

HYMAN: Well I guess a lot of them were pretty important over there.

GELLBURG: I know, but they're supposed to be *refugees,* aren't they? With all our unemployment you'd think they'd appreciate a little more. Latest official figure is twelve million unemployed you know, and it's probably bigger but Roosevelt can't admit it, after the fortune he's pouring into the WPA and the rest of that welfare *mishugas.* —But she's not *annoying* me, for God's sake.

HYMAN: ...I just thought I'd mention it; but it was only a feeling I had...

GELLBURG: I'll tell you right now, I don't run with the crowd, I see with these eyes, nobody else's.

HYMAN: I see that. —You're very unusual— [*Grinning*] — you almost sound like a Republican.

GELLBURG: Why? — the Torah says a Jew has to be a Democrat? I didn't get where I am by agreeing with everybody.

HYMAN: Well that's a good thing; you're independent. [*Nods, puffs.*] You know, what mystifies me is that the Germans I knew in Heidelberg... I took my M.D. there...

GELLBURG: You got along with them.

**Hyman:** Some of the finest people I ever met.

**Gellburg:** Well there you go.

**Hyman:** We had a marvelous student choral group, fantastic voices; Saturday nights, we'd have a few beers and go singing through the streets... People'd applaud from the windows.

**Gellburg:** Don't say.

**Hyman:** I can't imagine these people marching into Austria, and now they say Czechoslovakia's next, and Poland... But fanatics have taken Germany, I guess, and they can be brutal, you know...

**Gellburg:** Listen, I sympathize with these refugees, but...

**Hyman:** [*cutting him off:*] I had quite a long talk with Sylvia yesterday, I suppose she told you?

**Gellburg:** [*a tensing:*] Well... no, she didn't mention. What about?

**Hyman:** [*surprised by* Sylvia's *omission:*] ... Well about her condition, and... just in passing... your relationship.

**Gellburg:** [*flushing:*] *My* relationship?

**Hyman:** ... It was just in passing.

**Gellburg:** Why, what'd she say?

**Hyman:** Well that you... get along very well.

**Gellburg:** Oh.

**Hyman:** [*encouragingly, as he sees* Gellburg's *small tension:*] I found her a remarkably well-informed woman. Especially for this neighborhood.

**Gellburg:** [*a pridefully approving nod; relieved that he can speak of her positively:*] That's practically why we got together in the first place. I don't exaggerate, if Sylvia was a man she could have run the Federal Reserve. You could talk to Sylvia like you talk to a man.

**Hyman:** I'll bet.

**Gellburg:** [*a purse-mouthed grin:*] ... Not that talking was all we did—but you turn your back on Sylvia and she's got her nose in a book or a magazine. I mean there's not one woman in ten around here could even tell you who their Congressman is. And you can throw in the men, too. [*Pause.*] So where are we?

**Hyman:** Doctor Sherman confirms my diagnosis. I ask you to listen carefully, will you?

**Gellburg:** [*brought up:*] Of course, that's why I came.

**Hyman:** We can find no physical reason for her inability to walk.

**Gellburg:** No physical reason...

**Hyman:** We are almost certain that this is a psychological condition.

GELLBURG: But she's numb, she has no feeling in her legs.

HYMAN: Yes. This is was we call an hysterical paralysis. Hysterical doesn't mean she screams and yells...

GELLBURG: Oh, I know. It means like... ah... [*Bumbles off.*]

HYMAN: [*a flash of umbrage, dislike:*] Let me explain what it means, okay?—Hysteria comes from the Greek word for the womb because it was thought to be a symptom of female anxiety. Of course it isn't, but that's where it comes from. People who are anxious enough or really frightened can imagine they've gone blind or deaf, for instance... and they really can't see or hear. It was sometimes called shell-shock during the War.

GELLBURG: You mean... you don't mean she's... crazy.

HYMAN: We'll have to talk turkey, Phillip. If I'm going to do you any good I'm going to have to ask you some personal questions. Some of them may sound raw, but I've only been superficially acquainted with Sylvia's family and I need to know more...

GELLBURG: She says you treated her father...

HYMAN: Briefly; a few visits shortly before he passed away. They're fine people. I hate like hell to see this happen to her, you see what I mean?

GELLBURG: You can tell it to me; is she crazy?

HYMAN: Phillip, are you? Am I? In one way or another, who isn't crazy? The main difference is that our kind of crazy still allows us to walk around and tend to our business. But who knows?—people like us may be the craziest of all.

GELLBURG: [*scoffing grin:*] Why!

HYMAN: Because we don't know we're nuts, and the other kind does.

GELLBURG: I don't know about that...

HYMAN: Well, it's neither here nor there.

GELLBURG: I certainly don't think *I'm* nuts.

HYMAN: I wasn't saying that...

GELLBURG: What do you mean, then?

HYMAN: [*grinning:*] You're not an easy man to talk to, are you?

GELLBURG: Why? If I don't understand I have to ask, don't I?

HYMAN: Yes, you're right.

GELLBURG: That's the way I am—they don't pay me for being easy to talk to.

HYMAN: You're in... real estate?

GELLBURG: I'm head of the Mortgage Department of Brooklyn Guarantee and Trust.

HYMAN: Oh, that's right, she told me.

**GELLBURG:** We are the largest lender east of the Mississippi.

**HYMAN:** Really. [*Fighting deflation.*] Well, let me tell you my approach; if possible I'd like to keep her out of that whole psychiatry rigamarole. Not that I'm against it, but I think you get further faster, sometimes, with a little common sense and some plain human sympathy. Can we talk turkey? *Tuchas offen tisch,* you know any Yiddish?

**GELLBURG:** Yes, it means get your ass on the table.

**HYMAN:** Correct. So let's forget crazy and try to face the facts. We have a strong, healthy woman who has no physical ailment, and suddenly can't stand on her legs. Why?

[*He goes silent.* GELLBURG *shifts uneasily.*]

I don't mean to embarrass you . . .

**GELLBURG:** [*an angry smile:*] You're not embarassing me.—What do you want to know?

**HYMAN:** [*sets himself, and launches:*] In these cases there is often a sexual disability. You have relations, I imagine?

**GELLBURG:** Relations? Yes, we have relations.

**HYMAN:** [*a softening smile:*] Often?

**GELLBURG:** What's that got to do with it?

**HYMAN:** Sex could be connected. You don't have to answer . . .

**GELLBURG:** No-no, it's all right . . . I would say it depends—maybe twice, three times a week.

**HYMAN:** [*seems surprised:*] Well, that's good. She seems satisfied?

**GELLBURG:** [*shrugs, hostilely:*] I guess she is, sure.

**HYMAN:** That was a foolish question, forget it.

**GELLBURG:** [*flushed:*] Why, did she mention something about this?

**HYMAN:** Oh no, it's just something I thought of later.

**GELLBURG:** Well, I'm no Rudolph Valentino but I . . .

**HYMAN:** Rudolph Valentino probably wasn't either.—What about before she collapsed; was that completely out of the blue or . . .

**GELLBURG:** [*relieved to be off the other subject:*] I tell you, looking back I wonder if something happened when they started putting all the pictures in the paper. About these Nazi carryings-on. I noticed she started . . . staring at them . . . in a very peculiar way. And . . . I don't know. I think it made her angry or something.

HYMAN: At you.

GELLBURG: Well... [*Nods, agreeing.*] In general. — Personally I don't think they should be publishing those kind of pictures.

HYMAN: Why not?

GELLBURG: She scares herself to death with them — three thousand miles away, and what does it accomplish! Except maybe put some fancy new ideas into these anti-Semites walking around New York here.

[*Slight pause*]

HYMAN: Tell me how she collapsed. You were going to the movies...?

GELLBURG: [*breathing more deeply:*] Yes. We were just starting down the porch steps and all of a sudden her... [*Difficulty; he breaks off.*]

HYMAN: I'm sorry but I...

GELLBURG: ... Her legs turned to butter. I couldn't stand her up. Kept falling around like a rag doll. I had to carry her into the house. And she kept apologizing...! [*He weeps, recovers.*] I can't talk about it.

HYMAN: It's all right.

GELLBURG: She's always been such a level-headed woman. [*Weeping threatens again.*] I don't know what to do. She's my life.

HYMAN: I'll do my best for her, Phillip, she's a wonderful woman. — Let's talk about something else. What do you do exactly?

GELLBURG: I mainly evaluate properties.

HYMAN: Whether to grant a mortgage...

GELLBURG: And how big a one and the terms.

HYMAN: How'd the Depression hit you?

GELLBURG: Well, it's no comparison with '32 to '36, let's say — we were foreclosing left and right in those days. But we're on our feet and running.

HYMAN: And you head the department...

GELLBURG: Above me is only Mr. Case. Stanton Wylie Case; he's chairman and president. You're not interested in boat racing.

HYMAN: Why?

GELLBURG: His yacht won the America's Cup two years ago. For the second time. The *Aurora*?

HYMAN: Oh yes! I think I read about...

GELLBURG: He's had me aboard twice.

HYMAN: Really.

GELLBURG: [*the grin:*] The only Jew ever set foot on that deck.

HYMAN: Don't say.
GELLBURG: In fact, I'm the only Jew ever worked for Brooklyn Guarantee in their whole history.
HYMAN: That so.
GELLBURG: Oh yes. And they go back to the 1890s. Started right out of accountancy school and moved straight up. They've been wonderful to me; it's a great firm.

[*A long moment as* HYMAN *stares at* GELLBURG, *who is proudly positioned now, absorbing his poise from the evoked memories of his success. Gradually* GELLBURG *turns to him.*]

How could this be a mental condition?

HYMAN: It's unconscious; like ... well take yourself; I notice you're all in black. Can I ask you why?
GELLBURG: I've worn black since high school.
HYMAN: No particular reason.
GELLBURG: [*shrugs:*] Always liked it, that's all.
HYMAN: Well it's a similar thing with her; she doesn't know why she's doing this, but some very deep, hidden part of her mind is directing her to do it. You don't agree.
GELLBURG: I don't know.
HYMAN: You think she knows what she's doing?
GELLBURG: Well I always liked black for business reasons.
HYMAN: It gives you authority?
GELLBURG: Not exactly authority, but I wanted to look a little older. See, I graduated high school at fifteen and I was only 22 when I entered the firm. But I knew what I was doing.
HYMAN: Then you think she's doing this on purpose?
GELLBURG: —Except she's numb; nobody can purposely do that, can they?
HYMAN: I don't think so. —I tell you, Phillip, not really knowing your wife, if you have any idea why she could be doing this to herself...
GELLBURG: I told you, I don't know.
HYMAN: Nothing occurs to you.
GELLBURG: [*an edge of irritation:*] I can't think of anything.
HYMAN: I tell you a funny thing, talking to her, she doesn't seem all that unhappy.

GELLBURG: Say!—yes, that's what I mean. That's exactly what I mean. It's like she's almost...I don't know...enjoying herself. I mean in a way.

HYMAN: How could that be possible?

GELLBURG: Of course she apologizes for it, and for making it hard for me—you know, like I have to do a lot of the cooking now, and tending to my laundry and so on...I even shop for groceries and the butcher...and change the sheets...

[*He breaks off with some realization.* HYMAN *doesn't speak. A long pause.*]

You mean...she's doing it against me?

HYMAN: I don't know, what do *you* think?

[*Stares for a long moment, them makes to rise, obviously deeply disturbed.*]

GELLBURG: I'd better be getting home. [*Lost in his own thought.*] I don't know whether to ask you this or not.

HYMAN: What's to lose, go ahead.

GELLBURG: My parents were from the old country, you know,—I don't know if it was in Poland someplace or Russia—but there was this woman who they say was...you know...gotten into by a...like the ghost of a dead person...

HYMAN: A dybbuk.

GELLBURG: That's it. And it made her lose her mind and so forth.—You believe in that? They had to get a rabbi to pray it out of her body. But do you think that's possible?

HYMAN: Do I think so? No. Do you?

GELLBURG: Oh no. It just crossed my mind.

HYMAN: Well I wouldn't know how to pray it out of her, so...

GELLBURG: Be straight with me—is she going to come out of this?

HYMAN: Well, let's talk again after I see her tomorrow. Maybe I should tell you...I have this unconventional approach to illness, Phillip. Especially where the mental element is involved. I believe we get sick in twos and threes and fours, not alone as individuals. You follow me? I want you to do me a favor, will you?

GELLBURG: What's that.

HYMAN: You won't be offended, okay?

GELLBURG: [*tensely:*] Why should I be offended?

HYMAN: I'd like you to give her a lot of loving. [*Fixing* GELLBURG *in his gaze.*] Can you? It's important now.

GELLBURG: Say, you're not blaming this on me, are you?

HYMAN: What's the good of blame? — from here on out, *tuchas offen tisch,* okay? And Phillip?

GELLBURG: Yes?

HYMAN: [*a light chuckle:*] Try not to let yourself get mad.

[GELLBURG *turns and goes out.* HYMAN *returns to his desk, makes some notes.* MARGARET *enters.*]

MARGARET: That's one miserable little pisser.

[*He writes, doesn't look up.*]

He's a dictator, you know. I was just remembering when I went to the grandmother's funeral? He stands outside the funeral parlor and decides who's going to sit with who in the limousines for the cemetery. "You sit with him, you sit with her..." And they obey him like he owned the funeral!

HYMAN: Did you find out what's playing?

MARGARET: At the Beverly they've got Ginger Rogers and Fred Astaire. Jimmy Cagney's at the Rialto but it's another gangster story.

HYMAN: I have a sour feeling about this thing. I barely know my way around psychiatry. I'm not completely sure I ought to get into it.

MARGARET: Why not? — She's a very beautiful woman.

HYMAN: [*matching her wryness:*] Well, is that a reason to turn her away? [*He laughs, grasps her hand.*] Something about it fascinates me — no disease and she's paralyzed. I'd really love to give it a try. I mean I don't want to turn myself into a post office, shipping all the head cases to specialists, the woman's sick and I'd like to help.

MARGARET: But if you're not getting anywhere in a little while you'll promise to send her to somebody.

HYMAN: Absolutely. [*Committed now: full enthusiasm.*] I just feel there's
   something about it that I understand. — Let's see Cagney.
MARGARET: Oh, no Fred Astaire.
HYMAN: That's what I meant. Come here.
MARGARET: [*as he embraces her:*] We should leave now...
HYMAN: You're the best, Margaret.
MARGARET: A lot of good it does me.
HYMAN: If it really bothers you I'll get someone else to take the case.
MARGARET: You won't, you know you won't.

[*He is lifting her skirt.*]

Don't Harry, come on.

[*She frees her skirt, he kisses her breasts.*]

HYMAN: Should I tell you what I'd like to do with you?
MARGARET: Tell me, yes, tell me. And make it wonderful.
HYMAN: We find an island and we strip and go riding on this white horse...
MARGARET: Together.
HYMAN: You in front.
MARGARET: Naturally.
HYMAN: And then we go swimming...
MARGARET: Harry, that's lovely.
HYMAN: And I hire this shark to swim very close and we just manage to get
   out of the water, and we're so grateful to be alive we fall down on the
   beach together and...
MARGARET: [*pressing his lips shut:*] Sometimes you're so good. [*She kisses
   him.*]

BLACKOUT

# SCENE 2

*The Lone Cellist plays. The lights go down...*

*Next evening. The Gellburg bedroom.* SYLVIA GELLBURG *is seated in the wheelchair reading a newspaper. She is in her mid-40s, a buxom, capable, and warm woman. Right now her hair is brushed down to her shoulders, and she is in a nightgown and robe.*

*She reads the paper with an intense, almost haunted interest, looking up now and then to visualize.*

*Her sister* HARRIET, *a couple of years younger, is straightening up the bedcover.*

HARRIET: So what do you want, steak or chicken? Or maybe he'd like chops for a change.

SYLVIA: Please, don't put yourself out, Phillip doesn't mind a little shopping.

HARRIET: What's the matter with you, I'm going anyway, he's got enough on his mind.

SYLVIA: Well all right, get a couple of chops.

HARRIET: And what about you. You have to start eating!

SYLVIA: I'm eating.

HARRIET: What, a piece of cucumber? Look how pale you are. And what is this with newspapers night and day?

SYLVIA: I like to see what's happening.

HARRIET: I don't know about this doctor. Maybe you need a specialist.

SYLVIA: He brought one two days ago, Doctor Sherman. From Mount Sinai.

HARRIET: Really? And?

SYLVIA: We're waiting to hear. I like Doctor Hyman.

HARRIET: Nobody in the family ever had anything like this. You feel *something*, though, don't you?

SYLVIA: [*pause, she lifts her face:*] Yes ... but inside, not on the skin. [*Looks at her legs.*] I can harden the muscles but I can't lift them. [*Strokes her thighs.*] I seem to have an ache. Not only here but ... [*She runs her hands down her trunk.*] My whole body seems ... I can't describe it. It's like I was just born and I ... didn't want to come out yet. Like a deep, terrible aching ...

HARRIET: Didn't want to come out yet! What are you talking about?

SYLVIA: [*sighs gently, knowing* HARRIET *can never understand:*] Maybe if he has a nice duck. If not, get the chops. And thanks, Harriet, it's sweet of you.—By the way, what did David decide?

**HARRIET:** He's not going to college.

**SYLVIA:** [*shocked:*] I don't believe it! With a scholarship and he's not going?

**HARRIET:** What can we do? [*Resignedly.*] He says college wouldn't help him get a job anyway.

**SYLVIA:** Harriet, that's terrible!—Listen, tell him I have to talk to him.

**HARRIET:** Would you! I was going to ask you but with this happening. [*Indicates her legs.*] I didn't think you'd ...

**SYLVIA:** Never mind, tell him to come over. And you must tell Murray he's got to put his foot down—you've got a brilliant boy! My God ... [*Picks up the newspaper.*] If I'd had a chance to go to college I'd have had a whole different life, you can't let this happen.

**HARRIET:** I'll tell David ... I wish I knew what is suddenly so interesting in a newspaper. This is not normal, Sylvia, is it?

**SYLVIA:** [*pause, she stares ahead:*] They are making old men crawl around and clean the sidewalks with toothbrushes.

**HARRIET:** Who is?

**SYLVIA:** In Germany. Old men with beards!

**HARRIET:** So why are you so interested in that? What business of yours is that?

**SYLVIA:** [*slight pause; searches within:*] I don't really know. [*A slight pause.*] Remember Grandpa? His eyeglasses with the bent sidepiece? One of the old men in the paper was his spitting image, he had the same exact glasses with the wire frames. I can't get it out of my mind. On their knees on the sidewalk, two old men. And there's fifteen or twenty people standing in a circle laughing at them scrubbing with toothbrushes. There's three women in the picture; they're holding coat collars closed, so it must have been cold ...

**HARRIET:** Why would they make them scrub with toothbrushes?

**SYLVIA:** [*angered:*] To humiliate them, to make fools of them!

**HARRIET:** Oh!

**SYLVIA:** How can you be so ... so ...? [*Breaks off before she goes too far.*] Harriet, please ... leave me alone, will you?

**HARRIET:** This is not normal. Murray says the same thing. I swear to God, he came home last night and says, "She's got to stop thinking about those Germans." And you know how he loves current events. [SYLVIA *is staring ahead.*] I'll see if the duck looks good, if not I'll get the chops. Can I get you something now?

SYLVIA: No, I'm fine, thanks.
HARRIET: [*moves upstage of* SYLVIA, *turns:*] I'm going.
SYLVIA: Yes.

[*She returns to her paper.* HARRIET *watches anxiously for a moment, out of* SYLVIA'*s sight line, then exits.* SYLVIA *turns a page, absorbed in the paper. Suddenly she turns in shock—*PHILLIP *is standing behind her. He holds a small paper bag.*]

SYLVIA: Oh! I didn't hear you come in.
GELLBURG: I tiptoed, in case you were dozing off... [*His dour smile.*] I bought you some sour pickles.
SYLVIA: Oh, that's nice! Later, maybe. You have one.
GELLBURG: I'll wait. [*Awkwardly but determined:*] I was passing Greenberg's on Flatbush Avenue and I suddenly remembered how you used to love them. Remember?
SYLVIA: Thanks, that's nice of you. What were you doing on Flatbush Avenue?
GELLBURG: There's a property across from A&S. I'm probably going to foreclose.
SYLVIA: Oh that's sad. Are they nice people?
GELLBURG: [*shrugs:*] People are people—I gave them two extensions but they'll never manage... nothing up here. [*Taps his temple.*]
SYLVIA: Aren't you early?
GELLBURG: I got worried about you. Doctor come?
SYLVIA: He called; he has nice results of the tests but he wanted to come tomorrow when he has more time to talk to me. He's really very nice.
GELLBURG: How was it today?
SYLVIA: I'm so sorry about this.
GELLBURG: You'll get better, don't worry about it. Oh!—there's a letter from the captain. [*Takes it out of his jacket.*]
SYLVIA: Jerome?
GELLBURG: [*terrific personal pride:*] Read it.

[*She reads, his purse-mouthed grin is intense.*]

That's your son. General MacArthur talked to him twice.

SYLVIA: Fort Sill?

GELLBURG: Oklahoma. *He's going to lecture them on artillery!* In *Fort Sill!* That's the field-artillery center.

[*She looks up dumbly.*]

That's like being invited to the Vatican to lecture the Pope.

SYLVIA: Imagine. [*She folds the letter and hands it back to him.*]

GELLBURG: [*restraining greater resentment:*] I don't understand this attitude.

SYLVIA: Why? I'm happy for him.

GELLBURG: You don't seem happy to me.

SYLVIA: I'll never get used to it. Who goes in the army? Men who can't do anything else.

GELLBURG: I wanted people to see that a Jew doesn't have to be a lawyer or a doctor or a businessman.

SYLVIA: That's fine, but why must it be Jerome?

GELLBURG: For a Jewish boy, West Point is an honor! Without Mr. Case's connections, he never would have gotten in. He could be the first Jewish general in the United States Army. Doesn't it mean something to be his mother?

SYLVIA: [*with an edge of resentment:*] Well, I said I'm glad.

GELLBURG: Don't be upset. [*Looks about impatiently.*] You know, when you get on your feet I'll help you hang the new drapes.

SYLVIA: I started to ...

GELLBURG: But they've been here over a month.

SYLVIA: Well this happened, I'm sorry.

GELLBURG: You have to occupy yourself is all I'm saying, Sylvia, you can't give in to this.

SYLVIA: [*near an outburst:*] Well I'm sorry—I'm sorry about everything!

GELLBURG: Please, don't get upset, I take it back!

[*A moment; stalemate.*]

SYLVIA: I wonder what my tests show.

[GELLBURG *is silent.*]

That the specialist did.

GELLBURG: I went to see Doctor Hyman last night.
SYLVIA: You did? Why didn't you mention it?
GELLBURG: I wanted to think over what he said.
SYLVIA: What did he say?

[*With a certain deliberateness,* GELLBURG *goes over to her and gives her a kiss on the cheek.*]

SYLVIA: [*she is embarrassed and vaguely alarmed:*] Phillip! [*A little uncomprehending laugh.*]
GELLBURG: I want to change some things. About the way I've been doing.

[*He stands there for a moment perfectly still, then rolls her chair closer to the bed on which he now sits and takes her hand. She doesn't quite know what to make of this, but doesn't remove her hand.*]

SYLVIA: Well what did he say?
GELLBURG: [*he pats her hand:*] I'll tell you in a minute. I'm thinking about a Dodge.
SYLVIA: A Dodge?
GELLBURG: I want to teach you to drive. So you can go where you like, visit your mother in the afternoon.—I want you to be happy Sylvia.
SYLVIA: [*surprised:*] Oh.
GELLBURG: We have the money, we could do a lot of things. Maybe see Washington, D.C.... It's supposed to be a very strong car, you know.
SYLVIA: But aren't they all black?—Dodges?
GELLBURG: Not at all. I've seen a couple of green ones.
SYLVIA: You like green?
GELLBURG: It's only a color. You'll get used to it.—Or Chicago. It's really a big city, you know.
SYLVIA: Tell me what Doctor Hyman said.
GELLBURG: [*gets himself set:*] He thinks it could all be coming from your mind. Like a...a fear of some kind got into you. Psychological.

[*She is still, listening.*]

Are you afraid of something?

**SYLVIA:** [*a slow shrug, a shake of her head:*] …I don't know. I don't think so. What kind of fear, what does he mean?

**GELLBURG:** Well, he explains it better, but…like in a war, people get so afraid they go blind temporarily. What they call shell-shock. But once they feel safer it goes away.

**SYLVIA:** What about the tests the Mount Sinai man did?

**GELLBURG:** They can't find anything wrong with your body.

**SYLVIA:** But I'm numb!

**GELLBURG:** He claims being very frightened could be doing it.—Are you?

**SYLVIA:** I don't know.

**GELLBURG:** Personally…. Can I tell you what I think?

**SYLVIA:** What.

**GELLBURG:** I think it's this whole Nazi business.

**SYLVIA:** But it's in the paper—they're smashing up the Jewish stores… Should I not read the paper? The streets are covered with broken glass!

**GELLBURG:** Yes, but you don't have to be constantly…

**SYLVIA:** It's ridiculous. I can't move my legs from reading a newspaper?

**GELLBURG:** He didn't say that; but I'm wondering if you're too involved with…

**SYLVIA:** It's ridiculous.

**GELLBURG:** Well you talk to him tomorrow. [*Pause. He comes back to her and takes her hand, his need open.*] You've got to get better, Sylvia.

**SYLVIA:** [*she sees his tortured face and tries to laugh:*] What is this, am I dying or something?

**GELLBURG:** How can you say that?

**SYLVIA:** I've never seen such a look in your face.

**GELLBURG:** Oh no-no-no…I'm just worried.

**SYLVIA:** I don't understand what's happening… [*She turns away on the verge of tears.*]

**GELLBURG:** …I never realized… [*Sudden sharpness*] …look at me, will you?

[*She turns to him; he glances down at the floor.*]

I wouldn't know what to do without you, Sylvia, honest to God. I… [*Immense difficulty.*] I love you.

SYLVIA: [*a dead, bewildered laugh:*] What is this?

GELLBURG: You have to get better. If I'm ever doing something wrong I'll change it. Let's try to be different. All right? And you too, you've got to do what the doctors tell you.

SYLVIA: What can I do? Here I sit and they say there's nothing wrong with me.

GELLBURG: Listen ... I think Hyman is a very smart man ... [*He lifts her hand and kisses her knuckle; embarrassed and smiling.*] When we were talking, something came to mind; that maybe if we could sit down with him, the three of us and maybe talk about ... you know ... everything.

[*Pause.*]

SYLVIA: That doesn't matter anymore, Phillip.

GELLBURG: [*an embarrassed grin:*] How do you know? Maybe ...

SYLVIA: It's too late for that.

GELLBURG: [*once launched he is terrified:*] Why? Why is it too late?

SYLVIA: I'm surprised you're still worried about it.

GELLBURG: I'm not worried, I just think about it now and then.

SYLVIA: Well it's too late dear, it doesn't matter anymore. [*She draws back her hand.*]

[*Pause.*]

GELLBURG: ... Well all right. But if you wanted to I'd ...

SYLVIA: We did talk about it, I took you to Rabbi Steiner about it twice, what good did it do?

GELLBURG: In those days I still thought it would change by itself. I was so young, I didn't understand such things. It came out of nowhere and I thought it would go the same way.

SYLVIA: I'm sorry, Phillip, it didn't come out of nowhere.

[*Silent, he evades her eyes.*]

SYLVIA: You regretted you got married.

GELLBURG: I didn't "regret" it ...

SYLVIA: You did, dear. You don't have to be ashamed of it.

[*A long silence.*]

**GELLBURG:** I'm going to tell you the truth — in those days I thought that if we separated I wouldn't die of it. I admit that.

**SYLVIA:** I always knew that.

**GELLBURG:** But I haven't felt that way in years now.

**SYLVIA:** Well I'm here. [*Spreads arms out, a wildly ironical look in her eyes.*] Here I am, Phillip!

**GELLBURG:** [*offended:*] The way you say that is not very...

**SYLVIA:** Not very what? I'm here; I've been here a long time.

**GELLBURG:** [*a helpless surge of anger:*] I'm trying to tell you something!

**SYLVIA:** [*openly taunting him now:*] But I said I'm here!

[**GELLBURG** *moves about as he speaks, as though trying to find an escape or a way in.*]

I'm here's for my mother's sake, and Jerome's sake, and everybody's sake except mine, but I'm here and here I am. And now finally you want to talk about it, now when I'm turning into an old woman? How do you want me to say it? Tell me, dear, I'll say it the way you want me to. What should I say?

**GELLBURG:** [*insulted and guilty:*] I want you to stand up.

**SYLVIA:** I can't stand up.

[*He takes both her hands.*]

**GELLBURG:** You can. Now come on. Stand up.

**SYLVIA:** I can't!

**GELLBURG:** You can stand up, Sylvia. Now lean to me and get on your feet.

[*He pulls her up; then steps aside, releasing her; she collapses on the floor. He stands over her.*]

What are you trying to do? [*He goes to his knees to yell into her face*]

*What are you trying to do, Sylvia?*

[*She looks at him in terror at the mystery before her.*]

BLACKOUT

# SCENE 3

*The lone cellist plays. Then lights go down...*

Dr. Hyman's *office. He is in riding boots and a sweater.* Harriet *is seated beside his desk.*

Harriet: My poor sister. And they have everything! But how can it be in the mind if she's so paralyzed?

Hyman: Her numbness is random, it doesn't follow the nerve paths; only part of the thighs are affected, part of the calves, it makes no physiological sense. I have a few things I'd like to ask you, all right?

Harriet: You know, I'm glad you're taking care of her, my husband says the same thing.

Hyman: Thank you...

Harriet: You probably don't remember, but you once took out our cousin Roslyn Fein? She said you were great.

Hyman: Roslyn Fein. When?

Harriet: She's very tall and reddish-blond hair? She had a real crush...

Hyman: [*pleased:*] When was this?

Harriet: Oh — NYU, maybe twenty-five years ago. She adored you; seriously, she said you were really *great.* [*Laughs knowingly.*] Used to take her to Coney Island swimming, and so on.

Hyman: [*laughs with her:*] Oh. Well give her my regards.

Harriet: I hardly see her, she lives in Florida.

Hyman: [*pressing on:*] I'd like you to tell me about Sylvia; — before she collapsed, was there any sign of some shock, or anything? Something threatening her?

Harriet: [*thinks for a moment, shrugs, shaking her head:*] Listen, I'll tell you something funny — to me sometimes she seems... I was going to say happy, but it's more like... I don't know... like this is how she wants to be. I mean since the collapse. Don't you think so?

Hyman: Well I never really knew her before. What about this fascination with the Nazis — she ever talk to you about that?

Harriet: Only this last couple of weeks. I don't understand it, they're in *Germany,* how can she be so frightened, it's across the ocean, isn't it?

Hyman: Yes. But in a way it isn't. [*He stares, shaking his head, lost*] ... She's

540

very sensitive; she really sees the people in those photographs. They're alive to her.

HARRIET: [*suddenly near tears:*] My poor sister!

HYMAN: Tell me about Phillip.

HARRIET: Phillip? [*Shrugs.*] Phillip is Phillip.

HYMAN: You like him?

HARRIET: Well he's my brother-in-law... You mean personally.

HYMAN: Yes.

HARRIET: [*takes breath to lie:*] ... He can be very sweet, you know. But suddenly he'll turn around and talk to you like you've got four legs and long ears. The men—not that they don't respect him—but they'd just as soon not play cards with him if they can help it.

HYMAN: Really. Why?

HARRIET: Well, God forbid you have an opinion—you open your mouth and he gives you that Republican look down his nose and your brains dry up. Not that I don't *like* him ....

HYMAN: How did he and Sylvia meet?

HARRIET: She was head bookkeeper at Empire Steel over there in Long Island City...

HYMAN: She must have been very young.

HARRIET: ... Twenty; just out of high school practically and she's head book-keeper. According to my husband, God gave Sylvia all the brains and the rest of us the big feet! The reason they met was the company took out a mortgage and she had to explain all the accounts to Phillip—he used to say, "I fell in love with her figures!" [HYMAN *laughs.*] Why should I lie?—personally to me, he's a little bit a prune. Like he never stops with the whole Jewish part of it.

HYMAN: He doesn't like being Jewish.

HARRIET: Well yes and no—like Jerome being the only Jewish captain, he's proud of that. And him being the only one ever worked for Brooklyn Guarantee—he's proud of that too, but at the same time...

HYMAN: ... He'd rather not be one.

HARRIET: ... Look, he's a mystery to me. I don't understand him and I never will.

HYMAN: What about the marriage? I promise you this is strictly between us.

HARRIET: What can I well you, the marriage is a marriage.

HYMAN: And?

HARRIET: I shouldn't talk about it.

HYMAN: It stays in this office. Tell me. They ever break up?
HARRIET: Oh God no! Why should they? He's a wonderful provider. There's no Depression for Phillip, you know. And it would kill our mother, she worships Phillip, she'd never outlive it. No-no, it's out of the question. Sylvia's not that kind of woman, although … [*Breaks off.*]
HYMAN: Come, Harriet, I need to know these things!
HARRIET: … Well I guess everybody knows it, so … [*Takes a breath.*] I think they came very close to it one time … when he hit her with the steak.
HYMAN: Hit her with a *steak*?
HARRIET: It was overdone.
HYMAN: What do you mean, hit her?
HARRIET: He picked it up off the place and slapped her in the face with it.
HYMAN: And then what?
HARRIET: Well if my mother hadn't patched it up, I don't know what would have happened and then he went out and bought her that gorgeous beaver coat, and repainted the whole house, and he's tight as a drum, you know, so it was hard for him. I don't know that to tell you. — Why? — you think *he* could have frightened her like this?
HYMAN: [*hesitates:*] I don't know yet. The whole thing is very strange.

[*Something darkens* HARRIET's *expression and she begins to shake her head from side to side and she bursts into tears. He comes and puts an arm around her.*]

HYMAN: What is it?
HARRIET: All her life she did nothing but love everybody!
HYMAN: [*reaches out to take her hand:*] Harriet.

[*She looks at him.*]

What do you want to tell me?

HARRIET: I don't know if it's right to talk about. But of course, it's years and years ago …
HYMAN: None of this will ever be repeated; believe me.
HARRIET: Well … every first of the year when Uncle Myron was still alive we'd all go down to his basement for a New Year's party. I'm talking like fifteen, sixteen years ago. He's dead now, Myron, but … he was … you

know… [*Small laugh*] …a little comical; he always kept this shoebox full of…you know, these postcards.

HYMAN: You mean…

HARRIET: Yes. French. You know, naked women, and men with these great big…you know…they hung down like salamis. And everybody'd pass them around and die laughing. It was exactly the same thing every New Year's. But this time, all of a sudden, Phillip…we thought he's lost his mind…

HYMAN: What happened?

HARRIET: Well Sylvia's in the middle of laughing and he grabs the postcard out of her hand and he turns around screaming—I mean, really screaming—that we're all a bunch of morons and idiots and God knows what, and throws her up the stairs. Bang! It cracked the bannister, I can still hear it. [*Catches her breath.*] I tell you it was months before anybody'd talk to him again. Because everybody on the block loves Sylvia.

HYMAN: What do you suppose made him do that?

HARRIET: [*shrugs:*] …Well if you listen to some of the men—but of course some of the dirty minds on this block…if you spread it over the back-yard you'd get tomatoes six feet high.

HYMAN: Why?—what'd they say?

HARRIET: Well that the reason he got so mad was because he couldn't…you know…

HYMAN: Oh, really.

HARRIET: …anymore.

HYMAN: But they made it up.

HARRIET: Listen, to be truthful you have to say it—although it'll sound crazy…

HYMAN: What.

HARRIET: You watch him sometimes when they've got people over and she's talking—he'll sit quietly in the corner, and the expression on that man's face when he's watching her—it could almost break your heart.

HYMAN: Why?

HARRIET: He adores her!

BLACKOUT

# SCENE 4

*The cellist plays, and is gone.*

STANTON CASE *is getting ready to leave his office. Putting on his blazer and a captain's cap and a foulard. He has a great natural authority, and almost childishly naïve self-assurance.* GELLBURG *enters.*

CASE: Good!—you're back. I was just leaving.
GELLBURG: I'm sorry. I got caught in traffic over in Crown Heights.
CASE: I wanted to talk to you again about 611. Sit down for a moment.

[*Both sit.*]

We're sailing out through the Narrows in about an hour.

GELLBURG: Beautiful day for it.
CASE: Are you all right? You don't look well.
GELLBURG: Oh no, I'm fine.
CASE: Good. Have you come to anything final on 611? I like the price, I can tell you that right off.
GELLBURG: Yes, the price is not bad, but I'm still…
CASE: I've walked past it again; I think with some renovation it would make a fine annex for the Harvard Club.
GELLBURG: It's a very nice structure, yes. I'm not final on it yet but I have a few comments… unless you've got to get on the water right away.
CASE: I have a few minutes. Go ahead.
GELLBURG: … Before I forget—we got a very nice letter from Jerome.

[*No reaction from Case.*]

My boy.

CASE: Oh yes!—how is he doing?
GELLBURG: They're bringing him out to Fort Sill… some kind of lecture on artillery.

544

CASE: Really, now! Well, isn't that nice!… Then he's really intending to make a career in the army.

GELLBURG: [*surprised Case isn't aware:*] Oh absolutely.

CASE: Well that's good, isn't it. It's quite surprising for one of you people— for some reason I'd assumed he just wanted the education.

GELLBURG: Oh no. It's his life. I'll never know how to thank you.

CASE: No trouble at all. The Point can probably use a few of you people to keep the rest of them awake. Now what's this about 611?

GELLBURG: [*sets himself in all dignity:*] You might recall, we used the ABC Plumbing Contractors on a couple of buildings?

CASE: ABC? —I don't recall. What have they got to do with it?

GELLBURG: They're located in the neighborhood, just off Broadway, and on a long shot I went over to see Mr. Liebfreund—he runs ABC. I was wondering if they may have done any work for Wanamaker's.

CASE: Wanamaker's! What's Wanamaker's got to do with it?

GELLBURG: I buy my shirts in Wanamaker's, and last time I was in there I caught my shoe on a splinter sticking up out of the floor.

CASE: Well that store is probably fifty years old.

GELLBURG: Closer to seventy-five. I tripped and almost fell down; this was very remarkable to me, that they would leave a floor in such condition. So I began wondering about it…

CASE: About what?

GELLBURG: Number 611 is two blocks from Wanamaker's. [*A little extra-wise grin.*] They're the biggest business in the area, a whole square block, after all. Anyway, sure enough, turns out ABC does all Wanamaker's plumbing work. And Liebfreund tells me he's had to keep patching up their boilers *because they canceled installation of new boilers last winter.* A permanent cancellation.

[*Pause.*]

CASE: And what do you make of that?

GELLBURG: I think it could mean they're either moving the store, or maybe going out of business.

CASE: *Wanamaker's?*

GELLBURG: It's possible, I understand the family is practically died out. Either way, if Wanamaker's disappears, Mr. Case, that neighborhood in my opinion is no longer prime. Also, I called Kevin Sullivan over at Title Guarantee and he says they turned down 611 last year and he can't remember why.

CASE: Then what are you telling me?

GELLBURG: I would not touch Number 611 with a ten-foot pole—unless you can get it at a good defensive price. If that neighborhood starts to slide, 611 is a great big slice of lemon.

CASE: Well. That's very disappointing. It would have made a wonderful club annex.

GELLBURG: With a thing like the Harvard Club you have got to think of the far distant future, Mr. Case, I don't have to tell you that, and the future of that part of Broadway is a definite possible negative. [*Raising a monitory finger:*] I emphasize "possible," mind you; only God can predict.

CASE: Well I must say, I would never have thought of Wanamaker's disappearing. You have been more than thorough, Gellburg, we appreciate it. I've got to run now, but we'll talk about this further... [*Glances at his watch.*] Mustn't miss the tide... [*Moves, indicates.*] Take a brandy if you like. Wife all right?

GELLBURG: Oh yes, she's fine!

CASE: [*the faint shadow of a warning:*] Sure everything's all right with you— we don't want you getting sick now.

GELLBURG: Oh no, I'm very well, very well.

CASE: I'll be back on Monday, we'll go into this further. [*Indicates.*] Take a brandy if you like.

[CASE *exits rather jauntily.*]

GELLBURG: Yes sir, I might!

[GELLBURG *stands alone; with a look of self-satisfaction starts to raise the glass.*]

BLACKOUT

# SCENE 5

*The cello plays, and the music falls away.*

Sylvia *in bed, reading a book. She looks up as* Hyman *enters. He is in his riding clothes.* Sylvia *has a certain excitement at seeing him.*

Sylvia: Oh, doctor!
Hyman: I let myself in, hope I didn't scare you...
Sylvia: Oh no, I'm glad. Sit down. You been riding?
Hyman: Yes. All the way down to Brighton Beach, nice long ride—
   I expected to see you jumping rope by now.

[Sylvia *laughs, embarrassed.*]

I think you're just trying to get out of doing the dishes.

Sylvia: [*strained laugh:*] Oh stop. You really love riding, don't you?
Hyman: Well there's no telephone on a horse.

[*She laughs.*]

Ocean Parkway is like a German forest this time of morning—riding
under that archway of maple trees is like poetry.

Sylvia: Wonderful. I never did anything like that.
Hyman: Well, let's go—I'll take you out and teach you sometime. Have you
   been trying the exercise?
Sylvia: I can't do it.
Hyman: [*shaking a finger at her:*] You've *got* to do it, Sylvia. You could end
   up permanently crippled. Let's have a look.

[*He sits on the bed and draws the cover off her legs, then raises the
nightgown. She inhales with a certain anticipation as he does so. He
feels her toes.*]

You feel this at all?

SYLVIA: Well ... not really.
HYMAN: I'm going to pinch your toe. Ready?
SYLVIA: All right.

[*He pinches her toes sharply; she doesn't react. He rests a palm on her leg.*]

HYMAN: Your skin feels a little too cool. You're going to lose your muscle if you don't move. Your legs will begin to lose volume and shrink ...
SYLVIA: [*tears threaten:*] I know ...!
HYMAN: And look what beautiful legs you have, Sylvia. I'm afraid you're getting comfortable in this condition ...
SYLVIA: I'm not. I keep trying to move them ...
HYMAN: But look now—here it's eleven in the morning and you're happily tucked into bed like it's midnight.
SYLVIA: But I've tried ...! Are you really sure it's not a virus of some kind?
HYMAN: There's nothing. Sylvia, you have a strong beautiful body ...
SYLVIA: But what can I do. I can't feel anything!

[*She sits up with her face raised to him; he stands and moves abruptly away. Then turning back to her ...*]

HYMAN: I really should find someone else for you.
SYLVIA: Why!—I don't want anyone else!
HYMAN: You're a very attractive woman, don't you know that?

[*Deeply excited,* SYLVIA *glances away shyly.*]

HYMAN: Sylvia, listen to me ... I haven't been this moved by a woman in a very long time.
SYLVIA: ... Well, you mustn't get anyone else.

[*Pause.*]

HYMAN: Tell me the truth, Sylvia. Sylvia? How did this happen to you?
SYLVIA: [*she avoids his gaze:*] I don't know. [*Sylvia's anxiety rises as he speaks now.*]
HYMAN: ... I'm going to be straight with you; I thought this was going to be simpler than it's turning out to be, and I care about you too much to play

a game with your health. I can't deny my vanity. I have a lot of it, but I have to face it—I know you want to tell me something and I don't know how to get it out of you. [SYLVIA *covers her face, ashamed.*] You're a responsible woman, Sylvia, you have to start helping me, you can't just lie there and expect a miracle to lift you to your feet. You tell me now— what should I do?

SYLVIA: I would tell you if I knew! [HYMAN *turns away defeated and impatient.*] Couldn't we just talk and maybe I could ... [*Breaks off.*] I like you. A lot. I love when you talk to me ... couldn't we just ... like for a few minutes ...

HYMAN: Okay. What do you want to talk about?

SYLVIA: Please. Be patient. I'm ... I'm trying. [*Relieved; a fresher mood:*] — Harriet says you used to take out our cousin Roslyn Fein.

HYMAN: [*smiles, shrugs:*] It's possible, I don't remember.

SYLVIA: Well you had so many, didn't you.

HYMAN: When I was younger.

SYLVIA: Roslyn said you used to do acrobatics on the beach? And all the girls would stand around going crazy for you.

HYMAN: That's a long time ago ...

SYLVIA: And you'd take them under the boardwalk. [*Laughs.*]

HYMAN: Nobody had money for anything else. Didn't you used to go to the beach?

SYLVIA: Sure. But I never did anything like that.

HYMAN: You must have been very shy.

SYLVIA: I guess. But I had to look out for my sisters, being the eldest ...

HYMAN: Can we talk about Phillip?

[*Caught unaware, her eyes show fear.*]

I'd really like to, unless you ...

SYLVIA: [*challenged:*] No! —It's all right.

HYMAN: ... Are you afraid right now?

SYLVIA: No, not ... Yes.

[*Picks up the book beside her.*]

Have you read *Anthony Adverse?*

HYMAN: No, but I hear it's sold a million copies.

**SYLVIA:** It's wonderful. I rent it from Womraths.
**HYMAN:** Was Phillip your first boyfriend?
**SYLVIA:** The first serious.
**HYMAN:** He's a fine man.
**SYLVIA:** Yes, he is.
**HYMAN:** Is he interesting to be with?
**SYLVIA:** Interesting?
**HYMAN:** Do you have things to talk about?
**SYLVIA:** Well... business, mostly. I was head bookkeeper for Empire Steel in Long Island City... years ago, when we met, I mean.
**HYMAN:** He didn't want you to work?
**SYLVIA:** No.
**HYMAN:** I imagine you were a good businesswoman.
**SYLVIA:** Oh, I loved it! I've always enjoyed... you know, people depending on me.
**HYMAN:** Yes.—Do I frighten you, talking like this?
**SYLVIA:** A little.—But I want you to.
**HYMAN:** Why?
**SYLVIA:** I don't know. You make me feel... hopeful.
**HYMAN:** You mean of getting better?
**SYLVIA:**—Of myself. Of getting... [*Breaks off.*]
**HYMAN:** Getting what?

[*She shakes her head, refusing to go on.*]

... Free?

[*She suddenly kisses the palm of his hand. He wipes her hair away from her eyes. He stands up and walks a few steps away.*]

**HYMAN:** I want you to raise your knees.

[*She doesn't move.*]

Come, bring up your knees.

**SYLVIA:** [*she tries:*] I can't!
**HYMAN:** You can. I want you to send your thoughts into your hips. Think of

the bones in your hips. Come on now. The strongest muscles in your body are right there, you have tremendous power there. Tense your hips.

[*She is tensing.*]

Now tense your thighs. Those are long dense muscles with tremendous power. Do it, draw up your knees. Come on, raise your knees. Keep it up. Concentrate. Raise it. Do it for me.

[*With an exhaled gasp she gives up. Remaining yards away...*]

Your body strength must be marvelous. The depth of your flesh must be wonderful. Why are you cut off from yourself? You should be dancing, you should be stretching out in the sun... Sylvia, I know you know more than you're saying, why can't you open up to me? Speak to me. Sylvia? Say anything.

[*She looks at him in silence.*]

I promise I won't tell a soul. What is in your mind right now?

[*A pause.*]

SYLVIA: Tell me about Germany.
HYMAN: [*surprised:*] Germany. Why Germany?
SYLVIA: Why did you go there to study?
HYMAN: The American medial schools have quotas on Jews, I would have had to wait for years and maybe never get in.
SYLVIA: But they hate Jews there, don't they?
HYMAN: These Nazis can't possibly last—Why are you so preoccupied with them?
SYLVIA: I don't know. But when I saw that picture in the *Times*—with those two old men on their knees in the street... [*Presses her ears.*] I swear, I almost heard that crowd laughing, and ridiculing them. But nobody really wants to talk about it. I mean Phillip never even wants to talk about being Jewish, except—you know—to joke about it the way people do...
HYMAN: What would you like to say to Phillip about it?

SYLVIA: [*with an empty laugh, a head shake:*] I don't even know! Just to talk about it ... it's almost like there's something in me that ... it's silly ...

HYMAN: No, it's interesting. What do you mean, something in you?

SYLVIA: I have no word for it, I don't know what I'm saying, it's like ... [*She presses her chest.*] —something alive, like a child almost, except it's a very dark thing ... and it frightens me!

[HYMAN *moves his hand to calm her and she grabs it.*]

HYMAN: That was hard to say, wasn't it. [SYLVIA *nods.*] You have a lot of courage. — We'll talk more, but I want you to try something now. I'll stand here, and I want you to imagine something. [SYLVIA *turns to him, curious.*] I want you to imagine that we've made love.

[*Startled, she laughs tensely. He joins this laugh as though it's a game.*]

I've made love to you. And now it's over and we are lying together. And you begin to tell me some secret things. Things that are way down deep in your heart. [*Slight pause.*] Sylvia —

[HYMAN *comes around the bed, bends, and kisses her on the cheek.*]

Tell me about Phillip. [SYLVIA *is silent, does not grasp his head to hold him. He straightens up.*] Think about it. We'll talk tomorrow again. Okay?

[HYMAN *exits.* SYLVIA *lies there inert for a moment, Then she tenses with effort, trying to raise her knee. It doesn't work. She reaches down and lifts the knee, and then the other and lies there that way. Then she lets her knees spread apart....*]

BLACKOUT

# SCENE 6

*The cellist plays, then is gone.*

*HYMAN's office. GELLBURG is seated. Immediately MARGARET enters with a cup of cocoa and a file folder. She hands the cup to GELLBURG.*

GELLBURG: Cocoa?

MARGARET: I drink a lot of it, it calms the nerves. Have you lost weight?

GELLBURG: [*impatience with her prying:*] A little, I think.

MARGARET: Did you always sigh so much?

GELLBURG: Sigh?

MARGARET: You probably don't realize you're doing it. You should have him listen to your heart.

GELLBURG: No-no, I think I'm all right. [*Sighs.*] I guess I've always sighed. Is that a sign of something?

MARGARET: Not necessarily; but ask Harry. He's just finishing with a patient.—There's no change, I understand.

GELLBURG: No, she's the same. [*Impatiently hands her the cup.*] I can't drink this.

MARGARET: Are you eating at all?

GELLBURG: [*suddenly shifting his mode:*] I came to talk to *him.*

MARGARET: [*sharply:*] I was only trying to be helpful!

GELLBURG: I'm kind of upset, I didn't mean any...

[HYMAN *enters, surprising her. She exits, insulted.*]

HYMAN: I'm sorry. But she means well.

[GELLBURG *silently nods, irritation intact.*]

HYMAN: It won't happen again. [*He takes his seat.*] I have to admit, though, she has a very good diagnostic sense. Women are more instinctive sometimes...

GELLBURG: Excuse me, I don't come here to be talking to her.

HYMAN: [*a kidding laugh:*] Oh, come on, Phillip, take it easy. What's Sylvia doing?

**GELLBURG:** [*it takes him a moment to compose himself.*]… I don't know what she's doing.

[HYMAN *waits.* GELLBURG *has a tortured look; now he seems to brace himself, and faces the doctor with what seems a haughty air.*]

I decided to try to do what you advised. — About the loving.
**HYMAN:** … Yes?
**GELLBURG:** So I decided to try to do it with her.
**HYMAN:** … Sex?
**GELLBURG:** What then, handball? Of course sex.

[*The openness of this hostility mystifies* HYMAN, *who becomes conciliatory.*]

**HYMAN:** … Well, do you mean you've done it or you're going to?
**GELLBURG:** [*long pause; he seems not to be sure he wants to continue. Now he sounds reasonable again:*] You see, we haven't been really … together. For … quite a long time. [*Correcting:*] I mean specially since this started to happen.
**HYMAN:** You mean the last two weeks.
**GELLBURG:** Well yes. [*Great discomfort.*] And some time before that.
**HYMAN:** I see. [*But he desists from asking how long a time before that. A pause.*]
**GELLBURG:** So I thought maybe it would help her if … you know.
**HYMAN:** Yes, I think the warmth would help. In fact, to be candid, Phillip — I'm beginning to wonder if this whole fear of the Nazis isn't because she feels … extremely vulnerable; I'm in no sense trying to blame you but … a woman who doesn't feel loved can get very disoriented you know? — lost. [*He has noticed a strangeness.*] — Something wrong?
**GELLBURG:** She says she's not being loved?
**HYMAN:** No-no. I'm talking about how she may feel.
**GELLBURG:** Listen … [*Struggles for a moment; now firmly.*] I'm wondering if you could put me in touch with somebody.
**HYMAN:** You mean for yourself?
**GELLBURG:** I don't know; I'm not sure what they do, though.
**HYMAN:** I know a very good man at the hospital, if you want me to set it up.
**GELLBURG:** Well maybe not yet, let me let you know.

HYMAN: Sure.

GELLBURG: Your wife says I sigh a lot. Does that mean something?

HYMAN: Could just be tension. Come in when you have a little time, I'll look you over. ... Am I wrong? —you look like something's happened ...

GELLBURG: This whole thing is against me ... [*Attempting a knowing grin.*] But you know that.

HYMAN: Now wait a minute ...

GELLBURG: She knows what she's doing, you're not blind.

HYMAN: What happened, why are you saying this?

GELLBURG: I was late last night—I had to be in Jersey all afternoon, a problem we have there—she was sound asleep. So I made myself some spaghetti. Usually she puts something out for me.

HYMAN: She has no problem cooking.

GELLBURG: I told you—she gets around the kitchen fine in the wheelchair. Flora shops in the morning—that's the maid. Although I'm beginning to wonder if Sylvia gets out and walks around when I leave the house.

HYMAN: It's impossible. —She is paralyzed, Phillip, it's not a trick—she's suffering.

GELLBURG: [*a sideways glance at* HYMAN:] What do you discuss with her?— You know, she talks like you see right through her.

HYMAN: [*a laugh:*] I wish I could! We talk about getting her to walk, that's all. This thing is not against you, Phillip, believe me. [*Slight laugh.*]— I wish you could trust me, kid!

GELLBURG: [*seems momentarily on the edge of begin reassured and studies* HYMAN'*s face for a moment, nodding very slightly:*] I would never believe I could talk this way to another person. I do trust you.

[*Pause.*]

HYMAN: Good! —I'm listening, go ahead.

GELLBURG: The first time we talked you asked me if we ... how many times a week.

HYMAN: Yes.

GELLBURG: [*nods:*] ... I have a problem sometimes.

HYMAN: Oh. —Well that's fairly common, you know.

GELLBURG: [*relieved:*] You see it often?

HYMAN: Oh very often, yes.

GELLBURG: [*a tense challenging smile:*] Ever happen to you?

HYMAN: [*surprised:*] ... Me? Well sure, a few times. Is this something recent?
GELLBURG: Well ... yes. Recent and also ... [*breaks off, indicating the past with a gesture of his hand.*]
HYMAN: I see. It doesn't help if you're under tension, you know.
GELLBURG: Yes, I was wondering that.
HYMAN: Just don't start thinking it's the end of the world because it's not — you're still a young man. Think of it like the ocean — it goes out but it always comes in again. But the thing to keep in mind is that she loves you and wants you.

[GELLBURG *looks wide-eyed.*]

You know that, don't you?

GELLBURG: [*silently nods for an instant:*] My sister-in-law Harriet says you were a real hotshot on the beach years ago.
HYMAN: Years ago, yes.
GELLBURG: I used to wonder if it's because Sylvia's the only one I was ever with.
HYMAN: Why would that matter?
GELLBURG: I don't know exactly — it used to prey on my mind that ... maybe she expected more.
HYMAN: Yes. Well that's a common idea, you know. In fact, some men take on a lot of women not out of confidence but because they're afraid to lose it.
GELLBURG: [*fascinated:*] Huh! I'd never of thought of that. — A doctor must get a lot of peculiar cases, I bet.
HYMAN: [*with utter intimacy:*] Everybody's peculiar in one way or another but I'm not here to judge people. Why don't you try to tell me what happened? [*His grin; making light of it.*] Come on, give it a shot.
GELLBURG: All right ... [*Sighs.*] I get into bed. She's sound asleep ... [*Breaks off. Resumes; something transcendent seems to enter him.*] Nothing like it ever happened to me, I got a ... a big yen for her. She's even more beautiful when she sleeps. I gave her a kiss. On the mouth. She didn't wake up. I never had such a yen in my life.

[*Long pause.*]

HYMAN: And?

[GELLBURG *silent.*]

Did you make love?

GELLBURG: [*an incongruous look of terror, he becomes rigid as though about to decide whether to dive into icy water or flee:*] ... Yes.
HYMAN: [*a quickening, something tentative in Gellburg mystifies:*] How did she react?—It's been some time since you did it, you say.
GELLBURG: Well yes.
HYMAN: Then what was the reaction?
GELLBURG: She was ... [*Searches for the word.*] Gasping. It was really something. I thought of what you told me—about loving her now; I felt I'd brought her out of it. I was almost sure of it. She was like a different woman than I ever knew.
HYMAN: That's wonderful. Did she move her legs?
GELLBURG: [*unprepared for that question:*] ... I think so.
HYMAN: Well did she or didn't she?
GELLBURG: Well I was so excited I didn't really notice, but I guess she must have.
HYMAN: That's wonderful, why are you so upset?
GELLBURG: Well let me finish, there's more to it.
HYMAN: Sorry, go ahead.
GELLBURG: —I brought her some breakfast this morning and—you know —started to—you know—talk a little about it. She looked at me like I was crazy. She claims she doesn't remember doing it. It never happened.

[HYMAN *is silent, plays with a pen. Something evasive in this.*]

How could she not remember it?

HYMAN: You're sure she was awake?
GELLBURG: How could she not be?
HYMAN: Did she say anything during the ... ?
GELLBURG: Well no, but she's never said much.
HYMAN: Did she open her eyes?

GELLBURG: I'm not sure. We were in the dark, but she usually keeps them closed. [*Impatiently:*] But she was ... she was groaning, panting ... she had to be awake! And now to say she doesn't remember?

[*Shaken,* HYMAN *gets up and moves; a pause.*]

HYMAN: So what do you think is behind it?

GELLBURG: Well what would any man think? She's trying to turn me into nothing!

HYMAN: Now wait, you're jumping to conclusions.

GELLBURG: Is such a thing possible? I want your medical opinion—could a woman not remember?

HYMAN: [*a moment, then:*] ... How did she look when she said that; did she seem sincere about not remembering?

GELLBURG: She looked like I was talking about something on the moon. Finally, she said a terrible thing. I still can't get over it.

HYMAN: What'd she say?

GELLBURG: That I'd imagined doing it.

[*Long pause.* HYMAN *doesn't move.*]

What's your opinion? Well ... could a man imagine such a thing? Is that possible?

HYMAN: [*after a moment:*] Tell you what; supposing I have another talk with her and see what I can figure out?

GELLBURG: [*angrily demanding:*] You have an opinion, don't you?—How could a man imagine such a thing!

HYMAN: I don't know what to say ...

GELLBURG: What do you mean you don't know what to say! It's impossible, isn't it? To invent such a thing?

HYMAN: [*fear of being out of his depth:*] Phillip, don't cross-examine me, I'm doing everything I know to help you!—Frankly, I can't follow what you're telling me—you're sure in your own mind you had relations with her?

GELLBURG: How can you even ask me such a thing? Would I say it unless I was sure? [*Stands shaking with fear and anger.*] I don't understand your attitude! [*He starts out.*]

HYMAN: Phillip, please! [*In fear he intercepts* GELLBURG.] What attitude, what are you talking about?

GELLBURG: I'm going to vomit, I swear—I don't feel well...

HYMAN: What happened... has she said something about me?

GELLBURG: About you? What do you mean? What could she say?

HYMAN: I don't understand why you're so upset with me!

GELLBURG: What are you doing!

HYMAN: [*guiltily:*] What am *I* doing! What are you talking about?

GELLBURG: She is trying to destroy me! And you stand there! And what do you do! Are you a doctor or what! [*He goes right up to Hyman's face.*] Why don't you give me a straight answer about anything! Everything is in-and-out and around-the-block!—Listen, I've made up my mind; I don't want you seeing her anymore.

HYMAN: I think she's the one has to decide that.

GELLBURG: I am deciding it! It's decided!

[*He storms out.* HYMAN *stands there, guilty, alarmed.* MARGARET *enters*]

MARGARET: Now what? [*Seeing his anxiety:*] Why are you looking like that?

[*He evasively returns to his desk chair.*]

Are *you* in trouble?

HYMAN: Me! Cut it out, will you?

MARGARET: Cut what out? I asked a question—are you?

HYMAN: I said to cut it out, Margaret!

MARGARET: You don't realize how transparent you are. You're a pane of glass, Harry.

HYMAN: [*laughs:*] Nothing's happened. *Nothing has happened!* Why are you going on about it!

MARGARET: I will never understand it. Except I do, I guess; you believe women. Woman tells you the earth is flat and for that five minutes you're swept away, helpless.

HYMAN: You know what baffles me?

MARGARET: ... And it's irritating.—What is it—just new ass all the time?

**HYMAN:** There's been nobody for at least ten or twelve years ... more! I can't remember anymore! You know that!

**MARGARET:** What baffles you?

**HYMAN:** Why I take your suspicions seriously.

**MARGARET:** Oh that's easy. — You love the truth, Harry.

**HYMAN:** [*a deep sigh, facing upward:*] I'm exhausted.

**MARGARET:** What about asking Charley Whitman to see her?

**HYMAN:** She's frightened to death of psychiatry, she thinks it means she's crazy.

**MARGARET:** Well, she is, in a way, isn't she?

**HYMAN:** I don't see it that way at all.

**MARGARET:** Getting this hysterical about something on the other side of the world is sane?

**HYMAN:** When she talks about it, it's not the other side of the world it's on the next block.

**MARGARET:** And that's sane?

**HYMAN:** I don't know what it is! I just get the feeling sometimes that she *knows* something, something that ... It's like she's connected to some ... some wire that goes half around the world, some truth that other people are blind to.

**MARGARET:** I think you've got to get somebody on this who won't be carried away, Harry.

**HYMAN:** I am not carried away!

**MARGARET:** You really believe that Sylvia Gellburg is being threatened by these Nazis? Is that real or is it hysterical?

**HYMAN:** So call it hysterical, does that bring you one inch closer to what is driving that woman? It's not a word that's driving her, Margaret — she *knows* something! I don't know what it is, and she may not either — but I tell you it's real.

[*A moment.*]

**MARGARET:** What an interesting life you have, Harry.

BLACKOUT

INTERMISSION

# ACT TWO

## SCENE 1

*The cellist plays, music fades away.*

STANTON CASE *is standing with hands clasped behind his back as though staring out a window. A dark mood.* GELLBURG *enters behind him but he doesn't turn at once.*

GELLBURG: Excuse me ...
CASE: [*turns:*] Oh, good morning. You wanted to see me.
GELLBURG: If you have a minute I'd appreciate ...
CASE: [*as he sits:*] — You don't look well, are you all right?
GELLBURG: Oh I'm fine, maybe a cold coming on ...

[*Since he hasn't been invited to sit he glances at a chair and then back at* CASE, *who still leaves him hanging—and he sits on the chair's edge.*]

I wanted you to know how bad I feel about 611 Broadway. I'm very sorry.

CASE: Yes. Well. So it goes, I guess.
GELLBURG: I know how you had your heart set on it and I ... I tell you the news knocked me over; they gave no sign they were talking to Allan Kershowitz or anybody else ...
CASE: It's very disappointing—in fact, I'd already begun talking to an architect friend about renovations.
GELLBURG: Really. Well, I can't tell you how ...
CASE: I'd gotten a real affection for that building. It certainly would have made a perfect annex. And probably a great investment, too.

561

GELLBURG: Well, not necessarily, if Wanamaker's ever pulls out.

CASE: ... Yes, about Wanamaker's—I should tell you—when I found out that Kershowitz had outbid us I was flabbergasted after what you'd said about the neighborhood going downhill once the store was gone— Kershowitz is no fool, I need hardly say. So I mentioned it to one of our club members who I know is related to a member of the Wanamaker board.—He tells me there has never been any discussion whatever about the company moving out; he was simply amazed at the idea.

GELLBURG: But the man at ABC...

CASE: [*impatience showing:*] ABC was left with the repair work because Wanamaker's changed to another contractor for their new boilers. It had nothing to do with the store moving out. Nothing.

GELLBURG: ...I don't know what to say, I...I just...I'm awfully sorry...

CASE: Well, it's a beautiful building, let's hope Kershowitz puts it to some worthwhile use.—You have any idea what he plans to do with it?

GELLBURG: Me? Oh no, I don't really know Kershowitz.

CASE: Oh! I thought you said you knew him for years?

GELLBURG: ...Well, I "know" him, but not...we're not personal friends or anything, we just met at closings a few times, and things like that. And maybe once or twice in restaurants, I think, but...

CASE: I see. I guess I misunderstood, I thought you were fairly close.

[CASE *says no more; the full stop shoots* GELLBURG'*s anxiety way up.*]

GELLBURG: I hope you're not...I mean I never mentioned to Kershowitz that you were interested in 611.

CASE: Mentioned? What do you mean?

GELLBURG: Nothing; just that...it almost sounds like I had something to do with him grabbing the building away from under you. Because I would never do a thing like that to you!

CASE: I didn't say that, did I. If I seem upset it's being screwed out of that building, and by a man whose methods I never particularly admired.

GELLBURG: Yes, that's what I mean. But I had nothing to do with Kershowitz...

[*Breaks off into silence.*]

**CASE:** But did I say you did? I'm not clear about what you wanted to say to me, or have I missed some ... ?

**GELLBURG:** No-no, just that. What you just said.

**CASE:** [*his mystification peaking:*] What's the matter with you?

**GELLBURG:** I'm sorry. I'd like to forget the whole thing.

**CASE:** What's happening?

**GELLBURG:** Nothing. Really. I'm sorry I troubled you!

[*Pause. With an explosion of frustration,* CASE *marches out.* GELLBURG *is left open mouthed, one hand raised as though to bring back his life.*]

BLACKOUT

# SCENE 2

*The cellist plays and is gone.*

SYLVIA *in a wheelchair is listening to* EDDIE CANTOR *on the radio, singing "If You Knew Susie Like I Know Susie." She has an amused look, taps a finger to the rhythm. Her bed is nearby, on it a folded newspaper.*

HYMAN *appears. She instantly smiles, turns off the radio, and holds a hand out to him. He comes and shakes hands.*

SYLVIA: [*indicating the radio:*] I simply can't understand Eddie Cantor, can you?

HYMAN: Cut it out now, I heard you laughing halfway up the stairs.

SYLVIA: I know, but I can't stand him. This Crosby's the one I like. You ever hear him?

HYMAN: I can't stand these crooners—they're making ten, twenty thousand dollars a week and never spent a day in medical school. [*She laughs.*] Anyway, I'm an opera man.

SYLVIA: I never saw an opera. They must be hard to understand, I bet.

HYMAN: Nothing to understand—either she wants to and he doesn't or he wants to and she doesn't. [*She laughs.*] Either way one of them gets killed and the other one jumps off a building.

SYLVIA: I'm so glad you could come.

HYMAN: [*settling into chair near the bed:*] —You ready? We have to discuss something.

SYLVIA: Phillip had to go to Jersey for a zoning meeting...

HYMAN: Just as well—it's you I want to talk to.

SYLVIA: —There's some factory the firm owns there...

HYMAN: Come on, don't be nervous.

SYLVIA: ...My back aches, will you help me onto the bed?

HYMAN: Sure.

[*He lifts her off the chair and carries her to the bed where he gently lowers her.*]

There we go.

[*She lies back. He brings up the blanket and covers her legs.*]

What's that perfume?

SYLVIA: Harriet found it in my drawer. I think Jerome bought it for one of
my birthdays years ago.

HYMAN: Lovely. Your hair is different.

SYLVIA: [*puffs up her hair:*] Harriet did it; she's loved playing with my hair
since we were kids. Did you hear all those birds this morning?

HYMAN: Amazing, yes; a whole cloud of them shot up like a spray in front
of my house.

SYLVIA: [*partially to keep him:*] You know, as a child, when we first moved
from upstate there were so many birds and rabbits and even foxes here—
Of course that was *real* country up there; my dad had a wonderful
general store, everything from ladies' hats to horseshoes. But the winters
were just finally too cold for my mother.

HYMAN: In Coney Island we used to kill rabbits with slingshots.

SYLVIA: [*wrinkling her nose in disgust:*] Why!

HYMAN: [*shrugs:*] — To see if we could. It was heaven for kids.

SYLVIA: I know! Brooklyn was really beautiful, wasn't it? I think people were
happier then. My mother used to stand on our porch and watch us all the
way to school, right across open fields for—must have been a mile. And
I would tie a clothesline around my three sisters so I wouldn't have to
keep chasing after them!—I'm so glad—honestly … [*A cozy little laugh.*]
I feel good every time you come.

HYMAN: Now listen to me; I've learned that these kinds of symptoms come
from very deep in the mind. I would have to deal with your dreams to
get any results, our deepest secret feelings, you understand? That's not my
training.

SYLVIA: But when you talk to me I really feel my strength starting to come
back …

HYMAN: You should already be having therapy to keep up your circulation.

[*A change in her expression, a sudden withdrawal which he notices.*]

You have a long life ahead of you, you don't want to live in a wheelchair,
do you? It's imperative that we get you to someone who can …

SYLVIA: I could tell you a dream.

HYMAN: I'm not trained to …

SYLVIA: I'd like to, can I?—I have the same one every night just as I'm
falling asleep.

HYMAN: [*forced to give way:*] Well ... all right, what is it?

SYLVIA: I'm in a street. Everything is sort of gray. And there's a crowd of people. They're packed in all around, but they're looking at me.

HYMAN: Who are they?

SYLVIA: They're Germans.

HYMAN: Sounds like those photographs in the papers.

SYLVIA: [*discovering it now:*] I think so, yes!

HYMAN: Does something happen?

SYLVIA: Well, I begin to run away. And the whole crowd is chasing after me. They have heavy shoes that pound on the pavement. Then just as I'm escaping around a corner a man catches me and pushes me down ... [*Breaks off.*]

HYMAN: Is that the end of it?

SYLVIA: No. He gets on top of me, and begins kissing me ... [*Breaks off.*]

HYMAN: Yes?

SYLVIA: ... And then he starts to cut off my breasts. And he raises himself up, and for a second I see the side of his face.

HYMAN: Who is it?

SYLVIA: ... I don't know.

HYMAN: But you saw his face.

SYLVIA: I think it's Phillip. [*Pause.*] But how could Phillip be like ... he was almost like one of the others?

HYMAN: I don't know. Why do you think?

SYLVIA: Would it be possible ... because Phillip ... I mean ... [*A little laugh*] ... he sounds sometimes like he doesn't like Jews? [*Correcting.*] Of course he doesn't *mean* it, but maybe in my mind it's like he's ... [*Breaks off.*]

HYMAN: Like he's what. What's frightening you? [*Sylvia is silent, turns away.*] Sylvia?

[HYMAN *tries to turn her face towards him, but she resists.*]

Not Phillip, is it?

[SYLVIA *turns to him, the answer is in her eyes.*]

I see.

[*He moves from the bed and halts, trying to weigh this added complication. Returning to the bedside, sits, takes her hand.*]

I want to ask you a question.

[*She draws him to her and kisses him on the mouth.*]

SYLVIA: I can't help it.

[*She bursts into tears.*]

HYMAN: Oh God, Sylvia, I'm so sorry...
SYLVIA: Help me. Please!
HYMAN: I'm trying to.
SYLVIA: I know!

[*She weeps even more deeply. With a cry filled with her pain she embraces him desperately.*]

HYMAN: Oh Sylvia, Sylvia...
SYLVIA: I feel so foolish.
HYMAN: No-no. You're unhappy, not foolish.
SYLVIA: I feel like I'm losing everything, I'm being torn to pieces. What do you want to know, I'll tell you!

[*She cries into her hands. He moves, trying to make a decision...*]

I trust you. What do you want to ask me?

HYMAN: —Since this happened to you, have you and Phillips had relations?
SYLVIA: [*open surprise:*] Relations?
HYMAN: He said you did the other night.
SYLVIA: We had *relations* the other night?
HYMAN: But that... well he said that by morning you'd forgotten. Is that true?

[*She is motionless, looking past him with immense uncertainty.*]

SYLVIA: [*alarmed sense of rejection:*] Why are you asking me that?
HYMAN: I didn't know what to make of it... I guess I still don't.
SYLVIA: [*deeply embarrassed:*] You mean you believe him?
HYMAN: Well... I didn't know what to believe.

**SYLVIA:** You must think I'm crazy,—to forget such a thing.
**HYMAN:** Oh God no!—I didn't mean anything like that...
**SYLVIA:** We haven't had relations for almost twenty years.

[*The shock pitches him into silence. Now he doesn't know what or whom to believe.*]

**HYMAN:** Twenty...? [*Breaks off.*]
**SYLVIA:** Just after Jerome was born.
**HYMAN:** I just...I don't know what to say, Sylvia.
**SYLVIA:** You never heard of it before with people?
**HYMAN:** Yes, but not when they're as young as you.
**SYLVIA:** You might be surprised.
**HYMAN:** What was it, another woman, or what?
**SYLVIA:** Oh no.
**HYMAN:** Then what happened?
**SYLVIA:** I don't know, I never understood it. He just couldn't anymore.

[*She tries to read his reaction; he doesn't face her directly.*]

You believe me, don't you?

**HYMAN:** Of course I do. But why would he invent a story like that?
**SYLVIA:** [*incredulously:*] I can't imagine...Could he be trying to...
[*Breaks off.*]
**HYMAN:** What.
**SYLVIA:** ...Make you think I've gone crazy?
**HYMAN:** No, you mustn't believe that. I think maybe...you see, he mentioned my so-called reputation with women, and maybe he was just trying to look...I don't know—competitive. How did this start? Was there some reason?
**SYLVIA:** I think I made one mistake. He hadn't come near me for like— I don't remember anymore—a month maybe; and...I was so young...a man to me was so much stronger that I couldn't imagine I could...you know, hurt him like that.
**HYMAN:** Like what?
**SYLVIA:** Well...[*Small laugh.*] I was so stupid, I'm still ashamed of it... I mentioned it to my father—who loved Phillip—and he took him aside

and tried to suggest a doctor. I should never have mentioned it, it was a terrible mistake, for a while I thought we'd have to have a divorce...it was months before he could say good morning, he was so furious. I finally got him to go with me to Rabbi Steiner, but he just sat there like a...[*She sighs, shakes her head.*]—I don't know, I guess you just gradually give up and it closes over you like a grave. But I can't help it, I still pity him; because I know how it tortures him, it's like a snake eating into his heart...I mean it's not as though he doesn't like me, he does, I know it.—Or do you think so?

HYMAN: He says you're his whole life.

[*She is staring, shaking her head, stunned.*]

SYLVIA: [*with bitter irony:*] His whole life! Poor Phillip.

HYMAN: I've been talking to a friend of mine at the hospital, a psychiatrist. I want your permission to bring him in; I'll call you in the morning.

SYLVIA: [*instantly:*] Why must you leave? I'm nervous now. Can't you talk to me a few minutes? I have some yeast cake. I'll make fresh coffee...

HYMAN: I'd love to stay but Margaret'll be upset with me.

SYLVIA: Oh. Well call her! Ask her to come over too.

HYMAN: No-no...

SYLVIA: [*a sudden anxiety burst, colored by her feminine disappointment:*] For God's sake, why not!

HYMAN: She thinks something's going on with us.

SYLVIA: [*pleased surprise—and worriedly:*] Oh!

HYMAN: I'll be in touch tomorrow...

SYLVIA: Couldn't you just be here when he comes. I'm nervous—please—just be here when he comes.

[*Her anxiety forces him back down on the bed. She takes his hand.*]

HYMAN: You don't think he'd do something, do you?

SYLVIA: I've never known him so angry.—And I think there's also some trouble with Mr. Case. Phillip can hit, you know. [*Shakes her head.*] God, everything's so mixed up! [*Pause. She sits there shaking her head, then lifts the newspaper.*] But I don't understand—they write that the Germans are starting to pick up Jews right off the street and putting them into...

HYMAN: [*impatience:*] Now Sylvia, I told you...

SYLVIA: But you say they were such nice people—how could they change like this!

HYMAN: This will all pass, Sylvia! German music and literature is some of the greatest in the world; it's impossible for those people to suddenly change into thugs like this. So you ought to have more confidence, you see?—I mean in general, in life, in people.

[*She stares at him, becoming transformed.*]

HYMAN: What are you telling me? Just say what you're thinking right now.

SYLVIA: [*struggling:*] I...I...

HYMAN: Don't be frightened, just say it.

SYLVIA: [*she has become terrified:*] You.

HYMAN: Me! What about me?

SYLVIA: How could you believe I forgot we had relations!

HYMAN: [*her persistent intensity unnerving him:*] Now stop that! I was only trying to understand what is happening.

SYLVIA: Yes, And what? What is happening?

HYMAN: [*forcefully, contained:*] ...What are you trying to tell me?

SYLVIA: Well...what...

[*Everything is flying apart for her; she lifts the edge of the newspaper; the focus is clearly wider than the room. An unbearable anxiety...*]

What is going to become of us?

HYMAN: [*indicating the paper:*]—But what has Germany got to do with...?

SYLVIA: [*shouting; his incomprehension dangerous:*] But how can those nice people go out and pick Jews off the street in the middle of a big city like that, and nobody stops them...?

HYMAN: You mean *I've* changed? Is that it?

SYLVIA: I don't know...one minute you say you like me and then you turn around and I'm...

HYMAN: Listen, I simply must call in somebody...

SYLVIA: No! You could help me if you believed me!

HYMAN: [*his spine tingling with her fear; a shout:*] I do believe you!

SYLVIA: No!—you're not going to put me away somewhere!

HYMAN: [*a horrified shout:*] Now you stop being ridiculous!

SYLVIA: But... but what... what... [*Gripping her head; his uncertainty terrifying her:*] What will become of us!

HYMAN: [*unnerved:*] Now stop it—you are confusing two things...!

SYLVIA: But... from now on... you mean if a Jew walks out of his house, do they arrest him?

HYMAN: I'm telling you this won't last.

SYLVIA: [*with a weird, blind, violent persistence:*] But what do they do with them?

HYMAN: I don't know! I'm out of my depth! I can't help you!

SYLVIA: But why don't they run out of the country! What is the matter with those people! Don't you understand...? [*Screaming:*]... This is an *emergency*! What if they kill those children! Where is Roosevelt! Where is England! Somebody should do something before they murder us all!

[SYLVIA *takes a step off the edge of the bed in an hysterical attempt to reach* HYMAN *and the power he represents. She collapses on the floor before he can catch her. Trying to rouse her from her faint...*]

HYMAN: Sylvia? Sylvia!

[GELLBURG *enters.*]

GELLBURG: What happened!

HYMAN: Run cold water on a towel!

GELLBURG: What happened!

HYMAN: Do it, goddam you!

[GELLBURG *rushes out.*]

Sylvia!—oh good, that's it, keep looking at me, that's it dear, keep your eyes open...

[*He lifts her up onto the bed as* GELLBERG *hurries in with a towel.* GELLBURG *gives it to* HYMAN, *who presses it onto her forehead and back of her neck.*]

There we are, that's better, how do you feel? Can you speak? You want to sit up? Come.

[*He helps her to sit up. She looks around and then at* GELLBURG.]

GELLBURG: [*to Hyman:*] Did *she* call *you?*
HYMAN: [*hesitates; and in an angry tone:*] ...Well no, to tell the truth.
GELLBURG: Then what are you doing here?
HYMAN: I stopped by, I was worried about her.
GELLBURG: You were worried about her. Why were you worried about her?
HYMAN: [*anger is suddenly sweeping him:*] Because she is desperate to be loved.
GELLBURG: [*off guard, astonished:*] You don't say!
HYMAN: Yes, I do say. [*To her:*] I want you to try to move your legs. Try it.

[*She tries; nothing happens.*]

I'll be at home if you need me; don't be afraid to call anytime. We'll talk about this more tomorrow. Good night.

SYLVIA: [*faintly, afraid:*] Good night.

[HYMAN *gives* GELLBURG *a quick, outraged glance,* HYMAN *leaves.*]

GELLBURG: [*reaching for his authority:*] That's some attitude he's got, ordering me around like that. I'm going to see about getting somebody else tomorrow. Jersey seems to get further and further away, I'm exhausted.
SYLVIA: I almost started walking.
GELLBURG: What are you talking about?
SYLVIA: For a minute. I don't know what happened, my strength, it started to come back.
GELLBURG: I knew it! I told you you could! Try it again, come.
SYLVIA: [*she tries to raise her legs:*] I can't now.
GELLBURG: Why not! Come, this is wonderful...! [*Reaches for her.*]
SYLVIA: Phillip, listen...I don't want to change, I want Hyman.
GELLBURG: [*his purse-mouthed grin:*] What's so good about him?—you're still laying there, practically dead to the world.
SYLVIA: He helped me get up, I don't know why. I feel he can get me walking again.

GELLBURG: Why does it have to be him?

SYLVIA: Because I can talk to him. I want *him*. [*An outburst:*] And I don't want to discuss it again.

GELLBURG: Well we'll see.

SYLVIA: We will not see!

GELLBURG: What's this tone of voice?

SYLVIA: [*trembling out of control:*] It's a Jewish woman's tone of voice!

GELLBURG: A Jewish woman...! What are you talking about, are you crazy?

SYLVIA: Don't you call me crazy, Phillip! I'm talking about it! They are smashing windows and beating children! I am talking about it! [*Screams at him:*] I am talking about it, Phillip!

[*She grips her head in her confusion. He is stock still, horrified, fearful.*]

GELLBURG: What... "beating children"?

SYLVIA: Never mind. Don't sleep with me again.

GELLBURG: How can you say that to me?

SYLVIA: I can't bear it. You give me terrible dreams. I'm sorry, Phillip. Maybe in a while but not now.

GELLBURG: Sylvia, you will kill me if we can't be together...

SYLVIA: You told him we had relations?

GELLBURG: [*beginning to weep:*] Don't, Sylvia...!

SYLVIA: You little liar!—you want him to think I'm crazy? Is that it? [*Now she breaks into weeping*].

GELLBURG: No! It just... it just came out, I didn't know what I was saying!

SYLVIA: *That I forgot we had relations?! Phillip?*

GELLBURG: Stop that! Don't say anymore.

SYLVIA: I'm going to say anything I want to.

GELLBURG: [*weeping:*] You will kill me...!

[*They are silent for a moment.*]

SYLVIA: What I did with my life! Out of ignorance. Out of not wanting to shame you in front of other people. A whole life. Gave it away like a couple of pennies—I took better care of my shoes. [*Turns to him.*]—You want to talk to me about it now? Take me seriously, Phillip. What happened? I know it's all you ever thought about, isn't that true? *What happened?* Just so I'll know.

[*A long pause.*]

GELLBURG: I'm ashamed to mention it. It's ridiculous.
SYLVIA: What are you talking about?
GELLBURG: But I was ignorant. I couldn't help myself.—When you said you wanted to go back to the firm.
SYLVIA: What are you talking about?—When?
GELLBURG: When you had Jerome... and suddenly you didn't want to keep the house anymore.
SYLVIA: And?—You didn't want me to go back to business, so I didn't.

[*He doesn't speak; her rage an inch below.*]

Well what? I didn't did I?

GELLBURG: You held it against me, having to stay home, you know you did. You've probably forgotten, but not a day passed, not a person could come into this house that you didn't keep saying how wonderful and interesting it used to be for you in business. You never forgave me, Sylvia.

[*She evades his glance.*]

So whenever I... when I started to touch you, I felt that.

SYLVIA: You felt what?
GELLBURG: That you didn't want me to be the man here. And then, on top of that when you didn't want any more children... everything inside me just dried up. And maybe it was also that to me it was a miracle you ever married me in the first place.
SYLVIA: You mean your face?

[*He turns slightly.*]

What have you got against your face? A Jew can have a Jewish face.

[*Pause.*]

GELLBURG: I can't help my thoughts, nobody can... I admit it was a mistake, I tried a hundred times to talk to you, but I couldn't. I kept waiting for myself to change. Or you. And then we got to where it didn't seem to matter anymore. So I left it that way. And I couldn't change anymore.

[*Pause.*]

SYLVIA: This is a whole life we're talking about.
GELLBURG: But couldn't we... if I taught you to drive and you could go anywhere you liked... Or maybe you could find a position you liked...?

[*She is staring ahead.*]

We have to sleep together.

SYLVIA: No.

[GELLBURG *drops to his knees beside the bed, his arms spread awkwardly over her covered body.*]

GELLBURG: How can this be?

[*She is motionless.*]

Sylvia? [*Pause.*] Do you want to kill me?

[*She is staring ahead, he is weeping and shouting.*]

Is that it! Speak to me!

[SYLVIA's *face is blank, unreadable. He buries his face in the covers, weeping helplessly. She at last reaches out in pity toward the top of his head, and as her hand almost touches...*]

BLACKOUT

# SCENE 3

CASE's *office.* GELLBURG *is seated alone.* CASE *enters, shuffling through a handful of mail.* GELLBURG *has gotten to his feet.* CASE's *manner is cold; barely glances up from his mail.*

CASE: Good morning, Gellburg.
GELLBURG: Good morning, Mr. Case.
CASE: I understand you wish to see me.
GELLBURG: There was just something I felt I should say.
CASE: Certainly. [*He goes to a chair and sits.*] Yes?
GELLBURG: It's just that I would never in this world do anything against you or Brooklyn Guarantee. I don't have to tell you, it's the only place I've ever worked in my life. My whole life is here. I'm more proud of this company than almost anything except my own son. What I'm trying to say is this whole business with Wanamaker's was only because I didn't want to leave a stone unturned. Two or three years from now I didn't want you waking up one morning and Wanamaker's is gone and there you are paying New York taxes on a building in the middle of a dying neighborhood.

[CASE *lets him hang there. He begins getting flustered.*]

Frankly, I don't even remember what this whole thing was about. I feel I've lost some of your confidence, and it's ... well, it's unfair, I feel.

CASE: I understand.
GELLBURG: [*he waits, but that's it:*] But ... but don't you believe me?
CASE: I think I do.
GELLBURG: But ... you seem to be ... you don't seem ...
CASE: The fact remains that I've lost the building.
GELLBURG: But are you ... I mean you're not still thinking that I had something going on with Allan Kershowitz, are you?
CASE: Put it this way—I hope as time goes on that my old confidence will return. That's about as far as I can go, and I don't think you can blame me, can you. [*He stands.*]

**GELLBURG:** [*despite himself his voice rises:*] But how can I work if you're this way? You have to trust a man, don't you?

**CASE:** [*begins to indicate he must leave:*] I'll have to ask you to...

**GELLBURG:** [*shouting:*] I don't deserve this! You can't do this to me! It's not fair, Mr. Case, I had nothing to do with Allan Kershowitz! I hardly know the man! And the little I do know I don't even like him, I'd certainly never get into a deal with him, for God's sake! This is... this whole thing is... [*Exploding:*] I don't understand it, what is happening, what the hell is happening, what have I got to do with Allan Kershowitz, just because he's also a Jew?

**CASE:** [*incredulously and angering:*] What? What on earth are you talking about!

**GELLBURG:** Excuse me. I didn't mean that.

**CASE:** I don't understand... how could you say a thing like that!

**GELLBURG:** Please. I don't feel well, excuse me...

**CASE:** [*his resentment mounting:*] But how could you say such a thing! It's an outrage, Gellburg!

[GELLBURG *takes a step to leave and goes to his knees, clutching his chest, trying to breathe, his face reddening.*]

**CASE:** What is it? Gellburg? [*He springs up and goes to the periphery.*] Call an ambulance! Hurry, for God's sake. [*He rushes out, shouting:*] Quick, get a doctor! It's Gellburg! Gellburg has collapsed!

[GELLBURG *remains on his hands and knees trying to keep from falling over, gasping.*]

BLACKOUT

# SCENE 4

SYLVIA *in wheelchair,* MARGARET *and* HARRIET *seated on either side of her.* SYLVIA *is sipping a cup of cocoa.*

HARRIET: He's really amazing, after such an attack.

MARGARET: The heart is a muscle; muscles can recover sometimes.

HARRIET: I still can't understand how they let him out of the hospital so soon.

MARGARET: He has a will of iron. But it many be just as well for him here.

SYLVIA: He wants to die here.

MARGARET: No one can know, he can live a long time.

SYLVIA: [*handing her the cup:*] Thanks, I haven't drunk cocoa in years.

MARGARET: I find it soothes the nerves.

SYLVIA: [*with a slight ironical edge:*] He wants to be here so we can have a talk, that's what it is. [*Shakes her head.*] How stupid it all is; you keep putting everything off like you're going to live a thousand years. But we're like those little flies — born in the morning, fly around for a day till it gets dark — and bye-bye.

HARRIET: Well, it takes time to learn things.

SYLVIA: There's nothing I know now that I didn't know twenty years ago. I just didn't say it. [*Grasping the chair wheels.*] Help me! I want to go to him.

MARGARET: Wait till Harry says it's all right.

HARRIET: Sylvia, please — let the doctor decide.

MARGARET: I hope you're not blaming yourself.

HARRIET: It could happen to anybody — [*To* MARGARET.] Our father, for instance — laid down for his nap one afternoon and never woke up. [*To Sylvia.*] Remember?

SYLVIA: [*a wan smile, nods:*] He was the same way all his life — never wanted to trouble anybody.

HARRIET: And just the day before he went and bought a new bathing suit. And an amber holder for his cigar. [*To* SYLVIA] — She's right, you mustn't start blaming yourself.

SYLVIA: [*a shrug:*] What's the difference? [*Sighs tiredly — stares. Basically to* MARGARET.] The trouble, you see — was that Phillip always thought he was supposed to be the Rock of Gibraltar. Like nothing could ever bother him. Supposedly. But I knew a couple of months after we got married that he... he was making it all up. In fact, I thought I was stronger than him. But what can you do? You swallow it and make believe you're weaker. And after a while you can't find a true word to put in your mouth. And now I end up useless to him... [*starting to weep*] just when he needs me!

HARRIET: [*distressed, stands:*] I'm making a gorgeous pot roast, can I bring some over?

SYLVIA: Thanks, Flora's going to cook something.

HARRIET: I'll call you later, try to rest. [*Moves to leave, halts, unable to hold back.*] I refuse to believe that you're blaming yourself for this. How can people start saying what they know?—there wouldn't be two marriages left in Brooklyn! [*Nearly overcome.*] It's ridiculous! —you're the best wife he could have had! —better! [*She hurries out. Pause.*]

MARGARET: I worked in the pediatric ward for a couple of years. And sometimes we'd have thirty or forty babies in there at the same time. A day or two old and they've already got a personality; this one lays there, stiff as a mummy... [*mimes a mummy, hands closed in fists*] a regular banker. The next one is throwing himself all over the place... [*wildly flinging her arms*] happy as a young horse. The next one is Miss Dreary, already worried about her hemline drooping. And how could it be otherwise—each one has twenty thousand years of the human race backed up behind him... and you expect to change him?

SYLVIA: So what does that mean? How do you live?

MARGARET: You draw your cards face down; you turn them over and do your best with the hand you've got. What else is there, my dear? What else can there be?

SYLVIA: [*staring ahead:*] ... Wishing, I guess... that it had been otherwise. Help me! [*Starts the chair rolling.*] I want to go to him.

MARGARET: Wait. I'll ask Harry if it's alright. [*Backing away.*] Wait, okay? I'll be right back.

[*She turns and exits. Alone,* SYLVIA *brings both hands pressed together up to her lips in a sort of prayer, and closes her eyes.*]

BLACKOUT

# SCENE 5

*The cellist plays, the music falls away.*

GELLBURG's *bedroom. He is in bed.* HYMAN *is putting his stethoscope back into his bag, and sits on a chair beside the bed.*

HYMAN: I can only tell you again, Phillip, — you belong in the hospital.

GELLBURG: Please don't argue about it anymore! I couldn't stand it there, it smells like a zoo; and to lay in a bed where some stranger died ... I hate it. If I'm going out I'll go from here. And I don't want to leave Sylvia.

HYMAN: I'm trying to help you. [*Chuckles.*] And I'm going to go on trying even if it kills both of us.

GELLBURG: I appreciate that. I mean it. You're a good man.

HYMAN: You're lucky I know that. The nurse should be here around six.

GELLBURG: I'm wondering if I need her — I think the pain is practically gone.

HYMAN: I want her here overnight.

GELLBURG: I ... I want to tell you something; when I collapsed ... it was like an explosion went off in my head, like a tremendous white light. It sounds funny but I felt a ... happiness ... that funny? Like I suddenly had something to tell her that would change everything, and we would go back to how it was when we started out together. I couldn't wait to tell it to her ... and now I can't remember what it was. [*Anguished, a rushed quality; suddenly near tears.*] God, I always thought there'd be time to get to the bottom of myself!

HYMAN: You might have years, nobody can predict.

GELLBURG: It's unbelievable — the first time since I was 20 I don't have a job. I just can't believe it.

HYMAN: You sure? Maybe you can clear it up with your boss when you go back.

GELLBURG: How can I go back? He made a fool of me. It's infuriating. I tell you — I never wanted to see it this way but he goes sailing around on the ocean and meanwhile I'm foreclosing Brooklyn for them. That's what it boils down to. You got some lousy rotten job to do, get Gellburg, send in the Yid. Close down a business, throw somebody out of his home ... And now to accuse me ...

HYMAN: But is all this news to you? That's the system, isn't it?

580

GELLBURG: But to accuse me of double-crossing the *company!* That is absolutely unfair ... it was like a hammer between the eyes. I mean to me Brooklyn Guarantee—for God's sake, Brooklyn Guarantee was like ... like ...

HYMAN: You're getting too excited, Phillip ... come on now. [*Changing the subject:*]—I understand your son is coming back from the Phillipines.

GELLBURG: [*he catches his breath for a moment:*] ... She show you his telegram? He's trying to make it here by Monday. [*Scared eyes and a grin.*] Or will I last till Monday?

HYMAN: You've got to start thinking about more positive things—seriously, your system needs a rest.

GELLBURG: Who's that talking?

HYMAN: [*indicating upstage:*] I asked Margaret to sit with your wife for a while, they're in your son's bedroom.

GELLBURG: Do you always take so much trouble?

HYMAN: I like Sylvia.

GELLBURG: [*his little grin:*] I know ... I didn't think it was for my sake.

HYMAN: You're not so bad. I have to get back to my office now.

GELLBURG: Please if you have a few minutes, I'd appreciate it. [*Almost holding his breath.*] Tell me—the thing she's so afraid of ... is me isn't it?

HYMAN: Well ... among other things.

GELLBURG: [*shock:*] It's me?

HYMAN: I think so ... partly.

[GELLBURG *presses his finger against his eyes to regain control.*]

GELLBURG: How could she be frightened of me! I worship her! [*Quickly controlling:*] How could everything turn out to be the opposite—I made my son in this bed and now I'm dying in it ... [*Breaks off, downing a cry.*] My thoughts keep flying around—everything from years ago keeps coming back like it was last week. Like the day we bought this bed. Abraham & Strauss. It was so sunny and beautiful. I took the whole day off. (God, it's almost twenty-five years ago!) ... Then we had a soda at Schrafft's—of course they don't hire Jews but the chocolate ice cream is the best. Then we went over to Orchard Street for bargains. Bought our first pots and sheets, blankets, pillowcases. The street was full of pushcarts and men with long beards like a hundred years ago. It's funny, I felt so at home and happy there that day, a street full of Jews, one Moses after another. But they all turned to watch her go by, those fakers. She was a knockout; sometimes walking down a street I couldn't believe I was married to her. Listen ... [*Breaks off, with some diffidence:*] You're an educated man, I only went to high school—I wish we could talk about the Jews.

HYMAN: I never studied the history, if that's what you ...

GELLBURG: ... I don't know where I am ...

HYMAN: You mean as a Jew?

GELLBURG: Do you think about it much? I never ... for instance, a Jew in love with horses is something I never heard of.

HYMAN: My grandfather in Odessa was a horse dealer.

GELLBURG: You don't say! I wouldn't know you were Jewish except for your name.

HYMAN: I have cousins up near Syracuse who're still in the business—they break horses. You know there are Chinese Jews.

GELLBURG: I heard of that! And they look Chinese?

HYMAN: They are Chinese. They'd probably say you don't look Jewish.

GELLBURG: Ha! That's funny. [*His laugh disappears; he stares.*] Why is it so hard to be a Jew?

HYMAN: It's hard to be anything.

GELLBURG: No, it's different for them. Being a Jew is a full-time job. Except you don't think about it much, do you.—Like when you're on your horse, or ...

HYMAN: It's not an obsession for me ...

GELLBURG: But how'd you come to marry a shiksa?

HYMAN: We were thrown together when I was interning, and we got very close, and ... well she was a good partner, she helped me, and still does. And I loved her.

GELLBURG: —a Jewish woman couldn't help you?

HYMAN: Sure. But it just didn't happen.

GELLBURG: It wasn't so you wouldn't seem Jewish.

HYMAN: [*coldly:*] I never pretended I wasn't Jewish.

GELLBURG: [*almost shaking with some fear:*] Look, don't be mad, I'm only trying to figure out ...

HYMAN: [*sensing the underlying hostility:*] What are you driving at, I don't understand this whole conversation.

GELLBURG: Hyman ... Help me! I've never been so afraid in my life.

HYMAN: If you're alive you're afraid; we're born afraid—a newborn baby is not a picture of confidence; but how you deal with fear, that's what counts. I don't think you dealt with it very well.

GELLBURG: Why? How did I deal with it?

HYMAN: I think you tried to disappear into the goyim.

GELLBURG: ... You believe in God?

HYMAN: I'm a socialist. I think we're at the end of religion.

GELLBURG: You mean everybody working for the government.

HYMAN: It's the only future that makes any rational sense.

GELLBURG: God forbid. But how can there be Jews if there's no God?

HYMAN: Oh, they'll find something to worship. The Christians will too—
maybe different brands of ketchup.

GELLBURG: [*laughs:*] Boy, the things you come out with sometimes ... !

HYMAN: —Some day we're all going to look like a lot of monkeys running
around trying to figure out a coconut.

GELLBURG: She believes in you, Hyman ... I want you to tell her—tell her
I'm going to change. She has no right to be so frightened. Of me or anything else. They will never destroy us. When the last Jew dies, the light of
the world will go out. She has to understand that—those Germans are
shooting at the sun!

HYMAN: Be quiet.

GELLBURG: I want my wife back. I want her back before something happens.
I feel like there's nothing inside me, I feel empty. I want her back.

HYMAN: Phillip, what can I do about that?

GELLBURG: Never mind ... since you started coming around ... in those
boots ... like some kind of horseback rider ... ?

HYMAN: What the hell are you talking about!

GELLBURG: Since you came around she looks down at me like a miserable
piece of shit!

HYMAN: Phillip ...

GELLBURG: Don't "Phillip" me, just stop it!

HYMAN: Don't scream at me Phillip, you know how to get your wife
back! ... don't tell me there's a mystery to that!

GELLBURG: She actually told you that I ...

HYMAN: It came out while we were talking. It was bound to sooner or later,
wasn't it?

GELLBURG: [*gritting his teeth:*] I never told this to anyone ... but years ago
when I used to make love to her, I would almost feel like a small baby on
top of her, like she was giving me birth. That's some idea? In bed next to
me she was like a ... a marble god. I worshipped her, Hyman, from the
day I laid eyes on her.

HYMAN: I'm sorry for you Phillip.

GELLBURG: How can she be so afraid of me? Tell me the truth.

HYMAN: I don't know; maybe, for one thing... these remarks you're always making about Jews.

GELLBURG: What remarks?

HYMAN: Like not wanting to be mistaken for Goldberg.

GELLBURG: So I'm a Nazi? Is Gellburg Goldberg? It's not, is it?

HYMAN: No, but continually making the point is kind of...

GELLBURG: Kind of what? What is kind of? Why don't you say the truth?

HYMAN: All right, you want the truth? Do you? Look in the mirror sometime!

GELLBURG: ... In the mirror!

HYMAN: You hate yourself, that's what's scaring her to death. That's my opinion. How it's possible I don't know, but I think you helped paralyze her with this "Jew, Jew, Jew" coming out of your mouth and the same time she reads it in the paper and it's coming out of the radio day and night? You wanted to know what I think... that's what I think.

GELLBURG: But there are some days I feel like going and sitting in the *schul* with the old men and pulling the *talles* over my head and be a full-time Jew the rest of my life. With the sidelocks and the black hat, and settle it once and for all. And other times... yes, I could almost kill them. They infuriate me. I am ashamed of them and that I look like them. [*Gasping again:*] — Why must we be different? Why is it? What is it for?

HYMAN: And supposing it turns out that we're *not* different, who are you going to blame then?

GELLBURG: What are you talking about?

HYMAN: I'm talking about all this grinding and screaming that's going on inside you — you're wearing yourself out for nothing, Phillip, absolutely nothing! — I'll tell you a secret — I have all kinds coming into my office, and there's not one of them who one way or another is not persecuted. Yes. *Everybody's* persecuted. The poor by the rich, the rich by the poor, the black by the white, the white by the black, the men by the women, the women by the men, the Catholics by the Protestants, the Protestants by the Catholics — and of course all of them by the Jews. Everybody's persecuted — sometimes I wonder, maybe that's what holds this country together! And what's really amazing is that you can't find anybody who's persecuting anybody else.

GELLBURG: So you mean there's no Hitler?

HYMAN: Hitler? Hitler is the perfect example of the persecuted man! I've heard him — he kvetches like an elephant was standing on his pecker!

They've turned that whole beautiful country into one gigantic kvetch. [*Takes his bag.*] The nurse'll be here soon.

GELLBURG: So what's the solution?

HYMAN: I don't see any. Except the mirror. But nobody's going to look at himself and ask what am *I* doing—you might as well tell him to take a seat in the hottest part of hell. Forgive her, Phillip, is all I really know to tell you. [*Grins:*] But that's the easy part—I speak from experience.

GELLBURG: What's the hard part?

HYMAN: To forgive yourself, I guess. And the Jews. And while you're at it, you can throw in the goyim. Best thing for the heart you know.

[HYMAN *exits.* GELLBURG *is left alone, staring into space.* SYLVIA *enters,* MARGARET *pushing the chair.*]

MARGARET: I'll leave you now, Sylvia.

SYLVIA: Thanks for sitting with me.

GELLBURG: [*a little wave of the hand:*] Thank you Mrs. Hyman!

MARGARET: I think your color's coming back a little.

GELLBURG: Well, I've been running around the block.

MARGARET: [*a burst of laughter and shaking her finger at him:*] I always knew there was a sense of humor somewhere inside that black suit!

GELLBURG: Yes, well ... I finally got the joke.

MARGARET: [*laughs, and to* SYLVIA:] I'll try to look in tomorrow. [*To both:*] Good-bye!

[MARGARET *exits.*]

[*A silence between them grows self-conscious.*]

GELLBURG: You all right in that room?

SYLVIA: It's better this way, we'll both get more rest. You all right?

GELLBURG: I want to apologize.

SYLVIA: I'm not blaming you, Phillip. The years I wasted I know I threw away myself. I think I always knew I was doing it but I couldn't stop it.

GELLBURG: If only you could believe I never meant you harm, it would ...

SYLVIA: I believe you. But I have to tell you something. When I said not to sleep with me ...

GELLBURG: I know ...

SYLVIA: [*nervously sharp:*] You don't know!—I'm trying to tell you something! [*Containing herself:*] For some reason I keep thinking of how I used to be; remember my parents' house, how full of love it always was? Nobody was ever afraid of anything. But with us, Phillip, wherever I looked there was something to be suspicious about, somebody who was going to take advantage or God knows what. I've been tip-toeing around my life for thirty years and I'm not going to pretend—I hate it all now. Everything I did is stupid and ridiculous. I can't find myself in my life.

[*She hits her legs.*]

Or in this now, this thing that can't even walk. I'm not this thing. And it has me. It has me and will never let me go.

[*She weeps.*]

GELLBURG: Sshh! I understand. I wasn't telling you the truth. I always tried to seem otherwise, but I've been more afraid than I looked.
SYLVIA: Afraid of what?
GELLBURG: Everything. Of Germany. Mr. Case. Of what could happen to us here. I think I was more afraid than you are, a hundred times more! And meantime there are Chinese Jews, for God's sake.
SYLVIA: What do you mean?
GELLBURG: They're *Chinese!*—and here I spend a lifetime looking in the mirror at my face!—Why we're different I will never understand but to live so afraid, I don't want that anymore. I tell you, if I live I have to try to change myself.—Sylvia, my darling Sylvia, I'm asking you not to blame me anymore. I feel I did this to you! That's the knife in my heart.

[GELLBURG's *breathing begins to labor.*]

SYLVIA: [*alarmed:*] Phillip!
GELLBURG: God almighty, Sylvia forgive me!

[*A paroxysm forces* GELLBURG *up to nearly a sitting position, agony on his face.*]

SYLVIA: Wait! Phillip!

[*Struggling to break free of the chair's support, she starts pressing down on the chair's arms.*]

There's nothing to blame! There's nothing to blame!

[GELLBURG *falls back, unconscious. She struggles to balance herself on her legs and takes a faltering step toward her husband.*]

Wait, wait ... Phillip, Phillip!

[*Astounded, charged with hope yet with a certain inward seeing, she looks down at her legs, only now aware that she has risen to her feet.*]

[*Lights fade.*]

THE END